ALSO BY GARY MARMORSTEIN

The Label: The Story of Columbia Records

Hollywood Rhapsody: Movie Music and Its Makers

A Ship

Without a

Sail

The Life of
LORENZ HART

GARY MARMORSTEIN

SIMON & SCHUSTER

NEW YORK   LONDON   TORONTO   SYDNEY   NEW DELHI

Simon & Schuster
1230 Avenue of the Americas
New York, NY 10020

First Simon & Schuster hardcover edition July 2012

SIMON & SCHUSTER and colophon are registered trademarks
of Simon & Schuster, Inc.

Credits and permissions appear on page 503.

For information about special discounts for bulk purchases,
please contact Simon & Schuster Special Sales at
1-866-506-1949 or business@simonandschuster.com.

The Simon & Schuster Speakers Bureau can bring authors
to your live event. For more information or to book an event,
contact the Simon & Schuster Speakers Bureau at
1-866-248-3049 or visit our website at www.simonspeakers.com.

Designed by Ruth Lee-Mui

Manufactured in the United States of America

2   4   6   8   10   9   7   5   3   1

Library of Congress Cataloging-in-Publication Data
Marmorstein, Gary.
A ship without a sail : the life of Lorenz Hart / Gary Marmorstein.
        p.   cm.
Includes bibliographical references, discography, and index.
1. Hart, Lorenz, 1895–1943.   2. Lyricists—United States—Biography.   I. Title.
ML423.H32M37   2012
782.1'4092-dc23
        [B]   2011040654

ISBN 978-1-4165-9425-3
ISBN 978-1-4165-9843-5 (ebook)

To my mother

Wits are never happy people. The anguish that has scraped their nerves and left them raw to every flicker of life is the base of wit—for the raw nerve reacts at once without any agent, the reaction is direct, with no integumentary obstacles. Wit is the cry of pain, the true word that pierces the heart.

—Dawn Powell's diaries, March 1, 1939

You remember
When Beauty said "I love you" to the Beast
That was a fairy prince, his ugliness
Changed and dissolved, like magic . . . But you see
I am still the same.

—Cyrano de Bergerac to Roxane

Author's note: Preference for a biographical subject's first name is often characteristic of hagiography and meant to demonstrate the author's coziness with the subject. But Lorenz Hart was known even to strangers as "Larry." And so, for the most part, he is here.

Contents

A Ship Without a Sail

I'm a Sentimental Sap,
That's All

O N   T H E   morning of November 29, 1943, one week after the death of Lorenz Hart at age forty-eight, several people gathered at the Guaranty Trust Company, on the southwest corner of Forty-Fourth Street and Fifth Avenue, to open the decedent's safe-deposit box. Hart was considered by many to be the greatest of all American lyricists. Hart's attorney Abraham M. Wattenberg arrived with his young associate Leonard Klein, bearing an order, duly made by Surrogate James A. Foley, to open the box with the express purpose of removing Hart's will. A representative of the state tax commission agreed to be there at 11:45 A.M. to oversee the task. Already present were the two executors named in the will: William Kron, who had been Hart's accountant for the past five years; and Richard Rodgers, the composer with whom, over the course of twenty-five years, Hart had written more than eight hundred songs, including "My Funny Valentine," "Isn't It Romantic?," "My Heart Stood Still," "Blue Moon," "My Romance," "With a Song in My Heart," "The Lady Is a Tramp," "Thou Swell," "I Didn't Know What Time It Was," "Mountain Greenery," "Manhattan," "Bewitched, Bothered and Bewildered," "I Could Write a Book," and "Where or When."

Expected at the bank were Hart's younger brother, Theodore, an actor known personally and professionally as Teddy, and Teddy's wife, Dorothy. Teddy had lived with Lorenz—or Larry, as he was called—and their mother until January 1938, when he married Dorothy Lubow and the couple moved to an apartment in the West Fifties. Never living far from Larry, the Harts often looked after him—and few intelligent, able-bodied men have needed such looking after—especially in the six months following the death of the boys' mother, Frieda, in April 1943. When they arrived at Guaranty Trust, they did not know what was in the will. The others did.[1]

The state tax commission representative was delayed. Teddy Hart, who had always played up his lack of book knowledge in clowning contrast to the erudition of his brother, now asked Abe Wattenberg if he had a copy of the will. Wattenberg, in fact, was carrying two copies, and he gave one to Teddy and one to Dorothy. Sitting side by side in the funereal hush of the bank, the Harts read through Larry's will, dated June 17 of that year. The high-ceilinged space had not always felt so sepulchral; decades earlier it had been occupied by the opulent restaurant Sherry's, where Charles Pierre, who later built the Hotel Pierre, was captain, and diners were serenaded by live music and the clatter of silverware and crystal.[2]

"Do either of you have any questions?" asked Wattenberg.

Dorothy Hart finally looked up from her copy. "Does this mean that if I have any children, they're cut off?" Yes, said Wattenberg, that's what it meant. "That's hardly fair," Dorothy said. She pointed out that Larry's estate ought to remain in the family; given the way the will was worded, if she were to have children, they would have no share in his legacy.

By then Teddy and Dorothy had been married for nearly six years; to Abe Wattenberg, a Hart child seemed an improbability. Nevertheless, Wattenberg assured her that the Harts would be ably supported by the $100,000 life insurance policy that Larry had left to Teddy—more than enough to take care of the Harts and any children they might have. "In any case," Wattenberg went on, "I followed your brother's instructions to the letter. This is what he wanted." Wattenberg, a music publishing insider who over the years had represented John Philip Sousa, George Gershwin, Jerome Kern, and Vincent Youmans, had been Larry Hart's attorney since 1925 and, as he reminded Teddy and Dorothy, every legal action he'd taken had been in his client's best interests. Wattenberg produced a waiver of citation that, if signed by Teddy, would enable probate to go through within three or four days.

Anxious about holding up the proceedings, Teddy signed.

The state tax man appeared. The safe-deposit box was extracted from the vault and taken to a conference room. The will inside it was compared with the copies read by the Harts, and everyone agreed the copies matched the original document. Wattenberg gave the original to a bank representative, who would forward it to the Surrogate's Court. At this point Richard Rodgers, having no reason to remain, left the bank.

Wattenberg led the Harts, both groping for purchase in a fog of legalese, up to the second floor to get Teddy Hart's signature notarized. Wattenberg then handed the notarized waiver and the petition to probate to his associate, who took the documents away to file with the court.

The Harts remained in the conference room with Wattenberg, who did his best to placate the befuddled couple, and with Larry Hart's financial manager, William Kron, whose position in the decedent's will was its most perplexing aspect. A full 30 percent of the Lorenz Hart estate was to go to Kron; when he died, that same 30 percent would pass on to his children, and then to his children's children, and so on, presumably until the family stopped reproducing. Although the will bequeathed Teddy Hart 70 percent, with his share going to his wife when she was widowed, no provision was made for their issue; the Harts' participation in Lorenz Hart's future royalties, which were sure to be considerable, would end with Dorothy's death. Then the 70 percent share would be payable, in perpetuity, to the Federation of Jewish Philanthropic Societies (later known as the United Jewish Appeal).

This was curious, because Larry Hart—although he'd been bar mitzvahed at Mt. Zion synagogue in Harlem and been generous to several Jewish organizations, notably the Jewish Theatrical Guild—was not known to have been devoted to Jewish causes. If the Federation of Jewish Philanthropies maintained a strong link with anyone even remotely involved in the proceedings, it was with Rodgers's wife, Dorothy. Felix Warburg, a close friend of Dorothy Rodgers's family, had been first president of the Federation, and Dorothy Rodgers's mother, May Adelson, was a founder of the Federation's thrift shops. If Dorothy Rodgers had a lifelong cause, it was the battle against anti-Semitism and raising funds to help in that battle. Larry was sympathetic, but the cause wasn't his. William Kron was said to be an ardent supporter of the Federation. It was just as likely, however, that the Federation's inclusion in the will had been engineered by Rodgers to acknowledge his wife's profound interest in the organization.

As they left the bank that day, the Harts were drifting into shock. Dorothy knew at least one thing that Wattenberg and the others did not. One week earlier—on the day her brother-in-law died, in fact—she had gone to her doctor, concerned about abdominal discomfort that she thought was an ulcer, only to learn she was pregnant.

❦   ❦   ❦

Larry Hart's will, dated June 17, 1943, was filed in New York City's Surrogate's Court on November 30. The will named Rodgers and Kron as coexecutors and trustees and instructed them to form two trusts out of the residuary estate—the Teddy Hart share and the William Kron share. Before there was a residuary estate, however, bequests had to be made. Teddy Hart was bequeathed $5,000 outright, with another $2,500 going to Dorothy. The other legatees were Hart's cousin Sidney Hertz (the family surname before Hart's father changed it); his friend Irving Eisenman; Mary Campbell, known to the Hart family as "Big Mary" and in their employ as housekeeper for twenty years; and Dr. Milton ("Doc") Bender, a dentist turned talent agent who had been as close to Hart as anyone for more than twenty years. These legatees received $2,500 each. Hart's aunts Emma Kahn and Rose Elkan were to receive $2,000 each, as was his uncle William Herman, but Elkan predeceased Hart by six weeks, and the bequest did not pass through to her two children.[3] Herman, too, died before probate, his share going back to the residuary estate. Bequests of $2,000 also went to Irene Gallagher, who had spent years with Chappell & Company, one of the more powerful music publishers, and to Rodgers's two daughters, Mary and Linda.

As executors, Kron and Rodgers legally seized control of the Rodgers & Hart copyrights and could direct payouts from various income sources, particularly the American Society of Composers, Authors and Publishers, better known as ASCAP. What made Kron's position as a primary beneficiary so baffling, however, was that he had been imposed as accountant on Hart by Rodgers only a few years earlier. Hart was known to be a big spender; so, although he was never poor after 1925, when Rodgers and Hart's Revolutionary War–era musical, *Dearest Enemy*, became a hit, he was frequently broke. In Rodgers's eyes, Kron, who had handled the financial affairs of playwright Edna Ferber and composer Jerome Kern, was the antidote to Larry's devil-may-care attitude about money. The Rodgerses saw Kron as saving not only Larry's money but saving Hart from himself. Dorothy Rodgers said, "Willy Kron, Larry's good friend and financial advisor, went away with him for short trips and played endless card games to keep him from drinking."[4]

In 1929, Rodgers and his father, William, a prominent obstetrician known as Will, had opened a savings account for Hart at a bank at Eighty-Sixth and Broadway; Hart's royalty checks, according to Rodgers, went directly into that account. This was something of a hedge against not only Larry's profligate ways but also his generosity—supporting his mother and brother for many years, routinely picking up checks for people he barely knew, and being widely known as the softest touch on Broadway. "Later on, when there was a great deal more money available," Rodgers remembered, "what [Willy Kron] did was virtually the same thing that my father and I did, with one exception. He took Larry's money and distributed it in savings accounts all over the city, in Larry's name. There was no way for Larry to get at it, and no way for anybody else to get at it."[5]

Not everyone saw Kron's caretaking as magnanimous. Kron often appeared in the lobby of the Ardsley, Larry's apartment house on Central Park West, and someone down there—a doorman or a friend—would phone upstairs to the penthouse to signal that the accountant was on his way up "ostensibly to discuss business," as the Hart biographer Frederick Nolan has said, but really to check out the evening's festivities. Everyone tried to scatter before Kron made it up there. "It was like dodging the truant officer," Nolan has written. "Larry loved it."[6]

"The relationship between Kron and Lorenz Hart was, as far as I could see, purely a business relationship," Mary Campbell, the Hart family's devoted cook and housekeeper, testified in New York's Surrogate's Court. "Lorenz never expressed any affection for Kron. Kron's children visited very rarely and only when Kron brought them there." If Campbell's testimony suggested that Kron's closeness to Larry had been inflated by the coexecutors, other remarks she made were more troubling.

"I also heard Kron tell Lorenz Hart that Dorothy Hart, Theodore's wife, was planning to put him in an insane asylum because Dorothy wanted Theodore to inherit Lorenz's money and when he did she would take the money away from Theodore Hart and leave him. On each occasion Kron said he would protect Lorenz against any such acts on the part of Dorothy and that he would see to it that Dorothy would not put him away.

"Lorenz Hart frequently repeated these statements, more particularly when he was under the influence of liquor."

Campbell, however, emphasized the Hart brothers' mutual fraternal devotion. "I have never known two brothers who were more attentive to each other and who loved each other more. When Lorenz spoke of Teddy he frequently cried. Lorenz, during his lifetime, frequently said that whatever he had in life was for his mother and Teddy and when his mother died he said that everything was for Teddy."[7]

If the testimony sounded coached, there was still ample evidence, pictorial as well as written, of how close the brothers were. Larry did not hang photographs of himself, whether pictured alone or with others, in his various residences, but he kept a photograph of Teddy's appearance in the play *Three Men on a Horse* in his bedroom. Even as adults the two famously undersized men—at five feet one or so, Teddy was slightly taller than his older brother—had lived and occasionally worked together. Teddy's leading role in *The Boys from Syracuse* was created for him by Larry. Kron's accusation that Teddy and Dorothy Hart were planning to put Larry away by declaring him insane sounded wild on its face and was almost certainly false.

It would be more reasonable to conclude that Larry Hart was being manipulated by Kron, and probably at the direction of Rodgers. Yet Larry drank, according to Doc Bender, "morning, noon, and night," and the paranoia that often accompanies such chronic alcoholism had kicked in, exacerbated by the loss of the one person—his mother—who had given him unconditional love.[8]

It was rumored that Larry was bankrupt—that those deposits in "savings accounts all over the city" had vanished. Teddy and Dorothy Hart suspected that all that cash had gone into Willy Kron's pocket. According to an Order to Show Cause for Approval of Compromise Agreement, not counting two insurance policies—$100,000 from New York Life, and a separate $10,000 policy that turned up—the estate showed a total of $33,462.69—more than $29,000 in ASCAP royalties and $4,000 from a checking account.[9] But this wasn't enough to pay immediate expenses, including $22,500 in bequests; costs incurred from Larry's last illness and burial, which amounted to $16,500; and Larry's bequest of $1,000 to Mt. Zion Cemetery, in Maspeth, Queens, for the perpetual care of the Hart family plot. (The will makes no mention of cemetery space for Teddy or Dorothy Hart.) It also turned out—a shock to the Harts—that the New York Life policy erroneously named the estate as beneficiary, not Teddy.

This was not even the final insult to the Harts. In the last week of 1943, given the stunning insurance policy mistake and now desperate to slow the probate process, Teddy Hart filed an affidavit in Surrogate's Court stating that his brother had been "an alcoholic addict" and was subject to undue influence when he had revised his will the previous spring, shortly after the death of his mother. Teddy Hart's affidavit declared: "In the last three years of his life he acted like a man mentally unbalanced and one who did not know what he was doing and did not understand the nature of his acts. His friends and business associates recognized this."[10] Acknowledging his brother's alcoholism was painful for Teddy, but it was necessary to challenge the will.

In a counter-affidavit, Rodgers wrote, "If I did not think Lorenz Hart was physically and mentally capable of carrying on with his part in the production of [the revival of *A Connecticut Yankee*], which required an investment of $100,000, I never would have risked the investment of that large sum nor would I have risked my own professional standing and reputation."[11]

Rodgers was in a tricky position. Through years of Larry's alcoholism, Rodgers had gone to great lengths to get him to work. As early as 1938, during the writing of the stage version of *I Married an Angel*, Hart's long unexplained absences had greatly truncated the team's writing sessions. Rodgers, if pressed, could write lyrics, sometimes even good lyrics, but they were not Hart lyrics. For two decades Rodgers had hung in, forgiving Hart's tendency to vanish and trying to get him to see a psychoanalyst. If Rodgers and Hart were hardly (as one admiring newspaper profile put it) the Castor and Pollux of Broadway, they had loved each other. "Part of it was Dick really adored Larry," said costume designer Lucinda Ballard, "and he would get frantic with worry because Larry was always getting half drunk across the street with somebody; he would disappear from his cronies as well as from everybody else. He might disappear just at a time when a lyric was desperately needed or a change or something. Their relationship was more like brothers who are fond of each other but become estranged by different lifestyles. You know how in families people can still love each other, and I think Dick wanted to protect Larry."[12] When the success of *Oklahoma!*, written by Rodgers with Oscar Hammerstein II after Hart had expressed no interest in it, had quietly but obviously pierced Hart, it was Rodgers who pushed to revive their 1927 hit *A Connecticut Yankee* so that Hart would have work to focus on.

But Rodgers also wanted control of the works he'd produced with Hart. "There is a statute of limitations on gratitude," Rodgers said of the artistic debt he owed Larry.[13] Fed up with decades of worry and anxiety, of playing the responsible, chiding brother to an erratic imp, Rodgers figured it was time to get something back for his suffering. Given that Larry Hart had to be practically locked in a room to write a lyric, it's astounding that he and Rodgers wrote any shows at all. As it was, they produced nearly thirty shows and some eight hundred songs in twenty-five years (with additional "lost" lyrics still turning up now and then). At least fifty of those songs are among the finest American songs ever written.

Further countering Teddy Hart's accusation of undue influence on his brother, Rodgers tiptoed along the precipice of perjury. "The new *Connecticut Yankee* has been received with great acclaim and is one of the current New York hits," Rodgers testified (though the revival was not a hit). "Its present success depends in a large measure upon the excellence of the lyrics for which Mr. Hart was solely responsible and to the brilliance of the book which he assisted in rewriting." Among those lyrics was "To Keep My Love Alive," one of the wittiest songs written in the twentieth century, about an oft-married queen ("I'm never the bridesmaid / I'm always the bride") who kills off each and every one of her imperfect husbands—a list that Larry Hart kept expanding as delighted audiences demanded additional choruses. "From the foregoing I can unhesitatingly state that between May and October, 1943," Rodgers went on, isolating the period when the team was revising its 1927 show, "Lorenz Hart was never under the influence of liquor in my presence and that at all times during that period as far as I know he was in complete possession of all of his mental faculties and aware of his every act and competent to understand the nature of same."[14] The kindest thing to say about that closing sentence may be that Rodgers was being technical. His claim was supported by Dr. Jacques Fischl, the young Doctors Hospital resident who had seen Larry on June 17, 1943, the day he signed the last will, and testified that the lyricist had shown "not the slightest trace of intoxication."

The Harts' jaws could not have dropped lower. Although the Harts were hardly genteel Upper East Side people who aspired to Society—the kind of which Dorothy Rodgers might have approved—Dick Rodgers carried no animosity toward them. What he coveted was revealed in the Fourth Part of the June 17 Hart will:

> In this connection I respectfully request those persons who are authorized to renew copyrights of any of my literary compositions, dramatic compositions, dramatico-musical compositions, musical compositions and songs pursuant to rights of renewal of such copyrights, to procure such renewals of copyrights and after they have done so to assign them to my Trustees hereunder, or to the legal entity which may be organized by them under the provisions of this, my Will.
>
> I also respectfully request that all sums that may be payable to me by the American Society of Composers, Authors and Publishers be paid to my Executors and Trustees hereunder or to the legal entity which may be organized by them under the provisions of this, my Will.

The underlining was done by Abe Wattenberg, who took pains to emphasize the assignment of copyrights to the will's Trustees—the control that Trustee Rodgers had wanted all along. It was the last paragraph, directing that all of

Larry's ASCAP royalties be paid to the Trustees, that set Teddy Hart off on another round of litigation.

The will's Trustees, Rodgers and Kron, were represented by the white-shoe law firm of O'Leary and Dunn. Teddy was represented by the scrappy Louis Brodsky, who found himself in something of a bind: he did believe that Larry Hart had been a victim of undue influence in signing the June 17 will; he also believed that Teddy Hart's consent to go ahead with probate was not made under duress, and there was only so much that could be done in light of that fact. Prepared to compromise, Brodsky wrote a letter to Emil Goldmark, attorney for the Federation of Jewish Philanthropies, reviewing the situation:

> The decedent undoubtedly believed that the $100,000.00 [New York Life policy] was payable to his brother. This belief was shared by his attorney, and immediately after the death of Larry Hart, the policy was delivered to Teddy Hart for the purpose of cashing the same, but when he attempted to do so and filed the necessary papers, he was told that the policy was payable to the estate.

Brodsky went on at some length about Larry's alcoholism and pushed for a compromise:

> I have suggested, subject to the other elements that may enter into it, such as taxes, etc., that the Federation be paid the sum of $10,000.00 in cash in lieu of their interest in the policy of $100,000.00, and if such a proposition is acceptable to the Federation then Mr. Dunn and I can resume our talks with a view to straightening out the whole matter.

Brodsky sent the letter to Goldmark's office and kept his fingers crossed. The Federation, as it turned out, was prepared to compromise; Brodsky's client, Teddy Hart, was not.

The first Surrogate's Court judge on the Hart case was James A. Foley, a veteran of the so-called New Tammany. When Foley stepped down, he was replaced by James A. Delehanty. Sixty-four years old when the case came into his courtroom, Delehanty seemed to give Teddy Hart every legal opportunity to challenge the legitimacy of the June 17 will.

Meanwhile, Larry Hart was remembered in a March 5, 1944, memorial service, organized by Oscar Hammerstein II, at the Majestic Theatre.

Proceeds went to Armed Forces Master Records, which supplied servicemen with records (and sometimes the phonographs to play them on). Although Hart had made it clear he did not want a funeral, he would have been proud, as a patriotic American deemed too small to serve in the First World War, of the $6,000 raised that day at the Majestic.[15] The opening speaker was Deems Taylor, president of ASCAP, who would be named within the year as part of Teddy Hart's complaint against ASCAP. Six days after the memorial service, the revival of *Connecticut Yankee* ended a Broadway run of less than four months. *Oklahoma!* was entering its second sold-out year, its authors reaping the fruits of the new all-American brand known as Rodgers & Hammerstein.

On April 28, Louis Brodsky, at his wits' end, tried one last time to persuade Teddy to accept $86,250.00 out of the insurance fund: $50,000.00 in cash and $36,250.00 set aside to pay federal and state taxes, with the excess eventually returned to him. In addition, the Harts would get back property—furniture, silver, many personal effects, etc.—which had been seized by the Trustees' agents as collateral against the estate. "I believe that this settlement is as fine a settlement, short of winning the case itself, as could possibly be made," Brodsky concluded.[16]

Regarding Brodsky's eagerness to compromise as a betrayal, Teddy fired him. Teddy hired Arnold Weissberger, an attorney based on Madison Avenue. The Surrogate's Court judge, tolerating Teddy's apparent intractability, came up with yet another compromise, but that too proved inadequate. "Mr. Theodore Hart has asked me to advise you that he is not prepared to accept the modifications of the proposed settlement agreement suggested by Your Honor," Weissberger wrote, "and requests that the agreement be withdrawn."[17]

In early June Teddy had pulled out of the cast of the Kurt Weill–Ogden Nash musical *One Touch of Venus*, though the show would continue to run for a while. Lorenz Hart II was born that summer. And Rodgers and Hammerstein were preparing their second musical collaboration, *Carousel*, which Rodgers would claim to be his favorite of all his shows. *Carousel* was based on Ferenc Molnár's *Liliom*, which was first produced in 1909 in Budapest, where it bewildered audiences because the playwright killed off his hero in the fifth scene. More than a decade later, when the Theatre Guild presented an English-language version of *Liliom*, the translation was signed by Benjamin F. Glazer, a literary agent with ambitions to write and direct. Unacknowledged in public was that the translation used for the 1921 production—a theatrical run so successful that it kept the Theatre Guild afloat through bad times—had been made by Larry Hart as part of his routine work for Shubert associate Gustave Amberg. Larry received $200 for four weeks at $50 a week. Although never credited, Larry didn't make an issue of the fact that the translation was his.

Throughout 1945 Teddy Hart lost one appeal after another. Rodgers secured what he'd wanted: control of the copyrights to those extraordinary songs.

It is pointless to suggest that Larry Hart's lyrics would have gripped us as they have without their marriage to Rodgers's music. No American composer is so frequently recorded as Rodgers. Noël Coward said of Rodgers that the man positively pees melody (Rodgers did not, as some antagonistic critics have claimed, say it of himself), and if the line is hardly elegant, it is metaphorically accurate. Though Rodgers's music has been sometimes derided for having no discernible style—unlike, say, the constantly shifting rhythms of George Gershwin or the absolutely right blue notes of Harold Arlen—that is more a testament to his fecundity than to his limitations. Larry Hart, annoyed by the lack of depth and adventurousness in American lyric-writing, overhauled the art—but he probably needed the disciplined, endlessly imaginative Rodgers to succeed.

In his seminal study, *American Popular Song*, the composer-lyricist Alec Wilder wrote about Rodgers: "Though he wrote great songs with Oscar Hammerstein II, it is my belief that his greatest melodic invention and pellucid freshness occurred during his years of collaboration with Lorenz Hart. . . . I have always felt that there was an almost feverish demand in Hart's writing which reflected itself in Rodgers's melodies as opposed to the almost too comfortable armchair philosophy in Hammerstein's lyrics."[18] In their collaboration Rodgers's music usually came first and Hart's lyric second, but Wilder is surely referring to Hart's high standards, which pushed Rodgers to create fresh, memorable melodic lines.

The longtime music director Buster Davis said something similar about Hart inspiring his more disciplined collaborator. "Rodgers & Hart: I put them a little bit ahead of George and Ira. Musically, Rodgers, though not given to the rhythmic variation of Gershwin, had an incredible harmonic sense; his melodies go places the Gershwins never thought of. The reason: Rodgers *catered* to Hart—and Hart's lyrics, especially the later ones, are complex, multidimensional and unique." Like tobacco or alcohol, a tune, Rodgers said, was a stimulant to Larry—he needed it to get started. "Hart was a mercurial, thoroughly unreliable tortured genius who drove Rodgers up the wall," Davis said. "Finally it was too much. Rodgers behaved with great cruelty but he certainly had been provoked." [19]

There is plenty of evidence that Rodgers did not intend to be cruel. Two years after Larry Hart's death, Metro-Goldwyn-Mayer put a biopic about Rodgers and Hart into development. Rodgers could have quashed the project immediately but signed off on it because he wanted the Harts to reap the payoff that came with it. Or so he claimed. Rodgers's go-ahead benefited him and Kron as well, of course, because the money paid by MGM for what are called "grand rights" or "cavalcade rights," to depict the songwriters' lives and use their musical compositions, would be considered income and thereby apportioned to the estate.

Apprised of the lucrative movie contract, Teddy Hart still could not rest. He contended that the right to privacy—his as well as his brother's—was being sold, along with a permit to have his brother represented by an actor, and therefore should be considered principal, payable to him. But Teddy was manacled by a provision in Larry's will, cleverly inserted by Abe Wattenberg six months before Larry's death, which stipulated that if Teddy were to anticipate income from the trust, or if he became so financially overburdened that creditors would attempt to reach into the trust, Teddy's share would be eliminated. [20] Challenging MGM's legal department as well as the trustees' attorneys, Teddy had to be cautious.

MGM turned to Guy Bolton, Rodgers and Hart's collaborator from the 1920s, to sketch the story. By July 1946, Bolton had turned in the outline of *With a Song in My Heart*, a biography of the songwriters that was almost dizzying in its fictions. Bolton provided the sober Larry with a girlfriend he never had; Larry's swift decline, in Bolton's version, is due to heterosexual romantic grief that Larry never suffered, so far as is known—the first stirrings of portraying the lyricist, in the words of Wilfrid Sheed, as a "lovelorn dwarf." [21]

Bolton was replaced by other scenarists. The project's title for a while became *Easy to Remember*. To coproduce, MGM brought in Rodgers's brother-in-law Ben Feiner, who had known Rodgers since boyhood and Hart since adolescence. When the biography was finally filmed and renamed *Words and Music*, script credit went to Feiner and Fred Finklehoffe, whose play *Brother Rat* had been a smash hit in 1937. That may partially explain why Feiner himself is a character in the movie, while more important characters from Hart's life—notably his father, Max, and Teddy and Dorothy Hart—are omitted.

Despite its myriad inaccuracies, *Words and Music* offers some significant pleasures. It contains the extravagant, accelerated rendition of that marvelous song "Where's That Rainbow?," led by Ann Sothern (whose early career got a tremendous boost from her appearance in the 1931 Rodgers & Hart show *America's Sweetheart*). "Slaughter on Tenth Avenue," rechoreographed and danced in the film by Gene Kelly, had been conceived by Larry Hart, even though it was an instrumental piece with no lyrics. And Judy Garland and Mickey Rooney appear together on-screen for the last time, trading lines in "I Wish I Were in Love Again," easily the best lyric ever written about the sometimes violent, sometimes out-of-control rush of romance.

In fact it is Mickey Rooney who rises above *Words and Music's* infelicities. Despite obvious differences between actor and role—Rooney is light and Irish where Larry was dark and Jewish; Rooney is irrepressibly heterosexual where Larry was quietly, discreetly homosexual—Rooney captures many of Larry's mannerisms and much of his personality: the way he rubs his face or his hands, his easy laughter at other people's jokes, his delight in the big black cigars he smokes, his generosity, and the dynamic way he moves. "I think of him as always skipping and bouncing," Hammerstein wrote of Larry, and he might as well have been describing Rooney's version of him. "In all the time I knew him, I never saw him walk slowly. I never saw his face in repose. I never heard him chuckle quietly."[22]

However entertaining Rooney's performance might have been, *Words and Music* left a sour taste in the mouths of its primary beneficiaries. In early July 1948 Rodgers sent a telegram to producer Arthur Freed full of praise for the picture, but secretly he hated it. Teddy Hart—no surprise—lost his case against MGM in New York's Supreme Court, which decreed that:

> the showing of a motion picture in which the compositions of Rodgers and Hart will be made known to a wider audience than they have hitherto enjoyed will result in larger sales of sheet music and phonograph records and in a larger use by musicians of the music and words and in a larger use of the compositions in radio performance and in television shows.[23]

Teddy and his wife would have to be content with 25 percent of the contract proceeds, while the remaining 75 percent went to the estate.

Perhaps that was all that could be hoped for. The motion picture, a photographic medium before it is a dramatic or philosophical one, has always struggled to show what's internal and complex; why expect it to be able to cope with Larry Hart's work, which was interior and often too clever by half, the lyrics spinning with what Rodgers referred to as their "pinwheel brilliance" and much more dazzling than the narratives they were set in?

"There is more going on inside a lyric, and inside Hart's head, than in anybody else's," the performing arts critic Gerald Mast wrote. "Hart was the most confessional of theater lyricists—the most able and willing to put his own feelings, thoughts, pains, sorrows, fears, joys, misery into the words of songs for specific characters in musical plays. What he could never say aloud, even to his closest friends in private, he let characters sing in public. He was a gay bachelor who wrote the best love lyrics for women and the most joyous lyrics about falling in love and the most melancholy lyrics about falling out of love." [24]

Such encomiums suggest that Larry Hart was a poet, as he's often been called. His friend Henry Myers thought otherwise. "Larry in particular was primarily a showman," Myers wrote. "If you can manage to examine his songs technically, and for the moment elude their spell, you will see that they are all meant to be *acted*, that they are part of a play. Larry was a *playwright*." [25]

Hart usually wrote for specific characters, and his lyrics often take on even greater depth when we return to their original settings. "You Are Too Beautiful," for instance, was written to be sung to an amnesiac. "Have You Met Miss Jones?" was originally addressed to Franklin Delano Roosevelt. "This Can't Be Love" was sung by two relatively new acquaintances who fear they might be already related by marriage, if not by blood. "I Could Write a Book" was a pickup line of Pal Joey's. As fast as Larry Hart wrote, he always kept his characters in mind.

Ben Feiner, as writer and associate producer on *Words and Music*, thought Hart's energy—if only it could be captured on the screen—would make the picture irresistible. "At no time was Larry ever an ordinary conventional human being. He was always tremendously high-strung, and consequently either way up or way down. His dialogue was extremely dynamic and colorful. It was never bland, and he never indulged in clichés or even the usual patterns of speech." He was a curious contradiction, this man whose lyrics could be so nuanced and indirect, his behavior so direct—shouting when he was angry, laughing when he was pleased, crying openly when he was displeased.

"Remember that living with Larry for a protracted period of time," Feiner wrote, "would be something like existing in the midst of a continuous demonstration of brilliant and varicolored fireworks. At times they are totally extinguished. And then the silence and the darkness become that much more emphatic."[26]

Part I Harlem to Camelot

CHAPTER 1

Life Is More Delectable
When It's Disrespectable

*L*ORENZ HART was the second child born to German-Jewish immigrants Frieda Isenberg Hertz and Max Meyer Hertz. Max (born 1866) and Frieda (1868) had met in New York City and married in 1887 and had their first child in 1892. Both families were large—there were nine Hertz children, ten Isenberg kids—and lived near each other in the heart of the Lower East Side.[1] Like so many other immigrants, Max and Frieda clung to Jewish tradition, its religious practices and language and food, but were also determined to assimilate and get ahead. Toward that end, Max had ingratiated himself with the Irish and German Catholic men who played key roles at Tammany Hall, the New York political machine.

Max and Frieda gave their first child the decisively Anglo-Saxon name James and referred to him as Jimmy. After fire raged through the Harts' tenement house on Allen Street—surely one of the 86,000 buildings that would have been decreed substandard when the Tenement House Law was passed eight years later—Frieda grabbed her baby boy and escaped out into the frigid air. Jimmy, nine months old, died of pneumonia within the week.[2]

Is there any grief more unyielding than grief over the death of one's child? In an attempt to quell Frieda's inconsolability, Max was determined to provide a change of scene. Although Allen Street was still home to their respective families, it was among the more clotted, shadowy streets of the densely populated Lower East Side, its air filled with soot from the elevated trains' coal exhaust. Friends who had the means to escape the immigrant-packed

Fourth Ward were moving to the inexpensive, open streets of Brownsville, across the East River in Brooklyn, where one could see the sun rise and set. But that wasn't practical for Max, who preferred to be headquartered in Manhattan to pursue various schemes, most of them involving real estate.[3] Max sensed that the place to go was Harlem, where a Jewish community was sprouting.

The Metropolitan Street Railway Company had built elevated trolley lines connecting Battery Park and the upper reaches of Central Park West. Max learned that these lines would soon be extended into Central Harlem, enabling residents to commute downtown for a nickel.[4] Synagogues began to dot the neighborhood. In the spring of 1893, Max and Frieda moved into a brownstone on East 105th Street, a slice of East Harlem bordering on what was then an uptown "Little Italy." When Frieda's depression failed to lift, Max applied for naturalization in the city's Common Pleas Court, procured passports for both of them, and took Frieda to Hamburg, their common birthplace, for the summer.[5]

Returning to New York, they moved another block north. Max leased an office at 115 Nassau Street, where he listed himself as a notary and real estate broker. Before prosperity enabled him to hire a car—later, he would own as many as three cars at once—Max took the Elevated downtown each day. A decade before the subway system was in place, you could ride the El and see much of the city spread before you, the encircling rivers glinting in the distance as though Walt Whitman himself were guiding the tour ("what can ever be more stately and admirable to me than mast-hemm'd Manhattan?").[6] Max had reason to study the island's grid; even when he dipped into other schemes, real estate was his business. He largely shunned the Jewish Harlem brokers, the Yiddish-speaking real estate speculators who convened at the corner of Fifth Avenue and 116th Street, preferring to be downtown each day.[7]

By the time Lorenz was born, on May 2, 1895, Max had changed the family name from Hertz to Hart (*Herz* is German for *heart*) and moved the family still farther uptown, to 173 East 111th Street. The name on their second child's birth certificate is *Laurence*, but to Frieda the boy would be *Lorry* for the rest of his life; to the rest of the world, after adolescence, he was Larry.[8]

Citizenship enabled Max Hart to vote and conduct real estate transactions that would have been otherwise denied him. He spent an increasing amount of time at Tammany headquarters, on Fourteenth Street, hard by Huber's

Fourteenth Street Museum ("The legless man!" "The bearded lady!") and Tony Pastor's music hall. The Harts' third son, the second to survive infancy, was born on September 25, 1897, and named Theodore Van Wyck Hart, after two important political leaders of the time: Theodore Roosevelt, the Republican police commissioner who had been supported by Tammany Democrats; and Robert A. Van Wyck, who would be elected the first mayor of Greater New York a few months later, when all five boroughs were joined together. Growing up, Theodore Van Wyck Hart would stick close to his older brother.

Just before the beginning of the twentieth century, the Harts moved to West 119th Street, bordering Harlem's idyllic Mount Morris Park (Marcus Garvey Park today), which interrupts Fifth Avenue between 120th and 124th Streets. In August 1903, the *New York Herald* reported: "Unquestionably the choicest section of private dwellings in Harlem is that in and to the west of Mount Morris Park, between 119th and 124th Streets, over to Seventh Avenue."[9] Max bought the brownstone at number 59—three floors and a finished basement. As Dorothy Hart pointed out, it was a gemütlich household—warm and embracing, with an abundance of food and affection.[10] The Hart boys' aunts and uncles came up from downtown and Brooklyn to visit, often towing along friends from the worlds of business, finance, and theater. Although Frieda had had theatrical ambitions before coming to America, neither of the Harts showed much artistic inclination. Max, however, was descended on his mother's side from the German poet Heinrich Heine.[11]

"Larry was a great-grandnephew of Heinrich Heine," Richard Rodgers recalled for Columbia's oral history program. "[The family] had an intellectual background, which was pretty well submerged until Larry came along and started to write."[12]

"Max Hart was a book in himself," Rodgers said. Built close to the ground and wide—some documents generously give his height as five feet four, and over the years his weight fluctuated between 260 and 290 pounds—Max Hart was a voluptuary whose appetites defined the 119th Street household. "If Larry had written dirty lyrics," his classmate Morrie Ryskind said, "his old man would have sold them."[13]

Max Hart wanted action, and he got plenty of it. He brokered whatever he could; sometimes it was coal, sometimes insurance, more often it was real estate. He was hauled into court by business associates as early as 1897 and frequently hid behind his wife's name in legal matters. Although there is no evidence that Frieda Hart ever had any more involvement than signing where Max told her to, in 1902 the Bowery Bank of New York sued both adult Harts to foreclose a mortgage.[14] The Broadway Trust Company sued over another mortgage.[15] In late February 1903 in a Manhattan courtroom, an assemblyman punched Max in the kisser for insulting him.[16] What Max might have said can only be guessed, but there's no mystery about why he was in court that day: two weeks earlier, the Abbey Press, a vanity press with offices on lower Fifth Avenue, had burned shortly after closing for the day, and Max, recently hired to put the company's affairs in order, was accused of setting the fire. In that case, arson was only the punctuation to larceny. Max and a brother-in-law had arranged to buy $10,000 worth of silk to manufacture book bags, with the promise of payment in several months, and then turned around and had the silk auctioned off at fifty cents on the dollar. The insurance company, declining to pay claims on $60,000 worth of policies, won its lawsuit, and Max subsequently spent a few weeks in the Tombs—the only time he was known to be in jail in New York.[17]

It was all for Frieda and the boys, Max would insist. Larry's was very much a Gutenbergian education, the printed word being paramount at elementary school and throughout the house on 119th Street. He was already reading Shakespeare and Walter Scott, Byron and the young Yeats. And atop the upright piano the Harts kept in the sitting room there were all those Gilbert & Sullivan operettas to pore over, the librettos studied time and again.

> *O amorous dove, type of Ovidius Naso,*
> *This heart of mine is soft as thine*
> *Although I dare not say so.*

The lyric from "The Fairy Queen's Song" in Gilbert and Sullivan's *Iolanthe* sent Larry to Ovid's *Heroides*. No one wrote lyrics quite like W. S. Gilbert; sometimes it seemed as if no one would ever come close to their sophistication and wit.

Discouraged by the tepid reception of his own musical play *The Sultan of Sulu*, George Ade lamented that the days of the Gilbertian comic opera were over. "But the truth is, we've never had another Gilbert to find out," the comedian Peter F. Dailey told the *New York Tribune*, "especially another Gilbert in conjunction with another Sullivan, for one was just as important as the other."[18] In June 1905, when the producers Klaw & Erlanger offered a Gilbert & Sullivan revue at the New Amsterdam Aerial Theatre and Gardens, one of the largest venues in the city, the public response was rabidly enthusiastic. "The little taste of Gilbert and Sullivan provided at the Aerial Gardens," said the *Tribune*, "has whetted our appetite until Oliver-like we cry for 'more.'" [19]

If Max and Frieda were reluctant to take their boys to what few Gilbert & Sullivan productions appeared in New York, they were not ambivalent about having them attend entertainments performed in Yiddish or German. It might be said that the bedrock of the American musical comedy was the Yiddish theater, its language uniting German-Jewish immigrants with Eastern European–Jewish immigrants. Among Jewish New Yorkers, the actors Boris and Bessie Thomashefsky were as venerated as, say, Ellen Terry was in London. The People's Music Hall on the Bowery was only one of many theaters below Fourteenth Street that catered to Jewish audiences. The Hebrew Actors Union, founded in 1899, was one of the first artists' unions in the nation, and demonstrated its muscle five years later when it called successfully for an actors' strike. By 1905, the United Hebrew Trades had even managed to unionize theater ushers. The Yiddish theater proved an essential training ground for countless craftspeople whose skills later became the lifeblood of the English-speaking Broadway theater.[20] It was also where Larry and Teddy were first bitten by the acting bug.

The Hart boys' desire to perform was burnished by attending the Irving Place Theatre, a stone's throw from Gramercy Park, where German plays and musicals were performed in German by stars like Agnes Sorma and Adolf von Sonnenthal.[21] When he had cash to fund an evening's lavish entertainment, Max Hart made sure that actors like these, as well as producer Gustave Amberg, were guests at West 119th. The preadolescent Larry could talk theater with Amberg, in German as well as English.

In May 1906 Larry turned eleven. The following month his father was prosecuted for kiting checks, in particular taking $600 from a man who could neither read nor write English, promising him a stake in a Philadelphia property and then using that check to pay interest on another mortgage. Max was convicted on two counts of grand larceny and sentenced to state prison for seven years and six months. The prosecuting attorney was John R. Dos Passos, father of the novelist, who knew the Harts socially. (According to his son, the elder Dos Passos liked to sing Gilbert & Sullivan, knew the entire score of Offenbach's *La Belle Hélène*, and could act out scenes from Shakespeare's plays without missing a line.) Max appealed and won a reversal.[22] And on it went, with Frieda's presence often demanded in court because her name had been on the papers Max had drawn up.

Now and then, Rodgers remembered, "Mrs. Hart's jewelry would disappear, because the old man had it." Eventually the jewelry would reappear. The house was usually appointed with expensive furniture, china, and silver. The Harts, said Rodgers, "were unstable, sweet, lovely people."[23] In an attempt to create stability, Max, boorish and profane as he was, was committed to providing his family with the best food and furnishings, his boys with the best education.

By 1908, as Larry was preparing to enter secondary school, much of the New York metropolitan area had been transformed by new transportation links. The Williamsburg Bridge and the Blackwell Island Bridge (soon to be renamed the Queensboro Bridge) had been finished, with completion of the Manhattan Bridge imminent; the Pennsylvania East River Tunnel, the Hudson River Tunnel, and the New Jersey and New York Trolley Tunnel had also made travel into and out of the city considerably easier.[24] The new subway system connected parts of the city that had been thought of as being prohibitively distant from one another. This provided Larry with a choice of schools he would not have had four or five years earlier.

From 1908 to 1910 Larry attended DeWitt Clinton, then at Fifty-Ninth Street and Tenth Avenue. He made several close friends there, among them Arthur Hornblow, Jr., son of a staff critic at *Theatre* magazine. Young Hornblow was a member of the Dramatic Society at DeWitt Clinton and associate editor of *The Magpie*, the school's literary magazine. Hornblow ushered into print Larry's first published piece of fiction, a short story called "Elliot's Plagiarism." Running just under a thousand words, it appeared in a 1910 edition of *The Magpie* and was signed Lorenz Milton Hart.

In "Elliot's Plagiarism," Mr. Baker, faculty adviser to the student magazine *Longfellow Chronicle*, is greatly impressed with Elliot Larned's short story "Sentiments." When he reads a sensational new novel titled *The Sentimentalists*, authored by a man named Craig, Mr. Baker suspects that Elliot's story was plagiarized from it. Confronted by Mr. Baker, Elliot refuses to confess to plagiarism, and later, humiliated before the entire student body of Longfellow High, he faints. Next morning his father, Dr. Larned, comes to his bedside and asks him what happened. Elliot swears he plagiarized nothing, but that he did use the basic outline of a broken romance of his brother's. Dr. Larned laughs and says, "That's the plot of *The Sentimentalists*"; he should know because he's the author, writing under the name Craig. Elliot happily returns to school but vows to never again write a story about a domestic incident.[25]

"Elliot's Plagiarism" is a mature story for a fifteen-year-old to compose, and it glances at themes Larry would be working through, in one form or another, for the next several years: a "cheery" young hero suffering a false accusation and becoming "downcast," ambivalence toward a powerful father who is as deceptive as he is authoritative, a brother whose emotional state is significant to the hero, and how much literary theft was considered acceptable.

In the first decade of the twentieth century, New York was rapidly becoming cleaner and safer. At thirteen and eleven, the Hart boys could move around the city with a freedom and a sense of security that would have been denied them only a few years earlier. The historian David Nasaw has pointed out that incandescent lighting transformed the city "from a dark and treacherous netherworld into a glittering multicolored wonderland." The notorious wonderland known as Longacre Square—renamed Times Square in April 1904 after *The New York Times* moved into its new twenty-five-story building at the Forty-Third Street junction of Broadway and Seventh Avenue—was dubbed the Great White Way for the density of its incandescent light. Most streetcars had been electrified. Subways were all-electric; if you could navigate the underground trip, it was possible to ride from Morningside Heights in Manhattan to Coney Island in Brooklyn for a nickel.[26]

On summer days Coney Island could be impassable, with millions of visitors swarming to the ocean. If you had the means and the time—and as a result of union struggles, more workers were being paid for holidays and vacations—it was imperative to get out of the city to escape the heat.

New York Jews, ghettoized even at summer resorts, had more limited options. They were not welcome, for instance, at Saratoga Springs, long considered the gateway to the Adirondacks, to say nothing of the eastern Long Island coastal towns like Southampton and Bridgehampton. If it was beach weather they wanted, a Jewish family could get a summer place at Far Rockaway, or travel down to the Jersey Shore, where Atlantic City was the center of the action. The great Jewish exodus each summer, however, was to the Catskill Mountains. Max sent his boys to the Weingart Institute, the Catskills summer school that served as an annex to the New York City elementary school of the same name.

"Weingart Institute was a forerunner of the modern camps," said the playwright-scenarist Sig Herzig, who was there when Larry and Teddy attended in 1908 and 1909, "and was patronized mostly by the sons of well-to-do German-Jewish families."[27] Myron and David Selznick would spend adolescent summers there, and so would Oscar Hammerstein, Richard Rodgers, and Harold Hyman, who became the Harts' family doctor many years later.[28] School founder Sam Weingart mixed a military-style camp—reveille, lineups, and regular bunk inspections—with rigorous studies every morning, followed by sports and other activities. Larry joined the institute's Literary Society, which published *The Weingart Review* and often sponsored dramatic entertainments. It was in one of those entertainments—a farce called *New Brooms*, according to Sig Herzig—that Larry got his first experience on the stage, singing "Pass It Along to Father" (music by Harry Von Tilzer, lyrics by Vincent Bryan). Even at thirteen, Larry didn't think much of the Literary Society's readings—recently anointed classics by Robert Louis Stevenson and Edward Everett Hale. He contributed his own material to *The Weingart Review*. The unsigned "An Interview with Mr. Lorenz Hart" was supposed to be the work of a classmate, but it has Larry's stamp on every line as he pokes fun at his own stature and at the pretentiousness built into the position of boy editor—in this case, as dramatic editor of the *Highmount Daily Dope-Sheet*. The "reporter" makes clear he's taking down the speech of "the diminutive Mr. Hart," otherwise known as "Professor Lorenzo Hart," at the rate of "five paragraphs a second." "I was small then, and am still small, because my heavy brain does not permit me to grow in a vertical direction."[29]

Chafing under Weingart's relatively strict in loco parentis regulations, Larry spent subsequent summers at Camp Paradox. Because Lake Paradox was in the Adirondacks—considerably farther from New York than the Catskills, and of higher elevation—the trip there was more complicated: you boarded a boat at 125th Street and sailed, overnight, up to Ticonderoga; after disembarking, you were taken by horse-drawn wagon or car some twenty-five miles to the camp. That first glimpse of the lake, though, made the journey worthwhile. Larry was the charge of Mel Shauer, a Paradox veteran, who was Larry's age but looked and acted older. (Most campers looked older than Larry.) Other kids packed clothes in their camp trunks; Larry packed a complete set of Shakespeare and whatever additional books he could fit. After a while counselors and fellow campers referred to him as Shakespeare Hart.[30]

In his first summer at Paradox, Larry met Herbert Fields, the younger son of the vaudevillian Lew Fields (of Weber & Fields) and older brother of the future lyricist Dorothy Fields. "It was the first season of the camp," Herb

Fields said many years later, "and we were only small boys. Larry was thirteen and I was eleven. They had no dramatics, so Larry and I wrote sketches and put them on ourselves. Every week we had something else."[31] In fact, Larry was at least fifteen—his first year at Paradox was 1910—but he appeared much younger. Herb, like Larry, was well read and quick with a quip, but his love of the theater was something his parents were doing their best to discourage.[32] Lew Fields did not want his children to go into the family business.

Larry's younger brother, Teddy, had followed him to both camps. Although Larry still wanted to perform even more than he wanted to write, it was Teddy who was all clown all the time. Teddy and Larry developed a twin-brother routine that both flummoxed and amused the campers. "Larry had his hair and we both wore big black beards," Teddy said. "Larry used to go off the stage on one side and then I would pop on from the other side."[33]

Of the brothers, Teddy took the brunt of Max Hart's ire. (The clown so often does.) Mel Shauer remembered the day Max arrived unannounced at Paradox and shattered the sylvan quiet by bellowing for his sons as he huffed his way up the hill. Spotting the two boys, he bawled them out for failing to greet him, and he swatted Teddy. Max did not touch Larry, who was the older (but smaller and more "sensitive") son.[34] Frieda would not have tolerated it.

While Larry was at DeWitt Clinton, the renowned anthropologist Franz Boas began a study for the U.S. Immigration Commission to investigate how the recent influx of immigrants had affected the average physique of the American population. Nearly eighteen thousand immigrants and their American-born children were interviewed and measured; data was collected from New York City schools, including DeWitt Clinton. Larry himself might not have been interviewed, but the study's results, later published as *Changes in Bodily Form of Descendants of Immigrants*, upset the received idea that the size of a racial or ethnic type was fixed—suggesting and sometimes demonstrating outright that birth and rearing in America were making most children larger. According to data collected for Boas by Dr. Maurice Fishberg (who had published *The Jews: A Study of Race and Environment*, a couple of years earlier), this turned out to be true even among Jewish immigrants of a European background.

> Among the east European Hebrews the American environment, even in the congested parts of the city, has brought about a generally more favorable development of the body, which is expressed in the increased height of body

(stature) and weight of the children. . . . It seems that the change in stature and weight increases with the time elapsed between the arrival of the mother and the birth of the child.[35]

So what happened to Larry, who grew up slightly taller than his mother but not as tall as his squat father? As an adolescent his stature was beginning to make him self-conscious. Eugenics—the "science" of selective breeding of desirable genetic traits—had been in the public consciousness for several decades and been embraced by some intellectuals (George Bernard Shaw among them) long before the Nazis applied it so ruthlessly and horrifically. Increasingly, Larry felt that his peers regarded his looks as undesirable. "We are socialized to value cultural factors such as intelligence, creativity, empathy, and perseverance," Stephen Hall wrote in *Size Matters*, his tough-minded study of short stature in America. "But the society of children does not always embrace these values—especially when the adults are not looking. Kids are keenly aware of big and small, short and tall, strong and weak. Indeed, these categorizations are among the earliest organizing principles in how children see the world and their place in it. Before we ever utter a word, other people think they know something about us."[36] Because Larry's stature was considered extreme, assumptions were made about him, especially among boys meeting him for the first time.

Max Hart's own diminutive stature didn't seem to bother him. Larry's friend Henry Myers described Max as a "vociferous walrus," bellowing behind his mustache, his methods informed by misrepresentation, generosity, and an unapologetic coarseness.[37] Teddy took delight in the crudeness and trickery of Max, whom the boys referred to as the O.M. (Old Man). As an actor all his life, Teddy aspired to putting his gags and impressions over on audiences, and that's what Max did so well—he conned people. That same behavior often made the more sensitive Larry wince. Something of a mama's boy, sharing her gentler temperament, Larry loved the O.M. but didn't always like him.

Some of the more outrageous stories might have been true, such as the time Max, who claimed to have worked as assistant to a coroner, demanded and got a ten-thousand-dollar bribe to keep quiet about the suicide of a Vanderbilt.[38] Cantor Yosele Rosenblatt, one of the key Jewish musical figures of the twentieth century, made early recordings for Victor and its subsidiary Camden that had enthralled Eastern European immigrants. He kept a house for his wife and children on 114th Street and one for himself on 120th Street, north of the Harts' house on 119th. According to family lore, during one summer heat spell, the world-famous *chazen* was singing in the backyard they shared, when Max, unable to stand the noise any longer, leaned out a second-story window and poured a bucket of water on the cantor's head.[39] The writer Milton Pascal, visiting Larry at 119th Street, remembered Max coming into Larry's bedroom on the third floor and, without a trace of self-consciousness, urinating out the window.[40]

Boorish behavior isn't necessarily criminal. Max's financial dealings took care of that part.

"There were some awful consequences, for other people as well as for him," Geoffrey Wolff wrote of his own father in his memoir, *The Duke of Deception*. Like Max Hart, the elder Wolff lived beyond the law when it suited him to do so. "He was lavish with money, with others' money. He preferred to stiff institutions: jewelers, car dealers, banks, fancy hotels. He was, that is, a thoughtful buccaneer, when thoughtfulness was convenient. But people were hurt by him."[41] Max's depredations were similarly hurtful, and for a while they were sanctioned by his friends at Tammany Hall, particularly the cronies of Martin Engel, longtime boss of the Eighth Assembly District (known to constituents as "De Ate"). There is no evidence that Max participated in Tammany profits from its most sordid activity, its well-organized slave trade—the barely hidden recruiting and sale of Jewish immigrant girls and women—with the New York Police Department said to be well paid to look the other way.[42] Even if Max had had no moral objection to slave-trading, it would have involved more labor than he liked. Since the birth of his sons and the ascension of the Van Wyck administration—an administration so nakedly corrupt that a group known as the Committee of Fifteen was organized to investigate its abuses—Max preferred trading favors with Tammany associates until, inevitably, the capital of that association ran out. "Be you guarded in your relations with the ruling power," cautions the Talmud, "for they who exercise it draw no man nigh to themselves except for their own interests. They appear as friends when it is to their advantage, but they stand not by a man in his time of stress."[43] In the 1910 U.S. Census, with Larry about to transfer out of DeWitt Clinton, the Harts' Head of Household listed his occupation simply as "Real Estate."

CHAPTER 2

I Read My Plato

*I*N THE fall of 1910 Larry transferred to Columbia Grammar School, which was considerably smaller than DeWitt Clinton and closer to home. Originally founded in 1764 just north of City Hall, when Columbia College was downtown, Columbia Grammar kept relocating farther uptown. The Melville brothers, Gansevoort and Herman, were among its alumni. By 1905, the school had settled on West Ninety-Third Street.[1]

There were twenty other students in the Columbia Grammar class of 1913. Larry's confidence was bolstered at the smaller school. A year after he transferred, he was placing poems, stories, and essays in the monthly *Columbia News*, where he served as associate editor. Reading Larry's paean to the Bible (presumably the Old Testament, though he doesn't say), one waits in vain for the kind of adroit twist he would dash off in his maturity. The same issue includes "The Goobergoo and the Kantan," a two-hundred-word allegory in which a wood-pond dries up, to be replaced by "a vaudeville theater managed by George M. Cohan."[2]

On May 28, 1911, at the fourth annual Frolic of the Friars' Club, George M. Cohan sang Irving Berlin's "Alexander's Ragtime Band." Cohan's rare rendition of another man's composition was the ultimate stamp of approval. The Berlin song became as inescapable as the street organ-grinder had been, heard throughout the city. For the Harts' celebration of their silver wedding anniversary, Larry wrote his own words to "Alexander's Ragtime Band" and performed them, on November 6, 1911, at the Bronx hall his family had rented for the occasion. His version probably qualifies as his earliest surviving lyric:

So clink your glass,
Each lad and lass,
For Max and Frieda's wedding day.
Put on a smile,
Make life worthwhile—
Let each wrinkle shout hooray!

In this anniversary song, Larry is already employing tools he would use for the next thirty years: warmth; gallantry ("And Mrs. Hart still plays her part / Though her age I dare not tell"); repetition when it's called for; a reference or two to booze; colloquial English and German that landed easily on the ear.[3] It might not have been up to the level of Gilbert's "When a Merry Maiden Marries" toast from *The Gondoliers*, but, coming from a sixteen-year-old, it was impressive.

A month after the anniversary celebration, *The Columbia News* published Larry's sliver of a story "The Long Line," about a wealthy, egotistical young man who wanders on Christmas Eve from Times Square down to the Bowery Mission, where he identifies with the men, women, and children waiting on the bread line. "What is a hungry stomach in comparison with a hungry heart?" asks the "ugly" little preacher.[4]

From his adolescent apprenticeship right up to his last shows—particularly *The Boys from Syracuse*, *By Jupiter*, and the revival of *A Connecticut Yankee*—Larry pranced along a high wire linking classical references with contemporary show business. Here is the fourth stanza of "The Modern Student," published in *The Columbia News* in January 1912:

At Homer who told tales of Troy
We raise an awful din,
We'd rather hear Sir Eddie Foy
Sing "Ragtime Violin."
Salome too was not the whirl
The Semites used to think,
Why Miss Deslys could make that girl
Sit down and take a drink.

Eddie Foy was the popular vaudevillian, of course, and Gaby Deslys was a French-Czech celebrity whose recent appearance at Yale had caused a riot.[5] Such topicality would become a Hart trademark. For the 1912 month of presidential birthday celebrations, Larry wrote quatrains in homage to Washington ("Father of our Country!") and Lincoln ("Savior of our Country!").[6] One month after the *Titanic* went down, Larry published "Balm," a eulogy for the ship's dead.[7] Although his writing would take years to mature, his preoccupations were, for the most part, already in place. Chronically dismayed with vaudeville, with popular music that was indiscriminately labeled "ragtime," and with the musical comedies that he regarded as pandering, he also had little patience for classics he found dull. Early and late, Shakespeare was his man.

In the autumn of 1912 the Harts went to Germany, arriving at Bremen on October 12 and then spending a month in Hamburg before going on to Berlin. "Though the life at the German Capital is fascinating and gay," Larry wrote from the Savoy in Berlin to *The Columbia News* editors, "Teddy and I are homesick. We long for our New York friends, and especially for those at old C. G. S. I never was patriotic till a German band irritated me by playing 'Die Wacht Am Rhein.'" Larry wrote that he hadn't given much thought to women's dress until confronted by German women's lack of chic. But beer was cheap, which presumably made up for the insult to his eyes, and he was looking forward to being home in New York. Larry now signed himself "Lorenz Hart, '14," because the semester of travel would push his graduation from Columbia Grammar back at least half a year.[8]

The Berlin trip inspired Larry's story "The Mummer," which *The Columbia News* ran in its December 1912 issue. The story is about a German actor (or mummer) whose grief-stricken performance as Shylock, only hours after the death of his young American wife, is the beginning of a great theatrical career.[9] In Larry's story "Baseball and the Exams—A 'Mix-up,'" the narrator neglects his schoolwork while he dreams of being New York Giants pitching star Christy Mathewson. The celebration of baseball is all the sweeter in the middle of winter, when the diamond is covered by snow. Throughout his childhood, Larry was a Giants fan, in part because it was the oldest Manhattan team and, more significantly, because Giants manager John J. McGraw cultivated actors and journalists.[10]

"We have an excellent tragedian in Hart," the *News* declared in its February 1913 issue. In that same issue, Larry was given several pages for a story called "The Man Model," about someone who models as Hamlet but doesn't earn enough to win the woman he loves. The painter he models for boldly decries the woman's acquisitiveness:

> One fool steals himself away from Art to make money and the other won't marry him because he hasn't made enough of it. Money, money! God! Those who chase it are crazy! If they make it, they speak of what they gain, they never think of what they lose. The fools, they lose the best years of their lives.[11]

The model finally wins her by becoming a moving picture star, appearing in the new film version of *Hamlet*. The story seems all the more original when we remember that there was no on-screen *Hamlet* until 1915, when J. Forbes-Robertson, considered the greatest Hamlet of his time, appeared in a three-reel version.

The following month, in an unfinished confection titled "Comus at C. G. S.," ostensibly about basketball, Larry was already mixing the Arthurian idiom with contemporary slang ("Nay, Lady Bertie—if I but wave this wand / Your nerves are all chained up in tutti frutti").[12]

That spring Larry took second prize in the English department's competition of 1913 for his essay "Falstaff." Acknowledging that there are two Falstaffs in Shakespeare—in *Henry IV* and *The Merry Wives of Windsor*—and that they differ in many ways, Larry regarded his hero as a rascal "fond of sack, of repartee, and the smile of a pretty lass." His analysis is remarkable, particularly for a boy not yet out of adolescence. Shakespeare knew, Larry wrote, "that real love was impossible for Falstaff," whose abiding affection for wine was one of the things that precluded it. There is Falstaff's extreme size—Falstaff is enormous, of course, Larry tiny—he is "carelessly but richly dressed," his hose "very dirty and worn." (Larry could have been describing his own sartorial style.) "This blustering, boisterous boy of Bacchus" could have been a statement of what Larry himself aspired to, though he was shyer and quieter.[13]

Larry returned, with Teddy, for a final summer at Camp Paradox. His one Paradox verse that survives is called "The Tale of the Lone(some) Pine," in which he rhymes *snoozing* with *schmoozing* and throws in names of fellow campers—an audience-pleasing practice he would continue for the next thirty years.[14]

In that last season at the camp, one of his campmates was Herbert Marks, son of the song publisher Edward Marks. Larry, Herbert Marks remembered, was a "very special camper, because he wrote camp shows that were really remarkably good. He had that wonderful gift for lyric writing even then." Edward Marks would be impressed enough to subsequently hire Larry to make lyric translations for the publishing firm.[15] They were probably Larry's first show business work for pay.

At night in camp, by lantern light, Larry read Boccaccio, Maupassant, and Chaucer's "The Miller's Tale," and took great delight in recounting the more suggestive passages to Teddy, who was not much of a reader but enjoyed his older brother's confidence.[16] Larry was developing his own sense of the Falstaffian, which he mixed with everyday burlesque humor. Henry Myers remembered that Larry liked to regale Paradox campers with the joke about the train stopping on a bridge above a stream where two boys are swimming: a proper dowager looks down through her lorgnette and expresses shock that the boys are nude; she looks for another moment and adds, "And Jewish boys, too!"[17] Larry laughed at his own jokes as easily as he laughed at his friends' jokes. And, by all accounts, he had a lot of friends.

Larry never thought seriously about leaving New York to attend college. His plan was to enroll at the School of Journalism, the new undergraduate school at Columbia. (It was not yet a graduate school.) The campus was only half a mile west of his 119th Street house, in Morningside Heights—so named because the steep western cliff of the park now known as Morningside Park glowed from the morning rays of the rising sun.

Larry could live at home and would still be only a subway ride away from the theater district. In the fall of 1913 he finished his classes at Columbia Grammar and enrolled in a Columbia extension class in dramatic technique taught by Hatcher Hughes, then in his early thirties. Hughes had been a prize student of Columbia's Brander Matthews, who was widely regarded, along with Harvard's George Pierce Baker, as one of the nation's preeminent teachers of drama, and Hughes was now giving classes on his own. Like his mentor, Hughes idolized Ibsen and promoted the so-called "well-made play." Larry, preferring Shakespeare, perhaps because Shakespeare's dialogue often rose to the level of poetry, didn't think much of Hughes's ideas. But he warmed immediately to his classmate Henry Myers, a composer who also wrote plays. A mutual friend told Larry that Henry was "the dirtiest slob" he knew—"dirty" meaning lewd. Larry would befriend almost anybody willing

to be befriended, but Myers, with his own considerable knowledge of the theater (and a mother who thought him a genius), was heaven-sent.[18]

Myers became part of the Harts' open house at 59 West 119th. Larry's
friends met in the basement, where there was a modicum of privacy. It was a
group of formidable young men, and Larry, sharing cigars and food and his
father's liquor and cash, was the one who held it all together. Over time, the
group grew to include Larry's old Paradox friend Mel Shauer; Irving Strouse,
who would become a publicist and a producer; Herbert Schloss, who would
produce plays under the name Herbert Castle; Milton Winn, who was preparing to be a lawyer; and an oversize figure with the classic Anglicized name Jake
Robbins, or John Jacob Robbins. (His birth name was Rabinovich.) Two years
older than Larry, Jake Robbins lived a few blocks from the Harts, and enjoyed
writing plays and epic poetry, often of an erotic nature, in Russian and Yiddish.
He considered himself a master chess player, but only because nobody else in
the group played. (For Larry, chess required a sustained concentration he could
rarely summon.) Robbins would sit in the center of the room and, arranging
a dim light on his face, declaim his latest work.[19] He would go on to become
head of translation for the *Jewish Daily Forward*, a tireless producer-director of
Jewish theater in New York and New Jersey, and the translator of *My Life in
Art*, the autobiography of his old mentor Konstantin Stanislavski.

But then most of these boys were on their way somewhere.

"The Hart house on 119th Street was, compared to the Shauer household,
bohemian and kind of shocking in that era," Mel Shauer recalled. "The rest
of us came from conventional homes of conventional parents. At all hours of
the night the house in Harlem was open to any and all of Larry's and Teddy's
friends. No matter where any of us went for an evening, we'd often wind up
there at one or two in the morning. Nobody had to let us in. The door was
always open and there was always something going on in the living room or
kitchen."[20]

Myers, forewarned by Larry about the ribald character of those late-night
gatherings, participated on his first night there by pulling a recently completed bit of verse from his pocket. "Will you fellows stand for a clean poem?"
he asked the others. Prompted by Larry, Myers began to read several bawdy
stanzas, made all the more hilarious because he'd composed them in the style
of a classical pastoral. Soon the others were screaming with laughter. "Stop!
Stop!" pleaded Milton Winn, pounding the table. "This is the filthiest thing
I ever heard!" By the time he came to the end of his poem, Myers knew he'd
been accepted.[21]

College-age men often have the stamina to talk and drink well into the morning. One night Max Hart, wearing a nightshirt that emphasized his girth, came roaring down the stairs to curse out the young men for the noise they were making. One of them had the presence of mind to say they'd been talking about show business, which softened Max immediately. He seated himself at the table, informed everyone present that his son Lorenz knew everything there was to know about the theater, poured himself a glass of beer, and said, "Gentlemen, I ask you all to join me in a toast to Lorenz's mother." Then he excused himself, reminding the boys that some people had to get up in the morning to go to work.[22]

"Larry loved it all," Mel Shauer said. "He loved having people around him. Loved to see them eat and drink. Everybody was welcome at all times. His father would give him a hundred-dollar bill. Larry would gather a group and we'd all go out on the town. Nobody else was allowed to pick up a check— not that any of us had any real money to spend."[23] The families of those boys considered the Hart household eccentric, perhaps also a bad influence. But the open-house policy was generous rather than sinister. It was natural for young men to want to gather there.

Columbia Journalism was only a year old when Larry entered with the class of 1918. The school, funded in large part by a bequest from Joseph Pulitzer, was founded on the principle that the newspaper profession was a scholarly one. Talcott Williams, who had been editor of *The Philadelphia Press*, was named Journalism's first director.

There's no evidence that Larry ever wanted to be a journalist per se. He did want to write, however, and the infant School of Journalism enabled him to write for most of his classes and avail himself of the most renowned courses and teachers at Columbia: the philosopher John Dewey; Charles Beard and his course in American politics; James Harvey Robinson and his History of the Intellectual Class in Europe; and Walter Pitkin's The Psychology of News Interest.[24] Some college campuses lend themselves to leisurely study; this one, with a student body more localized than those of other Ivy League schools, was never one of them.

"You don't saunter at Columbia," the critic James Huneker wrote a few months after Larry Hart matriculated; "there is too much intellectual ozone in the air, even on hot days."[25]

But Larry also wanted to be part of the theater, whether as actor, producer, director, or playwright. At the time, the American theater suffered from an inferiority complex. Ibsen was recognized as the single greatest influence on the drama of the era. Hungarian dramaturgy, also derived from Ibsen but emphasizing a kind of comic naturalism, was beginning to dominate contemporary drama. Ferenc Molnár was already on his way to international fame. The Irish playwrights Shaw, Synge, Wilde, and Lady Gregory had made their mark. In England, John Galsworthy and Arthur Wing Pinero were hitting their stride. America had William Vaughn Moody, Augustus Thomas, and Percy Mackaye—none of them in the same league as the Europeans. Even the absurdly prolific Clyde Fitch, who made his name writing to order for the actor Richard Mansfield and died young in 1909, larded his plays with expository dialogue. During the 1914–15 academic year, Eugene O'Neill had not yet arrived in New York but was studying playwriting in George Pierce Baker's 47 Workshop at Harvard. (The number stood for the class catalogue number: English 47.) When Augustus Thomas came to Baker's class as a guest lecturer, he suggested that playwrights tailor their plays to a star—a practice that O'Neill found abhorrent. Thomas had a formula, precisely the thing that O'Neill was determined to discard.[26]

Finding both American contemporary drama and American musical theater emotionally flat and theatrically timid, Larry turned to more eccentric entertainments. He and his pals were delighted by an ongoing program at the Princess Theatre, produced by and starring actor Holbrook Blinn, in which risqué comedies alternated with macabre one-acts known as Weirdies. Blinn was hoping to establish a kind of American Grand Guignol. At first these one-acts seemed easy to produce because they were so brief, but once Larry and his friends analyzed the structure of the Weirdies, that equation broke down.[27]

Larry was also excited by the February 1914 arrival in New York of William Butler Yeats. In New York, Yeats stayed at the Algonquin Hotel and met the press. Over the next several weeks he lectured in Chicago and Canada, his lyrical power not only undiminished in middle age but gathering force. His poems were brimming with music. The music is what Larry, who heard him speak in New York, found missing from contemporary American theater.

New York, in fact, was *starved* for good theater. In spring 1914, J. J. and Lee Shubert, the most successful theatrical impresarios of the period, retained the Harts' old friend Gustave Amberg to scour Europe for plays that could be translated and produced by them. Amberg's scouting proved frustrating. Copyrights were a frequent problem, and the Shuberts rarely advanced him enough money to lock up the rights to European plays he found desirable.[28]

Although there wasn't much the Shuberts successfully imported in 1914, they were not deterred; their dominance of theater in America had hardly begun. It was the year *The New York Times* brought the rotogravure process from Germany, a development closely examined at Columbia's School of Journalism. In the coming years newspapers would gradually adorn their columns with reproduced photographs, often replacing the old Yellow Journalism with a new kind of sensationalism.

Max Hart's tribulations were sensational even without the rotogravure. He kept more or less permanent headquarters at 51 Chambers Street while maintaining a business, M. M. Hart, Inc., with offices at 115 Nassau Street and 280 Broadway. Nobody could ever figure out what kind of work M. M. Hart, Inc., actually did. In the early weeks of 1914 checks drawn on the account of the Oneida Milling Company at the First National Bank of Bayonne were issued to M. M. Hart, Inc., and to the J. C. Jaffe Company. The payments were the hard evidence of Max Hart's defrauding of Oneida, which had been a legitimate, well-respected company. "J. C. Jaffe" turned out to be Max's former stenographer Jeanette C. Jaffe. The embezzlement ruined Oneida and closed the First National Bank of Bayonne. Max was convicted in federal court in Watertown, New York, of fraudulent use of the mails and sentenced to five years in prison. Once again, however, he won on appeal.[29]

His older son was getting a hell of an education: in the morning, another analysis of *All's Well That Ends Well*; in the afternoon, another indictment of the O. M.

And then the semester was over. On July 28, Archduke Franz Ferdinand, heir to the Austrian throne, was assassinated in Sarajevo. War began in Europe. Eventually it would ensnare America and change just about everything, including American theater and song.

CHAPTER 3

The Rhyme Is Hard to Find, My Dears

D URING THE summer when war broke out across the Atlantic, Larry stayed in the city. He must have figured that now that he was a college man, his camp days were over. At Larry's old outpost in the Catskills, twelve-year-old Richard Rodgers, who grew up barely two blocks from Larry but had never met him, was expanding his musical education by taking piano lessons from Stella Weingart. This was the summer when Rodgers began to compose. He had been able to reproduce melodies on the piano since he was a tot, encouraged by his mother—"the best sight-reader I ever knew," he said of her—and he began to get a sense of harmony when he was six or so. But formal lessons didn't take. Until this hardheaded child permitted Stella Weingart to show him a thing or two, the closest he came to accepting musical instruction was after the family would come home from a Broadway show, bearing, in the tradition of the time, the score of the show in book form, which his mother would proceed to play on the Steinway.

Dick's mother, Mamie, was born a Levy in New York; his father, William, born an Abrams in Missouri. Will Abrams (a shortened version of Abraham) was rejected by a medical school because, he believed, he had a distinctly Jewish name, so in 1892 he legally changed it to Rodgers, an Anglicized version of the family's original name, Rogozinsky.[1] Will Rodgers became a general practitioner with a specialty in obstetrics; he maintained his medical office on the ground floor of the family's house, which stood at the corner of 120th Street and Mt. Morris Park Way. The large household included Mamie's parents, an unmarried great-uncle, and Dick's older brother, Mort. In fact, the house was owned by the Levys, and the three generations that were jammed in it together—not to save money but to placate the Levys, who had not wanted to see their daughter move away—created a much cooler atmosphere than that in the Harts' household. The relatively rural neighborhood was white, middle class, neither German nor overwhelmingly Jewish, with each house facing the small, lovely park.[2] During the war in Europe, the Rodgers family would finally move out of Harlem to the Upper West Side.[3] It was remarkable, though, that Dick Rodgers had not met Larry Hart while the two families were living in the same neighborhood, not least because Mort Rodgers knew some of the people Larry knew.

By any measure, Larry knew a lot of people. The gang continued to convene at 119th Street. Now it included new friends from Columbia Journalism as well as Columbia Grammar, Camp Paradox as well as Weingart. Among the new friends was Milton Bender, a Baltimore native who had moved with his family to 111th Street. (In *Lorenz Hart: A Poet on Broadway*, Frederick Nolan suggests that Bender didn't meet Hart until later, in the Adirondacks. Bender's *Herald Tribune* and *Variety* obituaries said they met when Hart was Bender's dental patient in the late 1920s. But Hart pal Henry Myers remembered Bender being on the scene much earlier.) A year older than Larry, Bender was at Columbia College and, like so many in the gang, was interested in the theater. He was lanky, nearsighted, already showing signs of baldness, and didn't hide his sexual preference for men. Perhaps encouraged by his father to "have something to fall back on," Bender would enter the New York College of Dentistry and eventually become a practicing dentist, earning the sobriquet "Doc" for the rest of his life.[4] In the meantime he played piano and promoted the operatic gifts of his older brother, Charles, a tenor who aspired to sing at the Met. Something about Bender did not invite affection, but Larry liked having him around. When it came to music and theater, Bender had great taste.

Max Hart still spread the word that his older son knew more about theater than anyone, that he wrote marvelous stories and poems. Max heard that David Segal, an attorney and fellow tenant at 51 Chambers Street, was acquainted with the pint-size young entertainer Georgie Price. Years earlier, Price had been part of *Gus Edwards' Song Revue*, along with George Jessel and Walter Winchell (a boy hoofer before he became the most widely read and feared columnist in New York), and was now doing his own shows for the Shuberts. Max pressed comedy material by his son on Segal to pass on to Price, who read it, then wrote Larry a check for $150 and ordered more.[5]

Max's old friend Gustave Amberg continued to roam Western Europe as a theatrical scout. Into the first few months of 1915, however, the war was making it ever more difficult to option anything with the hope of bringing it to New York. Communications with the brothers Shubert had to go through Denmark; by the time a letter arrived, whether in Europe or New York, the business at hand was moot. On March 15, 1915, J. J. Shubert wrote to Amberg, "There is a great scarcity of plays in America at the present time now that we do not receive anything from Paris or London, and we don't hear from Berlin or Vienna, which makes it all the harder."[6] Amberg had been delighted to be home in Europe, but the war was infecting everything, even the theater, and he returned to New York discouraged.

Increasingly, New York was coming to seem a political and cultural island as well as a geographic one. On August 16, 1915, a Georgia lynch mob seized the pencil factory superintendent Leo Frank, who was awaiting execution for a murder he almost surely did not commit, and hanged him. From the point of view of many New Yorkers reading the news accounts, Frank had been murdered by the mob because he was a Brooklyn Jew working in the Deep South. The lynching blasted open a long-closed door between American blacks and Jews, who had been living in close proximity in several New York neighborhoods, and nowhere more closely than in the uptown area that took in central and lower Harlem, where the Harts lived, just when the great Negro migration from the South to the North was cresting. On November 19, Industrial Workers of the World organizer Joe Hill was executed by firing squad, politicizing hundreds of thousands of American workers, many of them singing IWW songs like "Hallelujah, I'm a Bum" ("Why don't you work like other folks do? / How the hell can I work when there's no work to do?").

Popular song had hardly turned radical, though. Hits from the previous year, still heard on pianos and ukuleles throughout the city, included "By the Beautiful Sea," "There's a Long, Long Trail," and W. C. Handy's "St. Louis Blues." The lyricist Howard Johnson collaborated on two 1915 songs that quickly became standards: "M-O-T-H-E-R, a Word that Means the World to Me" (music by Theodore Morse) and "There's a Broken Heart for Every Light on Broadway" (music by Fred Fisher). "The Colonel Bogey March," imported from England, took its title from the golf course where its composer conceived the melody as a march. (The song would become popular later as the theme of *The Bridge on the River Kwai*). The war gave rise to military-inflected lyrics. "Pack Up Your Troubles in Your Old Kit Bag" and "I Didn't Raise My Boy to Be a Soldier" were sung all over New York, even though America had not yet entered the war.

Larry was still pursuing, or pretending to pursue, a degree. He banked his greatest enthusiasm for the theater, and for drink. When Larry wasn't drinking at home in the cellar, sharing Max's expensive pinch-bottle spirits with his friends, he was out drinking with them. He and Morrie Ryskind, who by then had become editor of Columbia's humor magazine *Jester*, drank at the Lion Saloon, at Broadway and 110th Street.[7] Descended from Russian Jews, Ryskind grew up on 145th Street in Washington Heights in what was still considered, half a century after the Civil War, "out in the country." Like Larry, Ryskind was enamored of Gilbert and Sullivan and was an even more ardent New York Giants fan. He was vociferously left-wing in the years before he moved far to the right, and, despite his round face and wire-rimmed glasses, intimidating. (The *Columbia Spectator* referred to him as "the well-known apostle of bitterness.") Ryskind was soon expelled from Columbia Journalism after publishing a scathing *Jester* editorial attacking President Nicholas Murray Butler and Journalism director Talcott Williams for failing to support the right of Count Ilya Tolstoy, son of the great Russian novelist, to speak at the Cosmopolitan Club.[8]

As a student, Ryskind was ardently political. Herman Mankiewicz, another drinking pal of Larry's, thumbed his nose at campus politics and other students' earnest literary efforts. When Ryskind and Max Schuster (later cofounder of Simon & Schuster) helped start a campus magazine called *Challenge*, Mankiewicz parodied it with a journal called *Dynamite*.[9] If Larry was delighted by the more ribald classics, Mankiewicz went him one better, running a lending library of erotica: *Fanny Hill* for a buck an hour, a mere four bits for *Josephine Mutzenbacher*.[10] Known on Morningside Heights as Mank the Tank, Mankiewicz was as devoted to booze as Larry was, but probably possessed double Larry's weight and tolerance. Some nights when the boys failed to report home at a reasonable hour, Max Hart would telephone Mankiewicz's father, Franz, and the two men would search together for their errant sons.[11]

Mank (class of '16) and his friend Ray Perkins ('17), said to be the "most red-headed man" at Columbia, wrote a musical show for the 1916 Varsity Show competition. Apart from athletics, the Varsity Show was the most anticipated university event of the year, the chosen production said to be the best of the shows—all of them written by men who were matriculating at Columbia or had done so in the past—submitted each winter for consideration. In March 1916, the Mankiewicz-Perkins show, *Peace Pirates*, was selected over eighteen other candidates and became the first politically tinged Varsity Show presented at Columbia. The previous year's Varsity Show, *On Your Way*, had been cobbled together by Herman Axelrod ('15), who had been a couple of years ahead of Larry at Columbia Grammar, with some additional material by Oscar Hammerstein II. Hammerstein took a role in *Peace Pirates* as "Washington Snow the Darkey," in blackface. Larry played "Mrs. Rockyford," a Mary Pickford parody and surely a variation on a skit he'd contributed to *On Your Way*.[12] The loose "plot" of *Peace Pirates* involved the Rockyfords and their party as refugees on Captain Kidd's island—*Gilligan's Island* with an antiwar message. *Peace Pirates* gave Ray Perkins an opportunity to play his own music onstage, and for Larry to do some outrageous celebrity impressions—not just Pickford, America's Sweetheart, but actor George Monroe, Ethel Barrymore, and vaudevillian Louis Mann. The *Columbia Spectator* critic reported, "We had sixteen nightmares after seeing Larry Hart as that golden haired western dream, Chick a boom, Chick a boom, the pirates are coming the injuns are running—Larry's a nut, he's a nut."[13] *Peace Pirates* was sold out for a solid week at the Hotel Astor. It was Larry's headiest experience yet in making an audience laugh and beg for more.

At twenty-one Larry was increasingly preoccupied by the idea of making new theater. He could write clever, topical verse, and he could tailor lyrics, in German as well as in English, to just about any musical setting. With this in mind, he became reacquainted with his parents' old friend Amberg, who had returned to New York to run his own company, United Plays, which bought theatrical properties and had what amounted to a first-look deal with the Shuberts. When German producer Samuel Rachmann was looking for someone to translate the lyrics of a show called *Die Tolle Dolly* into English, Amberg had just the boy for the job. *Die Tolle Dolly*, translated alternately as *Crazy Dolly* and *Madcap Dolly*, with the German star Mizi Gizi in the title role, opened in October 1916 at the Yorkville Theatre at Eighty-Sixth Street between Lexington and Third Avenues. The song that everyone made much of was "Meyer, Your Tights Are Tight." This could have been a sly reference to Max Meyer Hart, but in any case Larry's translated lyric fit the character—a wealthy, stout gentleman who's falsely arrested for train robbery, in part because his trousers, like those of the real robber, are too small.[14] After *Die Tolle*

Dolly, Larry would translate for Amberg's United Plays for the very respectable salary of fifty dollars a week.

On April 6, 1917, the United States, having edged for months toward participation in the Great War, finally declared war on Germany. The Selective Service Act was passed on May 18. Previously, Larry had identified himself as a pacifist, and he might have also winced at his native country going to war with his parents' native country. In June 1917, a few weeks after he turned twenty-two, his draft registration card listed him as "Playright" [*sic*] and his height as "SHORT." The draft was on his mind when he went to camp for the first time as a counselor.

A year earlier, three physical education teachers from New York—Bob Gerstenzang, Jack Molloy, and "Unc" Joe Eberly—each of whom had been a counselor at Paradox, had purchased a farm near Chestertown, also in the Adirondacks but an hour or so closer to the city, and founded their own camp on Brant Lake, almost equidistant from Lake George to the east and Schroon Lake to the west. With Brant Lake Camp ready to open, Larry was invited to be its dramatics counselor and serve as adviser to the camp newspaper.

His old Paradox friends Mel Shauer and Eugene Zukor also joined the Brant Lake staff. Mel and Gene would be linked, personally and professionally, for decades. In 1903, when Gene's father, Adolph, was leaving the fur business to devote himself to his popular new penny arcades, he hired Mel's father, Emil, a buyer for Mandel Brothers in Chicago, to manage the arcades there. After his unprecedented success in 1912 distributing the Sarah Bernhardt film *Queen Elizabeth*, with producer Daniel Frohman, Adolph oversaw a burgeoning movie empire at Paramount Pictures. Emil Shauer soon joined the studio in an executive capacity and, after a divorce from his first wife, would marry Julie Kaufman, sister of Lotte Kaufman Zukor.[15] For several years the back-page ad in *Bee Ell See*, the Brant Lake Camp yearbook, was underwritten by Paramount Pictures, "Controlled by Famous Players Lasky Corporation," whose president was Zukor.

The trip to Brant Lake was another night boat ride up the Hudson. At Albany the campers and chaperoning counselors caught the train to Riverside, where the boys were picked up in a caravan of cars organized by the camp's travel director, Manny Litt [Littauer], which took them the rest of the way to the camp. Brant Lake Camp was smaller than Paradox. The lake was stocked with pickerel, perch, and bass. Campers enjoyed the loosely structured freedom of long evenings, water and land sports, and minimal clothing.

Counselors, though, were anxious about going to war—most of them had registered for the draft, as Larry had—especially since the reasons for America's entering the war were not always clear to them.

If Larry wrote a lyric for the camp that summer of 1917, there is no record of it. When he returned to New York at the end of summer, he spent more time translating for United Plays than attending class. For all intents and purposes, he had dropped out of Columbia Journalism.

An operetta called *Hello Central*, registered for copyright in 1917 by Lorenz M. Hart, could be said to have been partly original. There was already a libretto, credited to Franz Arnold and Georg Okonkowki, with music by the German popular composer Jean Gilbert (né Max Winterfeld). There is no evidence that Larry ever met Gilbert; the adaptation was an assignment from United Plays, with Larry writing lyrics that were more original than adaptive. Through Gustave Amberg, the Shuberts got a look at Larry's version. *Hello Central*—the title would have been immediately familiar to anyone who used a telephone at the time—is about the complications involving secret newlyweds Robert, a handsome young sculptor, and Marie, a former telephone operator. One song, about the end of bachelorhood ("Bid Farewell to Midnight Maidens"), is interspersed with the lovers singing of their mutual devotion ("Deep in your eyes, love I surmise"), barely able to wait till midnight to consummate their marriage. Robert's uncle Felix, unaware that Robert has married, wants him to marry Elsie, whose father is Felix's business partner. Robert humors his uncle. "Has she a figure?" he asks Felix. "Three million, my boy—maybe four," replies Felix, and it becomes apparent why he wants this match to go through. By the end of act 1, Marie has gotten wind of Felix's scheme and, playing along, pretends she's married to another man, Billy. Singing to Felix about how she met Billy, she makes up a story about a spirited call she took from him while she was working:

> *So one day he shouted so mightily,*
> *That I almost fainted—and I*
> *Told him that at Central we're ladies,*
> *And told him where he'd go when he'd die,*
> *And then he said without regret,*
> *"You little Aquab—I'll get you yet.*
> *I'll be at the Ritz at a quarter to eight,*

I'll wear a gardenia, and I shall not be late.
You darling—do not be unforgiving—
To-night's the night, the two of us start living."

In act 2 of *Hello Central*, Robert, late coming home to Marie, explains that Felix dragged him and the other young men all over town for a floating stag party. Marie's mother, Betty, shows up and is furious at this marital ruse. Another complication is introduced when Felix comes to believe that Marie is really the daughter of his beloved Agatha Blueblossom, of Yonkers, whom he's never actually met but has fallen in love with through her poetry. Felix loves Agatha, he tells the others, "like the White Rock people love Billy Sunday, like the lawyers love [Harry] Thaw, like Douglas Fairbanks loves the side of a house." At the end of act 2, Betty takes daughter Marie away, leaving Robert bereft.

Act 3 makes everything all right again. Poetess Agatha Blueblossom turns out to be Aloysius Seller, a tall blond man wearing tortoiseshell glasses, using a female nom de plume. Felix realizes that, much as he adores his poetry and letters, he can't marry a man. Billy and Elsie, after pretending to be paired off with the principals, now have eyes for each other. And Robert and Marie are reunited.[16]

This was Larry Hart at twenty-two, putting his characteristically nutty stamp on a musical show that was presented to him for an adaptation in English. Many songs are marked "to be written"; of the lyrics Larry completed, one faintly resembles "Dancing on the Ceiling," which Rodgers and Hart would not complete for another thirteen years. Several lyrics combine, in Larry's characteristic fashion, classical and biblical allusions with current popular references. In one lyric, Vernon and Irene Castle whirl their way out of the Garden of Eden.

The Shuberts passed on producing *Hello Central*. Larry was paid by Amberg for the adaptation as part of his weekly wage.

Although Larry no longer registered for classes, he was still on campus most days. Columbia had become a lightning rod of opinion about the war. At the beginning of October 1917, James McKeen Cattell of the psychology department and Henry W. L. Dana of English and Comparative Literature were fired for speaking out against America's participation in the war. Charles Beard, one of the more popular professors at Columbia, resigned in sympathy. Campus agitation was threatening to cancel the year's Varsity

Show.[17] While everybody was arguing about the conduct of the war, Larry received word from his draft board that he was being rejected for military service on account of his height. So it was official: Lorenz Hart was too small to serve his country. As science writer Stephen Hall has suggested, "cultural fascination with extremes of physical size" trespasses on human dignity.[18] Somehow—by channeling all his energies into the theater?—Larry kept his dignity. The cost of his brave face, though, would emerge over the next twenty-five years in dozens of lyrics that were less about being small than about what it's like to *feel* small—to be dismissed, excluded, denied admission, and left standing out in the cold.

Then again, everybody was cold that winter. By January 1, 1918, twelve New Yorkers had died of weather-related causes. Tugboats on the Hudson were locked in; for more than a week there was no ferry service between New York and New Jersey. Larry had often taken the eight-minute ferry ride from 125th Street to Fort Lee, where the bars were far from the vigilant eyes of his parents and his more puritanical friends, but his New Jersey escapes ceased that winter.

So did Fort Lee's moviemaking industry—at the time the largest in the world. From 1910, when the Champion studio opened for business—the studio was the location for *The Perils of Pauline*, with Pearl White famously hanging from the side of a cliff—to that brutal winter of 1918, Fort Lee thrived on moviemaking, and moviemaking thrived in Fort Lee. For moviemakers Fort Lee had been an incomparably versatile location, with woods, farms, streets, and the Palisades. But the arctic impounding of New York combined with an influenza epidemic to close the Fort Lee studios and send many of the moviemakers to Southern California.[19] A few studio owners, like Lewis J. Selznick, resumed Fort Lee operations that spring. But the movies had migrated to Hollywood more or less permanently, leaving only the jetsam of the industry in New Jersey.

The winter didn't cripple all activity. In New York, there was still theater—if you could get to it—including new musical theater. Since 1912 Jerome Kern had been composing complete musicals, and since 1915 he had been collaborating with the English librettist Guy Bolton. Their first show together, *Nobody Home*, opened at the Princess Theatre, the theater district's precious jewel box (it seated fewer than three hundred), as would most of the subsequent Kern-Bolton musicals. In February 1917 the English lyricist P. G. Wodehouse joined them on *Oh, Boy!* At the time the very mention of a Princess show implied high musical ambition. The shows "were intimate and uncluttered," Richard Rodgers wrote, "and tried to deal in a humorous way with modern, everyday characters. They were certainly different—and far more appealing to me—from the overblown operettas, mostly imported, that dominated the Broadway scene in the wake of *The Merry Widow* and *The Chocolate Soldier*."[20] Seeing the Princess shows as an adolescent, Rodgers recognized them as a native form of musical theater. So did Larry Hart, who wore out one phonograph needle after another listening to the Victor Light Opera Company recordings of many of the shows' songs.

The Kern-Bolton-Wodehouse show in the spring of 1918 was *Oh, Lady! Lady!* The show was not as beloved as earlier Princess shows—certainly not the way its predecessor, *Leave It to Jane*, had been beloved. But the show's cast included a twenty-one-year-old Philadelphia girl named Vivienne Segal, whose importance to Larry Hart would grow over the next twenty-five years. Columbia Journalism student Bennett Cerf, known around campus as "Beans," gushed in *The Jester*: "You'll hear a rustle offstage. Miss Vivienne Segal enters—smiles at the audience—and—Oh Lady! Lady!"[21]

There was also something called the 1918 Campus War Show, *Ten for Five*, "A Musical Farce in Two Acts," by Oscar Hammerstein II. Hammerstein was twenty-three, just a few weeks younger than Larry Hart, pre-law at Columbia but so immersed in the theater—the world of his grandfather, his father, and his uncle—that it was only a matter of time before he too dropped out of school. The music for *Ten for Five* was composed by Robert Lippman, who had earlier encouraged the fourteen-year-old Dick Rodgers to write a song extolling the joys of Camp Wigwam, the Maine boys' camp where Lippman was a counselor and Rodgers a camper.[22] When these young, gifted New York men weren't hailing each other on Morningside Heights, they seemed to be finding each other at summer camps throughout the Northeast.

In the summer of 1918, Larry Hart returned to Brant Lake for a second year. Mel Shauer and Gene Zukor had each gone to war—Mel into the Army, Gene into the Navy. Mel was especially missed because he was a strong swimming instructor and composed music for the camp's Sunday night entertainments.

Those nights now belonged to Larry, who wrote skits for the campers and occasionally adapted longer shows. Bob Gersten, nephew of Brant Lake Camp's founder Bob Gerstenzang, recounts his uncle's recollections: "To put on a show, Larry would take anything he needed from wherever he could find it—the head counselor's office, the infirmary, the kitchen—and never returned anything."[23] About the first production of the summer of 1918, on July 7, the *Bee Ell See* reported, "We had with us our experienced coach, 'Lorry' Hart, and all praise is due to him for the way he 'pulled it through.' If the first show is to be taken as a standard, the shows this year should rank favorably with the amateur performances of the city." For the following Sunday, Larry wrote two sketches: "Deaf and Dumb," about a bootblack who's supposed to play deaf and mute to help catch some kidnappers; and "Fifty-fifty," about a Jewish sausage manufacturer. For the July 21 show, Teddy Hart showed up in camp to appear in a dramatic, O. Henry–like sketch (on Christmas Eve an orphaned messenger boy steals a doll to present to his sister), and Larry did some of his patented singing impressions: Al Jolson; the character actor David Warfield; and the music hall star Jack ("Take Me Out to the Ball Game") Norworth. Did the Brant Lake boys know the voices of these men? If not, Larry imitated them with such gusto that it didn't matter.

On July 28, Larry staged *Leave It to Jane*, the recent Kern-Bolton-Wodehouse musical based on George Ade's *The College Widow*. Camper Milt Breslauer took the leading role of Jane Witherspoon; Teddy Hart was recruited to play Flora Wiggins, "world's champion waitress," and Larry was Stub Talmadge, "manager and little fixer." It was the largest-scale production Larry had ever taken on.

There was more to his summer than Sunday night plays. He played right field for Litt's Durhams, one of the camp's baseball teams, and was considered a great fielder—laterally quick, low to the ground, unafraid of a hard-hit ball. Wednesday nights were Short Story Nights. On the first night, after campers read Balzac and O. Henry, Larry read what he referred to as "an exemption skit" about the war, concluding with a call for patriotism. As faculty adviser to *Bee Ell See*, he didn't bother to sign the verse, "To Eugene Zukor (to the tune of K-K-K Katy)":

Z-Z-Z Zukie, sleepyhead Zukie,
You're the only g-g-g-guy that's on the sea;
When the t-t-t-taps blows into the tent flaps
We'll be thinking of your pop-popularity.

It certainly sounds like Larry. So does this unsigned poem:

I've dined on frankfurters and cream,
On rarebits and pastrami,

But none of these can make me dream
Like Lucy Litt's salami. . . .

A Horicon cigar I've smoked,
And hardtack in the army,
On onion soup I've never choked—
But that was not salami.

The rhyme is hard to find, my dears,
My head is getting balmy,
Or else I'd write for fifty years
My poem about salami.

With a tweak or two, it could be an additional verse to "The Lady Is a Tramp," which wouldn't show up in Larry's catalogue for another nineteen years.

Such prodigious talent! If only Larry, back in New York and translating for United Plays, could put it all to patriotic use. Curiously, he got his chance at Columbia, where the Varsity Show was on wartime hiatus and the campus had turned into a veritable army post. Morningside Heights, dotted with plaques commemorating Revolutionary War battles, was aswarm again with men in uniform. In late October 1918 the *New York Tribune* reported that Columbia was home to at least five distinct military groups. The Army's G Company had taken over the old Speyer School for Nurses, on 128th Street. G Company's commander answered to the marvelously knickerbockerish name of Lt. Cortland Van Winkle. The company was sponsoring an Army-Navy Christmas week revue scheduled for Broadway, tentatively titled *Forward, March!*, "which, it is assured, will knock the spots off *Yip, Yip, Yaphank* and *Biff, Bang!* and the other service shows that have lured New Yorkers from professional performances to S.R.O. houses."[24] Private Herbert Fields was assigned to select and drill the chorus and take the principal male part. Private Philip Leavitt, a DeWitt Clinton graduate who had played the comely "Dorothy Fairface" in *Peace Pirates*, would take the principal female role. Writing the *Forward, March!* libretto was Lorenz Hart, who had no military affiliation.

The *Spectator* published a casting call: "Men who have stunts of any type, dancers, jugglers, magicians, artists, musicians, and the like, as well as candidates for the cast should report today in Earl Hall between 4 and 5 P.M. If this time is not suitable they may report any day at 4 P.M. to Lorenz M. Hart or Private Herbert Fields in Earl Hall."[25] Lieutenant Van Winkle was trying to induce Jerome Kern and Irving Berlin to contribute songs for *Forward, March!* If asked, Larry was ready to write lyrics.

Teddy Hart got word that he, too, was deemed too small for the armed forces. His draft card said that he was employed by Leffler Bratton, a theatrical company that built musicals around popular songs. (John Bratton composed the children's melody "The Teddy Bears' Picnic.") Decades later Teddy would tell his son that Max had fixed things with the draft board so that neither of his boys would be accepted.[26]

On November 11, an armistice was announced. "The terror had gone out of the landscape," George Seldes wrote. "Every tree, every bush, every little rise in the ground, every little gulley, everything in nature had been evil in the days and nights of four years of trench warfare, and now sometimes a brave little bird might come over and perhaps even sing."[27]

It's likely that Larry celebrated by drinking with his friends. It's also likely that a part of him was disappointed. With the end of the war, *Forward, March!* was rendered superfluous. A complete script, if there ever was one, has not survived. But it's probable that *Going Up*, a brief musical that Larry sketched out, with dialogue and at least two sets of lyrics, was written to be part of the Army-Navy show. (The title might have been Larry having fun with the theater term that denotes an actor forgetting his lines or losing his way.)

The *Going Up* characters are known as The Aeronuts: Fifi Lamonte, of the French Aerial Corps, and Dick Hire, "who flies for Uncle Sam." Fifi enters in a French dirigible above the audience—Larry must have been thinking of ways to stage it—singing "Take a Little Breath of Air."

Take a little breath of air,
Dickie birdie, won't you dare?
I'll fly high.
My limit is the sky.
If your heart is young and strong,
You can take your heart along.
Kisses are the only fare.
Take a little breath of air.

The dialogue includes a few wince-inducing jokes about Fifi's French accent, a pun involving Pershing and *perishing* ("that's what the Kaiser will be doing"), and a swipe at High Society. Then comes Larry's lyric for "A Subway Bungalow (Somewhere in France)," the one part of *Going Up* that links the boy playwright to the witty, mature lyricist:

> *When the spring lambs start their bleating, and the skeeters start their skeeting,*
> *And the summer sun's some summer sun, you bet.*
> *When the Reverend Billy Sunday makes each day seem like blue Monday*
> *Then you put your little city-flat to let.*
> *Every lounging-lizard bummer says that summer is a hummer*
> *And the Levys leave for Arverne by the sea.*
> *How'd you like a small vacation with the transport population*
> *In the trenches on the firing line with me?*

And:

> *When you wake up in the morning and you find the day is dawning*
> *At the time you used to think of going to bed,*
> *You find Jakie Cohen is dreaming of gefilte fish a-steaming*
> *And his mouth is filled with mud-pudding instead.*
> *Jones and Smith are traitorous weasels*
> *For they've got the German measles,*
> *And they look at pretty nurses with a grin.*
> *I think Clifton Crawford oughter run around and carry water,*
> *It's the best place to revive his Gunga Din.*

With references to Broadway and the subway, the lyric is suffused with longing to be home in New York. *Going Up* ends when the Franco-American lovers climb into Dick's plane, which drops bombs that "burst in mid air, scattering tiny American and French flags, with which they were filled."[28]

There is no record of *Going Up* ever having been produced. The Army-Navy show was canceled. Herb Fields was released from the Corps and was rolling up his sleeves to go to work in his father's business, show business. Larry's old friend Irving Strouse, who was to have stage-managed *Forward, March!*, was trying to obtain a discharge from the Navy.[29]

But now a victory celebration, sponsored by G Company, was in order. Three weeks after the armistice, a variety show was produced at the Columbia gym. There was no music by Kern and Berlin, and stars like Al Jolson and Belle Baker—the two greatest song pluggers of the era, in fact—begged off from appearing. Besides Army and Navy performers, the show boasted theatrical stars Clifton Crawford, Emily Stevens, and Jean Southern—all of them active on Broadway during the war. The hit of the evening, however, was Larry imitating Jolson and doing his version of a George M. Cohan production, its irony-free Americanism rendered without derision. Larry had his public patriotic moment after all.[30]

With the war over, it seemed as if everyone was passing grandly through Manhattan. "New York had all the iridescence of the beginning of the world," F. Scott Fitzgerald wrote about the winter of 1918–19. "The returning troops marched up Fifth Avenue and girls were instinctively drawn East and North toward them—this was the greatest nation and there was gala in the air." Edna Ferber described New York that winter as "a dazzling kaleidoscopic world center. Just to walk on the street—practically any street—was an emotional experience. Fifth Avenue had a look of perpetual carnival with the flags of all the Allies flying brilliant in the winter sunshine."[31]

The pageantry drew the wealthiest Americans—Society, if you will—to town. On one sleeting February night in 1919, the columnist Maury Paul, who wrote under the name Cholly Knickerbocker, was at his usual station in the downstairs dining room of the Ritz-Carlton when he noticed some mingling without precedent: Newport socialites were talking with people from Tuxedo Park; Southampton residents deigned, for the first time in the reporter's experience, to hold a conversation with New Jersey plutocrats. Despite the ferocious weather, Society wasn't staying home, Paul marveled; Society was *going out*. In his column the next morning Paul coined the term "Café Society."[32] Years later, the phrase was picked up by *Herald Tribune* nightlife columnist Lucius Beebe, who thereafter employed it almost daily.

Larry Hart never had much use for Café Society, High Society, or the so-called Four Hundred, except as a dartboard, its members largely figures of fun. But the teenage Dick Rodgers was fascinated by that world, which remained exclusive, open only to the wealthiest Americans of the "highest" (i.e., invariably Caucasian, usually with English derivation) pedigree, although a pass was occasionally given to those who combined talent and style. Rodgers knew he had the talent but was still, like most adolescents, searching for his style.

Near the end of that winter Rodgers, not yet seventeen, contributed sixteen numbers to *Up Stage and Down*, an amateur show, presented by the Infants Relief Society, at the Waldorf-Astoria's Grand Ballroom. The sixteen numbers comprised Rodgers's first published songs, including "Love Me by Parcel Post," with the lyric by his brother, Mort. Three other sets of lyrics were by that ubiquitous man of the theater Oscar Hammerstein II, and another lyric or two were by Benjamin Kaye, an attorney who was a patient of Dr. Rodgers.[33] By the time *Up Stage and Down* was staged for its one performance, Dick Rodgers was an amateur show veteran, having written the melodies for *One Minute, Please*, presented at the Grand Ballroom of the Plaza to benefit *The Sun* Tobacco Fund, near the end of 1917. (The Tobacco Fund sent cigarettes to American troops in Europe.) That earlier show had been a production of the Akron Club, an all-male social-athletic club whose ragtag shows had been using stale vaudeville acts, pirated jokes, and popular songs of the day—until, that is, the members heard Mort Rodgers's younger brother play his own melodies on the piano. There was something thrilling about the Club having an in-house composer, even if he could barely shave. "Here was a composer of songs," Akron member Philip Leavitt recalled. "In order to completely round out an original score it was necessary to find a suitable lyricist."[34] So lyricists were recruited, some almost as good as the poetic Hammerstein, but no single partnership seemed right. To save money on *One Minute, Please*, the Akron Club had Dick Rodgers conduct *and* play piano. He conducted *Up Stage and Down* as well, learning that the reaction of a live audience, positive or negative, was more telling than your friends' or your brother's compliments for the songs you played at home.

Phil Leavitt was Mort Rodgers's age. He had graduated from Columbia with the class of 1917 and, despite his desire to be on the stage, was working in the paint business. One day Leavitt realized that he knew the right lyricist for Dick Rodgers. The Rodgers family now lived on West Eighty-Sixth, between Columbus and Amsterdam Avenues, with Dr. Rodgers still maintaining his medical office on the ground floor of their residence. Leavitt took Dick to 59 West 119th Street to meet Larry Hart, then a college dropout of twenty-three.

The Harts' door was opened probably by their cook, Rosie, who had one bad eye but knew how to make the German food that Max liked, or by their housekeeper Kathryn Queen, an Irish immigrant, the same age as Larry, who lived with them.[35] One of them escorted the visitors inside to meet Larry.

"This was a curious character," Rodgers said of Hart many years later.

His appearance was so incredible that I remember every single detail. The total man was hardly more than five feet tall. He wore frayed carpet slippers, a pair of tuxedo trousers, an undershirt and a nondescript jacket. His hair was unbrushed, and he obviously hadn't had a shave for a couple of days. All he needed was a tin cup and some pencils. But that first look was misleading, for it missed the soft brown eyes, the straight nose, the good mouth, the even teeth and the strong chin. Feature for feature he had a handsome face, but it was set in a head that was a bit too large for his body and gave him a slightly gnome-like appearance.[36]

Larry led Dick and Phil into the parlor. "He was shy," Rodgers remembered, "and I don't believe the ice was broken until a disreputable cat ambled into the room. 'That's Bridget,' said Mr. Hart. 'She's an old fence-walker!' He chortled with glee at the joke and rubbed his hands furiously together, a nervous habit of his. There was a sudden crashing BONG that lifted me out of my chair. Hart told me not to be frightened. It was his mother's clock."[37] Recovering, Dick sat down at the upright and began to play some of his melodies. Larry's ears pricked up like a startled deer's.[38] After that Phil receded into the background, and Dick and Larry talked. That is, Larry talked. "He knew a great deal about lyric writing," Rodgers said years later. "Of course, he was seven years older than I, so this was like talking theater with an old man. . . . He knew a great deal about rhyming, about versification, and I thought he was wonderful. He felt that lyric writers didn't go far enough, that what they were doing was fairly stupid and had no point, didn't have enough wit, they were too cautious, and he felt that the boundaries could be pushed out a good deal."[39]

Hart and Rodgers had each grown up in the environs of Mt. Morris Park. Each man had been taken with the Princess musicals—the Kern-Bolton-Wodehouse shows that they admired but figured they could top. Each had come from secular Jewish households—Rodgers's the more severe, Hart's the more disreputable. Each attended the opera—Rodgers on a regular basis, Hart when he was in the mood. Otherwise they were hardly alike. Rodgers, an indifferent student, had recently transferred from Townsend Harris Hall to the less demanding DeWitt Clinton High School. Hart, though failing to earn a degree from Columbia (as Rodgers would also fail to do), was one of the best-educated young men in New York, with an encyclopedic knowledge of literature and fluency in at least four languages. (He knew French as well as German and Yiddish.) Rodgers was heterosexual, already "seeing" (Rodgers's word) girls he found attractive, and very handsome. Hart's sexuality was still a puzzlement to many of his friends, though he had once confided to Henry Myers that he had a crush on a Columbia extension class-mate named Miss Langevin. And despite the "handsome face" that Rodgers generously described, Hart was all too often referred to as a troll, a dwarf who, like the recently deceased Toulouse-Lautrec, spent too much time with his mother and drank in excess. "My favorite blight and partner," was how Rodgers would refer to Hart much later, when their professional relation-ship had turned 180 degrees and the younger man had become the dominant partner. If Hart fell in love with Rodgers that spring day in 1919, he did not express it directly. Instead he and the younger composer worked out an in-formal schedule—meeting today at 119th Street, tomorrow at Eighty-Sixth Street—rolled up their sleeves, and went to work.

CHAPTER 4

I'll Go to Hell for Ya

WITH THE Great War over, the 1919 Varsity Show at Columbia was back on again, though in a dialed-down production. This was *Take a Chance*, with music by Roy Webb (class of 1910) and lyrics by his older brother Kenneth. *Take a Chance* played at the Plaza for five performances, from April 28 through May 3, rather than the customary three. Most of the songs were about the end of the war as it was experienced on Morningside Heights. Asked to supply something along the lines of a lullaby, Larry Hart contributed the only non-Webb lyric, "Sandman." ("On twilight's wings / The cricket sings—/ The Sandman's coming / With shades of night.")[1]

The last production Larry directed before returning to Brant Lake for the third summer was a benefit for the Soldiers and Sailors Welfare Fund. As if to reaffirm his commitment to Dick Rodgers, Larry restaged *Up Stage and Down*, which was presented this time as *Twinkling Eyes* (the title of one of Rodgers's songs) at the Forty-fourth Street Theatre on May 18, under the auspices of the Brooklyn YMHA.

Larry and Dick could get work done in either household, for each included a piano where Dick could compose. Larry just needed pencil, paper (he preferred yellow foolscap), ashtray, and, of course, the promise of liquor if not necessarily the liquor itself. After hearing something he liked, Larry would make a lead sheet, comprising the skeletal melody and rhythm, so he could work on a lyric away from the piano. They started late in the morning and usually worked till 5 or 6 P.M., when Larry could take his first drink. But sometimes he couldn't wait, helping himself to his father's liquor or surreptitiously pouring something at Dick's house to tide him over. "I don't remember where he got what he did have to drink," Rodgers recalled about one afternoon when Larry began drinking in the middle of their work session, "but he left and my mother said to me, 'That boy won't be alive five years from now.'"[2]

Phil Leavitt, having introduced Rodgers to Hart, was now eager to promote this fertile new partnership. For the summer his family rented a cottage on Franklin Street in Far Rockaway, where the Lew Fields family was also spending the summer. Leavitt already knew Herb Fields and also had a thing for Herb's younger sister, Dorothy.[3] Lew Fields, whose vaudeville partnership with Joe Weber had dissolved without acrimony, had recently opened at the Shubert Theatre in a musical called *A Lonely Romeo*.

Twenty years earlier, before Larry Hart had begun school, Joe Weber and Lew Fields had been at the peak of their stardom. Both partners were sons of Polish immigrants, both born on the Bowery in 1867. (Lew Fields was born Moses Schoenfeld.) In 1884, shooting pool in a hall adjacent to Miner's Bowery Theatre, at Broome and Delancey Streets, they were spotted by the Miner's stage manager, who asked them if they wanted to go to work for the Ada Richmond Burlesque Company. In a matter of weeks Weber and Fields had developed what came to be called their Dutch knockabout act— *Dutch* a corruption of *deutsch* (i.e., the German-Jewish immigrant accents so prevalent on the Lower East Side), *knockabout* for their mutual, not-always-harmless physicality.[4]

Before they parted for the summer it's probable that Dick and Larry saw *A Lonely Romeo*. Herb Fields had a small role in which he got walloped, one performance after another, by his fifty-two-year-old dad, who could still do handsprings onstage. Heywood Broun probed the heart of Fields's art when he wrote, "One of his assets is his comic sincerity. He never patronizes a scene nor does he ever get out of it into a winking mood. Moreover, in his broadest burlesques he preserves a glint of infinite sadness."[5] *A Lonely Romeo* was considered one of the best entertainments in town, and yet there was little memorable about it besides Lew Fields being Lew Fields.

The state of the theater that late spring and early summer was everything Larry Hart had scoffed at. After the Great War there was a period of retrenchment, even in drama. The horrors of the war, the first in which airplanes became weapons and American corpses were shipped home by the boatload, had been made vivid in newspapers through the recently imported rotogravure process, and through moving pictures. Death on a massive, international scale, even death "over there," had been inescapable as never before. The old ways of play-making now seemed artificial if not downright phony. Even the hugely successful playwright Owen Davis was troubled by such artificiality. "After the war a writer faced a new world," wrote Davis, who was forty-two, portly, and comfortable when America entered the war. "The changes in the form of play writing speak volumes of the change in our own mode of thought and our standards." On the stage, freely spoken asides now sounded laughable; you could no longer get away with long narrative solilo-quies or even the quick expository monologue, e.g., "Poor John, I wonder if he knows I have been untrue to him."[6]

As if recognizing the gulf between what American drama might be and what it was, the judges of the 1918–19 Pulitzer Prize in Drama, for the second time in three years, decided that no play merited the award. The Pulitzer Prize was administered by Columbia University, where the Varsity Show remained the Holy Grail—so much so that alumni like Kenneth Webb (class of '07) were still writing Varsity Shows more than a decade after they'd graduated.

On June 30, 1919, Talcott Williams, director of the School of Journalism since its founding, retired. Larry was still very much a part of campus activi-ties. Just as he hung around Columbia as an older dropout, using the libraries and seeing his friends, so he returned to Brant Lake Camp as an older coun-selor, an alarmingly erudite twenty-four-year-old man who by then had years of experience translating from the German, directing stage shows, and writing original material for anybody who could use it, whether or not he was paid.

"The first thing that encouraged the prediction that this year's entertainments would be well worth seeing was Lorry Hart's decision to be with us again," the Summer 1919 edition of *Bee Ell See* reported. "This able playwright, lyri-cist, actor, and coach was somewhat handicapped by the absence of some of last year's talent. New talent, however, partially offset this misfortune, and the first entertainment of the season was undoubtedly better than the one of 1918." *Bee Ell See* also mentioned the high proportion of Columbia men at the camp. "If George the Third were alive today, he would look with favor upon Brant Lake Camp, for there he would see several followers of Colum-bia College's banner. Even though Nicholas Murray Butler never smiles, he would feel some glow of satisfaction when he glances at the roster of faculty."

Among the Columbia men serving as counselors in 1919 were Milton K. Breslauer, who would later transfer to Princeton and eventually found the Famous Artists School, and Donald Klopfer, who would cofound the Modern Library and Random House with the slightly older Columbia alumnus Bennett Cerf. Morrie Ryskind, invited up to Brant Lake as a guest, still regarded himself as a Columbia man despite having been asked to leave the university. After his visit he sent in a poem, "This Is the Life," about leaving a broiling New York City to take refuge in the Adirondacks. "This Is the Life" anticipates the pine scent of "Hello Muddah, Hello Faddah," the Allan Sherman classic that hit the charts more than forty years later:

The rain had made me shiver, and I had a stomach ache, too,
And Milton Levy sympathized, and threw me in the lake, too,
Then Larry called rehearsals, and he put me in the chorus,
And called me lots of nasty names, and added to my tzoris.

With Mel Shauer still not returning to Brant Lake Camp, Milton Thomashefsky, more popularly known as Mickey Thomas and son of the great Yiddish actors Boris and Bessie Thomashefsky, took possession of the recreation hall's piano. Mickey Thomas and Larry Hart went to work on a "Crazy Musical Comedy" called *B-R-A*, which was staged on Sunday, July 13, 1919. "B-R-A" was a peppy camp song. Larry used the word "boys" as punctuation ("B-R-A for brawn will stand, boys") and rhyme, just as he had often used "dear" or "dears" in his earliest lyrics. "Green and Gray" celebrated the camp's colors, while "He Lights Another Mecca" celebrated camp director Joe Eberly. "Old Brant Lake" was a rhapsody about the camp's sylvan setting. "Our Cheerleader" raised its glass to Brant Lake camper Eddie Gittler. ("A hula dancer has nothing on Eddie / When the team's going smooth / And the pitcher is steady.")

B-R-A was the high point of the summer's entertainment. On July 20 there were two skits, each written by Larry and unfavorably reviewed by *Bee Ell See*. Larry was out of the picture on July 27. "Misfortune overtook us on the eve of our entertainment," *Bee Ell See* reported, "when two hours before the show was scheduled to begin, Lorry Hart was taken sick. The situation was indeed serious, as Lorry had the principal part in a sketch, which as a consequence could not be put on."

It's not clear whether Larry went home to New York or remained at Brant Lake. What is certain is that Dick Rodgers, who harbored his own crush on the adolescent Dorothy Fields, appeared with Leavitt at the Fieldses' summer home in Far Rockaway one sweltering Sunday afternoon in August.[7] Lew Fields, who was still dining out on his notices for *A Lonely Romeo*, had already been primed by Dorothy and Herb about this new team, Rodgers and Hart. He listened politely as Rodgers began his selling audition with "Venus" ("There's no difference between us"), Larry's favorite song of the moment. Fields barely reacted. Most of the songs that followed sounded no more promising to him. But he warmed to "Any Old Place with You," with its vaudeville jocularity. The line frequently quoted from it is "I'll go to hell for ya, / Or Philadelphia," but just as cute are "I'm goin' to corner ya / In California," and "I've got a mania / For Pennsylvania." Fields bought the song and made plans to insert it in *A Lonely Romeo*, to be sung by his young costars Alan Hale and Eve Lynn. Rodgers was pleased and, once he got word to him, Hart was pleased. By the end of the year, "Any Old Place with You" would become the first copyrighted Rodgers & Hart song.[8] As far as its being heard on Broadway, however, there was a small hitch. The American Federation of Labor arrived in town. The Actors' Equity Association, which had been formed in 1913 but come under AFL auspices only that July, began a strike on August 8.

A Lonely Romeo, which had transferred from the Shubert to the Casino, remained open for the time being; Actors' Equity would grant it an exemption from the strike, along with a handful of other productions, for various reasons. But theatergoers with tickets for other shows were usually turned away. The theater district was known to take a nap after curtains rose, its streets drowsing until curtains fell two to three hours later. On August 6, however, when the first unofficial actors' walkout took place, the district snapped awake in mid-evening. Lines of disgruntled theatergoers formed at ticket windows demanding their money back. Cabdrivers rushed back from half-eaten meals. Streets between Broadway and Eighth Avenue were soon packed with pedestrians looking to salvage the evening.[9] Most of the theaters north of Forty-Second Street had gone dark. The fabled Princess Theatre, south of Forty-Second, was scheduled to house the new play *Nightie Night*, and its title was proving all too descriptive.

It was the first actors' strike in the history of the American theater, and the wonder is that it had taken so long. Actors' Equity was fighting not for more money for its members, nor for a completely closed shop, which would have forbidden any nonmember from appearing onstage. Instead it simply wanted to be recognized as the representative entity of stage actors; it wanted to be taken seriously.

Actors had always been hired by producers and had to answer to their every demand. A producer with the power of, say, William A. Brady could call rehearsal after rehearsal without paying a performer, dock a performer's pay for the slightest infraction, and fire a performer on a whim. As a manager-producer, Chamberlain Brown could take a cut of an actor's salary, citing the "personal direction" he provided, then take a percentage of the box office of that actor's show. Brown might have been the most egregious offender of such double-dipping, but there were many others, and it was considered standard business on Broadway.

Pro-strike performers dropped their usual stage demeanor to help organize. Among the most passionate of these was Ed Wynn, the comedian with the "serious sensahuma," who saw nothing funny about exploitative producers. Every Lady of the Chorus had stories of suffering sexual indignities at the hands of a predatory producer. Consequently, the nonprofessional public began to equate chorus girls and loose morals. Old joke about two New York chorus girls who arrive in Boston for a musical comedy tryout:

> First Chorus Girl: "Gosh, we're in Boston! Let's get scrod!"
> Second Chorus Girl: "Okay. But let's have dinner foist." [10]

Marie Dressler, who had already been on the stage for two decades, was elected president of the Chorus Equity Association, the new union formed in support of Actors' Equity. Ethel Barrymore drove in from Mamaroneck to encourage the chorines. [11]

The anti-Equity faction tended to be older and more conservative but no less vociferous. William A. Brady, who prided himself on never backing away from a fight—in fact he also managed prizefighters—kept his own show, *At 9:45*, open by appearing as the butler when the original actor walked out. Brady's ally and friend George M. Cohan emerged as the storm center of the strike. Loathing the idea of actors unionizing, Cohan sensed the times were passing him by—which made him only more defiant. He resigned from the Lambs, where he had held court at least once a week when he was in town, and from the Friars, where he had attained the lofty position of abbot. "I am not going to associate as a fellow club member with actors who give me the raspberry on the street and insult me and my family," Cohan told reporters.

"'Every dollar I have in the world—and I have a few—is on the table in this fight against the actors who are being misled by the Actors' Equity Association.'"[12]

Cohan was the driving force behind the founding, on August 23, of the Actors Fidelity League, organized in direct opposition to Actors' Equity. The Fidelity League regarded Equity as "Bolshevik," unapologetically socialist and therefore wrong for the theater. The prominent actress Minnie Maddern Fiske, more popularly known as Mrs. Fiske, published a defiant defense of the Fidelity League: "Manual labor has found it advantageous to unionize. Acting is not manual labor and the pay of actors cannot be scaled as the pay of manual labor is scaled. Actors, it should be needless to point out, are paid according to individual abilities. Peculiar talent, skill and genius are not susceptible of a uniform wage." Mrs. Fiske stirred the pot. "In certain instances it is possible that chorus girls have suffered great wrongs," she acknowledged. "No one will deny that they should have protection against these wrongs, but it is an unfortunate attempt to effect this reform when it becomes a factor in disrupting an entire profession."[13]

The entire profession *was* disrupted as actors discovered how much power they had if, like workers in various industries and crafts, they organized. In the final tally, the strike halted sixty shows in rehearsal and closed thirty-five theaters.[14]

At the beginning of September a settlement seemed to be at hand. Actors' Equity would be formally recognized, and managers would not discriminate against its members or in favor of Fidelity members. The Equity victory provided a bonus for stage writers, who now had a contract stipulating that a producer could no longer lay claim to a property's film rights and cut out the playwright.[15] (Although they had yet to have a commercial show produced under their own names, this stipulation would become significant to Rodgers and Hart in less than a decade.)

The strike ended on September 6. Brady would bait Actors' Equity for the next few years; Cohan would continue to grouse about Equity for the rest of his career. Performers sympathetic to the Fidelity League claimed they had been harassed by Equity members throughout the strike. Bessie McCoy, the musical comedy beauty and widow of journalist Richard Harding Davis, was appearing in *Greenwich Village Follies* when she reported that she entered her dressing room to find the word *SCAB!* written in soap on her makeup mirror. McCoy told of other threats and humiliations at the hands of Equity members, but the rest of the cast dismissed her account as fiction because

Greenwich Village Follies was, along with a handful of other shows, exempt from the strike, with every cast member encouraged to go onstage without interference of any kind.[16]

During the matinee performance of one of the other exempt shows, *A Lonely Romeo*, on August 26, at the Casino Theatre, Fields allowed Eve Lynn and Alan Hale to sing "Any Old Place with You." "It wasn't much of a splash," Rodgers wrote in his autobiography, *Musical Stages*, "but to Larry and me Niagara Falls never made such a roar as the sound of those nice matinee ladies patting their gloved hands together as the song ended."[17] The song could be heard at the Casino for six weeks, until Fields, citing disappointing box office numbers, decided to close the show.[18]

It would be nice and orderly to say that, after "Any Old Place with You" made it to Broadway, Dick and Larry devoted all their energies to writing songs together. It only seemed that way because they were so productive, turning out completed songs and bits of songs that would be put to use later. Larry was still living at home—if home means living with one's mother, he would do so for all but the final seven months of his life—and still translating for Amberg's United Plays. Apparently he had a crack at writing English lyrics to Offenbach's *La Belle Hélène*. The show was a burlesque of Homer's Helen of Troy. Henry Myers remembered Larry singing, or trying to sing, the German version of King Menelaus's number. Whether or not anything Larry wrote was used, the lyrics credit for *Fair Helen*, as the modernized English version was titled, went to Charles Hudson Towne, editor of *McClure's Magazine*.[19]

Amberg took a look at Larry's one-act play *The Reality*. After a too quick reading, the play might be dismissed as juvenilia, but that would be a mistake. Aiming high—certainly higher than the plays and musicals of 1919—Larry, inspired by Brieux's *Damaged Goods*, wrote a nifty little drama about syphilis. *Damaged Goods* had been banned for years in England because of what Shaw called "the childishness of our theater," and its fearlessness in the face of conventional morality must have appealed to Larry, who almost certainly had seen the English-language production in 1914 at New York's Academy of Music.[20] In *The Reality*, journalist Dobson Brakefield rails against *Weekly American* owner Philip McClinton for refusing to run his story about syphilis. "People don't like it to be known that they have it," Brakefield says, trying to make his case to McClinton. "They conceal the fact, because they know that its discovery means shameful condemnation." The discovery of penicillin was still twenty years away, but the treatment of venereal disease had come a long way since the days when most doctors prescribed silver nitrate and exile. McClinton reminds Brakefield that he puts out a family magazine. But when he believes that his college-age son, tortured by his own diagnosis of syphilis, has shot himself to spare his family shame, he is inconsolable—until he learns the son and the journalist have faked the suicide to make a point. "The reality comes upon us like a flash of lightning," Brakefield says to the relieved, enlightened editor, "and we see what was hidden in our hazes of theory, the truth, Mr. McClinton, the truth."

Never again would Larry write anything that could be remotely called a problem play in the Brieux mode, either alone or with Rodgers. He didn't see himself as a muckraker or a social reformer; he was, first and last, an entertainer. Writing *The Reality*, though, he must have figured he was standing up, like the Doctor in *Damaged Goods*, to the "rigid moralists, who are so choked with their middle-class prudery." [21]

Middle-class prudery poured off most Prohibitionists. Minnesota Republican congressman Andrew Volstead sponsored the Eighteenth Amendment, which would prohibit the sale and distribution of liquor for all but strictly medicinal purposes. It became federal law on January 16, 1920, enforcement beginning at midnight. [22] Despite high-flown speeches by politicians and church organizations, many Americans saw right through the Prohibitionists' self-righteousness. "Prohibition was the rearguard action of a still dominant, overwhelmingly rural, white Anglo-Saxon Protestant establishment," Edward Behr wrote in his book *Prohibition*, "aware that its privileges and natural rights to rule were being increasingly threatened by the massive arrival of largely despised (and feared) beer-swilling, wine-drinking new American immigrants." [23]

Prohibition turned every drinker into an outlaw. In this unsettled climate of suppression and new acceleration—the airplane, the automobile, and wireless news gathering, to name just three examples—the arts were ready to break out. After the last of the returning doughboys had been delivered back to the States, "How Ya Gonna Keep 'Em Down on the Farm, After They've Seen Paree?" was the applicable hit song, and most people knew that the reference to Paris meant more than just a three-day pass to the City of Light. Paul Gallico, then a junior at Columbia, wrote that it was "not only a period of license following upon restraint; it was far more a time of emancipation from outworn and outmoded ideas, and an evolution." [24]

Having been rejected by the U.S. Army, Larry Hart had spent the war either in Manhattan or in the Adirondacks. He was not yet even on the front lines of battle in the theater. In the late winter of 1920, he and Dick worked on two shows that would overlap. *You'd Be Surprised*, billed as "an atrocious musical," was another Akron Club presentation and pretty much Doc Bender's show as book writer, co-lyricist, and director. Its first performance was given at the Plaza Hotel on March 6, and its cast included Phil Leavitt, Etta Leblang (daughter of theater owner and ticket broker Joe Leblang), sixteen-year-old Dorothy Fields, and seventeen-year-old Elise Bonwit (born Elise Bonnit), whose dancing Larry particularly admired. Bender was in his junior year at the New York College of Dentistry, but the musical stage was what he lived for. Lew Fields was credited with "professional assistance," which might mean simply that he contributed money. In any case, Lew was impressed by the songs in *You'd Be Surprised*. Most of them have been lost. But one that survived—perhaps because it was recycled for the next show—was "Don't Love Me Like Othello." "You may not be handsome, like a Grecian frieze" is a line from the first verse, and it anticipates "My Funny Valentine," written in the middle of the next decade. Larry was already sharpening his use of repetition and triple rhymes in this, from the refrain:

Don't love me like King Bluebeard,
His technique was risqué.
And never try to be a caveman—
Don't rave, man,
Behave, man.
But you can treat me like a slave, man,
If you will love and obey.

Dick conducted *You'd Be Surprised*, and he also conducted *Fly with Me*, the Columbia Varsity Show of 1920, which opened two and a half weeks after *You'd Be Surprised*. *Fly with Me* took off from a sketch by Milton Kroopf (years later Kroopf would become counsel to the Securities and Exchange Commission, though he still kept one toe in the theater); the sketch was fleshed out by Larry Hart and Phil Leavitt. Two and a half years after the Russian Revolution, Larry and Phil decided the time was right to poke fun at Americans' fear that Bolshevism might jump across the ocean like an airborne virus. The action is set on an island "ruled by Soviets" off the coast of North America—that is, Manhattan—fifty years in the future. Many of the songs were sung in the Love Laboratory of Bolsheviki University. In the opening chorus, "Gone Are the Days," the Professor tells his students:

Down with all eccelesiastics,
Moral teachings by bombastics,
We've our own iconoclastics,
Teaching plastics, by gymnastics.

The "futuristic" love song "Inspiration" teases the pretensions of Modern Art. In "A Penny for Your Thoughts" monetary value rises, or only seems to, as the singer gets closer to his beloved: a dime for every word; a quarter for every blush; a dollar for every smile; but a kiss is priceless. "A College on Broadway" may be the only great college song that never mentions the name of the college (the title is enough).

The Varsity Show Approval Committee, which included Oscar Hammerstein and Ray Perkins, took a look at what Hart, Leavitt, Kroopf, and Rodgers had on the page, and made arrangements to send *Fly with Me* into the Grand Ballroom of the Hotel Astor in late March.

Leonard Manheim, who knew Rodgers at DeWitt Clinton, played Mrs. Haughton, who teaches a class in lovemaking. "Hart was a little man," Manheim recalled nearly half a century later. "He sat on the upright piano and fed Rodgers lyrics while Rodgers was playing the music. Sometimes he would rewrite them a bit later on. I remember learning lyrics and having them changed on me right after." [25] When *Fly with Me* opened at the Astor, on March 24, 1920, Rodgers was once again in the pit, with twenty musicians under his baton. Much of his music was jaunty and march-like—"A College on Broadway" was marked Tempo di Marcia—and sounded more like the syncopated rhythms of Irving Berlin and George M. Cohan than the more subdued, waltz style that Rodgers was moving toward. But it all fit a Varsity Show. [26]

It's possible that Lew Fields was taken with the songs that Richard C. Rodgers (as he was still known) and Lorenz Hart had written for *both* shows, *You'd Be Surprised* and *Fly with Me*. Above and beyond "Any Old Place with You," the boys had proven themselves to Fields. In April, Fields, figuring he was getting a bargain, hired them to write half a dozen songs for his new show, *Poor Little Ritz Girl*. "News that Fields was entrusting his score to a pair of college kids was greeted with skepticism," wrote Armond and L. Marc Fields in *From the Bowery to Broadway*, an exhaustive study of Lew Fields's career and his place in the American theater. [27] But Lew had confidence in Dick and Larry, in part because he already knew the melodies: he wanted Larry to revise his lyrics to several of the *Fly with Me* songs, with one or two left over from *You'd Be Surprised,* and slide them right into *Poor Little Ritz Girl.* This made the boys' assignment relatively uncomplicated. Just as *You'd Be Surprised* was the first complete amateur score by Rodgers and Hart, *Poor Little Ritz Girl* would be their first complete *professional* score.

One month later they had finished most of their work for Fields. Larry had just turned twenty-five but, apart from his swiftly receding hairline and the frequency with which he needed to shave, he still looked like a boy; Dick was a Columbia freshman and not yet eighteen.

For an actor trained in vaudeville in the last third of the nineteenth century, Lew Fields was particularly attuned to currents in contemporary theater. Perhaps Lew was *too* attuned, for he often chose projects on the basis of their similarities to other plays. Fields had his writers, Harry B. Stillman and William J. O'Neil, give him a story based on the Cinderella archetype, and what they produced for him was simple enough: chorus girl Barbara is struggling to keep up with rehearsals at the Frivolity Theater for a revue titled *Poor Little Ritz Girl*; she goes home to the Riverside Drive apartment she's renting, unaware that the place really belongs to the handsome, wealthy Pembroke, who falls in love with her when he returns to New York.[28]

Rehearsals for *Poor Little Ritz Girl* were held at the Central Theatre, at Forty-Seventh and Broadway. The boys stayed out of the way until the Boston tryouts, beginning on May 29. They took the night train to Boston with the rest of the company. As Rodgers told it in his memoir *Musical Stages,* it was the next morning before he realized that Larry was missing. "It seems that he was so small that the porter couldn't find him in his upper berth to wake him in time," Rodgers wrote, "so he slept his way out of the train yards. He didn't make it to the theater until the afternoon."[29] At Boston's Wilbur Theatre, the stage was supposed to be split into two sets—one half the drawing room of the Riverside Drive flat, the other a portion of the stage of the Frivolity Theatre—but when the curtain rose on May 29, the audience saw a platoon of stagehands still attempting to maneuver the sets into place. Humiliated, Dick and Larry left the theater and walked the Boston Common till long after the curtain fell.

There was nothing for the boys to fix at that point. They could only wait till midsummer when the show would be in good enough shape to open on Broadway.

So Larry went back to Brant Lake in 1920 for a fourth summer. By then he had something of a reputation as a lyric writer and dramatics counselor.

The recent New York University graduate Arthur Schwartz had heard about Hart from his new acquaintance Milton Bender. At NYU's University Heights campus in the Bronx, which was often referred to, in the casual anti-Semitism of the era, as "Kike's Peak," Schwartz had been all over campus—active in the Dramatic Society, the Glee Club, the Varsity Quartet, and the Sandham Oratorical Contest, and served as captain of the Debating Team and editor in chief of *The New Yorker*, the university's literary magazine (no relation to the popular magazine that would be founded five years later). He was also a self-taught pianist whose melodies inclined toward minor-key melancholia. Schwartz got himself hired at Brant Lake specifically so he could write songs with Larry.[30] "In the summer when I was [on my way] to law school," Schwartz said, "I was a counselor in a summer camp. I chose the camp because Larry Hart was there. I knew he was writing with Rodgers, but they had not yet succeeded. I thought I could learn something about song writing, and wrote those camp shows which everybody writes."[31] Schwartz could produce new melodies almost as easily as Rodgers could, but he tended to be dissatisfied with his own work. When he and Larry wrote a show for the camp titled *Dream Boy*, about a camper who prefers staying in his tent and reading, the song that proved the catchiest was "I Love to Lie Awake in Bed," the melody surely familiar from its subsequent lyric, provided by Schwartz's longtime collaborator Howard Dietz, as "I Guess I'll Have to Change My Plan." Later, Larry told Henry Myers, "Don't worry about Arthur Schwartz getting there!"[32]

Theatrical apprenticeships at summer camps have been a peculiarly American phenomenon, and Arthur Schwartz wasn't the only New Yorker to seek out Larry that summer of 1920. Shortly before Larry first worked at Brant Lake Camp, in 1917, a teenager named William Rosenberg dropped out of the High School of Commerce and set about making his fortune with his facility at shorthand. In Washington he found a job as stenographer with the War Industries Board, whose chairman, Bernard Baruch, took a shine to him and hired him as his personal stenographer. Baruch, one of the keenest financial minds in the nation, opened several doors for Rosenberg, and the younger man eagerly stepped through them. Barely taller than Larry Hart, Rosenberg wasn't burdened by Hart's self-consciousness about his height. "It's not much fun being five-three in a five-nine world," he once wrote, elongating his own frame by a couple of inches, but that's about as troubled by it as he would publicly admit to.[33] Rosenberg shared with Hart a warm embrace of the city and all its crud, and an energy that made both men seem motorized. "[Rosenberg] loved many things," Ben Hecht wrote, "but the deepest of his loves was the city of New York. Fame lay hidden in it, to be gone after with pick and shovel." Billy Rosenberg saw it and went for it. "I was never conscious of his shortness until I read about it," Hecht swore. "This was due to the way he walked—with the bounce of an overwound toy; and to the way he stood still, head raised, face expectant, like a man about to climb a flagpole."[34] One persistent dream of Billy Rosenberg's was to impress his old boss, Barney Baruch. In New York a date steered Billy to Wolpin's, a delicatessen at 1216 Broadway, where she pointed out songwriters like Fred Fischer and Walter Donaldson. Learning that some of these guys pulled down two grand a week for their labors, Billy thought, This is for me. Someone must have told Billy—as someone evidently told Arthur Schwartz—about Larry Hart, who had no compunction about helping out with a lyric. Rosenberg was soon making pilgrimages up to Brant Lake Camp—four hours each way—and writing under the name Billy Rose.

Within a couple of years, Billy had written the lyric to one of the first singing commercials, "Does the Spearmint lose its flavor on the bedpost overnight?" Rose would soon marry Fanny Brice and remain close, professionally if not personally, to Rodgers and Hart.

The boys had spent their summers apart—Larry at Brant Lake, Dick and Herb Fields at Paradox. Meanwhile, *Poor Little Ritz Girl* had moved from Boston to Stamford to Atlantic City, undergoing the alterations that almost every show must before it reaches Broadway. Two months after its initial Boston tryout, *Poor Little Ritz Girl* was ready to open at the Central. Larry, who wasn't officially on the Brant Lake Camp payroll in 1920, had no trouble returning to the city; Dick and Herb were given a royal send-off by Paradox director Ed Goldwater.[35] Through his father, Herb had experienced the rush of a Broadway opening night, but Dick had not.

Gathering at the Central Theatre, the boys saw immediately that Lew Fields had changed the show considerably. Among his changes were getting rid of Victor Moore, who was just about everybody's favorite stage comic, and installing Charles Previn (older cousin of André) as musical director. Most shocking to Rodgers and Hart, though, was that Fields had cut out half their score and replaced it with songs by Sigmund Romberg and Alex Gerber. There were now eight Romberg tunes to Rodgers's seven. Fields, preoccupied with getting the show on its feet, had neglected to tell the boys about the changes. Herb Fields was embarrassed.[36] Romberg's participation was especially hard to swallow because he was thought to be indifferent to lyricists. (When Gus Kahn wrote his first lyric for Romberg, he expected Romberg to say, "Gus, that's wonderful," but all Rommy said was, "Mmm, that fits," which was his response to all his collaborators.)[37]

The alterations ordered by Fields made the show amusing but never really exciting. The Romberg-Gerber songs were widely seen as pleasant in their familiar, sentimental way. Reviewing the show for the *Tribune*, drama critic Heywood Broun had special praise for the boys' "What Happened Nobody Knows," though the lyric has been missing ever since; for "Mary, Queen of Scots," though the lyric was actually written by Herb Fields; and for Larry's "You Can't Fool Your Dreams," which used the musical refrain of "Don't Love Me Like Othello" to make the debatable point, "When a maiden is asleep / All she says is true." Broun wrote, "One of the lyric writers has gone far enough away from Forty-second Street to have heard Dr. Freud, and has composed a song called 'You Can't Fool Your Dreams,' which shows at least a working knowledge of the theory of the unconscious."[38] It was a working knowledge but hardly a profound one. In the coming decade Larry would find ways to say epigrammatic things about dreams that even the most critical psychoanalyst would approve of. For now, though, Broun's assessment went a long way toward assuaging the boys' disappointment. From other quarters there was praise for the song "Love's Intense in Tents," which recycled music from *Fly with Me* and which sounds, in writer Ethan Mordden's phrase, "like a freshman warm-up for 'Mountain Greenery.'"[39] ("Summer breezes blowing, / Soon we will be going / Camping!")

Larry soaked up whatever encomiums came his way. But the moments from *Poor Little Ritz Girl* that made the deepest impact on him were only partly his: "The Daisy and the Lark," a song that he and Dick wrote for the show, was sung and danced by Elise Bonwit. "Elise is always the hit of the show," Larry told Henry Myers.[40] This teenager's performances impressed upon him the notion that a dance inserted into a musical play—not the high kicking of chorus girls, but a choreographed dance that advanced the narrative—could be very effective, even on Broadway.

CHAPTER 5

The Great Big City's a Wondrous Toy

ISAPPOINTING THOUGH the *Poor Little Ritz Girl* experience was, Dick and Larry were in for the long haul—and it would be a very long haul, fraught with rejection and humiliation. By the fall of 1920, Dick was wondering what he was doing at Columbia College, struggling with academic classes while his mind was always on a new melody. He had used Columbia for what had most interested him—writing not one but *two* Varsity Shows, the first one without Larry—and he was considering the counsel of two young women he was seeing at the time about transferring to the Institute of Musical Art.

One of those women was almost certainly Helen Ford, an actress from Troy, New York. Shortly after the end of the war, Helen appeared in several amateur productions in and around Albany, where she met and married George Ford of the theater-owning family that included among its properties Washington, D.C.'s Ford's Theatre.[1] A month or so after their wedding, Ford was back on the road to oversee his theatrical concerns. In the closing weeks of 1919, Helen went to New York to begin rehearsals for *Always You*, Oscar Hammerstein II's first Broadway show, and it was probably around this time that she and Rodgers met. Over the next few months, she became the most important person to him. "Because her husband was continually away on lengthy business trips," Rodgers wrote, "it was possible for us to spend many hours together, mostly walking in Central Park discussing our two favorite topics, ourselves and music."[2] Slightly older than Rodgers, Helen was, for a while, his teacher as well as his lover. Wouldn't it be great, they sometimes wondered, if Dick and Larry wrote a show for her?

As it happened, a new idea for a show was rolling around in Larry's mind. One day in the late summer or early fall of 1920, Larry came upon a bronze tablet made in 1903, nailed over a door frame on a house near the corner of Lexington Avenue and Thirty-Seventh Street, in the heart of the Manhattan district long known as Murray Hill. Etched into the tablet was a rendering of "Mrs. Murray Receiving the British Officers," a scene from 1776 based on a painting by Jennie Brownscombe. The tablet described the scene:

> [British generals] Howe with Clinton, Tryon and a few others went to the house of Robert Murray, on Murray Hill, for refreshments and rest. With pleasant conversations and a profusion of cake and wine, the good whig lady detained the gallant Britons almost two hours, quite long enough for the bulk of [Continental Army general] Putnam's division of four thousand men to leave the city and escape the heights of Harlem by the Bloomingdale Road, with the loss of only a few soldiers.

Already enamored of the Revolutionary War period, Larry figured this story had possibilities. Although there were variations on the episode, it was widely known among historians of the era as "Mrs. Murray's Tea."

According to *New York Chronology* author James Trager, General Howe arrived at Kips Bay on September 15, 1776, his infantry climbing the steep rocks at the foot of what would become East Thirty-Fourth Street. Howe stopped for lunch at the home, called Iclenberg, of Mary Murray, who entertained him and his troops with help from her beautiful daughters. Consequently, Howe missed apprehending General Washington, who had galloped down from the Jumel Mansion, overlooking the Harlem River, to hold off the British until general Putnam could withdraw troops trapped at the Battery; Washington retreated to Harlem Heights and the next day repulsed a British attack. In political journalist Will Irwin's version, Dame Murray was entertaining generals Howe and Cornwallis and had her serving maid sing them the new London song "Sally in Our Alley," delaying them just long enough to allow the Continental Army to slip through and make a stand at McGowan's Pass (near what is now 105th Street and Fifth Avenue).[3]

Whichever version was the more accurate, Larry was intrigued. Harlem and Morningside Heights were rich with Revolutionary War lore; the action of Mrs. Murray's Tea was only a few miles to the south. Larry shared the history with Herb Fields, who was familiar with at least one version and was ready to work on it for the stage. Larry remained so fixated on the era that when Gustave Amberg assigned him to adapt Jean Gilbert's musical version of *The Lady in Ermine*, he set aside the Mrs. Murray's tea story and turned *The Lady in Ermine* into a Revolutionary-era story.

The Lady in Ermine was originally a two-act play, by Rudolph Schanzer and Ernst Welisch, set in northern Italy "about eighty years ago." Larry moved it back another sixty years or so and changed the locale to colonial New York. In an "Adapter's Note," he explained the new background:

> In 1777, the Continental Congress closed all the theaters in the Colonies. When the British occupied New York, they reopened the Nassau Theatre and rechristened it the Theatre Royal. Colonel Williams, an actual character in our history, was the officer in love with the leading lady of the company. Major John Andre, as in my adaptation of *The Lady in Ermine*, was actually engaged with preparing the performances. He designed the scenery. The masculine roles were assumed by the officers themselves. The producer will find little of an anachronistic nature in the historical detail concerning Burgoyne, Clinton, and the others mentioned in the adaptation.[4]

Larry's principals are Harry and Marie Hastings, the American commander at Saratoga and his wife. They're aided by the Lady in Ermine, an amalgam of Meridiana, the Lady of the Lake, and maybe also Washington Irving's Sleepy Hollow characters. Apart from his wholesale shift in time and locale, Larry completed several lyrics. "The Belle of Other Days" introduces the title character as something of a phantom:

> *Milady fair in ermine*
> *Keeps safeguard o'er all*
> *Convictions I am firm in*
> *That something must befall.*
> *When'er she walks into the night,*
> *Beware the legend says,*
> *Resplendent in her ermine white,*
> *The belle of other days.*

"A Soldier's Song" is a conventional drinking song:

> *Oh, wine, you are the truest of lovers*
> *To wine, I never say nay*
> *In wine, one never discovers*
> *That passion has gone its way.*

The drinking song had been a hardy tradition for centuries, but Larry's seems to be an homage to Yeats's 1910 "A Drinking Song":

> *Wine comes in at the mouth*
> *And love comes in at the eye;*
> *That's all we shall know for truth*
> *Before we grow old and die.*
> *I lift the glass to my mouth,*
> *I look at you, and I sigh.*

The lyric he would later recycle so effectively is "When the Boys Are Older," which demonstrates that, when it comes to pleasing a lover, maturity trumps youth:

> *Romeo was very youthful,*
> *But unskillful to be truthful*
> *Couldn't love her, under cover, though he tried.*
>
> *Don Juan was over fifty,*
> *With a great romantic gift, he*
> *Had it in 'em, he could win 'em till he died;*
>
> *Youth in love may be the fashion,*
> *Young men may excel in passion,*
> *They begin it, love a minute, then depart.*
>
> *Though an old boy may be shopworn*
> *And his hair a little topworn,*
> *He'll be much more settled when he'll lose his heart. . . .*

It's not clear whether Amberg liked Larry's adaptation, but the Shuberts didn't use it in any case. Retaining Gilbert's music, the Shuberts brought in other lyricists and had the locale restored to Italy during Napoleon's invasion. Amberg had another assignment waiting for Larry, however, and this one would stick in Larry's smoke-filled craw longer than any mere rejection.

Ferenc Molnár, born to a Hungarian-Jewish family, was thirty-one when his play *Liliom: A Legend in Seven Scenes and a Prologue* premiered in Budapest in December 1909. Even the most sophisticated European theatergoers were accustomed to protagonists surviving through most, if not all, of a play, so the act 1 death of Molnár's protagonist confused audiences and froze ticket sales. It wasn't until after the terrors of the Great War, when so many Europeans were newly sensitized to death on a massive scale, that the play's dark blend of love and death, the two great themes of literature, began to make sense. *Liliom*—in Hungarian the hero's name means "lily" and is also a slang term for "tough"—was revived to great acclaim. A German copy of the play landed in the hands of the actor Joseph Schildkraut—the same version that Larry Hart was working with at Amberg's behest. Benjamin (Barney) Glazer, then employed by a literary agency, extracted from Schildkraut a promise that if Schildkraut wanted to play Liliom, he would arrange for Glazer to get the job translating it.[5]

This is where versions of the story collide. Schildkraut wrote that he kept his promise and engaged Glazer to make the translation. A few weeks later Schildkraut, affectionately known as Peppy in the theater world, took the translation to Theresa Helburn, one of the founders of the Theatre Guild, a permanent acting company still in its infancy that had modeled itself on the Moscow Art Theatre. "It's wonderful," Schildkraut said to Helburn, "and I want to play the lead." Helburn and the Guild's cofounder Lawrence Langner gave him the go-ahead. Peppy immersed himself in the role and, during rehearsals, moved fluently from English to German to Hungarian. With Peppy as the tough but ultimately tender Liliom, and Eva La Gallienne as Liliom's young widow, Julie, *Liliom* proved to be a smash in New York when it opened in April at the Garrick Theatre. The show, revived several times over the years, provided the Guild with a substantial annuity. Glazer got the credit for the translation, and it enabled him to start his career as a translator-producer, continuing with Molnár's next two plays, *Fashions for Men* and *The Swan*. After that, Glazer went to Hollywood, where he became a dialogue writer for the movies and a founding member of the Motion Picture Academy of

Arts and Sciences. As a successful movie producer, particularly at Paramount Pictures, he often requested the services of Rodgers and Hart.[6]

Glazer might have paid Larry for his translation of *Liliom* and to keep mum about it. "Only a few privileged friends know *Liliom* was Larry's work," Samuel Marx and Jan Clayton wrote in their book about Rodgers and Hart, "and they were sworn to secrecy."[7] Dorothy Hart wrote, "Schildkraut told me—and Teddy, Arthur Schwartz, and several other knowledgeable Broadwayites have confirmed—that Larry did some work on *Liliom*. And who knew better than Schildkraut? But Larry didn't mind too much." "Even if Glazer did 'lift' [the translation]," Frederick Nolan wrote recently, "Larry never badmouthed anybody."[8] Yet eight years after the fact, Larry was irritated enough to mention to *Dance Magazine* that he received no royalty for his translation, just the $200 from Amberg for four weeks' work.[9] It's odd: in the second paragraph of *Liliom*'s Prologue, as translated by Larry, the stage direction identifies the "merry-go-round at the Center," the carousel that would become the musical and narrative nucleus of what turned out to be Richard Rodgers's favorite of all his shows—but written without Larry Hart.

The Akron Club's eighth annual "original" (in its broadest sense) musical comedy was *First Love*, with songs by Rodgers and Hart. Staged by Herb Fields, *First Love* was first performed at the Brooklyn Academy of Music, on February 10–11, 1921, then transferred to the Plaza in Manhattan for the next nine days, where it was known as *Say Mama*.[10] The cast included Elise Bonwit, Phil Leavitt, and large-eyed sixteen-year-old Dorothy Fields, who, like her brother Herb, was ignoring her parents' entreaties to stay out of show business. Of the surviving lyrics, the most interesting was probably "Priscilla," about the object of desire of Pilgrims John Alden and Miles Standish.

Before the boys sat down to write another Varsity Show for the spring, they went to the movies. On a cold day in March, Rodgers and Fields went to see the new Fox release *A Connecticut Yankee at King Arthur's Court*, based on Mark Twain's 1889 novel. (Rodgers remembered it as showing at the Capitol, though it was actually at the Selwyn.) There had been a 1910 adaptation. Neither man was prepared for the liveliness of this new screen version, which starred Harry C. Myers—no relation to Hart's playwright friend Henry Myers and best remembered as the wealthy drunk who matches Chaplin scene for scene in *City Lights*. The movie pulsated with anachronistic, up-to-the-minute comedy based on American slang, motorcycles, and references to cowboy literature and Prohibition. Among the inside jokes: a Model T driven by the Yankee (Myers), with Sandy (Pauline Starke) riding shotgun, bears the license plate number 528, the year of its manufacture, A.D. 528. "We laughed for nearly two hours," Rodgers recalled more than two decades later, "and walking home decided that there, by cracky, was the perfect idea for a musical comedy. Mr. Hart thought so too, so a couple of days later I walked into the office of the lawyer for the Mark Twain estate to try to get the necessary permission to make a musical version of the novel. The lawyer was Mr. Charles Tressler Lark." [11]

Lark, deeply involved in the cultural life of the city—he was on the Board of Trustees of the Music Lovers' Foundation, which sponsored "musical mornings" at the Waldorf—was considered an authority on wills and estates; the first will he drew up was Twain's. [12] He must have been amused by the eighteen-year-old Rodgers, who said he wrote songs with the Columbia Varsity Show writer Lorenz Hart and asked about rights to *Connecticut Yankee.* Rodgers left Lark's office that day carrying a free—free!—six-month option on the book.

Herb Fields went to work on an adaptation. He was still fiddling with "Mrs. Murray's Tea," keeping Larry's basic outline and also keeping Dick's girlfriend Helen Ford in mind.

A month into the spring of 1921, Dick and Larry's second Columbia Varsity Show, *You'll Never Know,* was staged in the Grand Ballroom of the Hotel Astor, with a book credited to four alumni and direction by three, including Oscar Hammerstein II. Columbia senior Paul Gallico had won his varsity letter at crew, and now he wanted the college's silver King's Crown watch charm, which he could earn by serving as press agent for the Varsity Show. [13] All he had to do was sell Rodgers and Hart:

> The Varsity Show is Here! The Varsity Show is Here! The Varsity Show, the one and only, the great, the gay, the social event of the Columbia year, the realization of months of drilling, the grand carnival of frolic and banter as the phrase has it—the Varsity Show has come to town. *You'll Never Know* we enjoyed thoroughly; and we fling aside criticism for enthusiasm to strum its praises. It is a very good show. [14]

Meanwhile, Rodgers joined the Musicians' Union so he could conduct Winkler's Orchestra, which provided the music for the three nights at the Astor. Two months shy of nineteen, Rodgers must have been the youngest conductor in midtown Manhattan that week. For *You'll Never Know,* songs from *Say Mama* and *Poor Little Ritz Girl* were recycled. But there were nearly a dozen new songs, some of them charming. In the introductory "Don't Think That We're the Chorus of the Show," the young men suggest the importance of the Varsity Show when they sing, "Oh, please applaud us, and we'll know / We'll all get parts in next year's show." Of the two songwriters, the lyricist had stopped attending classes years earlier, and the composer already had one foot out the door—and yet they were still writing for the annual extravaganza. In the verse to "I'm Broke," Larry wrote:

> *Dreams are ethereal*
> *But not material.*
> *Aesthetic thrills*
> *Today won't pay my bills.*

And in the title song, which is about the Mona Lisa–like inscrutability of the female gaze, Larry rhymes "Da Vinci" with "cinch, he."

You'll Never Know was Rodgers and Hart's Columbia swan song. Columbia classmates would stay in their lives, but the campus would no longer be a daily destination for either of them. That spring Dick was accepted at the Institute of Musical Art, the forerunner of the Juilliard School of Music, only a few blocks from Columbia in Morningside Heights. As if to welcome him, the Institute staged *Say It with Jazz*, a potpourri of Rodgers & Hart songs from previous shows, with other lyrics by Rodgers's new classmate Frank Hunter.

Then came a period of frustration and education. There was work done intermittently on the Mrs. Murray's Tea musical comedy, tentatively titled *Sweet Rebel*, and Fields worked, off and on, on a *Connecticut Yankee* adaptation, even after the free option period was over. While Dick pursued his musical studies at Musical Art, Larry had his hand in several projects. He was impressed by *The Blond Beast*, a play written by his friend Henry Myers, who said he was under the spell of Schopenhauer when he composed it: "It was about a philosopher who doesn't believe in women. Not that there's anything queer about him, but he considers himself above human emotion. He can manage not to feel anything—this was the philosophy. The story was about how this girl makes him feel something." [15] Larry decided *The Blond Beast* wasn't yet produceable, so he threw his energies into another full-length Myers play, *The First Fifty Years*. In seven scenes, the play followed a Harlem couple, Anne and Martin Wells, from the beginning of their marriage, during the Hayes presidency, and ending with their fiftieth anniversary in the same Harlem brownstone.

Raising money for *The First Fifty Years* began with the O.M. writing a check for $1,500—but it was *not to be cashed under any circumstances!* Instead, the $1,500 was meant to draw other producers. These turned out to be the more stagestruck friends from the 119th Street gatherings, including Herbert Schloss and Irving Strouse, who, after contributing an aggregate sum of $5,000, insisted on accompanying Larry to every audition and theatrical interview he could scare up. For the way his uptown pals followed him around, Larry named his production company Caravan, Inc., aware they were sticking close to him to make certain he wasn't running off, à la Hart père, with the dough. Now the play needed a star.

George Greenberg, one of the 119th Street gang and later to become a stage manager for the Theatre Guild, was stage-managing Susan Glaspell's *The Verge* at the Provincetown Playhouse on MacDougal Street. Greenberg arranged for Myers to give the script to the show's star, Margaret Wycherly, a respected English actress whose recent appearance as queen to Paul Robeson's king in the play *Voodoo* had won her some notoriety.[16] (Even productions of *Othello* rarely risked using an interracial couple in the leads. Most Othellos of the era were white men who blackened their faces for the role.) Larry got wind of this and, reminding Myers that *he* was the producer, also took the script to her and told her he hoped she would do it. If they could get Wycherly to star, they could get it on the boards fast. Wycherly read *The First Fifty Years* and soon invited the producer, the playwright, and her current stage manager to her Greenwich Village apartment to discuss it. After a Sunday dinner—there was no performance of *The Verge* that night—Wycherly expressed interest in the play. The actress had put an enormous amount of time into making revisions. She proudly showed Larry, Myers, and Greenberg the changes she'd made: every single speech was altered. Myers was devastated. To break the awkward silence, Larry said to Wycherly, "It's wonderful of you to give Henry the benefit of your judgment and experience. I think he should take it home and study it."[17] Pleased, Wycherly saw the three men out and expected to hear from them. On the sidewalk, safely out of earshot, Larry turned to Myers and Greenberg and said, "Fuck her. We'll do it without her."[18]

It's not as if Larry believed Myers's play was untouchable. In fact, he had already arranged with Max Simon (a play doctor known as "Doc" decades before playwright Neil was born), to be ready to help revise *The First Fifty Years*. But Larry was loyal. It simply wasn't kosher for Miss Wycherly, star or no star, to rewrite his friend's play like that.

Then Caravan, Inc., got lucky. Livingston Platt, who had been designing scenery and costumes for the actress Margaret Anglin, agreed to direct the play. Platt's participation lured actors Clare Eames and Tom Powers, and the theater they got was the Princess, at Thirty-Ninth Street, east of Broadway, with only 299 seats.[19] It's where Larry and Dick had sat in awe of so many Jerome Kern musicals.

Rehearsals commenced in February 1922. George Greenberg was set to stage-manage, Morrie Ryskind to serve as press representative. When Myers didn't like the way the rehearsals were going, he recommended they pull the plug. Furious, Larry said, "If you ever again mention stopping this production, I'll kill you." Larry had had translation work first performed in Yorkville (*Crazy Dolly*), his lyrics performed in a dozen Varsity and amateur shows; but this was *Broadway*, baby! He wasn't going to let an overanxious playwright ruin the experience. In the back of Larry's mind, though, was the schedule: the play's opening coincided with Lent, which tended to keep more observant Christian theatergoers at home.

The New York Times ran its first ad for the play on March 5:

PRINCESS
Opening Mar. 14 Seats
Tuesday   Thurs.

Lorenz M. Hart and Irving S. Strouse Present

"The First Fifty Years"

A New Play by Henry Myers—with

CLARE EAMES and TOM POWERS

STAGED BY LIVINGSTON PLATT

After a run-through in Allentown, Pennsylvania, the play opened in New York to not-bad reviews. Alexander Woollcott seemed to like it, though without much enthusiasm. Percy Hammond praised it for the cynicism at its core.[20] Myers, still jittery after opening night, never stopped second-guessing everyone and was getting in Larry's thinning hair.[21] Although Ryskind still officially represented the play in the press, it was Larry who cooked up a publicity stunt to have the playwright suddenly become "lost": Myers would hole up with a cousin of Larry's in Paterson, New Jersey, until the Princess box office buzzed with scandal. Myers dutifully went out to Paterson but lasted there only a day because his mother demanded he come home at once. So the twenty-seven-year-old Myers slouched back to Manhattan. "For twenty-four hours I had some peace," Larry sighed.[22]

Larry and Myers considered *The First Fifty Years* a flop. In fact, the play ran for forty-eight performances—a respectable showing for a new playwright.[23]

Playwright and producer remained friendly, even close. So, for a while, did the producer and his press representative, who was waiting to get paid for the work he'd done. Georgie Price, who had bought material earlier from Larry through the Old Man, asked for a sketch to try out at a Keith vaudeville theater in Brooklyn. Larry brought Morrie Ryskind in on the assignment and offered their completed material to Price, who agreed to buy it on the condition that they stay away from the theater because their presence would make him nervous. Naturally, Larry and Morrie went anyway, buying seats in the gallery and listening to the audience laugh at their gags. The following day Price, unaware the boys had attended, described their material as amateurish and offered Larry and Morrie $100. Irked by Price's attempt to manipulate them, Morrie said no thanks, but Larry kicked him in the shin and thanked Price for offering to pay. Later, on the street, Larry advised Morrie that this could lead to other offers. In fact, Price used their material, a mass of Shakespeare- and baseball-inspired jokes and lyrics that became known as *Shakespeares of 1922*, throughout the vaudeville season.[24] The stuff seems to have been almost equal parts Hart and Ryskind—"They named a vegetable for a baseball player, Corn on Cobb!"—and an IOU from Price for $200 suggests that Larry subsequently persuaded Herb Fields and Dick Rodgers to participate.[25]

Larry, Herb, and Dick were still tending several irons at once. For the late spring Musical Art production *Jazz à la Carte*, Rodgers and his friend Gerald Warburg (son of the banker Felix) wrote the music, Fields did the choreography, and three of Larry's lyrics were recycled. Sometime during that summer, work began on a show titled *Winkle Town*.

The idea was cooked up by Larry and Herb. In the Connecticut village of Winkle Town, a young man invents a new "electronic" system that makes electrical wires unnecessary—a development to please everyone, including, presumably, the girl he loves.[26] If the idea sounds at once corny and prescient—it was the boys' "wireless" piece—it came out of their determination to get away from the conventions of the era and devise a more cerebral kind of musical comedy. The premise was so intriguing to Oscar Hammerstein II, who was a Broadway veteran by 1922, that he offered to work with Herb Fields on a book for the show. Fourteen or fifteen *Winkle Town* songs were written on the top floor of the Lew Fields house at 307 West Ninetieth Street, between West End Avenue and Riverside Drive.[27]

But there were no takers. In a profile of Rodgers and Hart in *Collier's*, a simple explanation was offered:

> [The producer] yearns for lyrics replete with such rhymes as "love," "above" and "dove," or "moon," "June" and "swoon." He demands a plot in which the Handsome Hero (tenor) arrives in Bulgravia on a walking trip and falls in love with the Village Maiden (soprano). She reciprocates his passion (duet at this point) but her angry father (baritone) insists that she marry the local elderly Rich Man (second baritone). The situation clears up in time for the final curtain, when the Handsome Hero reveals that he is the Crown Prince of Czechogavinia in disguise. A couple of Jewish comedians appear and disappear at regular intervals throughout the show and the producer assures himself that all this is Good Box Office.
>
> Such was the case, at all events, when Rodgers and Hart were attempting to find a backer for *Winkle Town*.[28]

One of the songs written at the Fields house was called "Manhattan." The immortal verse begins:

> *Summer journeys to Niag'ra*
> *Or to other places aggra-*
> *Vate all our cares,*
> *We'll save our fares!*

Unable to get the show financed, the boys auditioned "Manhattan" for Max Dreyfus, who owned T. B. Harms, one of the two or three most powerful music publishing concerns. Dreyfus listened and said, "There's nothing of value here."[29] "Manhattan" and several other songs written for *Winkle Town* would be heard on the stage eventually, but *Winkle Town* itself was dead.

On October 2, 1922, *The Lady in Ermine* opened at the Ambassador Theatre, stripped of Larry's Revolutionary-era New York setting and his lyrics.

There was Romberg again—not displacing Larry per se, but composing the show's hit, "When Hearts Are Young." Musical comedies were already dominating the season. Top ticket prices for musicals hit $4.40, and audiences were paying it. The Ziegfeld *Follies* and the *Scandals* of 1922, starring Ann Pennington, were selling out nightly. *The Gingham Girl*, starring Dick's secret girlfriend Helen Ford; *Molly Darling*; and *Sally, Irene and Mary* were enjoying brisk business.[30] In November, Adele and Fred Astaire opened in *The Bunch and Judy*, by Jerome Kern and Anne Caldwell. The *Bunch and Judy* plot touched on the current fashion of rich American women partnering with English royalty. "There was a terrible self-consciousness of Americans at the time about the British," Alice Roosevelt Longworth said. "They adored and *aped* everything British. It was a time when all those young (and sometimes not so young) American heiresses were leaping across the Atlantic to marry European aristocracy."[31] The Astaire siblings played romantic partners, although their characters' romance doesn't bloom until the chaste closing scene. Several years later Adele Astaire would take an English lord as a husband.

Bert Lahr in *Keep Smiling* and Willie and Eugene Howard in *The Passing Show* were doing their patented comedy routines to packed houses. Broadway welcomed a revival of light operas, including *Blossom Time*, DeKoven's *Robin Hood*, and several Gilbert & Sullivan shows. On November 16, John Barrymore opened in *Hamlet*, with Tyrone Power, Sr., as Claudius and incidental music by Robert Russell Bennett, whose orchestrations would prove so essential to Richard Rodgers's work in the future. Opening that same week was the less serious but no less successful *Merton of the Movies*, by George S. Kaufman and Marc Connelly, which might have been the first major comedy to track a movie fan (Merton Gill) who takes Hollywood gossip seriously. Movies, along with the increasingly ubiquitous presence of radio, were insinuating themselves into American culture with alarming rapidity.

At 119th Street, a force of nature named Maria Campbell, who preferred to be called Mary, came to work for the Harts and quickly made herself indispensable. Born in Jamaica, Big Mary, as she would be known, was respectful but took no guff from the Hart men. Under Frieda's tutelage, she learned to cook the heavy, *geschwollene* German food favored by the Harts. She remembered a guest's name after one introduction and got the lazybones Hart brothers out of bed most mornings.

Larry had a lot to wake up for. He still worked now and then for Amberg and United Plays. He remained interested in producing and directing. As a lyricist he was more determined than ever to leave Victorian clichés behind and instead exploit the crackling American idiom. The postwar years had brought new colloquial phrases—"Make it snappy!" "Get a load of this!" "It's a howl!"—into the lexicon. This is the way we speak, Larry thought; why not use it? As Yeats had directed while sitting in the Algonquin back in 1914, why not be natural with everyday speech?

In the winter of 1923 Larry decided Henry Myers's comedy *The Blond Beast* was in shape to produce. Larry's old friends Milton Winn, who would soon graduate from law school, and Edwin Justus Mayer, working as a press agent but an aspiring playwright himself, put up seed money with the intent of taking the play to Broadway. Larry directed. To play the Schopenhauer-influenced iconoclast, Larry and Myers hired the young Hungarian actor Bela Lugosi. But Lugosi couldn't quite handle Myers's lines in English, and he was soon replaced by Arthur Hohl. Hohl was among the most respected actors of the decade. One imagines the twenty-seven-year-old Larry at the edge of the stage, a cigar between his fingers and sleeves rolled up, laughing supportively at his friend's dialogue. *The Blond Beast* had had one performance at the MacDowell Club, 108 West Fifty-Fifth Street, which went well enough that Eddie Mayer's client Arthur Hopkins, who controlled the Plymouth Theatre, agreed to give over his theater for a matinee performance. Larry's idea was to show it during the day, when producers or their representatives would be less likely to have another commitment. It was a brilliant idea. But in the third week of February, with the Plymouth booked for a March 2 performance, there was an ominous rumbling in the theater district. The pugnacious William A. Brady had appeared in his own production of *La Flamme* at the Playhouse, three blocks north of the Plymouth, and had done so for a Sunday performance in February, forcing everyone else in the cast to appear that day. Brady's defiance drew the ire of the Lord's Day Alliance and Sabbath Societies, as well as a rebuke from Actors' Equity, which put out the statement, "We believe in the age-old principle, 'Six days shalt thou labor.'"[32] Larry knew how these rumblings could turn into quakes. As predicted, the most prominent producers showed up for the March 2 matinee performance of *The Blond Beast*. "Just before the curtain went up," Frederick Nolan wrote, "word arrived at the theater that there might be another actors' strike," and the place emptied of the few people who had had enough clout to ensure at least a trial Broadway run. Not a single backer stepped up to invest in *The Blond Beast*.[33]

Larry and Myers felt they were batting 0 for 2. Myers went to work for the Shuberts as a publicist.

The Fields family was still very much in Larry's life. In Dick's, too. For the fetching Dorothy Fields, then a senior at the Benjamin School for Girls, Dick wrote several songs for an adaptation of Justin McCarthy's 1902 play *If I Were King*. Dorothy, sporting a beard, played the protagonist, fifteenth-century French poet-thief François Villon. Larry contributed one lyric, "The Band of the Ne'er-Do-Wells," its Gilbertian patter beginning with "Ev'ry honest thief has entry / Break the law and pass the sentry." The show was performed at the Thirty-ninth Street Theater, with Dick conducting the orchestra, on March 25, 1923. Producer Russell Janney—he would publish the best-selling *The Miracle of the Bells* more than twenty years later—approached Rodgers about writing a full-length adaptation of *If I Were King* for Broadway, with Larry. A producer was coming to *them* for a change! When they never heard again from Janney, Rodgers screwed up his courage and called the producer, who told him his partners couldn't take a chance on "inexperienced" songwriters. Inexperienced? The guy had to be kidding! Janney's enthusiasm for a musical adaptation, however, was sincere: before year's end, Rudolf Friml and Brian Hooker (translator of *Cyrano de Bergerac*) were in place to write another version of *If I Were King*.[34]

Herb Fields had worked out bits and pieces of a *Connecticut Yankee* musical. When Rodgers needed a show that June for Musical Arts, Fields's work was edited into *A Danish Yankee in King Tut's Court*, joined to a script by a Rodgers classmate, Dorothy Crowther. The book was Mark Twain sifted through the dust of the recent discovery, by Egyptologist Howard Carter and his patron, the Earl of Carnarvon, of the tomb of Tutankhamen. Leading the young cast was a Musical Arts piano student named David Buttolph, who would eventually go west to score films and television (notably the Seven Arts western series *Maverick*). Four of Larry's lyrics were used, though a couple of these were recycled from *Poor Little Ritz Girl* and *Winkle Town*. Unlike the earlier Fields-Rodgers-Hart show for Musical Art, which had one night on Broadway, this was done in the school's auditorium on Claremont Avenue. No matter what was happening in Larry's life, he couldn't get far from Morningside Heights.

There was always *Sweet Rebel* to tinker with. Helen Ford was obviously too young to play Mrs. Murray, so the boys came up with an ingenue role for her: Betsy Burke, Mrs. Murray's niece. Meanwhile, in the spring, Helen had signed on to play Helen McGuffey, a stenographer from Troy (Helen Ford's hometown), in *Helen of Troy, N.Y.* The title had been cooked up by agent turned producer Rufus LeMaire—or so LeMaire blared. (In a lawsuit filed later that year, Elaine Sterne Carrington claimed that her play *Helen of Troy, N.Y.* had been submitted to LeMaire in the fall of 1922 and promptly rejected.)[35] The title was a perfect fit for Helen Ford. Bert Kalmar and Harry Ruby wrote the score, but Larry contributed a song called "Moonlight Lane" with slightly older composer W. Franke Harling (who had written the music for the West Point hymn "The Corps" in 1910) that was interpolated in the show during its Newark tryout.

> *Love calls deep in the night,*
> *Moonlight caresses the air*
> *We'll be lost in delight*
> *While moonbeams dance in your hair.*

It's the kind of pop song sentiment Larry had always made fun of. "Even with his name appearing incontrovertibly on the sheet music," Frederick Nolan wrote, "it is still difficult to believe the lyric was written by Lorenz Hart."[36] Several songs were mentioned in the *New York Times* review, but "Moonlight Lane" was not among them.[37] Helen Ford received kind notices, but it was Queenie Smith, as Helen's little sister, who got most of the raves. Larry probably didn't care much about his own lyric—who knows why he agreed to write it, anyway—but went to the theater to cheer on Helen. Once again, for him the highlight of the show was Elise Bonwit's dancing. Opening June 19, 1923, *Helen of Troy, N.Y.* was considered a "summer show." But for several weeks, along with that season's *Follies* and *Scandals*, it was more profitable than any drama on Broadway.[38]

Helen Ford's romance with Dick Rodgers might have still been going on. George Ford was frequently back in town, however, so they had to be discreet. Larry was no less discreet. He was already a habitué of the city's bathhouses, some of which catered to a homosexual clientele. But he kept quiet about practically everything else. The climate in New York City in the summer and fall of 1923 was informed by open hostility as expressed by the Society for the Suppression of Vice, which, under its second leader, John Sumner, launched a campaign in cooperation with the New York Police Department to root out homosexuality in bathhouses, on the piers and in the shadowy streets beneath the Elevated where men congregated for sex, and in saloons.[39] The north end of The Ramble in Central Park was already known as "the Fruited Plain." Drag balls were advertised as being for "Tom Boys and Girls" so that the publications that ran the ads could disavow their meaning if readers complained. The ominous climate made even the theater timid, despite a tradition of tolerating homosexuals. Discounting plays featuring an English fop (who was not necessarily homosexual anyway), there was probably not even an overtly effeminate male character, let alone an openly homosexual character, on the American stage until Frederick Lonsdale's *Spring Cleaning* opened in November 1923. "How divine!" chirps the character Bobby Williams, a dandy who's had a terrible row with his hosier. If Larry Hart was private about his sexuality, he had every reason to be.

Henry Myers, having got his feet wet in the world of theatrical publicity, invited Larry to see *The Dancers*, Lee Shubert's English import of the season. In London, the leading role was played by actor-producer Gerald du Maurier. In New York, Richard Bennett took over the lead. The play, which purported to be a tragic romance peculiar to the Jazz Age, failed to impress Larry, who was more intrigued by the likelihood that Bennett was having sexual relations with his leading lady, Jean Oliver. "Don't you *know* if they're fucking?" asked Larry. Myers claimed not to know; he was a publicist, not a *yenta*. "And you call yourself a playwright!" said Larry in mock disgust.[40]

While old Morningside Heights friends were going to work in the movies—Morrie Ryskind on and off for decades, Herman Mankiewicz and Howard Dietz for the rest of their professional lives—Dick and Larry remained committed to Broadway. They were writers, too, yes, but they were also musical theater writers, and music still hadn't come to the movies, only to the orchestra pits of the theaters that showed them.

In the spring of 1924 they caught a break. Once again it was the Fields family providing the employment.

Lew Fields was determined to remake himself into a tragedian—a virus that has afflicted, among many comic actors, Woody Allen, Jerry Lewis, and Bill Murray. Fields and son Herb drafted an idea along the lines of *The Music Master*, which had run in New York in 1904. David Warfield, who had enjoyed a career as one of New York's leading dialect comics—Larry Hart had even done his Warfield impression at summer camp—transformed himself into a formidable tragedian in *The Music Master*, which was about a German musician who tracks his wife and daughter across the Atlantic, where they've been taken by another man. Lew Fields, like Warfield, had made audiences laugh uproariously; now, as Warfield had done in *The Music Master*, he wanted to make them cry. So Fields and his second son concocted something along the same lines.[41]

The Jazz King was to star Lew Fields as Franz Henkel, an Austrian composer whose Dresden Sonata is turned into a popular song. Dick and Larry were invited onto the project. Emphasizing the contrast between Henkel's serious music and the manufactured frivolity of Tin Pan Alley, "Herbert Richard Lorenz"—the pseudonym combined the writers' three first names— might have had in mind Dr. Albert Sirmay, the classically trained Hungarian composer who, having had nearly a dozen musical scores produced in Budapest and Vienna, had come to America the previous year and become a staff writer for the music publisher T. B. Harms. (Rodgers referred to Sirmay as "the Irving Berlin of Budapest.")[42] Larry was eager to send up the burgeoning practice of turning classical pieces into pop songs. In 1917, Chopin's Fantaisie Impromptu, Op. 66 was recolored as "I'm Always Chasing Rainbows," and in 1920 listeners could discern in the hit "Avalon" the aria "E Lucevan le Stelle" from Puccini's *Tosca*. One can imagine Larry rubbing his hands together as he devised the lyric to show that Henkel's "Dresden Sonata" would be turned into "Moonlight Mama":

> She's just a love physician,
> Makes me obey,
> And there's never a fight.
> Here's why I'm in condition,
> An apple a day
> And a peach every night.

As sung in the show, the song was meant as a travesty of popular songwriting, yet it had to be, at its core, better than a travesty. In the way the lyric anticipates Larry's "I Could Write a Book," it almost *was* better.

> I have never studied art,
> I've never read a book,
> But I've learned about my heart
> In Mama's night school
> That's the right school.

After tryouts in Pennsylvania, in late March 1924, *The Jazz King* became *Henky* (a diminutive of the main character's surname), reaching Chicago in late April, and then, finally, *The Melody Man* when it opened at the Ritz Theatre in New York on May 13. "Moonlight Mama," as it turned out, didn't bear a reprise. Neither did "I'd Like to Poison Ivy"—everything the song had to say could be found in its title. Yet Eva Puck and Sammy White, married to each other offstage and blessed with that peculiar capability of conveying affection through mutual sniping, put the number across so entertainingly that Rodgers and Hart promised to write an entire show around them someday.[43]

The other lasting thing to emerge from *The Melody Man* had little to do with Larry. The young violinist hero was played by twenty-seven-year-old Fredric March. Only two and a half months before *The Melody Man* opened, he had been Frederick McIntyre Bickel, president of the class of 1920 at the University of Wisconsin. Applying for a legal name change, Bickel claimed he was often mistaken for George Bickel, a *Follies* comedian whose specialty was yet another Dutch act. More likely, he simply liked the way Fredric March sounded.[44]

The Melody Man won no prizes. The Pulitzer for the 1923–24 season went to Larry's former playwriting teacher, Hatcher Hughes, for *Hell-Bent for Heaven*. Forty when the play was produced, Hughes was still on the Columbia faculty. *Hell-Bent for Heaven* was a comedy about religious fanaticism, and it was championed by Hughes's longtime mentor, Columbia professor Brander Matthews, whose influence on the Drama committee outweighed that of the three jurors who wanted to give the award to George Kelly's *The Show-Off*.[45] Few decisions for the Drama award have been greeted with such cynicism.

Larry regarded the *Hell-Bent for Heaven* award as further evidence that Broadway was starved for good writing. For the dozenth time, he excavated *Sweet Rebel* from the mound of projects he had worked on, either with Dick Rodgers or other collaborators. He was aware how few musical plays there had been about the emerging national identity in an American setting. Apart from two Victor Herbert shows from 1910, *Natoma* (which took place in California while still under Spanish rule) and *Naughty Marietta* (set in New Orleans, also under Spanish rule), what was there? The British-versus-American theme yielded some ensemble pieces in the style of Gilbert and Sullivan, with Larry writing rhyming couplets in quasi-dialogue. Armed with carbon copies of the latest draft of *Sweet Rebel*, Larry, Dick, and Herb Fields made the circuit looking for a backer.

Lew Fields had the right of first refusal. He listened to the songs and said no, probably because he had lost money on *Jack and Jill*, which was set in Old New York, and blamed its historical setting.[46] The boys rode the train out to Great Neck to play the *Sweet Rebel* material for several would-be angels. No sale. Going in another but equally familiar direction, Dick and Larry persuaded a music publisher in midtown to sit and listen; if the songs could be published in sheet music form, they might prove more attractive to producers. The publisher kept them waiting for hours until he deigned to come in and take a seat. Larry went to Dick's side at the piano to sing, explaining that this opening number, "Heigh Ho, Lack-a-Day," was a "charming pastoral." The publisher, not having the vaguest idea what Larry meant, nervously burst into laughter, stood up, and, while Dick was playing the introduction, chided them for taking up his time. It would not be the last time Rodgers and Hart would be dismissed.[47]

Released from *Helen of Troy, N.Y.*, Helen Ford got into the act. "We auditioned for every Tom, Dick and Harry, every cloak and suiter down on Seventh Avenue who would listen to us," Ford recalled. "Finally, we found that we were doing it for the gangsters. They were beginning to put money in the business."[48]

The process turned 1925 into a winter of discontent. Dick was self-conscious about his father's opinion of him, not to mention the opinions of the women he was dating. He had left Columbia without a degree, devoted himself to music, and all for what?

But Larry pulled the discouraged Dick into one last one-night stand. *Bad Habits of 1925* sounded at once naughty and inviting, a more prosaic variation on theatrical titles—follies, vanities, scandals—that refract the lower forms of human behavior. The revue was put together by Larry and his old pal Irving Strouse for the benefit of the Evelyn Goldsmith Home for Crippled Children. For the night of February 8, 1925, Strouse arranged to use the Children's Theatre of the Heckscher Foundation, at 104th Street and Fifth Avenue. (It is currently part of the Museo del Barrio.) For *Bad Habits*, Dick and Larry used a couple of the old *Winkle Town* songs and wrote five or six new ones. The title "Mah-Jongg Maid" survives, but its lyrics are missing. "I'd Like to Take You Home to Meet My Mother" is a tour de force of vernacular, with allusions to Irving Berlin, George M. Cohan, *The Merry Widow*, Rudolph Valentino, Al Jolson, and Metropolitan Opera general manager Giulio Gatti-Casazza. It is a remarkable imitation of Gilbert and Sullivan ("If you'd only meet the mater / I'm convinced it would elate her"), but it is unmistakably Hart, with patter that contains crossword clues: "A word of thirteen letters, starts with X and ends with I." (Xanthomelanoi?) Was anyone else writing lyrics like that?

Bad Habits of 1925 was no more than an uptown blink during what Harold Clurman would later refer to as possibly the best theatrical season ever, 1924–25: O'Neill's *Desire Under the Elms*; Philip Barry's comedy *The Youngest*; the Kaufman-Connelly *Beggar on Horseback*; *What Price Glory?* by Laurence Stallings and Maxwell Anderson; the Astaires in the Gershwins' *Lady Be Good*; Molnár's *The Guardsman*; and Sidney Howard's *They Knew What They Wanted*.[49]

These last two were produced by the Theatre Guild, which was managed with frightening efficiency. Movies had crushed old stock companies, but the Theatre Guild survived on a combination of pluck, literary acumen, and a strong permanent company that was advised by Margaret Wycherly. Since 1919 the Guild had worked primarily out of the Garrick Theatre—closer to Herald Square than to Times Square—and was now moving to a new theater on Fifty-Second Street, west of Broadway, next to a skating rink called Iceland, Inc. In December 1924, New York governor Al Smith had laid the building's cornerstone. Four months later the Theatre Guild held a Vaudeville Tapestry Ball and Buffet Supper at the Hotel Commodore abutting Grand Central Terminal. The evening's program announced: "This year we are going to have a Vaudeville, followed by a Ball and Buffet Supper. We call it the Tapestry Ball, because we want those who come to vote upon the selection of the tapestries for the new Guild Theatre."[50]

The selection of tapestries might have been made that night, but there wasn't enough money raised to buy them. To accomplish that, the Guild would have to put on another show.

Even if Dick and Larry had been invited to the Guild's Vaudeville and Tapestry Ball, they didn't have much money to contribute. Larry was contemplating turning thirty with no prospects. Dick, defeated and desperate, was considering an offer from a Mr. Marvin, for fifty dollars a week, to train in the business of manufacturing children's underwear. Broadway and Seventh Avenue—the world of the theater and the world of *shmatte*—were only blocks apart; if Dick, for all his musical talent, couldn't master one, he'd master the other. Though it cracked Dr. Rodgers's heart to see his son in this state, he figured it was the right move for him.

One of Dr. Rodgers's patients was the attorney Benjamin Kaye. And one of Kaye's clients was the Theatre Guild. Kaye mentioned that the Guild was considering producing a revue to be written and performed primarily by its junior members. Dick was thrilled by the prospect. Larry, on the other hand, was not interested in reverting to writing songs that were not part of a story; a revue meant it was back to amateur time. Dick persuaded him to reconsider by suggesting they write a jazz opera that would be wholly theirs; the opera would become the center of the revue.[51] All right, Larry was in. So, in April 1925 Kaye brought Dick and Larry to the Garrick to meet its directors, Lawrence Langner and Theresa Helburn.

"Sitting on the empty stage of the Garrick," Helburn wrote, "Dick Rodgers played the songs and Larry Hart, a slight frail youth, not over five feet in spite of his elevator shoes, sang them for us. When they came to the song 'Manhattan' I sat up in delight. These lads had ability, wit, and a flair for a light sophisticated kind of song."[52]

Helburn looked over at Langner; Langner looked back at her. *Well?* Because the new Guild Theatre wasn't ready, Helburn and Langner promised the boys a budget of $5,000 and free use of the Garrick for two performances and two performances only. They had a month to put it all together.

CHAPTER 6

You Mustn't Conceal Anything You Feel

T H I S W A S more like it. Dick Rodgers went to the piano to work out new tunes for the show, which would be performed by the junior members of the Guild. Edith Meiser, a sloe-eyed Vassar graduate who had already written a sketch called "Gilding the Guild," was under the impression that she would write the lyrics to Rodgers's tunes. Rodgers gently disabused her of the notion.

"I generally work with a guy named Larry Hart," he said to Meiser, suggesting she hear some of the songs they'd already hammered out.

Meiser remembered:

A few days later Dick brought in the lyrics. Well, I did have the sense to know when I was outclassed. Those lyrics were so absolutely sensational! I remember Larry Hart coming into the theater. This little bit, almost a dwarf, of a man. I always thought he was the American Toulouse-Lautrec. He was that kind of personality. But an enchanting man. He had what is now called charisma. He had such appeal. He was already balding. He had this enormous head and a very heavy beard that had to be shaved twice a day.[1]

Meiser contributed material anyway, and served as director for many of the skits. Ben Kaye, who had brought Rodgers and Hart around in the first place, wrote several skits. On the street, Larry and Philip Loeb, a young Philadelphian who had directed several Guild plays, ran into Larry's old writing partner Morrie Ryskind and asked him for a skit. Morrie, dyspeptic as ever, agreed to write something and said he would try to make it to Larry's thirtieth birthday party. He was sore at Larry because he still hadn't been paid for his press work on *The First Fifty Years.* "If a man is going to cheat you," Ryskind wrote in his diary, "he does it just as easily, even though there be a [*sic*] contract." [2] *Like father, like son,* he must have thought.

Harold Clurman had initially been hired by the Guild as a play reader, although, like many professorial types, he was not averse to appearing on the stage. Beginning in April he had a bit part in the Guild's *Caesar and Cleopatra.* Sandy Meisner and Lee Strasberg, who would become New York's most prominent acting teachers, played soldiers that winter in John Howard Lawson's comedy *Processional,* along with future screenwriter (and later one of the Hollywood Ten) Alvah Bessie. These junior players were asked to sing for Dick, Larry, and Loeb. Auditioning at the Garrick, Strasberg preceded Clurman, who heard him try a verse of "My Wild Irish Rose." Strasberg did well enough to be given a singing part; Clurman was less impressive, so he was assigned to stage-manage *The Garrick Gaieties.* [3]

Rehearsals commenced in Helburn's old attic office and continued in cast members' apartments. The twenty-one-year-old Mexican caricaturist Miguel Covarrubias was commissioned to design a set for the show. Costumes came from the Brooks Costume Company. Herb Fields consulted on the dances.

It was a dynamic few weeks. These weren't the rehearsals of their grandmother's era, when usually one or two men—an actor-manager or variation thereof—ran everything. This was a give-and-take work environment where conversation was charged by philosophy and politics—this was the first generation of theater people who had been to college. Edith Meiser said, "Suddenly colleges were giving courses where the theater was a serious educational process." [4] Ben Kaye provided a wealth of material. Morrie Ryskind didn't appear at Larry's thirtieth birthday party but turned in a skit he wrote with Arthur Sullivan (no relation to one half of the Gilbert & Sullivan team). The skit ran four pages; the Theatre Guild's participatory contract ran twelve.

The Garrick Gaieties was performed on Sunday, May 17, 1925, in what was meant to be the first of two Sunday shows, presumably producing enough box office revenue to buy those coveted tapestries for the new Guild Theatre. Nobody, however, could have predicted the warmth with which the revue was received.

"The music by Richard Rodgers, and the lyrics, by Lorenz Hart, both of whom are still remembered at Columbia University, were well above the average Broadway output," hailed the *Daily News*.[5] The show was divided into two acts and twenty-three scenes, which, during the revue's run, would be altered now and again, but usually to conform to political or cultural news.

In act 1, "Soliciting Subscriptions" made it clear what the *Gaieties* was about. Larry rhymes "avenue" with "have in you" and "never see 'em" with "a museum." And there's the glinting double-rhyme welcome of "We like to serve a mild dish / Of folk-lore, quaintly childish / And sometimes, Oscar Wilde-ish." This opening rolled into "Gilding the Guild," a Meiser idea, with lyrics by Larry, which introduced the charming Betty Starbuck, who had an act with her brother, lately at the Waldorf. A characteristic Hart lyric was "April Fool," sung by Betty Starbuck and Romney Brent.

> My poor heart goes
> Any way the wind blows,
> Spring is a habit with me;
> Girls refuse me
> But they cannot lose me;
> Plato and I can't agree.

His lines were becoming tighter, more succinct, packing more emotion into fewer words. One popular spoof by Ben Kaye was of Sidney Howard's Pulitzer Prize–winning romantic comedy *They Knew What They Wanted* (thirty years later the basis for Frank Loesser's musical *The Most Happy Fella*), here known as *They Didn't Know What They Were Getting*. The story about a California-Italian bootlegger whose young bride falls for a migrant worker was an instant classic—and ripe for parody.

TONY

> Dis place mucha too quiet. I wanna have roun'
> here a woman, an' bambino—babies—eight,
> ten, twelve lil' babies, heh?

"The Joy Spreader," the piece that mollified Larry about participating in the *Gaieties*, was a warm-up for the recitative style Dick and Larry would perfect in the movies several years later. The early verdict on "The Joy Spreader" was that it was too long and indifferently performed.

"Ladies of the Box Office" includes Larry's old rhyme of "hell for ya" and "Philadelphia," and also anticipates Johnny Mercer's "Hooray for Holly-wood":

> *If your nose will photograph well*
> *And your pearly teeth will laugh well*
> *Though you only can act half well*
> *You'll put Barrymore on the blink.*

"Manhattan," left over from *Winkle Town,* was introduced by June Cochrane and a red-haired, froggy-voiced young Georgian, Sterling Holloway, who would become familiar to moviegoers of the 1930s as a Paramount con-tract player and the voice of several Disney characters. The *Gaieties* playbill, though not the lyric, drolly connected "Manhattan" to John F. Hylan, the mayor of Greater New York for the past eight years, a Tammany politi-cian widely believed to be the marionette of newspaper publisher William Randolph Hearst. At the hint of a crisis, particularly anything involving the subway system, Hylan and his wife would bolt to Florida for a month's vacation.[6] "Do You Love Me?" (not to be confused with the better-known Bock-Harnick song from *Fiddler on the Roof*) was, the authors explained, the revue's obligatory "reference to the rapidly disappearing emotion known as love."

Work on the *Gaieties* forged some durable relationships. Harold Clurman and Lee Strasberg became close friends, and the Group Theatre emerged out of that friendship. Like the various editions of Gerard Alessandrini's *Forbid-den Broadway* that began running in 1982, *The Garrick Gaieties* was conceived for audiences in the know—people who read every week about Grover Wha-len (police commissioner and former president of Wanamaker's department store), people familiar with the subway to Coney and eating baloney on a roll, people who appreciated the sly ribbing of more affluent New York denizens who wouldn't be caught dead on Mott Street in lovely October, never mind in the canicular days of July.

"A considerable part of the undeniable fun of the *Gaieties* hinges on the personal and technical activities of the Guild itself," *The Wall Street Journal* reported after the second Sunday performance. "In this the entertainment recalls college productions in which the whole audience grows gleeful over 'grinds' and jokes on the local faculty and other matters familiar to a limited public." If the show were to continue through summer, the *Journal* said, its more inside material would have to be modified for summer patrons, who tended to be from out of town.[7]

And would the *Gaieties* continue? What about it? Rodgers went to Helburn.

"What would you have us do?" said Helburn, citing the popularity of Alfred Lunt and Lynn Fontanne in the Guild's current hit, *The Guardsman*.

"Pack up the Lunts," Rodgers said, with the kind of confident authority he would begin to wield over his partner.[8]

So the Theatre Guild packed up the Lunts, and the regular New York run of the *Garrick Gaieties* began on June 8. In opening up the show to out-of-towners and keeping current, Larry's beloved jazz opera "The Joy Spreader" was dropped. Larry didn't mind; if a number didn't work, it didn't work. (In the coming years Rodgers would be a particularly ruthless editor of their material.) Other songs were jettisoned. The Hart lyric "Black and White," which suggests that sentiments are best appreciated when recorded on the page, was replaced by "On with the Dance," which counsels shedding one's inhibitions. "You mustn't conceal / anything you feel" goes one line, and it seemed to be a lifetime removed from the self-pity and self-protectiveness that so many Hart characters would give voice to in the coming years. A song called "Sentimental Me," which might also have been recycled from *Winkle Town*, was added to good effect; as in so many Hart lyrics, it had one sincerely ardent refrain and one comic refrain. "And Thereby Hangs a Tail," by Ryskind and Loeb, with lyrics by Hart, was inserted at the beginning of act 2. The Scopes "Monkey Trial" was under way in Tennessee; John Scopes, about to be tried for violating a state law prohibiting the teaching of evolution, was reported to have seen the show and roared with laughter. The scene: a jungle courthouse, with everybody wearing a monkey mask and Philip Loeb impersonating William Jennings Bryan, who enters the courthouse singing:

> I'm sure I'd rather prosecute this case
> Than run another presidential race;
> For the Congo's greatest menace is
> A monkey who will not believe in Genesis.

Dick had to be at the Garrick every night to conduct. For weeks, Larry also attended every performance. "His special job, self-invented," reported *New York Amusements*, "is to run back stage with a report of the celebrities nightly found in the audience. Lately he has tailored a line in one of his lyrics to fit some one well known with a high visibility, and the singer has to memorize the new sparkle at once." Lyrics to go. "The cast say they expect any night to walk right on with Hart hanging to a coat tail, murmuring thus and thus to the audience because he didn't get a chance to tell the singer."[9]

Whether he wanted a vehicle for his wife after *Helen of Troy, N.Y.*, or because he too could hear all the talent behind the songs in *The Garrick Gaieties*, George Ford decided he would produce *Sweet Rebel*. Lacking enough money to plan for a Broadway run, however, Ford called on his family—in this case his brother Harry, who directed the stock company at the Colonial Theatre in Akron, Ohio. Harry said he would do what he could. By promising to get his boss's sister-in-law to appear in *The Gingham Girl* at the Colonial, Harry won approval for use of the theater in midsummer. By the time the show played on July 25, it was retitled *Dear Enemy*.

The performance went well. *Dear Enemy* was *Romeo and Juliet* at the American Revolution, and audiences of the 1920s hadn't seen anything quite like it—a native operetta that went so far as to suggest that proper colonial women were interested in sex. It played in Akron for one night. The Fords and Rodgers and Hart decided they might be able to bring this show to Broadway after all. George Ford began to arrange for another tryout.

Then two related events put their enthusiasm in new perspective. A verdict came in on the so-called Monkey Trial in Tennessee: John Scopes was found guilty of breaking state law by teaching Darwinian evolution; prosecutor William Jennings Bryan had triumphed over Scopes's lawyer Clarence Darrow. Before Bryan could savor his victory, however, he dropped dead.

While Bryan's body lay in state in Dayton, Tennessee, the *Garrick Gaieties* players quickly eliminated "And Thereby Hangs a Tail."[10] The program was reassembled. Had some of the charm worn off? The show was panned in the humor magazine *Judge* by George Jean Nathan, the most acerbic of critics, who wrote that "for all its Homeric striving, it contains nothing that Ziegfeld, White and Charlot do not do fifty times better. Its singing is bad; its comedy is poor; its dancing is commonplace; its pictorial quality is nil."[11]

"Most good artists begin by getting bad reviews," Edmund Wilson wrote.[12] A review like that didn't wound Larry the way it would in later years. Larry might have also been considering the source: it was George Jean Nathan who once declared, "Intelligence ruins a pretty woman, as intelligence ruins a pretty lyric."[13]

❧   ❧   ❧

In the pre–air-conditioning era, the theater district in midsummer broiled. After performances on especially hot nights, Dick would take the train out to Long Beach to spend the next day swimming with his parents before returning to Manhattan to conduct again that evening. Larry would hire a limousine and take cast members for long drives, the night air cooling the car, bootlegged booze and songs flowing. Although Rodgers and Hart rarely socialized together away from first nights at the theater, they occasionally attended the same parties. One smitten host was Jules Glaenzer, by then vice president of Cartier, New York, who held cocktail parties at his apartment on East Sixty-Fifth Street, where George Gershwin played *Rhapsody in Blue*, Vincent Youmans sang his latest songs, and Larry did his Al Jolson imitation.[14]

Rodgers was dining alone one July night at Rudley's, in the theater district, when he met the "very attractive" English actress Gladys Calthorp and her escort, Noël Coward. Coward's *The Vortex* had already enjoyed commercial success in London and was weeks away from opening in New York. The two songwriters complimented each other's recent triumphs. Coward soon became a fixture at the Glaenzer parties.[15]

On August 6, Dick was still conducting the *Gaieties*, so he could not have attended the opening of the musical *June Days*, to which he and Larry had contributed one song, "Anytime, Anywhere, Anyhow." (The lyric is missing.) Most of the *June Days* music was written by J. Fred Coots.

One evening later that month, Coots was drinking at the Woodmere Country Club, on Long Island, when he heard the bar's pianist playing a medley of songs that made him sit up. The songs were by Rodgers and Hart; the pianist was Dorothy Fields.

Coots approached her. "Have you ever written lyrics?"

Fields said she had, but, in fact, she hadn't; she meant she *felt* like she had. Coots introduced Fields to his composer friend Jimmy McHugh: maybe they could write something together? "I was so impressed with the inter-rhyming and the feminine hybrid rhymes of Larry Hart," Fields said, "that [at first] I was not writing like anybody but trying to be like Larry, and consequently they weren't very good."[16]

George Ford arranged for further *Dear Enemy* tryouts in September at Ford's Opera House, in Baltimore, but he began to worry about money. Helen Ford was still carrying around the script, figuring she might inveigle some sucker into investing. She even moved out of the Algonquin, where it seemed like *everybody* was in show business or publishing, to the nearby Roosevelt, which attracted a broader (and sometimes more naïve) clientele.

Sure enough, riding down in the elevator, Helen was taken aback when a middle-aged man said hello and told her he was from New Hampshire.

"What a coincidence!" said the alluring actress. "My husband went to school there, at Dartmouth."

"Not Gink Ford!" said the man from New Hampshire, who introduced himself as Robert Jackson. His brother had roomed with George Ford at Dartmouth. In fact, Jackson had also attended Dartmouth, albeit several years earlier than Ford, before obtaining a law degree and becoming chairman of the New Hampshire Democratic Party. It wasn't his Dover-based law practice, however, that enabled Jackson to travel first class but his sizable stake in Dominion Stores Ltd., a grocery chain founded in Ontario in 1919. (Decades later Dominion would be acquired by A & P.) "I see you have a script under your arm," Jackson said, pointing to the latest typescript of *Dear Enemy.*

"Do you know anyone who'd want to put money in a show?" said Helen.

"Well, I might," said Jackson, who turned out to be utterly stagestruck.[17]

Helen introduced Jackson to Dick, Larry, and Herb Fields. Jackson checked out *Garrick Gaieties* and loved it, loved it, thought it was marvelous. Through early September, while he considered investing in *Dear Enemy,* Jackson took Helen and the boys to nightclubs. A frequent stop was Texas Guinan's, on West Forty-Eighth Street. Guinan had been the hostess at the El Fey Club, on West Forty-Fifth, but the El Fey, owned by bootlegger Larry Fay, tended to be padlocked every few weeks by Prohibition agents. Hart admired the ease with which Guinan created pandemonium in the room, spraying a stylized condescension at just about everybody, without regard to attire or income. Her popularity was multiplied exponentially by customers who wanted the experience of being ordered about by her. She famously addressed prospective big spenders with "Hello, sucker!" Whenever a drunk became boisterous, she would say, "Make all the noise you want, sucker—it will all be on your check."[18] Jackson, like so many customers with cash to throw around, proceeded to act the role Guinan had assigned him.[19]

Still, Jackson wouldn't make a commitment. Helen Ford went to Baltimore for a week to star as Betsy Burke in the retitled *Dearest Enemy,* at Ford's Opera House there. A few days later, on September 18, the show opened at the Knickerbocker in New York.

With Rodgers conducting the orchestra, *Dearest Enemy* garnered wonderful reviews. "Baby-grand opera," wrote Percy Hammond in the *Herald Tribune.* "More than a chance flavor of Gilbert and Sullivan," said the *Times.*[20] Despite notices like these, George Ford didn't know how long he could keep the show running. Jackson suddenly announced that he wanted to see the new George S. Kaufman comedy, *The Butter and Egg Man.* Rodgers, Hart, and Fields, sensing this was the *worst* play for a prospective angel to see, did what they could to dissuade him. But Jackson stole away one night to take a look.

The Butter and Egg Man is about young naïf Peter Jones, who comes to New York and, eager to "stake a show" on Broadway, is persuaded by fast-talking impresario Joseph Lehman into investing in a show that's certain to flop. (If Mel Brooks hadn't read the play when he wrote the movie *The Producers*, he must have been channeling Kaufman.)

Jackson laughed throughout the play and told Helen Ford that the young hero was "an awful fool"; then he announced he was putting his money into *Dearest Enemy*, which could then be kept running while it built an audience. She passed the news on to Larry. Frederick Nolan's snapshot of the moment is delightful: "He took hold of her hands and danced her around, ring-a-rosy style, chanting, 'We've found a butter-and-egg man, we've found a butter-and-egg man!'"[21]

Garrick Gaieties, fun and successful as it was, still had the personality of a revue, of a varsity show in long pants. *Dearest Enemy*, on the other hand, was the genuine article—a Broadway musical that was all of a piece and demonstrated what its creators were capable of. John Murray Anderson, who had tried his hand at musical comedy with an earlier edition of the *Greenwich Village Follies*, directed. Anderson brought in two of his *Follies* artists, Reginald Marsh and James Reynolds, to work on *Dearest Enemy*. Marsh was drawing a column of sketches for the *Daily News* and illustrating book jackets. No painter captured Larry Hart's perspective of New York's ugly beauty quite as vividly as Marsh. Many of the figures in Marsh's paintings are bawdy, overripe, anxious, frenetic, and terribly lonely—much like the characters singing Larry's lyrics. For *Dearest Enemy*, Marsh designed the intermission curtain, which drew as much attention as any stage picture. James Reynolds, though also a scenic designer, worked primarily on the late-eighteenth-century costumes.

Dearest Enemy opens at the Murray mansion in 1776. Mrs. Murray and the young wives and daughter who lodge with her sing "Heigh-Ho,

Lackaday," the "charming pastoral" that so embarrassed the music publisher years earlier. (Ira Gershwin used *lackaday,* too. The word probably comes from *alack the day,* an archaic phrase that Larry employed to express the women's sorrow.) Larry knew the effectiveness of sweet and sour, pinning the regretful "Lackaday" like a tail to the self-consciously cheery "Heigh-Ho." There are marvelous rhymes in the song:

We have learned from observation
The creation of a nation
Comes to better consummation
Born in joy!
So let us quit,
And dance a bit!

While their men are at war, these women have been stitching their hearts out and long for some fun! Who can blame them? But Mrs. Murray is there to bring order:

I behold in consternation
You have taken a vacation.
Fingers in your occupation
Please employ!
The creation of a nation
Comes of steady application.
Vain sensation of elation
Please destroy!

But the British are coming, and their imminent arrival is a two-edged sword. "Hooray, we're going to be compromised!" the men-starved ladies cry out in "War Is War." (In a later version "compromised" became "fraternized.")

As the heroine Betsy Burke, Helen Ford made one of the sauciest entrances in the history of musical theater—emerging from the riverbank wearing a barrel because she's lost her clothes while swimming. British Captain Copeland gets an eyeful of Miss Burke, and romance blossoms. After a few meetings, Copeland will sing "Here in My Arms" to Betsy, as she does eventually to him. Their duet "Bye and Bye" sounds like it could have been a Revolutionary Era song, even when Hart rhymes "sorrowful" with "tomorrow full" and "flies on" with "horizon." Betsy, confiding in her friends, sings "I'd Like to

Hide It," meaning her attraction to Captain Copeland, whose close proximity makes her "blood turn into wine."

The British officers are humanized in "Cheerio," for they too leave mothers, wives, and children at home. Hart's intense feeling for Manhattan is evident in "Where the Hudson River Flows," which reminds us that the great river has always been romantic as well as magnificent. In "Old Enough to Love," the lyric Larry had first written for *The Lady in Ermine* as "When the Boys Are Older," General Howe supplies the reasons why a more mature man is the better lover (though he runs out of steam before he finishes the song). There's a marvelous variation on the theme when the British officers praise the mature beauty of Mrs. Murray in "Full Blown Roses," and in the reprise General Tryon sings:

> *I prefer the riper charms*
> *That the autumn years disclose.*
> *Your equator may be greater,*
> *But I like to fill my arms*
> *With the most substantial foes.*[22]

"Sweet Peter" was a comedy number about Peter Stuyvesant, who was already part of ancient New York history by the time of the American Revolution. In the song, which cleverly echoes the nursery rhyme "Peter Peter Pumpkin Eater," the wooden leg of the governor of New Amsterdam alerts his wife every dawn as he hobbles home drunk. The song, as music scholar Graham Wood has pointed out, is also about deception: although the clumping of Peter's wooden leg makes it impossible to deceive his wife, the song is sung by another pair of nation-crossed lovers, Jane Murray and Captain Henry Tryon, while they deceive Mrs. Murray into thinking they're sitting far from each other when they're actually close enough to kiss.[23] Larry might have conceived the song after years of passing the wooden statue known as Peg-Leg Peter, in front of the Stuyvesant Insurance Company, at 157 Broadway, not far from Max Hart's office downtown.

One night after a performance of *Dearest Enemy*, a disgruntled audience member was ushered backstage to speak to Larry. Observing the man's distress, Larry asked what the problem was.

"That song of yours, 'Sweet Peter,' is not very considerate," the man said. "I mean, if a one-legged man were in the audience, don't you think his feelings would be hurt?"

Larry's patience with such delicate sensibilities would grow thinner each year. ("Always the dullness of the fool is the whetstone of the wits," says Celia in *As You Like It*.) He pushed his hat back, tilted his head up to the man, and said, "If you went to the theater and saw an idiot on the stage, would your feelings be hurt?"[24]

Through the fall of 1925, *Dearest Enemy* was at the Knickerbocker—a most appropriate venue, given the musical's Old New York setting—at Thirty-Eighth and Broadway, so Larry could saunter up from the Garrick, at Thirty-Fifth. If he walked an extra block, though, he might grit his teeth at the marquee for the Friml-Hooker version of *The Vagabond King*, at the Casino Theatre. *The Vagabond King* had been one of the shows that got away.

That lingering disappointment was buried under much happy activity. "Manhattan" and "Sentimental Me" were interpolated in the *Greenwich Village Follies* on tour. "Sentimental Me," "April Fool," "On with the Dance," and "Manhattan" were orchestrated for fox-trot by Arthur Lange and published by Marks. Paul Whiteman recorded "Sentimental Me" and "Manhattan" for the Victor Talking Machine Company.[25] *Rodgers & Hart* began to appear on record labels. In a diary entry from 1925, Edmund Wilson tracked the flow of a popular song through the tributaries of American culture:

> Harlem cabarets, other cabarets, Reisenfeld's classical jazz, the Rascoes' private orchestra, the hand organs, the phonographs, the radio, the Webster Hall balls, other balls (college proms), men going home late at night whistling it on the street, picked out on Greenwich Village ukuleles, sung in later motor rides by boys and girls, in restaurants—hotel restaurants, Paul Whiteman and Lopez, vaudeville, played Sundays by girls at pianos from sheet music with small photographs on the cover, of both the composer and the person who first sang it—first sung in a popular musical comedy (introduced several times—at the end of the second act pathetically—and played as the audience are leaving the theater)—pervading the country through the movie pianists, danced to in private houses to the music of a phonograph—the Elks fair—thrown on the screen between the acts at the National Winter Garden Burlesque and sung by the male audience—Remey's Dancing Academy (decayed fairies).[26]

Since 1925 the technology has changed immeasurably, of course, and Broadway is rarely the source of hit songs these days. But the distribution of pop music became viral very quickly, even without the electronic advantages of the present day.

The Garrick Gaieties and *Dearest Enemy* played to packed houses in the same year as the publication of F. Scott Fitzgerald's *The Great Gatsby*, which was not a commercial success at the time but, like "Manhattan," would outlive its era. Budd Schulberg wrote:

In 1925 alone, when *The Great Gatsby* confirmed Scott as the Prodigy of American letters, other books published that year included Dreiser's *An American Tragedy*, Dos Passos's *Manhattan Transfer*, Lewis's *Arrowsmith*, Hemingway's astonishing collection of short stories, *In Our Time* (with *The Sun Also Rises* close behind). Faulkner was beginning, Frost was coming into his maturity, O'Neill had a new play ready every season, Dorothy Parker was at the top of her Emily Dickinsonian form, Ring Lardner's latest book of short stories was coming off the presses, and there were volumes of poetry by Ezra Pound, Archibald MacLeish, Edwin Arlington Robinson, Amy Lowell . . . the list went on. Not to mention the movies, Chaplin and all the wonderful silent comedians.[27]

It was a heady time to visit New York and attend the theater. The writer Lincoln Barnett showed up after midterm exams in his freshman year of college and bought a ticket to *The Garrick Gaieties*. "Nothing I have witnessed in the theater since has touched it," Barnett wrote.

The skits were distilled satire; the girls were my dream girls—every one of them; and the music—the bewitching, irresistible music seemed to embody everything that was wonderful and exciting about New York—spangled towers against the evening sky, the great audacious ships moving out to sea, the golden portals of theaters and hotels, mirrored avenues glittering in the rain, the red-lit mists of March, the street-gray dusk of November, and Central Park muffled in snow; it lifted me right up into the stars, filled me with inquietude and longing and discontent, set my feet twitching, and made me want then and there to get up on the stage and sing and dance and win applause as an integral member of that happy and attractive company.

Years later Barnett told Richard Rodgers, "*The Garrick Gaieties* was the best time I ever had at the theater."

"Oh, yes," said Rodgers. "Me, too."[28]

❧   ❧   ❧

The three *Dearest Enemy* creators at last had money in their pockets. One evening Richard Rodgers, who was not yet drinking with either the openness or eagerness of his writing partner, went to pick up his slightly younger friend Ben Feiner at his apartment so they could go to the movies. There Rodgers caught a glimpse of Ben's willowy younger sister Dorothy, who was going on a date with Andrew Goodman, of the Bergdorf Goodman family, to see the new show *Sunny*.[29] The image of this beautiful young woman would stay with him.

Herb Fields had no equivalent romantic preoccupation. For a while Herb was in thrall to Larry, parroting Larry's cigar-smoking and night-crawling.[30] But it was impossible for Herb to follow his idol around because Larry was there one minute and gone the next, vanishing into the shadows of the city. In December, Larry and Dick took a week in Havana, at the time probably the most licentious city in the hemisphere, sampling Cuban cocktails and making notes for another musical Herb had cooked up. They were home a few days before Christmas.

Larry was presumably sober when Rodgers told him how Max Dreyfus had summoned him to his office at T. B. Harms and eaten crow. A few years earlier, Dreyfus had dismissed the song "Manhattan," and now he wanted to publish Rodgers and Hart, even offering them an office and an account from which the boys could draw advances against royalties for their works in progress. Rodgers had told Max no, that wasn't the way they worked, and Larry, toughened by seasons of uncredited labor for United Plays, concurred. Nevertheless, Harms became the boys' music publisher. Dick and Larry were always welcome at the Brewster, New York, estate that Max shared with his brother Louis. And it was Louis, no less impressed with the team than Max, who recommended them to English music hall star Jack Hulbert.[31] Hulbert and his wife, Cicely Courtneidge, were appearing at the Gaiety in a revue called *By the Way*, which they had imported from London, and made it known they were looking for songwriters for a new show.

CHAPTER 7

It's So Good It Must Be Immoral

FIRST THE boys had two other commitments—one of them to Larry's old client Billy Rose. By 1925 Rose had had his name on more than a hundred songs, including "Barney Google," co-credited to Con Conrad and an enormous success (and, in the view of critic-composer Deems Taylor, "the worst song in the history of the music business").[1] With an annual income climbing into six figures, Rose put $50,000 into the second floor of a mansion at 683 Fifth Avenue, at Fifty-Fourth Street—then, as now, among the most expensive real estate properties in the United States—to convert it into a club. Simulating the interior of a theater, the club was meant to show the world—and maybe his mentor, Barney Baruch—that Billy Rose had class. The five-dollar cover charge was supposed to keep out the riffraff. "It exhaled so much fake swank," Rose wrote, "that on opening night my French headwaiter suggested I stay out of sight in the office."[2] Rodgers and Hart, whom Billy still referred to as "a couple of college kids, fresh out of Columbia," wrote several songs that became *The Fifth Avenue Follies*, presented at the Fifth Avenue Club beginning in late January 1926. The Fifth Avenue Club soon encountered a problem that had nothing to do with Dick and Larry or their work: the BYOB policy, which was considered prudent in the middle of Prohibition, was meaningless to customers who wanted to be served someone *else's* booze. Billy sold the place before *The Fifth Avenue Follies* could benefit from the word of mouth that most shows need to keep running.

The Girl Friend opened on March 17, 1926. It was the show Dick and

Larry had promised those entertaining spouses, Eva Puck and Sammy White. Lew Fields produced. Herb Fields wrote the book. This one was about bicycle racing. Lenny Silver (White) trains on Long Island for an important six-day race. His girlfriend Mollie (Puck), meaning well, forges letters that get Lenny into trouble with his trainer; then Lenny gets out of trouble. Love and marriage ensue. It wasn't much, but it was enough. Audiences were expecting big things from Rodgers and Hart, in part because of the married headliners. They sing the title song ("She's knockout, / She's regal, / Her beauty's illegal") and, after Mollie produces blueprints drawn by her late dad, an architect who had wanted to design the house she'd be happy in, "The Blue Room," which Stanley Green referred to as "that classic of city-life contentment."[3] "The Blue Room" was probably written in early March 1926, in Atlantic City, just before tryouts of the show. In *The Rodgers and Hart Song Book*, Margery Darrell analyzed its deceptively simple construction:

> With only a few exceptions all the rhymes and inner rhymes [in "The Blue Room"] occur in the same note, C. Every time you are going to hear the half note which is the center of the melody, it is preceded by the repetition of C and the rhyme. And this same half note is always the note which carries (each time higher) the word *room*, the most important word in the song.[4]

Eva Puck had a delightful comic waltz, "The Damsel Who Done All the Dirt," that anticipates the more well-known "Guys and Dolls" and shows Larry at his slyest:

> *When one guy kills the other guy,*
> *"Find the woman" is the cry.*

And:

> *The rise and fall of every nation*
> *Allows a sex interpretation.*

And:

> *When Washington crossed the Delaware,*
> *It wasn't for the ride.*

He had a date with a Jersey flapper
On the other side.

A few days after *The Girl Friend* opened, the *Herald Tribune* ran a piece focusing on Larry and how he worked. In the unsigned "If You Must Write Lyrics, Be Natural," the reporter said, "To watch Lorenz Hart write a lyric such as 'The Girl Friend' number in the show of that name now playing at the Vanderbilt Theater is to become as exasperated as is possible to a mortal man who is also a writer."[5] Pressured to write an additional chorus, the reporter observed, Larry seemed to be disappearing behind pieces of the set; while dancers in rehearsal pounded the floor, furniture was being moved, lights were adjusted, and cast and crew were calling out to one another, he would finish the thing in minutes. Lighting a cigar and tossing away the match, Larry told the *Herald's* man that it was about spontaneity. "Watch music phrases!" he said. "Pick out the essential phrase in the first line of a hit song. Don't try to find the most trite word or words to fit that phrase. Find something living, a word everyone uses. People don't go around talking about 'love' and 'dove.' They do talk about 'blue rooms,' so I wrote a song of that name. And boys do have girl friends, and a fellow is apt to say: 'I give in to you? Why do I?' So I have a song of that name."

The reporter, absorbing Larry's emphasis on using everyday language, said it reminded him of when Yeats last visited New York and told his audience that "the poet should be natural above all things." "You're only half right in your quotation," Hart replied. "Yeats writes back to the beginnings of all things poetry. Popular song should go back to the origins, too. But the comedy song, the satirical song—that can afford to be a bit smart. And I think one can drop a bit of satire, fling a daring rhyme even into the popular song, provided it doesn't rise too close to the surface." The *Herald* piece acknowledged Larry's ability to make the creation of a lyric appear effortless. (Yeats: "A line will take us hours maybe; / Yet if it does not seem a moment's thought, / Our stitching and unstitching have been naught.")[6]

In *Life*—the weekly that predated the photograph-swollen, Henry Luce *Life*—critic Robert Benchley tipped his hat to Larry's work. "And those of us calamity-howlers who have been worrying about the low state of musical comedy lyrics ought to take up quite a lot of space in hailing young Mr. Lorenz Hart, whose words have graced the deft and melodious music of Richard Rodgers in *The Garrick Gaieties*, *Dearest Enemy*, and recently in a very satisfactory show called *The Girl Friend*. Mr. Hart's lyrics are both facile and funny, and . . . show unmistakable signs of the writer's having given personal thought to the matter."[7]

Benchley was a funny man with an incisive wit, but, unlike Larry Hart, unfamiliar with the pleasures of alcohol until Prohibition was in force. Apparently it was the popular cocktail known as the Orange Blossom, in vogue since the Great War, which hooked Benchley one night in 1922.[8] Prohibition had a way of doing that to some people. By the end of 1926, New York City's Health Department would record 750 deaths by alcohol poisoning.[9] The semisecrecy required by the Volstead Act, even in spirits-soaked Manhattan, suited Larry fine. He had his favorite speakeasies, including wherever Texas Guinan was cracking her whip that week, and he had his special hideaways. Photographs suggest that he sometimes went off to the Jersey side of the Hudson, catching one of the ferries at 125th Street to Fort Lee, and drinking there, far from his family and his increasingly disapproving writing partner.

After two shows running simultaneously on Broadway, with countless amateur shows behind him and more projects on the way, Larry was getting something of a reputation—one both connected to, and disconnected from, his father. By early 1926 Larry's protégé Arthur Schwartz had set up a law practice at 299 Broadway and taken on Max Hart as a client. There was always action from Max and money to be made, but Schwartz wanted, more than anything, to make *music*. He wrote to Larry's former Columbia classmate Howard Dietz, who had gone to work in the publicity department of Metro-Goldwyn-Mayer:

> As I told Beans [Bennett Cerf], I think you are the only man in town to be compared with Lorry Hart and from me, that's quite a tribute because I know almost every line Lorry has written. I think that three or four tunes of mine will be riots in the Grand Street Follies this year IF they have lyrics such as only Lorry and you can write.[10]

Dietz declined that invitation. But before too long he would agree to write with Schwartz.

Those early Dietz-Schwartz shows were revues. *The Garrick Gaieties* of 1926 continued the revue tradition. Returning were many of the previous year's participants. Rodgers conducted on opening night, May 10, 1926, and then turned the baton over to the older Columbia Varsity Show composer Roy Webb. The Rodgers & Hart song that achieved classic status almost instantly was "Mountain Greenery," sung by Sterling Holloway and Bobbie Perkins. In addition to well-known lines like "While you love your lover let / Blue skies be your coverlet" and "Beans can get no keener re- / Ception in a beanery," "Mountain Greenery" includes the lesser-known lines "Here a girl can map her own / Life without a chaperone" and "Life is more delectable / When it's disrespectable." This paean to the great outdoors—and it's easy to envision the Adirondacks of Larry's camp days—contains some pine tar. A few years after the 1926 edition of *The Garrick Gaieties*, a critic for *Theatre Magazine* wrote of "Mountain Greenery," "There is in the Hart lyrics an occasional tendency toward wickedness that has not been detrimental," and he cites the leer beneath some of the more innocent-sounding lines.[11] But there's also Larry's maturing use of American slang owing little to the polite, continental lyrics of operetta:

> *Eat and you'll grow fatter, boy,*
> *S'matter, boy?*
> *'Atta boy!*

A most adult kind of wickedness pervades one of the encores Larry wrote for the song "Queen Elizabeth":

> *They say he [Sir Walter Raleigh] discovered tobacco*
> *And that I made him smoke—it is true.*
> *For my tresses so Titian*
> *Gave him the ignition*
> *And one must have a moment or two.*

Reviews were enthusiastic, though most critics regarded the sequel as inferior to the original. In the *Times*, drama critic Brooks Atkinson didn't think the Rodgers & Hart songs had attained the high level of the first *Gaieties*, though he admired "Tennis Champs," with its very current references to Bill Tilden and Helen Wills, and "Queen Elizabeth." One month later Atkinson revisited the show and wrote an essay about how the order of a revue's material is critical to its effectiveness.[12] Since the revue is, by definition, lacking a sustained narrative, the balance of the sketches must be periodically weighed. The primary naysayer was, once again, George Jean Nathan, who wrote, "The audience at the opening applauded everything but the hat-holders under the seats."[13] (Beneath every theater seat there was, in fact, a place to put one's hat during the performance.)

❧   ❧   ❧

Almost precisely ten years earlier, in 1916, a revue called *The Light Blues* opened in London. That show, about May week at Cambridge, was produced by the renowned theater manager Robert Courtneidge and included his daughter Cicely in the cast. (Noël Coward appeared in a small role.) The show had been written in part by Jack Hulbert, who, unlike so many British music hall entertainers of the era, had been to university. The popular music scholar Dennis Moore wrote that Hulbert "always carried a slight 'I'm-only-an-amateur, chaps' air of embarrassment, which was sometimes painful to watch."[14]

During the 1920s Cicely Courtneidge and Jack Hulbert became one of the most beloved couples in British musical theater, although they had rarely appeared together until their success in *By the Way*, in 1925. For a follow-up, Hulbert and his producing partner Paul Murray were looking to drive their new vehicle with American music—or at least with energetic show music that was the province of American songwriters.

Because neither of the Rodgers & Hart shows then running on Broadway seemed appropriate—Hulbert and Murray weren't about to import a musical romance about the American Revolution, and a six-day bicycle race, set on Long Island, seemed so bloody quaint—Hulbert turned to much of the team that had assembled *By the Way*: the American librettists Bert Kalmar and Harry Ruby and the Englishmen Guy Bolton and Ronald Jeans. What emerged was *Lido Lady*, a trifle about a tennis champion whose father wants her to marry an athlete of equal or greater accomplishment. With a boost from Louis Dreyfus, who was now managing Chappell in England, Dick and Larry were invited to write the songs.

Since the show was set on the Lido, the boys came up with a nifty idea: they'd go to Venice and, intending to meet up with Dick's brother Mort and his new bride on their honeymoon, soak up some atmosphere. So the songwriters sailed to the Mediterranean aboard the *Conte Biancamano*, Larry rolling the name around his tongue with glee.[15] While Dick scoured the decks for attractive, unattached young women, Larry hoisted himself onto a bar stool and stayed there for hours.

And the bar was where he headed as soon as they arrived at the Lido. There Noël Coward introduced Rodgers, still on the prowl, to Linda and Cole Porter (Rodgers called Linda "the most beautiful woman I had ever seen"). Once Porter heard that Rodgers was there with Hart, he invited them to dinner, sending his private gondola to their hotel. At dinner each composer played some of his songs, and Rodgers was surprised by how gifted Porter was, though the privileged Episcopalian Hoosier had not yet had a complete show succeed on Broadway. In fact, Porter confessed his ambition of writing for Broadway while living in Europe.

"I have discovered the secret of writing hits," Porter confided.

Dick and Larry waited to hear the magic formula.

"I'll write Jewish tunes," Porter said.[16]

After Italy, Rodgers and Hart went to Paris ("every Parisian . . . was trying to take advantage of a couple of innocents abroad") and were happy to finally get to England. Hulbert and Paul Murray booked accommodations at the Savoy for Dick and Larry, who found the rooms disappointingly dark and small. "Mr. Hulbert brought [back to London] with him two American authors," *The New York Times* reported, "both in their teens, who are locked in a flat working out the music and lyrics of a new revue which he will present in New York soon. They are Lorenz Hart and Richard Rodgers. Mr. Hulbert says they recall Gilbert and Sullivan more than any couple he knows."[17]

The "teenagers" did what they could. In "A Cup of Tea," Larry teases the English for their five o'clock custom (he was now rhyming "Philadelphia" with "well f'ya" and "yell f'ya"). "A Tiny Flat in Soho" was tailor-made for the show, with Larry transferring the urban coziness of "Blue Room" to London. They churned out more than a dozen songs for *Lido Lady*. The boys were used to writing with Herb Fields's input, however—lyricist, composer, and librettist knowing each other so well, tossing ideas back and forth—and they missed Herb. They were perplexed by the relatively leisurely, long rehearsal time—nine weeks' worth, or three times longer than an American musical might get—and suspected that Hulbert's leading lady Phyllis Dare (Courtneidge had the more amusing but lesser role as Hulbert's sister) might not be credible as a coltish young tennis star: Dare had played debutantes on the London stage twenty years earlier.

Weeks before *Lido Lady* was to open, Dick and Larry decided to go home and resume work on a Herb Fields story set almost entirely inside a dream. They had been away from New York when the frenzy of the showing of Rudolph Valentino's dead body at the Campbell Funeral Home in Lincoln Square had pushed all other late-summer news off the front pages, and they'd only heard rumors about a new citywide discontent with Mayor Jimmy Walker. In early September, from Southampton, they took the *Majestic* to Cherbourg. On that leg of the voyage, Dick and Dorothy Feiner—tall and elegant in manner, she would have been perfect for the Phyllis Dare role—noticed each other again.[18] Dick's girl-chasing days were ostensibly over.

Home in New York, Dick and Larry went to work on Herb Fields's most recent idea—turning Mack Sennett's classic movie *Tillie's Punctured Romance* into a musical play. The material was in the family: Lew Fields had produced the movie's source material, the 1910 *Tillie's Nightmare*, with the young, pre-battle-ax Marie Dressler and sixteen songs to boot. *Tillie's Punctured Romance* did without the sixteen songs, of course, but Charlie Chaplin and Mabel Normand were aboard, with Dressler dominating the screen as she had dominated the stage. The Sennett movie took a whopping fourteen weeks to shoot—an unconscionably long time for a smallish comedy of the period.[19] Herb Fields's notion—he had been writing steadily since returning from his own European holiday in mid-August—was to change the overwhelming Tillie Blobbs into the young and pretty Peggy Barnes, from Glens Falls, New York. As it developed after many conferences with Dick and Larry, Fields's script, now called *Peggy*, would take the spirited ingenue into an extended dream of going to New York and Havana, where the Glens Falls people turn up.

This was right up Larry's alley. He had written the "You Can't Fool Your Dreams" lyric before he was twenty-seven. Now he was working with one big, overarching dream. Meanwhile, he contributed several paragraphs to *The New York Times* about the boys' experiences in London, much of the piece graciously but firmly acknowledging the gulf between British musical comedy and American musical comedy:

> English musical comedies are too light. Their music is too feathery. The English composer strives to imitate American jazz, and because his feet do not touch American soil, he falls just short. Whether we live in the North or the South, the American Negro's music has influenced us. Lacking that influence, the English musical writer can only echo an echo.[20]

It's curious that Larry would acknowledge the influence of the music of the American Negro, because he seems to have had mixed feelings about jazz and blues. Yet his analysis is spot-on.

Peggy, in its new form, began to take shape. Lew Fields would produce again, this time with his friend Lyle Andrews. Tracking the title character from her break with her bumpkin boyfriend Guy, who really loves her, to her fever-dream of meeting him again in New York, Dick and Larry wrote several songs but dispensed with the usual opening chorus, letting the dialogue provide the necessary exposition. ("I'd love to see New York," Peggy says, although she's in love with Guy, who makes twenty bucks a week and doesn't have a prayer of getting there.) While the action is still upstate, we hear "Hello," a familiar Hart theme that shows the singer's life as barren before the lover came along, and "A Tree in the Park," about the lovers' meeting place:

> Meet me underneath our little tree in the park,
> No one else around but you and me in the dark,
> Just five minutes from your doorstep.
> I'll wait for your step to come along
> And the city's roar becomes a song.

Feeling unappreciated, Guy walks out on her, and the dejected Peggy falls asleep reading the papers. She dreams of searching for Guy in Manhattan.

In "A Little Birdie Told Me So," Peggy, alone in the big city, reminds herself of her mother's warning about getting pregnant out of wedlock. (It would not be the last time Larry would extol the wisdom of maternal advice.)

> He'll say his love is mental
> And very transcendental.
> His talk will soon get boorish
> And very ostermoorish.

The Ostermoor had been a popular mattress since the late nineteenth century, and using a brand name—in this case, to imply the lulling language of seduction—was a Hart trait. (In "You're the Top," Cole Porter mentioned the Simmons mattress, though there was nothing sexy about the reference.) Peggy has learned to be chary: "A little word called 'Yes!' / Can make an awful mess. / The answer to 'Giddap' is 'Whoa!'" She finds Guy, who has become the prosperous owner of Guy Pendleton's Dry Goods, but, feeling a little sorry for herself, sings "Where's That Rainbow?," which telescopes the increasingly embittered irony of the lyricist: "Fortune never smiles, but in my case, / It just laughs right in my face."

In act 2, Peggy and Guy, whose attempt to wed in Manhattan has been interrupted, find themselves on a yacht bound for Havana. Invaded by "We Pirates from Weehawken," Peggy averts disaster by charming them. But disaster strikes anyway: the yacht is wrecked, forcing Peggy and Guy and two other characters to get on a lifeboat out on the open sea. Along comes a giant silver fish—a *talking* giant silver fish—to tow them to shore. "I'd be delighted to take you all the way," says the fish. "Were you going to the main dock, or did you want to get off at 125th Street?" In Havana, Peggy wins at the race track and, on the lawn of the track's clubhouse, her friend Mrs. Frost redeems herself by singing "Give This Little Girl a Great Big Hand," another Texas Guinan phrase. Peggy and Guy find a Cuban judge to marry them. Before the judge can complete the ceremony, he rushes out to place his own bet, leaving Peggy and Guy still unwed. Peggy wakes up and, after a scene and a song or two, is reunited with the real Guy, who suddenly has prospects.

The dreamscape is jagged and outlandish, like a real dream. The songs, particularly the longing "Where's That Rainbow?" and the salacious "A Little Birdie Told Me So," are broken into shards of melody, as they might sound in a dream. And Peggy's encounters in exotic settings with people from her hometown are dream flashes that everyone has had.

Would Helen Ford play the part? Rodgers was now enthralled by Dorothy Feiner, writing to her almost every day; the romance with Helen had either ended or gone deeper underground. If Helen wouldn't play Peggy Barnes, who would? Just when the boys were considering their casting options, near the end of October 1926, the telephone rang. If Dick and Larry, with four Broadway shows on the boards in a year and a half, hadn't thought of themselves as having arrived, they did now: Florenz Ziegfeld wanted them to write *his* new show.

The Shuberts had amassed the most real estate in the theater, but Flo Ziegfeld had made the most of glamour, serving grateful audiences since the first decade of the century. His annual *Follies* were loosely based on the Folies Bergère. Sometimes they were funny (as in Fanny Brice funny) and occasionally tuneful; mostly they were eye-popping. The lavish productions were about abundance, specifically American abundance, which is really all Flo Ziegfeld had known since he'd grown up in Chicago in the privileged, rarefied world of successful theater.

Once Dick and Larry recovered from the pleasurable shock of having the most powerful producer of musicals request their services, they had to keep their own counsel when Ziegfeld said he didn't want the new songs for at least two weeks. *Two weeks?!* The boys were fast, but not *that* fast. In fact,

Ziegfeld knew they were working on *Peggy*. Sounding at once generous and wise, he informed the boys that the title of their work-in-progress would have to be changed because his present wife, Billie Burke (most famous as the good witch in *The Wizard of Oz* some years later), had starred in the film *Peggy* in 1915, and audiences were likely to think the musical comedy was based on the film story.

For Ziegfeld, Dick and Larry had to write songs to a libretto being assembled not by Herb Fields but by others—in this case, Irving Caesar, who had just scored big with *No, No, Nanette*, and David Freedman. Caesar and Freedman had been childhood friends on the Lower East Side. The slightly older Caesar had quickly focused on songwriting, had hits with lyrics for Gershwin's "Swanee" and Vincent Youmans's "Tea for Two"—probably the most famous dummy lyric deemed right enough to go unrevised. Freedman, a chess prodigy and the son of a Romanian political refugee who lived by the El on Allen Street, had begun writing stories early. Concurrently with the Ziegfeld assignment, Freedman published *Mendel Marantz*, about a Lower East Side peddler fed up with his *gonif* landlord.[21] Freedman was only one of a large congregation of first-generation Jewish-American writers whom Walter Winchell referred to as "dialecticians," their characters speaking English in Yiddish accents the way their parents did—only a slight, literary variation on the "Dutch" dialects of vaudeville.

Although Caesar and Freedman were having a troubled collaboration, they came up with a musical book called *Betsy Kitzel*. The plot is simple, if not also simplistic: Brothers Louie, Joseph, and Moe Kitzel want to marry their respective girlfriends, but Mama insists they must first find a husband for their sister Betsy. The brothers try to pawn off Betsy to Archie, but Archie has eyes only for Betsy's sister, Ruth.[22] In the end everything works out for all the Kitzel kids. If the material was not Rodgers's cup of tea, it was poison to Larry—everything he found toxic and pandering about the contemporary theater. Still, if he had to write this stuff, he would do so without condescension or—please, God—making it "too Jewish."

On November 3, after Rodgers and Hart's attorney, Abe Wattenberg, and Ziegfeld's attorney had shouted across the table for three hours, the songwriters and the producer signed a contract, calling for them to write songs for a show for Belle Baker, who would play Betsy Kitzel.

Belle Baker's participation ought to have ensured a popular show. Born Bella Becker on Orchard Street, one of eight surviving children of Russian-Jewish émigrés, Baker was only nine years old when the great Jacob Adler began to give her small roles in his shows. When she wasn't acting, she worked as a newsboy—wearing boys' work shoes, her hair tucked under a cap—shouting the headlines. As a teenager she got work in vaudeville shows singing originals by Irving Berlin. "I Want to Go Back to Michigan (Down on the Farm)" was a sheet music smash after Baker introduced it.[23] "Next to Jolson," songwriter Harry Ruby remembered years later, "Belle Baker was the biggest songplugger there was. If she introduced [a song] on Monday (in those days the show started on Monday for the week), your publishing office the next day was crowded with actors coming in to ask for it."[24]

There were other things for the boys to worry about. There was a plan in the air to go to London to see *Lido Lady*, which was still volleying its way through tryouts in Liverpool and Manchester. The impresario Arthur Hammerstein (uncle of Oscar II) asked Dick and Larry for a show to inaugurate his new theater, the Hammerstein Temple of Music, at Broadway and Fifty-Third. Unlike Ziegfeld, Hammerstein wanted a show in a matter of months, not two weeks. (Nothing came of the request. An Emmerich Kalman show titled *The Golden Dawn* became the first show at the Temple of Music.) And then there was the question of who would star in the newly titled *Peggy-Ann*. Helen Ford, on tour with *Dearest Enemy*, cited professional reasons for being unavailable. Rodgers was quite taken with Ona Munson—her most famous role would be as Belle Watling in *Gone With the Wind*—finding her ravishingly beautiful and a pretty fair dancer. But Munson, too, declined. Ada-May, a dancer since childhood and formerly known as Ada Mae Weeks, said no, then yes. *Peggy-Ann* rehearsals began November 8, with Seymour Felix, one of the best in the business, as dance director. Four days later Ada-May left the show to sign with, of all people, Ziegfeld. Dorothy Dilley was signed to replace Ada-May, but nobody was too happy about it.

Meanwhile, rehearsals had now begun for *Betsy Kitzel*, and Rodgers and Hart were auditioning fifty people a day for the two shows. They often had to remind each other which theater they were in. At night they relaxed by going to the theater. They enjoyed the Gershwins' *Oh, Kay!* with the magnificent Gertrude Lawrence and not one but *two* pianos in the pit. The boys had a special interest in the show. Wodehouse and Bolton, the wordsmiths on those seminal Jerome Kern musicals, had written the *Oh, Kay!* book; when Ira Gershwin had an attack of appendicitis, George Gershwin asked not Wodehouse but Howard Dietz to lend a hand. Dietz came up with the title "Someone to Watch over Me" and wrote a couple of lyrics without credit. Dick and Larry didn't have a monopoly on collaborations gone flooey.[25]

Peggy-Ann was being well-cast and -staffed with people Rodgers and Hart had worked with before: Edith Meiser, Betty Starbuck, and Lulu McConnell (of *Poor Little Ritz Girl*). Larry brought in Arthur Schwartz, Max Hart's young attorney, as rehearsal pianist so he could be at the center of the action. Roy Webb was hired as music director. By the end of November, however, Dorothy Dilley had dropped out, and once again there was no Peggy. June Cochrane, another *Garrick Gaieties* alumna, was a possibility. Herb Fields got Helen Ford on the phone in Cincinnati, where she was wrapping up *Dearest Enemy*, and this time she agreed to take another look at *Peggy-Ann*. Fields took the train to Ohio armed with a manuscript and a contract.

There wasn't much time. *Peggy-Ann* was to begin tryouts at the Walnut Street Theatre in Philadelphia on December 13, the Ziegfeld show at the Forrest in the same city on the same night. "*Peggy* is such a daring idea," Rodgers wrote to his new sweetheart, "and is being done to the limit, while the other is so much applesauce that it's impossible to tell."[26] That other show was now retitled *Betsy*—"I know it's a bit startling, but then you have to be different nowadays," Rodgers wrote drily—and was already scheduled to go to Washington the week before Christmas.[27] Tensions were running high on both shows. *The Girl Friend* was in its final week at the Vanderbilt; *Lido Lady* was about to open at the Gaiety in London; *Peggy-Ann* and *Betsy* had rounded the turn and were running neck and neck toward the finish line; and Flo Ziegfeld was spending less time on his new show—leaving the organization of it to his bickering songwriters and librettists, now joined by veteran Broadway writer William Anthony McGuire—than on the construction of his new theater. Designed by the architect Thomas W. Lamb and by Joseph Urban, at the time America's most prominent scenic designer, the building was being erected at the northwest corner of Sixth Avenue and Fifty-Fourth Street. When completed in early 1927, it would have classical figures above its fourth floor and Ziegfeld's name engraved right below them.[28] More than any of his shows, the theater would exhibit the great in The Great Ziegfeld.

In London, *Lido Lady* opened on December 1, 1926, though it was not quite the same show that the boys had worked on. Several of their original songs were dropped; Con Conrad's "But Not Today" and the DeSylva-Brown-Henderson "It All Depends on You" were interpolated. But "Here in My Arms," which Courtneidge and Hulbert had so admired in New York, was still the show's centerpiece, sung by Hulbert and Phyllis Dare. *The Observer* called the revue "a good-tempered musical comedy" and singled out Jack Hulbert, "of the lyrical feet, jutting jaw, and light comedy genius," as adding luster to the proceedings.[29] *The Times* of London was also favorable (though it mentioned Rodgers and not Hart). It was James Agate's review in the London *Sunday Times* that wrenched the celebrations. Agate, who covered film and classical music with the same acidic insight with which he covered the theater, took aim at America—"Happy is the country which has no history, and happier still is that musical comedy about which one can find nothing to say"—and then got the lyricist in his sights for committing his leading lady to singing, "Here in my arms it's adora*bull*, it's deplora*bull*," the melodic accent falling on the last syllable.[30] It was a fair criticism, though it might have had as much to do with the way Phyllis Dare was directed, or the way the song had been orchestrated, than with Hart's failure to find the appropriate accent. It might also have been the awkwardness of bringing American enunciation into the English theater. Irving Berlin's "What'll I Do?" had gone over well in the *Music Box Revue* in New York, but when Norah Blaney sang it in the British revue *The Punch Bowl* in 1924, audiences were puzzled by the phrase "waddle I do?"[31]

It appeared that *Lido Lady* would be around for a while. The boys would eventually get to see it, and with pleasure—crossing the Atlantic on one of the new ocean liners was still the height of glamour—but these two American shows had to be put on. At first the *Peggy-Ann* rehearsals went badly. Dick and Larry spent more time with it, figuring this one was *their* show and wanting to please their longtime benefactor Lew Fields at least as much as they wanted to please Ziegfeld.

But Ziegfeld was not pleased. On December 5 he publicly bawled out Rodgers for not appearing at enough rehearsals. Rodgers, not used to being addressed this way, told Ziegfeld he was through with his lousy show. Ziegfeld's general manager made some crack—either about *Peggy-Ann* or about Larry—which only redoubled Rodgers's fury. Max Dreyfus, true to his word about protecting the boys, summoned the general manager to the Harms office to apologize to Rodgers. The following evening Rodgers and Ziegfeld walked around the stage arm in arm. The incident was forgotten.[32]

There was one more significant episode before *Betsy* went to Washington. Calling a meeting about the production, Ziegfeld sent a chauffeured Rolls-Royce to bring Dick and Larry to Burkeley (for Billie Burke) Crest, his estate in Hastings-on-Hudson. The hosts were gracious, dinner was fine, but there was no discussion of *Betsy*. Then Ziegfeld steered the songwriters into the drawing room and asked them to perform all the songs they'd written for the show to entertain his nine-year-old daughter.[33] It was the kind of display of executive power Rodgers and Hart would experience several more times during their career together—but more frequently in Hollywood than in New York.

Ziegfeld also neglected to tell the boys that he had booked Borrah Minevitch's Harmonica Playing Orchestra for the show. Minevitch, born in Russia in 1902, was known as the Pied Piper of harmonic-playing boys. Over the years the Orchestra—a dozen harmonicas humming at once—hired out as a specialty act. Because the Musicians' Union categorized the harmonica as a toy rather than a professional instrument, Ziegfeld obtained the Orchestra's services on the cheap.[34]

Peggy-Ann opened in New York on December 27 at the Vanderbilt, *Betsy* at the New Amsterdam the following night. *Peggy-Ann* was hailed a fine show, Freudian in its outlook (it was not), adventurous (it was)—a successful adaptation by Herb Fields, who took a successful Marie Dressler vehicle, split the character in two—Peggy was one half, the more outrageous Mrs. Frost the other—and made the whole thing new. "Where's That Rainbow?" was noted as one of the finer Rodgers & Hart songs up to that point. *Peggy-Ann* would run a respectable 197 performances.

Betsy wouldn't make it to forty. It's tempting to say that *Betsy*'s failure somehow demonstrated the superiority of Rodgers and Hart as masters of their own work, that they were better when they weren't compromised by the demands of a theatrical Gargantua like Flo Ziegfeld. But Dick and Larry felt the failure was theirs as well. And they were right to. They had written at least fifteen songs for *Betsy*, but the story material they had to work with remained uninspiring, especially to Larry. Most of the lyrics seem trapped in a Lower East Side airshaft. In "My Missus," Larry rhymes "rather" with "father" and "feel inside" with "blushing bride." In the "Stonewall Moskowitz March" (which Irving Caesar claimed to have had a hand in), the litany of "witz" rhymes sounds more juvenile than the Jewish-name verses Larry had written at school and at camp. "The Kitzel Engagement," which opens the show, is done in recitative, some of it clever, some of it banal; but in the middle of it the character Levi responds to the line "She kissed him" with "Is dis a system?"—a reference to cartoonist Milt Gross's recurring character Isidore, who frequently proclaims, "Is dissa system?"[35]

Betsy's one masterpiece is "This Funny World," the lyric suggesting that we must mask our sorrows in order to get by.

A mop! A broom! A pail!
The stuff my dreams are made of!
You hope, you strive, you fail!
The world's a place you're not afraid of.
But soon you are brought down to earth,
And you learn what your dream was worth.

In the Hart-wired central nervous system, every slight is experienced as a wound. "If you're beaten, conceal it, / There's no pity for you" emerged from Larry's diamond-hard lack of illusion: "For the world cannot feel it. / Just keep to yourself. / Weep to yourself." Wedded to Rodgers's music box melody, it's a great lyric.

But right up to the night before the opening, Belle Baker was uncomfortable with the song's darkness. She phoned her old friend Irving Berlin and asked him to write her a new song. What he gave her next morning—on the day of *Peggy-Ann*'s triumphant opening—was "Blue Skies." The lyric's sunniness felt right to Baker, who sold the hell out of it—much to the shock of both Dick and Larry, who were seated in the back of the house that first night. Irving Berlin, it turned out, was also in the house, and after the audience exhorted Baker to sing the song several more times, Ziegfeld ordered a spotlight on Berlin, who stood up in acknowledgment.[36] It was especially embarrassing for Rodgers and Hart, who tasted not only Baker's rejection but the enormous goodwill the audience felt for Berlin and his fairy-tale romance with Ellin Mackay.

Practically everyone at the New Amsterdam that night knew the story. Three years earlier, Clarence Mackay, president of the Postal Telegraph Company, had broken up the romance for classic reasons: his daughter was Catholic, a beautiful, privileged New York aristocrat; the songwriter was Jewish, raised in poverty on the East Side, and a widower. Ellin was sent abroad to "forget," while Berlin, filled with desperate longing, turned out "All Alone," "Don't Wait Too Long," and "Remember"—all for her. On January 4, 1926, deciding to marry without Mackay's blessing, the lovers left Irving Berlin, Inc., at Forty-Ninth and Broadway, and took the subway—it was said to be Ellin's first time underground—to the Municipal Building. Although he had a view of the Municipal Building from his office, Clarence Mackay was unaware that his daughter was going against his wishes.[37]

In the month that *Betsy* ran on Broadway, Berlin, Baker, "Blue Skies," and Borrah Minevitch's Harmonica Playing Orchestra stole all the attention from the show's main composer and lyricist. Ziegfeld still lost more than $100,000 on *Betsy*—a considerable sum even for the Great Glorifier. Rodgers and Hart lost only some face. Rodgers wouldn't speak to Irving Berlin for years, but Hart shrugged it off. Within a year or two he was publicly praising Berlin and meaning every word of it.

In January 1927, it was time for Dick and Larry to back go to Europe, checking out *Lido Lady* in London and continuing on to Paris. They booked a flat to share on St. James's Street.[38] In the middle of the month they sailed on the *Aquitania*, leaving their respective families and *Peggy-Ann* in New York. The Theatre Guild wanted an operetta from them for next fall. And Harms had just bought London rights to *Peggy-Ann* on excellent terms. So what was there to complain about?

PART II TO *London* and *Los Angeles*

CHAPTER 8

A House in Iceland Was My Heart's Domain

ODGERS AND Hart arrived in England on January 21, 1927, to find that *Sunny*, by their old friend Oscar Hammerstein II, and *Lido Lady* were the biggest hits in town. The boys, settled into their service flat (a private apartment with housekeeping and meals provided by the management) at 29 St. James's Street, were busy—meeting British musical stars like Jack Buchanan, going to the theater most nights, arranging for London productions of *The Girl Friend* and *Peggy-Ann*, seeing the head man at Chappell, and again talking over *Polly with a Past*, the operetta they had proposed for Arthur Hammerstein, based on a play by George Middleton and Guy Bolton. If everything panned out, Dick and Larry would have *three* shows running in London by fall. Two songs from *Betsy*, "Sing" and "If I Were You," were to be interpolated in *Lady Luck*, an upcoming show featuring Cyril Ritchard, ensuring a bigger audience than they received in the Ziegfeld debacle.[1] R. P. Weston and Bert Lee bought the *Girl Friend* score but made clear their intention to jettison the bicycle-racing book and include new material by veteran musicals writer Vivian Ellis.

Then came the call that was at least as thrilling as that first one from Flo Ziegfeld. In fact, Charles B. Cochran was sometimes referred to as the Ziegfeld of London; the Cochran Young Lady was the British counterpart of the Ziegfeld Girl. As a producer of musical productions in Great Britain, only André Charlot, for whom Cochran had once toiled as press agent, approached Cochran's dominance. "One popular comment on the British scene,"

Robert Baral wrote, "was that Charlot would discover ace talent only to lose the stars to Cockie, who gave them plusher settings." Cochran was always on the hunt for new talent, often sailing to New York to see what was on Broadway. He also stayed in close touch with John Murray Anderson and James Reynolds since employing them years earlier for his lavish 1921 revue *The League of Notions*, and it's likely that he heard of the boys' work from one or the other, or from both.[2]

Cockie wanted Dick and Larry to write the songs for an "ultra-smart 9:30 P.M. revue," to be produced in the spring, and offered the highest royalty rate they had ever earned. On the eve of departure for a vacation on the Continent they enjoyed a bacchanalian send-off from the *Girl Friend* producers.

In Paris they checked into the Hotel Raphael. This was a more rewarding trip; Dick and Larry had less to prove, and they were sitting on top of the world. They ran into New York friends Rita Hayden and Ruth Warner, who were with them during a near collision that has acquired the status of legend. Despite conflicting details, it's generally agreed that Rodgers and Hart were in a taxicab with Hayden and Warner when another vehicle missed them by inches. The taxicab stopped and everyone tried to calm down. "Oh, my heart stood still!" exclaimed Hayden or Warner. "That's a great song title!" said Larry. Rodgers wrote down the phrase, to be extracted for later use.[3]

After traveling on the Continent, the boys were back in St. James's by March 15. There Dick played for Larry the melody he'd composed to accompany the phrase "My Heart Stood Still"; Larry had no recollection of the phrase, but grabbed a pencil and wrote the lyric. The partners winced for their friends back home when largely negative reviews came in from the New York papers for *The New Yorkers*, a revue assembled by Doc Bender; Henry Myers had a hand in the book and lyrics; Arthur Schwartz, in whom Larry had every confidence, wrote the music, along with Edgar Fairchild, who would assist Rodgers on their shows through the 1930s. In *The New York Times*, Brooks Atkinson had called *The New Yorkers* a "frail and awkward revue" consisting of "song numbers of mediocre quality."[4] Staging a musical was never easy, although Rodgers and Hart's productivity since the first *Garrick Gaieties* made it appear so. At the St. James's Street service flat, Larry's snoring and frequent trips to the bathroom—his favorite activity, according to Rodgers—prompted Dick to take another room several yards away. There were no hard feelings.

Enjoying their own brand of domestic contentment, they got a dog—a wire-haired terrier they named John. "He has a nice face and he likes Jews,"

Rodgers told Dorothy. "As I write now, he's licking my left hand."[5] On April 7, Dick, Larry, and Fred Astaire attended the London opening of *The Desert Song*, by (among others) their old friends Ockie and Rommy—that is, Oscar Hammerstein and Sigmund Romberg. Although it was impossible to hold any ill will toward Hammerstein—no man was ever the object of so little schadenfreude—Dick and Larry hated the show. But they agreed that London had become so enamored of American musicals—even those with North African settings—that it could run a year.

One night the boys were at a party when someone requested "Queen Elizabeth," from the second *Garrick Gaieties*. To Dick's merry accompaniment, Larry began to sing:

I'm Elizabeth, the Virgin Queen.
Don't laugh!
On my title I stand firm,
Though it's just a technical term.
My royal bed was only used by half!

The door opened and in walked the Prince of Wales. Oops.[6] But the Prince of Wales, Cochran told the boys, was to be the new revue's chief patron because he knew so many of their songs by heart. You couldn't take royal fans for granted.

At the end of April, carrying the new songs for Cochran's revue ("My Heart Stood Still" among them), Rodgers went to Paris to persuade Robert Russell Bennett to orchestrate the whole affair. He left Larry behind. They needed a break from each other.

By the time it opened, on May 19, at the London Pavillion, Cochran's show was titled *One Dam Thing After Another*. Starring Mimi Crawford, Richard Dolman, Edythe Baker, Sonnie Hale, Jessie Matthews, and 20 Girls 20!, it attracted special interest because: (a) it was Cockie's latest show, and (b) the Prince of Wales attended opening night. The eccentric spelling in the title was a nod to more delicate sensibilities. Just the previous year, future poet laureate John Masefield published a novel, *ODTAA*, and he didn't have to spell out what the letters stood for. Even the fearless W. S. Gilbert had refrained from using the word "damn," referring instead to "the big, big D." Once again, Ronald Jeans handled most of the script. "Cochran, for all his fine showmanship, sometimes puts a great strain on his author," Jeans griped, "for he tends to swamp his work by the very lavishness of his productions."[7] Reviewers could see that the lanky, innocent-looking Jessie Matthews was going to be a star. Matthews and Richard Dolman introduced "My Heart Stood Still." Matthews grabbed everyone's attention singing the naughty "Gigolo," which was written for the 1926 *Garrick Gaieties*, Larry Hart addressing a theme he would circle back to in *Pal Joey*:

> *If you are fat and forty,*
> *You can be just as sporty,*
> *Look for a young Gigolo.*
> *Girl friends of Booth and Barrett*
> *Stay up and guzzle claret*
> *With boys of twenty or so.*
> *Diet and weigh yourself,*
> *Turn your fantastic face*
> *Into a plastic face.*
> *Oh listen to the band, Ma,*
> *Don't always be a grandma.*
> *Go get yourself a Gigolo!*

Mimi Crawford sang "My Lucky Star" (not to be confused with the Freed-Brown song "You Are My Lucky Star"). Edythe Baker, an American showgirl with porcelain skin and black bangs that made her resemble Louise Brooks, played her trademark white piano. Those striking contrasts embellished Baker's most popular number, "I Need Some Cooling Off," one of Rodgers's jazziest tunes, the singer burning up so fast that she's headed straight for hell. One of the Cochran Young Ladies was billed as Sheilah Grahame, with an extra *e*; hired by Cochran at four pounds a week, she would fill in for Mimi Crawford for several days, be voted England's "most beautiful chorus girl," and eventually move to Hollywood, where she would become an upstart gossip columnist and see her lover F. Scott Fitzgerald through the final months of his life.[8]

With all that talent onstage and behind the scenes, however, *One Dam Thing*'s first night proved oddly subdued. Everyone in the audience seemed to be watching the Prince of Wales rather than the business onstage. Reviews were mostly positive. *The Observer* said, "There are scenes in this revue which deserve to be called beautiful, in which colour and group are mingled and composed with artistry." *The Guardian*'s critic was smitten with Edythe Baker but otherwise had nothing good to say about the production. Almost everyone admired "My Heart Stood Still," though. Even James Agate, who had been so hard on *Lido Lady's* American aspects, referred to "My Heart Stood Still" as a "delicious scena."[9] With all that, ticket sales were anemic. Cochran, despite his kindness toward his artists, could be ruthless when appraising the future of his own productions. He considered closing the show and bringing a film into the theater. Was it the Prince's fault for drawing attention away from the show that first night?

If it had been, then the Prince redeemed himself the following month when he attended a dance at the Royal Western Yacht Club, in Plymouth. Between numbers the Prince asked the evening's bandleader, the American xylophonist-saxophonist Teddy Brown, to play "My Heart Stood Still." Brown and his musicians were unfamiliar with the song, so His Highness taught it to them by humming several bars. After that night the song was all over England.[10]

By then Dick and Larry were back in New York, having headed home on the *Berengaria* on Saturday, May 28.

In New York, the *Polly with a Past* project quickly dissolved, either because of Larry's lack of enthusiasm or a return to his old dissolute ways, thus making progress impossible. Although it makes for a wonderful story to have Larry rejecting every new idea that Rodgers and Herb Fields came up with and then blurting out that he really wanted to do *A Connecticut Yankee*, the notion probably came to him during *One Dam Thing After Another*.[11] The Cochran revue had two costume designers, Kitty Shannon and Doris Zinkeisen, and Zinkeisen's gorgeous medieval costumes, in particular for a sketch called "Progress," sent Larry back to Camelot.[12] That draped, colorful clothing looked great onstage and evoked a literary period that had always fascinated him.

But the option on the Twain novel was no longer free. Since 1921, when that first option had run out, Twain's attorney Charles Tressler Lark had handled hundreds more estates and learned the value of licensing. What's more, Rodgers and Hart were considerably more successful since the struggling years between *Poor Little Ritz Girl* and *The Melody Man*, the two shows starring Lew Fields. But Larry persuaded Dick and Herb that *Connecticut Yankee* was the show they should do. Toward that end, Herb sent the Twain book to Lew, who had arrived in England to superintend the London version of *Peggy-Ann* just about when the boys were arriving in New York. Lew said he didn't see a musical in the book. Disappointed but undaunted, Herb Fields, without his father's support, updated the contemporary part of *Connecticut Yankee* and used the long dream sequence as a clothesline on which to hang a score or two of anachronistic jokes. Herb's revised adaptation, which reached Lew in England right around the time *Peggy-Ann* opened there, apparently did the trick: Lew now wanted to produce *A Connecticut Yankee*.

Max Hart, the "vociferous walrus" who had shouted obscenities like a steam whistle, was having an increasingly painful time negotiating a flight of stairs. So Larry moved his family from the 119th Street house, where the Harts had lived for nearly thirty years, to an elevator building at 415 Central Park West, at 101st Street. The elevator went all the way to the top—to the penthouse. Larry could afford it, just as he could afford to reverse the filial flow of cash and give Max a weekly allowance. An old Jewish proverb goes: "If the father shares his money with his son, both may laugh; if the son shares his money with his father, both may weep."[13] Yet there seemed to be no shame or self-consciousness in the Hart household. Max used some of his allowance each week to play pinochle and kibitz at the Cayuga Club, a Tammany Hall headquarters close to his old neighborhood, at 122nd Street and Seventh Avenue. But his declining health—arteriosclerosis had put a huge strain on his body—prohibited him from going out and turning a profit, legal or otherwise.[14] Larry was still living with his parents (so, by the way, was Dick Rodgers, and Herb Fields had a room on the same block as *his* parents, on West End Avenue), but now the Harts all lived in penthouse splendor, with Mary Campbell coming each morning from her own place in Harlem.

Max's health, however, might not have been the sole impetus for the move. As Jeffrey Gurock recorded in *When Harlem Was Jewish*, restrictions and a labor shortage during the Great War had halted tenement starts, with a fixed number of dwellings housing a rapidly expanding population. After the war, black Harlem was moving south and Jewish Harlem was dissipating. Jews were taking advantage of the housing boom in previously inaccessible communities like Flatbush, Jackson Heights, and the Grand Concourse, moving to the outer boroughs or creating new suburbs altogether. These weren't for Larry or, for that matter, any of the Harts. Since *Dearest Enemy*, however, Larry had money to burn, and one of the new luxury apartment houses on Central Park West—they were also rising every month on Riverside Drive and on Park Avenue below Ninety-Sixth—was where he chose to burn some of it.[15]

❧   ❧   ❧

In the late summer of 1927, Larry Hart was known around Broadway by pretty much everybody. He was thirty-two, nowhere near the peak of his abilities. He could usually be found in his own bed in the morning, in the bedroom he shared with brother Teddy, but where was Larry in the wee small hours? His nocturnal disappearances, usually starting after post-curtain drinking had stopped, were acquiring folds of mystery. In November of the previous year the Paramount Building had been opened in Times Square at Forty-Third Street, "leaning indulgently" (in Stephen Graham's description) over the Hotel Astor like "some great coconut palm," its big clocks at the top visible from practically any angle until 12:30 A.M. when their lights were turned off.[16] Larry was like the Paramount clocks: illuminating Broadway till after midnight, then gone. He often arrived home as the milkman was making his rounds.

In the evenings he could be seen at first nights and at the opera, dressed formally like everyone else, though he detested the air of ostentation. "Larry Hart has a silk hat that is as tall as he is," Walter Winchell cracked in his column.[17] In late August of 1927, Democratic Party organizer Ernest Harvier supplied Winchell's paper, the *Evening Graphic*, with a list of "native New York arts notables"; Larry was on this exclusive list, probably because the Harts were so well known in Tammany circles in the first place, and Richard Rodgers was not.[18] But Larry's position as the older, dominant writing partner was already beginning to erode. In the next couple of years Rodgers, whom Larry began referring to (behind his back) as The Principal, would watch over his lyricist partner, chiding him every few days for his tardiness, for his disinclination to write without pressure, and for his need for a drink. What Larry did in the middle of the night, however, was his business, as long as it didn't interfere with work.

But it would interfere, and to Rodgers's increasing agitation.

With most of the *Connecticut Yankee* songs written, Dick and Larry were faced with another problem—one that would cost them the way the Mark Twain rights now cost them. Dick and Larry had been in discussions with American producer Charles Dillingham to do a show with him. Dillingham had promised his longtime client, the incomparable Beatrice Lillie, that she could introduce to American audiences the boys' "My Heart Stood Still" which, thanks mostly to the Prince of Wales's enthusiasm, was just about the hottest song in England. Much as both Dick and Larry loved Lillie as a performer, they felt she wasn't right for the song. (Lillie often added a layer of irony to a lyric, and it would have backfired on "My Heart Stood Still.") To short-circuit her plans to sing it, they told Dillingham it was already part of *A Connecticut Yankee*. But they had to back up the lie by negotiating for the song, which was still being sung in *One Dam Thing*.

C. B. Cochran, though, wasn't going to let them just *have* it. Doing what a hardheaded impresario is supposed to do, he had paid Rodgers and Hart up front for the rights, including the American rights. Were the boys prepared to buy back their own song? Deliberately complicating matters, Flo Ziegfeld made an offer to Cochran so *he* could use the song in the upcoming *Follies*. To his credit, Cochran refused Ziegfeld, either because he had no intention of giving his American counterpart such gold or because the boys were still deciding.

Over the summer, *Peggy-Ann* had opened at Daly's Theatre in London. The reviews were respectful, but not much more than that. Although Lew Fields had gone to some pains to make the references more English—"A Little Birdie Told Me So" was rewritten by Larry Hart's lyricist friend Desmond Carter as "Country Mouse," and the upstate locale changed to an English boardinghouse—the show seemed intractably American. Still, this *Peggy-Ann* would stay at Daly's for 134 performances.[19]

Then, at the beginning of September, Albert Sirmay's *Princess Charming* vacated the Palace Theatre after a profitable run and made room for *The Girl Friend*. As the producers had warned, the show was unrecognizable, for it now included songs by Con Conrad, with lyrics by Otto Harbach and Gus Kahn, some of which were drawn from *Kitty's Kisses*, which had opened on Broadway a couple of months after *The Girl Friend*. Despite the hodgepodge, the show would play to excellent business for more than 400 performances.[20] Dick and Larry could disown it—or they could claim it as partly theirs. "Although it comes from America," *The Guardian* reported, "one was not drenched in the inescapable American vocal tones"—another dig at the "slanguage" of songs imported from Broadway.[21]

As for "My Heart Stood Still," Dick and Larry recognized that Cockie had them boxed in. Believing the song would work well for *A Connecticut Yankee*, Rodgers and Hart purchased American rights. Word on the street was they had paid $10,000 to buy back their own song.[22]

It is, by any reckoning, a powerful song—and, according to Hart, the only one he wrote that was inspired by a memorable incident (the near collision in France). It is probably insignificant that the first six lines of the refrain are composed entirely of one syllable words ("I took one look at you / That's all I meant to do"), except that they're clear and easy to sing, just as the *oo*, *ill*, and *awk* sounds close out each line so definitively ("My feet could step and walk / My lips could move and talk"). In *One Dam Thing After Another*, the opening of the verse was obviously for British audiences:

> The boys at Harrow
> Would always say
> That Cupid's arrow
> Couldn't fly my way.

For *A Connecticut Yankee*, Larry changed the lines to:

> I laughed at sweethearts
> I met at schools;
> All indiscreet hearts
> Seemed romantic fools.

The female counterpart implies she learned that love is a sin by reading Plato. ("I read my Plato, / Love I thought a sin.") There is no concept of sin in Plato, of course, the idea sounding more Nietzchean; but "I read my Nietzsche" probably wouldn't sound right. Stunned by romance, the singer is devouring the works of Elinor Glyn, author of *Three Weeks* and other novels considered risqué at the time. ("But since your kiss / I'm reading Missus Glyn.") Once again Larry was right up to the minute: the popular movie version of Glyn's *It*, starring Clara Bow, had been released three months before *One Dam Thing* opened.[23]

"My Heart Stood Still" didn't make it into the Stamford tryouts of *A Connecticut Yankee*, but by the time the show caravanned to Philadelphia, it was beating soundly there. William Gaxton, a veteran trouper whose musical comedy career was still in the ascendant, and Constance Carpenter were in the leads as the Yankee (or, in 1927 Connecticut, Martin) and Demoiselle Alisande (known as Sandy in the year A.D. 528 and Alice in 1927 Connecticut). Lew Fields was sharing producers' chores and credit with Lyle D. Andrews because Andrews owned the Vanderbilt Theatre, while Herb Fields was fine-tuning the book. Along with *Peggy-Ann*, it is his funniest. Rodgers and Hart wrote nearly a dozen new songs.

A Connecticut Yankee could have posed an enormous challenge to Hart, because he had to include the idioms of two epochs, fourteen hundred years apart, and make them blend so that the result was comprehensible, funny, and still pleasing to the ear. Moreover, the language of the Mark Twain novel, like that of Herb Fields's book, is really a pseudo-Elizabethan English.[24] But Larry dashed off the lyrics to Rodgers's jumpy melodies as though he'd written varsity shows for King Arthur. In "At the Round Table," Larry rhymes "flagon" and "dragon," a combination made famous nearly thirty years later when Panama and Frank wrote the marvelous knight competition scene for Danny Kaye in *The Court Jester.* "On a Desert Island with Thee" is insistently bawdy as Galahad and his lady Evelyn rhapsodize about being far from their mothers, about where they will eat before they dress, and about how the island's population next year just might go from two to three. (A depressive but never a misanthrope, Larry returned time and again to the idea that lovers expanded the human race.) "I'll dress the way that Adam did," Galahad declares, and Evelyn replies, "And I the way his madam did!" And then Hart, as he did so often, closes with a salacious kicker for Galahad: "I'll see enough of thee!" "It's done so pleasantly," recalled Larry's fraternity brother Robert M. W. Vogel, who edited the *Columbia Spectator* and became chief of MGM's international unit. "I don't think anybody else could have written that lyric and gotten away with it, on the New York stage or anywhere else."[25] In rehearsal, "My Heart Stood Still" was placed near the beginning of the show, when Martin, engaged to Fay Morgan, sees his old flame Alice at a reception in present-day Connecticut. "Thou Swell" was the show's most debated song, with half the production staff believing the lyric was too complex for the audience to understand. "Babe, we are well met," begins the first verse, which pokes ancient England with the needle of contemporary Manhattan:

> As in a spell met—
> I lift my helmet.
> Sandy,
> You're just dandy
> For just this here lad.
> You're such a fistful,
> My eyes are mistful—
> Are you too wistful
> To care?

It was to be sung in Camelot by the Yankee (Martin) and Sandy (Alice), who don't recognize each other from their twentieth-century lives but know they're in love.[26]

Thou swell!
Thou witty!
Thou sweet!
Thou grand!
Wouldst kiss me pretty?
Wouldst hold my hand?
Both thine eyes are cute, too—
What they do to me.
Hear me holler
I choose a
Sweet lolla
Palooza
In thee.

Despite its comic idea and the jokes built into each anachronism, *A Connecticut Yankee* doesn't really have an out-and-out comedy song as so many other Rodgers & Hart shows have. The closest to a comic number is "The Sandwich Men," in which the knights appear wearing sandwich boards advertising contemporary products like Lux soap and Coca-Cola.

Between these boards called sandwiches
We're such a sorry sight.
We troop throughout the land, which is
A hell of a job for a knight!

In "I Feel at Home with You," lovers Galahad and Evelyn hash out their differences, reaffirming their mutual love while acknowledging that neither of them is an intellectual. "Your brain needs a tonic, / It's still embryonic," Evelyn tells her knight, adding, "Our minds are featherweight, / together their weight / Can't amount to much." The Hart lyric doesn't patronize the lovers' slowness but reminds us that these two belong together—that everyone belongs to someone out there.

A Connecticut Yankee went to Philadelphia on October 3, 1927. Two days later Sam Warner, the moviemaking brain of the Warner brothers, died suddenly. The following night Sam's movie *The Jazz Singer* opened at the Warner Theatre in Manhattan and turned American culture topsy-turvy. Sound had come to the movies—not as a novelty anymore but as an inevitability that affected not only the movies but radio, the recording industry, the press, and, of course, the theater. *The Jazz Singer*, based on the Samson Raphaelson play that starred George Jessel, had Al Jolson singing right to the audience. Since childhood, Larry Hart had been imitating Jolson, unaware that Jolie would make his most significant contribution to the arts after he was forty.

But even on the screechy sound track, Jolie's cantorial projection came through. And Larry must have reacted with a jolt when Warner Oland, playing Jack Robin's cantor father, opened his mouth to sing the "Kol Nidre" and "Yahrzeit" and out came the dubbed voice of the Harts' former neighbor Yosele Rosenblatt.

Through the rest of October, Dick and Larry shuttled between Philadelphia and New York, making changes to the show. On October 13 they went together to see Adele and Fred Astaire rehearsing the new Gershwin show *Funny Face*, and found it a disappointment. On October 24 the boys went to Atlantic City to concentrate on some new songs—not for *Connecticut Yankee* but for the upcoming Beatrice Lillie show, tentatively titled *That's My Baby*.[27] Meanwhile, Larry, aware that his father's health was irrevocably declining and that he had become the family's primary support, took out his first life insurance policy, with New York Life, designating Frieda as beneficiary.[28] The policy would have repercussions not only for the remainder of Larry's life but for the remainder of Teddy Hart's life. But then Larry was only thirty-two.

When *A Connecticut Yankee* opened at the Vanderbilt on November 3, 1927, Richard Rodgers was in the pit conducting. (Roy Webb would take over the second night.) The acid test was the much-debated "Thou Swell." When William Gaxton and Constance Carpenter got about eight bars into the song, Rodgers felt something at the back of his head: the audience reacting. Rodgers could feel it as though it were a material thing.[29] From that moment he knew the show was in good shape.

There was an ambivalent evaluation that couldn't be ignored, much as Rodgers and Hart tried, and it came from Franklin P. Adams, more popularly known by his readers as F. P. A. Author and administrator of a "colyum" (as he called it) in *The World*, F. P. A. was considered to have the most literate standards of any taste-maker and, many years earlier, had often published the light verse of Larry Hart's classmates, including Morrie Ryskind, who signed himself "Morrie"; Robert Simon, who contributed as "Leoceles"; and Howard Dietz, who signed himself "Freckles."[30] F. P. A. encouraged these young men because lyric writing was the craft he most admired, but he also became increasingly envious when several of them had begun to get their lyrics into Broadway shows.[31] Wanting to contribute *something* to popular song, F. P. A. had even gone so far as to recruit the best, writing "Keep Your Rabbits, Rabbi, We Have Rabbits of Our Own" in 1920 to music by Jerome Kern and getting the song published by Harms. After he'd attended the *Connecticut Yankee* first night, he wrote up his reaction:

[Thursday, November 3, 1927]: So home to dinner, and thence to the theatre with Miss Edna Ferber, to see *A Connecticut Yankee at King Arthur's Court*, invested with great panoply and all accoutered with beauty, but I wearied early of the many attempts at comick anachronisms, and it all seemed to me a high school show well staged. And I thought, too, that the songs were too much repeated, in especially "My Heart Stood Still," a good song but to my notion too pretentiously done. And I was deeply interested in the lyrics wrote [sic] by Mr. Lorenz Hart, whose rhyming agility meseems is a liability to him, and I wish he would lean more to simplicity, forasmuch as his gifts are great . . . So to bed, and lay there thinking how easy it is to write these feminine rhymes, and how hard to listen to, and I dreamed:

I find the triple rhyme
A stamped and stipple rhyme;
I deem no miracle
The super lyrical;
A bard who bangs the lyre some—
What's hard I find is tiresome—
Oh, Mr. Hart, stand still![32]

But Larry could not stand still. He and Dick were committed to too many projects to dwell on criticisms of his penchant for rhyme. After a year's run *Peggy-Ann* was about to go on the road with Helen Ford remaining in the title role. As written, "A Little Birdie Told Me So" would not play in Boston, the city where *Leaves of Grass* had been pulped and used for mulch by the Watch and Ward Society in 1878. So Larry wrote a more anodyne version of "Little Birdie"—but on a roll of toilet paper, which he presented to Helen Ford, hoping to shock her.[33]

Abie's Irish Rose was finally shuttered after a six-year run. Oscar Hammerstein, writing both book and lyrics to Jerome Kern's music, had his greatest triumph yet with *Show Boat*, which opened on December 27 and managed to integrate songs and narrative more fluidly than any American show before it. Almost as surprising was that it was presented by Flo Ziegfeld, who saw the show's possibilities even if it meant forgoing much of the glamour he promoted. *Show Boat* essentially turned musical comedy into musical drama—in this case a peculiarly American one with racism and miscegenation among its themes. Kern's music was first-rate till the day he died, but Hammerstein's growth, from the Columbia Varsity Shows through 1927, could be charted as a steady climb up the mountain. It was impossible for the boys not to be pleased for him. *A Connecticut Yankee* was not in *Show Boat's* league—it still relied heavily on vaudeville-derived humor—but it became one of the hits of the 1920s, not just the 1927–28 season. Soon after New Year's 1928 there were recordings of "My Heart Stood Still" by Jessie Matthews and Edythe Baker. When Edmund Wilson, that most unsentimental of writers, went to Santa Barbara to visit his future wife, Margaret Canby, he felt puzzled and alienated by West Coast culture. To stay calm, he played "My Heart Stood Still" over and over on Canby's phonograph.[34]

CHAPTER 9

You've Cooked My Goose

After trying out at the National Theatre in Washington, at Ford's Theatre in Baltimore, and at the Shubert in Newark, *She's My Baby*—the new title for the Beatrice Lillie show—opened at the Globe Theatre, at Broadway and Forty-Sixth Street, on January 3, 1928. Considering the talent involved, the show ought to have been a smash. Guy Bolton, annually logging tens of thousands of miles on what people now thought of as Lindbergh's ocean, contributed to the book. Most of that book was by Bert Kalmar and Harry Ruby. The veteran songwriters ("Three Little Words," "Who's Sorry Now?") had discovered it was less taxing to write jokes than songs. Kalmar & Ruby and Bolton came up with a story that went back to *Madame Sherry*, before World War I: to raise enough money to put on a musical starring his sweetheart, Polly, Bob has to persuade his wealthy uncle that he has a family, so Tilly the maid masquerades as Bob's wife. *She's My Baby* had the services of Jack Whiting, the elegant Clifton Webb, already refining that superior air of his, the young Irene Dunne, and the show's reason for being, Beatrice Lillie.

To say there was no one else like Bea Lillie at the time suggests there is someone like her now; there is not. The Chicago theater critic Charles Collins set down Lillie's appeal more precisely than anyone else:

> She is the Fairy Queen of wise-crackers, the Ariel of burlesquers, the Puck of parody. . . . Her humor is so quaint, her wit so zigzag, that she passes outside

familiar human categories and becomes a sprite. Her clowning is always wildly eccentric, and yet it never loses its mental delicacy. Her slap-stick is cerebral. She is a thirty-second degree kidder, dealing in lunatic tidbits of that pastime. Her mirth is given special zest by her personal allurement. She is unconquerably pretty, even in the craziest of costumes. A boyish-form sweetheart, obsessed by the imp of the ridiculous—that is Beatrice Lillie.[1]

Collins made this important qualification: "She is so fantastic that she destroys the plots of musical comedies. Hence the French farce frame-work of *She's My Baby* never seems substantial in a story-telling way." Known to royals-watchers and theatergoers alike as Lady Peel, wife of M.P. Sir Robert, the Ontario-born comedienne was usually more memorable than the vehicles she rode in.

Still, if little of the music from *She's My Baby* has remained in the popular repertoire, Larry Hart does some typically clever work in it. The boys recycled "A Tiny Flat in Soho" as "A Little House in Soho" and several other numbers. But there were new numbers designed expressly for Lillie—lyrics that few others could have pulled off. In "When I Go on the Stage," Tilly (Lillie), in full self-deception regalia, compares herself to the great female theater, opera, and movie stars of the era, naming more than a dozen. She flicks off an inside joke about the show's producer, Charles Dillingham, "As a willing ham for Dillingham / I'll pack the Globe." As Ethan Mordden has pointed out, "This spendthrift cataloguing of celebrities, unheard of before the end of the mid-1920s, was like a verbal jazz, improvisations by youngsters eager to blow their elders away. Hart used it best. Ira Gershwin thought it a little vulgar; his idea of celebrity was Heinrich Heine. Cole Porter was a thoroughly committed adherent, though he adulterated the mix by citing also his froufrou society friends. Who was the Duke of Verdura, anyway?"[2] (For the record, the Duke of Verdura was an aristocratic Sicilian jewelry designer.) "A Baby's Best Friend" is a perverse lullaby, a parody of the kind of best-selling melodramas so in vogue, ending with a recitation in which the beaten-down defendant in a court case is given another chance by the judge who, removing his wig and mustache, reveals himself to be—the defendant's mother! "Whoopsie," which was dropped from the show soon after the New York opening, gave rhyme and rhythm to Lillie's distinctive brand of impishness. Lillie sits out the closing number, "Wasn't It Great?," while the other players attempt to indemnify the show from criticism; most, though not all, of the New York critics are mentioned, and Larry rhymes "faith in" with [George Jean] "Nathan." We might recall that in his charming lyric "Sarah Jackman," sung to the tune of "Frère Jacques," Allan Sherman employs the same rhyme.

Perhaps Lillie's and Hart's comic sensibilities were both so strong that they whizzed right past each other. It could be that *She's My Baby* emerged as just another revue, with a skeleton of a hoary story and no place for the great, lantern-jawed comedienne to take it. Or it might even be simpler than that: Rodgers and Hart had done the show, as they had worked on *Betsy*, without Herb Fields, who hadn't sulked when excluded from the Ziegfeld project but found work writing the book for the Vincent Youmans show *Hit the Deck*. If Herb Fields's writing never seemed terribly original, it was usually efficient in its showbiz carpentry. He knew all the old jokes and told them without getting in the songwriters' way.

With *She's My Baby* quickly marked as an undistinguished evening with Bea Lillie, Larry took a vacation to Bermuda—he appears to have traveled by himself—and was home in New York on January 26. Rodgers, meanwhile, sailed to Europe with his parents, took a quick detour to Algiers, and wouldn't be back till the end of February. During that time Sidney Skolsky, then a young Broadway columnist at *The Sun*, published a profile of Larry suggesting the lyricist was an original character. Hart's only exercise, Skolsky wrote, was laughing. "When he does he sways and twists his entire body," and

He always needs a shave. . . .

He is dissatisfied with himself and when alone is very melancholy. . . .

When in his cups he sings the lyrics of his latest songs. He's a terrible singer. . . .

He hates first nights, the radio, vaudeville, society, plays with a message and home cooking.

His favorite song is Irving Berlin's "Oh, How I Hate to Get Up in the Morning," which he considers a masterpiece. Of his own, he likes "Mountain Greenery" the best.

Suffers from insomnia, but finds it helps him with his work.

Is very nervous at his own opening nights. Paces the back aisles continuously.

Asks standees, "How do you like it?" and won't take no for an answer. During intermission he shaves himself to look neat for the second act. Stays up all night waiting for the reviews.

Is especially fond of mountains, good cigars, Beatrice Lillie, tropical scenery, Shelley and chop suey.[3]

It was characteristically generous of Larry to say he was fond of Bea Lillie. And it's almost certain he meant it when he cited the Berlin song, written for the show *Yip, Yip, Yaphank* when Berlin was a sergeant at Camp Upton, Long Island, in 1918.[4] The lyric is modest, earthy, and true—qualities Larry valued. If, more than a year after being upstaged by "Blue Skies," Rodgers hadn't forgiven Berlin, Larry had.

Max Hart's body began to deteriorate. The family felt an eerie foreshadowing when the prominent clothier of Hart, Schaffner & Marx was reported dead in Chicago on February 22. That Max Hart was, like Max Meyer Hertz, born in Germany, brought to the United States by his parents, and had a brother named Harry.

Three days later Rodgers returned from the holiday with his parents and was ready to go back to work, with Herb Fields prepared to write the next musical book. Prior to *A Connecticut Yankee*, Fields had enjoyed a huge hit with his book for *Hit the Deck*, with music by Vincent Youmans ("More Than You Know" and "Hallelujah" were the two most memorable songs), which might have suggested that Rodgers and Hart needed Fields more than Fields needed Rodgers and Hart. Their new show, with the equally snappy military phrase *Present Arms* as the title, was about marines rather than sailors and was set in Pearl Harbor rather than China. And maybe it was supposed to make a difference that in the new show the hero pursues the heroine rather than the other way around?[5]

Present Arms tried out in Wilmington, Delaware, and Atlantic City before settling in at Lew Fields's Mansfield Theatre in New York on April 26. As it happened, most theatergoers and practically every critic who saw *Present Arms* cited *Hit the Deck* as the obvious comparison. (The word "rip-off" was still a good forty years away from entering the lexicon.) It probably didn't help Rodgers, Hart, and Fields that they'd selected Charles King, who had starred in *Hit the Deck*, as their leading man. Still, it was a professional job. Roy Webb was on hand as musical director, and the Viennese émigré Hans Spialek was becoming indispensable to Rodgers, orchestrating those lovely melodies with his eyes closed. There were high hopes for a ballad called "Do I Hear You Saying 'I Love You'?" though, unlike Cole Porter, Larry was never at his best when employing that universal declaration. "A Kiss for Cinderella," sung by a quartet of marines encouraging Chick, a private in love with a society girl, was more impressive because it mixed sweet and sour, the innocent and the salacious, the elegant and the piss-elegant:

A Jane was once called Cinderella,
Whose life wasn't much of a panic.
She kept under the thumbs of her sisters, two bums;
Poor kid was their kitchen mechanic.

And:

Here is Cinderella's shoit,
Stiff and clean from doit,
And here's a little kiss for Cinderella.

Although he's about to attend the equivalent of a royal ball, masquerading as a captain, Chick obviously ain't no Cinderella:

Her foot was so tiny to fit it was hard.
Her foot was a foot, but your foot is a yard.
She had a complexion as smooth as vanilla.
And Chick has a skin that is draped in chinchilla.

"A Kiss for Cinderella" anticipates Rodgers's "There Is Nothing Like a Dame," though that was by another lyricist, in another lifetime. Joining leading man Charles King on "Cinderella" was the choreographer Busby Berkeley, who had won the second lead as Sergeant Atwill. Berkeley and Joyce Barbour (English and, in Rodgers's words, "a juicy little grape of a girl"), playing ex-spouses who still have a thing for each other, had a duet in what proved to be the show's most popular song, "You Took Advantage of Me." "So what's the use? / You've cooked my goose" is one example of Larry's delineation of sexual enthrallment, "I'm so hot and bothered that I don't know / My elbow from my ear" another. Alas, Berkeley could move dancers around the stage with more finesse than he moved himself. On opening night he launched into his half of "You Took Advantage of Me" and promptly (in theatrical parlance) "went up," his mind drawing a blank. Ever the trouper, Berkeley made up a lyric that went something like:

When I was walking down the street,
I saw a little bird who called tweet-tweet,
I shook my head and said instead,
'Cause you took advantage of me.

"It was awful," Berkeley admitted in his memoir, "but I got through it. I can still see poor Larry Hart running up and down in the wings almost apoplectic. He already had a reputation for witty, poetic lyrics, and here I was ruining his marvelous lines. But I drew a lot of laughs that night from the audience and he later forgave me."[6] Larry forgave everybody.

There was one other notable feature of *Present Arms*: the chorus boys were among the burliest men that could be found—more marine-like than marines. Whether Larry Hart had a say in this decision is anybody's guess. Rodgers claimed this development was altogether different from other shows. In fact the practice of hiring such bruisers for the chorus was not new. Years earlier the Shuberts had decided that too many of their musicals had been cast with insufficiently masculine chorus men. The corrective had simply found its most outrageous expression in *Present Arms*, in which the chorus men's antics, according to George Jean Nathan, were "enough to bring the blush of discomfort to a longshoreman."[7]

For a while the chorus men's attempts at daintiness were a hoot. (The dance critic Arlene Croce once wrote, "A heavy thing trying to become light is automatically funnier than a light thing trying to become heavy.")[8] Then, too, just a few days before *Present Arms* opened on Broadway, heavyweight champion Gene Tunney had lectured on Shakespeare to an overfilled auditorium at Yale. Brawn and brains were being jammed together in culture high and low.

On May 9, Lew Leslie's *Blackbirds of 1928* opened at the Liberty Theatre after a popular stay at a Fifty-Seventh Street nightclub. There was Adelaide Hall singing "Diga Diga Do" and forty-nine-year-old Bill "Bojangles" Robinson—largely unfamiliar then to New York audiences, he claimed never to have had a dance lesson—crossing the stage on his own invisible stairs. The music was by Jimmy McHugh; the lyrics were by the lovely young Dorothy Fields, who had found her own voice. "I Can't Give You Anything But Love," which commenced Dorothy Fields's personal colloquial style, became one of that summer's most ubiquitous popular songs. Larry's ardent student was on her way.

Larry told the evening *Post* that he and Rodgers were not aiming to do "high brow" work in the commercial theater but strove "to write for the public consumption and this means not to the intelligentsia but to men, women, girls and boys from every walk of life." If they were lampooning aesthetes in the first *Garrick Gaieties*, Larry said, they had to allow the *Present Arms* marines to use the comic vernacular, because that's what was appropriate for the show. "With this," the *Post* reporter noted, "young Hart quickly rubbed his hands together, puffed on a cigar almost as big as himself and ran down the theater aisle to chat with Lew Fields. Together they walked in the box office and registered pleasure when informed by Manager Niemes that the S. R. O. sign would again adorn the front of the theater."[9]

In June, while *Present Arms* was being sold to the movies, Larry found what he wanted to do next. Published a year earlier, Charles Pettit's novel *Son of the Grand Eunuch* was one of the more eccentric comic novels of the decade. Set in ancient China, it presents the Grand Eunuch (a real position in China's Imperial Court, by the way, and still influential as late as 1900), whom Pettit names Li Pi Siao (an inversion of the name of an actual Grand Eunuch). The gluttonous Grand Eunuch is despised by the Peking populace, which refers to neuters as "Lao Korn," or impotent old roosters. Li Pi Siao proposes that his son Li Pi Tchou, who has a wife, Chti, and a son, succeed him as Grand Eunuch; but Li Pi Tchou loves Chti passionately and sexually, so he's not happy at the prospect of being castrated. His father asks him if he's "mentally deficient" and accuses him of loving his wife "in the unseemly and foolish manner of the pale-face Barbarians." "At your age!" the Grand Eunuch ridicules. "At over forty years old! . . . To aspire to being loved for oneself!" Rejecting the Grand Eunuch's offer, Li Pi Tchou and Chti leave their little boy behind and cast out on a series of adventures. So rebuffed, the Grand Eunuch makes his *second* son his heir. On the road it becomes clear that Li Pi Tchou is part poet, part clown, while Chti is (using Jack Conway's word) a bimbo—but a bimbo with considerable cunning. To save Li Pi Tchou from a beheading, Chti gives herself (with fewer objections than her husband might like) to a threatening Tartar. Most of the couple's subsequent encounters close like that one, with Chti saving the hapless Li Pi Tchou from execution. In the end the Grand Eunuch orders the beheading of his daughter-in-law, exacts revenge on the tribes that menaced his family, and installs his son, neutered after all, as his successor.

Whew. This is what Larry took to Dick Rodgers and Herb Fields. Herb, who tended to be just a half step behind Larry's enthusiasms, was excited, but Dick was having none of it. A musical comedy about castration?! Lew Fields was already committed to the next Rodgers & Hart show, however, and Fields in turn had a commitment from Helen Ford, script unseen, so Dick went along. It's possible, as Frederick Nolan has speculated, that Larry responded to the novel because he saw himself as a eunuch, sexually inactive while observing the sex play of others through a keyhole, and was delighted by the possibility of "getting his sexual innuendoes past Mrs. Grundy," the fictional embodiment of the censorious personality.[10] It's also possible that Larry—and Dick would come around to his way of thinking—saw *Present Arms* as entertaining but safer than a marine barracks at Pearl Harbor, while *Show Boat's* thematic risks had paid off, and he was ready to take a similar risk on idiosyncratic material. Asked why, against all advice, he wanted to adapt *The Son of the Grand Eunuch*, Larry replied, "It's got balls!"[11]

Making the show for Helen Ford, the boys turned the vapid Chti into the kinder, more thoughtful Chee-Chee. But as they worked, the city began to bake. You could see waves of heat rising from construction sites along Eighth Avenue, parts of which were still being torn up for new subway lines, and rippling across the theater district. For the theaters open on Independence Day, Knickerbocker Ice would park its trucks out front and deliver blocks of ice to the back rooms of each building; huge fans were positioned behind the blocks and switched on, sending cool air through the theater. (Once the ice melted—usually well before the curtain came down—the second or third act became intolerable to sit through.) To beat the heat, Rodgers, Hart, and Fields fled Manhattan to work on *Chee-Chee* at the Valley View Farm Inn, in Hawthorne, New York, in Westchester County—a few degrees cooler than the city but close enough in case of an emergency.[12]

On the fifth of July, the *New York American* ran a piece by Larry—the accompanying photo of him in a hat makes him look like Eddie Cantor—about the state of American musical theater. "America," he wrote, "may become a satellite of London tomorrow, as it was yesterday, but today it is a Ziegfeldian Parnassus. The taste in this form of entertainment moves in cycles. Central Europe was, perhaps, the first home of what is known as the modern musical comedy." Insisting that American musical comedy gets better every day (though he claims no credit for himself), Larry reminds his readers of the sameness of the old Viennese operetta, and invokes W. S. Gilbert as the savior of the libretto. "With the exception of Richard Wagner, [Gilbert] is the only librettist whose work has lived for itself alone. That is not merely because of the music." Praising Jerome Kern as a guiding light to younger composers, Larry insists that Gershwin and Youmans are not imitators of Kern but originals, and he has extravagant praise for the stage designers Josef Urban, James Reynolds, and Leon Bakst. Audiences might argue about the stage design of a musical play, Larry says, but not, surprisingly, about the musical's book. "Rather, I have heard them discuss the music, the comedy, the actors and the chorus, but never have I seen anyone agitated by the turn of the story. The answer is that we need new stories. There is no reason to assume that music, if decently interpolated, would mar the continuity of any story."[13]

This might have been Larry justifying his interest in *Son of the Grand Eunuch*; certainly the Charles Pettit source material qualified as new. For all his immersion in the theater—for all his *knowledge*, period—Larry was an oddly contradictory creature. He was only thirty-three, had demonstrated he could write lyrics, and while doing so had been dizzyingly productive (even if much of that productivity had been driven by his younger, workaholic collaborator). All those shows since *Garrick Gaieties*, which had been only three years earlier! And yet Larry hadn't changed. He remained a devoted son, gentle and kind, shy and private, yet willing to express his opinion in print and always, always ready for a party. He was more self-conscious than ever about his physical stature, for even Rodgers had begun to make jokes about it. In his letters to Dorothy Feiner, Rodgers often referred to Hart as "the shrimp." Larry felt himself to be an outsider even though, in 1928, he was about as inside as one can get in the American musical theater.

Before summer's end, *Chee-Chee* went into the Forrest Theatre in Philadelphia. It was more ambitious than anything Rodgers and Hart had previously tried, because each song, each patch of music, was meant to advance the story. Just as Rodgers's music for *The King and I* more than twenty years later would give only an *impression* of Bangkok, his music for *Chee-Chee* was an impression of China rather than an attempt to re-create the *yayue* (elegant music) or the *sayue* (popular music) of ancient China. "I pulled my usual preopening stunt of becoming good and sick a few days ago," Rodgers wrote to Dorothy Feiner. "I've managed to do that before every opening except *Present Arms* and that was a flop."[14]

Philadelphia audiences didn't know what to make of the ancient China setting or the hero with the indelicate dilemma. Of the musical numbers that were to be sung in full, everyone had high hopes for "I Must Love You," and then the boys wrote a new song, "Dear, Oh Dear," in Philadelphia, and figured the latter would complement the former. Both were to be sung by William Williams and Helen Ford, as Li Pi Tchou and Chee-Chee. In "Dear, Oh Dear," Chee-Chee sings to her husband:

Once a kiss was just a kiss,
A smile was just a smile.
To hold a manly hand like this
Was hardly worth the while.
Each boy was like a brother,
And one was like the other,
Your kisses seem to be
Not brotherly to me.

Increasingly, Larry's lyrics were not avoiding clichés so much as inverting them.

While *Chee-Chee* was still in tryouts, the busiest season for the performing arts was just starting in New York. *Manhattan Serenade*, the new jazz concerto by Louis Alter, who had been solo pianist for the *Greenwich Village Follies*, was being played all over town and would join Gershwin's *Rhapsody in Blue*—and, later, Earle Hagen's *Harlem Nocturne*, Alfred Newman's *Street Scene*, Aaron Copland's *Quiet City*, and Rodgers's *Slaughter on Tenth Avenue*—as anthems blowing through the city's canyons. On September 19 *The Singing Fool*, Al Jolson's follow-up to *The Jazz Singer*, opened at the Winter Garden, where the top orchestra ticket for the premiere was a bank-breaking eleven dollars. Audiences couldn't get enough of Jolson singing "I'm Sitting on Top of the World." What had been novelty the previous year was now cozily familiar.

Six days after Jolie took the Winter Garden in his arms, *Chee-Chee* opened at Lew Fields's Mansfield Theatre. "Rodgers and Hart invade the Orient" was how the musical director Buster Davis described it—"The Orient wins." Commercially, that was true. Critically, the show's reception was more complicated. The all-important *Times* review by Brooks Atkinson was undeniably negative, though he meant it as a compliment when he compared the show's look to that of Winthrop Ames's production of Gilbert and Sullivan's *The Mikado*—the Chinese and Japanese settings, one supposes, coming from the same design grab bag—and Atkinson had kind words for William Williams, who had sung Gilbert & Sullivan for Ames. A notoriously angry review by guest critic St. John Ervine in *The World* evaluated *Chee-Chee* as "Nasty! Nasty! . . . there can rarely have been a play so ornately produced to so little effect." Some critics who weren't offended by the not wholly printable plot still found it dull. But some of the best reviewers found plenty to admire. In *The Sun* Gilbert Gabriel—Rodgers's favorite theater critic, because he knew about music as well as drama—called the show "charming" and said, "I find

Hart's lyrics going in for purposely simple and easier rhymes than he has used before. I like them."[15] Collating the notices decades later, Ethan Mordden wrote, "The myth of *Chee-Chee*, which lasted a month and then vanished, is that the critics recoiled from its subject matter and fell on it like the fold on the wolf. In fact, it got five pans, two half-and-halfs, and six raves. The *Daily Mirror* called it 'a revolutionary musical show,' *The Evening World* saw 'a rousing tale of stage adventure with a finale that was greeted by rousing cheers.'. . . But the book, almost all felt, was slow going, and, indeed, the subject gave more than a few viewers the feeling that the musical had become not so much liberal as pointlessly smutty."[16] But *Chee-Chee* didn't receive the kind of word of mouth that smut can command. The day after its opening it was all too easy to buy a ticket.

Chee-Chee's failure led into a sad autumn. Although *Chee-Chee* would not be the last time Rodgers and Hart would work with Herb Fields, it put a crimp in the collaboration, and it was no longer assumed that Herb would write the book for each show. In this period he went off to write something with his sister, Dorothy, for Lew, who had expressed a desire to go back on the stage himself. Roy Webb, the older Columbia alumnus who had taught Rodgers so much, packed up and went to Hollywood, where they were putting music into pictures. (By the end of the following decade, Webb would be the default composer at RKO.) With *Chee-Chee*, Helen Ford had done her final Rodgers & Hart show, though she and George Ford would remain friendly with both writers for the rest of their lives.

In the days before Lew Fields's press agent announced *Chee-Chee's* closing, Max Hart's sixty-two-year-old body was shutting down. On the night of October 8, Max was in bed—he could no longer lie prone without agony—with Larry and Teddy on either side of him. Like so many people near the end of their lives, he felt death enter the room and wait politely to approach. "I'm going to die tonight," Max said to his sons. "Don't wake your mother, though. Let her sleep." Sensitive to the boys' reactions, he added, "Don't grieve for me. I haven't missed a thing!" He was still breathing until just after seven the next morning.[17]

There was no obituary. Frederick Nolan has suggested that Larry hated obituaries and declined to alert the newspapers. Max was buried in a family plot at Mt. Zion Cemetery in Maspeth, Queens, a sprawling Jewish cemetery where corpses from the tragic Triangle Shirtwaist Company fire in 1911 were buried after they had lain unclaimed in Manhattan.[18]

Max's death left the Harts with more financial tsuris. Through the rest of October and all of November, representatives of the Eagle Indemnity Company hounded the family for money that Max was said to have owed them. "Stand in line," Larry might have responded, except he declined to make himself available. On November 8, Howard Myers, attorney for Eagle Indemnity, arrived at 415 Central Park West to serve a citation ordering the family to pay Max's debt. "I was informed by the colored maid in charge of the apartment," Myers testified in Surrogate's Court, "that the Harts were not at home. She further stated that she did not know when any one of the Harts would be home. After waiting several hours and not seeing any of the Harts, I left." Eagle Indemnity wanted $10,000? Good luck! Well, that's how the O. M. would have handled it, wasn't it? Howard Myers repeated the procedure the following day, with the same results. On November 28 he returned, accompanied by a New York County deputy sheriff. Once again Big Mary stonewalled them. On December 18 the doorman stopped them and, making a show of phoning up to the Harts' apartment, made it clear that no Hart was in residence. Next day Myers requested the Surrogate's Court to issue an order authorizing court service of the citation to the Harts, whom he believed to be "hiding" in their apartment. Finally served, the Harts—or Larry, anyway—wrote the check.[19]

While Eagle Indemnity was demanding its money, *Chee-Chee* closed, followed in short order by *A Connecticut Yankee*. The former had had the briefest run—31 performances—of any Rodgers & Hart show up to that time, the latter the longest: an astonishing 418. What remains striking about *Chee-Chee* is the same thing that's striking about so many of the shows Herb Fields wrote with Rodgers and Hart: how swiftly they went from conception to execution, with a first night often occurring in a matter of weeks. ("It has nothing to do with conquering the world," Duke Ellington said of putting on one of his shows. "You write it tonight and play it tomorrow, and that's it!")[20]

In the first few weeks of 1929 Rodgers and Hart teamed up with the absurdly prolific playwright Owen Davis to create a new show, *Spring Is Here*. It was a return to conventional fare—comfort food after the exotic indelicacies of *Chee-Chee* and the loss of a life force like Max Hart. Alex A. Aarons and Vinton Freedley ushered the show into the Alvin Theatre (so named for the combined first names of the producers) on March 11. Based on Davis's play *Shotgun Wedding*, its plot was a throwback to the nineteenth-century comedy-melodrama—the kind of play Davis himself had renounced after the Great War: Terry (Glenn Hunter) loves Betty (Lillian Taiz), but Betty thinks she loves Stacy (John Hundley); Stacy and Betty are preparing to elope when her father interferes, enabling Terry to prove he's the right man for Betty.[21]

Davis regarded musical comedy writing as something he had to try. Near the close of 1928 he had participated in the Ziegfeld–Eddie Cantor version of *Whoopee*, adapted from his own play *The Nervous Wreck*, and a few weeks later had a hand in *Lady Fingers*, the musical adaptation of his comedy *Easy Come, Easy Go*. The collaboration with Rodgers and Hart was his third crack at a book musical, and the third time, apparently, was not a charm. "[William Anthony] McGuire and Otto Harbach need not worry," Davis wrote; "they can have the musical comedy field so far as I am concerned. Of all the forms of writing I find it the least interesting and the most difficult; to me it remains a trick like putting peas up your nostrils, not at all impossible, but why do it? . . . That the properly concocted musical show must be dominated by its score and not by its book is explanation enough as to why a vain old dramatist can't rave about this form of expression."[22]

Davis was correct: the shows that clicked commercially were memorable for their musical scores. But if Davis would have preferred it otherwise, so did Larry Hart, who had argued repeatedly for more attention to be paid to a musical's book. Given *Spring Is Here*'s mundane, overly familiar plot, it boasted some wonderful assets, including the director Alexander Leftwich, who had previously worked so well with Rodgers and Hart's material; Alfred Newman taking over for Roy Webb (and soon to follow Webb to Hollywood and emerge as one of the three or four most commanding film composers in the business); the pianists Arden and Ohman in the orchestra pit; Charles Ruggles as Betty's father; that "grape of a girl," Joyce Barbour; and the show's secret weapon, the lovely-funny Inez Courtney, inevitably compared to Beatrice Lillie and playing Betty's clever sister Mary Jane.

The "Spring Is Here" that became a standard isn't from *Spring Is Here*—the boys wouldn't write that song for several more years, and it wouldn't be heard onstage for nearly another decade—but "Spring Is Here in Person" from the 1929 show is a much lighter thing. Encouraging sis Betty to get out there and make Terry jealous, Mary Jane sings "Baby's Awake Now" ("Ready to shake her chassis, / Baby has new springs"). Although the sisters' approach to romance is different, they share a lament in "Why Can't I?" The lyric shows Larry Hart working at top speed. "Only my book in bed / Knows how I look in bed" sings Betty, a "nice" but bewildered young woman, who's alone when she lowers her lamp but—unlike the lady who's a tramp, still eight years away from bursting into the Hart canon—would rather not be.

Leading man Glenn Hunter had been appearing in Broadway dramas since the war, and he was not by any definition a singer. Consequently, "Yours Sincerely" was written to be declaimed by both Betty and Terry, writing letters to each other with very different agendas, and it's been sung that way (notably by Rosemary Clooney) ever since. The lyric is deliberately crammed with epistolary clichés—"tears of love," "hoping to find the phrase," "groping to find each word," etc.—but the feeling behind the awkward expressions is itself messy: leave it to Larry to have his singer declare, "My passion is unruly"; if it weren't it wouldn't be passionate. Betty tells Terry that not only does he not stand a chance with her, but she will use his semi-poetic declarations of love, Cyrano-style, on Stacy, whom she thinks she loves.

And then there's "With a Song in My Heart," which requires a wide tessitura (the particular range of a vocal part), not necessarily by a baritone (is there a greater version of the song than Ella Fitzgerald's?) but so written for the show. Because Glenn Hunter was not up to the task, the song went to his rival John Hundley. The refrain is stirring operetta, with the word "song" given the highest note in the melody. It's in the two verses that the song packs a wallop. The first verse, the singer Mary Cleere Haran pointed out, "floats around in a lovely, unresolved netherworld of anticipation and excitement, the way you feel when you're about to see the one you love. When he or she finally appears, the verse simply melts into the gorgeous melody and audiences never fail to grasp when that happens."[23] Standing beside the anticipation is the lyric's sense of renewal, for each meeting of the lovers brings "a new kind of love at first sight": for the bond to hold, it must keep changing. Not for Larry Hart the sentiment of Irving Berlin's "Always" (whose refrain George S. Kaufman corrected as "I'll be loving you—Thursday!")[24] In the second, less familiar verse—"an air that I'll live to repeat"—the cycle of renewal begins all over again.

> Oh, the moon's not a moon for a night
> And these stars will not twinkle and fade out
> And the words in my ears
> Will resound for the rest of my years.

In the morning I'll find with delight
Not a note of our music is played out.
It will be just as sweet,
And an air that I'll live to repeat:
I greet you . . .

Although there's always the danger of it turning cloying, "With a Song in My Heart" remains a marvelous piece of work.

Spring Is Here was favorably reviewed, though no critic mistook it for groundbreaking musical theater. George Jean Nathan singled out the monkeyshines of Charles Ruggles and seemed to like the show, but he mentioned neither Rodgers nor Hart.[25] Every second or third reviewer referred to Glenn Hunter's inability to sing.

It was a tough time for any play, musical or straight, that failed to dazzle. Talking pictures were roaring from every cinema and audiences preferred their cheaper ticket prices and more convenient showtimes. In his 1929 novel, *Hangover*, Max Lief wrote, "One newspaper statistician took the trouble to discover that every legitimate playhouse on Broadway from Forty-second to Fiftieth Street had gone talkie, although there were numerous [legitimate theaters] left in the side-streets. . . . Even the Theatre Guild, presided over by its sextuple hierarchy with a list of 25,000 subscribers, was unable to extend many of its plays beyond the usual six-week subscription period."[26]

And yet Broadway glittered more than ever. Advertisements for Squibb's Dental Cream, Maxwell House Coffee, and Lucky Strike emblazoned Times Square. After the British writer G. K. Chesterton got his first look at the Square, he wrote, "What a garden of earthly delights this would be if only one had the gift of not being able to read."[27]

When it came to Broadway musicals, it seemed that theatergoers had been bitten by Gershwinitis, with *Oh, Kay!*, *Funny Face*, and *Rosalie* recently given extravagant (and profitable) productions. *Strike Up the Band* and *Girl Crazy* waited in the wings. For the more serious-minded, radical theater struggled way uptown and in the Village. In 1928, New Playwrights, housed on charming Commerce Street, staged John Howard Lawson's *The International* and Michael Gold's *Hoboken Blues*. Literate as they were, these plays tended to preach to the converted, had little or no ambition to entertain, and were quickly forgotten. E. E. Cummings mimicked New Playwrights by imagining two radical theater compatriots sitting around: "When does the strike begin?" asks the first man, with dripping sincerity, and the second man replies, in a falsetto voice, "Mother's at the house sewing her eyes out!"[28] It was mean but not so far-fetched. Sympathetic as he was to New Playwrights' politics, Larry wanted no part of it.

CHAPTER 10

My Head Is Just a Hat Place

BY THE time *Spring Is Here* opened in 1929," Margery Darrell wrote in the 1951 *Rodgers and Hart Song Book*, "Rodgers & Hart were celebrities. Reporters had begun to follow them around on their semi-annual jaunts to the Continent. Richard Rodgers no longer had to struggle with the newspapers to keep the 'd' in his name. And stories began to be told about the way the diminutive Larry Hart got folded up in upper berths and put away by porters who didn't know he was there."[1]

Despite its conventionality, or maybe because of it, *Spring Is Here* was doing well at the box office, and the sale of its movie rights to First National made further collaboration with the tireless playwright Owen Davis advisable. An early April item in the *Times*, referring to Davis as "the speediest of the playwrights," reported that Davis had already completed a libretto for the next Rodgers & Hart musical, to be produced by Sam H. Harris and tentatively titled *Two Is Company*.[2]

It's not clear what *Two Is Company* was about; Davis didn't use the title again. While the libretto's fate was being considered, however, Dick and Larry were asked to appear in a Paramount Famous Lasky two-reeler called *Makers of Melody*, to be shot in Astoria, Queens. The head of the music department at Astoria was the Englishman Frank Tours, and it was under Tours's aegis that musical stars like Duke Ellington came in and performed while the cameras rolled.

Makers of Melody was shot in April 1929 and released a few weeks later. The short subject was conceived by S. Jay Kaufman, a peripatetic show business journalist who would subsequently try his hand at feature-length movies and radio. The twenty-minute film is a curiosity piece—quaint and awkward but chock-full of information, particularly about the evolving relationship between the two songwriters.

The framework of *Makers of Melody* is that of Rodgers and Hart telling the story of their partnership to a feature writer, Miss Merrill. The songwriters' accents betray their Manhattan upbringing. They begin with the days when they were rejected by every music publisher in town. "Now you'll *have* to go into the real estate business with your father," Dick says to Larry. (Would that Max Hart had been alive to hear it.)

An obvious reference to Manhattan leads into Allan Gould and Ruth Tester singing "Manhattan" on a tiny stage while a montage of skyscrapers flickers on the screen. In the next scene, the boys are writing "Here in My Arms," and although Dick's role as the sterner partner is supposed to be fictional, it plays as uncomfortably authentic. To fit Dick's melody as he plays it on the piano, Larry tries the lyric, "Here in my arms I think it's adorable," as if he's making it up on the spot. "Not bad," says Larry. "Not good," Dick admonishes. Of course the line doesn't fit anyway, and we're reminded that in most songwriter biopics the writing process is reduced to such silly, perspiration-free stops and starts. In the next five minutes Larry appears in checked pajamas, looking vaguely like a jailbird, with a big black cigar between his fingers, and then he's dressed in top hat and tailcoat but no pants—the alternately mischievous and petulant little boy to Dick's chiding parent. In between there's some business with Inez Courtney dancing to "The Girl Friend," and an almost surreal account of the boys writing "The Blue Room" while they were in Washington. When Larry fails to recall this detail, Dick rebukes him, "You forgot to remember!" Is it far-fetched to suggest the line was authored by Rodgers and meant as a dig at Irving Berlin, whose song "Remember" includes that phrase?

After viewing *Makers of Melody*, one takes away not a refreshed appreciation of the songs but a queasily accurate glimpse of the way the songwriters—the younger but more authoritative Rodgers, the older but still irrepressible, irresponsible Hart—related to each other. In any case, an early June edition of *Variety* gave *Makers of Melody* an indifferent review and, contrary to what Margery Darrell wrote about this period in their lives, misspelled the songwriters' names as Richard Rogers and Lawrence Hart.[3]

✵   ✵   ✵

Makers of Melody was a two-reeler meant to pass away twenty minutes as part of a longer program in the cinema. But movies with sound had become a powerful new force. Many movies photographed without sound the previous year were quickly refitted with sound tracks—some with music but no spoken dialogue, some with only snippets of dialogue. It was hard to keep track of the changing formats. William R. Weaver, film critic for *The Chicagoan*, divided 1929 pictures under his consideration into Vocal, Quasi-Vocal, and Mute. Film purists lamented the coming of sound, insisting it robbed the medium of its unique imagination, but even purists didn't deny that sound was creating new jobs. The economic devastation of the stock market crash was still months away, but playwrights and newspapermen were leaving employment in the East and Midwest to accept writing contracts with motion picture studios that were (in Ian Hamilton's phrase) buying dialogue by the ton.[4] Vincent Lawrence, whose plays were often running down the block from Rodgers & Hart shows, went to Hollywood and never returned. Riding on the good notices for his musical *Good Boy*, Henry Myers signed a contract with Paramount. Myers's friend Jo Swerling, Chicago correspondent for *Variety*, went west to get a look at the place he'd been writing about, and soon began a decades-long career as a screenwriter. Larry Hart's old classmate and drinking partner Herman Mankiewicz was already ensconced in Los Angeles and imploring his pals to come join him. (Three years earlier Mankiewicz had sent Ben Hecht what remains the most famous telegram to come out of the movie business: WILL YOU ACCEPT THREE HUNDRED PER WEEK TO WORK FOR PARAMOUNT PICTURES? ALL EXPENSES PAID. THE THREE HUNDRED IS PEANUTS. MILLIONS ARE TO BE GRABBED OUT HERE AND YOUR ONLY COMPETITION IS IDIOTS. DON'T LET THIS GET AROUND.)

The demands of the microphone, however, were quite different from the demands of the movie camera. Everyone knows a version of the story of silent screen star John Gilbert, who was said to have a voice that miked poorly and made his high-flown dialogue in *His Glorious Night*, his first talkie, sound ridiculous.[5] "My *dear*," says one woman to another in *Hangover*, "imagine [Jeanne Eagels, star of the Broadway play *Rain*] trying to get into the talkies with that lisp of hers!"[6] Theatergoers were afraid there'd be such a mass exodus to Los Angeles that there'd be no actors left for the stage; maybe there'd be no *stage*. "Thousands of play actors have deserted like mercenaries to the tents of Hollywood," wrote the *Chicagoan* theater critic Charles Collins, "and the Broadway producers are groaning that they are unable to find casts for the master-pieces on which they have paid advance royalties."[7] *Makers of Melody* had hardly constituted a desertion of Broadway. Dick and Larry were still musical play writers and had every intention of remaining so.

In the meantime they seemed to have written at least three songs for a musical version of Ferenc Molnár's 1926 hit *The Play's the Thing*. Whether this was on speculation or on assignment is hard to say—Dick and Larry would often write several songs before funding for a show was found—though it must have given Larry a strange buzz to be adapting Molnár again after getting no credit for the *Liliom* translation. In any case the *Play's the Thing* musical was dropped.

Owen Davis's *Two Is Company* was also dropped. *Spring Is Here* closed on June 8, 1929. By then Davis was deep into a musical book called *Me for You*, with Dick and Larry writing songs through the first half of the summer. *Me for You* was about a bootlegger, to be played by the gentle, bleating comic actor Victor Moore (perhaps best remembered today as Fred Astaire's sidekick in *Swing Time*), whose daughter is unaware of how he really makes his living. Drifting out from the plot was a wispy seafaring romance involving Jack Whiting (then appearing in *Hold Everything*). It sounded fine on paper. Most nights Dick would file updates by telegram with Dorothy Feiner, who was in Europe for the summer. Herb Fields was living in Chappaqua and working on at least two projects—a new play for his father, in collaboration with sister Dorothy, and, for Cole Porter, *Fifty Million Frenchmen*. (One of the quintet of that show's producers, which included Irving Berlin, had persuaded Porter to omit the rest of the phrase, "Can't Be Wrong," from the title.) Considering that he was teaming up these days with Porter, Herb had little reason to feel bad that his pals were working without him again.[8]

By June 3, Dick and Larry had completed "A Ship Without a Sail." One of the first great American lyrics to sustain a vivid metaphor, "A Ship Without a Sail" evokes a vast, empty horizon where laughter echoes as hollow and hope is futile.

> *All alone, all at sea!*
> *Why does nobody care for me?*
> *When there's no love to hold my love,*
> *Why is my heart so frail,*
> *Like a ship without a sail?*
> *Out on the ocean*

Sailors can use a chart.
I'm on the ocean
Guided by just a lonely heart.

The title phrase was not Larry's invention. Sometime before 1908 the popular American song "Silver Dollar" began, "A man without a woman is like a ship without a sail, / Is like a boat without a rudder, a kite without a tail." And in 1920 several singers recorded a new song called "I'm Like a Ship Without a Sail."

But no earlier song containing the phrase approached the lyrical and emotional sophistication of the Rodgers & Hart song. Graham Wood has mentioned that the simile of "*Like* a ship without a sail" is displaced by the completed metaphor of "*For* a ship without a sail": "The singer has *become* the ship, and although life (and time) has moved on, this particular metaphorical journey (the song) has come to an end."[9]

Still alone, still at sea!
Still there's no one to care for me.
When there's no hand to hold my hand
Life is a loveless tale
For a ship without a sail.

Writing to Dorothy Feiner, Dick pronounced the song "pretty hot."[10] Oddly, it was Larry who almost didn't know what they had. Frederick Nolan tells the story of Larry calling his old friend Milton Pascal to read him the lyric over the phone; Pascal was impressed and said so. Some hours later, though, Larry phoned again, this time in a panic, because he had misplaced the scrap of paper containing the lyric. No need to worry: Pascal remembered every word.[11]

Among the other songs completed for *Me for You*, "As Though You Were There" imputes a mature sexual knowingness to lovers when they're apart:

Brush my hair and dress with care
Though no one's around to crave my face,
Shave my face
As though you were there.

And:

Every day when you're away
And others ask me, "Why behave?"
I behave
As though you were there.

Larry makes fidelity funny but not dull (and no other lyricist so consistently employed the subjunctive mood properly).

Me for You was almost set. From out of nowhere, the producer Philip Goodman announced he had engaged Maxwell Anderson and Otto Harbach as librettists for an untitled musical drama set in New York City on New Year's Eve—with Rodgers and Hart writing the score.[12] Did Dick and Larry know about it? Goodman's announcement could have been based on little more than a brief exchange at Sardi's, which had settled into its current location on West Forty-Fourth Street three years earlier.

By midsummer of 1929 Larry Hart had become a regular at the restaurant. Vincent Sardi had stood up to the feared Owney Madden and other bootlegging gangsters who demanded a piece of the action. But Sardi remained concerned about his family's safety. He said as much to Texas Guinan, who apparently got her underworld pals off Sardi's back. Sardi quietly kept whiskey in the restaurant and served it to customers he knew and liked, including Larry. "I remember particularly one young and brilliant lyricist," Sardi wrote, "whose songs were later to be hailed far and wide as ranking with the best musical-comedy tunes ever written in this country. My wife [Jenny] treated him like a son. Unfortunately he did not have much will power. He would promise my wife that he was going to stop drinking so much, and then friends of his would arrive and ask him to sit down, and the next thing he knew he would be drinking again. Some nights when he would fall asleep, exhausted, my wife would make a bed for him in the back of the restaurant." There would have been little doubt that the young and brilliant lyricist was Larry Hart even if Sardi's son Vincent Jr. had not clarified the omission of the name: "When Dad wrote his autobiography in the 'fifties, he referred to Larry's drinking, but after the book had gone to press, he paid to have all copies of the book recalled and reprinted without the revelation about Hart's drinking."[13]

This was the period when Larry began to come into Sardi's with Doc Bender, who made Vincent Sr. nervous—a response to the dentist many people shared. Sardi declined to cash Bender's check for any sum over five bucks.[14] Not that it mattered: Larry always picked up the bill anyway.

Sardi allowed actors to keep charge accounts—they always paid him, eventually—and set up some tacit rules to protect them from autograph hounds and favor-seekers. (Customers were not permitted to send drinks from one table to another.) Sardi liked newspapermen, too. Seated most days for lunch were members of the Cheese Club, so named not for the snacks on the tables but because each newspaperman thought of himself as the Big Cheese. One member of the Cheese Club, Irving Hoffman, brought around the young Russian émigré Alex Gard. Gard was not a writer, but he could draw dead-on caricatures in a matter of minutes. Showing Sardi what he could do with charcoal and a piece of paper, Gard entered into an agreement: the restaurateur would pay Gard two meals a day for drawing caricatures, which would become Sardi's property; Sardi was not to criticize the caricatures, Gard was not to criticize the food. By the time Gard died in 1948, he had drawn nearly seven hundred caricatures for Sardi's—Larry Hart's among them.[15]

Gard decided whom he drew, but his choices were frequently directed by Renee Carroll, perhaps the most famous hatcheck girl in New York at the time. A redhead who referred to herself as Sardi's "ex-chequer of top pieces," Carroll was born Rebecca Shapiro on the Lower East Side. She went to work at Sardi's in 1927 and, although her official position was supposed to keep her out of the dining room, she came to know even more than Vincent Sardi did about the diners present on any given evening.

Max Lief described a typical lunch at Sardi's in 1929:

> Pencil in hand, a twenty-three-year-old producer was figuring out on the tablecloth the expected profits of a five-character play with only one set. At another table George Abbott, playwright, was outlining the plot of his latest melodrama to Ward Morehouse, who ran the *Sun*'s daily column of dramatic news. A couple of ticket brokers were loudly bemoaning the terrific heat which was decimating theater attendance and were considering dumping their tickets into the cut-rate agencies . . . and in a far corner Al Woods and Lee Shubert were wrangling over the luncheon check, the latter beating his fellow-producer to the draw by handing the waiter a hundred dollar bill, the smallest he had.[16]

Larry Hart could feel safe at Sardi's. The family recognized his gifts, fed him, left him alone, put him to bed if necessary, and put him in a cab after dawn.

In a mid-July 1929 letter to Dorothy Feiner, Dick reported that the Fox studio had made Rodgers and Hart an offer to bring them to the West Coast and put them to work; but the boys had said no, committed as they were to Aarons & Freedley for *Me for You*. They weren't turning their backs on the movies, however. Laurence Schwab, who had coproduced the musical *Follow Thru* with Frank Mandel, asked them to contribute songs for the movie version, which Schwab would not only coproduce but codirect at the Paramount studios in New York. Although it was in the tradition of *Good News*, *Follow Thru* was about golf rather than football and boasted the winsome "Button Up Your Overcoat," by DeSylva, Brown & Henderson. Dick and Larry had heard that movie producers routinely threw out songs from a stage play and brought in other writers. They decried the practice but, like so many other writers, couldn't turn down the money that was offered.

To celebrate the *Follow Thru* assignment, Larry held an open house at 415 Central Park West. "Larry Hart threw an endurance party at his place the other a.m.," *Variety* reported. "Broke all pent-house records." [17]

Rodgers, now twenty-seven, practically (though not yet officially) engaged to be married to Dorothy, decided it was time to move out of his parents' apartment off Amsterdam Avenue and get his own. He took a nineteenth-floor apartment in the Lombardy Hotel, on East Fifty-Sixth Street, on the same floor as the novelist-playwright Edna Ferber, whose prolific career was cresting as the author of the source material for *Show Boat*. Rodgers would remain an Upper East Side resident, even if eventually part-time, for the rest of his life. The affluent neighborhood was home to the Right People. Larry Hart didn't care about the Right People; he just wanted to be in the company of women and men who were talented and funny.

In mid-September *Me for You* opened in Detroit, with the Rodgers & Hart alumna Betty Starbuck and a comic dancer from Boston named Ray Bolger added to the cast. The songs went over well, but the musical as a whole seemed to come at the audience all wrong. The problem, Rodgers wrote, was that nobody could accept the lovable Victor Moore, whose befuddlement was often expressed in cracked-voice one-liners, as a bootlegger. After some gloom-laden conferences—and there is no more entertaining depiction of these interminable hours of defeat than the scene in the movie *The Band Wagon*—the story was twisted around by two new writers, John McGowan and Paul Gerard Smith, and several songs were scrapped, including the delicious "As Though You Were There." In the revised version, now known as *Heads Up!*, Victor Moore becomes the cook on a yacht that's being used— unwittingly by its owners, it turns out—for booze smuggling. Moore's cook passes the long hours on the water by inventing things; one of his prize inventions is a fluid that's supposed to kill flies. "Did it kill 'em?" he's asked. "Well, no," he replies, "but it mixes nicely with ginger ale." [18] Among the few new songs written specifically for *Heads Up!*, "Why Do You Suppose?" recycled the music and the same five beats of "How Was I to Know?" from *She's My Baby* and declares the universal you-and-only-you sentiment in a lovely way. "You've Got to Surrender" folds in a variation on Gilbert and Sullivan's "Twenty Love-Sick Maidens We" (from *Patience*), adding thirteen maidens who expect to be courted by "a delegation / From the naval station." "Ongsay and Anceday" is Larry having fun with pig Latin several years before Ginger Rogers sang "We're in the Money" in *Gold Diggers of 1933.* And "Knees" was a takeoff on Rudyard Kipling's "Boots."

While *Heads Up!* was trying out at the Shubert Theatre in Philadelphia, the stock market crashed. On Tuesday, October 29, a then record 16.4 million shares were traded, with some $30 billion vanishing overnight. WALL STREET LAYS AN EGG was *Variety*'s banner headline the following day. The wild party that was the Roaring Twenties was over. It was natural for the *Heads Up!* principals to assume audiences wouldn't show up anymore.

But *Heads Up!* had some extra coal in the engine room. Besides Victor Moore, Jack Whiting, and Whiting's number "A Ship Without a Sail," it had Betty Starbuck, who was transferred to a comic role to make way for the conventionally prettier Barbara Newberry; the baritone John Hundley; the delectable Alice Boulden; and the rubbery, "skin-and-boneless" Ray Bolger, who could move across the stage as though dangled by a puppeteer, giving the illusion that his feet were never touching the floor. When *Heads Up!* opened at the Alvin on November 11, just two weeks after the crash, the reviews were okay, and the audiences kept coming. In *The World*, Frank Sullivan said that "A Ship Without a Sail" was the best song written since "Ol' Man River." The most prominent naysayer was—as usual—George Jean Nathan, who found the show's book much too familiar but praised Victor Moore, admitted there'd be a "future popular phonograph record" from the show, and mentioned Rodgers but not Hart, the omission apparently deliberate. [19]

When Nathan reviewed *Fifty Million Frenchmen*, he was unusually hyperbolic: "When it comes to lyrics, this M. Porter is so far ahead of the other boys in New York that there is just no race at all." [20] It was only Porter's second full Broadway show, but Nathan had already placed Porter in the winner's circle.

Porter had moved to New York but was not yet occupying his famous aerie in the Waldorf Towers, the lights of Greater New York twinkling below; the Waldorf Towers hadn't been built yet. But several of New York's other songwriters lived high above Manhattan, and the question was why. In a late November piece in *The Sun*, probably intended to advertise *Heads Up!*, songwriters were said to be attracted to penthouses. "This on the authority of a young fellow named Larry Hart, whose first name is Lorenz on programs," the piece began, and then let Larry pinpoint which songwriter was where. While he occupied a penthouse at 101st and Central Park West, his partner Richard Rodgers had a terrace on the nineteenth floor of the Lombardy. Irving Berlin owned a penthouse near the East River. Sigmund Romberg and Buddy DeSylva were perched in tall buildings on the Upper West Side. Vincent Youmans went home to the penthouse above his office on West Forty-Fourth Street, smack in the middle of the theater district. And the Gershwin brothers shared a twelve-room penthouse at Seventy-Fifth and Riverside. "The idea seems to be, as Hart works it out, that the higher these composers get in the air the higher will be their notes."[21] Larry was only half serious. Naturally, a penthouse signified robust earnings. It's also an inversion of the consumptive poverty suggested by, say, the low-ceilinged garrets of *La Bohème*: a songwriter drawing from the deep well of ASCAP royalties and box office percentages is shouting to the world that he may be a commercial success but *he's still an artist*.

But proclaiming himself an artist wasn't Larry Hart's style, and most of the skyscraper songwriters did not have such an extended family to support. He was just a breadwinner who knew a lot about the theater.

And a lucky one. In "A Lesson in Song Writing," in *The World*, Larry suggested that getting the right lyric was sometimes a matter of circumstance. He came to write "Why Do You Suppose?" because he had used the phrase in a question to Dick, who replied, "There! That's your title!"[22]

In late summer, Flo Ziegfeld had asked the boys to consider writing a musical for the comic Ed Wynn. They had put Ziegfeld off, citing possible commitments to a movie studio in California (half-true) and to C. B. Cochran in London (true, though there was no contract yet). After *Heads Up!* appeared poised to run for a while, Ed Wynn invited Dick and Larry to his apartment on East End Avenue and told them that if Ziegfeld was the cause of their reluctance he would handle him. Wynn could be the saddest of comedians, casually breaking your heart with his sweetness, and also the giddiest, sharing the equivalent of nitrous oxide with his audience—more than thirty years later, his rendition of "I Love to Laugh" in *Mary Poppins* would be done in his unique key—but he was also a tough professional, and the boys wanted to believe he would not be cowed by Ziegfeld. Rodgers, who had run interference with Ziegfeld during the making of *Betsy*, knew that the Great Glorifier was unafraid of, even thrived on, litigation; but Rodgers was also aware of the authority wielded by the Dramatists Guild, which had installed a new royalties system and could close down a production faster than the courts could.[23] Thus assured, Rodgers and Hart went to work on a show for Ed Wynn, with the ubiquitous Guy Bolton collaborating with Wynn on the script.

In the meantime, Dick and Larry were trying to get a handle on how the picture producers exploited songs. The film version of Cole Porter's *Paris* had just opened, denuded of practically the entire Porter score. The lovely, mildly suggestive "Don't Look at Me That Way" was still part of it, but that's about all. The boys could understand why the censors would forbid the inclusion of "Let's Do It," the wittiest of all the euphemistic "It" songs (and famously embellished later by Noël Coward); but *Paris* now featured a song called "I'm a Little Negative (Looking for a Positive)," with a lyric by Al Bryan that was no less salacious. What, the boys wondered, gives with these guys?

Rehearsals for *Simple Simon*—the Ed Wynn vehicle—began December 20 in New York. The show was scheduled to go into the Ziegfeld Theatre, which remained a grand palace nearly three years after its opening, and Joseph Urban himself was designing the show's scenery. (Urban's professional stationery was marked "By Grace of Joseph Urban.")[24] Disappointments had already begun—first Wynn's inability to keep Ziegfeld out of the way, then Wynn and Bolton's script, which turned out to be a grab bag of Ed Wynn routines and not much of a story. Rodgers and Hart sensed that *Simple Simon* would be a regression for them.

The plot went like this: Simon Eyyes owns an information and newspaper kiosk on the midway at Coney Island, but Simon reads only fairy tales because he can't bear bad news. Falling asleep in front of his shop, he dreams that his fellow merchants are fairy-tale characters—Cinderella, Old King Cole, Jack and Jill, Snow White, etc.—and that he is the hero. (Ed Wynn's dream of Cinderella was quoted thirty years later by Jerry Lewis in his movie *Cinderfella*.) The names of the fairy-tale characters are only slight variations on the "real life" characters in Simon's world. Tempting as it is to blame the story on the overemployed Bolton, this was typical Ed Wynn stuff. Simon's friend Olee King (the same actor plays Old King Cole in Simon's dream, of course) exclaims, "Did you see the advertisement? Fifty beautiful girls, forty-five lovely costumes! I hate to miss that!" Simon is given to making vaudeville puns that were worn out before Weber met Fields. "An amethyst is a man who doesn't believe in God!" Ed Wynn shoehorned into the show his patented "I love the woods" routine, which usually came out as "I love the woodth!" (The goodwill that Wynn had built up over the years tended to indemnify him from negative reactions to such antique gags.) Wynn's other routines included his imitation of twenty horses running through a field and a piano-bicycle—a keyboard mounted atop the handlebars—which he rode wearing sunglasses with tiny windshield wipers.[25]

Yet the hoariness of the material didn't deter Rodgers and Hart from writing some of their greatest songs yet. Although Larry again rhymes "Coney" with "baloney," as he did so memorably in "Manhattan," his lyric for "Coney Island" re-creates the teeming weekend activity on the boardwalk, as Reginald Marsh did in so many of his illustrations—New Yorkers reveling cheek by jowl on "Good old phony Coney Isle." In hands other than Larry's, "Sweetenheart" would have been rendered as a common profession of love between two young lovers, but here the lovers compare their words to Shelley's, Keats's, Sappho's, and Edna St. Vincent Millay's and, inevitably, find their expressions wanting; everything that needed to be said was in the simple declaration "I love you." Dorothy Parker had ridiculed the wave of I-love-you movie theme songs by imagining the title lyric to a new Norma Talmadge picture as "Woman Disputed, I Love You!"; Larry tosses Parker's joke right into the lyric.[26]

"Dancing on the Ceiling" gives us the ectoplasmic hovering of a young woman's lover as she lies in bed, and the alternating frustration and exhilaration of not being able to sleep because of it. "Say When, Stand Up, Drink Down" is a comically misogynistic toast that prefers the temporary headache wrought by liquor over the interminable headache of a woman's love. "He Was Too Good to Me" remains the most plaintive expression of regret by a lover who has ended a romance—a theme running through American popular song. "He Was Too Good to Me" has been claimed by some listeners to be subtly directed at homosexuals; "I was a queen to him" and "Who's going to make me gay now?" are two Hart lines often invoked as gay code. But Larry Hart wrote specifically for a stage character—in this case, a singer and dance hall girl called Sal—and the song was meant to be Sal's lament that she had broken off her romance. (Searching for gay code within a Hart lyric can turn into an absurd game. One could argue, for instance, that "A Little Birdie

Told Me So" is about gay gossip because "little birdie" translates in Yiddish as *faygeleh*.) In "Hands," for which no music survives, Larry conveys the entrapped feeling of the manicurist whose livelihood depends on the mutual touch of her clients:

> *I do men's nails for seventy-five cents*
> *And I guess I earn my pay.*
> *Kindly realize that a heel or two*
> *Get a manicure plus a feel or two.*
> *God, how I hate their hands!*

These were some of the songs *Simple Simon* went to Boston with. Meanwhile, the *Times* had announced that C. B. Cochran in London had officially engaged Rodgers and Hart to write his next revue.[27] Cochran wanted something along the lines of Noël Coward's *Bitter Sweet*, which was really all in the family because Coward had become a good friend to both Dick and Larry, Cochran produced it, it had been running at the Ziegfeld Theatre since early November, and it starred Evelyn Laye, the beautiful English actress married to Sonnie Hale, who had appeared in *One Dam Thing After Another*. *Bitter Sweet* was told through the eyes of the elderly Marchioness of Chayne recalling her youth, and the role for an actress playing the same woman in youth and dotage had proved so winning to audiences that Cochran figured a similar role would be right for Jessie Matthews, who had also appeared to such acclaim in *One Dam Thing*. The request must have warmed Larry, who always appreciated the appeal of mature women ("I prefer the riper charms / That the autumn years disclose"). It didn't take long for Dick and Larry to come up with an outline about a young woman passing herself off as her own grandmother, whose youth has supposedly been preserved by cosmetics, until she falls in love with a young man close to her actual age. Nor did it take long for Cockie to approve the outline.

But now Rodgers and Hart were in Boston and *Simple Simon* began to change quickly—not the Bolton-Wynn script, but the music and the dances. Among the casualties were "Dancing on the Ceiling," "Say When, Stand Up, Drink Down," "He Was Too Good to Me," and "Hands." A melody from *Chee-Chee* was reused as "I Still Believe in You" (not to be confused with Frank Loesser's "I Believe in You"). The refrain from *Chee-Chee*'s "I Must Love You" was rewritten as "Send for Me." The idea behind "Hands" was retained for "Ten Cents a Dance," written at the Ritz-Carlton where the boys were staying, with Sal transformed from a manicurist to a dance hall hostess.

The Ritz-Carlton was where Larry first sat for an interview with Isaac Goldberg for the *Boston Evening Transcript*. Larry tended to be polite with reporters, tolerant of their ignorance of musical theater, but he had special respect for Goldberg, who had written extensively about Gilbert and Sullivan and the New York theater and had contracted with Simon & Schuster to write a biography of George Gershwin. Goldberg, in turn, was in awe of Larry. "There is an air about successful youth that is subtly electric," Goldberg wrote later. "Hart is short, not much over five feet. He is dark, even Oriental, with deep eyes that belong anywhere except in a 'lyric writer's' head. His manner is more nervous than Rodgers's, and he covers far more territory during an afternoon or evening in the theater."[28] *Heads Up!* had been recently sold to Paramount Pictures for a lot of money, Goldberg reported, and then he floated a rumor, preposterous as it sounded, that F. P. A., Franklin P. Adams, would write the book for the boys' next musical. Larry didn't dispel the rumor but, while he and the writer walked from the Ritz-Carlton to the Colonial Theatre, expounded on how the theater would benefit from the talkies. "Here is the way I see it," he said. "In the long run, the films will prove a boon for the finer things of the playhouse. You see, the cheaper stuff finds its natural audiences now in the picture houses." This might have sounded uncharacteristically elitist, but it was consistent with views Larry had held since he was an adolescent. The theater, he felt, was baggy with tired humor and condescension toward its audience, who could, if given half a chance, appreciate "smart" material. If audiences wanted to be patronized or take in their daily quotient of vulgarity, well, the movies could provide all that and then some.

Goldberg didn't record whether or not he agreed with Larry's theory, but he took his measure as a practitioner of his craft. "If words are being listened to once again in the musical playhouse, Hart is among those who recaptured the straying ear. Of course, like those of his tribe, he committed murder now and then, dispatching his constabularies in search of wild vocabularies." Larry had been warned about his rhyming crimes; even an admirer like Goldberg wasn't going to pronounce him perfect.

Dick and Larry had to see how "Ten Cents a Dance," the song revamped for Sal in *Simple Simon*, would go over. Contracted to play Sal was Lee Morse, who was known as "the little girl with the Swanee voice." Through the second week of February 1930, Morse stopped the show each night by posing, à la Helen Morgan, atop Ed Wynn's piano-bicycle. The story of Morse's firing in Boston has been told many times; here is Rodgers's version: "The first evening ["Ten Cents a Dance"] was to be performed, Ziegfeld, in an unprecedented show of friendliness, invited me to sit with him in the audience. Wynn, the bicycle-piano and Lee Morse made their entrance and were greeted with applause. Everything would have been fine except that Miss Morse had had a few too many and couldn't remember the words or the music."[29] Ziegfeld, uneasy about delegating decisions to others and inclined toward apoplexy, immediately fired Morse and signed the singer Ruth Etting. Pretty, svelte, and sober (at least when it mattered), Etting had scored with New York audiences by singing Harold Arlen's "Get Happy" in the *9:15 Revue*, which had just closed. She had already shown what she could do in the 1927 Ziegfeld *Follies* and, the following year, in *Whoopee*, which Ziegfeld also produced. Etting took the train to Boston and reported for work at the Colonial Theatre, where sheet music for some of the *Simple Simon* songs was being sold in the lobby. Sure enough, Etting's rendition of "Ten Cents a Dance" was special—everybody knew it—even though "I Still Believe in You," which Etting also sang, was the one the critics wrote about.

If it took a few weeks for "Ten Cents a Dance" to be noticed, that could be expected. *Simple Simon* opened at the Ziegfeld Theatre on February 18. First night was an elegant affair befitting the venue, the producer, the star, and the songwriters. "You went deaf from the crunching of starched shirts," Walter Winchell wrote.[30] No critic except, curiously, George Jean Nathan, refrained from ridiculing the book. Ed Wynn was perhaps (as the Chicago-based critic Charles Collins put it) "too good-natured to be a satirist."[31] But critics seemed to love the dancer Harriet Hoctor, and most of them had praise for the Rodgers & Hart score, with "Ten Cents a Dance" getting extraordinary word of mouth. On March 4, Etting went into a Columbia Records studio and recorded "Ten Cents a Dance."

Seven to midnight, I hear drums.
Loudly the saxophone blows.
Trumpets are tearing my eardrums.
Customers crush my toes.
Sometimes I think
I've found my hero,
But it's a queer romance.

All that you need is a ticket.
Come on, big boy, ten cents a dance!

Two days later *The New York Times* reported that Dorothy Feiner and Richard Rodgers were married at the home of the bride's parents, at 270 Park Avenue, the twelve-story building known as The Marguery, which housed the exclusive French restaurant of the same name and took up the entire block between Forty-Seventh and Forty-Eighth and Park and Madison, looming over Vanderbilt Avenue. The ceremony was performed by Stephen S. Wise, at the time the most prominent Reform rabbi in New York, who had married the parents of both bride and groom; the groom's brother, Mort, and his wife; and Ben Feiner, Jr., and *his* wife. Mort was Best Man, with Larry and Herb Fields serving as unofficial ushers. The *Times* got the Rodgers spelling correct but mistakenly reported that the groom had graduated from Columbia.[32] The newlyweds sailed the Atlantic on the *Roma*, visited Taormina and Rome, then were joined in Cannes by Larry Hart. This odd trio—the Rodgerses and the stag Hart—went to London and rented a house from the daughter of a friend of Dick's. Dick and Larry had another Cochran show to write.[33]

For a while in London everything was good. *Simple Simon* was pedaling along at home in New York. Cockie's new show, the *Cochran Revue of 1930*, opened the following week and included "With a Song in My Heart," with Eric Marshall singing it to the American star Ada-May (Cochran's new mistress). Soon that gorgeous song was being heard all over London. Etting's recording of "Ten Cents a Dance" had already become a hit record there.

The public responds to torch songs if they sound sincere and not overwhelmed by self-pity. "Ten Cents a Dance" was not only sincere but honest, bracingly so. Everybody could relate to "trumpets are tearing my eardrums" and "customers crush my toes"—sensual assaults more vivid than what Larry had attempted in "Hands"—and to the touching resignation of the dance hall hostess, who can't help daydreaming that one of her clients will turn out to be The One.

If you were male and single in New York City and no longer a minor, it was likely you had visited a dance hall like the Palace Ballroom, where Sal is employed. "There are eight taxi-dance ballrooms between Forty-Sixth and Fiftieth streets, on Broadway and Seventh Avenue," Leonard Q. Ross (Leo Rosten) reported, "and they are singularly alike. All are on a second floor. All fill their entrances with semi-provocative pictures of their 'hostesses.' Each has a uniformed barker on the sidewalk who passes out special-rate cards and baits lonely men with hints of the feminine miracles at one's beck and call upstairs. All are invested with the same spurious romanticism." Yet the taxi-dancers, Ross amplified, were a friendly voice amid the desolation and impersonality of the city. Ross turned in his special-rate card and paid thirty-five cents, for which he received an admission ticket and one "Free" dance. A burly bouncer checked him out from head to toe and permitted Ross to step in to have a look.[34] (It's delightful to contemplate Larry Hart going through such motions in the guise of research.) Ross saw eighteen girls in evening gowns, lined up behind a low rail, and most of them beckoned. "Dance, honey? Me!" Ross selected a hostess named Jean, from Brooklyn, and after that the other hostesses ignored him because he was considered hers.

Rodgers's boyhood idol Jerome Kern told him that "Ten Cents a Dance" was not only the best song Rodgers and Hart had yet written but the best character sketch since *Camille*.[35] In December 1930 Columbia Pictures was preparing to release *Anybody's Girl*, starring Barbara Stanwyck as a dance hall hostess, when it changed the title to *Ten Cents a Dance*.[36] And in 1933, Reginald Marsh completed his painting *Ten Cents a Dance*, done in tempera, the hostesses blowzy with makeup, their eyebrows plucked, their slinky dresses clinging to their curves. What Larry Hart's lyrics evoked, Marsh showed on the canvas—a gritty, grotesque, gorgeous New York that now and then offered up the appropriate body to help assuage one's loneliness.

With Rodgers and Hart far away in England, Ruth Etting persuaded Ziegfeld to let her interpolate Walter Donaldson and Gus Kahn's "Love Me or Leave Me" into *Simple Simon*. The song was written for *Whoopee*, and Etting recorded it, too, for Columbia. Although *Simple Simon* was on its last legs, Etting's new version of "Love Me or Leave Me" won her a contract to make short musical films for Vitaphone.[37] Hearing about the interpolation, Dick and Larry must have had a "Blue Skies" déjà vu. You labor on a show for weeks or months, grabbing food and sleep when you can; you come up with a dozen songs, and after a while you admit that some of them are damned good; and then your leading lady charms the producer and gets to sing whatever she pleases.

From London, Larry accompanied C. B. Cochran to Berlin to meet with the British playwright Benn W. Levy, who had had a string of successes, most recently with *Mrs. Moonlight*, and was now writing a picture for the German film studio UFA. They all went to see the first screening of Marlene Dietrich in *The Blue Angel*.[38] If Larry resented Cochran's recruitment of Levy to write the script for the new collaboration, titled *Ever Green*, he didn't say so. *Mrs. Moonlight*, which had opened at the Kingsway Theatre in early December 1928, had a plot that was a sibling, if not a twin, to Larry's idea for *Ever Green*. In Levy's play, Sarah Moonlight wears a necklace with the power to grant her one wish: to never grow old. Twenty years later Sarah returns to town posing as the daughter of her sister—that is, as her own niece.[39]

Mrs. Moonlight was considered a comedy-fantasy, with sparklings of A. A. Milne and J. M. Barrie, but it reached for tragedy in its theme of the desire to remain young at all costs.[40] Larry had something decidedly less tragic in mind: a woman ending a profitable masquerade as a well-preserved senior so she can be with the man she loves. However Larry reconciled Cochran's choices in his head, he was thinking about new lyrics as he occupied the floor above the newlyweds' at 11 York Terrace. It was the beginning of an affectionate but ambivalent relationship between Larry and Dorothy Rodgers, who used the words "lovable" and "difficult" when describing him but was put off by his lack of polish. At York Terrace, Larry often appeared in the morning in a stained bathrobe smoking a cigar. Dorothy was mortified. In the second day of residence at the house, Larry left his bath running because he was immersed in a book, and soon bathwater was dripping onto the rooms below, down the steps, and into the street. Admonished by Dorothy for his negligence, Larry was contrite. She forgave him as she might have forgiven a child who will make the same mistake again and again.[41]

CHAPTER 11

I Try to Hide in Vain

S HORTLY BEFORE the Feiner-Rodgers wedding in the late winter of 1930, Rodgers and Hart had been invited by Warner Bros. to come west and write songs for three pictures; as an added inducement, Herb Fields's services were thrown into the mix. Fields was to write a screenplay for Ziegfeld star Marilyn Miller; Rodgers and Hart would write the songs.[1] The old trio would be back in harness, the money was good, and by the time Dick and Larry were home from London, the only reason to cancel the trip west was Dorothy's pregnancy. But that wasn't reason enough. Dorothy was in no condition to travel but gave her blessing. Besides, the dog days were setting in, and the Central Park Reservoir between Eighty-First and Eighty-Fourth Streets—due west from the Metropolitan Museum of Art—was being drained and the earth around it torn up, making a walk across the park to work a treacherous commute. (After years of municipal wrangling, the old reservoir would be transformed into the Great Lawn.)[2] Why not avoid the heat and the rubble this summer?

Larry and Herb Fields went west and were greeted by the news that Marilyn Miller, at Flo Ziegfeld's behest, had chosen to make the film version of *Sunny* instead of Herb's screenplay. Mildly disappointed, Herb decided to try horseback riding and promptly broke his leg.[3] A few days later—it was the third week of June 1930—Dick arrived. As the Santa Fe Chief approached its terminus in Pasadena, Dick arrived in Pullman-ironed clothes— a man had to make an impression when reporting for work—but was soon surprised at how casually everyone dressed. After checking into his hotel, Dick met Larry and, taking a hired car over the Hollywood Hills to get to Burbank, reported to First National. Along the way they crossed the Los Angeles River, which looked less like a river than a concrete gully dotted with puddles.

Los Angeles was in the midst of extraordinary transformation. The population of the City of Los Angeles had recently passed 1.2 million—and with the surrounding Southland region, the number was closer to 2.2 million. The streets were designed for cars rather than pedestrians. Drive-in architecture was everywhere. Stores like Bullock's, part of Wilshire Boulevard's Miracle Mile, were meant to be approached by automobile, a pedestrian entrance appearing to be an afterthought. In 1928 the city's Metropolitan Water District was founded—a major step in turning the arid land green—and three years later a bill authorizing the district to bring water and power from the Colorado River went through.

The movie industry was far and away the largest employer in Los Angeles, but the aircraft industry would soon settle there, with oil production in Wilmington (at the southern tip of Los Angeles County) providing tens of thousands more jobs. Ralphs Grocery Company, eventually to morph into the chain of Ralphs supermarkets, was already in place. So was the famed Brown Derby. The Wiltern Theatre towered above the intersection of Wilshire and Western Boulevards. MacArthur Park, with Wilshire bisecting it, led into the downtown area—one of the few neighborhoods with pedestrians on the sidewalks. In the other direction, toward the Pacific Ocean, Wilshire paused at the purlieus of Westwood Village, which embraced UCLA and some of the most magnificent picture palaces in the city.[4]

The boys' current employer, Warner Bros., was expanding at an alarmingly rapid rate. Warners had just acquired the Crescent Amusement Company, which operated more than sixty theaters in Tennessee, Alabama, and Kentucky. Although Warner Bros. Pictures would not officially merge with First National Pictures, Inc., and Vitaphone Varieties until that November, the three companies were already operating as divisions of the same empire, which now included music publishers—Harms (Dick and Larry's publisher) was the most important—and the Brunswick Radio Corporation.[5]

And there was the First National motion picture studio, spread across a half mile in the southern foothills of the San Fernando Valley. Rodgers felt like he was on another planet. His former collaborator Owen Davis had been there recently and would write of Los Angeles, "It is a bee hive of activity; it is the most cosmopolitan city in the world—and the dullest. For some reason one comes away from Hollywood with that impression stamped firmly in the memory. It's a bore."[6]

That was Rodgers's impression as well. So he was appalled when Larry spread his arms wide, Jolson style, and said, "I want to stay forever!" The most New York of all New York songwriters, Larry loved the weather (seventy-eight degrees and clear in June, seventy-two and clear when it was said to be cool), the palm trees, the hours each day in a car and the privacy they afforded, and, maybe most of all, the distance from Frieda, to whom he was devoted but who was incessantly watching him.

First National was eye-opening. Rodgers and Hart were given a large office with a view of the hills, an excellent Chickering piano, and a comely secretary. What did they need her for? They were there to write a few songs for Herb Fields's screenplay *The Hot Heiress*, about a romance between a debutante and a dese-dems-and-dose riveter. They had the secretary reassigned. Bobby Crawford, the head of the music department, came by to introduce himself and tell them how much he loved their work; he let them know that "Ten Cents a Dance" was a *huge* hit on the Coast. Larry had already made fun of Hollywood in several songs, recently in "They Sing! They Dance! They Speak!" and knew movie-biz hyperbole when he heard it. Dick liked to think of himself as immune to such compliments. But when you have just arrived in a new place and your employer is not only gushing about your past work but paying you premium prices, the flattery lights up your brain like a pinball machine. Crawford called in the New York refugee Ernö Rapée to discuss orchestration. Rapée had come to town in February to head up musical direction at the studio. He claimed to have originated the movie theme song with "Charmaine" for *What Price Glory*, and knew that the scoring of movies was a mixed blessing for musicians: on one hand, there was constant work in Los Angeles, with studios organizing orchestras and hiring almost anyone who could read music; on the other, movie sound equipment had put eight thousand New York musicians out of work, and few of them could afford to travel west on their own.[7] In his new capacity as head of music, Rapée pronounced one Rodgers tune perfect, and soon Rodgers was feeling pretty good—maybe not yet warming to the place as Larry had, but keeping an open mind.

"Larry's working on the lyric in the next room," Rodgers wrote to Dorothy. It was probably a tune Rodgers had worked out on the Santa Fe Chief. "He's less crazy than usual and has been working like the devil. It must be in the air."[8]

On the second or third afternoon at the studio, Dick and Larry were summoned to the executive dining room to meet Jack Warner. Larry seemed to be as curious and quizzical as Dick was. They found Warner seated at the head of the table drinking coffee with a spoon in the cup, its gaucheness making Rodgers wince.

In a thick Jewish accent, Warner said to Rodgers, "How do you do, Mr. Hart?" Then, apparently catching his mistake, he said, "Oh, no, you're the odder man!"

Rodgers was surprised that this handsome, well-tailored fellow sounded like a newly arrived immigrant. Warner made stupefying small talk with department heads, who seemed to be hanging on his every mangled word, then he turned back to Rodgers.

"Now vat ve vant is some sonks vit guts, like 'Yiddishe Momme,' Sophie Tucker's sonk!" Never mind the train; Rodgers wondered how soon he could get a *flight* home. Warner took a swallow of coffee, dropped the cup with a bang, and yelled, "Dis visa-versa coffee is so God darnt hot it boined my mouse!"

The dining room erupted in laughter. Larry grinned at Rodgers and lit a cigar. Warner grinned at his minions and also lit a cigar.

"I've never been taken over so completely in my life," Rodgers admitted, "and I loved it. It was actually Warner giving me a personal greeting."[9]

The boys were invited to the Warner Bros. Jubilee Dinner celebrating the studio's twenty-fifth anniversary, the figure based on the opening of its first film exchange in 1905.[10] Fields, Rodgers, and Hart took out an ad in that week's *Variety*, the entire issue given over to the Jubilee, and the copy has Larry's handprints all over it.[11]

Those Hot Boys from Tin Pan Alley

FIELDS, RODGERS AND HART

*Wish a happy birthday to WARNER BROS. in order
to tell them what the leading critics say about:*

MR. FIELDS'S BOOKS	MR. RODGERS' MUSIC	MR. HART'S LYRICS
Poems of jeu d'esprit	*Music of the Spheres*	*If he were a girl,*
—SAINT BEUVE	—ORPHEUS	*I would love him*
		—SAPPHO!

MR. FIELDS'S BOOKS	MR. RODGERS' MUSIC	MR. HART'S LYRICS
Who is Herbert Fields?	*Here in my Harms,*	*Mein Herz stand stille*
What is he?	*it's adorable.*	*ist ein Gedicht*
—WILLIAM SHAKESPEARE	—MAX DREYFUS	—GOETHE
Nasty! Nasty!	*Shows very little progress.*	*Every lyric writer except*
—ST. JOHN IRVINE [SIC],	—GOLDSMITH,	*Cole Porter should*
The World	*The Tribune*	*commit suicide.*
		—GILBERT SELDES,
		The Graphic

Dick and Larry wore dinner jackets to the event and were seated together. Seated nearby was the thirty-one-year-old Jimmy Cagney, well into his second feature at the studio and silently registering everything the executives said in Yiddish, which he'd picked up growing up in Yorkville on Manhattan's Upper East Side.[12] Rodgers was pleased that guest Ona Munson, who had gotten away before she could appear as *Peggy-Ann*, was signed to play *The Hot Heiress*'s title character at $1,000 a week. In addition, Hal Wallis, already considered among the best in the business, was assigned as producer under the First National banner.[13]

Larry was reveling in this temperate paradise—he could go *anywhere* and nobody would know but his driver! A swimmer—since summer camp, it was his only physical recreation—he enjoyed the consistently dry, warm weather and partook of the hotel swimming pool. He found cardplayers.

But Rodgers could think only about what he and Larry were missing—apart from Dorothy, that is—in New York. Howard Dietz was said to be compiling a score for a new show for Max Gordon, the follow-up to the successful *The Little Show*. For the time being this would be known as the *Second Little Show* (later it became *Three's a Crowd*). Toward that end, Dick and Larry arranged for the music and lyrics of "He Was Too Good to Me" to be messengered to Dietz at the Warwick Hotel, at Fifty-Fourth Street and Sixth Avenue.

The boys had already completed three songs for *The Hot Heiress* and were getting a crash course in how sound movies were made. "Nobody Loves a Riveter" was to be sung by Ben Lyon. When it came time to shoot the "Riveter" scene, Dick and Larry were intrigued by the necessity of recording Lyon and the thirty-piece orchestra separately, because the script called for Lyon to drive rivets into a building while he sang. In the theater, of course, there was no way to do that. "Like Ordinary People Do" was a sort of working-class "Blue Room" extolling the joys of domestic devotion:

> *Of seven nights a week*
> *I'll spend all seven at home.*
> *And that's the way we'll seek*
> *To make our heaven at home.*

The boys were particularly interested in this number because their old friend Inez Courtney sang along with the leads. When Ernö Rapée played the recording back for them, they were astounded by the fidelity. And they were impressed by the way Ben Lyon and Ona Munson seemed to click in their mutually admiring duet "You're the Cats," anticipating Cole Porter's unforgettable "You're the Top" (published in 1933).

With one or two more songs to write, Dick and Larry took back "He Was Too Good to Me" to revise for *The Hot Heiress*. Dick wrote to Dorothy: "I think we're going to use 'He Was Too Good to Me' as Larry doesn't want to give it to Max Gordon for his revue and they're crazy about it here. If we do, that only leaves one more number to write as there are only five in all. It's not so hard, is it?"[14] Larry had known Howard Dietz since both men were at Columbia, and he adored Dietz's songwriting partner, Arthur Schwartz. But he had become wary of revues consisting of numbers by several writers, even if some terrific songs had come out of these revues. In New York the third edition of *The Garrick Gaieties* had been staged in early June, not at the old Garrick—earlier in the year it had been transformed into a burlesque house and renamed the New Columbia—but at the Guild on Fifty-Second Street.[15] Like the first edition in 1925, this one was ignited by the desire of some Guild members to put on their own revue, and they did so with the blessing of the Guild board, with some members and skits from the *Grand Street Follies* folded into the mix. Rodgers and Hart were conspicuously absent.

So "He Was Too Good to Me" was touched up for *The Hot Heiress* as "He Looks So Good to Me"—a diminishment of the lyric that turned out to be moot when the number was dropped from the picture.

Although their work on *The Hot Heiress* seemed to be finished, Rodgers and Hart were obliged to stick around for a while and see what their second assignment would be. But the writing was on the wall. The glut of musicals was keeping audiences away. In 1929 it had been estimated that 50 percent of all American pictures were either musicals or semi-musicals, with more than 130 songwriters under contract at the nine leading studios; by the summer of 1930, following an industry-wide housecleaning, the number of musicals was down to 5 percent, with half the number of songwriters (including Dick and Larry) still under contract.[16] "The present demand for entertainment is centered on comedy," *Variety* reported. "Musicals of any kind are dead, say the neighborhood managers. Question often asked the exhibitor by the patron is: 'Is it a musical?' If it is, there's a dropoff."[17] Easel boards out front of movie houses would advertise "This Is Not a Musical!" Larry, though tirelessly supportive of fellow lyricists, began to make fun of the low level of the craft in the picture business. He told Dick about a lyric for another Warners picture that rhymed "desirable" with "admirable." Even the moon-June-spoon writers of early Tin Pan Alley days could do better than that.

Still, while they awaited a decision on their fate, the boys—and, by extension, Herb Fields—could work in Los Angeles as productively as they had worked on the East Coast or in Europe. They had been warned that the Southern California climate was lulling and soporific, antithetical to the creative impulse. "The weather is beautiful and all the days are exactly alike," was how Edmund Wilson described the place to his editor, Maxwell Perkins. "The calm Pacific spaces are excellent for work—I always feel cramped in New York. But if you stayed out here for very long, you would probably cease to write anything, because you would cease to think—it isn't necessary out here and the natives regard it as morbid."[18] But L.A. hadn't had that effect on Larry, who wrote in an explosion of scribbling when Dick pushed him, nor on Dick, who was as melodically fertile as ever. Moreover, the Warners' publicity department was planning a far-reaching ad campaign for *The Hot Heiress*, which would be released as a First National and Vitaphone Picture in early 1931. *What would you do with a lover who was an expert at slinging rivets but who bungled his forks at the Ritz?* went one ad. *Suppose you were a Park Avenue debutante. . . . See what charming Ona Munson does when Park and Third Avenues meet.*

Believing he and Dick might be on the West Coast for a while, Larry hired New York transplant Bert Allenberg as his business manager. Four years younger than Larry, Allenberg knew Hollywood as well as he knew Wall

Street. Larry, never much of an accountant, sent charge statements for even the smallest sums to Allenberg, who paid them without complaint and billed Larry later.

The movie version of Rodgers and Hart's *Present Arms* was in the can at RKO and retitled *Leathernecking*. After several weeks of editing, *Leathernecking* previewed in San Bernardino. Eddie Foy, Jr., starred opposite Irene Dunne, with the vaudeville comedian Ken Murray in Busby Berkeley's old role and the fashion plate Lilyan Tashman in the role of the principals' mutual friend. Since appearing in Rodgers and Hart's *She's My Baby*, Dunne had toured with the road company of *Show Boat* and attracted the attention of RKO production chief William LeBaron; this was her first film role. The *Leathernecking* preview confirmed everyone's worst fears about the state of the movie musical. There had been rumors that producer Louis Sarecky had thrown out the entire Rodgers & Hart score and hired Oscar Levant to write new songs. In the end two Rodgers & Hart songs were retained from *Present Arms*—"You Took Advantage of Me" and "A Kiss for Cinderella"—with the rest of the score written by Harry Akst and Benny Davis. At the preview Irene Dunne, realizing her numbers had been deleted, burst into tears. The audience laughed derisively at the chorus of marines and not at all at the scripted attempts at humor. When Sarecky told the *Los Angeles Times* that war pictures had entered the realm of burlesque—that, a dozen years removed from the Great War, armed-forces movies had become apolitical entertainment—it was hard to tell if he was being critical of those pictures, defensive about *Leathernecking*, or merely promoting it.[19]

When *Leathernecking* opened in September, it was quickly dismissed, as was *Follow Thru*, which left out all but one of the four songs Rodgers and Hart had written for it. At least *Follow Thru* had Technicolor going for it. A few weeks before those pictures opened, however, the anticipated edict had arrived from New York by telegram: NO MORE MUSICALS.[20] So the boys could fulfill their contracts, Bert Allenberg negotiated a deal whereby Fields, Rodgers, and Hart would write an original musical for the stage, to be produced by Warners on Broadway during the winter. A week later, Warners decided to halt their financing of Broadway musicals, but the deal stayed in the lap of the Warners-backed producers Arthur Swanstrom and Bobby Connolly. So Herb Fields was still obligated to start a new script.[21]

With Cochran beckoning from London, Larry went east, followed in short order by Dick and Herb Fields.

⚓ ⚓ ⚓

Larry dodged one of the worst heat waves on record in the eastern United States by stopping in New York just long enough to check in with his family, repack, and catch the *Europa* to Southampton, to resume work on the C. B. Cochran show *Ever Green*.[22] Cochran had delayed mounting the show for several months while his two stars, Jessie Matthews and Sonnie Hale—they had fallen in love while appearing in *One Dam Thing After Another*—unhitched themselves from their respective spouses, Harry Lytton, M.P., and the exquisite musical comedy actress Evelyn Laye. Although Cochran knew the value of publicity, he had staked his career on being a Gentleman Producer and thought it best to allow the scandal to burn itself out.

Before Larry left New York, he sat for a quick interview with the *Telegram*. Hollywood thus far had taught him that a musical play doesn't need the tagline of a lyric for the prima donna to break forth into song. "The songs are going to be a definite, essential part of the progress of the piece," Larry said, still determined to write lyrics that always advanced, or at least commented on, the musical's plot.[23] With *Show Boat*, Oscar Hammerstein II had done so, if imperfectly; Larry wanted to do it more perfectly, and with more wit.

Herb Fields remained in New York where, the newspapers reported, he had a "new production pending," although the production wasn't named.[24] Once again leaving Dorothy in New York, Rodgers sailed with his parents on the *Olympia*. Rodgers did not like to compose in front of anyone except Larry, but he found time during the crossing to sit down for an hour at one of the ship's pianos and work out a melody that would become, after Larry's lyric for it, "If I Give In to You." The lyric shows Larry tinkering with a theme—how even the most misshapen appearance is immaterial if one can love and be loved—that would reach its deepest articulation in "My Funny Valentine":

> *Though your profile's all awry*
> *And you are no Apollo,*
> *And you wear a beastly tie,*
> *You're the one I'll follow.*

Meanwhile, Larry had taken a suite at the Savoy—parlor, bedroom, and bath at sixty-five shillings a day.[25] Waiting for Dick (sans Dorothy) and his parents to arrive, he persuaded C. B. Cochran that *Ever Green* could benefit mightily by using a revolving stage. Several theaters in Berlin had employed revolving stages; for productions of Wagner's operas in Bayreuth they were now almost routine. Although the Yiddish Art Theatre in New York had one, a revolving stage was still a rare thing in Manhattan's theater district, where few playhouses had strong enough floors or large enough stages to accommodate one. It's possible that Larry had seen at least one revolving stage on a visit to Germany. It's more probable that while he was in Hollywood he had seen what hydraulics could accomplish—not only on film sets but with a moving platform traversing and then withdrawing from the sorry-looking Los Angeles River, which ran through the First National property. In any case, Cochran immediately ordered a revolving stage from the manufacturer that had outfitted so many Berlin theaters, and arranged for delivery to the King's Theatre in Glasgow by October 1. Cochran's decision to hold *Ever Green* tryouts in Glasgow, far from Grub Street's magnifying glass, was meant to be protective of his scandal-scarred stars, Matthews and Hale. Cockie knew that theater people and journalists were gunning for all of them, especially with such an expensive show at stake.

On August 28, when the Rodgers family docked in Southampton, Larry was there to meet them, delighting even Mamie Rodgers, who had so heartily disapproved of his drinking. Dick was also happy to see him but quietly arranged for his own suite at the Savoy. "Thank God I didn't agree to live with Larry!" he wrote to Dorothy. "He's worse than ever and if he doesn't go completely mad soon, I will! However, I must admit he works hard and hasn't held me up a bit." [26] Cockie and his wife owned a Broadwood grand piano whose action Rodgers enjoyed; he'd finish a melody there and take it to Larry, who went to work on it. [27] They had already decided to reuse "Dancing on the Ceiling," which had been cut from *Simple Simon*, because it sounded right for Jessie Matthews.

Cochran hired two gifted black American choreographers, Buddy Bradley and Billy Pierce, and they staged "Dancing on the Ceiling" quickly and imaginatively. In an American show, even in New York, an integrated staff might have caused some tension, but there seemed to be little of that in London. The presence of Bradley and Pierce inspired the boys to write "Harlemania," a testament to uptown dancing ("With the best of intentions, / Folks who used to be nice / Shake what nobody mentions"). Bradley and Pierce staged the number for maximum scorching. Rodgers and Hart wrote "Nobody Looks at the Man" for Sonnie Hale:

Nobody looks at the man.
Nobody knows that he's there.
You only hear, "What a beautiful girl!"
And that's why I dance with a chair!

Written for Hale and Matthews, the lyric of "Dear! Dear!" returns to Larry's familiar theme of sizzling heat created by two formerly cool people who have found each other. Larry also has the singers refer obliquely to their real-life tribulations:

All of our transgressing
Seems such a blessing;
Am I bad?

They had certainly been made to feel that way. Referring to Matthews's love letters to Hale, the judge in Hale's divorce case pronounced Matthews "to be a person of odious mind."[28]

Sometimes Larry went off to investigate the shows in town. He was particularly proud that the Jewish-American chanteuse Sophie Tucker, appearing in *Follow a Star*, and the Pulitzer Prize–winning play *Street Scene*, by the Jewish-American Elmer Rice, were scoring so well in London.[29]

Larry and Dick met the Dreyfus brothers, Max and Louis, for lunch. Since Warner Bros. had bought T. B. Harms the previous year, the brothers had aligned themselves with Chappell, the British music publisher that had had a New York presence since 1906. Louis acquired the company in 1929; Max became chairman of the associated but independent Chappell & Co. in New York. Unlike the Shuberts, the Dreyfuses were close if not inseparable. Apart from Max's early regrettable rejection of "Manhattan," the Dreyfus brothers had done right by them. There was no question that Chappell would now become their publisher.

The boys also went out with the Hulberts (Jack Hulbert and Cicely Courtneidge), for whom they had written their first English show (*Lido Lady*), and the Hulberts' good friends Irene Russell and Ivor McLaren. They made a curious sextet. Larry was still the little boy looking through the keyhole, his eye taking in everything. "Larry tells me that there's an *entente cordiale*," Rodgers wrote, "and that Jack and Irene are one pair and Cicely and

McLaren the other. They always appear in public that way. It's odd, to say the least, and makes me a bit fidgety." [30]

Rehearsals for *Ever Green* were being held at a theater in Poland Street, with the mass migration to Glasgow only a week away. Cochran told Rodgers and Hart he was very pleased with their work; they could relax a bit. He had arranged for *Ever Green*'s credits to read "Book by Benn Levy, Based on Idea by Rodgers & Hart," so that they wouldn't be relegated to the subsidiary role of songwriters (though, of course, that's what they were). That was good enough for Larry. At a party thrown by Noël Coward and Gladys Calthorp, the boys played their latest songs. A few days later, when Coward opened opposite Gertrude Lawrence in his play *Private Lives*, at the beginning of the second act he sat down at the piano onstage and played the opening bars of "Dancing on the Ceiling." [31] Dick and Larry took it as the tribute it was meant to be.

At the Savoy one evening, Larry threw a party where the guests included Dick; Dick's brother, Mort; Joyce Barbour; and Beatrice Lillie. They were soon joined by Buddy Bradley and Billy Pierce, who brought along two young black British women. Neither woman had ever been to America; one of them had a Jewish mother. "She spoke Yiddish to Larry and used several words which even I understood," Rodgers reported. "It was terribly interesting and all very polite. They had one drink each and left early, saying their thanks and goodbyes in the best Mayfair manner." [32]

Rehearsals outgrew the Poland Street theater and moved to the oversize Alexandra Palace in the suburbs, the two-hundred-plus members of the company and staff conveyed there each morning by charabancs. [33] With the huge show on its feet the next step was the move to Glasgow's King's Theatre. "The main trouble will come in Glasgow when we get on the revolving stage," Rodgers wrote. [34] No; the main trouble was that there was no revolving stage, and no confirmation about when it might be delivered. The delay made everyone tense and a little bit paranoid. When Larry arrived in Glasgow, he couldn't believe that his hotel was directly opposite the railway station, so he insisted that his cabbie drive him to the proper location, realizing only in midride that it was his mistake. Whether he was saving face or just wanting to give the press a readable item, he turned the anecdote into a tourist's shakedown. LARRY HART WAS "TAKEN FOR A RIDE," blared *Zit's Theatrical Newspaper*; "Glasgow Cabbie Knew All the American Tricks, Author Found":

Lawrence [*sic*] (Larry) Hart returned last week from Glasgow, where his latest musical collaboration *Evergreen* [*sic*] got under way to a record advance sale of $50,000 with a tale of having been "taken for a ride."

It was a Scottish taxi-driver who took Hart for the ride, proving that the species abroad is no different than here. In driving Hart to his hotel, which he afterwards learned was directly opposite the railway station, the cabbie circled around for a mile or so before putting Hart down at the hostelry.[35]

Cochran and his company had to scramble. The revolving stage finally arrived and was installed, accommodating, as Larry knew it would, the show-within-a-show structure. Rehearsals were configured for the King's Theatre. The opening tryout, on October 13, 1930, went surprisingly well.

Ever Green's author was Benn Levy, but there's too much of Larry Hart in it to ignore. Its story, sprinkled with Levy's pixie dust and Larry's sawdust, is more integrated with its songs than any Rodgers & Hart show up to that point.

Ever Green's heroine, the twenty-three-year-old entertainer Harriet Green (Jessie Matthews), has conspired with her mother, Mrs. Platter, to pretend to be her own grandmother, a beautiful sixty-year-old. The masquerade has enabled Harriet to lend her name to a highly profitable line of cosmetics. Her manager, Mary, is in on the masquerade; otherwise no one else knows Harriet's secret.

The opening scene is of a beauty contest—Harriet was supposed to judge it, but she will arrive in time only to present the award—at Albert Hall. "Be on your toes!" calls the Head Usher—it's a phrase Larry Hart will use again, to greater resonance—to the Beauties in competition. In that opening number, Larry rhymes "dressing rooms" with "distressing rooms" and "[Cochran's] Young ladies" with "go to Hades!"

Harriet attracts young entertainer Tommy (Sonnie Hale), who is unaware that she's the famously well-preserved "sixty-year-old." Following a breakup and reconciliation, the lovers sing "No Place but Home," suggesting that wherever they are together, whether Cairo or Rome, they'll be at home. At the Casino de la Folie, in Paris, Harriet is grandly introduced to the audience as La Belle de Soixante Ans. Stupefied, Tommy bolts from the theater. End of act 1.

In act 2, Harriet has finally located Tommy at the Cabaret Tenorio and intends to confront him the next night. After she and her mother, Mrs. Platter, retire to their hotel bedrooms, Harriet turns out all but one reading lamp and begins "Dancing on the Ceiling," the room turning upside down but also enlarging somehow, and Tommy (in fantasy) joins her, until the song is over and the room diminishes to its actual size. This woman, fraught with her own sense of fraud, is haunted by the love she feels for the man she will see again at last tomorrow.

Folie director St. Didier comes to Harriet to ask if he might marry her "daughter," Mrs. Platter, though he finds her "ugly." This is a man surfeited with beauty—Ziegfeld buffeted by his Girls; Cochran smothered by his Young Ladies. St. Didier explains in "Je M'en Fiche de Sex Appeal":

> *The first little sweetheart is charming,*
> *The second, ah well, she is belle!*
> *The third is a little alarming*
> *As for the fourth—the fourth is hell!*
> *Too many curves are bad for the nerves,*
> *Too much chicken just ruins the meal.*
> *I've drained the whole cup*
> *J'en ai marre—I'm fed up!*
> *Je m'en fiche de sex appeal!*

A stranger fails to blackmail Harriet but does expose her as a fraud to Tommy. At the Cabaret Tenorio the tables have turned. Harriet sits in the audience while Tommy performs the "Talking Song," pointing out notables among the crowd:

> *Table C—a welcome sight,*
> *The only Yankee here tonight!*
> *The Yankees are so broke today,*
> *They all stay in the U.S.A.*

Tommy reserves his vitriol for the unsuspecting Harriet:

> *I ask you now to gaze upon*
> *La Belle Charmante de soixante ans.*
> *All hail—she wears fair Helen's wreath*
> *Yet her heart is falser than her teeth.*

His attack shocks the audience. Any chance of romance appears to have been crushed.

But later, Tommy comes around to Harriet's dressing room and, despite their supposed age difference, professes his love for her. "I'm not a freak," says Harriet, "I'm worse! I'm a fraud, a fake. I'm not sixty, really—I'm twenty-three!" He doesn't believe her. So when she's next onstage she removes her clothes to show Tommy, and everyone else, that hers is hardly the body of a sixty-year-old. There goes the lucrative cosmetics line; there goes her career. She goes to Tommy, who reprises "No Place but Home."

While *Ever Green* was still trying out in Glasgow, there was little doubt it would be a hit when it opened in London at the new Adelphi Theatre, and even less doubt that Jessie Matthews—lanky and wasp-waisted—would become a bigger star than ever. Cockie had deftly managed the scandal involving his costars and slipped most of the show past the scissors of the Lord Chamberlain, who snipped no more than a few minutes from the original script. So Rodgers and Hart went home to New York.

The film version of *Heads Up!*, with only two of their songs remaining, had just been released in the States and caused barely a ripple. *The New York Times* said that Victor Moore stole the picture (a redundancy: Moore stole *every* picture). The *Chicago Daily Tribune* referred to it as "an amiable nonentity." The *Hartford Courant* praised Moore and Helen Kane and her boop-boopa-doops, but made no reference to the boys. In fact only Philip K. Scheuer of the *Los Angeles Times* mentioned the songs: "These, the output of that talented pair, Richard Rodgers and Lorenz Hart, abound in superior lyrics (what you can hear of them) and at least one exceptional melody, called 'A Ship Without a Sail.'"[36]

A few weeks later, when the *Manchester Guardian* raved about *Ever Green*, Rodgers was mentioned ("engaging tunes") but not Hart.[37] If Larry cared, he didn't show it.

On November 24, 1930, in New York, Dick and Larry, in association with Max Dreyfus, established their publishing firm Rodart (an acronym of their surnames) Music. It was the first major business move that would enable Dick to gain control of so much of his own work—control that Larry had little or no interest in.

In Glasgow, Dick and Larry had read the outline of Herb Fields's "pending production," initially meant to play at Warners' Hollywood Theatre in

New York, its performance rights still controlled by the production firm of Swanstrom and Connolly. The boys had not been especially impressed.[38] By the time they were home in New York, however, Fields had somehow extracted from his outline a musical play they were willing to work on. It would be Fields's seventh collaboration with Rodgers and Hart.

The plot was simple. Just before the advent of the talkies, Geraldine March and Michael Perry have hitchhiked from St. Paul to Hollywood to get into the movies, intending to marry as soon as they can afford to. Geraldine, having won the admiration and ardor of a studio chief, becomes a silent screen star and, believing the studio hype about her, is ready to cast off Michael. But when the talkies arrive, Michael becomes the star—he has a *voice*—while Geraldine is considered untouchable because of a lisp. Michael forgives her earlier treatment of him and arranges for her to appear in his next movie.

The theme of the talkies destroying and making movie careers was already in the air. The theme would be used for *Singin' in the Rain*, one of the best movie musicals ever made, and for *The Artist*, which won the Oscar for Best Picture of 2011.

After several more changes, Fields's script came to be called *America's Sweetheart*, the affectionate (if sometimes mocking) nickname for Mary Pickford during her silent screen stardom. But the firm of Swanstrom and Connolly was disbanding, turning *America's Sweetheart* into an orphan.

Not for long, however. After enjoying an impressive string of Broadway hits, Laurence Schwab and Frank Mandel had signed a contract with Paramount to produce movies. The honeymoon lasted until Schwab realized that, quite unlike their positions in the theater, he and Mandel were not the bosses; in fact, once audience apathy toward movie musicals had taken hold, they weren't even producers anymore. They went home to New York. Schwab and Mandel's frequent choreographer Bobby Connolly offered them *America's Sweetheart* for a decent price. Schwab and Mandel agreed to produce it.[39]

While Dick and Larry wrote songs, mostly at Dick's apartment in the Lombardy, the producers began to pull the show together. Monty Woolley, who had taught drama at Yale, was signed to direct. Rodgers and Hart had been impressed by a young actress named Harriette Lake in the Boston tryout of the Vincent Youmans show *Smiles*.[40] (In Hollywood, she would change her name to Ann Sothern.) *Smiles* opened at the Ziegfeld Theatre in New York with the Astaires and Marilyn Miller—but without Lake, so she was available.

In the middle of these preparations for *America's Sweetheart*, Dorothy Rodgers gave birth to the Rodgerses' first child, Mary, at Lenox Hill Hospital on January 11, 1931, with her brother-in-law Mort attending the delivery. The Lombardy apartment began to look like a storybook nursery. Dorothy could barely tolerate Larry's near-continuous cigar-smoking in the best of times, but now, with the baby in the house, it was getting to her. And Larry was reverting to his old form, often arriving from Central Park West much later than he was expected, stopping to pick up cigars for himself and—a lifelong habit—presents for Mary Rodgers.

As usual, Larry's favorite lyric was the one he had just finished. His friend Larry Adler, the harmonica virtuoso, had only recently closed in *Smiles* when he ran into Hart, who was now particularly enthusiastic about his latest lyric, "A Cat Can Look at a Queen." The song was to be sung in *America's Sweetheart* by Jeanne Aubert as the French movie star Denise, who's reminding hero Michael that, although he loves Geraldine, there's no harm in looking at another woman. But the song was dropped during the Pittsburgh tryout in mid-January. Music and lyrics to "A Cat Can Look at a Queen" have been lost, but Larry Adler remembered this fragment:

> *Though it may be dark at night,*
> *A cat can see*
> *More than you,*
> *More than me!*[41]

It doesn't sound like much. But who would want a collaborator who was chronically unenthusiastic about his latest creation?

Jack Whiting was on board again to play opposite Harriette Lake, and the comedian Gus Shy would be assigned the second banana role of Larry Pittman, with the reliable Inez Courtney as his partner. Instead of writing the head of Premier Pictures as Jewish, which would have been hackneyed but accurate, Fields gave him the Irish name Dolan but imbued him with the coarseness of the first- or second-generation Jewish immigrant—the furrier or shoe salesman turned studio chief. Dolan's Premier Pictures is preparing to turn *Camille* into *Lovey Dovey* and *Othello* into *Hot Lips*. Larry Pittman recommends Jolson for the role of the Moor; Dolan promptly gives him a raise.[42]

At the Shubert Theatre in Pittsburgh, "I've Got Five Dollars," sung by Geraldine and Michael to each other after they arrive broke in Hollywood— she has $4.75 in her pocket, he has an even $5.00—was already being hailed as the one everyone would listen to. (In "I've Got Five Dollars," Larry was already trying out the phrase "Everything I've got belongs to you.") Jeanne Aubert got plenty of attention with "A Cat Can Look at a Queen" before it was dropped. And Gus Shy and Inez Courtney practically brought down the house with "You Ain't Got No Savoir Faire":

HE
A lady must have savoir faire.
That means she knows her eggs,
Tells risqué stories with an air,
And she has limbs not legs.

SHE
Lord Chesterfield would be distressed
To hear you pull that bunk.
You're not Beau Brummel or Beau Geste,
Tom, you're plain Beau Hunk.

Along the way there are references to Agua Caliente (at the time the closest racetrack and legal casino near Hollywood, though it was across the Mexican border more than a hundred miles away); movie fan magazines; the Beverly-Wilshire Hotel; coast-to-coast radio hookups; Hollywood bungalows; raising cash from party guests to pay for bootleg whiskey; and the preparation of a golf picture—an obvious nod to the producers' *Follow Thru*. Writing to his exhausted wife, Rodgers thought things were going rather well and that what wasn't going well was at least fixable.

After quick tryouts in Washington and Newark, *America's Sweetheart* opened on February 10, 1931, at the Broadhurst, the show's title blazing in a thousand-plus lightbulbs. Larry knew he'd done some of his best, if most salacious, writing for the show, and was eager to see it in New York. But he hated first nights and told *Cinema* magazine so:

A Broadway first night is agony. Everything goes wrong. The actors are so nervous their greasepaint melts. . . . The juvenile goes up in his lines and the leading lady has hysterics and weeps mascara on her costume.[43]

The New York notices were at least respectful. Writing in the *New York American*, the dependable Gilbert Gabriel was taken with "I've Got Five

Dollars" and "the even prettier" "We'll Be the Same," with special praise for "The Innocent Chorus Girls of Yesterday":

> *We all got stinkin' last night!*
> *It's the nuts the way we're leaping!*
> *It sure was an orgy all right,*
> *Men didn't know who they were keeping.*

Other critics echoed Gabriel's belief that some of the songs (which benefited from the orchestrations of Robert Russell Bennett and the conducting of the young Alfred Newman) were among the "pleasantest" Rodgers and Hart had composed.

But Dorothy Parker, during a long interval substituting for her friend Robert Benchley as theater critic of *The New Yorker*, was offended. Parker took off on Jeanne Aubert, whose husband had recently pled in the French courts that he be permitted to restrain her from appearing on the stage. "Professional or not, the man is a dramatic critic," Parker wrote. She labeled Fields and Hart "extraordinarily over-rated young men" and suggested that Hart's rhymes were "less internal than colonic; they also have a peculiar, even for Broadway, nastiness of flavor. What, by the way, has ever become of that little thing called taste?"[44] (Parker's polished talons grew sharper each week. One month after her review of *America's Sweetheart*, Parker panned Channing Pollock's *The House Beautiful* as "the play lousy.")[45] In *The World* Charles Darnton wrote, "Smut leaves its mark on any book by Herbert Fields and the lyrics of Lorenz Hart."[46] He was surely referring to at least one of Jeanne Aubert's songs, "A Lady Must Live," the rhymes of which were not printable in Darnton's newspaper, including "With my John and my Max / I can reach a climax" and "What's the siren song for? / What's my chaise longue for?"

Some attacks were less direct. Perhaps Owen Davis, completing his memoirs in early 1931, was aiming at Fields and Hart when he wrote, "I have the masculine man's contempt for dirty plays, arising, I suppose, from the fact that masculine men do not write them. Dirty plays are always written either by women or by effeminate men, and always have been."[47]

As the Depression set in, so too did an inescapable personal depression for Dick and Larry. Dick's family needed more space than his terraced apartment at the Lombardy afforded. As it happened, Dorothy's parents needed *less* space. Benjamin Feiner, an attorney so walloped by the stock market crash that he eventually needed close medical supervision, and his wife, May, gave up their apartment at the Marguery and took over their son-in-law's lease at the Lombardy. At the same time, the younger Rodgers family moved into the apartment-house part of the Carlyle Hotel, at 50 East Seventy-Seventh. Rodgers, inexorably drawn to that exotic intersection of theater and Society, was becoming more Upper East Side by the minute. Larry, on the other hand, had no interest in Society, and had even begun to keep his distance from the Jules Glaenzer soirees where black tie became de rigueur. He was still in the penthouse at 415 Central Park West. Teddy, often billed in those days as Theodore Hart, was frequently away upstate or in New England playing vaudeville venues. "Big Mary" Campbell ran the household and was becoming popular with the friends Larry gathered at night, who were both intimidated by and appreciative of her straight-shooting. And then there was Frieda, whom her elder son referred to as a "sweet, menacing old lady."[48] (She was sixty-three at the time.) Frieda regarded Larry as a genius—it is the advantage and curse of the Jewish son to have such a mother—and fervently wished he would meet a nice Jewish girl and get married.

"First I need to meet the girl, Mama," Larry would say. "Then I'll need a stepladder."

It was all rather unlikely. (Later there would be evidence that Frieda knew it was unlikely.) Larry kept his sexual preferences quiet. Cole Porter, his closest rival when it came to lyric ribaldry, was married, but it was hardly a secret that Porter was homosexual. Larry's sexuality was more complicated—or, rather, more cloaked.

Where did Larry go at night when he hadn't invited half the theater district back up to his place? In his masterful biography *Lorenz Hart: A Poet on Broadway*, Frederick Nolan speculated that Larry might have spent some nights where nobody knew who he was—in the kind of elegant brothel that catered to an affluent clientele, as Polly Adler did, and one that provided male rather than female company.[49] It's possible that in 1931 Larry had a second apartment someplace. Max Hart had liquidated his real estate holdings at least two years before he died; it's unlikely there was a Hart-owned building left in the city. But Larry could have rented a place on his own.

He did visit the city's Turkish baths. Many men, heterosexual or homosexual, went to the baths at one time or another. In *Can't Help Singin',* his study of the American musical and its impact on the nation's culture, Gerald Mast suggested that Larry was a regular at the Luxor Baths, a popular bathhouse of the era, which welcomed patrons of either sexual orientation. The baths offered the possibility of a quick sexual encounter and provided a pore-opening bromide for too much booze. "The best thing for a hangover (next to not drinking)," wrote Ned Rorem about his early days in New York in the 1930s, "is that Manhattan array of rhapsodic turkish baths which answer so well to your one-track carnal awareness the afternoon after. Days, days can be spent there in the sensual naked steam of anonymity disintoxicating the body (always the body), while outside it ceaselessly rains, glumly rains to your total disinterest."[50]

Despite his discretion, Larry never pretended an aversion to homosexual performers if they were talented. He was particularly intrigued by the female impersonator Jean Malin, who had taken New York by storm in the past two or three years. Born in Brooklyn in 1908 to Polish and Lithuanian parents, Victor Eugene James Malin had gone from chorus boy to headliner, sometimes using the name Imogene Wilson, appearing first at the Rubaiyat Club, in Greenwich Village, and then later at the uptown Club Abbey. Malin, large and physically imposing, married a woman, Christine Williams, in January 1931. The columnist Mark Hellinger liked to refer to Malin as "a professional pansy." After a while Malin stopped wearing women's clothes, yet his impersonation of a woman was complete and utterly sincere. His authority as a club's master of ceremonies was no less impressive than Texas Guinan's.[51]

Malin represented the most theatrical—consequently the most acceptable—corner of the homosexual subculture in New York. Other corners of that culture had been hammered deeper underground. There were the various outposts of Childs, which Larry had referred to in his lyric for "Manhattan," that were hospitable to a homosexual clientele. "The Childs under the Paramount," wrote Renee Carroll, the famous hatcheck girl of Sardi's, "used to be the hangout for the theatrical fraternity and the more squeamish of the uncertain sex. The latter had headquarters for a time in the Fifth Avenue Childs, near 45th Street, until police began warning them."[52] Larry—much more Cafeteria Society than Café Society—might have been a regular patron if only it hadn't marked his sexuality one way or the other. Throughout Prohibition and later, Larry was a Lindy's man, preferring the company of other writers and showbiz folk, including the horse-playing, cigar-smoking characters that Damon Runyon was immortalizing with each new story he published.

During Prohibition the State Liquor Authority enforced its jurisdiction over what it regarded as lewd or intemperate behavior. The Authority could shut down a saloon or a restaurant on the mere suspicion of employing a homosexual. At the same time, Prohibition provided cover for women and men, including Larry, who wanted to keep their sexuality under wraps. "We lived not in closets but in an underground world that had many parallels with the life of a drinker during the fourteen years of Prohibition," Donald Vining has written in *How Can You Come Out?* "Even the speakeasy passwords even had a parallel in the gay world. . . . Just as the drinkers of the prohibition era enjoyed mocking and defying the forces of the law, so we relished the sub rosa aspects of gay life, feeling we were outwitting our opponents. Gay bars and baths could be raided, yes, as speakeasies and stills could be raided and even demolished by revenue officers. When they were, the scene of action simply moved elsewhere." Vining has also referred to the isolation that homosexual men feel after adolescence, when they are sure of their sexuality, and then the subsequent delight at finding "so many gorgeous men eager to climb into our beds."[53]

It's debatable whether Larry Hart, a man referred to by others as "ugly" and a "troll," found many gorgeous men eager to go to bed with him. That might account, in part, for the early and chronic drinking that, as Gerald Mast wrote, eased the transport between glittering Broadway and the midnight world of hustlers on the waterfront and under the El.[54] Even in the theater, to be openly homosexual was to invite scorn. It was only a few months later that same year when the theater column in *Zit's*, a publication that might have been expected to be relatively enlightened, reported, "Bryant Park may change its name to Pansy Park, for the darlings are meeting there in droves every midnight."[55] In Larry's case, he was protecting not only himself but his family, especially his mother.

Frieda didn't join Larry on his next trip west, in late March 1931. She and Teddy would eventually travel out to California when Larry was settled there. For now, though, the idea was for Larry and Herb Fields to go west, a few days ahead of new father Dick, to report to Warner Bros., where all three were assigned to write music, lyrics, and screenplay for *Love of Michael*. The picture would reunite the boys with Ben Lyon and Ona Munson, who would reverse class roles: she would be the working girl, he the college boy.[56] It was a curiously considered reunion, however, since *The Hot Heiress* had just been released to thoroughly unenthusiastic reviews. As Larry and Herb approached Los Angeles, they read—as if they needed confirmation of their jaundiced view of picture-making—that Warner Bros. had just released a film version of *Fifty Million Frenchmen*, with comedians Olsen and Johnson and in glorious color, but again without its Cole Porter score. The ghost of Herb Fields's book could still be discerned in the screenplay, but not a single Porter song remained—not even the instant classic "You Do Something to Me." Larry might have taken comfort, however modest, that same week from *The New Yorker*'s review of the Columbia release *Ten Cents a Dance*, which said the picture "projects the theme and the milieu of the poignant lyric of that title."[57] In less than two years Larry's four-word title had become a catchphrase.

As they approached Los Angeles, Larry and Herb were tracking a couple of other newspaper stories. The first was about New York mayor Jimmy Walker, who had just become the subject of an investigation by the State Legislature on charges of graft and corruption.[58] Walker had survived several challenges to his power, including the opposing candidacy in 1929 of Fiorello La Guardia, with rare political flair. But astute City Hall observers could read the handwriting on the wall.

The second story was of no political consequence but unnerving in the way it kept changing. On February 14, in Havana, Lewis Warner, the twenty-two-year-old son of Warner Bros. president Harry M. Warner, had come down with septic poisoning after a tooth extraction. On March 4, accompanied by his parents and an aunt and uncle, Lewis was flown to Miami, then carried by train to New York and admitted to Doctors Hospital, at East End Avenue and Eighty-Seventh Street, which was said to provide the best medical care in the city. On April 4, the family announced some improvement. But Lewis died the next day. The news of his death was pushed to the back of the papers to make room for rolling tributes to Knute Rockne, the Notre Dame coach killed in an airplane crash in Bazaar, Kansas, on March 31. Larry and Herb's arrival coincided with the studio's decision to close all Warner Bros. theaters for a day.[59]

If there really had been room for another innocuous musical picture to be made at Warner Bros., the death of young Lewis walled it off. *Love of Michael* was pulled from development. By the time Dick arrived in Los Angeles, all they could do was accept the end of the Warners contract, turn right around, and go home.

America's Sweetheart was flickering at the Broadhurst, but not with enough illumination to make a difference in the careers of Rodgers and Hart. Playing over at the Paramount was Chaplin's *City Lights*, a masterwork in which his characters, more than three years after the advent of talkies, remained silent but hardly speechless. Fox released another version of *A Connecticut Yankee in King Arthur's Court*, starring Will Rogers and Maureen O'Sullivan, the story employing contemporary references like the latest Dunhill lighter and a Baby Austin car. While Dick and Larry were kicking around several ideas, Joe Leblang, the theater owner and discount ticket broker—often credited with keeping Broadway shows running by offering cut-rate ticket prices (a practice that thrives to this day)—died in New York. Leblang's memorial service drew three thousand mourners to Temple Emanu-El. Then David Belasco, the last of the great playwright-showmen from the nineteenth century, died after a theatrical career of nearly sixty years. Rodgers and Hart had written innumerable songs that described and then subverted Victorian-era mores, and now that era was fading fast.

That anti-Victorian Billy Rose phoned the boys to ask them to write something for his wife, Fanny Brice. This was the period when Rose was still referred to as "Mr. Brice" because his wife's fame was so much greater. But Rose was also a conscientious, hardworking producer, and Fanny was the star of his latest revue, which had originally opened the previous fall in New York as *Sweet and Low*, with a script by David Freedman. In mid-May 1931 Rose brought a greatly revised version of the show back into town under the title *Crazy Quilt*. The uncontested hit song of the show was Brice's number "I Found a Million Dollar Baby (in a Five and Ten Cent Store)," by Rose, Mort Dixon, and Harry Warren. Nearly a month into the show's run, Brice remained dissatisfied with her material, so Rose bought three new numbers for her, including a Rodgers & Hart ballad, tailor-made for Brice, titled "Rest Room Rosie." Brice was appeased, but *Crazy Quilt* closed before midsummer.[60]

The Third Little Show opened on June 1, 1931, and was built around Beatrice Lillie. On June 3 Max Gordon opened *The Band Wagon*, with the Astaires, the lovely Tillie Losch, and Frank Morgan (who would impersonate the Wizard of Oz near the end of the decade). *The Band Wagon* could also boast the comic services of Helen Broderick—as deft a satirist as Lillie, though less physical—and the use of a revolving stage. As *Ever Green* was completing its London run, *The Band Wagon*'s revolving stage was seen as precluding a Broadway run.[61] But *Ever Green* was probably not only too cumbersome but too Continental for a strong New York showing. Larry knew that. Besides, Benn Levy's *Mrs. Moonlight* was still playing at the Charles Hopkins Theatre; hauling *Ever Green* and its huge cast and stage apparatus overseas would have seemed redundant.

Billy Rose was trying to get Rodgers and Hart to complete another few songs for a musical version of *The Play's the Thing*, with P. G. Wodehouse said to be interested in doing the adaptation. To sweeten the pot, Rose claimed to be negotiating with Ernst Lubitsch to direct.[62] The boys would believe it when they saw it.

What to do, then? Walter Winchell liked to refer to Broadway as "The Long Lane of Short Careers." If it applied to Dick and Larry, well, they had had a commendable six-year run. Out west, the status of movie musicals remained unclear. Some Hollywood observers argued that the recent cycle of gangster films had run its course, and that musicals were due for a comeback, albeit on a smaller, more intimate scale.

In the last week of October, Larry made his first solo radio appearance as a guest on a weekly show hosted by S. Jay Kaufman, who had originated the *Makers of Melody* short for Paramount two years earlier. Larry proved to be a hit—a raconteur who, even though he disliked radio, didn't talk down to the radio audience.[63]

Then Mel Shauer called Larry from his office at Paramount Pictures, in Los Angeles. He wasn't calling about the guest appearance on radio, nor to reminisce about their days at Brant Lake Camp.

CHAPTER 12

I'm Not Afraid of My Own Creation

M EL SHAUER was calling about a performer he had discussed with Larry nearly a year earlier. Maurice Chevalier was a Paramount star. Shauer had recommended the boys to Chevalier, but a combination involving the glut of movie musicals and the shaky financial condition of Paramount Publix—as of April 15, 1930, the new corporate title of Paramount Famous Lasky—had put the idea on hold. By late autumn 1931, Rodgers and Hart went to the West Coast—it was their third trip in eighteen months—to see about writing for Chevalier.

Was there ever another entertainer like Maurice Chevalier? Born September 12, 1888, in Menilmontant, France, he was the son of a braid-trimmer and a housepainter. As a boy, Chevalier had held several jobs. He got his break at age thirteen, when he went on at the Casino des Tourelles for twelve francs a week. At the time he still worked occasionally as a mechanic. But after World War I, having played the Folies Bergère and already begun to use his trademark straw hat, Chevalier became, along with the chanteuse Mistinguett (who introduced *"Mon Homme,"* among many other classic songs), the dominant entertainer of the French music hall.[1]

Mel Shauer had met Chevalier in Paris, almost surely through Jesse Lasky, and was instrumental in the arrangements, from 1927 to 1928, for Chevalier to make movies for Paramount. The Paramount brass didn't want Chevalier at first. In the late 1920s he had made a screen test in London with the music hall star Elsie Janis, but it had not gone well. In addition, Irving Thalberg and

Louis B. Mayer had tried and failed to sign Chevalier to MGM, negotiations breaking down when Chevalier asked for the studio to pay his assistants and household help. By 1928 Chevalier was forty—a year younger than Al Jolson but, by screen star standards, ancient to be making his debut. Adolph Zukor cabled Lasky to remind him of the public's rejection of sound performers with the slightest hint of an accent. "Coming from Zukor, whose Hungarian accent was the delight of Hollywood," wrote Chevalier's biographer Edward Behr, "the comment must have amused Lasky." [2] When Chevalier, signed by Lasky over Zukor's objections, and his wife, Yvonne Vallée, arrived in New York, Mel Shauer met them there. The Chevaliers appeared in front of various New York landmarks for the four-day shoot of *Bonjour New York!*, a Paramount News documentary, and made a much-publicized visit to Sardi's.

Chevalier's first talkie feature, *Innocents of Paris* (1929), marked him as a star of film as well as of the music hall. Paramount staff writers Richard Whiting (music) and Leo Robin (lyrics) wrote "Louise" for him ("Ev'ry leetle breeze seems to wheesper Louise"), along with a barrowful of other songs. *Love Parade* (1929), directed by Ernst Lubitsch, paired him with Jeanette MacDonald. The all-star *Paramount on Parade* (1930) had Chevalier as a chimney sweep singing "Sweeping the Clouds Away."

As sound became the industry standard, many foreign stars—Pola Negri and Camilla Horn, to name only two—left Hollywood because their English was barely intelligible; others, like Greta Garbo and Vilma Bánky, remained to play foreign women (Garbo's voice was pleasingly husky, while Bánky's was acceptable as long as she played a Hungarian). Of all the foreign stars whose post-sound English proved to be heavily accented, Chevalier thrived like no other. "Chevalier's success has given new hope to many foreign stars," the *Los Angeles Times* proclaimed, "but the Chevaliers of the profession are rare. And even Chevalier will need carefully selected vehicles." [3]

Paramount had another relatively recent hire. Earlier in 1931 the young director Rouben Mamoulian signed a long-term contract with the studio. Slender, dark-haired, wearing horn-rimmed glasses, Mamoulian had amicably bidden good-bye to the Theatre Guild, which had used him several times (*Porgy*, *Marco Millions*, etc.), and then directed Laurence Stallings's adaptation of Hemingway's *A Farewell to Arms*. At Adolph Zukor's behest, Mamoulian looked over the new script for Chevalier's next slated picture, *The Grand Duchess and the Waiter*, and, much as he admired screenwriter Samson Raphaelson—*everybody* admired Raphaelson—said it wasn't for him. It was rare for a director, after only two films (*Applause*, shot in Paramount's Astoria studio, and the Fredric March version of *Dr. Jekyll and Mr. Hyde*), to deny the studio bosses, but Mamoulian's contract permitted him considerable latitude and he was not afraid to use it. Zukor implored Mamoulian to come up with *something*, even a musical, for Chevalier, who was being paid $5,000 a week with nothing to do.

At a dinner party one night, French playwright Leopold Marchand gave Mamoulian a synopsis of a play he'd written with Paul Armont. Mamoulian thought the play, *Le Tailleur au Chateau* (*The Tailor in the Castle*), had possibilities and arranged for the studio to buy it. Once the purchase was made, he kept the play's outline and threw out most of its dialogue. This is, essentially, what Mamoulian handed to Rodgers and Hart (who were already on the Paramount payroll), giving them carte blanche to organize the piece as they saw fit.

This was more like it! Rodgers and Hart were "to get to work on the words and music immediately," *Variety* reported on December 1, 1931. Once the boys had structured the movie, George Marion, Jr., was brought in to pull a script together. The Lithuanian-born newspaperman-turned-light-verse-poet Samuel Hoffenstein added his two cents. (Although the line has been attributed to many others, it was Hoffenstein who said, "In Hollywood we writers work our brains to the bone. And what do we get for it? A fortune.") Also credited was Waldemar Young, a descendant of Brigham Young, who had been one of the most popular journalists in San Francisco before moving south to Hollywood to write for the silents. Samson Raphaelson and Vincent Lawrence did some uncredited script work as well.

For the last few weeks of 1931, Larry lived with the Rodgers family, which was deep in mourning. On October 22, just before the songwriters' latest trip west, Dorothy's father, Benjamin Feiner, was on the terrace of the Lombardy apartment that had formerly belonged to his daughter and son-in-law when he stepped over the terrace wall and fell to his death.[4] One month after the suicide, Feiner's widow, May, joined her daughter, infant granddaughter, son-in-law, and the son-in-law's writing partner for the trip west. Along with Mary's nurse and a young housekeeper, they all moved into a house at 724 North Linden Drive, in the heart of Beverly Hills.

For Dorothy Rodgers, any other municipality in Southern California would have been unthinkable. Less than a half hour's drive from downtown Los Angeles, but cooled by the ocean's breeze, Beverly Hills had been incorporated in January 1914. There were sidewalks, but it was not a walking town; the streets were there to showcase the houses—"homes," as they were advertised by local realtors. The Rodgers home happened to belong to Elsie Janis, she of the poorly received Chevalier screen test.

The Rodgerses hired a cook to help them entertain and were soon on the movieland party circuit. It was strange to be welcoming the Christmas holidays in Los Angeles, where nobody walked, everybody drove (even to the corner), and the sun's glare made it seem to be perpetually high noon. One mile of Hollywood Boulevard, between Vine Street and La Brea Avenue, was dubbed Santa Claus Lane and decorated with Christmas trees illuminated by thousands of blinking lights—an eerie spectacle for Easterners who associated the season with snow and starkly beautiful bare trees.[5] The Southern California yuletide season depressed the hell out of Dick; it cheered Larry immensely.

Larry did not suffer even the expected twinges of jealousy when the New York papers reported that *Of Thee I Sing*—the Gershwins' latest musical, written by George S. Kaufman and Morrie Ryskind—which opened the day after Christmas, was so entertaining. The upcoming year was a presidential election, and the show's lighthearted, politically themed book and songs, including "Who Cares?" and "Love Is Sweeping the Country," satirized the entire process. On North Linden Drive, Dick and Larry paced the living room swapping the reviews.

"Because Larry had lived with us in London," Dorothy Rodgers wrote with her peculiar, brittle understatement, "I knew there could be problems." The flammable mixture of Larry's cigars and his absentmindedness was one of them. Another, not surprisingly, was booze. As the stag member of the household, Larry decided that it was his responsibility to keep the house stocked with liquor. "[In Los Angeles] almost every home had a bar," Harry Ruby said of entertaining in that town. "Whatever drinking you did—your mild normal drinking, the cocktail before dinner—was done at home. That brought about a kind of social thing. Where in New York, you'd go out."[6] For each Rodgers dinner party when he was in residence, Larry would insist on tending bar, mixing martinis out of the pantry.

"Ready for a sample?" Larry would say to the cook. Several samples later, with dinner still in midpreparation, both men would be on the floor. Dorothy Rodgers was not amused.[7]

Her patience reached its limit one morning when the Rodgers family was awakened by noises from downstairs. Dick descended to find Larry mixing cocktails for his guests, actors Jack Oakie and Joan Marsh, who had not been informed that Larry shared the house with others. They departed immediately. Larry, embarrassed, also fled and was gone for two days; in the interim he apologized for his gaffe by sending Dorothy flowers. According to Rodgers's biographer Meryle Secrest, after Larry brought home an entire jazz band in the middle of the night, Dorothy gave Dick an ultimatum: "It's Larry or me."[8]

Larry went looking for a place. Mel Shauer had been living apart from his wife, Miriam, and son, Kenneth, staying in a modest Hollywood apartment, and he suggested to Larry that they take a house together. Larry liked the idea. After all, they knew each other's habits from camp in the Adirondacks twenty years earlier. What Larry ended up renting, much to Mel's astonishment, was an extraordinary house, only two and a half blocks from the Rodgerses' house at 724 North Linden, and designed by the fabled architects Greene & Greene.

Designed in the Greenes' Arts and Crafts style, the house, originally built at the corner of Wilshire Boulevard and Berendo Street, was the firm's only Los Angeles dwelling of the period and considered its final masterwork. By 1923, however, the new Miracle Mile traffic along Wilshire had made single-family residences there less desirable, and the house was earmarked for demolition until silent screen star Norman Kerry grabbed it. Kerry had the house trucked from its original location to a lot he owned at 910 North Bedford Drive, in Beverly Hills. Dorothy Rodgers recorded the tale that the house's slow-speed transport to Beverly Hills took three days during which its interior was the site of a nonstop party.[9] But that's surely fanciful. (Plumbing, anyone?) Instead Kerry hired Henry Greene to "re-site" the house—Greene, who knew the structure better than anybody, did it in three sections—and then landscaped the Beverly Hills property. It must have been from Kerry, Frederick Nolan has suggested, that Larry Hart rented the house.[10]

Larry had less interest in the house's provenance, however, than in the sixty-foot-long swimming pool that Kerry had had dug on the property. Swimming was the one physical activity Larry could abide. And Mel had been a swimming instructor at Brant Lake.

At a party Larry spotted Henry Myers, who was also under contract at Paramount. "You fabulous sonofabitch!" cried Larry, throwing his arms around Myers. At the time Myers was working on a project called *Million Dollar Legs*, which Joseph L. Mankiewicz had cooked up in response to B. P. Schulberg's request that the studio have something ready to release in time for the 1932 Olympic Games, to be held in Los Angeles. Myers felt guilty about not yet bringing his devoted mother out to the West Coast. Larry, no less a mama's boy than Myers, was racked by a similar guilt. "When the mother comes," Larry told Myers, "no more freedom." [11]

Nevertheless, Larry soon sent for Frieda, Teddy, and Big Mary, along with his six-year-old, black-tongued red chow, Kiki, which was probably named for the title character of an old French play about a Parisian chorus girl. [12] (Larry had written the lyric "Kiki" for the 1922 Columbia Varsity Show *Steppe Around*, and a reference in it to David Belasco was surely a reference to the play.) The Hart brood arrived in the grip of national anxiety over the kidnapping of the Lindbergh baby, twenty-month-old Charles Jr., on March 1, from the family home in Hopewell, New Jersey, near Princeton—one of the biggest stories of the twentieth century. It would be seventy-two days before the child's body was discovered (in the woods, not far from the Lindbergh home), but by then fear had infected every state in the union. From his jail cell, Al Capone declared the abduction an "atrocious" crime and offered a $10,000 reward for the apprehension of its perpetrators. Will Rogers wrote that the nation had "but a single thought," the welfare of the Lindbergh baby. [13] Citizens saw kidnapping plots everywhere. Some commentators blamed the grim realities of the Depression; some blamed Prohibition. In that dread-filled late winter and early spring, children—particularly children of the affluent— were more closely watched than ever. ABDUCTION OF LINDBERGH BABY IS WARNING TO HOLLYWOOD was the banner headline of the March 12 edition of *Zit's Theatrical Newspaper*. [14]

There was no child in the Hart household, but the national gloom was inescapable. To cut through it, Larry decided to replicate his family's weekly Sunday dinners, but with an aquatic theme: guests could dine, drink, and swim, if not necessarily in that order, throughout the day. Exhibiting his typically excessive check-grabbing, Larry paid for everything—even most of Mel Shauer's expenses. [15]

If Larry Hart was the most generous of men, Maurice Chevalier was among the least. In early 1932 he probably qualified as the highest-salaried performer in Hollywood, but he was loath to part with a dollar. He would cadge a cigarette, only to put it behind his ear for later. He drove to Paramount each day not in a gleaming new car that might advertise his princely salary, as well as the studio that paid it, but in a dusty used Ford, which he would then park across the street, where it was free, instead of paying a quarter to keep it in the studio parking lot.[16] For *Love Me Tonight*, which was scheduled to begin shooting at the end of March 1932 (it would actually begin a week late), Chevalier's contract called for him to be paid $159,041.67, though that would eventually rise to over $200,000, an astronomical sum at the time. Jeanette MacDonald was receiving $5,000 a week, which came to about a third of Chevalier's weekly salary. The young minx Myrna Loy was loaned to Paramount by MGM for $1,800 a week, with MGM keeping $1,200 and letting Loy pocket $600.

Dick and Larry wrote most of the *Love Me Tonight* songs in the first three months of 1932, sometimes working at the North Linden Drive house but more often working out of a dreary Paramount cell, the antithesis of the luxurious quarters they had been given at Warner Bros. "If we went over to the tiny window and stuck our noses right up against the glass," Rodgers wrote, "we could see a patch of about six inches of sky." One afternoon Chevalier, dressed entirely in blue (including the shoes), knocked on the door and asked if he could hear some of the songs the boys had written. Dick and Larry took turns presenting each song. Chevalier sat there without expression and, after the final song, departed without a word. The boys were stunned. The black cloud that hung over them—would they be replaced? would they ever work again for the film studios?—did not blow away until well into the next day, when Chevalier came through the cell door, threw an arm around each of them, and said, "Boys, I couldn't sleep last night because I was so excited about your wonderful songs!"[17]

Almost immediately, however, there were problems with the Hays Office, the movie industry's self-monitoring censor. Every now and then, wrote columnist Llewellyn Miller, "Hollywood suffers from an attack of Hays fever, accompanied by chills, inter-office communications, and other manifestations of a code going to the head."[18] The Hays Office was named for Will Hays, an Indiana attorney and elder of the Presbyterian Church who, a decade earlier, had served as chairman of the Republican National Committee. Warren G. Harding named Hays U. S. Postmaster General. In 1922, with Hollywood reeling from publicity that made it sound like Sodom-by-the-Sea—the murder of director William Desmond Taylor was only one of several recent sensational scandals—the Motion Picture Producers and Distributors of America lured Hays into its presidency. In 1930 an official Motion Picture Code, written by *Exhibitors' Herald* publisher Martin Quigley and the Reverend Daniel Lord, a Jesuit priest, was adopted by the industry. By dint of his position as MPPDA president, Hays became the Code's enforcer.[19]

Hays's headquarters were at 28 West Forty-Fourth Street in New York, but most of his deputies were based in Hollywood, under the supervision of Joseph I. Breen, where they could evaluate a script or lead sheet sent by messenger, or review a film's rushes after no more than a half hour's drive. On March 8, 1932, Jason Joy of the MPPDA wrote to Paramount production chief B. P. Schulberg:

> I have read the lyrics of the song, "A Woman Needs Something Like That," to be used in *Love Me Tonight*. The lyrics are as amusing as they can be and as sung by Chevalier and Jeanette MacDonald they probably wouldn't be offensive to many people. However, coldly read they seem to me to go a little too far in innuendo. It isn't a question of individual words of course but of the thought itself.[20]

The thought itself was about sex, expressed with such cleverness that Larry Hart must have figured he was slipping it past Breen's people. The song was written for MacDonald, playing the ailing Princess Jeanette, and Joseph Cawthorne as the physician who comes to the house to examine her. At first Jeanette, unaccustomed to the touch of a commoner, resists the examination:

> *Before a single instrument you cram in me,*
> *Tell me, are you a man of noble birth?*

If Larry knew he was crossing a line, he did so with the full support of Mamoulian, who pushed the studio bosses' tolerance to the limit. In "A Woman Needs Something Like That," the physician tells Jeanette to remove her dress—a command that drew more tut-tutting from the Hays Office. The song remained in the film, including such suggestive rhymes as "A doorbell needs tinkling,/ A flower needs sprinkling" and "A car needs ignition / To keep in condition," but the first quarter of the lyric was chopped out to make it acceptable.

Larry's bawdier lyrics might have been his way of thumbing his nose not only at the censors but at the more restrictive aspects of life in Los Angeles. Larry had been at once amused and alarmed when, a month before the Hays Office draped his lyrics with a fig leaf, the LAPD shut down a production of *Lysistrata* at the Fox Carthay Circle Theater for its risqué dialogue.

Such censorship wasn't restricted to Los Angeles. By late March 1932, Billy Rose's *Crazy Quilt*, which still included Rodgers and Hart's "Rest Room Rosie," had been on tour for six months and was scheduled to open in Minneapolis. *Crazy Quilt's* ad campaign featuring seminude women was so provocative, however, that the Minneapolis mayor banned the show before it opened. *Crazy Quilt* moved over to St. Paul, where it drew capacity crowds for a week. It's delightful to imagine Larry's long-lost "Rest Room Rosie" lyric as being so salacious that the authorities demanded the song's removal from the show. But the Minneapolis episode had less to do with Rodgers and Hart than with Billy Rose's increasingly canny showmanship.

In Southern California in mid-April, Rouben Mamoulian began filming in several locations—the Sherwood Forest stage at Paramount, Busch Gardens, MGM, Fox Hills, and Chatsworth. *Love Me Tonight* opens with a rhythmic "symphony of sounds" beneath atmospheric images of Paris: smoke-belching chimneys; boot-makers and knife-grinders at work; the beating of a blanket; the honking of an automobile's Klaxon, etc. Richard Rodgers and Frederick Nolan have each correctly likened this aural montage to the opening of Dorothy and DuBose Heyward's play *Porgy*, which Mamoulian had directed for the Theatre Guild (and which was the basis for the Gershwin opera *Porgy and Bess*). *Porgy* opens on Catfish Row, a tenement in the fallen quarter of Charleston, South Carolina, and as the curtain rises, we hear, in gentle succession, the bells of St. Michael's church in the distance chiming the hour; the court echoing with laughter and banter in "Gullah," the African-spiced dialect of the Charleston Negro; the twanging of a guitar, followed by the dancing shuffle of an urchin; and then the rolling of dice. These are Saturday night sounds on Catfish Row, but Mamoulian applied the same idea to frame morning in Paris.[21] "That's the Song of Paree" introduces the tailor Maurice Courtelin (Chevalier), whose straw hat is the first thing we notice. Maurice sings the song, which paints a picture of a messy but incomparably romantic city, and on his way to the shop he encounters several people, including the grocer to whom he owes ten francs. (The grocer is played by Gabby Hayes, the old codger sidekick of two generations of westerns, though he might be hard to identify without whiskers and cowboy hat.)

Maurice is not just any tailor but a master tailor, although he owes everybody money, and pride in his work leads him into "Isn't It Romantic?" In one of the more bravura filmmaking passages in all movie musicals, the song travels from Maurice's shop to a taxi driver outside, whose new fare is a composer en route to the railroad station. Each line of theirs is spoken or sung to the lilting Rodgers melody. The composer boards the train, where he adds words he began in the taxi, and the song is taken up by soldiers who are soon marching to its beat through the countryside. Gypsies play the song, which wafts along the evening breeze to the château balustrade of the lovelorn Princess Jeanette:

Isn't it romantic? / Music in the night: / A dream that can be heard.

The hero, of course, will turn out to be only a Parisian tailor. For the moment, however, the princess's pursuer is the milquetoast Count de Savignac (Charles Butterworth), who has climbed a ladder to court her. Larry Hart's lyric performs the difficult feat of making the princess self-involved yet sympathetic. Sometime later, when Paramount's music publishing arm, Famous Music, published "Isn't It Romantic?," Rodgers and Hart added a verse that glints like an emerald, but it would have stopped the action cold in the movie. They would do that for several songs they wrote for movies, embellishing the lyrics later.

What follows in *Love Me Tonight* is a series of delectable movie moments, indoors and out. The sumptuous interiors were designed by Hans Drier, Paramount's longtime art director, who had trained as an architect before arriving in Hollywood. When Maurice arrives at the château, having been induced by the Vicomte de Vareze (Charles Ruggles) to impersonate a baron—an appropriate title to court a princess—he cannot keep away from Jeanette. Since she's on horseback and believes she's out of human earshot, Jeanette sings "Lover" to the unnamed swain who has yet to find her, but the increasingly swift ride causes her to call out to the horse—and to enable Hart to sidestep the censors: "He'll be my lord and my master, / I'll be a slave to the last. / He'll make my heartbeat go faster— / NOT TOO FAST!"

But Maurice has in fact overheard some of this. In contrast to the way Jeanette sings "Lover" without another human in sight, Maurice sings "Mimi" directly to her—introductory dialogue explains why he's addressing Jeanette as Mimi, which seems to have been drawn from the Mimi in *La Bohème*— but not before several other characters have passed the song around in a way similar to that of "Isn't It Romantic?" At the beginning of the song, C. Aubrey

Smith is putting a hand into the wrong sleeve of his robe, but Mamoulian regarded the blooper as natural and kept it. Even Myrna Loy, as the stunning, man-crazy Countess, tries a line of "Mimi"—probably the only time she ever sang in the movies.[22]

At the center of *Love Me Tonight* is a deer hunt scored by Rodgers. It was rare for the songwriter to be assigned underscoring of a picture—songwriting and underscoring were considered vastly different skills—but Mamoulian knew what Rodgers was capable of. Composing crosscutting themes for the frightened deer (strings) and two dozen or so pursuing dogs (brass), Rodgers contributed to one of the most shimmering hunting scenes in the movies, predating and ranking with those in Jean Renoir's *Rules of the Game* (1937) and Tony Richardson's *Tom Jones* (1963). What gives it a special kick is that Maurice saves the terrified stag, keeping it safe in a detached house, while the dogs yap and run wild.

The charming "A Woman Needs Something Like That," despite the censorial intrusions, reaffirms our sympathy for the princess, a twenty-two-year-old widow who has been wasting away in self-imposed solitude. Even in the movies, the tradition of the end of act 1 requires that the lovers separate; in *Love Me Tonight* they do so after Jeanette insults Maurice. Maurice's "The Poor Apache," photographed in low light with shadows flickering in the background (in contrast to the white, sumptuous open spaces of the rest of the movie), is filled with post-breakup bitterness and refers not to the American Indian nation but to the French career criminal. Apaches tended to operate in gangs, and Chevalier's childhood town of Menilmontant was an apache stronghold. "The apache type is far from being the romantic figure which novelists and film producers have made so popular all over the world," Georges Parcq wrote in *Crime Reporter*. "Neither does he spend his life falling in love with rich American heiresses, and revealing himself to be an impoverished French aristocrat in disguise!"[23] Chevalier's delivery is charming, but "The Poor Apache" is really an angry lament of self-reproach.

"Love Me Tonight" is the principals' duet, each one longing for their hearts and lips to meet. In 1932 the song was sometimes confused with one number from *The Vagabond King*, and was even more often confused with the Bing Crosby song, "Love Me Tonight" (music by Victor Young, lyrics by Ned Washington).

To make Jeanette a new riding habit, Maurice rips off her dress and pulls out—his tape measure! The finished riding habit fits so perfectly that Jeanette realizes something's not right, prompting Maurice's confession that he is not, after all, a baron. "The Son of a Gun Is Nothing but a Tailor" is passed around by practically the entire cast, most of them indignant, and it's Larry Hart at his most Gilbertian: "I'd rather throw a bomb in her / Than have her wed a commoner." After a period of shock and dismay, Jeanette will realize she's in love with the tailor anyway and, in a scene startling for the physical risks taken by MacDonald, who refused a stunt double, she's on horseback again when she chases down and halts his departing train. It's a satisfying if incredible ending.

Love Me Tonight, still among the most modern of movie musicals, has so much else going for it: a bit of the Strauss waltz "A Thousand and One Nights"; fine underscoring by staff composer Ralph Rainger and Larry Hart's onetime collaborator W. Franke Harling; Robert Greig, as the major-domo, recognizable from so many Paramount movies as the jowly butler or valet; and a split screen that slyly shows the lovers sleeping as though they're sleeping *together*. All of this was masterfully coordinated by Mamoulian. But it was Rodgers and Hart who made *Love Me Tonight* so much more than another generic kitschy romance. Even one of the songs deleted from the picture, "The Man for Me," is so much smarter than just about anything else written for the movies—a dizzying number in which Maurice acts as Cyrano for himself, instructing Jeanette what to write about him in a letter to a friend: "He is so distinguished and sweet, / Very debonair yet discreet!" Hart knew Chevalier pretty well—his professional side, at any rate—but it's debatable whether Chevalier knew Hart. Rampantly homophobic, perhaps due to the apache neighborhood he grew up in, Chevalier knew Larry's preference for men but made no remark about it. That would come later.

Love Me Tonight wrapped in late spring of 1932, with a George M. Cohan picture next. Hart family members had begun to acclimate themselves to California living. Larry brought friends around to play cards with Frieda. Mary Campbell fed and watered guests who streamed through the house to visit, but wondered about the birdlike appetites of movie actors. "They don't eat in California," Big Mary would tell the *World-Telegram*, "just sandwiches and bread."[24] Through Larry's connections Teddy won a role in *Million Dollar Legs*, the comedy cobbled together by Henry Myers and Joe Mankiewicz, about to be filmed on the Paramount lot. Described by the *Los Angeles Times* as four-foot-eight, Teddy, playing secretary of the navy of a fictitious republic sending its athletes to the Olympics, was paired with seven-foot-tall actor Tex Madsen, the contrast meant to be a sight gag in itself.[25] Now

Mel Shauer asked Larry for a favor: to write a lyric to a tune composed by Ralph Rainger for Lyda Roberti, playing a particularly vampy Mata Hari type, to sing. Larry came up with the lyric "It's Terrific When I Get Hot," though he was not credited, either by studio policy or by his own request, for such moonlighting would not have been acceptable to Dick.[26]

But Larry helped *anybody* who asked. After *Love Me Tonight* was screened to general executive approval, Dick and Larry were given a much nicer office in the two-story music building. There Larry was as restless as ever. Bandleader-lyricist Sam Coslow occupied the office next to Larry's and remembered him being too frantic to work during daylight hours, always dropping by to kibitz "mostly about the good old days back on Broadway, which he sorely missed."

> Sometimes, when I was working against time, Larry would offer to help on my lines—for free. He would say, "What are you trying to come up with there? Can I hear it?" I would read my pencil-scribbled lyrics to him, and on more than one occasion he would pace up and down, digging for a good punchline for me, just as if he were collaborating on the song. I used a few of his suggestions, happy to get them. Many writers would have asked for a cut on the royalties, but not Larry. That's the kind of guy he was. He loved his craft, and he felt a fraternal kinship to everyone else who worked in it.[27]

Each day Dick and Larry would enter Paramount through its massive iron gates to write songs for the new George M. Cohan picture. But Paramount couldn't make up its mind—one week the picture was a musical comedy, the next week it was a straight comedy—prompting Larry's college drinking pal Herman Mankiewicz to resign from the studio, to be replaced by none other than Barney Glazer.[28]

A huge neon sign went up in Hollywood: 1932 COME TO LOS ANGELES XTH OLYMPIAD GAMES—STANDARD OIL COMPANY OF CALIFORNIA. Larry had the wherewithal—that is, the money and the swimming pool—to host a party at the North Bedford house for the Olympic swimming team. Its current star was Eleanor Holm, who had been attracting the attention of movie producers since she had come to town.[29]

The George M. Cohan picture was called *The Phantom President*, based on a novel by George F. Worts, and its story will seem familiar. Medicine show entertainer Doc Varney (Cohan) is the exact double of presidential candidate Theodore K. Blair; because Blair has a charisma quotient of zero, his handlers recruit the more appealing Doc to stand in for him. Managing Doc's campaign is his medicine show partner Curley Cooney (Jimmy Durante). When Blair's girl Felicia (Claudette Colbert) is presented to Doc Varney, complications ensue, although there is little doubt that Doc will win Felicia's heart. Norman Taurog, who had just won an Academy Award for *Skippy* and whose career would last well into the 1960s, was slated to direct. Dick and Larry were assigned to write the songs for Cohan and Durante, with input from each.

This was an honor. No one else had ever written for Cohan, who had been a Broadway star since *Little Johnny Jones* in 1904, and whose own songs— "Yankee Doodle Dandy," "Over There," and "Give My Regards to Broadway," to name only three—were brash and enduring. Dick and Larry were aware of the responsibility they'd been handed.

But Cohan was already wary when he arrived in Pasadena right after Memorial Day in 1932. *The Phantom President*, timed to be released as the real presidential campaign reached the boiling point, would be Cohan's first picture. Two years earlier he had been on his way to Hollywood to make a movie but, realizing he would have no control over the movie's direction or marketing—control that he contractually demanded on his Broadway shows—he turned around in Chicago. What might have lured him to Paramount in 1932 was the promise that the studio would film a project he had in mind called *Song of the Eagle*, with an all-star Paramount cast.[30]

Although Cohan's irascibility hardly invited sympathy, there was something sad about him. The world of show business he had conquered decades earlier was spinning away from his grasp. In *Can't Help Singin'*, Gerald Mast has written of Cohan, "Not only was [Cohan] not Jewish; like many of his generation, he was anti-Semitic and, feeling himself shoved aside by newcomers, reacted against the new generation of immigrants like any established member of society. He was also, to use an unlovely but functional term of a much later generation, homophobic. He openly despised the new breed of showfolk who were seeping into the profession through the union that protected all actors equally."[31] The latter point is certainly true—and Rodgers and Hart represented that new, college-educated breed—but the former is debatable. Cohan had been around Jews in the theater all his life, often performing for—and being feted by—organizations like the Jewish Theatrical Guild. Legend has it that Cohan was once denied a room at a restricted hotel because the manager mistook his name for Cohen. Cohan said to the manager, "You thought I was a Jew. I thought you were a gentleman. We were both mistaken," and then proudly walked out of the hotel. Still, Cohan was perplexed by the waning of his authority, and his perplexity was compounded by the factory-town hours of Los Angeles. "Say, that's right about these people going to bed so early," he told the *Los Angeles Times*. "Why, you've got to when you're up and on the lot at eight in the morning." [32]

It was at Cohan's urging that Paramount borrowed Jimmy Durante from MGM. With Durante often sitting at the piano, where he was comfortable, Rodgers and Hart and staff songwriter Arthur Johnston went to work in late spring 1932. Larry had a chance to write something politically biting. In a time of unprecedented national deprivation, he might still not have had the chance to see the Gershwins' *Of Thee I Sing*, which had won the Pulitzer Prize for Drama—the first musical to be so honored—but Larry was known to admire Ira's spare, pungent lines from the Gershwins' *Strike up the Band*:

> We're in a bigger, better war
> For your patriotic pastime.
> We don't know what we're fighting for—
> But we didn't know the last time.

But such sentiments might have been too pointed for the Yankee Doodle Dandy. What Larry came up with wasn't bad, but the gums were soft. In "The Country Needs a Man," portraits of Washington, Jefferson, Lincoln, and Teddy Roosevelt—a talking Mount Rushmore—fawn over each other's ability to lead the country. Larry still gets in some smart lines in which he rhymes "King George" with "seldom gorge" and "Valley Forge," and couples "Mr. Volstead's famed amendment" with "To our liberty the end meant." "Give Her a Kiss" is the one song from the film that's occasionally revived, perhaps because it's romantic rather than political, and in the original it's sung by birds, bees, and frogs encouraging Doc Varney to kiss the fetching Felicia. (Cohan could put across a love song as long as it didn't require passion. Taurog and the cautious Paramount brass must have figured it was more effective to have the screen fauna handle it.) There's a political convention entirely in recitative. The most Hart-like number of all, which included critical input from Durante, is "The Medicine Show," which kicks off with the carnival barker's come-on and ends with the plot—Doc Varney's recruitment to stand in for Theodore K. Blair—clicking into place.

Durante always addressed Rodgers as "Roger," even after being corrected several times. Rodgers, like just about everybody else in show business, respected Durante's easy professionalism, gifted as he was at piano playing, writing, and, with that unavoidable proboscis and New York–inflected growl, joke telling. (Rodgers recorded a characteristic Durante gag: "Jimmy Durante says he got a post-card from his girl saying that she had a room with running-water. He wired her, 'Get rid of that Indian!'")[33] Durante and Larry also worked well together, which might have come as a surprise, considering this remark in Durante's 1931 book *Night Clubs*: "The sudden featuring of the horticultural young man as a night-club feature is no more new than it is pleasing. . . . As pathological examples they may be interesting. As entertainers they are not." (To be fair, that section of the book was authored by Durante's collaborator Jack Kofoed, who was writing specifically about his reaction to cross-dressing entertainers.)[34]

"A Schnozzola," one of the lyrics Hart and Durante worked on together, was to music by Arthur Johnston, who enjoyed the sauce as much as Larry did. In New York, Johnston had been Irving Berlin's arranger, turning so many of Berlin's one-fingered melodies into fully developed songs. Tagging along with Berlin to California, Johnston had helped Chaplin with the music on the 1931 *City Lights*. At Paramount he was paired with Sam Coslow, who, reacting to his collaborator's alcoholism and resulting absenteeism, was no less irritated than Dick Rodgers could be. "I am by no means saying," Coslow wrote, "that my problem with him was as acute as Dick Rodgers's similar one with Larry Hart, or that Arthur's binges were even in the same league with Larry's. Arthur in fact eventually licked his problem. But in many ways his drinking was just as difficult to cope with."[35] Alcoholics don't necessarily recognize each other instantly—they are birds not of a feather but of many feathers—but one wonders if Johnston and Hart had a drinking session or two. Johnston would go on to write "Pennies from Heaven" with another champion drinker, Johnny Burke.

Coslow, meanwhile, recorded Rodgers and Hart's "Isn't It Romantic?" for RCA Victor in Hollywood, with the full Paramount studio orchestra, and soon followed that up with "Give Her a Kiss."[36] Paramount, like Warner Bros. and MGM, maintained strong music publishing links and liked to exploit them whenever possible. Between March 29 and August 5, 1932, just over a third of a year, Paramount paid Rodgers and Hart $37,333.33—more than *forty* times the average annual American salary that year—for their work on *Love Me Tonight* and *The Phantom President*.[37] "Hollywood money isn't money," Dorothy Parker famously said. "It's congealed snow, melts in your hand, and there you are."[38] But the money Larry had earned on Broadway melted, too. That tends to happen when you pick up every check. That summer Larry invited practically everyone he met back to his place for a swim and a drink. As in New York, however, he did like to get away from Frieda and go out. The El Capitan, one of the opulent theaters on Hollywood Boulevard, was hosting a show called *Hullabaloo*, a spoof of *Grand Hotel*, which included a rendition of "Manhattan."[39] Larry checked that out and took a look at the new Sardi's on Hollywood Boulevard, housed in a building that was not an outpost of the New York Sardi's so much as an independent imitation.[40] Pari-mutuel betting beckoned Larry to Agua Caliente—the beautiful Santa Anita racetrack was still under construction—and to the nearby Stud Saloon in Tijuana, also frequented by Larry's fellow lyricist Al Dubin, who was then writing lyrics (to music by Harry Warren) for the songs for Warner Bros.' *42nd Street*, including "You're Getting to Be a Habit with Me" and "Shuffle Off to Buffalo." Dubin's daughter, Patricia McGuire, wrote that her father regarded Larry as the greatest American lyricist.[41]

In Beverly Hills it was necessary for Larry to telephone his partner almost daily. These communications went something like this:

"Rodgers residence."

"Is Mr. Rodgers in?" said Larry.

"No, sir, he's not. Would you care to leave a message?"

"Please tell him 'Rimsky-Korsakov' called."

Dick caught on quickly, and soon figured that any message from a celebrity he didn't know personally was really from his puckish partner.

One day that summer the Rodgerses' housekeeper approached Dick.

"Mr. Rodgers, Mrs. Roosevelt is on the telephone."

Dick was dumbfounded. Could it be the wife of the New York governor who was running for president? Could it be the widow of the twenty-sixth president? Of course not! It had to be Larry! Dick took the handset. "Hello, Larry," he said.

But it was the young wife of the son of President Theodore Roosevelt.[42] Whenever Dick subsequently told the story in his presence, Larry would laugh and rub his hands together.

Rodgers and Hart had written the songs for two Paramount pictures in 1932. One of them, *Love Me Tonight*, was innovative and thoroughly enjoyable to work on. The other, *The Phantom President*, had been soured by George M. Cohan's undisguised contempt for the moviemaking process and was a disappointment. For the year, Paramount was on track to lose a staggering $21 million, with mountains of debt accrued when the company had gone on a theater-buying spree two years earlier.[43] Under pressure, Paramount slashed its production slate, with little chance there'd be another assignment for the boys.

A few months earlier, Joe Schenck and United Artists had signed Al Jolson to star in three pictures, at $25,000 a week. As with Chevalier's original Paramount contract, Jolson's signing did not please the other UA executives, who regarded Jolson's cinematic fame as *yesterday*. After several false starts, UA settled on a project called *Happy Go Lucky*, with a script by Ben Hecht, based on a story by Harry D'Arrast. A Frenchman who had worked in Hollywood for many years, D'Arrast had been Chaplin's assistant director on *A Woman of Paris* and *The Gold Rush* and had directed at least three silent pictures starring Adolphe Menjou, as well as the ahead-of-its-time talkie, *Laughter* (1930). In self-imposed exile in France, D'Arrast told Lewis Milestone a story about a New York tramp. Milestone had directed the Academy Award–winning *All Quiet on the Western Front* and, more recently, the first film adaptation of the Ben Hecht–Charles MacArthur *The Front Page*, its dialogue coming off the screen at such a rapid clip that it muffled arguments against the talkies. Picture people spoke of "Milly," as he was called, with the reverence with which they had mentioned Ernst Lubitsch and now Mamoulian. Milestone liked the tramp idea so much that he persuaded D'Arrast to return to Hollywood and direct it with Al Jolson in the role. Because D'Arrast hadn't worked in nearly three years, Milestone offered to serve as "supervisor"—a go-between position, rapidly becoming defunct, that would allow UA to feel it had some insurance.

Ben Hecht heard D'Arrast's idea and jumped at the chance to write the first draft. Everyone seemed to be delighted with Hecht's script, which was retitled *The New Yorker*, except Jolson, who felt he had too few lines and no opportunity to sing. Veteran librettist William Anthony McGuire came in for a draft but quickly gave way to playwright S. N. Behrman. Irving Caesar arrived in Los Angeles and was said to be writing songs "between sun baths" for the new Jolson picture. Titles were shuffled like a deck of cards. By May 1932 *The New Yorker* had become *The Duke of Central Park* and then *Heart of New York*; a week later the phrase "Hallelujah, I'm a Bum," which appeared in Hecht's script, emerged as the latest title. Derived from a nineteenth-century folk song, "Revive Us Again," the lyric "Hallelujah, I'm a Bum" ("If I didn't eat I'd have money to burn") had been picked up by the Industrial Workers of the World as a protest anthem. As a movie title, *Hallelujah, I'm a Bum!* would be scrapped more than once.

Then, by the second week in July, D'Arrast was gone, too. Jolson still couldn't see himself as a sensitive, laconic hobo. The proud D'Arrast told the press that he had walked off the set to maintain his "artistic integrity." Along with D'Arrast went Irving Caesar's songs.[44]

So it was up to Milestone to direct. But Milestone was still mopping up problems with *Rain*, the Joan Crawford–Walter Huston melodrama, so he assigned stage director Chester Erskine, who had his own contract with UA, to begin filming some preapproved shots. On August 3, 1932, with Erskine essentially overseeing second-unit work, UA signed Rodgers and Hart "to write all music and lyrics for photoplay *The New Yorker* for $15,000, plus $2500/week for services in excess of four weeks."[45]

As usual, Dick and Larry roamed across the set for song ideas. Erskine recruited his friend the Broadway columnist Sidney Skolsky, who was in town collecting movie material for his column in the *Daily News*, to appear as a bank customer. Among the extras in the scene, the five-foot Skolsky felt absurdly small, until Larry Hart agreed to play opposite him as a teller.[46] Their six-second scene went smoothly. "Will you cash this check for five dollars?" asks Skolsky, and Larry replies, "No." The single word of on-camera dialogue was almost enough to get excited about.

Considerable excitement, though, was generated by strong notices for *Love Me Tonight*. The *Los Angeles Times*'s chronically withholding critic Philip K. Scheuer called the film "close to perfection," described the "photographic music" of the "Isn't It Romantic?" sequence in admiring detail, and, fifty years before a moviegoer could carry the product home, wrote, "It is, in substance, a picture I would like to take home with me, so that on dull evenings I could bring it out and display it to my friends, and make them happy, too."[47] *The New Yorker* (the magazine, that is) panned the picture—"it isn't bright and it isn't witty"—but Larry must have gotten a kick out of the phrase "Wagner gone chichi!" that ended the review.[48] *The Boston Globe* praised *Love Me Tonight* as "poetic and important," while Mordaunt Hall of *The New York Times* couldn't seem to get the lyric, "The Son of a Gun Is Nothing but a Tailor," out of his head.[49]

The boys' celebratory mood was dampened in August when the pregnant Dorothy Rodgers, experiencing premature contractions, was rushed to Cedars of Lebanon (now Cedars-Sinai) and gave birth to a baby girl who lived only a few minutes.[50]

The loss of a child cries out for a change of scene; it's what Frieda and Max Hart had tried when their firstborn son had died. Dorothy arranged to take twenty-month-old Mary home to New York, with Dick and Larry to follow when they could. For now, though, the songwriters had obligations to meet. Paramount needed them on the lot to supervise the recording of the *Phantom President* numbers. They were up for contract renewal at the studio. The gushing reviews for *Love Me Tonight* might have provided some leverage for negotiations. But an ad the boys placed in *Variety* in September seems less tough-minded or manipulative than jokey in the Hart manner: "Mr. Richard Rodgers [the likeness above his name is Beethoven's] and Mr. Lorenz Hart [Shakespeare's] enjoyed writing the songs and rhymed dialogue for Mr. Mamoulian and Mr. Paramount in *Love Me Tonight*. They thank all the cast, from Mr. Chevalier down to Mr. Remus, the deer, for their magnificent co-operation."[51]

Charged with writing for the many-titled hobo project at UA, Rodgers and Hart were trying to hold the line against Jolson's insistence on including two songs written by a friend of his.[52] This was particularly irritating to Larry, who, while he admired George M. Cohan, positively worshipped Jolson. With Milestone's support, the boys won that battle. They had four weeks to complete their own songs on what would prove to be one of the most interesting—and commercially dismal—movies of the decade.

CHAPTER 13

I Am Too Drunk with Beauty

WHILE RODGERS and Hart worked on the Jolson project, employing the half-rhyme and recitative that had served so well in *Love Me Tonight*, there were distractions. Jolson went to New York to sign an eight-week contract with NBC radio, sponsored by Chevrolet.[1] Roland Young, who was to costar in *Hallelujah, I'm a Bum!* as New York mayor Hastings, dropped out, to be replaced by Frank Morgan. In the third week of October, the boys were gratified that "Love Me Tonight"—but, surprisingly, not "Isn't It Romantic?"—was listed by *Variety* as one of the top ten sheet music sellers of the week. Taking a break, Dick and Larry drove (or, more likely, were driven) to Tijuana and checked into the Hotel Agua Caliente. "As usual, I haven't gambled at all," Dick wrote to his wife. "I just can't make myself do it. However, I watched Larry win two-hundred bucks in nine straight passes. He's about three-fifty up on the trip and if only I could kidnap him all would be well. He'll probably lose it all and more tonight."[2]

The boys were on the set to observe principal photography on *Hallelujah, I'm a Bum!* Their old friend Alfred Newman was on hand with his orchestra. The Riviera Country Club in Pacific Palisades, which had been completed six years earlier for the Los Angeles Athletic Club, stood in for Central Park. Lewis Milestone kept a tight rein on the schedule and managed to get Jolie, who was undergoing public marital troubles with Ruby Keeler, to finish the picture in his dependably professional way, even agreeing to work on Sundays to get a negative in under budget. Meanwhile, Metro's boy genius, Irving Thalberg, impressed by *Love Me Tonight,* was trying to throw an assignment to Rodgers and Hart. On November 6, 1932, Dick wrote to Dorothy that they had finally filmed a critical scene around their song "You Are Too Beautiful," strains of which would run throughout the picture. "That's the scene on the fire-escape which had to be re-made. It's much cuter this way and Jolson looks less like a monkey."[3] But the title song—and the title itself—could not be released in England because the word "bum" denoted not a derelict but a derriere. The song had to be rerecorded as "Hallelujah, I'm a Tramp."[4]

At last, Milestone permitted the boys to go home if they wanted to. Dick did, Larry did not.

On Election Day 1932, Dick boarded the Santa Fe Chief to head home to Dorothy and Mary in New York, promising to stay at least four weeks but not more than seven, after which they would report to work on a new picture for MGM, in Culver City. Thalberg had come through after all. When the day was done, Franklin Delano Roosevelt was elected president. Neither partner was in New York that night, when the Jerome Kern–Oscar Hammerstein musical *Music in the Air* opened. The show's semi-operatic style suggested that its creators had taken a close look at *Love Me Tonight* when it was released that August. "The Song Is You" and "I've Told Ev'ry Little Star" would emerge from *Music in the Air* as standards, the latter sung by ingenue Katherine Carrington, who would marry Larry's old friend Arthur Schwartz nearly two years later.[5]

Larry wanted to maintain the privacy afforded by Southern California distances and automobile travel, even though Frieda, Teddy, and Big Mary were still living with him in Beverly Hills and utterly dependent on him. Once you got away from its Puritan ethos, Los Angeles could be liberating. There were parties in Santa Monica and Malibu to drive out to, the revelers usually working, or trying to get work, at one of the studios and in no position to judge the behavior of anyone else. Several places in Hollywood quietly catered to a homosexual clientele; one of them was the New Yorker (that evocative phrase again!), housed in the Christie Hotel on Hollywood Boulevard at McCadden, which opened in September 1932 and was decorated in a black and silver motif. Former female impersonator and beloved cabaret star Jean Malin had been lured west to serve as master of ceremonies. Appearing there every night in those opening months were the identical Rocky Twins, Paal and Lief, Norwegian female impersonators.

The Rocky Twins had worked the Casino de Paris with Mistinguett, but their talents, beyond their impersonations, were elusive. Larry became a regular patron at the New Yorker, once caravanning an entire dinner party, including special guest Fanny Brice, to the club and picking up the tab for everybody in the joint.[6]

There were thousands of young men in town waiting for a break. Larry had become smitten with the young actor Tyrone Power, Jr. Despite his black-Irish handsomeness and his father's success as a Shakespearean actor, Power was having trouble getting so much as a screen test. Try as Larry might to help Power's career, he had no influence at the studios. Power biographer Hector Arce wrote, "Basically a New Yorker temporarily working in an alien medium, Hart didn't possess the clout of resident Californians whose entire lives were devoted to the business of motion pictures."[7]

Through newspapers and long-distance phone calls, Larry's connection to the East Coast remained strong. While wrapping *Hallelujah, I'm a Bum!*, he had noticed a lyric by E. Y. Harburg (the music was by Jay Gorney), "Brother, Can You Spare a Dime?" Harburg's lyric approached the devastation of the Depression by showing one man's distress—the kind of distress that Larry's hobos laughed through. The song went into a revue called *Americana*. Larry kept an ear open for Harburg's latest work. When Harburg's show *Walk a Little Faster*—this time Vernon Duke was the composer—was opening in Boston, Larry sent him a telegram: HEARD SOME OF YOUR LYRICS THE OTHER DAY AND I HOPE THEY'LL BE AS SUCCESSFUL AS I THINK THEY WILL BE.[8] One of those lyrics was "April in Paris."

Larry began to spend an increasing amount of time with the young producer Leonard Sillman, whose *New Faces* franchise—an extension of the *Garrick Gaieties* type of revue, always cast with the best players Sillman could find—would kick off any year now. "Naturally I had met the fabulous pair," Sillman wrote.

> No theatrical celebrity of any stature was safe from my assiduous wooing in those days, and Rodgers and Hart were then at Peak 4 in their steady assault on Olympus. Rodgers, the family man, the dedicated musician, was but a nodding acquaintance of mine. But Larry Hart—a stay-up-late, a jack-in-the-box, restless, nervous, impatient, buzzing into every corner like a bumble bee—was infinitely more my dish of tea. Between us there had sprung up a friendship that only high-strung insomniacs can understand. Larry was the most generous, the most gentle of geniuses.[9]

Sillman accompanied Larry on his nightly rounds and looked for new talent for a revue he was planning. Larry was concerned about Teddy, who had
long since completed his turn in *Million Dollars Legs* and needed a new role.
Could Sillman give Teddy a break? Sillman regarded Larry's younger brother
as nowhere near as talented as Larry, just with a lot more hair and a comical
lisp that was appropriate for a limited number of roles. But Sillman promised
to keep Teddy in mind.

After Thanksgiving 1932, Larry finally went to New York. His native city
had transformed in ways visible and invisible. The long-embattled Jimmy
Walker had finally resigned as mayor on September 1, replaced by Surrogate
Judge John (Boo Boo) O'Brien, a Tammany yes-man down to his fingertips,
to fill out Walker's unexpired term. Flo Ziegfeld had died during the summer and the Shuberts were moving in on his *Follies* franchise. Lew Fields had
gracefully retired. The new Waldorf-Astoria, forty-one stories high, had been
erected on Park Avenue at Fiftieth Street. Radio City Music Hall, anticipated
to become the greatest of all Art Deco theaters, was nearing completion. The
city's steel-and-concrete muscularity was softened here and there by vestiges
of an older New York: hansom cabs clustering along Central Park South;
bishop's-crook lampposts still lining many of the avenues and recalling an
Edwardian elegance; cast-iron arcades and kiosks that hadn't yet been torn
down; and tugboats, beautiful in their squat, unprepossessing way, pushing
along the Hudson.

In early December, in a botched—or corrupted?—attempt to further provide
for Teddy Hart, Larry agreed to a significant change (probably through his
attorney Abe Wattenberg) in the New York Life insurance policy he had first
taken out in October 1927. Larry changed his beneficiary from Teddy to his
"Executors, Administrators or Assigns," providing that New York Life, as
trustee, would receive the proceeds of the policy and pay it out according to the
following schedule: first Frieda would receive $10,000 and the income on the
balance of the trust for the rest of her life; upon her death, the trustee would
then pay Teddy Hart the balance in installments—but only until the age of
forty, after which he would have no stake in the proceeds of the trust.[10]

If Larry agreed to this, it was because he didn't understand it.

Hallelujah, I'm a Bum! was released on February 8, 1933, in the waning weeks
of the Hoover presidency, as banks around the country fell like dominoes.
Its theme could not have been more timely—nor more wrong for movie

audiences starved for visions of comfort and opulence as well as food. Still, it was something to see.

The movie opens in Florida, where the white hobo Bumper (Al Jolson) and his black sidekick, Acorn (Edgar Connor), run into Mayor Hastings of New York (Frank Morgan). Curiously, Bumper, leader of an encampment of Central Park hoboes, is a derelict version of Hastings. Bumper and Acorn sing "Gotta Get Back to New York," and though it's not a song that can be readily adapted to a nightclub act—indeed, it was written expressly for these displaced characters—it's filled with Larry Hart's love of his native city.

> I want to move these feet
> On each old dirty street.
> New York is New York and that's all you can say.
> It gets in your blood and it's in there to stay.
> I'm one of six million who can't keep away.
> I gotta get back to New York.

Before Bumper and Acorn get home, we see the Mayor playing on a piano the melody of what we will learn is "You Are Too Beautiful." He seems wistful, maybe sadly in love.

In "Bumper's Home Again," Bumper is greeted by his fellow tramps, including the socialist Egghead, played by Harry Langdon. Up to this point the movie—with its gray-toned photography, rhymed dialogue, and always mesmerizing Jolson—has been distinctive enough; but when Langdon enters the picture, it becomes positively eccentric, for the great comic appears in the white makeup he wore during the silent era. Chester Conklin, with his bushy mustache and slightly crossed eyes, is another silent-film great who shows up.

Mayor Hastings lays the cornerstone for P.S. 44, in New York, with everyone in motion and singing "My country 'tis of thee . . ."; and yet the first three familiar notes—"Have . . . you . . . heard?"—of what would become "I Married an Angel" can be made out with each pounding into the ground.[11] There's Dick Rodgers standing next to a photographer!

Mayor Hastings gives his girlfriend, June, a thousand-dollar bill and does so in a way that keeps her dignity intact. But June soon loses her handbag. The Mayor refuses to believe she has lost the money—"I must draw my own conclusions," he says sadly—and chooses instead to believe she has given the money to a friend, a man he mistakes for an old flame. He's devastated. In a garbage bin in Central Park, Bumper, Acorn, and Egghead find the handbag because of the ticking of the little clock inside it—it serves as a metronome for their song, called "Tick Tock"—and, amid the squabbling about what to do with the money, there are wry comments on the gulf between the haves and the have-nots and Egghead's political leanings, which bend to the right once he believes the thousand-dollar bill is real.

"It's from Cartier's," Bumper says of the clock.

"What's Cartier's?" says Acorn.

"Our favorite jewelry store," says Bumper. "The one we patronize."

"We?" says Acorn.

"We?" echoes Egghead.

"The Vanderbilts and me," rhymes Bumper. Larry manages to give a plug for his old friend Jules Glaenzer, who ran Cartier in New York, while invoking the name of one of the knickerbocker families equated with New York wealth.

When Egghead demands half of the $1,000 (not a third, mind you, since the black Acorn is visible to Egghead only insofar as he's linked to Bumper), Bumper has "three little words" for him: "screw, bub, screw." Bumper also finds a postcard in the handbag that provides evidence of the owner's generosity, along with an address on East Fifty-Second Street. In "Bumper Found a Grand," however, even Acorn proves he can be as greedy as any hungry tramp, and no one among the hoboes believes Bumper is correct to return the money to the "lady" who lost it; a thousand bucks will feed the entire encampment for a year. "Money is a curse," sings Bumper; "it's risky business and worse." ("Money, money!" wrote the teenage Larry Hart in his story "The Man Model." "Those who chase it are crazy!") How does one say such things to starving women and men? The hoboes' antagonism prompts the levelheaded Bumper to first sing "What Do You Want with Money?," which might be said to be Larry's variation on "The Best Things in Life Are Free." "Hallelujah, I'm a Bum" reaffirms Bumper's appreciation of those things, and the lyric contains one of Larry's most characteristic images: "The moon's your chandelier." Bumper, who has fallen for June from afar, takes a job in a bank to get close to her and is put on trial by a kangaroo court of his fellow tramps for betraying their cause.

A suicide attempt by June has caused her to lose her memory. Bumper rescues her and addresses her as Angel. In "You Are Too Beautiful," Bumper is singing to a woman who doesn't know who she is. "You are too beautiful, my dear, to be true" goes the opening line of the refrain, and surely Larry, who would take a taxi to the Bronx for a double entendre, meant "true" not only as real but as faithful. (Larry does not stand in judgment.)

Bumper returns the lost handbag and the $1,000 to June. Mayor Hastings, suffering exquisitely from his broken romance with June, arrives home and proclaims, "There's no place like home!"—a familiar maxim even then, six years before *The Wizard of Oz*. Bumper realizes that he and the Mayor are in love with the same woman ("You are too beautiful for one man alone") and effects a reconciliation of the lovers. When Angel recognizes the Mayor, she recovers her identity as June and no longer recognizes Bumper, the shadow mayor. (As young mistress of the prominent Mayor, June anticipates the Sam Coslow song "I'm in Love with the Honorable Mr. So and So," one of the more poignant lyrics of the 1930s.) Bumper, dejected but knowing he did the right thing, slips down a fire escape and strolls back into Central Park, to be welcomed by Acorn and their friends.

Hallelujah, I'm a Bum! aims high and, perhaps even more than *Love Me Tonight*, hits its target, its recitative style absolutely right for its story and its star. Of course, for a moviegoer allergic to Jolson's eager-to-please style, the movie doesn't work. And there have been reams of criticism for the way Edgar Connor's Acorn is portrayed—as little more than a rib to Jolson's Bumper. In an incisive analysis of Connor and his role, the scholar Elizabeth Abel suggested that Connor "comes only to [Jolson's] shoulders and follows him around like a diminutive shadow in all but the love scenes."[12] This is accurate and has sad implications (which Abel teases out) for African-American screen performers of the 1930s, who were usually relegated to playing servants or, like Acorn in *Hallelujah, I'm a Bum!*, sidekicks. But Connor, who had enjoyed a lauded career in vaudeville and burlesque, in some scenes *overshadows* Jolson. Although he was about the size of Larry Hart, it's often Connor you look at, not the attention-grabbing Jolson.

Despite all that extraordinary talent on the screen and all those memorable Rodgers & Hart numbers moving through the movie, *Hallelujah, I'm a Bum!* was a colossal flop. Jolson plugged the picture on his Chevrolet show by singing "You Are Too Beautiful," and then having NBC ban it because the lyric was "too warm for home consumption."[13] But nobody wanted to step into the cinema to look at characters even hungrier than they were. In the face of ongoing bank closings, rampant unemployment, and the ascendancy of Adolf Hitler, who had been named chancellor of Germany on January 30, the movie's failure was hardly noticed outside of United Artists. In New York, it played for a miserable two weeks at the Rivoli before UA yanked it and replaced it with the new Gloria Swanson picture, *Perfect Understanding* (remembered now, if at all, for a turn by the very young Laurence Olivier).[14]

But even before *Hallelujah, I'm a Bum!* proved to be a nonstarter, Dick and Larry were well into their commitment to Metro-Goldwyn-Mayer and Irving Thalberg.

Thalberg's was among the more story-savvy minds in the business. Early in his tenure at MGM, he had distributed his "Ten Commandments for Studio Readers":

1. Your most important duty is to find great ideas. You'll find them buried under tons of mediocre suggestions.
2. Read at least two newspapers daily. Photoplays sell best which are based on timely topics.
3. Analyze all material on the basis of the players working for us. . . .
4. Remember you are dealing with a pictorial medium. . . .
5. Make a close notation of all books you see the public reading.
6. See at least two full-length motion pictures each week, one from this company, one by a competitor. . . .
7. Everything else is secondary in your work to the finding of a strong dramatic situation . . . an interesting clash between the principal characters. . . .
8. Prove your ability to recognize creative material by writing and submitting to us stories of your own.
9. Be proficient in one language besides your own. The competition for good stories is so keen that the supply written in English was long ago insufficient.
10. Above all, train yourself to recognize sincerity in a story. Talking pictures, particularly, have made the public very sensitive to false notes in plots.[15]

Thalberg was intrigued by a story from the Continent—a play titled *Angyalt Vettem Feleségül*, written by Hungarian painter-playwright János Vaszary. The play had come into the studio the previous spring in English translation as *I Married an Angel*. Although Hungarian dramaturgy for decades had been as influential as any contemporary playwriting philosophy, with Ferenc Molnár its exemplar, Vaszary's play was hardly more than a sweet fantasy—"pure Hungarian pastry," in the phrase of theater scholar Mary C. Henderson.[16] The play was about a Budapest banker who, disillusioned by acquisitive women, swears he could marry only an angel—an impossibility, thereby protecting him from marriage after all. Yet an angel does descend into his life and he does indeed marry her. Because she must always tell the truth, however, she turns his life upside down.

The MGM reader assigned to cover it called it "a brilliant and witty comedy."

> The story is new and interesting, the situation humorous, the dialogue excellent, and the moral a pointed one. It would be a "riot" on the screen. One possible objection may arise. What are the ministers going to say to such a film? To this I can only say that in Hungary, a very religious Catholic country, the play was a hit, and the clergy raised no objection to it. I highly recommend it for production.[17]

That the clergy in Hungary raised no objection might have appeared to indemnify the play from American censorship. Thalberg evidently thought so and, believing the project might be right for Jeanette MacDonald, who was now under contract at Metro, brought in the boys who had written such successful songs for *Love Me Tonight*.

The young playwright Moss Hart, who went west after his success with the play *Once in a Lifetime* to investigate the movie business, had signed with Metro a few months earlier and was now assigned to adapt the Vaszary play. The joke around town was that the studio had locked Moss in an office to prevent him from writing another satire on the industry, just as Columbia had locked up Norman Krasna, whose own movie parody was called *Louder, Please*.

Moss Hart worked on *I Married an Angel* well into February, consulting frequently with Dick and Larry while they were writing the songs. By February 24, the boys had written the title song as we know it, but also more than a dozen others. Along the way they were also assigned to write a song for *Peg o' My Heart*, starring Marion Davies, based on the 1912 play by J. Hartley Manners. "When You're Falling Love with the Irish" went no deeper than its title, however, and it was (probably wisely) dropped from the completed film.

Of the *I Married an Angel* songs, several were done in the recitative style that Dick and Larry had honed in *Love Me Tonight* and *Hallelujah, I'm a Bum!* But the most interesting of the other songs is a straight ballad, "Tell Me I Know How to Love," perhaps less for its grounded lyric—there is little of Hart's dazzle—than for the way it so plaintively reveals how the outsider reaches for reassurance.

> *Tell me I know how to love,*
> *Let me hear it from you.*
> *Tell me I know how to love,*
> *And your words will come true.*

And there's a song called "Face the Facts," congested with Hart's trademark cynicism:

> *They sing of springtime*
> *In each cadenza.*
> *It's just a season for catching influenza.*
> *Marriage is surely a space between divorces.*
> *Horses don't divorce.*
> *Let's face the facts.*

In Larry Hart's world, spring brings on not romance and joy so much as hay fever and loneliness. The moon isn't all it's cracked up to be, either. One of Larry's lines in "Face the Facts"—"What is a moon but an ad for propagation / Paid for by the nation?"—drew the ire of James Wingate of the Hays Office.[18] While these songs were being written, Metro and Paramount argued over the title because Paramount had *I'm No Angel*, Mae West's follow-up to *She Done Him Wrong*, ready to go.

Thalberg had suffered a heart attack during holiday festivities at the end of 1932, and was slowly recuperating; since then he had not been seen on the Metro lot. *I Married an Angel* was held in limbo. On the late afternoon of March 10, the boys were waiting for the next assignment when the story editor Sam Marx, who had gone to summer camp with Rodgers and had edited *New York Amusements* before moving to Hollywood, paid a visit to their tiny office.

Not to waste the moment, Dick and Larry launched into "I Married an Angel," Dick seated at the scratched-up baby grand that came with the office, Larry singing the lyric. "Have you heard . . . ?" Suddenly the building began to move.

Larry stopped singing. Dick stopped playing. They both turned to Marx, who had been living in Los Angeles far longer than either of them. "What the hell is that?" asked Larry.

"How the hell should I know?" said Marx.

The rumbling erupted into a kind of shaking that none of them had previously experienced. Dick and Larry were aware that a piano had recently been installed in the room right above them; it could fall right through the ceiling.[19] There was a moment of helplessness before Larry—this is how Sam Marx remembered it—picked up the piano stool, threw it through a window, and then jumped out, with Rodgers and Marx following in his wake. The building they had just exited was still swaying. The largest earthquake to hit Los Angeles in decades, it was all over before 6:00 P.M.[20] The earthquake was responsible for the deaths of approximately one hundred people.

The earthquake also interrupted a conference, held on the top floor of the Hollywood Roosevelt, of studio heads attempting to respond to the March 5 decision made by the newly inaugurated Franklin Delano Roosevelt to close the banks. The result of that conference was a new wave of movie industry unemployment and a 50 percent pay cut—a development that would give new momentum to the formation of the Screen Actors Guild.[21] In April the Screen Writers Guild, responding to the salary cuts made seemingly by fiat, would become a closed shop. Lingering was the question of whether studio heads had been moved to do their part in the national belt-tightening or were attempting, clumsily, to sabotage the new president.

Industry gossip about Irving Thalberg was rampant. One insider would insist the Boy Genius would be back in the studio any day now; the next insider would whisper that Thalberg was through. Offering $4,000 a week and production budgets topping half a million dollars, Louis B. Mayer brought in his son-in-law, David O. Selznick, from RKO. Selznick, who had attended Weingart Institute after Larry and before Dick, was already known as one of the most dynamic, take-charge executives in the industry. After venting his spleen at Mayer, who had handled the transition of power with characteristic indelicacy, Thalberg departed on February 27 with his wife, Norma Shearer, for New York, as far from Culver City as he could get, and from there sailed alone to Europe.

❧   ❧   ❧

I Married an Angel was still alive, although, without Thalberg on the lot, it was hard to tell for how long. Word was out that FDR had personally phoned Will Hays wanting to know what these industry-wide, 50 percent salary cuts were meant to accomplish—and also wondering if the Republican Will Hays had met with ex-President Hoover at the Waldorf-Astoria to cook up this very ruse, which did nothing to boost the national economy and everything to consolidate power among the top movie executives.[22]

In mid-April the Nazis halted imports of American movies, closed every German film studio that was not conforming to Nazi dogma, and scrubbed its film industry of "all Jewish elements," which would leave it as dry and desiccated as old nitrate film stock.[23] In the third week of April the studio bosses, intimidated by Roosevelt, announced that full salaries would be restored to all contract employees.[24] The pay reduction had lasted for eight weeks.

MGM began to toss assignments at Rodgers and Hart like paper airplanes. The studio needed songs for *The Hollywood Revue*, and it was never a secret that Rodgers & Hart was simply one team of many. The all-star theme of the movie was illustrated by a memo Howard Dietz sent to Louis B. Mayer: "Essential to get as many prominent players in this scene as possible, just filing into the party. Myrna Loy, Madge Evans, Jack Oakie, Wallace Beery, etc. etc."[25]

"We're working hard at the studio trying to finish up," Rodgers wrote to his wife, "but Larry is hell. Luckily Dietz realizes that I'm not to blame, but it's worse than pulling teeth to get a lyric from him. When it comes it's good, but the aggravation!"[26]

Now Selznick wanted Dick and Larry for his new melodrama, *Dancing Lady*. The boys knew they were caught in the middle of a studio power struggle. Harry Rapf waddled through the hall, ranting that he was not going to share his songwriters with Selznick. Under other circumstances, the boys might have felt flattered. To calm Rapf, they took him back to their office and played him what they'd just completed, "You Are," a goofy love song written for the radio comedian Jack Pearl in his familiar ("Vas you dere, Sharlie?") dialect. Rapf screamed with joy over the song, but he was still burning about the way Louis B.'s son-in-law had marched onto the lot and taken over.[27]

Through most of this MGM chaos Dorothy Rodgers was in New York for surgery at Lenox Hill hospital, having left daughter Mary with Dick in Beverly Hills. Larry was still overseeing a Beverly Hills houseful. One evening, after ducking the executive cross fire at Metro, Dick drove over to Larry's to review the situation. On North Bedford Drive jacaranda blossoms were sprinkled across the roofs and hoods of the cars; the sweet aroma of honeysuckle filled the air. Dick went inside and found "a terrifically wild party in progress, consisting of Mrs. Hart, Mel [Shauer], and a few harmless boys playing twenty-one at a penny a chip! Mrs. H lost seventy-five cents, and was she burned!"[28]

A couple of nights later Larry dragged Dick out to Pasadena to see *Low and Behold*, the Leonard Sillman revue that had been gestating for so long. Larry wanted to be there not only to support Sillman but to cheer on his brother, Teddy, whom Sillman had cast in the revue after all. Sillman was intent on tweaking "morally hidebound" Pasadena.[29] Toward that end his skits were risqué, if not terribly witty. Holding the train of the gown worn by one of the Rocky Twins was a young dancer named Chuck Walters, who would become a frequent guest at Larry's house and eventually, with a letter of introduction from him, move to New York to act.[30] All this drag material left Rodgers cold, but Larry, as usual, was having a fine time.

The following week both men attended the first night of the Pacific Coast production of the Kern-Hammerstein *Music in the Air*, at the Belasco. The boys agreed the production was shoddy but swooned over Vivienne Segal, by now a seasoned trouper who seemed so much more carnal than the nice-virgin roles she usually played. Larry went to see her backstage. Small as Segal was, Larry was still looking up at her. "Kid, you've been miscast all your life," he said.

"Miscast?" said Segal with a half-smile, neither agreeing nor disagreeing.

"Producers think of you as an ingenue because you look like one. But you're siren through and through."

"Then write me a siren part," Segal said.

There were more songs to write for the all-star revue, which was now being called *Hollywood Party*. Two separate songs with that title were prepared by Rodgers and Hart and both of them were used in the completed movie. In one of these, Larry rhymes "At that crashing" and "Furniture-smashing" and double-rhymes "All the minks and sables, / Wine with labels, / Garbo-Gables." In that lyric, and in the one called "Baby Stars" ("Fresh from Peoria, Troy and Emporia"), Larry sounds once again like he's anticipating Johnny Mercer's more renowned lyric in "Hooray for Hollywood." A number called "I'm One of the Boys," meant for Marie Dressler to sing while dressed like

Marlene Dietrich (although triple her girth), was completed the second week of June:

> *I'm one of the boys, girls—just one of the boys.*
> *I go to the tailor that Marlene employs.*
> *No dresses from France are*
> *So modern as these,*
> *And under my pants are*
> *B.V.D.s*
> *I'm one of the boys, girls, I'm one of the boys.*
> *I handle a big cigar with manly poise.*
> *Once I was maternal,*
> *Now they call me Colonel.*
> *I'm one of the boys, one of the boys!*[31]

To present-day musical theater aficionados, the lyric might recall the Kander-Ebb song "One of the Boys," written for Lauren Bacall to sing in their 1981 show *Woman of the Year*, as well as its delicious parody in Gerard Alessandrini's *Forbidden Broadway*.

What Alessandrini could get away with in the 1980s, however, Rodgers and Hart could not in 1933. "With regard to 'I'm One of the Boys,'" the Hays Office's James Wingate wrote to Metro executive Eddie Mannix, "we would caution you against playing this in any way which might be suggestive of lesbianism—which we naturally assume you will do." [32] The previous year, when Dietrich strode through the Hollywood Roosevelt wearing a man's suit tailored to make her hips look like a man's, she didn't do it to attract the bellboys. The song was dropped. Also dropped was a bizarre rhumba for Lupe Vélez called "You've Got That." Writing for and with Jimmy Durante seemed almost second nature now to Dick and Larry, and so the trio came up with "Reincarnation," one of the many songs that Durante *owns*—nobody else can touch it.

There might have been as many as another dozen numbers written for *Hollywood Party*. "Fly Away to Ioway," which spoofed "Shuffle Off to Buffalo," from *42nd Street*, was dropped. The Durante number "Give a Man a Job," which celebrated FDR and the New Deal, was turned into a seven-minute short subject.[33] Another Durante number found its way into *Meet the Baron*, the Jack Pearl–Jimmy Durante comedy that grew out of the *Hollywood Party* project. (Pearl's MGM contract called for him to complete two pictures for the studio by December 31, 1933.)[34] The song that everyone remembers also did not, in fact, make it into the finished film. Written for Jean Harlow, it was called "Prayer," about a young woman who wants to be a movie star, and it had the melody of what we know as "Blue Moon."

Simultaneously, Dick and Larry were writing at least three songs for Selznick's *Dancing Lady*. The source material, written by James Warner Bellah, had been serialized in *The Saturday Evening Post* a year earlier. It chronicled the misadventures of a slum girl who works as a call girl, attracts and marries a millionaire playboy, goes through financial havoc with him, then is widowed and resumes her former career. The shooting script probably ripped off bits from *Our Dancing Daughters*, one of the semi-talkies to be released in 1928, starring Joan Crawford. For *Dancing Lady*, in fact, Selznick signed Crawford, who was reluctant to play a hooker until Selznick implied that Jean Harlow wanted the role. "I was playing hookers before Harlow knew what a hooker was!" snapped Crawford.[35] Set with his leading lady, Selznick subsequently signed her new fiancé, Franchot Tone, to play the millionaire. "Get a load of Park Avenue, will you?" sneers Crawford when she first encounters the nattily dressed Tone in the movie. The leading man is actually Clark Gable, but Tone's ophidian grin may be the most memorable thing about the movie. Also in the mix were the Three Stooges (who were then attached to comic Ted Healy), an unbilled Eve Arden, and, in his screen debut, Fred Astaire.

Of the songs Dick and Larry wrote for *Dancing Lady*, a version of the title song bore a stark resemblance, in its depiction of round-the-clock performing and resulting weariness, to "Ten Cents a Dance." That song, as well as a later version, would not be used, but Selznick's first response to it was so enthusiastic that he asked Dick and Larry to commit to writing the songs for his upcoming production of *The Prisoner of Zenda*. For a minute or so, the boys felt pretty good. "Lover," from *Love Me Tonight*, had hit the charts. And Samuel Goldwyn was calling to see if they'd be available late in the summer to write songs for his new picture, *Nana*. Goldwyn said he would negotiate with MGM for their services. For Selznick's *Dancing Lady*, they knocked out "That's the Rhythm of the Day," introduced by Nelson Eddy, who was also making his screen debut. But the song from the movie that was heartily embraced was "Everything I Have Is Yours," by Burton Lane and Harold Adamson, who had just been sent out by Irving Berlin Music on a six-week contract.

⚓   ⚓   ⚓

At the Cocoanut Grove, actor-singer Art Jarrett, who introduced the McHugh-Fields "My Dancing Lady" in the Selznick picture—and who had recently become engaged to swimming star Eleanor Holm—sang "I Married an Angel" on radio station KHJ, which was suddenly deluged with requests for the music. *Where can I find that song?* It was right around then—midsummer, shortly before Irving Thalberg returned to his office—that Louis B. Mayer scrapped *I Married an Angel*. Mayer was offended that the principal characters would cohabit without being married.[36] The Hays Office, too, would have had a fit. Those fresh, startling songs? Gone—at least for now.

But Dick and Larry hardly had a moment to sulk. With Arthur Hornblow running interference between them and Sam Goldwyn, they were soon preparing—with Metro's blessing, for they were still under contract there—to tackle the songs for *Nana,* adapted from Zola's 1880 novel about a young prostitute rising out of the slums of Paris. Larry, well-acquainted with the entire *Les Rougon-Macquart* series of novels—probably because they were considered "dirty" in their time—of which *Nana* was one, had already come up with the perfect song title: "Nana Loves Papa." Hornblow had a good laugh at that one.[37]

It was Hornblow, then serving as Sam Goldwyn's editorial chief, who had steered the project to United Artists. Originally owned by Paramount, the *Nana* adaptation had been slated in August 1931 to be the new Marlene Dietrich–Josef von Sternberg collaboration. The following year, fifty-two years after its publication in France, the novel went into public domain. Hornblow had the material overhauled by playwright George Oppenheimer until it proved cautiously satisfactory to Wingate of the Hays Office.

Although photography on *Nana* would not begin until August 1933, Dick and Larry worked on the songs. Near the end of June, they finally met actress Anna Sten—perhaps the object of Goldwyn's deepest (and to some observers most perplexing) crush. Sten was then thirty-two, a former student of Stanislavski's, with only the little English that Goldwyn's publicity chief Lynn Farnol had been able to teach her thus far. "Larry, I don't care what they write about me," Goldwyn said to Hart, "as long as they mention Anna Sten."[38] There was no secret about Goldwyn's enchantment. Even Cole Porter took a poke at it:

> *If Goldwyn can with great conviction*
> *Instruct Anna Sten in diction,*

Then Anna shows
Anything goes....[39]

Every minute all over the world, men become smitten with much younger women, but few of them can mount an entire film production around the object of their affection.

"We met Anna Sten yesterday and heard her sing," Dick wrote to Dorothy. "Her voice is like Dietrich's and not too hot, but the big disappointment was the lady herself. On the screen she's positively ravishing, but in a room all you see is a chunky peasant with tremendous hips and no breasts. She's a pleasant person, though."[40]

A few days later Dick went to Larry's house and, much to his shock, found that his partner had completed, without the usual prodding, a new lyric for "That's Love," to a "French type" tune Dick had written. They drove to United Artists and played the song for Hornblow and Alfred Newman. Both wildly enthusiastic, Hornblow and Newman ushered the boys in to see Goldwyn, who listened to the song and then phoned Anna Sten to tell her "That's Love" was the best song he had ever heard. "Boys, I thank you from the bottom of my heart!" he said to Dick and Larry. "Now I'm in love with Goldwyn," the not-easily-flattered Rodgers admitted later.[41]

Even if "That's Love" had been the loveliest song ever written, there was a limit to Sten's capabilities. Before *Nana* went into principal photography, George Oppenheimer, a Goldwyn aide, directed a trailer to advertise the film. Sten appeared first as herself and then dissolved into the character she was to play, with the lines, "Now I am Anna; now I am Nana." "Unhappily," Oppenheimer wrote, "her accent was so thick that 'Anna' and 'Nana' sounded identical."[42]

Dick and Larry were at once overworked and, by their lights, underemployed. They each spent time with Herb Fields, who was bunking in with his older brother Joe and Joe's wife. They saw a fair amount of Broadway refugee Edgar Selwyn, who had come west to rebuild the Selwyn brothers' fortune lost in the crash of '29. One evening Frieda Hart showed up at Dick's house on Angelo Drive and, as Larry always did, brought a present for Mary, who was not yet three.

"Thank you very much," Mary said as she inspected the little taffeta pocketbook. "Is there money in the pocketbook?"

"No, dollink," Frieda corrected. "That is a *poice!* Now you can go *chopping!*" [43]

Dick and Larry attended a party at Ernst Lubitsch's house, where the host played piano duets with one and smoked cigars with the other. Many of the guests, like Lubitsch, had fled Europe in recent years, and there was plenty of talk of the rise of Nazism. The jokes told around the wet bar had a peculiarly *Yiddishkeit* flavor:

> Two Jewish Sea Gulls are flying over Hamburg when they spy a parade.
>   First Jewish Sea Gull: "Morris, there's Hitler!"
>   Second Jewish Sea Gull: "Well, what are we waiting for?" [44]

At MGM the songwriters were stuck in another dingy office. To facilitate happier work time, Dick and Larry took a bungalow at the Beverly Hills Hotel. "Larry's already in the hands of the Little Folk," Dick wrote to Dorothy—meaning the gay friends who had been encouraged to drop in on him. The old pro Sigmund Romberg, it turned out, was in a bungalow across the court. Quite apart from the way his presence on or around various Rodgers & Hart projects of the past had signaled bad luck, Romberg, perhaps more than any other prominent composer in the theater, was often accused of appropriating the melodies of others. Working one afternoon in their bungalow, Dick and Larry could hear Romberg playing a Tchaikovsky piano concerto over and over. "Listen," said Larry, holding his cigar aloft, "Rommy's busy on another score." [45]

Although they shared many friends and professional acquaintances, Dick and Larry usually went their separate ways after dark. Dick dined and played piano at the homes of people he deemed important. Larry, usually wearing one of the white suits he thought appropriate for the Los Angeles climate, visited nightspots where he could find good conversation and drink. By midsummer of 1933, the question was no longer if Prohibition would end, but *when*; and whenever it ended, it would once again alter the way homosexual women and men congregated. For his part, Larry could have sneaked off to parties overlooking the ocean in Malibu or in the Hollywood Hills. But he leaned toward the comfort and companionability of nightclubs, even after favorite host Jean Malin accidentally drove off the Venice Pier in August and drowned.

One warm evening later that summer, while Larry was God knows where else, Dick attended a party in West Los Angeles. He was standing on the lawn in front of the house when the publisher of a Hollywood trade magazine—some evidence points to *The Hollywood Reporter*'s Billy Wilkerson, who was amassing his own string of clubs on the Sunset Strip—approached him.

"I've got to ask you something about Larry," the publisher said.

"What is it?"

"Is it true Larry's a fairy?"

Blood rushed to Rodgers's cheeks. "I never heard that," he said. He grabbed the man by the collar. "And if you print it," he said, "I'll kill you."

The publisher went pale and backed away. Was Dick being protective of Larry, or self-protective? Maybe a bit of both. While Larry was alive, no item about his homosexuality ever appeared in print. "Never a suggestion of it," Rodgers said, "and there was never anything in print about his drinking, either. And I know why: because the newspaper people were all crazy about him. They knew it would damage him."[46]

November turned out to be a thankless month. *Meet the Baron*—the title was a shortening of Baron Munchausen, Jack Pearl's radio character—was still in chaotic production, with a script assembled from bits and pieces by at least seven writers, including Dorothy Fields. (When it was finally released, the single most exciting thing about it was stock footage of the Hudson River and the Manhattan skyline.) *Dancing Lady* was released on November 1, and it was crushing to Dick and Larry to see all that pressurized work reduced to one Nelson Eddy number. They thought of walking away from their MGM contract. Fortunately, Irving Thalberg—back at work after several months' convalescence at Bad Nauheim, Germany—told them he had something for them: new songs were needed for Lubitsch's remake of Franz Lehár's *The Merry Widow*. This had been a dream project of Thalberg's since 1930, when he'd taken a look at Paramount's *Love Parade* and tried to borrow Ernst Lubitsch and stars Jeanette MacDonald and Maurice Chevalier for a Metro *Merry Widow*.[47] It had taken three years to make it happen. Even now, not everything was in place. Thalberg had wanted *The Merry Widow* filmed in the new three-color Technicolor process, but he was subsequently persuaded of the idea's unfeasibility.[48] It would be weeks before a leading lady was settled on, with Joan Crawford, Gloria Swanson, and Grace Moore all considered for the title role before MacDonald was signed. Then Thalberg had to muffle Chevalier's vocalized dismay at having to work again with either Lubitsch or MacDonald, with transatlantic and transcontinental phone calls to smooth things over. And Lehár rejected Metro's request to write new tunes for the *Merry Widow* remake; the old ones were just fine, thank you very much. Lehár would keep an open mind, however, about another composer contributing melodies.[49]

If this turned out to be not quite what Dick and Larry had in mind, they knew that the assignment, coming on the heels of the cross-eyed *Hollywood Party* and its idiot stepchild *Meet the Baron*, was a lucky thing to have.

During Thanksgiving week it was reported that the industry's weekly box office grosses had hit rock bottom, with losses for the previous two and a half months amounting to $10 million. Word came that Texas Guinan had died in Vancouver, of colitis, and her body was being shipped back to New York by train. Her fame coincided almost precisely with Prohibition, which officially ended on December 5, 1933, with legal-liquor celebrations across the nation.[50]

One morning a few days before Christmas, Dick went to the Beverly-Wilshire for breakfast. He had several newspapers with him. The New York papers were filled with stories about Eleanor Roosevelt's holiday plans; about the mayor-elect, Fiorello La Guardia; and about Broadway. Moss Hart, who went home to New York while Hollywood still wanted him, was enjoying the long run of his show *As Thousands Cheer*, with music by Irving Berlin. George M. Cohan's career was being given an enormous boost by his role as the leading man in the Theatre Guild's production of Eugene O'Neill's *Ah, Wilderness!* The Gershwin-Ryskind *Let 'Em Eat Cake*, the follow-up to *Of Thee I Sing*, was doing brisk business at the Imperial. And the Kern-Harbach musical *Roberta*, which could brag about "Smoke Gets in Your Eyes" and the young comic actor Bob Hope, had already been snapped up by the movies. Dick picked up the *Los Angeles Examiner* and turned to "Once Overs," the syndicated column by the New York–based writer O. O. McIntyre. For many years "Odd" McIntyre had presided over a Hearst column called "New York Day by Day" in a style that, when lined up alongside Winchell's rat-a-tat-tat prose, had come to seem quaint. "Once Overs" often included the phrase "what happened to?" in reference to people whose celebrity seemed to be in eclipse. Dick scanned the day's column:

One word description of Arthur Hopkins—dimply. What happened to Rodgers and Hart? Wonder how Irving Caesar would look in a monocle? Helen Mencken among the big stars again with renewed sparkle.[51]

Wait! What?! Dick reread the sentence, "What happened to Rodgers and Hart?" He asked his waiter for a telephone.

"Larry," he said urgently, "we've got to get out of here!"

CHAPTER 14

I Heard Somebody Whisper,
"Please Adore Me"

LEAVING HOLLYWOOD immediately was out of the question: the Merry Widow assignment had to be completed, with Larry translating the original German lyrics by Victor Léon and Leo Stein, and Dick providing some underscoring and, if asked, a few new melodies. On weekdays through February and March 1934, Larry met with Lubitsch, who did not happily tolerate his chronic tardiness and found his tendency to write lyrics on paper scraps—a cocktail napkin, a tissue, the back of an envelope—an appallingly disorderly practice.[1] They made an odd pair, Lubitsch and Hart, two squat, dark-eyed, cigar-smoking, cosmopolitan, highly literate men, each a potential poster boy for the physical traits Nazi eugenics targeted.

Rodgers liked to say that this period in Hollywood was idle for him—that Larry had to report to Lubitsch most days with new English lyrics, while Rodgers spent his afternoons at the Beverly Hills Tennis Club and nights playing bridge.[2] This was only half-true: Rodgers was composing for The Merry Widow, too.

Jeanette MacDonald arrived on the Paramount lot after canceling a world concert tour. Chevalier, chastened by Thalberg and on his best behavior, managed to mask his distaste for MacDonald. But he could barely hide his distaste for Larry's sexuality. Chevalier's assistant Robert Spencer, a dancer-model whom he had hired out of the chorus of Ballyhoo in 1931, recalled that his employer was always on the lookout for homosexuals, real or imagined. At the commencement of principal photography on The Merry Widow,

Chevalier warned Spencer to steer clear of Hart "or he'll try to get into your pants."[3] There's no evidence that Larry tried. If he had, it would have been that rare thing—a recorded attempt at seduction by a man who didn't believe himself capable of seducing his own shadow.

But Larry's lyrics could still be disarmingly seductive. None of the original songs that he and Dick wrote for *The Merry Widow* were kept in the released film, but the two written for Chevalier are infused with Hart's naughty-boy suggestiveness. In "It Must Be Love," the love-crazed Danilo (Chevalier) sings "I don't feel like drinking / Yet I keep drinking"—a familiar Hart kind of repetition in a lyric that seems like a rehearsal for "It's Got to Be Love" two years later. To Una Merkel's Dolores, Danilo professes his admiration for something in her that "has made a nation wild" and declares she has "something that beats any pen"—innuendo that puzzled censor Joe Breen, who interrogated Louis B. Mayer about what Larry had in mind.[4] (As if Mayer would know!)

The lyrics to the Lehár melodies were somewhat less risqué, most of them hewing close to the German originals. Yet many of these adapted lines contain Hart's patented wordplay. "When there's wine and there's women and song," goes the second refrain of "Girls, Girls, Girls!," "It is wrong not to do something wrong!" In the "Merry Widow Waltz," one of the most performed and recorded melodies of the twentieth century, is the couplet "I never knew before / How much I could adore"—a recurring Hart theme. "Maxim's," "where all the girls are dreams," is adapted from the original "I'm Off to Chez Maxime," and Larry retains the girls' names ("Lo-lo, Do-do," etc.) but—almost certainly with Lubitsch's approval, if not by his command—deletes the original's reference to the "beloved Fatherland," which in early 1934 already pulsated with Hitlerian hatred. And in "Vilia," Larry uses the Gypsy-evocative phrase "The song of the shepherd who cried for the moon." In the Hart solar system, the relationship between human and moon was continually revolving and evolving.

The Merry Widow was as bubbly as a glass of Moët & Chandon Imperial. "You knew [*The Merry Widow*] was a Lubitsch film before it started," S. N. Behrman wrote.[5] The credits are shown against a backdrop of half-notes and quarter-notes. Later, through a geographer's magnifying glass, we peer at a map of southeastern Europe to locate Prince Danilo's country, tiny Marshovia, tucked up against Romania, which Danilo will desert for Paris in pursuit of the merry widow (MacDonald) who owns 52 percent of the principality.

The action is set in the already long-ago of 1885. Besides the Lehár-Hart songs and the gorgeous production design by Cedric Gibbons, there is some very funny dialogue (probably written by Samson Raphaelson). In Marshovia, during the crisis created by the widow's defection to Paris, the principality's king (George Barbier) instructs his agent, "The opinion of the shepherd on the street—that's what I most want to know," and he dismisses "East Side shepherds" as intellectuals. Even in mythical Marshovia, we're never far from the crackling New York idiom.

Following Thalberg's suggestion, Lubitsch filmed *The Merry Widow* in French as well as in English. (Lyrics for the French version were probably translated by André Hornes.) Thalberg, ever mindful of foreign box office possibilities and aware that the film's two stars could sing in German, requested a German version, too. But Bob Vogel, head of Metro's international distribution arm, took Thalberg aside. "Mr. Hitler is starting to get very tough about Jewish names," Vogel told him, "and with Ernst Lubitsch's name up there on the masthead, and yours, I'm not sure the picture will be released."[6] No German version was filmed by MGM.

Lubitsch's *Merry Widow* turned out to be one of the last of the movie musicals set in mythic European kingdoms or in real capital cities rendered as they might exist in a pleasant dream. By 1934 the contemporary Hollywood musical belonged to Busby Berkeley. The tongue-in-cheek charm of a French career soldier gaily seducing a merry widow (or duchess or princess) had come from another era—one that Lubitsch preferred, perhaps, to his own.

After their work on *The Merry Widow* was completed, Dick and his family and Larry made plans to head home—at least for a while. In New York, on March 15, 1934, Leonard Sillman's *New Faces*, a thoroughly reworked (and cleaned-up) version of *Low and Behold*, opened at the Fulton Theatre, with a cast that included Imogene Coca, Henry Fonda, Larry's young friend Charles Walters—but no Teddy Hart. Actress–fashion plate Lilyan Tashman ("not kissed by an ashman," Larry wrote in "I've Got Five Dollars"), who was in New York making a picture at the Biograph studio on East 175th Street, died at thirty-four after an operation at Doctors Hospital.[7] The Nazis were on everyone's mind. The Jewish Theatre Guild was perversely pretending to enlist Father Coughlin, the Detroit radio priest who blamed Jews and "Franklin Delano Rosenfeld" for the Depression, to emcee an anti-Nazi fund-raising drive. One Guild member proposed buying space at the bottom of every newspaper's obituary page to read, "And Hitler lives!"

Right before Rodgers and Hart went east, Rodgers stopped by Thalberg's cottage on the MGM lot to thank him for his support. Rodgers found Thalberg seated at a conference table flanked by several executives. "Larry and I are leaving today and I just wanted to say good-bye," said Rodgers. Thalberg looked back at Rodgers with a glassy stare, and Rodgers realized that the young production head—foremost among the few men who could, in F. Scott Fitzgerald's words, "keep the whole equation of pictures in their heads"—did not have the vaguest idea who he was.[8]

It was a disappointing send-off from their longest stint in Hollywood. Larry went home to 415 Central Park West. Dick, Dorothy, and Mary reclaimed their East Seventy-Seventh Street apartment, which they had rented to another family during this most recent absence. The place had been left in such wretched condition that Dorothy spent weeks hunting down various kinds of craftsmen and fix-it shops to make necessary repairs. Both households—the Rodgerses' on the East Side, the Harts' on the West Side—attended the Shuberts' revival of Noël Coward's *Bitter Sweet*, which had performed so elegantly at the Ziegfeld in late 1929 before stepping aside for *Simple Simon*. Other than the Coward, there wasn't much in town they felt compelled to see. Expected back in Los Angeles to fulfill a commitment they had made to Arthur Hornblow and Paramount, they would have preferred to arrange something for themselves in New York.

During this brief spring interval, Larry saw a lot of his friend Nanette Guilford, the Metropolitan Opera star. Born in 1905, Guilford was one of hundreds of babies in the city delivered by Dr. William Rodgers throughout his long career. Grandniece of Lew Fields's partner Joe Weber, Guilford made her debut at the Met in 1923 in a minor role in *Rigoletto*. Less than three years later she appeared for the first time in a prima donna role, in Giordano's *The Jest*, and after that was known as the "baby star" of the Met. (Larry always called her "Baby," but then he called middle-aged men "Baby.") In 1928 Guilford married the violinist Max Rosen, who had grown up on the Lower East Side with David Freeman and Irving Caesar. Fifteen months later the marriage was over. Seeking a Mexican divorce, Guilford camped out in Beverly Hills while Rodgers and Hart were working at Warner Bros. She felt particularly close to Larry, who admired her musical gifts, her mastery of German, and her caustic humor. Referring to the way Max Rosen had so off-handedly proposed to her during a lunchtime walk down Seventh Avenue, Guilford liked to say that she "yawned" into the marriage.[9]

The Harts—Larry (then known as Lorry), Max, Frieda, and Teddy—photographed at the commencement of the twentieth century. The Hart parents were originally from Hamburg. Max worked as a coal broker, insurance broker, real estate broker, speculator, and scam artist. His older son loved him but didn't always like him.

Richard Rodgers and Larry Hart, 1925, on the eve of their first Broadway success with *The Garrick Gaieties*. Rodgers was about to turn twenty-three; Hart had just turned thirty.

3

Larry, in the first flush of theatrical fame, with his ever-present cigar, 1925.

4

Herbert Fields, Rodgers, and Hart, of the musical firm Fields, Rodgers, and Hart, late 1920s. Fields had known the other two men in childhood and remained friendly with them long after he began to write the books for Cole Porter's shows.

Maurice Chevalier, Jeanette MacDonald, and director Ernst Lubitsch on the set of *The Merry Widow*, celebrating MacDonald's thirty-first birthday, June 1934. Larry Hart wrote English versions of the original German lyrics, which Lubitsch loved, though he had little tolerance for Larry's chronic tardiness and disorganization.

Rodgers and Hart at work, 1936.

Myrna Loy, Maurice Chevalier, and Jeanette MacDonald in the great Rouben Mamoulian–Rodgers & Hart collaboration, *Love Me Tonight* (1932), among the few truly innovative musical films of the century. "Isn't It Romantic?" passes from Chevalier, as the poor but happy tailor, is picked up and relayed by several other serenading characters, and at last finds its way to MacDonald as the lovelorn princess in her château—and that's only the beginning.

Edgar Connor, Harry Langdon, Al Jolson, and Madge Evans in the charming, undervalued 1933 movie *Hallelujah, I'm a Bum!*, with songs and recitative by Rodgers and Hart. The Riviera Country Club, in Pacific Palisades, California, was meant to approximate the look of New York's Central Park.

Lew Fields and Joe Weber—Weber & Fields—among the most durable of vaudeville acts, officially parted after a twenty-year partnership but reunited frequently, on the stage and then on radio, for another thirty years. Lew Fields, Rodgers and Hart's theatrical father, was the biological father of the team's longtime partner, Herbert Fields, and of Dorothy Fields, who wrote in Larry Hart's voice until she found her own.

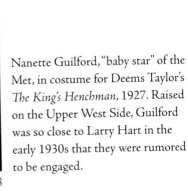

Nanette Guilford, "baby star" of the Met, in costume for Deems Taylor's *The King's Henchman*, 1927. Raised on the Upper West Side, Guilford was so close to Larry Hart in the early 1930s that they were rumored to be engaged.

Hart and Rodgers in *Makers of Melody* (1929), a two-reeler that purported to track their careers up till then. Filmed in Astoria, Queens, the shot shows the boys still looking at each other with affection.

The young Vivienne Segal, 1929. She and Larry Hart knew of each other at the time but wouldn't meet for another few years.

Ross Alexander, Lee Dixon, and Teddy Hart in *Ready, Willing and Able* (1937). Teddy, Larry's beloved younger brother, was frequently used by the movies for the physical contrast his diminutive size provided, and for a slight lisp that could add a kick to a line of dialogue.

Tamara Geva, George Church, and Ray Bolger in Rodgers and Hart's *On Your Toes*, 1936. It was probably the first Broadway musical to make the dancer—rather than the tenor or the baritone or the comic— the show's hero.

15

Wynn Murray and Alfred Drake, two of the gang of young performers in the original production of Rodgers and Hart's *Babes in Arms*, 1937. The musical featured primarily juveniles—all under twenty-six, anyway—but was squarely aimed at adults, and included five songs that became American standards.

Larry Hart and Richard Rodgers, probably at their favorite lunch spot, Dinty Moore, January 1938.

15

The Fields family, three of whom were professionally intertwined for many years with Rodgers and Hart. The photo was probably taken in the late 1930s. On the grass, left to right: Frances Fields Marcus, Dorothy Fields, Herb Fields. Seated: Lew Fields and Rose Harris Fields. Standing: Joseph Fields.

While Richard Rodgers preferred to stay with his family on Long Island, Vera Zorina, then starring in Rodgers and Hart's *I Married an Angel*, saw George Balanchine and Larry Hart onto the Grace liner *Santa Paula*, June 1938. The men were off on a sixteen-day cruise, intending to work on dance ideas and lyrics for what would become *The Boys from Syracuse*.

Marcy Wescott, Wynn Murray, and Muriel Angelus in the rousing "Sing for Your Supper," in Rodgers and Hart's *The Boys from Syracuse*, 1938.

Alex Gard's caricature of Larry hung among hundreds of other theater caricatures on the wall at Sardi's. Gard and Vincent Sardi, Sr., had an understanding: Sardi wouldn't criticize the drawings if Gard didn't criticize the meals he received as payment.

Richard Kollmar, Eddie Bracken, Hal Le Roy, and Desi Arnaz as the college footballers hired to protect coed Consuelo (Marcy Wescott) in Rodgers and Hart's *Too Many Girls*, 1939. The show made Arnaz a star, its film version introducing him to Lucille Ball.

"A Bevy of Beauties" surrounds Juana de Dios Castrello, also known as Diosa Costello, in *Too Many Girls*. Desi Arnaz wrote that the Guayama, Puerto Rico, native could "shake her ass better and faster than anyone."

Larry Hart and Richard Rodgers working on *Pal Joey*, autumn 1940,
in a bamboo chaise on the roof of 875 Park Avenue.

Shirley Paige and Gene Kelly in Rodgers and Hart's *Pal Joey*. Because Joey was amoral, Kelly's dancing had to be so dynamic and attractive that audiences would wait to see what the character did next.

Vivienne Segal and Gene Kelly in their little den of iniquity, *Pal Joey*, December 1940. By the time of the show's opening, Segal had a stronger rapport with Larry Hart than any woman except his mother.

Appearing at once dapper and Runyonesque, Hart posed for this photo in 1942, during rehearsals for *By Jupiter*, which he and Rodgers adapted from the play *The Warrior's Husband*.

During revisions of *By Jupiter*, a characteristic scowl from Rodgers while he and producer Dwight Deere Wiman (leaning against the cabinet) wait for a new lyric from Larry.

Ray Bolger and Constance Moore
in *By Jupiter,* 1942. It was the
last lavish Broadway musical
produced for the duration
of World War II.

A clerk (Clinton Sundberg) waits
on Larry Hart (Mickey Rooney) in
Words and Music, MGM's musical
biopic of Rodgers and Hart, produced
in 1948, five years after Hart's death.
For the last decade of his life, Larry
wore Adler elevator shoes; in the
movie they're known as Backett's Built
Up Shoes.

The Hart family plot at Mt. Zion Cemetery, Maspeth, Queens.

Now Guilford and Larry were both home in New York. They attended the theater together, and the opera, where Larry wore top hat and tails. "Those were dress-up days," Guilford remembered many years later, "and you wore formal clothes almost everywhere. . . . We were leaving the opera one night. As we waited for a cab, a couple of rowdies ridiculed and taunted him. Though he appeared to ignore them, he never wore a top hat again."[10]

In May 1934, Guilford was rehearsing a musical show called *Caviar*, in which she was to play an American prima donna who marries a Russian prince—solely, she believes, for the publicity value—until she realizes she really loves him. Guilford had become so distressed by the state of the show that Larry agreed to come to the theater in secret and rehearse the cast on his own.

Meanwhile, *Manhattan Melodrama* was released with that same stuck-in-the-head tune Rodgers had written for "Prayer." In the film, "The Bad in Every Man" was sung by Shirley Ross; a still earlier version was an attempt at a title song but dropped. If you sing the following lines to the refrain of "Blue Moon," you can hear what Larry was going for.

Act One:
You gulp your coffee and run;
Into the subway you crowd.
Don't breathe—it isn't allowed.

Act Two:
The boss is yelling at you;
You feel so frightened and cowed.
Don't breathe—it isn't allowed.

Manhattan Melodrama received a fair amount of attention not because of "The Bad in Every Man" but because it paired Clark Gable with William Powell, whose career had been faltering, and Powell with Myrna Loy—a couple so natural on-screen that they were soon paired again for the *Thin Man* series. On the day *Manhattan Melodrama* opened in New York, the *Times* reported that FDR had called for early enactment of twelve bills that would enlarge federal police powers, mostly to facilitate the FBI's pursuit of John Dillinger. The manhunt had already caused thirteen fatalities—one bystander, six Dillinger followers, and six federal employees.[11] The real-life gangster seemed to be no less exciting to Americans than Gable's movie gangster.

Also opening that month was MGM's *Hollywood Party*, which was received with utter indifference. Even the nervously vigilant Hays Office nodded off. "After months in production," Joe Breen reported to the boss, "*Hollywood Party* finally emerges as a somewhat mediocre musical hodgepodge, highlighted by a delightful Walt Disney Silly Symphony in color."[12] The kindest thing one might have said about *Hollywood Party* was that the time for its brand of studio showcasing had passed. Dick and Larry, soon to return to the West Coast, were hardly in a position to gloat.

Guilford's show *Caviar* was not helped by Larry's discreet direction. On opening night, June 7, 1934, Larry sent Guilford a wire: ONLY YOU CAN MAKE A SWAN OUT OF A TURKEY![13] Alas, the swan never took wing. "It would be hard to find a musical romance that said nothing with quite so much vigor and self-assurance as *Caviar*," Brooks Atkinson wrote. "Miss Guilford's acting is a concrete example of the fact that modern musical drama and grand opera are two different mediums."[14] The show closed after only eleven more performances but hardly affected the Guilford-Hart friendship, which some observers were determined to see as romance.

There was another opening on June 7, this one far more important to both Dick and Larry: the film version of *Evergreen* (the title now one word) opened in London, though it would not be seen in New York for another seven months. Produced by J. Arthur Rank and released by Gaumont, the film version starred the now-married couple Jessie Matthews and Sonnie Hale, with many of Buddy Bradley's dances retained. Because Dick and Larry had been in Hollywood during the filming and unavailable, the American songwriter Harry M. Woods ("Try a Little Tenderness," "What a Little Moonlight Can Do") was engaged to add songs to three of the boys' songs from the 1930 score. Most of the omitted Rodgers & Hart songs had been tied to Paris. In fact, all of the Paris material was removed in favor of a more tightly stitched backstage story (Emlyn Williams reworked Benn Levy's script) that stays in England. The theme of the hazards of toying with one's age is still there, and the picture is charming—no less entertaining than the best musicals then coming out of Hollywood. Oddly, the weakest minutes of *Evergreen* may be its most famous: Jessie Matthews's own literal-minded choreography to "Dancing on the Ceiling" as she twirls around a dining room, up a staircase, and into bed. Buddy Bradley ought to have put his foot down.

Dorothy Rodgers was pregnant again. Her husband rented a house in Rye, not far from the railroad station, so she and Mary, three and a half, might be cooler through the humid summer, although she had to come into the city each day to supervise the renovation of the East Seventy-Seventh Street apartment.[15] Larry had begun to make arrangements to move his family twenty blocks south, to the stately Beresford at Eighty-First and Central Park West. That could wait, though, until he and Dick returned from the Coast.

In the second week of July, Dick and Larry took the train across country to report for work at Paramount. In Los Angeles they checked into the Beverly Hills Hotel, which was expensive but convenient. "Larry gives every indication of being willing to work," Dick wrote to Dorothy, "and our surroundings are the best possible for it. He can come over here in a pair of trunks, so there isn't the waste of time while he gets dressed and we can sit out on the porch and discuss things when I don't have to use the piano. Fortunately his bungalow is far enough away to discourage him from dropping in with his friends. And so far the friends are not very much in evidence."[16]

The Paramount assignment was for an adaptation of a 1923 Booth Tarkington comedy, *Magnolia,* about young Tom, whose refusal to fight infuriates his bellicose father. Tom runs away to Natchez. A gambler teaches him that courage is merely preparedness: "The brave man is the man who feels he is safe." The play had already been adapted twice for the movies—first as a silent under the title *The Fighting Coward,* next as a talkie for Buddy Rogers.[17] A new screenplay was worked over by Claude Binyon and by Herb Fields. W. C. Fields was signed to star, at a salary totaling $31,250—not Chevalier money but enough to keep Fields in Tanqueray—as steamboat captain Commodore Jackson. The young radio singer Lanny Ross was to play Tom.[18]

Ross was a New Yorker with experience singing in the choir of the Cathedral Church of St. John the Divine and a law degree from Columbia, which he paid for by singing on the radio. Handsome and easygoing, Ross had signed a five-picture deal with Paramount, which positioned him to be the next Bing Crosby. (In fact the two men looked a bit alike.) He'd already made one movie, a throwaway called *Melody in Spring,* in which he played a guy who longs to sing on the radio and win the hand of Ann Sothern. There was some evidence in *Melody in Spring* that Ross on camera came off as stiff and uncomfortable in a way that Crosby did not.

Still, Paramount and producer Arthur Hornblow were going ahead with Ross for the *Magnolia* adaptation, now titled *Mississippi.* Norman Taurog got the directing assignment first, but by the time Dick and Larry arrived in town, Taurog had been replaced by Eddie Sutherland.

❧   ❧   ❧

During the first weekend back on the West Coast, Larry went to Agua Caliente to gamble; Dick stayed in Los Angeles, spending time with his parents, who had been out there for an extended period.[19] The following week Larry attended a *Merry Widow* wrap party at the home of composer Dmitri Tiomkin and choreographer Albertina Rasch.[20] Breathtaking news came out of Chicago: on the night of July 22, John Dillinger had been shot and killed by the FBI as he emerged from the Biograph cinema on Lincoln Avenue. He had just seen *Manhattan Melodrama*. It's not clear whether Dillinger, by then the FBI's Most Wanted man, identified with Clark Gable's gangster-gambler Blackie; what's certain, though, is that the last melody he heard in his brief life was "The Bad in Every Man."

When Larry, several hundred dollars ahead, returned from Mexico, Dick told him Metro's music publisher Jack Robbins had called. Robbins was on his way to London to handle music affairs from there, but first he wanted to encourage Larry to write a new lyric to go with the "Bad in Every Man" melody. Robbins had as much clout as anyone in music publishing and had given Rodgers and Hart a more than respectable bonus the previous year, so there was a sense of obligation.[21] Larry wasn't thrilled. All his life he had written lyrics for a specific character, or least for a specific occasion; this was something else.

"What are you looking for, Jack? Something like 'June / moon / spoon'?"

"Yeah, like that," Robbins said, letting Larry's sarcasm blow right by him. "Give me something commercial."

In an oddly prescient short story published earlier that spring in *The Saturday Evening Post*, Max Lief wrote about the embittered young songwriter Johnny Temple, whose latest lyric rhymes "peachy" with "Nietzsche" and who ridicules the more pedestrian inclinations of successful music publisher Dave Rodman. "Listen, wise guy," Rodman defensively tells Johnny Temple. "Do you know what those two little words—'love' and 'above'—did for me? . . . This beautiful office building you see here, a hundred employees, a catalogue of five thousand titles!"[22]

For Robbins, Larry came up with a lyric in which a blue moon—that rare thing, a *second* full moon in a calendar month, infrequent enough to prompt the phrase "once in a blue moon"—watches over the lonely singer, "the saddest of all men."

Blue moon,
You saw me standing alone,

Without a dream in my heart,
Without a love of my own.

It's a recurring Hart theme that goes at least as far back as the lyric for
"Hello," in *Peggy-Ann*: the lover's life barren—"I was as cold as the bear called
a polar"—until the loved one comes along. This blue moon has an almost
human consciousness, as if it *cares* what happens to the singer. The lunar link
is no less intense than Cyrano de Bergerac's—"Your other friend," says Le
Bret, of the moon, to Cyrano.[23] When a lover finally appears to the singer, the
blue moon turns to gold.

The melody had attracted attention in its earlier incarnations, but now
the deceptively simple lyric burnished it with a celestial shine. "Blue Moon"
would become the greatest hit of all Rodgers & Hart songs, though it was detached from any dramatic context—no show, no film, not even an anniversary
tribute—and would become much more deeply embedded in American culture than "Blue Skies" before it and "Blue Velvet" after it. For local color, John
O'Hara soon tossed it into one of his short stories.[24] It showed up in countless pictures released by MGM (which retained the rights), and its melody is
among the most recognizable guitar riffs in classic sixties rock: Eric Clapton's
direct quotation of it near the top of his famous solo in Cream's "Sunshine of
Your Love."

"Blue Moon" was written right in the middle of the boys' labors for *Mississippi*. Of the songs written for the picture that summer, two would make it
into the movie. Two that did not are more interesting. The mock-heroic "The
Steely Glint in My Eye" ("Every man is born a coward without a doubt / And
the hero's just a coward turned inside out") was meant for W. C. Fields to sing
to Lanny Ross. "Pablo, You Are My Heart" would be reworked more than
two years later into "Johnny One Note." Hornblow swore he was pleased with
the songs, but he was beginning to have doubts about how Lanny Ross was
coming through on film.

Because they were staying close to one another, and without their families,
at the Beverly Hills Hotel, Dick and Larry went out a lot together. In the
last week of July they attended a surprise party for Herb Fields. "Larry got
cockeyed and left early," Dick wrote, "and Herb had too much to drink and
got something like a crying jag over the sad fact that he was thirty-seven years
old."[25]

One midsummer evening Dick and Larry had Fred Astaire over to the hotel to listen to a two-page musical comedy idea, fleshed out with a couple of songs, about a young man who grows up in vaudeville and now teaches "polite" music, though he's also promoting a modern ballet on the side. The boys were well aware that Astaire and his sister, Adele, had been child performers in vaudeville, and also that Astaire appreciated classical ballet. There had been dramas with ballet done on Broadway; Archibald MacLeish's *Union Pacific*, with choreography by Leonide Massine and the young ballerina Irina Baronova in the leading role, had opened at the St. James that spring. But a balletic *comedy*? Astaire listened to the boys and said he'd get back to them. After losing Adele, his greatest dance partner, to marriage and retirement, Astaire had been scrambling to redefine himself. The scramble coincided with his entry into pictures. His supporting appearance in *Dancing Lady* had hardly made him a star, though audiences and critics couldn't help noticing him. Since then Astaire had been at RKO, partnered with Ginger Rogers in *Flying Down to Rio* and *The Gay Divorcee*. Frequently appearing in white tie and tails—and nobody, except perhaps Clifton Webb, wore a dinner jacket so well—Astaire had begun to click as the world's most romantic screen dancer. Why fiddle with this successful new image by pratfalling all over a stage? Astaire's response to Dick and Larry's idea came through his RKO producer, Pandro Berman. A DeWitt Clinton graduate with few enemies, Berman liked their idea but said that he had to decline for Astaire.[26]

Larry didn't need the excuse of a rejection to go on a bender; he just needed a bottle and a car and driver to make sure he got home all right. (Larry never did learn to drive.) On August 7 he missed an appointment with Dick, explaining that he had to go to Santa Monica to bail a friend out of jail. Reporting back to Dorothy, Dick mentioned rumblings at the studio—not the kind that make you jump out of a window to safety, but the kind that get you fired. "There seems to be a [Mack] Gordon and [Harry] Revel craze since the boys have written so many hits," Dick wrote, "and one faction, Manny Cohen and Lou Diamond, wants everyone to sound like G. and R. The other faction, Hornblow and Mel [Shauer], wants songs written according to the situation. Our side doesn't feel that 'Did You Ever See a Dream Walking' would be terribly appropriate for *Mississippi*, which is laid in 1858."[27] A local revival of *Peggy-Ann*, its cast appearing an exhausting four times a day, at Grauman's Million Dollar Theater did nothing to lift the songwriters' spirits.[28]

❧   ❧   ❧

With their work on *Mississippi* close to completed, Dick and Larry talked about going home. But Larry had a problem he didn't share with anyone except Dick. The newspapers were endlessly fascinated by Nanette Guilford, whose 1930 divorce was covered nationally, followed by her declaration of bankruptcy and a more recent report in which a weight doctor demanded payment for helping her to lose more than thirty pounds. Now the papers were marrying Guilford off to Larry Hart:

> Nannette [*sic*] Guilford, former Metropolitan Opera star and more recently engaged in musical comedy, today was getting her trousseau together for another try at matrimony, this time with Lorenz Hart, composer.
>
> The wedding bells will ring within two weeks, Miss Guilford told friends. Hart is now on the Coast, but plans an immediate return. He has been writing songs for motion pictures.[29]

"Larry is all upset about the account in the papers that he's going to marry Nanette the minute he hops off the [Super] Chief," Dick wrote. "I must say on his behalf that he has never worked so hard. I haven't had to wait for him once, he hasn't put me off at any time, and to top it all, he's done a grand job. Maybe he's sick."[30]

Whatever Larry and Guilford were communicating to each other, it did not include honeymoon plans. Larry was anxious enough about the situation—would this put a stop to rumors about his sexuality? would it hurt Frieda unduly to discover that the engagement was all a fiction?—to delay his trip home, encouraging Dick to go on ahead of him. In New York Larry's family waited for him on Central Park West. He had hundreds of friends there, including people he'd befriended on the West Coast: Leonard Sillman, Chuck Walters, and now Leonard Spigelgass, who'd moved to Manhattan to become East Coast story editor for Universal.[31] There was even work waiting: he and Dick had agreed to write a show (probably to a book by Philip Barry) for producer Max Gordon.[32] But, for whatever reasons, Larry needed an extra week alone in California.

Figuring *Mississippi* was on track, despite widespread dissatisfaction with Lanny Ross's performance, Dick took the Santa Fe Chief out of Pasadena. "I could remember everything about California, but I couldn't feel it," says the narrator of the unfairly neglected Hollywood novel *You Play the Black and the Red Comes Up*, by "Richard Hallas," the pen name of Eric Knight, a Philadelphia film critic who had gone to Hollywood to investigate the workings of the movie business. "I tried to get my mind to remember something that it could feel, too, but it was no use. It was all gone."[33] Dick was happy to be getting out of there. When he arrived in New York, he and Dorothy and Mary moved back into the East Seventy-Seventh Street apartment, now restored to its former elegance.

Before Larry got home, the Max Gordon project fell through. Still, there was plenty of excitement in and around Times Square. Film box office was booming again, particularly at the Broadway cinemas, long considered the show window of the industry. Radio City Music Hall, its six thousand seats making it the nation's largest movie house, was showing the Astaire-Rogers *Top Hat* five times a day; police were called in to keep order among people waiting to get in. At Loew's, at Forty-Fifth and Broadway, MGM's *Anna Karenina* (Garbo and Fredric March) was doing unprecedented business.[34] Theater folk were mourning the death of Charles Dillingham, who died at sixty-six, having produced two hundred shows on Broadway. With Dillingham's death the great theatrical triumvirate of Erlanger-Ziegfeld-Dillingham vanished. The day after Dillingham's funeral, Guilford put an end to the rumor that she was going to marry Larry Hart by disclosing she would instead marry British millionaire Martin Peck.[35] For all of his adoration of Guilford, Larry was relieved.

Martin Peck was described in the papers as "a polo enthusiast" and was not to be confused with Martin Beck, the eminent showman of the old Orpheum circuit. Shortly after Larry returned to New York, the theater named after Beck, on Forty-Fifth Street, began hosting the D'Oyly Carte Company, visiting from London's Savoy Theatre. One afternoon Warner Bros.' literary chief Jacob Wilk took his young son Max to a matinee there to see the first of several Gilbert & Sullivan productions. At intermission Jake took Max aside and presented a diminutive man badly in need of a shave.

"Max, this is Larry Hart. He's here every week." Even as a preadolescent, Max knew who the man was: the words half of Rodgers and Hart. "Larry, this is my son Max."

"It was my father's name!" said Larry. He shook hands with the boy. After he moved off to greet someone else, Max turned to Jake.

"I don't get it," he said. "What's he doing here every week?"

"Homework," Jake said. "You could say he's taking a refresher course."[36]

Larry and Dick were still walking around with the unglamorous music teacher idea—the one Astaire had rejected—in their pockets. They approached Harry Kaufman, a blocky, resolutely cheerful former sweater manufacturer and ticket broker who had recently gone to work for Lee Shubert as a kind of freelance producer, unsalaried amanuensis, and pinochle partner. The boys knew Harry from earlier days on Broadway; he also happened to be the younger brother of S. Jay Kaufman, who had talked them into making the 1929 short, *Makers of Melody*. Harry listened to the boys' story and said, "What about Ray Bolger?" Bingo! Bolger was under contract to Lee Shubert, so they all trudged up to Mr. Lee's office on the fifth floor of the Shubert Theatre. Mr. Lee periodically dyed his hair black and took sunlamp treatments that made him look like a forbidding Indian chief. Harry Kaufman urged the boys to make their pitch, which they were calling *Toe Business*. Mr. Lee, who rarely left his office before three or four each morning, promptly fell asleep.[37] (In a version Rodgers told two years later, undoubtedly to save Lee Shubert from embarrassment, he moved the locale of the pitch to the corner of Forty-Fifth and Broadway, where the four men supposedly stood in wide-awake fraternity.)[38]

Dick and Larry then took their idea to Dwight Deere Wiman, who had split off from his partner William A. Brady, Jr., and was happily producing on his own. Once Mr. Lee heard that Wiman was interested, he put *Toe Business* under Shubert contract and gave the boys an advance against royalties.[39]

Well, it *seemed* to be good news. So did word from Arthur Hornblow concerning *Mississippi*, although it had come about in a complicated way.

By 1933, Paramount-Publix was on the brink of collapse. The Publix part of Paramount's operations was the old Balaban & Katz theater chain, based in Chicago, and now it, too, found itself in the red. Sam Katz had resigned as a director and president of the theater chain in December 1932, but his brother-in-law Barney Balaban was more active than ever in the company's operations. Taking over from Katz was Emmanuel (Manny) Cohen, who was considered by most industry observers to be an excellent studio manager. Cohen supervised a slate of well-received but expensive pictures. In March 1933 Paramount-Publix entered into voluntary bankruptcy, placing the administration of its assets under jurisdiction of the bankruptcy court in New York. Five months later Paramount-Publix announced that its new subsidiary, Paramount Pictures, Inc., was operating at a profit. Reorganization of the company proceeded. Then, at the end of January 1935, Cohen was deposed, the board of directors citing his inability to rein in expenses. Dealmaker Henry Herzbrun and director Ernst Lubitsch were installed to replace Cohen, with Adolph Zukor surviving the board's wrath to be named chairman. It sounded impressive but effectively kept him from making significant production decisions.[40] (Zukor would be a Paramount figurehead for the next forty years.)

Barney Balaban would not become president of the studio until the following year but, while the board was conniving to remove Cohen, he supervised the production slate. When Balaban got a look at Lanny Ross in *Mississippi*, he confirmed what Dick and Larry had feared: Ross wasn't coming off well on film.

Bing Crosby was rapidly turning into Paramount's biggest star. The repeal of Prohibition had given him a push because saloons had installed jukeboxes in huge numbers—25,000 sold by 1934—and Bing's records—first on Brunswick, then on Decca—filled those jukeboxes. On October 15, 1934, Crosby was put on studio salary at $4,000 a week; reshooting of *Mississippi* with Crosby replacing Ross would begin November 26. As conflicting rumors about *Mississippi* swirled, Ross quietly fled to New York.[41]

One rumor was that Crosby didn't want to sing the songs Rodgers and Hart had written for the picture. That turned out to be true. Balaban was prepared to please his star, but Hornblow stood up for his old friends and said, "If the Rodgers & Hart songs go, I go." A compromise was reached: Crosby would sing the two Rodgers & Hart songs he deemed best, "Down by the River" and "Soon," but as a trade insisted on singing "Old Folks at Home," perhaps more widely known as "Swanee River." "Old Folks at Home" was one of Stephen Foster's unforgettable songs from the mid-nineteenth century, though Foster regarded it as frivolous. It had been played and sung in saloons and parlors throughout the rest of the nineteenth century, but there was scant evidence of it during the still-young recording era.

Apprised of Crosby's wishes, Dick and Larry were aghast. It was one thing for them to grudgingly accept the studios' practice of bringing several songwriters onto a movie, as they did screenwriters, but quite another to watch the studio brass acquiesce to the demands of a movie star. But Crosby got his way.

As shooting commenced in November 1934, *Mississippi* needed one more song. Dick and Larry conferred and decided, with Hornblow's support, to write the song in New York. If "A Ship Without a Sail" and "With a Song in My Heart" were earlier Rodgers melodies that would have been too pretty without Hart's stripped-down lyrics, the equally lovely "It's Easy to Remember" benefits from Hart's concision, in which the universal, obsessive reaction to a broken romance is captured in a twenty-three-word refrain. Dick and Larry went to the Paramount Building, where they were given a studio with a piano and a telephone, to play the song for Hornblow on the West Coast. Given his go-ahead, they brought in radio singer Jerry Cooper, who possessed a baritone eerily similar to Crosby's, to record "It's Easy to Remember," and they mailed the disk west.

Dick and Larry didn't have to be near the Paramount lot during reshooting. Crosby was also absent a number of days, whether because he was "ill," as he claimed, or because he was inspecting the stables and exercise track he owned at Rancho Santa Fe—not far from the Del Mar racetrack he would open with several partners in 1936. "Crosby wouldn't work," states the studio's Analysis of Loss in Schedule repeatedly.[42] After Santa Anita opened just east of Los Angeles on Christmas Day 1934, Crosby would spend much of his recreational time there. It's too bad Crosby and Larry Hart had so many fundamental differences, because they would have had a ball together playing the horses and drinking, one man writing expressly for the other.

In the early months of 1935 Dick and Larry waited to set up *Toe Business*, which was now being referred to as *On Your Toes*. On the night of February 24, 1935, playwright Marc Connelly gathered an all-star cast for *The Post-Depression Gaieties*, a single-performance revue presented at the New Amsterdam Theatre, for the benefit of the Authors League Fund and the Stage Relief Fund. The boys wrote something for it called "What Are You Doing in Here?"[43] (No music or words survive.) Two weeks later Dick and Dorothy Rodgers were blessed-evented by the arrival of their second surviving daughter, Linda. In late April Rodgers and Hart wrote a song called "You Are So Lovely and I'm So Lonely" for Hugh Sinclair to sing and accompany himself on piano, in the Broadway play *Something Gay*, produced by the Shuberts. The play starred Walter Pidgeon as a man who begins a romance with the widow upstairs while his wife (Tallulah Bankhead) is away. Presumably the song had been requested by either Lee Shubert or Harry Kaufman. The boys had come through with the song but still had received no word about *On Your Toes*.

By spring Larry had moved his family into the penthouse of the Beresford. Larry and Teddy still shared a bedroom, Mary Campbell slept in the maid's room when she preferred not to go home, and Frieda occupied a bedroom and adjoining bathroom across the landing. The Beresford was one of many majestic Manhattan apartment houses designed by the architect Emery

Roth, whose buildings, including the San Remo at Seventy-Fourth Street, were transforming Central Park West from a distant outpost to the West Side's showcase thoroughfare. The Roth buildings and others like them had been constructed with pre-crash money, their towers—the Beresford's three domed cupola towers made it impossible to miss from almost any angle in Central Park—meant to be symbols of glamour. But the apartments inside those buildings were something more modest and practical. "The designs [of the Beresford and its ilk] reflected a new concept of what home was supposed to be," cultural historian Mark Caldwell has written, "—neither a retreat for a family shutting out the world nor a fully staffed stackable mansion, but a pied-à-terre, a place to make forays from and come back to at all hours of the day and night." [44] That's how Larry used the apartment anyway—a place to retreat after his mysterious misadventures in New York.

CHAPTER 15

The World Was Younger Than I

D WIGHT DEERE Wiman still wanted to produce *On Your Toes*, which was mildewing in a pile of scripts in an office above the Shubert Theatre. Grandson of the steel-plow manufacturer John Deere, Wiman had attended Yale, where he studied with George Pierce Baker and his 47 Workshop, which swept into New Haven when Yale lured away several eminent Harvard professors at once. Wiman also took classes there with Monty Woolley before Woolley turned full-time to Broadway and Hollywood. During the Great War, Wiman left Yale without a degree to join the Navy. Returning to civilian life, he steeled himself to go to work at the family store, the John Deere Plow Works, in Chicago. His discontent was apparent to his older brother Charlie, who released him from company commitments and wished him well in his theatrical endeavors. During an apprenticeship with William A. Brady, Jr., son of the producer-actor, Wiman learned the business of presenting drama on Broadway.[1]

Rodgers and Hart were thrilled to have Wiman interested. But Lee Shubert intended to wait out the option, if only to keep the play off the market. With *On Your Toes* sitting in limbo, the boys were vulnerable to the exhortations of that overwound toy Billy Rose, who wanted them to write the songs for a musical about a circus. Billy had failed to pay them for previous work. But Larry usually laughed at being stiffed, and since the songwriters were already living well, they agreed to take another chance on Billy, who said he had investors lined up.

And oh, did Billy have them lined up! *New York World* publisher Herbert Bayard Swope, among the higher-rolling poker players in New York, had promised tens of thousands.[2] So had Barney Baruch. And then there was John Hay (Jock) Whitney, then the ambassador to the Court of St. James's and scion, along with his sister Joan, of one of the richest families in America.

Billy's Broadway circus sprouted from a December 1934 cable dispatch from King Boris of Bulgaria, published in the New York papers. Three royal elephants were beggaring the court; was there anyone out there willing to take one of the beasts off the king's hands? "Although he calls the animals his 'pets' and is deeply attached to them because of their tameness and intelligence," *The New York Times* reported, "Boris is willing to sell one or two of them to a circus—possibly an American one—at a bargain price. The circus will have to pay the freight." Rose, then immersed in a book about the exploits of nineteenth-century showman P. T. Barnum, cabled the king and put in a bid. He got no reply. But the following week brought news that Boris had changed his mind "despite a handsome offer from an American theatrical producer." Rose, according to his fifth publicist, Richard Maney—with each flop, the previous publicist had been shown the door—was irritated that his identity had remained masked. This was, after all, a man whose only preference to seeing his name in print was seeing it in electric lights.[3]

Rose procured one of the elephants, thereafter known as Big Rosie, and decided to call his show *Jumbo*, after the beloved elephant that was a star attraction of Barnum's circus as early as 1882, at Madison Square Garden.[4] He engaged Ben Hecht and Charles MacArthur to come up with a story for a musical about a circus. Hecht, in publicist Maney's enlightened opinion, often supplied Billy with the same material—an act he called "A Small Time Cavalcade."[5] Hecht was known to favor *Romeo and Juliet* as a model for practically anything. In the summer of 1932 Hecht and Gene Fowler had cooked up something called *The Great Magoo*, which was about a thwarted romance between two Coney Island vaudeville types, with a lot of pole-sitting and other stunts.

Billy Rose insisted that his oversize circus open at the Hippodrome. The Hipp, as Broadway insiders called it, was built in 1904 on the eastern edge of the theater district on Sixth Avenue between Forty-Third and Forty-Fourth Streets. It opened for business in April 1905 with *Yankee Circus on Mars*, an extravaganza with a cast and crew of five hundred (500!) and various acts that included horseback riders, jugglers, and, in one spectacular stunt, a giant-sized tapestry that, when rolled down from the rafters, revealed a portrait of President Theodore Roosevelt. Since then the Hipp had had a checkered history—managed for a while by the Shuberts, then by Charles Dillingham; bought and then unloaded by financier Otto Kahn; falling into disrepair and hosting wrestling matches and revival meetings. Rose, who had seen *Yankee Circus on Mars* as a boy, could not contain his eagerness to book the Hippodrome—a costly error, in the view of Maney. Rose had the theater gutted, "rendering it unfit for anything but *Jumbo*, a good six weeks before he had any right to enter the building."[6]

Rose's terms with Hecht and MacArthur were equally self-punishing. Inhaling the heady cologne of their reputation, he agreed to pay them 5 percent of the box office gross, though the going rate for the most reputable writers in a theatrical contract was 3 percent.[7] But he was aiming for an April 1935 opening and got the circus wheels rolling. Besides Hecht and MacArthur, Rose hired John Murray Anderson, almost exactly a decade after Anderson had directed *Dearest Enemy*, to stage the whole thing; James Reynolds, who had also worked on *Dearest Enemy* and had become one of the best costume designers on either side of the Atlantic; Raoul Pene du Bois and H. C. Wynn to cover the designs that Reynolds didn't have time for; and scenic designer Albert Johnson, who was charged with building a circus set smack in the middle of the theater—a tall order even for the man who had made the revolving stage for *The Band Wagon* operate so well.

And then Rose hired Rodgers and Hart. With some study of the Hecht and MacArthur script, the boys went to work. George Jean Nathan occupied an apartment in the Hotel Royalton, a mere fifty yards from the Hippodrome, and must have noticed all the activity going on there. At the time he was writing a foreword to the published version of *Of Thee I Sing*, by Kaufman, Ryskind, and the Gershwins:

> A glance backward over the modern American musical stage will disclose it to have followed, with little deviation, routine and rusty tracks. In endless succession that stage has given us the so-called romantic musical comedies with their proud princesses in love with humble naval lieutenants and their humble slaveys cinderellaed by proud princes, the revues with their vaudeville comedians and peafowl ladies, the shows laboriously manufactured out of dull comedies previously displayed on the legitimate stage, and the German and Austrian importations adapted to what has been believed to be the American taste by the insertion into their books of a sufficient number of facetious allusions to Congress, Yonkers, and Mrs. Aimee Semple McPherson.[8]

Curiously, although "Manhattan" makes mention of Yonkers, it was the Gershwins who were guilty of all three "facetious allusions." But Nathan's puckered catalogue of musical comedies certainly included most of Dick and Larry's shows. It was true that the integration of story and song that Larry Hart stood for had remained unrealized.

And yet *Jumbo*, though undistinguished as drama, would commence the major phase of Rodgers and Hart's career. If, as Rodgers's brother-in-law Ben Feiner suggested, the first Rodgers & Hart period ended with the success of *A Connecticut Yankee* and the second ended with their return from Hollywood after working on *Mississippi*, this third and final period would be marked by more autonomy, even more memorable songs, and, sadly, the steep decline of Larry Hart.

Billy Rose hired Jimmy Durante for $3,000 a week, and it's fair to say that without Durante there probably would have been no *Jumbo*.[9] Durante was given the plum role of Claudius B. Bowers (the B stood for Brainy), press agent for the Greater Considine Wonder Shows, which included this failing one-ring circus. Hecht and MacArthur tailored the role to Durante and his oversize coat—someone said that when he appeared on the Hippodrome stage, the diminutive Schnozzola seemed to be wearing the winter clothes of heavyweight boxer Primo Carnera—and may have colored the character with more than a dab of Dexter Fellows, the longtime advance man for Barnum & Bailey's Ringling Brothers circus.[10] Otherwise the writers were going to let Durante do his thing. "Is the robin connected with the springtime!" says Bowers to a U.S. Marshal visiting the circus. "Is the song of the lark connected with the twilight? That's how I'm connected!" The overcoat made Durante appear even more foreshortened as he circled the Marshal. "I'm used to sizin' people up in a twinklin,' stranger, but you got me baffled for the nounce."

The other celebrated member of the cast was bandleader Paul Whiteman. The King of Jazz had been recording Rodgers & Hart songs for Victor since the start of their Broadway career. Beginning a couple of years before he bought his Walking Horse Farm in western New Jersey, Whiteman would eat and drink at Colligan's Inn in Stockton, New Jersey, which had become popular with reporters covering the Lindbergh kidnapping trial in nearby Flemington in December 1934.[11] On one of his trips there, Whiteman was accompanied by Larry Hart, who noted the wishing well outside the inn. Out of that visit emerged the lyric "There's a Small Hotel," written to one of the few Rodgers melodies that annoyed Larry no end.

♦ ♦ ♦

The run-up to *Jumbo*'s premiere went on longer than the Hipp's construction. The April opening date came and went; midsummer was spent preparing for a Labor Day opening, which also passed. Parts of the show rehearsed in a Brooklyn riding academy, at the Manhattan Opera House, and in a church on Forty-Eighth Street.[12] Because Actors Equity classified *Jumbo* as a circus, the usual rehearsal regulations did not apply, so Rose could legally have his cast and crew rehearse night and day. Visitors streamed into the Hippodrome at all hours. Charles MacArthur cracked that the opening was being deliberately delayed until every potential paying customer had taken in a rehearsal.[13]

As summer turned to autumn and there was still no opening date locked in, Rose, surely on the counsel of Maney, bought a huge billboard space facing Broadway: SH-H-H-H! JUMBO IS IN REHEARSAL. A sign at the rear entrance of the Hippodrome read: THROUGH THESE PORTALS PASS THE MOST BEAUTI-FUL ELEPHANTS IN THE WORLD. Rose, who wrote speedily but did not read speedily, was blessed to have the most literate press agent in town working on his show. By the early thirties Maney had been immortalized by Hecht and MacArthur in *Twentieth Century* as the character Owen O'Malley, "truculent press agent."[14]

Rose offered George Abbott the job of staging the book. At forty-eight, Abbott was not yet even in midcareer, but he had never directed a musical comedy before. He couldn't bear to watch the aerialists for fear they would fall.[15] Thinking ahead to *On Your Toes*, Dick and Larry advised Abbott to learn a few musical comedy techniques by first doing *Jumbo*. So Abbott took the job and tried not to look up.

During the *Jumbo* delays, Paul Whiteman asked Rodgers for a "Nursery Ballet"; the resulting composition would not be performed until Christmas Day 1938, but patches of it would find their way into *Jumbo*. Jock Whitney had become fascinated by Technicolor and had recently invested in Pioneer Pictures, the latest enterprise of Merian C. Cooper (*King Kong*), which had made the Technicolor *Becky Sharp* and planned a 1936 slate to include *only* Technicolor films.[16] Jock Whitney asked Rodgers and Hart if they'd be interested in writing songs for a picture tentatively titled *Footloose*.[17] Unable to refuse the money, the boys said yes and made arrangements to go to Los Angeles at the end of the year.

Four weeks before *Jumbo* opened, the boys' songs for the radio musical *Let's Have Fun* were broadcast on CBS. The program begins with strains of "Blue

Moon" (Jack Robbins had, as promised, promoted it on two continents, on the air and in print) and follows songwriter Dick Ford (Ken Murray), through the "fourth dimension" back two thousand years to an Egypt ruled by Cleopatra (Helen Morgan). Ken Murray tries to find his way through the Rodgers & Hart originals "I'll Take a Little of You on Toast" and "Please Make Me Be Good," but on an air check of the program, he sounds confused or lost, or both.

Helen Morgan's version of "Please Make Me Be Good," is much better. Subsequent *Let's Have Fun* shows had been planned, but it appears the first one killed the others. Although Dick and Larry had previously appeared on the radio, separately and together, the *Let's Have Fun* songs were probably the first ones they'd written exclusively for a radio program.

In its final weeks of rehearsal, *Jumbo* picked up a major radio sponsor, Texaco, which hawked its dime gas on NBC as the "Jumbo" of power. But rehearsals yielded a new problem: at the far ends of the Hippodrome, it was impossible to hear a lot of the show's dialogue and even some of the songs. The book, already skeletal, was further trimmed, and Rose took the opportunity to throw out a couple of songs, including "There's a Small Hotel," which he apparently didn't care for any more than Larry did.

When *Jumbo* finally opened on November 16, 1935, there was relief that the gestation period was over. The delays and unprecedented radio blitz paid off, however—not enough to make *Jumbo* profitable but enough to fill the Hippodrome for a few months.

Several *Jumbo* songs were directly about the circus. The most memorable of these, "Over and Over Again," had been written for MGM's *Hollywood Party* as "The Party Waltz." "Stick to your trick and your trick will be art," the Ringmaster advises, and the Chorus agrees: "A star does not come out of the sky; / He starts to work at ten." Larry Hart demolishes the quaint notion that art can be achieved by anything other than hard work.

Larry could summon Jimmy Durante's peculiar vernacular quickly. His special lyric for Durante is called "Laugh," which Durante sings to Gloria Grafton, who plays the young heroine Mickey Considine, daughter of one of the warring circus owners. No matter how catastrophic things get, according to Durante/Bowers, you have to laugh. "Yes, I was off," he narrates about recovering from a fight, "off like a toupee in a windstorm." He reminds Mickey that whenever she's in trouble, she must "stand the gaff / Be a Pagliacci and laugh."

The reviews ranged from neutral to enthusiastic. Percy Hammond in the *Herald Tribune* praised "Little Girl Blue." John Mason Brown in the *Post* called the show a "super Bergdorf-Goodman circus." Robert Benchley in *The New Yorker* referred to *Jumbo* as "a circus deluxe." Most surprising of all was the *Life* review by the incorrigibly dame-crazy George Jean Nathan, who appreciated "the ringful of girls" and "a staff of girl ushers that are even better looking," though he also had praise for the songs.[18]

If *Jumbo* was more circus than musical, the boys had fulfilled their contract and shown Broadway that they weren't done there. Looking over the crowds at the Hippodrome, Rose—alternately dubbed "the basement Belasco," "the mighty midget," "the penthouse Cagliostro," and "the Sixth Avenue Aladdin"—wasn't displeased.[19] Why should he be? Although weekly expenses made a profit impossible, the house was full each night. The big money was lost by Jock Whitney. Just as Rose had seen *Yankee Circus on Mars* as a little boy, so little boys just before and after the New Year of 1936 were taken to *Jumbo*. One of them was the adopted son of vaudeville impresario E. F. Albee, a six-year-old named Edward, who came to regard *Jumbo* as the play that changed his life.[20]

Of the ten or so songs written for *Jumbo*, three have become standards. As Matt Mulligan, Jr., Donald Novis sang "The Most Beautiful Girl in the World" to Gloria Grafton (Mickey), who "isn't Garbo, isn't Dietrich / But the sweet trick / Who can make me believe it's a beautiful world." Larry invoked the names of the two greatest international movie stars, known by practically every theatergoer, and "trick," demeaning as it might sound today, was a compliment. The most beautiful girl's lack of pretense prefigures the lady who's a tramp. Matt and Mickey sing "My Romance," which doesn't need that "castle rising in Spain / Nor a dance / to a constantly surprising refrain," nor any other symbol or ritual of courtly love. The most plaintive of the standards is "Little Girl Blue," in which Mickey recalls being a child, when the world was "As merry as a carousel" and "The circus tent was strung / With every star in the sky." In contrast to the elegiac tone of the song, the space around her is filled with tightrope walkers, aerialists, tumblers, and clowns, all of them bathed in a dreamy blue light.

Dwight Deere Wiman outwaited Lee Shubert. In December 1935, the two producers agreed to share interest in Rodgers and Hart's *On Your Toes*: Wiman would have approximately two-thirds interest, Mr. Lee one-third. The contract wouldn't be signed until February 16, 1936. In December, with

Jumbo packing them in, Rodgers and Hart flew west to fulfill their assignment for Pioneer Pictures. The boys claimed they wrote two songs, "Are You My Love?" and "When You're Dancing the Waltz," on the plane, each of them working with pencil, paper, and a drink, for the Technicolor movie that was previously titled *Footloose* and was now *Dancing Pirate*.[21]

Once more they settled in at the Beverly Hills Hotel. With the *Dancing Pirate* songs pretty much out of the way, they spent most of their time working on songs for *On Your Toes*, with tryouts scheduled only three months hence. Together, Dick and Larry often went to the Trocadero, the Sunset Boulevard club owned primarily by *Hollywood Reporter* publisher Billy Wilkerson. In the year and a half since it opened, in September 1934, the Trocadero had become so popular that Jack Kreindler and Charlie Berns, the owners of "21" in New York, were angling to buy it. On one night when the boys were at the Troc with their good friends Edith Meiser and Helen Ford—both women were out from New York—Phil Ohman was at the piano playing nothing but Rodgers & Hart.[22] Larry warmed to the Trocadero because his songwriting friends were already hanging out there, and because there was something pleasingly kitchy about its shiny low ceiling and its artificial palm trees—and maybe, too, because the Trocadero was one of the few elegant nightclubs in the city where young homosexual men were not harassed, provided "they behaved with discretion: no touching, no flamboyant clothes, no effeminate gestures."[23] Larry, more voyeur than pickup artist, hardly minded the parading young men. Dick liked the Trocadero because he heard his melodies played, and because it was filled each evening with beautiful women.

Dorothy Rodgers had remained in New York to start a business that had grown out of her displeasure with their former tenants. The idea was to open a shop, in the heart of the neighborhood bordering Sutton Place, capable of repairing anything from a chandelier to a lace handkerchief—in general, "the slightly damaged possessions of the now thrifty rich."[24] After much debate, Dorothy named the shop Repairs, Inc. Larry, wishing Dorothy well in her new enterprise, sent her a telegram: CAN YOU FIX MINE? Dorothy wired back, IF YOU CAN SEND IT WE CAN FIX IT.[25] What did Larry own, one wonders, that wasn't broken?

As Hollywood assignments went, *Dancing Pirate* had been tolerable as well as lucrative. When the dance-inflected comedy, set in Old California, was released that spring, it was distinguished less by the Rodgers & Hart songs than by the Technicolor contrasts so carefully worked out by Broadway refugee Robert Edmond Jones. Meanwhile, after six weeks, *Jumbo* had counted 318,613 paying customers at the Hippodrome—an astonishing attendance figure at the time for a theatrical enterprise.[26] In the spring of 1936, when the show folded its Sixth Avenue tent and moved to Fort Worth, Texas, Eddie Foy, Jr., succeeded Jimmy Durante. Billy Rose soon eliminated the role of Claudius B. Bowers altogether and most of the already slim book, retaining Big Rosie and the shimmering Rodgers & Hart songs. Durante was gone but the tinsel and gold remained.

Part III **M**t. Olympus
to
Mt. Zion

CHAPTER 16

Unrequited Love's a Bore

B Y   T H E   winter of 1936, Rodgers and Hart had worked with some of the nation's greatest artists: entertainers Lew Fields, Ed Wynn, Maurice Chevalier, Jimmy Durante, and Al Jolson; stage designers Josef Urban and Robert Edmond Jones; and directors John Murray Anderson, Rouben Mamoulian, Lewis Milestone, and Ernst Lubitsch. But none of these men had their fields to themselves the way George Balanchine did. He had not yet achieved the absolute dominance of ballet and modern dance when he first worked with Rodgers and Hart, but he would do so soon enough. Balanchine's collaboration with the songwriters, beginning with *On Your Toes*, would lift their careers onto a higher plane.

Balanchine's participation in the show would not have occurred without Larry Hart's conviction that a ballet or a dance number, without lyrics, should advance the plot, and it would make *On Your Toes* unique. This idea had been in Larry's head since the early 1920s when he was so enchanted by the dancing of Elise Bonwit.

Balanchine first came to the United States in October 1933, sailing on the *Olympic* from Cherbourg to New York, but it's probable that Dick and Larry had been aware of his work since 1930, when C. B. Cochran employed him as choreographer for the London revue that interpolated "With a Song in My Heart." In New York Balanchine was soon in residence at the Metropolitan Opera, where his jazzy choreography immediately attracted attention, some of it not always positive. "He put a reptilian wiggle in the torsos of the *Aida* chorus," Dorothy Kilgallen wrote, "until the dowagers couldn't believe their lorgnettes. He staged an orgy in *Tannhauser* and was heard to remark: 'This scene is in hell and they don't dance the minuet.'" [1]

Balanchine made dances that were undeniably sexy. He had to be cautious, however, because the theater had its rules, many of them imposed by Mayor Fiorello La Guardia's office. A rider to the Select (Shubert) Theatre contracts with its artists precluded: lyrics that may be taken to be obscene; bare-legged female performers; "muscle dancing by either sex"; profanity; and "the portrayal of a moral pervert or sex degenerate." Balanchine's choreography was erotic but never degenerate or cheap. On August 13, 1935, having been recommended by Larry, he read an agreement with Lee Shubert that named him sole and exclusive dance director and paid him $250 per week during rehearsals and production of *On Your Toes*. Balanchine signed it. So did his agent, Doc Bender. [2]

If Balanchine was to enhance the careers of Rodgers and Hart from 1936 on, Doc Bender's position in their lives was more complex. Once Dick and Larry resettled in New York, never again to spend more than a few consecutive months in Hollywood, Doc Bender was on the scene. Certainly Bender—tall, balding, and googly-eyed—lacked the sort of presentability the Rodgerses required. Bender's homosexuality was less flamboyant than merely flagrant—he made no attempt to hide it, which offended Dick and Dorothy and their friends. Careful with money though hardly parsimonious, Dick didn't need Bender to look after his finances. Larry, on the other hand, spent everything in his pocket, was afflicted with a generosity that could only be deemed excessive, and craved company—if not necessarily Bender's, then the people Bender might bring to him. In January 1936, Bender declared bankruptcy, city records showing that his dental practice had unpaid bills amounting to nearly $10,000. [3] It was said he had been a terrible dentist; in fact, he was in his office all too rarely, preferring to survey performers on the stage rather than fill their teeth up close.

Bender has often been described as a procurer and a pimp, though those labels seem to be based on hearsay more than hard evidence. While he was still practicing dentistry, Doc had set himself up as a talent agent. He laughed, perhaps all too easily, at whatever Larry said and was known to entertain Frieda Hart at the Beresford apartment by playing the piano. Twenty years later, Bender would serve as the model for Dr. Kitchell, DDS, in the Comden-Green-Styne musical *Bells Are Ringing*, "a sweet, ineffectual-looking, balding young man with glasses" who interrupts his examination of patients to write down music he's just thought of. [4]

In the mid-1930s, having first stepped into the world of the arts promoting the opera singing of his brother Charles, Doc broadened his scope to include ballet. In America in 1935, ballet was still considered more exotic than absinthe or baccarat. The Ballet Russe de Monte Carlo had just ended its second New York season while Balanchine was still choreographing for the Met. Yet Bender was interested in dancers long before most readers of the Arts section of *The New York Times* could identify more than one or two.

"Balanchine was agented by that Bulwark of Broadway, the irrepressible 'Doc' Bender," wrote the Russian émigré composer Vladimir Dukelsky, better known in New York as Vernon Duke and also a theater world client of Bender's. "[Bender was] Larry Hart's aide-de-camp, troubleshooter and father confessor—a pushy and fast-talking character; his salesmanship was worthy of respect, because he only sold things he honestly and passionately believed in. He didn't have to sell Larry Hart, who was the best of all lyricists (not excluding Gilbert, in my opinion) but when he screamed at the top of his lungs that Balanchine was a god among choreographers . . . he was only voicing his inner beliefs and, being fanatically sincere, was undeniably convincing."[5]

Doc Bender and Vernon Duke encouraged Balanchine to sign on as choreographer of the 1936 edition of the *Ziegfeld Follies*, which was the second under Shubert management. (Since Flo Ziegfeld's death in 1932, the enterprise was often referred to as Billie Burke's *Follies*, for the beautiful, daffy-seeming widow had managed to slap away the palms of most of her husband's creditors.) Opening in January, well before *On Your Toes* rehearsals were under way, this *Follies* boasted Fanny Brice, Bob Hope, the Vernon Duke–Ira Gershwin song "I Can't Get Started," and Josephine Baker. Apart from making dances for the acrobatic Nicholas Brothers, it was a fairly thankless assignment for Balanchine. After years of starring at the Folies Bergère, Josephine Baker had become more of a presence than an entertainer, with a voice too small for the Broadway stage. As the dance scholar Emily Coleman pointed out, "Baker and her world-renowned derriere were hardly the blank canvas [Balanchine] preferred to work with."[6] It was while Baker was appearing in this *Follies* that she accompanied Fanny Brice to a party at Larry Hart's. Baker ventured into the Hart kitchen and, noting Mary Campbell in her apron, asked, *"Donnez-moi une tasse de café, s'il vous plaît?"* "Honey," said Big Mary, "you're full of shit. Talk with the mouth you were born with!"[7]

Mary's appealing, straight-shooting style, meanwhile, was being mined by George S. Kaufman and Moss Hart to create Rheba, the black maid of the wacky white family in *You Can't Take It with You*. Many of Rheba's lines now read as anachronistic minstrelsy and don't bear repeating. But when Rheba describes some guests by saying, "All those rich men are Elks or something," it's Mary Campbell all the way.[8]

Other impressive talents were lined up for *On Your Toes*. George Abbott had signed his agreement with Lee Shubert to direct even before *Jumbo* opened. For the show's scenic design, Dwight Deere Wiman brought in Jo Mielziner, who had trained with the best (Urban, Jones, and Lee Simonson) and had designed Wiman's *The Little Revue* and its second edition as well. Mielziner's style was implication rather than elaboration: a line here, a splash of color there, a piece of fabric to stand in for a roomful of furnishings.[9] Irene Sharaff had been a designer at the Brooks Costume Company, a Broadway institution for decades, owned and managed at the time by Jimmy Stroock (father of the actress Geraldine Brooks, who took the family store name for her stage name). Monty Woolley was engaged to play the Diaghilev-like impresario Sergei Alexandrovitch. And the beautiful Tamara Geva, who had married Balanchine in 1922, when she was fifteen and he eighteen, was engaged to play the Russian ballerina Vera Barnova. The character's name was surely a play on the name of Irina Baranova, who made her debut at thirteen dancing for Balanchine at the Theatre Mogador in Paris in 1932.[10] Geva, like Balanchine, was represented by Doc Bender.

Talent was shaking the floorboards. George Abbott exercised his characteristic authority, with everyone but Wiman, Rodgers, and Hart addressing him as "Mr. Abbott." Among Abbott's recent credits was revising and directing the comedy *Three Men on a Horse*, which had enjoyed a run through most of 1935, with Teddy Hart in the role of "Frankie" employing the lisp he couldn't hide but also appropriating his older brother's habit of rubbing his hands together in moments of anticipation.

As *On Your Toes* rehearsals progressed, there was more than the usual anxiety because it aspired to be the first musical comedy to incorporate ballet as part of its story. Rodgers was feeling particularly self-conscious about "Slaughter on Tenth Avenue." Balanchine, who was supposed to make a ballet out of it, was used to working with the music of Bach, Bizet, and Tchaikovsky; compared to them, Rodgers thought of himself as a *pischer*. In the first week of February, Rodgers went up to the apartment of the show's co-pianist Edgar Fairchild to play a four-handed version of "Slaughter" for Wiman and Balanchine. Wiman, Rodgers knew, would be enthusiastic, but Rodgers held his breath until Balanchine gave his verdict: excellent! Exhaling,

Rodgers admitted that, knowing nothing about ballet, he had winged it. "You write. I put on," Balanchine said.[11]

Some of the *On Your Toes* songs went back to the initial concept Dick and Larry had pitched to Astaire. With a couple of songs (probably "Too Good for the Average Man" and "Quiet Night") left to tweak, the boys took the train to Atlantic City—as much to shed their respective families as to be inspired by salt air and the stark midwinter seaside atmosphere—and took a suite at the Ritz, where they reworked the songs. "We always had a distaste for artistic self-pampering," Rodgers wrote, "and only rarely did we ever take one of those hide-out trips so popular with writers. . . . We returned to New York on Monday with [the songs] completed, and I remember that we felt happy and rested."[12]

But *On Your Toes* had just suffered a crippling defection. Even in the peaceful weeks before rehearsals, the gruff Mr. Abbott had regarded Wiman as a dilettante, a rich boy lacking the drive and know-how that come with scratching your way to the top. Wiman was indeed wealthy, and his entry into the hard-knocks world of theatrical producing, with its tiers of responsibilities and setbacks, had been relatively easy. His air of privilege—he was chauffeured in a Rolls-Royce equipped with a bar and wickerwork seats, wore Savile Row suits, and brought his dog to the theater as if he were going hunting—held special appeal to Dick Rodgers. But not to Abbott, who departed abruptly for Palm Beach to play golf and dance in the clubs there.[13]

Abbott ignored Wiman's pleas to return, so Wiman hired Worthington Miner—known by his colleagues as Tony—to take over. Miner had been staging plays on Broadway since 1930. Though widely liked, he was not a musical comedy director, and the Rodgers & Hart songs and Balanchine dances were soon running away from his reins like a team of spooked horses. "It was too much show for Tony," Ray Bolger said.[14]

Bolger's wife, Gwen Rickard, was, depending on who was doing the talking, another problem. Bolger and Rickard had met in vaudeville, married, and she had since devoted her energies to his career. When the troubled show arrived in Boston for tryouts, in mid-March 1936, Rickard, who made no secret of her displeasure with the dialogue, arrived at the Shubert Theatre brandishing typewritten pages. "Here's your new second act," she declared, thrusting the pages at Tony Miner.[15] Larry's eyebrows shot up. George Abbott would have let the pages fall to the floor, but Miner took them graciously.

Rickard knew she was out of her depth with Balanchine, who worked the dancers—and himself—until exhaustion set in. He had a nervous tic, which became more pronounced as rehearsals grew longer, of wrinkling his nose and sniffing. Grace Kaye, of the *On Your Toes* ensemble, couldn't take her eyes off Balanchine's nose.[16]

In Boston, as late as the day before the first tryout, Dick and Larry decided to excavate "There's a Small Hotel" for *On Your Toes*. Although Larry still didn't like the melody, he knew it would fit in the first act. "It was kind of cute yesterday when we played 'Small Hotel' for Ray," Rodgers wrote to Dorothy. "He started to cry and ran off the stage. It was pretty un-goy-like."[17]

Bolger's emotional reaction notwithstanding, there had been some ugliness involved in getting the music done. Wiman had agreed to the boys' request to hire Hans Spialek, "the bouncing Czech," to orchestrate the songs. Spialek, in turn, farmed out some of the work to two young men, Conrad Salinger and David Raksin. On one of the orchestrations, Raksin came across a chord change that made no harmonic sense to him, so he reversed the chords. Rodgers, hearing his song played back, was so incensed that he had Raksin fired.[18] Raksin wasted no time going to Los Angeles, finding employment at Universal Pictures, and helping Charlie Chaplin with the score for *Modern Times*, including the song "Smile." (Salinger would go west shortly after that and, along with Roger Edens, create the sound of the MGM musical.)

Nothing in the Boston opening quite worked. The audience didn't know what to make of Geva as a man-eating ballerina, and Gwen Rickard's changes for the second act just lay there, flat-footed and limp. Larry had intended to ride home so he could wake up at the Beresford, however late in the day, but it was evident the show had to be revamped, so he took a room at the Ritz-Carlton, where Dick was staying, and stayed up till 4 A.M. discussing fixes with Dick, Wiman, and Worthington.[19]

When the fixes failed, too, Rodgers wired Abbott in Palm Beach. IT'S YOUR SHOW, said the telegram, AND IT'S YOUR OBLIGATION TO COME AND PROTECT IT.[20]

Abbott flew to Boston, saw the show without taking a single note, and met backstage with the others. When Rodgers suggested that they all repair to the hotel to discuss the problems, Abbott waved that away and said, "Let's get some girls and go dancing."[21]

Tony Miner was out (although he would be paid the same share of the profits and movie rights as Abbott was), George Abbott back in. Abbott fixed the show largely by reverting to the original script. By the time *On Your Toes* opened at the Imperial Theatre in New York on April 11, almost everything was clicking. In the program, Miner's name was still listed as director, but everyone knew that Abbott had come to the rescue. In the world of musical comedy, the show's immediate distinction was its change of emphasis from the jester—the Lew Fields/Victor Moore/William Gaxton/Ed Wynn role—to the dancer. *On Your Toes* was less an evening of comedy than of dance, even if much of that dancing was comic. That was, in fact, Ray Bolger's specialty. On the night he opened at the Imperial, Bolger could also be seen in the premiere of MGM's *The Great Ziegfeld*, at the Astor on Broadway, in which he played himself. His appearance in *The Great Ziegfeld* was part of a seven-year Metro contract, which would cause them all some trouble the following year.[22]

In *On Your Toes* Bolger played Phil Dolan III, known to his friends as Junior. Having grown up performing "Two a Day for Keith" (as in the Keith vaudeville circuit) with his grandfather, father, and mother, Junior has kicked the entertainer's life aside to teach a WPA extension course in "polite" music at Knickerbocker University, somewhere on the Hudson. It's 1936, and the Soviets have become cultural darlings in New York, particularly among proponents of the Popular Front. Teaching his students, Junior sings them "The Three B's," which is meant to refer to the great classical composers but ends up including even the likes of the harmonica *mayvin* Borrah Minevitch. Junior looks over a song written by his adoring pupil Frankie Frayne and pronounces it "unimportant"—an evaluation that stings her. But Junior does help his students, for he has agreed to show his student Sidney Cohn's ballet, now titled "Slaughter on Tenth Avenue," to the Russian dance company, which is in need of new material.

Junior, believing he's alone and unaware Frankie is watching him, removes his professorial spectacles and does some fantastic steps; it's his "lower nature" that his feet simply start moving after a while. (It's worth remembering that this can't-help-dancin' character trait, older than vaudeville itself, was conceived by the boys for Fred Astaire, and that Astaire subsequently used it several times.) This dance breaks the ice between Frankie and Junior, who asks that she sing her "unimportant" song, "It's Got to Be Love":

> *It couldn't be tonsillitis;*
> *It feels like neuritis*
> *But nevertheless it's love.*

At the end of the song, Frankie is joined by Junior, who tosses his glasses across the stage and comes down "in-one" (i.e., in front of the proscenium). What Frankie and Junior can't yet acknowledge, but we as the audience can see, is that these two belong together.

But first Junior must encounter the dazzling Russian ballerina Vera Barnova, who's been faithful to her latest lover, dancer Konstantine Morrosine, *for a whole month*. Socialite-publicist Peggy Porterfield (Luella Gear) introduces Junior to her as "a school teacher." Because Vera likes what she sees, she's also willing to dance in the ballet he's brought, Sidney Cohn's "Slaughter on Tenth Avenue," in which she would be doing a striptease as part of a burlesque show.

Maestro Sergei Alexandrovitch arrives. He used to be married to Vera—*three times*, in fact. Sergei, with his nostalgia for pre-Revolutionary Russia, and Peggy, wistful for the fading British Empire, sing "Too Good for the Average Man." The "average man" phrase was often employed by FDR in his fireside chats, and the lyric permits Larry Hart to satirize not only the ex-spouses' smug class superiority—"Caviar for peasants is a joke," they declare—but the privileges of their ilk: crowded and overpriced supper clubs; casual infidelities; easy access to discreet abortions; and psychoanalytic sessions where it all spills out.[23] Larry was fascinated by Freudian probing, but not for himself.

Psychoanalysts are all the whirl,
Rich men pay them all they can.
Waking up to find that he's a girl
Is too good for the average man.

It's a wonderful punch line, "based on the oldest smoking room joke in the world," said *Cue*, "and not at all cleaned up, either."[24] The melody sounds like an old nursery rhyme while the lyric stings like a paper cut.

It was right before *On Your Toes* that Larry went in for what Dick referred to as "self-improvement."[25] He began treatments to fight hair loss. After every two or three treatments he would point out, without having to tip his head, new hair growing on his scalp. Observers could only nod. He also began to wear Adler elevator shoes—"two-inch cheaters," he called them. The shoes, which might have raised Larry to the five-foot mark, were used unselfconsciously in the *On Your Toes* script:

> VERA (furious)
>
> Do you think you can make rules for Vera
> Barnova, you jealous dwarf?
>
> MORROSINE
>
> Dwarf?
>
> VERA
>
> Yes! I've seen those lifts in your shoes. You lie
> about your height two inches.
>
> MORROSINE
>
> Shut up!
>
> VERA
>
> Two inch liar!

As a defiant rebuke to Morrosine, the internationally desired ballerina attaches herself to Junior, the nerdy schoolteacher. The seduction may be the first of several unlikely, cross-cultural couplings in American musical theater—*Madame Butterfly* could be seen as an antecedent—that provided the narrative pillars for some of the most celebrated musicals of the mid-twentieth century. *On Your Toes* preceded *South Pacific* (a French planter and an American nurse), *Guys and Dolls* (a gambler and a missionary sergeant), *The King and I* (a Siamese king and an English tutor), *My Fair Lady* (a refined professor and a Cockney gamine), and *The Sound of Music* (an Austrian aristocrat and a laicized nun). Like the couples in these shows, Vera and Junior, despite their vastly different backgrounds, appear to be right for each other.

But so do Junior and Frankie, who meet again in Central Park. Junior attempts to persuade Frankie that, although he intends to see the irresistible Vera again, Frankie's friendship is more important to him. This is where the boys inserted "There's a Small Hotel." Considering that Larry still couldn't abide the melody, he turned the lyric into an extraordinary paean to the pastoral getaway. Larry's facility with repetition was sometimes used as an example of "laziness," as in:

Looking through the window
You can see a distant steeple,
Not a sign of people.
Who wants people?

But this repetition is precisely what's called for. The charm of the small hotel is that there's nothing and no one around. And yet, in a comic reprise of the song, sung later in the show, Larry acknowledges the mundane matter of the expense of such a holiday:

There's a small hotel
Which we loved so well—
From there we'll get the air tomorrow.
One big bill to pay,
One old jazz ballet,
Is all we have to share tomorrow.
Looking through the window
Is a man with a subpoena.
If you lose that meanie
You're Houdini.

Thanks to Max, the Harts knew about process servers, and if there wasn't anything romantic about them, trying to lose them had been fun for a while.

"There's a Small Hotel" also showed off Hans Spialek's wit in orchestrating, alluding to bits of melody that the audience was familiar with. The conductor John Mauceri has pointed out that, when Frankie sings of the hotel's "moosehead on the wall," Spialek quotes Siegfried's hunting-horn call; and when she sings of "the cheerful prints of Grant and Grover Cleveland," a phrase from "The Battle Hymn of the Republic" blows by.[26] If either David Raksin or Conrad Salinger had inserted these pleasing allusions, he failed to get credit for them.

Poor Junior is in love with two women. At the Cosmopolitan Opera House—a real opera company; Nanette Guilford sang there after leaving the Metropolitan—Peggy Porterfield, counseling him on his emotional entanglements, sings "The Heart Is Quicker Than the Eye." All in love is fair? Peggy doesn't buy it. Like the mamas in Johnny Mercer's lyric for "Blues in the Night" (1941) and in Smokey Robinson's "Shop Around" (1966), Peggy's mother advised her child at an early age:

Mother warned me that fair play doesn't apply.
Turn your back
And love goes whack!
The heart is quicker than the eye!

If Peggy's mother made frequent appearances in Reno, it hardly mitigates her wisdom.

Junior, grateful for the counsel, is about to go on the Cosmopolitan stage as a Nubian slave alongside several Russian dancers. While the Russians "black up," he must pretend to Sergei that he too is Russian. "Slaves on stage in five minutes!" calls the Stage Manager. What follows is the "Princess Zenobia" number, Balanchine's first big dance in the show, in which Vera and Morrosine (as Abu the Beggar) play dirty tricks on each other, perversely demonstrating their mutual lust. The number was the talk of the town. "When Tamara Geva made her entrance, legs wrapped around her partner," Irene Sharaff remembered, "she thought the audience was laughing at her and immediately started to camp her dance, at first tentatively, then when the laughter engulfed the auditorium, with more abandon. The company followed her lead and the whole thing became like a version of *Hellzapoppin'*." Sharaff was standing in the back of the house with Larry, Dick, Abbott, and Balanchine, who had gone pale. After the audience broke into wild applause, though, Balanchine turned to the others and declared, "Exactly how I imagined dance."[27] Geva's appearance quickened the blood of audience members, though perhaps none so publicly as *The New Yorker's* Wolcott Gibbs, who wrote, "The vision of Miss Geva in net stockings with the seams running crooked up the backs is going to be one of my great emotional memories."[28]

The "Princess Zenobia" ballet, meant as a spoof of *Scheherazade* (though not everybody got the joke), is one of several examples in the show in which classical music competes with jazz and ballet competes with tap. Strands of Rimsky-Korsakov and Tchaikovsky imply seriousness of purpose. But then Junior, as a Nubian slave, disrobes and, aghast, reveals his own white body, for he has neglected to blacken his torso.

The ballet closed act 1 of *On Your Toes*, so its timing was crucial. But in the early performances, the entrance of Junior and the other Nubian slaves came later and later. Rodgers went backstage to see what the holdup was and found Doc Bender chatting up the chorus boys. Refusing to acknowledge Bender, Dick vented his anger at Larry, who was the reason Bender was there in the first place. Larry withstood Dick's rage and watched him storm out of the dressing room. Instead of feeling insulted, Larry laughed and ad-libbed a new lyric to "There's a Small Hotel":

> *Looking through the window*
> *You can see six slaves and Bender.*
> *Bender's on the ender—*
> *Lucky Bender.*[29]

Act 2 opens at the new Planetarium Roof Garden. The orchestra plays for dancers, and a tenor (or lyric baritone) comes out and sings "Quiet Night," an impossibly lovely song that vacuums all the tension out of the city air. It's one of Larry's more abbreviated, straightforward lyrics, deferring to Rodgers's crystal melody, but what makes it special is its setting: the Hayden Planetarium had opened the first week of October 1935 right across Eighty-First Street from the Beresford, so it would have been on Larry's mind. After it begins to rain, Frankie and Sidney Cohn are left alone at a table beneath a large umbrella. Sidney is pleased to have received a hundred-dollar advance for his ballet, which is in rehearsal, but Frankie is stuck on Junior and feeling blue. Sidney leaves for a moment to fetch Frankie's cape, giving Frankie enough time to sing "Glad to Be Unhappy," the exquisitely self-torturing lament that might be as close to Larry's bone as any lyric he ever wrote.

> *Unrequited love's a bore*
> *And I've got it pretty bad.*
> *But for someone you adore,*
> *It's a pleasure to be sad.*

But once again there's a kicker: Sidney is glad to be unhappy, too, because he's stuck on Frankie.

After Junior takes a look at Frankie's new song, he pronounces this one cheap. In songwriting, however, the word isn't necessarily pejorative. ("Strange how potent cheap music is," Noël Coward wrote.)[30] "But I like it," Junior adds. "I can see how it might be a very effective number in the theater." The new song is "On Your Toes," and Frankie begins to sing after Sidney and Junior imagine what the orchestra—really a pit band that Spialek's arrangement transforms into the Philharmonic—might sound like.

Impresario Sergei is forced into knocking out the jealous Morrosine. With his leading male dancer out of commission for the premiere of "Slaughter on Tenth Avenue," Sergei puts Junior—renamed Juniorvitch Dolansky—in the lead role. The ballet, which had originally been Larry's idea—or so said Balanchine—is surely what made *On Your Toes* so distinctive in the end.[31] "Slaughter on Tenth Avenue" was a stand-alone jazz ballet but also advanced the plot, even if in a goofy way, and served as a model for dances-within-a-show forever after. It revolves once more around Geva, the object of desire for the Big Boss, played by George Church, and the Hoofer, played by Ray Bolger. Church, who gave up an undefeated record in boxing (fifty-six bouts) shortly after he saw his first ballet, had danced for Balanchine in *Follies* and had unusual upper body strength, able to lift and toss anyone he danced with.[32] In the dance, Bolger was prohibited by Balanchine to touch Geva, going against the grain of musical comedy courtships and tightening the sexual tension until it threatened to snap. Thugs approach the stage and, mistaking Junior for Morrosine, prepare to kill him as soon as he stops dancing. Frankie warns Junior to keep dancing—and here Balanchine stepped back and let Bolger express his own brand of free-form desperation: dance, fool, dance! The police arrive and Junior can finally stop dancing. Recognizing that Vera's world is no more appropriate for him than the academic world his parents wanted for him, Junior settles on Frankie, grateful to her for saving his life and asking her never to leave him.

Audiences exited *On Your Toes* ready to dance, but it was usually "Slaughter on Tenth Avenue"—for many years the "Slaughter" sheet music outsold all other Rodgers compositions—that stayed in their heads for days thereafter.[33] (In *The Catcher in the Rye* Holden Caulfield tells us that his classmate Stradlater could *whistle* it.)[34] Among the audience members who went away knocked out by the dance was the struggling actor Gene Kelly. "Slaughter" has that elusive symphony-of-the-city quality. John O'Hara, writing after several skirmishes with Rodgers in the 1950s and '60s, suggested that "Slaughter on Tenth Avenue" was only "quasi-Gershwin, with 'An American in Paris' ringing in [Rodgers's] ear."[35] But "Slaughter" has its own urban style, at once propulsive and poignant. "When a violin player would play the solo in 'Slaughter on Tenth Avenue,'" Hans Spialek recalled years later, "it took your heart out."[36]

In late April 1936, two weeks after *On Your Toes* opened at the Imperial Theatre, Rodgers and Dorothy accompanied the Wimans to Bermuda. Larry went to Hollywood for a couple of weeks, staying at the Beverly Hills Hotel, probably because its bungalows opened out to other bungalows and made him less lonely.[37] Teddy Hart was there, reprising his role as Frankie in *Three Men on a Horse* for Warner Bros. and appearing as a shyster lawyer in *After the Thin Man*, with his *Three Men* costar Sam Levene, for MGM. Teddy also had a girl-friend, a writer named Dorothy Lubow, a Brooklyn native who had danced for a while and then begun to write. A novel, *Reckless Hollywood*, published when she was twenty-eight, had won her assignments for show business magazines. She had recently come to Los Angeles to interview Sam Levene and Teddy Hart, and had fallen in love with Teddy. Larry was delighted, even if it meant Teddy would be less available to him. As it happened, Dorothy was enchanted by Larry's staccato speech, his erudition, and his generosity.[38]

With *On Your Toes* drawing late spring audiences to the Imperial, it was time to think about the next show. The official public relations story about the seed for *Babes in Arms* has the songwriters taking a walk in Central Park and noticing some children amusing themselves with made-up games. It's a touching image, but Dick and Larry strolling together in the park, particularly at that late date, is a scene from a fairy tale. The idea of children of entertainers putting on their own show came to Larry after talking with Dr. Leo Michel, a popular physician in theatrical circles who'd been dubbed "the Angel of Broadway" by humorist Harry Hershfield. At his office, Dr. Michel treated members of the Friars Club *and* their frequently neglected kids, who were left at home when their folks went out on the road. His Fifty-Fifth Street apartment was open to anyone from Broadway; there was always a gin rummy game going and the gin was always flowing. "Dr. Michel's is undoubtedly the finest night club in New York," Renee Carroll wrote in *In Your Hat*. "Everyone knows everyone else. There are no butter-and-egg men, no country cousins with popping eyes, and best of all, no prudes." In a cage in a corner of the apartment perched a canary whose warbling of a composer's new tune meant it would be a hit. It was Larry's kind of place. When Dr. Michel referred to his patients as "the temperamental children of show business," Larry took the phrase to Dick.[39] The boys twisted and turned it into *Babes in Arms*.

By midsummer, *Babes in Arms* was announced as Alex Yokel's next production. FIFTY CHILDREN WILL PLAY IN FORTHCOMING MUSICAL, the *Los Angeles Times* reported. The eldest child would be no older than sixteen, the youngest only four—a cornet player, no less![40]

✣   ✣   ✣

That summer Larry spent several weekends on Cape Cod with Balanchine, Bender, and Vernon Duke. It might have been a motley quartet—two White Russians, two Jewish New Yorkers—but what fun they must have had! Balanchine, who was living higher than his earnings could keep up with, frequently borrowed money from Larry, who didn't expect to get it back. In Manhattan, Larry kept a Cadillac garaged for the use of himself and his friends, and Balanchine played chauffeur on these weekends, not because he felt he owed Larry but because the others couldn't drive and Larry's legs didn't reach the floor pedals. "George, the 'Doc' and I wore berets," Duke wrote of that summer, "whereas gnomelike Larry secured, God knows where, a bona fide admiral's cap and wore it at a 'salty' angle. We traveled about in Larry's big black limousine, and its owner's habitual luggage consisted of a pigskin week-end bag stuffed with fifths and quarts of every alcoholic classic, plus one diminutive toothbrush." On the Cape, Duke and Larry wrote a song, "Who the Hell Are You?"; but when it was pointed out that a title like that would never get airplay, Larry tore up the lyric. (Duke's musical idol was George Gershwin and he usually wrote music rather than lyrics. But in at least one lyric credited to Duke, the 1935 "Autumn in New York," he seems to be taking dictation from Larry, whether it's about turning "the slums into Mayfair," or the "lovers who bless the dark / On benches in Central Park.") Of those summer weekends, Balanchine remembered Larry as "happy and laughing. He was so full of fun and energy, throwing his money around. From every pocket would come money and he paid everyone's bills wherever he went."[41]

By summer's end *On Your Toes* had drawn interest from the movie studios. In the speculative casting game, Ginger Rogers's name was most often mentioned for Vera. Despite the scorn Dick and Larry had for the studio system, which essentially relegated them to writers-for-hire status, movie money remained impossible to refuse. Jerome Kern and Oscar Hammerstein II, the success of their landmark musical play *Show Boat* notwithstanding, had each come to the conclusion that only Hollywood work was consistently profitable, and bought houses in Los Angeles.[42]

For a few weeks, though, Hollywood was grim. On September 14, 1936, Irving Thalberg died of lobar pneumonia. "In a principality," Budd Schulberg wrote, "that had developed almost overnight the ability to create myths for mass production, Irving Thalberg had been installed as a demigod, a crown prince in command of Taste and the more serious aspirations of Our World."[43] But business had to go on. Teddy Hart, having already made two pictures in 1936, was announced as part of the cast of a third, *Ready, Willing and Able*, a Ruby Keeler picture remembered now for the Mercer-Whiting song "Too Marvelous for Words."[44]

On Your Toes was still doing great business at the Imperial, and would soon move to the Majestic to make room for another show. On October 10 the NBC Blue Network's weekly program *The Singing Story Lady* carried "The Story of Richard Rodgers," a biography of the composer's boyhood aimed at children. Narrated and sung by "The Singing Lady," Ireene Wicker, the biography didn't even mention Larry Hart.[45] By November, Rodgers and Hart were putting the finishing touches on *All Points West*, a musical narrative they had written at the request of Paul Whiteman.

Although Whiteman's moniker as the King of Jazz, promulgated by the early two-strip Technicolor movie of that title, has been widely ridiculed for eighty years, it would be foolish to minimize his importance to American popular music from the 1920s to the 1940s. His early recordings had already made an impact when he commissioned Gershwin's *Rhapsody in Blue* in late 1923, and he became the best-known proponent of "symphonic jazz," including Gershwin and, most recently, "Slaughter on Tenth Avenue." Whiteman asked Rodgers and Hart for a piece he could play with the Philadelphia Orchestra.

All Points West, which runs just over twelve minutes, premiered at the Academy of Music in Philadelphia on November 27 and 28, and also played at the Hippodrome in New York on December 1. The piece is about a New York City train announcer who looks out over the terminal's concourse at the flow of people walking and running to the trains.[46] Written to Dick's music for a baritone and orchestra, Larry's words are plain and familiar. "Leavin' track thirty-three," calls the announcer, "Great Lakes Express . . . and all points west!" The announcer can see a salesman heading for the road and a mother saying good-bye to her son. He ponders the possibilities of going west. He notices doughboys and college girls on their way to Boston—"How young they are / How sweet they are"—and then a handcuffed prisoner being escorted to Sing Sing. "No Niagara Falls for him! He'll get as far as Ossining! No honeymoon for him!" When the prisoner escapes custody, the policeman responsible for him accidentally shoots the announcer, mortally wounding him. "I'm goin'," he says, as though announcing his own departure, "track seven at twelve oh." And the whistle starts to blow, the tracks are all clear. The announcer dies.

All Points West might be heard as pretentious—Rodgers and Hart's attempt at Socially Significant Radio. But there's that recurrent Hart theme of the singer observing teeming city life and wishing he could participate without getting emotionally wounded. Larry knew the announcer's panoramic, voyeuristic angle all too well.

Nine days after the New York performance of *All Points West* came the unprecedented, hugely entertaining news that Edward VIII had renounced the throne after not quite eleven months as King of England; his brother, the Duke of York, also an avowed fan of Rodgers and Hart, became George VI.[47] By then, Larry was writing special material for Beatrice Lillie in the Shuberts' *The Show Is On*, and it's a wonder he didn't toss in the abdication. The previous February, just when Dick and Larry were turning all their energies toward *On Your Toes*, the Shuberts had asked them to write a revue for Lillie and Bert Lahr for a fall opening at the Winter Garden.[48] The boys had had to say no, but when *The Show Is On* finally reached the rehearsal stage, under the direction of the young Vincente Minnelli, Lillie knew she needed a socko lyric or two. Who better to turn to than Larry? He added a satiric second chorus to "Rhythm," which Lillie had originally sung in a 1933 revue called *Please.* The new Lillie-Hart combination threw darts (or were they cupid's arrows?) at Broadway showstoppers, including Irving Berlin's "Blue Skies," "This Heart of Mine," Larry's own "On Your Toes," and, most barbed of all, Ethel Merman's window-shattering "I Got Rhythm" ("I got AHH!!!").[49] Lillie's rendition of the "hot rhythm number," according to Brooks Atkinson in the *Times,* "destroy[s] that music hall staple from now on."[50]

The Show Is On opened on the same day that Warner Bros. released *Three Men on a Horse.* (In it, Teddy Hart can be heard saying "miwacle.") Warners had locked up the movie rights to *On Your Toes* for $60,000, divided like this: 41⅔ percent to Rodgers and Hart; 8⅓ percent to Worthington Miner; 8⅓ percent to George Abbott; two-thirds of the remaining 41⅔ percent to Dwight Deere Wiman; and one-third of the remaining 41⅔ percent to Select Theatres Corporation (Lee Shubert).[51] Warners' embryonic casting notions retained Geva but substituted James Cagney for Bolger, whose MGM contract would have required extra fees to borrow him.[52]

Meanwhile, the British stage rights to *On Your Toes* went to producer Lee Ephraim, with Louis Dreyfus grabbing the British music publishing rights for Chappell. On New Year's Eve 1936 the Lord Chamberlain's Office received the script for *On Your Toes.* The blue pencil began to scratch across the pages.

❧   ❧   ❧

The Lord Chamberlain's objections were often so petty as to be not worth fighting. Vera, for instance, would no longer be permitted to claim that she had known several Russian composers "intimately." The word "fiddle" in the line "Like Heifetz needs a fiddle lesson!" was deemed disrespectful, though that line and many others were merely a matter of translating the American vernacular to England. "Two a Day for Keith" had to be reworked to change its vaudeville references to the British music hall circuit. Not surprisingly, "Too Good for the Average Man," proved more objectionable, so Larry altered a number of lines for British audiences. The King and his cronies no longer "had cocktails at Tony's" but now preferred "biscuits tortonis." Instead of appending "cocky" and "mockey" to "Men of fashion," he rhymed "philander" and "gander." The line "Birth control and the modus operandi" had to be cut altogether, so, while he was at it, Larry dashed off whole new stanzas, including:

> *Super tax for the wages of sin come*
> *To the wealthy European,*
> *Income tax that is more than your income*
> *Is much too good for the poor plebian.*

In the comic reprise of "There's a Small Hotel," the reference to a subpoena would not have clicked with British audiences, so Larry came up with:

> *Looking through the transom*
> *Is a house detective peeping,*
> *While we two are sleeping,*
> *Only sleeping.*

Once again his use of repetition is anything but lazy: the last two words provide the perfect punctuation.

While the British production of *On Your Toes* was being prepared, other Rodgers & Hart projects were evolving. *All Points West*, with Whiteman conducting and baritone Ray Middleton in the role of the trainmaster, was broadcast on the NBC network on January 3, 1937; Rudy Vallee secured the film rights, to star himself as the trainmaster, but the film never materialized.[53] By then Alex Yokel's option on *Babes in Arms*, the show Dick and

Larry had cooked up featuring only kids, expired—it was never clear what might have spooked Yokel about the show—making it available to Wiman, who was still preoccupied with *On Your Toes*. On Broadway Wiman's first musical success had proved intimidating. When he and the Shuberts were competing for a musical called *Fiddlesticks*, the *Times* reported that "Mr. Shubert's interest is apt to grow in ratio to Mr. Wiman's, for Mr. S. can scarcely have forgotten that he once owned *On Your Toes* and then released it (all but a small interest) to Mr. W." [54]

The Shuberts' young director Vincente Minnelli, who had recently piloted Bert Lahr and Bea Lillie into the Winter Garden, accepted a forty-week contract with Paramount in Hollywood, so Harry Kaufman threw him a going-away party. [55] Larry wouldn't have missed that party for anything. With *On Your Toes* finally closing on January 23, 1937, after 318 performances— about two-thirds of them under the roof of the Imperial Theatre, a third at the Majestic, where it had moved in November—and about to go on tour, Ray Bolger was in a quandary: after signing a new three-year MGM contract worth $480,000—a contract that would take him through the making of *The Wizard of Oz*—he did not want to stay out on the road in *On Your Toes*. Bolger appealed to Actors Equity, which sent the matter to arbitration. The American Arbitration Association decided that Bolger's contract stipulated that he remain in *On Your Toes* through April 3. [56]

In London, on February 5, Lee Ephraim's production of *On Your Toes* opened at the Palace Theatre with Jack Whiting and a twenty-year-old dancer whose birth name was Brigitta Hartwig and who was subsequently given the name Vera Zorina by Colonel de Basil, of the Monte Carlo Ballet Russe. [57] Born in Berlin of German and Norwegian parents, Zorina was, by wide agreement, not the dancer Geva was, but an enchantress in and out of a theater. With his predatory enthusiasm, Doc Bender would sign her as a client. George Balanchine would fall in love with her. Rodgers and Hart would think of using her from show to subsequent show.

That same week Larry was walking on Sixth Avenue when he ran into Vivienne Segal. "Larry, darling, what about that part you were going to write me?" said Segal. "When the right part in the right play comes," Larry said, "you'll hear from me." [58]

CHAPTER 17

Is Your Figure Less Than Greek?

*B*Y NOW it was a given that Dwight Deere Wiman would open a new show in the spring, after the theatrical season's competition had fallen away. *Babes in Arms* would be his 1937 spring musical. George Abbott, distancing himself from Wiman, turned his energies toward bringing to Broadway the farce *Room Service*, which had played in Princeton and Philadelphia a couple of years earlier. Hoping to repeat the success of *Three Men on a Horse*, Abbott began to bird-dog that show's costars, Sam Levene and Teddy Hart. For *Babes in Arms*, Wiman brought in Robert Sinclair to direct.

Babes in Arms was the first Broadway show in which Dick and Larry assembled an entire libretto without Herb Fields, George Abbott, or anyone else. Some eighteen years into their partnership, they were still determined to unhitch their work from the predictable steam engine of the old-fashioned musical comedy story. *On Your Toes* had replaced vaudeville turns and wan jokes with dance at its most dynamic, and managed to sustain a vision of musical comedy throughout; but it was still old-fashioned in the way everything was resolved at the end of act 2. Since 1918, when they first met, Larry had insisted on the higher intelligence of theatergoers; now even Rodgers believed that audiences, as he and Hart told reporters, "were surfeited with the leading man in the musical show taking the first act to meet the girl and having a spat with her just before the first curtain, and then spending the second act singing his way into the heart of the frowning maiden."[1] Writing *Babes in Arms*, however, they hadn't thought through the possibility that in replacing one theatrical cliché, they would create another.

The new cliché—it is often formulated as "Hey, kids! Let's put on a show!"—would take hold during a run of 289 performances on Broadway and in an MGM movie version. Meanwhile the libretto would comment on racism and classism and on the youthful embrace of communism. Since Dick and Larry didn't want to be so conventional as having the kids' amateur show save the day, they searched for another resolution.

As the *Babes in Arms* script neared completion, casting went into high gear. The Nicholas Brothers were the first performers Dick and Larry thought of. Fayard and Harold Nicholas were known for their extraordinary timing and flying leaps. Whenever Harold jumped onstage, he practically had to be cleared at Floyd Bennett Field for landing. But the Nicholas Brothers were currently committed to a show at the Cotton Club, which was one of several Harlem establishments that had set up outposts on or around Broadway to take advantage of post-repeal liquor. That show was to feature Duke Ellington and Ethel Waters and would be in rehearsal for what seemed like years. So Wiman and Rodgers and Hart signed Kenneth Wilkins and LeRoy James to play the young black brothers Booker and Lincoln Vanderpool.

Among the producer and songwriters, the feeling was that, with only a few exceptions, the most talented kids had gone to Hollywood to work in pictures, where their youth was more in demand than it was on the Broadway stage. (The exceptions tended to be attached to radio talent shows like Major Bowes's *Amateur Hour.*) Hundreds of juveniles auditioned. Wearying of imitations of ZaSu Pitts, Mae West, and W. C. Fields, Rodgers came to hate the word "chickadee" even more than "Nazi." Larry thought "chickadee" was swell.

One of the teenagers they saw was Mitzi Green. Tutored by her parents, an itinerant vaudeville team with Brooklyn roots, Green hadn't even turned four when she was noticed by impresario Gus Edwards, who subsequently employed her for as many hours as the law allowed. Paramount Pictures plucked her off the four-a-day vaudeville circuit. In the 1930 film *Honey*, directed by Wesley Ruggles, she played Doris, a little girl who runs around shouting "I know a secret!"; the line became a national catchphrase. That same year Mitzi appeared as Becky Thatcher in Ruggles's film version of *Tom Sawyer*. At Paramount, where he was helping out most of the lyricists in the songwriters' corridor, Larry couldn't miss Mitzi's talent, and he remembered it. Mitzi arrived with a considerably more substantial résumé than the other kids but auditioned like everyone else. Her special impressions were of the actress Luise Rainer, who was then at the height of her fame (she had just received an Oscar for *The Great Ziegfeld*), and of the actor George Arliss (*Disraeli*).

Mitzi Green was then all of sixteen. So was Wynn Murray, a contralto from Scranton, Pennsylvania. Because of her girth, Murray was often referred to as a younger edition of Kate Smith. Doc Bender heard her sing two bars and signed her. Ray Heatherton, who grew up singing in New Jersey church choirs and had been lately singing on the radio—the Old Gold show, under Paul Whiteman's aegis, and lately on several NBC shows—was said to be the cast's old-timer at twenty-five.[2] (In fact he was twenty-eight. A few years later he would father a little girl who would grow up to be the actress-dancer Joey Heatherton.) Duke McHale, nineteen, had been dancing for years in his native Providence and had toured with the most recent edition of the *Follies*.

Of the other kids, Alfred Drake, singing at Brooklyn College and in the chorus of Gilbert & Sullivan revivals, would become musical comedy's leading baritone for a decade, beginning with *Oklahoma!* in 1943. Ray McDonald appeared in *Babes* with his sister Grace and would be cheered by movie audiences who saw him dance alongside Joan McCracken in MGM's *Good News*. And Dan Dailey had to be the lankiest of MGM's musical stars of the 1950s.

The median age of the performers hovered at twenty-one—not quite the adolescent age Dick and Larry had envisioned, but still the youngest aggregate cast ever in a Broadway show not aimed directly at children. A separate chorus of dancers was dispensed with; for the first time on Broadway, every dancer onstage was also a character in the play.

Rodgers and Hart turned out ten songs, with Rodgers adding a ballet number that connected to one of the songs. Once again Hans Spialek supervised the orchestrations. As rehearsals got under way, with Sinclair directing and Balanchine creating the ballet, the boys gave their usual complement of interviews. In these Hart emphasized their identities as working stiffs who just happened to write songs. "We are the only collaborators in the theater who don't consider ourselves possessed of genius," Hart said. "We work for our living. We meet at 11 A.M. and from then on it is hard work without a trace of genius to make it easier." It was refreshing to journalists and readers alike to hear Larry shirk the trite genius label. (Paul Valéry's definition of inspiration: "the act of drawing the chair up to the work table.")[3] Larry explained to another interviewer that he and Rodgers were still speaking to each other because "We are the only writers who are not geniuses. We are not inspired

artists, but just working men with our coats off." By the time they were in
the middle of *Babes* rehearsals, Rodgers and Hart had composed more than
twenty shows and worked on six produced movies. "Rodgers and Hart admit
they like shows better than the films," *The Boston Globe* reported, "yet they
maintain their limousines and their private chauffeurs with Hollywood
checks." Larry, plugging his brother's appearance in Warner Bros.' *Ready,
Willing and Able*, readily conceded the advantage of movies in staging. "When
the musical comedy films can show 50,000 chorus girls, all beautiful as hou-
ris, dancing on a typewriter, what more can the theater do?" he said. "But I'll
tell you now, we'd rather work for the theater, which may be a dying mistress,
yet our own, than for the pictures, which sends us to Europe for changing
commas to periods and buys us limousines for writing 'and' instead of 'or' and
for whatever success may be attained, twenty-five men take the credit instead
of two." [4]

During mid-March rehearsals, changes were being made by the hour. Wynn
Murray, though advised early that her rotundity would become part of the
libretto, hadn't counted on how many lines about it showed up in the script.
Remonstrating with her away from the other members of the cast, Larry, who
knew what it was like to inhabit a physique considered extreme, persuaded
her that if she could withstand the gibes, it would make both her and the
show that much more appealing. Murray had three songs—"Way Out West,"
"Johnny One Note," and "Imagine"; a sense of humor about herself would
help put them over. Duke McHale's character, Peter, a boy having a romance
with communism until he wins some money, was initially intended to be the
leading role. But McHale had come to seem too young to carry so much stage
time, while Ray Heatherton (as Val LaMar) proved to be a more confident
trouper. Wiman ordered Heatherton's part built up and McHale's trimmed. [5]
McHale, according to reports at the time, was not happy, and Larry couldn't
fix this one so easily. On March 16, 1937, Rodgers wrote to Dorothy, "Mitzi
sings 'Tramp' like a house on fire!" A couple of days later Rodgers reported,
"The 'Johnny One Note' things have great humor and color, and the ballet
clothes are charming." And the following day: "We had another run-through
last night and discovered a million more things that need fixing, and, what
with airplanes and sound effects to be done here, it's hard to find rehearsal
time to repair book and numbers." [6]

This was a rare period when Larry stayed put, making himself available
for rewrites, interviews, and coaching. Rodgers had taken to introducing him

as his son, because of his size, and the gag didn't seem to bother him.[7] The *Times*'s Drama section legman Mordaunt Hall attended a *Babes* rehearsal and sat next to Hart, "who is as genial as his writing." The youngest actor in the cast was Douglas Perry, seven at the time and, by law, too young to appear as Beauregard Calhoun in more than one performance on the same day. Hall asked Perry, "Who is your favorite actress?" Without batting an eyelash, Perry answered, "Mitzi Green." "Ha!" said Larry. "A diplomat!"[8]

When *Babes in Arms* opened at the Shubert in Boston on March 31, not all of the kinks had been worked out. Mitzi Green's singing got less of a reaction than her mugging, at least in part because audiences, deprived of well-known stars in the cast, were pleased to be treated to impressions of Fanny Brice. Ray Heatherton was hard to hear without being miked. The set decoration for "Johnny One Note" was done in an Egyptian motif, with Cannon bath towels—an attempt to show how the kids might make their own scenery and costumes, grabbing whatever was available—and it puzzled some audiences. *Variety*'s correspondent reported: "Comedy is okay, although brilliant lines are scarce. On the other hand, the gags are clean." It was a fair assessment, but with a warning tacked on: "No nudity, no show girls, no plush or gold plate may mean no sale."[9]

The all-kids cast had generated little enthusiasm among ticket brokers and at the box office. Then came a blessing: the Nicholas Brothers finally signed to do the show, though it made their workdays unconscionably long. Harold Nicholas was only fourteen, Fayard Nicholas eighteen. They saw a tutor every afternoon, went to bed for a few hours, then got up at night to prepare for their Cotton Club appearances. Now they'd have to fit nightly performances of *Babes in Arms* into that schedule.[10]

Dwight Wiman wasn't worried. As producers go, he possessed a serenity that kept even the toughest challenges in perspective. With *Babes* completing its Boston tryouts and scheduled to open on Broadway on April 14, Wiman was also sponsoring the Surry Players, a stock company from Surry, Maine, that included the young actors Shepperd Strudwick, Whit Bissell, Connie Nickerson, and Anne Revere—all of them to become familiar character actors to the next two generations of movie and television audiences. By the end of the year Wiman would have the Surry Players' version of *As You Like It* up and running at the Ritz, on Forty-Eighth Street.

Babes had roles for seven or eight adults, most of them as vaudevillians who must leave their children behind in Long Island in order to go out on the road. With their folks gone, the kids are threatened with consignment to the local workhouse. Show business was—in fact still is—solidly middle-class; many vaudevillians actually did go home to Long Island, which was considerably cheaper than Manhattan and also deemed a more hospitable place to raise children. Rodgers and Hart set the story in fictional Seaport, Long Island, which was modeled on Freeport, an actors' enclave. The Lights Club was Freeport's popular summer organization, presided over by that professional fumferer Victor Moore. *Babes in Arms* extended the vaudeville family material of *On Your Toes*, where the protagonist was the son of four-a-day performers; in *Babes*, most of the kids have this lineage. And since they can't get jobs, they have to create them.

The natural leader of these kids is Valentine LaMar. The Christian name will justify the famous song to come; the surname was probably borrowed from the publicist Richard LaMarr, who was in and out of the songwriters' lives for many years. Val becomes intrigued by Seaport newcomer Wilhelmina Smith, known to one and all as Billie. A radiant vagabond, Billie has just traveled all the way from California after being unable to find work in the movies. Billie thought she had a role in *Camille*, she tells Val, and even met Robert Taylor. "But Garbo put her foot down," Billie jokes.

The new acquaintances are clearly attracted to each other. Val explains that the field next to his family's house is worthless; his dad bought it because there was a rumor it would be turned into an airfield, but that plan fell through. Facing each other in his family's kitchen, Val and Billie sing "Where or When." At its simplest, "Where or When" suggests that old feeling of (re-) connecting with someone you've never met before ("We looked at each other in the same way then / But I can't remember where or when"). In nine lines of verse and a mere eleven in the refrain, the song describes the *anamnesis*—a recalling to mind—in which time is flighty and illusive ("Thought has wings, and lots of things / Are seldom what they seem"), but graspable at moments of overwhelming emotion. The verse sustains the metrical balance of the title with phrases like "things you think" and "dreams you dream," and the emotion is grounded ("The clothes you're wearing are the clothes you wore") in everyday reality. The most eloquent of all déjà vu songs, "Where or When" penetrates the daze of new romance—even as experienced by teenagers.

The local Sheriff warns Val and Billie that if they don't soon find work, they and their temporarily orphaned friends will be sent to the local work farm. Val pleads for more time. The work farm appears to have been partly modeled on the camps of the Civilian Conservation Corps (CCC), an early

New Deal program. The Sheriff, sympathetic because he's father to two of Val's friends, gives them two weeks—after that, he'll have no choice but to send them away.

Val decides the solution is to put on a show. "I'll get the gang!" With the deep-voiced Marshall (Alfred Drake) joining them, they sing "Babes in Arms." Larry had used the phrase *babe in arms*, which goes back to Middle English, in "You Took Advantage of Me" in 1928. Here it's a war cry of survival.

The kids still need money to mount the show. One potential angel, Lee Calhoun, is a child of southern aristocracy who provides $49 of the necessary $100. "My father made quite a fortune in Wall Street by selling short during the crash," Lee declares. "The man who makes more deserves more because he's superior. You've got to have superior men just as you have superior races." It's difficult to gauge which Val finds more offensive—the supercilious boy's undisguised bigotry or his buccaneer capitalism.

The hatred Lee spews is contrasted with the innocence of his younger brother, Beauregard, who (to paraphrase Oscar Hammerstein) hasn't yet been carefully taught, and with that of the two sets of black brothers, Lincoln and Booker Vanderpool and Ivor and Irving DeQuincy. Lee, finding his little brother hanging out with the brothers, grabs him by the collar and hauls him away.

The boys are quickly replaced onstage by the white kids Dolores and Gus (Grace McDonald and Rolly Pickert), who used to go steady and now sing "I Wish I Were in Love Again." Few other lyricists have insisted on properly employing the subjunctive in the title. Hart had used it in the ribald "As Though You Were There," which was dropped from *Heads Up!* Hart's friend Noël Coward wrote "If Love Were All"; Clifford Grey wrote "If You Were the Only Girl in the World"; and Hart's devoted student Sheldon Harnick wrote "If I Were a Rich Man." After that there aren't many examples. The triple rhymes and inner rhymes of "I Wish I Were in Love Again" are positively dizzying: "The sleepless nights, / The daily fights, / The quick toboggan when you reach the heights; / I miss the kisses and I miss the bites." The kids now crave the tumult of "The broken dates, / The endless waits" and "the conversation with the flying plates." Instead of being just friends, the kids would rather be punch-drunk, gaga (a favorite Winchellism), and with all the foolery the word implies; they would rather be vulnerable to what Larry nailed as "the self-deception that believes the lie."

Val and his friends call their show the *Follies*—or, more specifically, *Lee Calhoun's Follies* for its primary investor. In a discarded railway boxcar, the DeQuincy brothers sing and dance to "All Dark People (Is Light on Their Feet)," which showcased the Nicholas Brothers' airborne style. For the era, the cheerfully squalid setting was a familiar one for black performers on-screen or on the stage. (The "All God's Chillun Got Rhythm" number from the Marx Brothers' *A Day at the Races*, performed in a spotless barn, is an example.) "All dark people is light on their feet," the refrain declares, as well as the howler "Paleface babies don't dance in the street" (i.e., white folks have no rhythm). Lines like "Skeet-ski-daddle" and "Beedy, weedy, weedy" are meant to approximate scat singing, especially as practiced at the time by such jazzmen as Cab Calloway and Leo Watson. The Nicholas Brothers' mother, Viola, detested the lyric's "Negro grammar" and had her sons sing "All dark people *are*," infuriating the stage manager but not, apparently, Larry Hart.[11] Still, what later audiences came to regard as offensive—an edited, more politically correct version was titled "Light on Their Feet"—turned out to be a great, propulsive number for the brothers. The trumpeter Bunny Berigan had a hit record with his version, recorded two weeks before the show opened.

To persuade Lee Calhoun that he's not backing a bunch of amateurs, Billie flirts with him and does an elaborate imitation of Luise Rainer. Exiting, she inadvertently leaves behind her lipstick, which Lee promptly smears on his cheek, planting the seed of Val's jealousy.

Child movie star Baby Rose (Wynn Murray) has come to town. "Wait till you see her!" says Peter, anticipating a lyric that Larry wouldn't write for another five years. While they're waiting to get a glimpse of her, Lee makes clear his refusal to allow the DeQuincy brothers to appear in the *Follies*. Introduced to Baby Rose, whose girth has expanded considerably since childhood, Lee barely hides his revulsion. Baby Rose declares she's "so tired of the west, but I don't want to desert my public entirely." Here Larry had to tread lightly. The marketing of child performers was hardly new, but movie profits had made the stakes exorbitant. Only a few months after *Babes in Arms* opened, the British magazine *Night and Day* and its film critic Graham Greene were sued by Shirley Temple and Twentieth Century-Fox because Greene had reviewed *Wee Willie Winkie* and imputed to the nine-year-old star a fully developed, self-conscious sexuality at odds with the way the studio presented her. During the trial Greene was described as "beastly" for libeling the "infant"

Miss Temple, who probably never saw the article. Temple was awarded £2,000, with more modest awards going to the American and British divisions of the studio.[12] *Night and Day* ceased publication. Instead of shooting his own barbed arrow at child stars—this was, after all, a musical about and carried largely by children—Larry came up with "Way Out West" for Baby Rose to sing:

> *Git along little taxi,*
> *You can keep the change.*
> *I'm ridin' home to my kitchen range*
> *Way out west on West End Avenue.*

In American fiction Bret Harte and Zane Grey had romanticized the West; in drama David Belasco had made *The Girl of the Golden West* a hit on Broadway, adapted for opera by Giacomo Puccini; then came *Girl Crazy*, which satirized the notion that the bracing western terrain could turn a boy into a man, and Cole Porter's "Don't Fence Me In" in the Bing Crosby picture *Rhythm on the Range* (1936). But for Larry Hart, the Upper West Side offered all the tough living you could ask for:

> *There's not much buffalo but lots of bull*
> *Way out west on West End Avenue.*

Val doesn't want Lee Calhoun's money if it means leaving the DeQuincy brothers out of the show. "There are times when you have to compromise," Billie cautions Val. "You've got to play politics once in a while." Repelled, Val walks out on her. In his absence, humbled and in love, Billie sings "My Funny Valentine." As in "Thou Swell," the verse mixes Arthurian (really pseudo-Elizabethan) syntax with a contemporary idiom, so that terms that apply to, say, a knight in shining armor—noble, upright, virtuous, sincere— are lanced by words like "dim-witted" and "dopey." (Hammerstein and Hart each loved the word "dope" and its variations.) In the refrain Hart strikes a familiar chord in which the object of affection is less than perfect, neither terribly heroic nor self-aware—owner of the "less than Greek" figure, the "laughable" and "unphotographable" looks, the ill-considered words that emerge from his mouth. Still, Billie Smith wouldn't change a hair on Val's tousled head.

But Val isn't yet aware of that.

The *Follies* is produced in the old red barn. In the first number of this show within a show, Baby Rose rocks little Beauregard to sleep and tells him the bedtime story about "Johnny One Note." The melody is certainly an expansion of "Pablo, You Are My Heart," which went unused in the film *Mississippi*, and this new lyric turns it into a disquisition on opera and opera singers. "Johnny could only sing one note / And the note he sang was this: / Ah!" With the ability to airmail her contralto to the back of the balcony, Murray was the perfect singer for this lampoon of a guy (Dennis Moore suggested the boys had Allan Jones in mind) who could hold one note and one note only.[13] Hart placed old Johnny in a production of *Aida* (which he rhymed with *indeed a*), his singing making "Verdi turn 'round in his grave." When it comes his turn to sing, Johnny yells "willy-nilly," prompting awestruck silence throughout the land, and the lines describing it comprise one of Hart's most arresting headlong series:

> *Cats and dogs stopped yapping,*
> *Lions in the zoo*
> *All were jealous of Johnny's big trill.*
> *Thunderclaps stopped clapping,*
> *Traffic ceased its roar,*
> *And they tell us Niag'ra stood still.*
>
> *He stopped the train whistles,*
> *Boat whistles,*
> *Steam whistles,*
> *Cop whistles,*
> *All whistles bowed to his skill.*

The series simulates urban chaos *outside* the opera house; shattering glass is *nothing* compared to the disasters Johnny causes.

Before the *Follies* can proceed, Lee brutally informs Ivor that he won't appear in the show not because he's too young—this was the excuse the others had made—but because he's too black. Val socks Lee in the jaw. The kids are going to the work farm.

At the beginning of act 2, the kids are on the farm and predictably miserable. Baby Rose sings "Imagine," which has the harmonic texture of a nursery rhyme:

Imagine you're out of debt
And love brings you no regret.
If you can imagine this,
Then you must be nuts, my pet!

Val receives a letter from his parents saying they'll be out on the road for several more months. This prompts Billie and him to review, in "All at Once," how kids pretend to act as adults. "We grow no older through the seven ages," Billie declares, quoting Jacques in *As You Like It* and proceeding to at once compress and parody Shakespeare. If all the world's a stage, a barn serves as a theater just as well as a wooden O. "All at Once" is almost never sung outside of a *Babes in Arms* performance, but it shows Hart working at top speed.

The Sheriff, feeling bad for the kids, plans to throw them a party on the LaMar property on his first night off duty. Peter, meanwhile, has disavowed communism because he's just won $500 at the Bank Night at the Cinema Palace, providing him with more than enough money to leave the work farm. He has no intention of sharing the money with his friends, who remain stuck there. Instead he goes on "Peter's Journey," in which he imagines going first cabin to Europe—this is where Balanchine's ballet fantasia comes in—becoming a prince, attended by footmen, visiting Radio City and Hollywood and marrying Garbo and Dietrich. (If Garbo and Dietrich hadn't been the greatest international movie stars of the era, Larry Hart would have made them so.)

At the party, held there on the presumably worthless land, Billie declares her intention to go back on the road rather than return to the work farm. This leads her into "The Lady Is a Tramp," with a lyric that has no equivalent in American song. Misunderstood by each subsequent generation, the song isn't about a woman who views herself as beholden, or even available, to any man, but the contrary—a bohemian, a free spirit who pays little heed to prevailing social opinion. If she's regarded as a tramp ("I've wined and dined on Mulligan Stew, and never wished for turkey"), it's because she's a vagabond with no desire to be otherwise. "My hobohemia is the place to be," Billie declares. Larry has often been credited with inventing the word *hobohemia*, which sounds worthy of Lewis Carroll; in fact the word was first used by Sinclair Lewis in his 1917 short story of the same name—Lewis, who felt himself an outcast in Greenwich Village, did not mean it affectionately—and it's inconceivable that Larry was unaware of at least Lewis's dramatization of the story, which played at the Greenwich Village Theatre in February 1919.[14] Nevertheless, the lyric keeps providing fresh, ironic variations on the theme of the subject's independence. The Lady has missed the Beaux Arts Ball, the exclusive annual affair, conceived and orchestrated by Society tastemaker Gretchen Menken, where you dressed precisely along the lines of the motif she had coordinated. The Lady also likes the populism of Coney Island and doesn't mind sitting in the bleachers at the ballpark. She declines to gossip but loves reading Walter Winchell (who grew up less than a mile from Hart). She claims to prefer the Automat to the Ritz, and if there's any doubt she isn't a tramp in the promiscuous sense, she reminds us: "I'm all alone when I lower my lamp."

Mitzi Green put the song across with such blazing energy that Larry was called on, as he so often was, to compose additional lyrics. The opening lines of two appended refrains are worth quoting here:

> *Don't know the reason for cocktails at five.*
> *I don't like flying—I'm glad I'm alive.*
> *I crave affection, but not when I drive.*
> *That's why the lady is a tramp.*

And:

> *Girls get massages, they cry and they moan.*
> *Tell Lizzie Arden to leave me alone.*
> *I'm not so hot, but my shape is my own.*
> *That's why the lady is a tramp.*

Contest-winner Peter shows up at the party and, now that he's blown his windfall in the fourth race at Belmont, is embracing communism once more. On the radio comes a vocalist, accompanied by accordion, singing Irving Berlin's "I Want to Go Back to Michigan," and the kids lunge for the dial to change the station. From the radio they get the news of French flyer René Flambeau's attempt to land in Newark, but he can't make it the extra fifteen miles and is forced to land in Seaport, right there on the LaMar property. For more than a decade the transatlantic aviator had been a heroic figure, a daredevil ideal whose every triumph and failure was picked over by the newspapers. The Americans had Charles Lindbergh, the British had Noel Davis, and the French could brag of the ace flyer Charles Nungesser and the air-mail pilot and novelist Antoine de Saint-Exupéry. These fliers (not to mention Amelia Earhart, who would be presumed dead by the summer of 1937) were celebrities of the time. Employing the familiar image of a dashing French pilot was Hart's crude but effective way of connecting with the audience. The publicity resulting from Flambeau's crash, with a little extra push from Val, will turn that worthless piece of land, it's implied, into a major airport. No more work farm for the kids.

Almost every critic used a lot of ink on the youthfulness of the show and how it was handled. "Nowhere is there a coy exploitation of the juvenile angle," Stirling Bowen wrote in *The Wall Street Journal*. "No professional prodigy is in evidence. Everything is done in earnest and in the best of faith; and done, furthermore, exceedingly well." "Without condescending from the sublime heights of maturity," Brooks Atkinson said in the *Times*, "Mr. Rodgers and Mr. Hart have written a genial and buoyant show for [the youngsters]." In *The New Yorker*, Robert Benchley seemed to be writing for many other observers when he praised *Babes in Arms* but felt it had been built on nostalgia for the first *Garrick Gaieties*, which had also been carried by young performers.[15] "Too much youth," George Jean Nathan wrote, "is a bore, since youth lacks variety and has little to fall back on but animal spirits, which are an even greater bore." But Nathan had high praise for Grace McDonald.[16]

Annoyance ran through Charles E. Dexter's review of *Babes in Arms* in the *Daily Worker*. Dexter wrote that "the central idea of the show and the clever lyrics are from the mighty brain of little Mr. Hart," and took note of the book's references to communism, fascism, and work farms. "But Mr. Hart is not the kind of writer who wants to keep in step. He's satisfied to lay the groundwork for a swell entertainment and let it go at that. His disinclination to write a great musical show is not due to any lack of ambition. It's due to his carelessness and muddled thinking. As a result he builds a tower toward the sky and forgets to finish it." Hart's sardonic presentation of a boy's quick, untroubled conversion from communist to capitalist irked Dexter, as it surely would have any representative of the *Daily Worker*. Dexter also took Hart to task for the subplot of Lee Calhoun declining to have Negroes in the show, the boy so patently misguided that Hart wound up insulting white Southerners and patronizing Negroes.[17]

Months later, a piece in the *New York Amsterdam News* suggested that

Babes in Arms had, in fact, "more propaganda in it favorable to Negroes than any show that's been on the 'Main Stem' in a long time. . . . *Babes in Arms* is doing a good job toward breaking down racial prejudice. It would be a treat some day to see a Negro play depicting the white man favorably."[18] If the boys knew about this notice from New York's premier black newspaper, they must have regarded it as gravy.

Although nobody thought the *Babes in Arms* book—most of it Hart's work—had power or even cohesion, Larry's lyrics were singled out by several reviewers. In the *Herald Tribune*, Richard Watts, Jr., wrote, "Mr. Hart proves that he is the slyest and most ingenious of lyric writers." On April 26, *Time* published an unqualified (though also unsigned) rave, and one line in the notice caused a bit of a stir: "Lyricist Hart—never topped since he observed in 1925, 'beans could get no keener reception in a beanery,' etc.—still maintains the lightest touch in the business."[19]

Dwight Wiman's publicity machine, stoked by publicist Henry Spitzer, chugged on. The day after the show opened, two items appeared that promoted the show without mentioning songs or performers. In one, a female skeleton was reported to have been found beneath the foundation of the Wimans' house in Bermuda; although no foul play was said to be involved, the skeleton remained unidentified—a mystery just sordid enough to keep the story, and Wiman's name with it, in print for a while.[20] The other item was classic Broadway PR. In his "Lyons Den" column in the evening *Post*, Leonard Lyons wrote that as *Babes* was opening, ticket-holders were lingering across the street at Sardi's, despite ushers calling "Curtain going up!" outside on West Forty-Fourth Street; finally, Larry Hart shouted "Fire! Fire!" to get everyone out and over to the theater.[21] The story might have been true.

There was immediate movie interest. The scout for Metro producer Eddie Knopf raved that *Babes in Arms* had cornered the youth market—then as now, these were sorcerer's words to studio executives—and that "The Lady Is a Tramp" "ranks with the best Cole Porter has ever devised." But the cold, unforgiving evaluations by the Hollywood scout said more about the studio than the talent. Of Kenneth Wilkins, who played Booker Vanderpool, the scout wrote: "A funny little piccaninny—can't use." Of Bob Fishelson, who played Pinkie: "Jewish looking boy—unimportant—can't use." And of the *zaftig* Wynn Murray: "I had her in here about three months ago—she's sixteen years old, weighs about 190 lbs., and sings like Kate Smith—can't use."[22]

❧   ❧   ❧

The mid-1930s are often described as a period of frantic musical comedy activity on Broadway. But the description is deceptive. The greatest era in American musical theater was still more than a decade into the future. Meanwhile there were Broadway seasons in which the musical offerings were paltry. That there were fewer choices may not have been a bad thing. In the *World-Telegram*, Douglas Gilbert wrote that in 1927 there were twenty-four musicals on Broadway in midseason; in 1937 the number was three. When *Babes in Arms* opened on April 14, 1937, the only other musicals still selling tickets were *The Show Is On*, the Bea Lillie–Bert Lahr revue; and *Fredericka*, a Franz Lehár operetta—the young Goethe was the hero—adapted and supplied with English lyrics by Edward Eliscu. That was it for the competition. The popularity of the talkies was the most obvious reason, but Gilbert gave credit rather than blame to the movies by insisting that movies in general, and movie musicals in particular, had raised the standard of the Broadway show. To lure audiences away from the considerably cheaper cinema, a musical comedy had to offer things you couldn't get on the screen: immediacy, live performers energized by the stage, and a score untouched by directors, producers, or front office yes-men who claimed to know better.[23] Larry Hart had been saying that for years.

Exactly one week after *Babes in Arms* opened, Dick and Larry went to Hollywood to write the score for a Mervyn LeRoy picture, *Return Engagement*, which was to star Fernand Gravet and Ethel Merman. Their getaway was hardly a secret. On April 25, the *Times*'s theater gossip column reported:

> When [Rodgers and Hart] return from Hollywood in three months or so they should have gotten well into the revue they will write with George S. Kaufman and Moss Hart. Then it will be time to whip into shape *I Married an Angel*, though that won't be starting quite from scratch, because several songs from the unproduced picture version will hold over. Then they will be working with Clare Boothe on the musical that still has no title but does have a general idea: a satire on scientific research.

The startling thing about the squib was how accurate it all was. There was a musical idea they had kicked around with George S. Kaufman and Moss Hart; *I Married an Angel* remained a dream project if only Wiman could secure the rights; and Clare Boothe had recently scored a smash with her play

The Women and was indeed trying to shape a play that could be turned into a libretto for Rodgers and Hart.

Out on the Coast, Dick and Larry each took a suite at the Beverly-Wilshire for $300 a month. Immediately they plunged into deeper discussions of the new show with Kaufman and Moss Hart. The show was to be about two young people befriending President Roosevelt. Although presidents had figured in Broadway shows before—the "Mr. and Mrs." skit in *Garrick Gaieties* had lampooned the domestic life of the Coolidges—this would be the first time the incumbent would be the protagonist of a musical comedy.[24]

They had some anxiety, though, about *Babes in Arms*. Mitzi Green had come down with laryngitis after singing one night at the nightclub Versailles (Fifty-Ninth and Lexington), "a house where innocence is as rare as courtesy," and was now missing *Babes* performances. Ticket sales, already wobbly because of notices suggesting the show was "wholesome," plummeted and it wasn't clear if the show would stay open till summer. Fortunately, within two weeks of the show's opening, "Where or When" was becoming one of the best-selling songs in the nation. Rodgers and Hart signed a contract to appear twice in the coming weeks on radio's *The Chase and Sanborn Hour,* which would draw them publicity for *Babes in Arms.*

At Warners, the boys worked on the LeRoy picture each day. Larry had Teddy and Teddy's fiancée, Dorothy, nearby but was always ready for a party. He and Dick went together to the Hollywood Bowl to hear Ray Middleton perform *All Points West* with the Philadelphia Orchestra—a disappointment because Middleton went up on (i.e., forgot) the lyrics, and worrisome because he was scheduled to sing the piece on *The Chase and Sanborn Hour.*[25]

On May 2, 1937, Larry Hart turned forty-two. He attended a birthday party thrown for him in Beverly Hills. Early in the proceedings he vanished, never to return that night, and Rodgers went to the piano "to save myself from being bored to death." On May 4 the boys showed up at a party where George S. Kaufman, having just received word that he and Moss Hart had won the Pulitzer Prize in drama for *You Can't Take It with You,* stood among the guests with a determined nonchalance, as though a Pulitzer were no big deal. (Kaufman, without Moss Hart, had won the prize once before, for *Of Thee I Sing.*)

On May 5 Rodgers and Hart were thrown a huge party by Herb Fields. "Larry distinguished himself by getting cockeyed before the meat course," Rodgers wrote to his wife, "and having to be put to bed by Joe Fields where he spent the rest of the party and the night. Everyone thought he was very cute. I had to play all the stuff from the new show many times and the enthusiasm made me feel a little more like myself. A new record was broken. I played all evening and George [Gershwin] never got near the piano." Over the years there'd been waves of jokes about Gershwin's piano-hogging. In Morrie Ryskind's *The Diary of an Ex-President,* a comic prose sequel to *Of Thee I Sing,* Gershwin camps out in the White House for days playing *Rhapsody in Blue* even as a fire rages around him.[26] Gershwin's not getting to the piano would prove to be more significant than Rodgers knew at the time.[27]

Mitzi Green returned to *Babes in Arms* and business picked up. Dick claimed to be eager to get home to New York, but there was so much West Coast activity—the Mervyn LeRoy picture, discussions with Kaufman and Hart about the FDR show, parties and nightclubs and the racetrack—that it would be awhile. "Besides [Arthur] Hornblow," Rodgers reported to Dorothy, "Mr. Goldwyn also wants us for a picture, so I guess there'd be no trouble if we wanted to stay here. But we don't. Which reminds me, there's been no word from anyone regarding *Angel* and I'm just going to wait and see how long it takes them. All in all, I'm working up to a good boil at the Wiman organization."[28] Wiman had promised to get the rights to *I Married an Angel.* What was the holdup?

"Had dinner with the shrimp last night," Dick wrote, referring to Larry, "and hit the hay at a very early hour while he went about his ne*far*ious (get it?) business."[29]

On the LeRoy picture, Merman was replaced by Carole Lombard—not a singer but an irresistible creature—to star opposite Gravet. Because Gravet's role was a French chef, the title was changed from *Return Engagement* to *Food for Scandal.* It would eventually be changed again to *Fools for Scandal.*

One evening Dick and Larry went to the Trocadero, where pianist Phil Ohman played nothing but Rodgers & Hart songs. It was a heady thing to be made much of at the swankiest club in town, hearing your music treated like a national treasure. "Manhattan," "My Heart Stood Still," "With a Song in My Heart"—they rolled off Ohman's keyboard and swirled around the room. Meanwhile, Dwight Wiman was close to wresting *I Married an Angel* away from Metro so the boys could write the musical they'd been waiting years to write. Word got around. Vincent Price told Wiman he would do *anything* to appear in *Angel.* "Hear him in a theater," Rodgers suggested to Wiman, knowing that actors accustomed to being miked on soundstages often thought of themselves as singers, too.

Doc Bender arrived in Los Angeles. A day or two later, Larry checked out of the Beverly-Wilshire, claiming he couldn't stand its enforced quiet, and rented an apartment in Hollywood for $150 a month. Of course it's possible he wanted to save a bundle on rent; more likely, he just wanted more privacy. Although Rodgers was then, as always, grateful to have some distance from his collaborator during nonworking hours, he was suspicious that Larry decided to move only now that Bender had come to town.

Dorothy Rodgers must have been annoyed by her husband's earlier reference to Hart's "nefarious business" and given him hell, because Rodgers was soon backpedaling. "My crack about Larry was just for fun. I have no idea what he does with himself after I leave him, but according to his morning reticence I have to draw my own conclusions. However, he seems to be functioning quite well and that's my major concern unless he manages to get in trouble."[30]

Fred Astaire, stepping high after the admiring reviews of the new Astaire–Ginger Rogers picture *Shall We Dance*—songs by George and Ira Gershwin, with George writing the underscore and also orchestrating—decided to take the summer off from his weekly radio program. As he turned the show over to his bandleader Johnny Green, he sang a version of "Johnny One Note" that made his radio audience, including Dick and Larry, very happy.[31] No air check has turned up, but it must have been delightful to hear Astaire, who introduced more popular standards than anyone else in the movies, use his narrow-ranged, conversational voice to accomplish Johnny's big trilling "Ahh!"

Something else came out of nowhere that pleased Dick and Larry. James Agate, the London *Times* critic who had found "Here in My Arms" so displeasing a decade earlier, caught *Babes in Arms* in New York:

> I enjoyed every moment of this; the music by Rodgers and Hart is written in a fascinating idiom which is theirs and nobody else's. Haunting! The show cost comparatively little to stage—fifty-five thousand dollars only—and could be put on in London for a quarter of that sum. But I doubt whether it would be a profitable experiment. Seeing that it has been put together with many brains, I foresee flattering notices and empty houses. London likes its musical comedy to be solid, substantial, and thick; *Babes in Arms* is airy and fanciful, and the scenery is of the sketchiest. This is as it should be, since the whole notion is that a lot of actors' orphans will be sent to work on the land if they don't make good with a revue of their own concocting.[32]

In the coming weeks Agate—as hard to please, whether writing about music, theater, or films, as George Bernard Shaw had been fifty years earlier—wasn't able to get the show out of his head. Still filing from New York, he reported that "the lilt of Hart and Rodgers' score, which has danced its way through everything I have seen," had "given this hardboiled city a dreamlike quality." At the end of May, Agate and his companion, "B.," sailed out of New York harbor, heading to Southampton. "And now New York begins to fade from my consciousness," Agate wrote. "Or would do if B. were not whistling 'Where or When' from *Babes in Arms*, the first piece we saw and the one I enjoyed most, musical comedy though it is. I think its sixteen-year-old naïveté gave me some foretaste of this still new and still raw country."[33]

After returning to London, Agate wrote to Rodgers and Hart, charmingly introduced himself (as though he needed to) as a *Times* critic, declared he had fallen in love with *Babes in Arms*, and requested records of "Where or When" and "Imagine" (though he referred to it as "Just Imagine"). "I'm just crazy about this stuff," Agate wrote, "how crazy you just can't imagine." The letter was forwarded to the boys on the West Coast. Rodgers arranged for pianists Edgar Fairchild and Adam Carroll to make recordings of the two songs, presumably singing Larry's lyrics too, through the Liberty Music Shop at Fiftieth and Madison. "Guard [Agate's letter] with [your life], and put it away with the one from Prince George [*sic*]," Rodgers wrote Dorothy.[34] This was approbation of the highest order.

The second of the boys' two appearances on *The Chase and Sanborn Hour* was scheduled for June 13. *The Chase and Sanborn Hour* first percolated on the air in 1928, briefly starring Maurice Chevalier, then Eddie Cantor for several years, with David Freedman serving as head writer. In April 1937, coinciding with Rodgers and Hart's most recent West Coast stay, *The Chase and Sanborn Hour* was revamped, with Don Ameche as host, and Edgar Bergen and Charlie McCarthy—the only successful ventriloquist-dummy team in a nonvisual medium—providing much of the comedy every Sunday night. W. C. Fields and Rodgers and Hart had been the guests on this new version's debut, on May 9, when *All Points West* was performed, and now Dick and Larry were slated to reappear on June 13.

An air check from that evening demonstrates Dick and Larry fitting right in. Preparing the audience for "A Little of You on Toast," Charlie McCarthy is quickly disabused of his claim to have written the song. "After all, none of us are human," Charlie says. "None of us *is* human," Larry corrects. Larry and

Dick possessed pleasant tenor voices with heavy New York accents, though Larry's had a slightly more singsong quality. When Charlie declares that a couple of "mugs" took credit for writing "My Heart Stood Still," Larry says, "We were the mugs who wrote that song, Cholly." And when Charlie suggests that all four of them form a songwriting partnership, Larry says, "I think three names might look betta." "Oh, no, you don't!" Dick protests, inferring he'll be the one left out. The rendition of "Toast" that follows is delightful, partly because Ameche and Dorothy Lamour could really sing, partly because Larry wrote several new choruses poking gentle fun at a dozen celebrities. Everyone sounds to be having a swell time.[35]

The Chase and Sanborn Hour was heard on NBC stations coast to coast. For just about a month, through Dick's thirty-fifth birthday and for a couple of weeks after that, the boys were on top of the world. Finishing their work on *Fools for Scandal*, they learned that Wiman had finally secured the stage rights to *I Married an Angel*. They were contemplating a political musical with two men who had just won the Pulitzer Prize. And *Babes in Arms* was picking up business as spring turned to summer in New York. Across the Hudson, in Fort Lee, New Jersey, in a warehouse that was part of the old Paragon movie studios, the *On Your Toes* equipment and costumes, including more than eighty pairs of ballet shoes, were put in storage. The melodic lines of "Slaughter on Tenth Avenue" haunted the warehouse every night.[36]

CHAPTER 18

All at Once I Owned the Earth and Sky

PROFILES OF the songwriters and reviews of *Babes* were still coming in. In the *Brooklyn Daily Eagle* Irving Kolodin mentioned correctly that both Rodgers's and Hart's Columbia careers ended before either earned a degree. (Future commentators, determined to etch differences between the collaborators, would have Hart flailing and finally dropping out, while Rodgers was often said to have graduated.) Hart, Kolodin wrote, was given to "Rabelaisian witticisms" and to melancholia, which he relieved by throwing parties and singing before his guests "in a loud, unmusical voice, most frequently in ribald parodies." Crediting Hart with taking up W. S. Gilbert's mantle before and better than any other lyricist—and relying in part on the profile Sidney Skolsky had written of him a decade earlier for the New York *Sun*—Kolodin said, "Hart shrinks (if such a thought were conceivable) from the idea of the radio, first nights, vaudeville, society, and home cooking." Larry thought radio to be a conduit for a lot of yammering, and when he wrote the declarative "I'll use the radio!" in the lovely, undervalued "I'll Tell the Man in the Street," it was a grudging acknowledgment that it was the most effective way to spread the word. First nights and Society, with their required evening clothes and limousine exclusivity ("I was never at a party where they honored Noel Ca'ad"), were perennial Hart targets. (On first nights, Larry, like Max Beerbohm before him, observed "the familiar faces in the audience; the mutual bows, smiles, handshakes, hand-waves; the sprightliness of it all, and the frantic self-importance.")[1] Home cooking may have been only a reference to Hart's preference for staying out and drinking—eating being no more than a necessity—rather than a slur on Mary Campbell's cooking.[2]

Almost every reporter invited to see Hart at home was taken with Big Mary. Profiling Hart in the *World-Telegram* from notes he'd made before Rodgers and Hart went to Hollywood, George Ross recounted how Mary called out, "Hey, Mr. Lorry! Telephone!" Mary, according to Hart, refused to let him stay in bed late, sometimes yanking the bedcovers off him and yelling, "Hey, Mr. Lorry, you lazy good-for-nothing, get up!"[3] Reporting for *Cue Magazine*, Orville Prescott got a load of Doc Bender entering the Beresford apartment and couldn't resist taking a shot. Bender was, Prescott wrote, "an anomalous gentleman ... a tall, bespectacled person, he looks like a stooge, discourses volubly and insists he represents Mr. Hart." What, one wonders, does a stooge look like? Still, there was something in Bender that brought out an observer's contempt. Or perhaps Prescott, like so many others who met Larry Hart, felt the need to protect him, even though Bender *did* represent Hart and was his most frequent companion around town.[4]

This was all publicity that kept *Babes in Arms* toddling along. During the first week of July, however, *Babes* found itself to be the only musical left standing—a situation that spiked sales. Wiman claimed that had been his strategy since the show opened.

The new FDR musical, *Hooray for Our Side*, was coming together. It's not clear who thought of it, but the first casting idea for FDR was Charles Winninger.[5] If Winninger could pilot a show boat on Broadway, he could pilot the nation! Winninger said no, and the next casting idea made Dick and Larry each hold his breath: *what about George M. Cohan?* Cohan had overhauled his career in Eugene O'Neill's *Ah, Wilderness!*—only the second time in forty years he'd played a part he hadn't written—but he hadn't appeared in a stage musical in a decade. Maybe that's why, after receiving a cable in London outlining the story, Cohan said yes.[6] Maybe he just wanted to be back on Broadway.

Calling from New York, Wiman issued the boys a challenge: *get someone else* to write the book for *I Married an Angel* so they wouldn't be overtaxed while they wrote the songs. Accustomed now to receiving somewhere in the neighborhood of $20,000 for each movie assignment, which usually took them no more than a few weeks, they calculated that without authors' royalties, *I Married an Angel* would have to run a year before they earned that same $20,000. No, they told Wiman, *they* would write the show's book. The July 7, 1937, edition of *Variety* listed "Where or When" at number two in the nation in record sales; the Lucky Strike Hit Parade listed it at number five.

On July 9, at a dinner party in Los Angeles thrown by Mildred Knopf, there were murmurs that something was wrong with George Gershwin. "I don't like what I hear about George," Rodgers wrote to Dorothy. "He's had a complete mental collapse and they don't know what to do with him. They'd like to send him east to a sanitarium as they don't trust the ones out here, but he's too ill to be moved."[7]

The party had lighter moments. Rodgers wrote, "F. Scott [Fitzgerald] told me that he had seen *Babes* three times and thought it was the best musical show he'd ever seen."[8] Fitzgerald, writing later to his daughter, Scottie, confessed to being drawn to the kind of work Rodgers and Hart accomplished. "Sometimes I wish I had gone along with that gang, but I guess I am too much of a moralist at heart and really want to preach at people in some acceptable form rather than to entertain them."[9] Fitzgerald, in fact, had once referred to Hart as the poet laureate of America.

Gershwin died, of a brain tumor, a day and a half after the Knopf party. "I phoned the Cedars a little after ten-thirty and was told that George had just died," Rodgers wrote on the eleventh of July.[10] The next day Rodgers wrote: "The town is in a daze and nobody talks about anything but George's death. . . . It's just awful. There will be funeral services here Thursday morning and Larry and I are on the committee."[11]

In fact, funeral services were held almost simultaneously in New York and Los Angeles. In New York, Rabbi Nathan Perilman and Rabbi Stephen S. Wise, associate and chief rabbis, respectively, conducted services at Temple Emanu-El, with sixty honorary pallbearers in attendance. In Los Angeles, Rabbi Edgar F. Magnin presided at Temple B'nai Brith. Dick and Larry attended. Oscar Hammerstein gave a eulogy on behalf of the songwriters and film composers.[12] In the post-funeral days the gloom was unrelenting.

Before becoming sick, Gershwin had completed five songs for *The Goldwyn Follies*; one of them was "Love Walked In." Gershwin was irreplaceable, but his former protégé Vernon Duke was brought in to complete the songs with Ira Gershwin. For a few weeks, the old Cape Cod quartet—Duke, Balanchine, Bender, and Larry—was reunited in Hollywood.

With the assistance of London-born Adolph Deutsch, who had orchestrated for Paul Whiteman and worked on *Jumbo*, Dick and Larry spent a few days finishing work on the *Fools for Scandal* sound track. Herb Fields and his brother, Joseph, had written the screenplay, based on a Broadway play, and the brothers were at a career intersection: Herb had come to Hollywood only after writing several musical plays, mostly for Rodgers and Hart and Cole Porter; Joseph had started early with credits on *Flying Down to Rio* (1933) and *Annie Oakley* (1935), and only later, determined to win better contracts for cowriter Jerome Chodorov and himself, would he write profitably for the theater (e.g., *My Sister Eileen*). *Fools for Scandal* wouldn't be released until spring of 1938, but Dick and Larry already knew the shape it was taking. Carole Lombard, in the only Warners role of her career, plays the American film star Kay Winters. Traveling to Paris in disguise as Kay Sommers, she offers to hire French cook René, played by Fernand Gravet, unaware that he's a marquis. (Gravet bore an unnerving resemblance to the young Milton Berle.) Romance ensues. Despite Lombard's considerable appeal, the only part of the film worth remembering is a number by Jeni Le Gon, a tiny black dancer who had gained national attention after filming *Hooray for Love* with Bill Robinson and Fats Waller.[13] Le Gon sings Rodgers and Hart's "There's a Boy in Harlem," which sketches a Duke Ellington–like composer.

> There's a new dark music by a new dark man,
> And he writes his symphonies in black and tan.

In early August, after nearly four months on the West Coast, Dick and Larry took the Super Chief east, using the bar car to knock out the first of several songs for the new Kaufman and (Moss) Hart and Cohan musical, now titled *I'd Rather Be Right*.

The new title was suggested by Dorothy Rodgers, quoting Henry Clay's speech to the Senate defending his Compromise of 1850. "I would rather be right than be President," Clay had said.[14] The abbreviated phrase was hardly obscure. On the inside of the front cover of a January 1928 issue of *Judge*, for instance, there was Ed Wynn with a cartoon bubble above him containing the quote.[15] In any case, the boys' work on the songs proceeded through the end of summer, at Dick's summer home in Port Washington; at Larry's apartment at the Beresford; at a bay-front hotel in Atlantic Beach, Long Island; and in a booth at Sardi's.

The plot of *I'd Rather Be Right* was cute—given that the popular president was the starring role, how could it not be?—without being much more substantial than the Herb Fields books for earlier Rodgers & Hart musicals. Phil Barker won't get a raise until the national budget is balanced, thereby postponing marriage to his sweetheart Peggy Jones. Together they dream of meeting FDR in Central Park—depicted by a footbridge and an underpass, with tall buildings rising in the distance—and FDR and his cabinet do what they can to make things right for the young couple, who marry in the end. The idea sounds original enough. But a Damon Runyon story called "A Call on the President," about Runyon's recurring characters Joe and Ethel Turp, had first appeared in Hearst's *Pictorial Weekly* and was then republished in *The Saturday Evening Post* in mid-August of 1937—right around the time Kaufman and Hart were revising their FDR musical and Dick and Larry were working on the songs.[16] In Runyon's story the Turps, hoping to get their mailman Jim his job back, drive from their home in Brooklyn to Washington and talk their way into the White House. Out comes the President. The Turps' stories about the veteran mailman, told with that peculiar Runyon syntax, prove so charming that FDR invites them to stay for lunch and promises to reinstate Jim at the post office.

Whether or not "A Call on the President" was on the minds of Kaufman and Hart, Kaufman demanded higher royalties for the team because he wanted to prove that a musical comedy book was more important than music and lyrics—a question-begging argument if ever there was one. The conciliatory producer Sam H. Harris agreed to Kaufman's demands: Kaufman and Hart would get 8 percent of box office, Rodgers and Hart 5 percent. Larry took their inferior position with a laugh, but Dick seethed. "Moss had great enthusiasm and loved music and was highly approachable at all times," Rodgers said. "George was extremely difficult, bitter, sarcastic, and had no interest in music."[17]

Kaufman was an irritant, but essential to *I'd Rather Be Right*. Yet the same was true for George M. Cohan, who never gave Rodgers or Hart the time of day and referred to them, dripping with derision, as "Gilbert and Sullivan." The Boston tryout, at the Colonial Theatre on October 11, 1937, was highly publicized and glamorous as tryouts go. The show's second number, "Have You Met Miss Jones?," in which Phil (Austin Marshall) recounts to FDR the trajectory of his romance with Peggy (Joy Hodges), was sure to be a hit:

"Have you met Miss Jones?"
Someone said as we shook hands.

She was just Miss Jones to me.
Then I said, "Miss Jones,
You're a girl who understands
I'm a man who must be free."
And all at once I lost my breath,
And all at once was scared to death,
And all at once I owned the earth and sky!
Now I've met Miss Jones
And we'll keep on meeting till we die,
Miss Jones and I.

Later, Peggy and Phil project their married selves forty years into the future with "Sweet Sixty-five," in which uncooperative knees aren't so different from losing one's hair in Paul McCartney's "When I'm Sixty-four." "A Homogeneous Cabinet" presents FDR's various secretaries and advisers, their real names known by every audience member who read the papers, including Secretary of Labor Frances Perkins and Postmaster General James Farley. "Nine Young Girls and Nine Old Men," which matched courtesans to jurists of the U.S. Supreme Court and conceded that even the great George Washington sometimes needed "a little bit of not so innocent fun," was dropped after a few performances in Boston. It would make way for the more specific "A Little Bit of Constitutional Fun," which rhymed "John Marshall" with "impartial" and tossed up the issue of FDR attempting to pack the Supreme Court. "Tune Up, Bluebird" was about balancing the budget. For a show focused on the President and his cabinet, the ensemble was surprisingly large, filling the stage in several scenes.

But it was the long number called "Off the Record," sung by Cohan as FDR, which got the most attention that first night, particularly the stanza that goes:

If I'm not re-elected and the worst comes to the worst,
I'll never die of hunger and I'll never die of thirst.
I've got one boy with Du Pont and another one with Hearst.
But that's off the record.

"Off the Record" went on for four extended choruses that bubbled over with names of the great in literature, show business, and politics. The sultry, hard-drinking actress Tallulah Bankhead, born into one of Alabama's most politically prominent families, was touring at the time in *Antony and Cleopatra* when Cohan sang:

> *My messages to Congress*
> *Are a lot of boola-boola,*
> *I'm not so fond of Bankhead*
> *But I'd love to meet Tallulah—*
> *Don't print it—it's strictly off the record!*[18]

"Off the Record" was the flash point for the simmering enmity between Cohan and Rodgers and Hart. Cohan refused to sing a Hart-authored line about Al Smith (whom Cohan regarded as an intimate friend) and substituted his own line. Frederick Nolan, recounting the episode, has written that "Larry Hart demanded that either Cohan be taken to task for this insultingly unprofessional behavior or he would quit the show and take his lyrics with him." In this case Larry had the support of Kaufman, who made Cohan promise never again to alter Hart's lyrics.[19]

The enmity between star and songwriters pumped up advance sales. The *Times* took the opportunity to remind its readers that contemporary political satire tended to be crude. In the previous century there was W. S. Gilbert and his still pertinent lines from *Iolanthe*:

> *When in that house M.P.'s divide*
> *If they've a brain and cerebellum too,*
> *They've got to leave that brain outside*
> *And vote just as their leaders tell them to.*[20]

So when, asked the *Times*, "will some American Gilbert appear and cultivate the rich comic field that yet has been spaded here and there?"[21] Poor Larry Hart couldn't catch a break—referred to sarcastically as Gilbert by Cohan, while the *Times* wasn't prepared to acknowledge Larry as Gilbert's rightful heir, either.

On November 2, the night *I'd Rather Be Right* opened in New York, it seemed like half of Manhattan waited outside the Alvin Theatre to get a glimpse of Cohan. "From the Battery to the Bronx at the least, New York seemed completely overwhelmed by the return of Mr. Cohan," journalist Lucius Beebe reported, "and popular rejoicing and Morris dancing in Longacre Square complemented the most insufferable crush, confusion, and amiable uproar Fifty-Second Street has ever known."[22] As it happened, Cohan tripped over a cable backstage but, ever the trouper, played with his leg in a rubber cast.[23] Rodgers conducted opening night—he would subsequently turn the baton over to Harry Levant, brother of Oscar—using Hans Spialek's orchestrations. After the show, theatergoers gathered at the Stork Club, El Morocco, and the Kaufman-Rodgers party for the cast at the Carlyle.

If the show had been something of an anticlimax, critics seemed to regard it as a significant achievement—a satire that managed, like Cohan himself, to be light on its feet—but tempered their enthusiasm. In the *Times* Brooks Atkinson called it "a clever and likeable musical comedy. But it is not the keen and brilliant political satire most of us have been fondly expecting." Eleven days later Atkinson thought to add that "nearly every Washington column and editorial page is from time to time more caustic than this musical show."[24] Although Robert Coleman gushed in the *Daily Mirror* and Jack Pulaski had nothing but good things to say in *Variety*, Burns Mantle's notice in the *Daily News* was closer to the ambivalence most critics felt: "But it just isn't the greatest musical comedy ever written or the greatest political satire ever staged."[25] John Mason Brown, who had seen the show in Boston as well as in New York, gave the others their due:

> As all of us hoped it would, *I'd Rather Be Right* elects the nation to the Gridiron Club. The most significant thing about it is that it is at all. It does not hesitate to call high public officials by their right names, and, while doing so, call them laughingly to account. It is gay, witty, topical, and audacious—the kind of irreverent satire which could be written and seen only in these much-abused United States. . . . Mr. Kaufman and the Zwei Herzen—Moss and Lorenz—get many unsparing and uproarious things said. They have their laughs at the fireside chats, at the Federal Theatre, at the Wagner act, at Mr. Farley, and Secretaries Perkins and Morgenthau.[26]

Box office swelled. Gertrude Lawrence sent Dick and Larry a congratulatory telegram. On November 6 Rodgers wired back:

> *My thanks to you my darling*
> *And the heavens came across,*
> *We have got a hit like Susan,*
> *But, by Jesus, it's by Moss.*

Rodgers was referring to Rachel Crothers's play *Susan and God*, the comedy starring Lawrence, which had opened on October 8 to great acclaim.[27] The new guessing game was who might step in as FDR once Cohan, now fifty-nine, got tired. The only name mentioned more than once was that of Walter Huston, who had done plenty of hoofing in his vaudeville days. But Huston knew better than to follow Cohan.[28] Months later, when *I'd Rather Be Right* was winding down—it would, astonishingly, run one performance more than the far superior *Babes in Arms*—Larry, still declining to trade barbs with Cohan, who remained in the show to the end, told *The Boston Herald* that the show had been a stunt. "Without George M. Cohan there'd have been no show at all. We hadn't anything to do with making it a success—we couldn't have reached first base without him."[29]

The boys' pattern had been to leave town soon after a show opened. True to form, Dick and Larry each made plans to leave for Europe, but separately—Larry sailing on the *Rex* to Italy, where he anticipated working on *I Married an Angel*, Dick following ten days later aboard the *Normandie*.[30] Before sailing, Larry phoned Vivienne Segal.

"Hello, baby. Are you available in the spring?"

"Why do you ask?" said Segal.

"Because I've written a part for you," Larry said, though he hadn't yet.

Segal knew better than to say no. Larry could now tailor the role to her.

By the time he boarded the *Rex*, only two musicals were still running on Broadway, *Babes in Arms* and *I'd Rather Be Right*.[31]

Larry was scheduled to meet Dick in mid-December, after they'd had a good long break from one another; until then he was likely to write a lyric only under penalty of death. Instead he was skipping through Naples, Rome, Florence, Venice, Vienna, and—entirely for his amusement rather than research for *I Married an Angel*—Budapest. He also had Doc Bender in tow. Frederick Nolan has naturally wondered why, in talking of this trip months later, Larry appeared resolutely oblivious to the stirrings of war. "Four major Italian cities and nothing about Mussolini and the rising tide of fascism? A week in Vienna just three months before the *Anschluss* and nothing about war clouds?"[32] The closest Larry came to acknowledging a hostile atmosphere was describing Rome as filled with Germans. "Even the Catacombs," Larry said. "You could hardly get through the Catacombs for Germans. Capri, the same thing. Venice, the same thing. Germans, Germans, Germans. You'd think you were in Yorkville."[33]

In Florence, Larry and Bender stopped in at Chez Moi and there at the bar, with three rich American women on his arm, was bandleader Jimmy Rogers. Barely larger than Larry, Rogers had led the band at the Lombardy, the hotel in Manhattan where Dick and Dorothy Rodgers used to live, and was now breezing through Europe with baronesses and countesses draping themselves across the pianos he played. That night in Florence, everyone got good and tight. Doc Bender went to the piano and accompanied Larry on some of the songs he and Rodgers had completed for *I Married an Angel*. "Have . . . you . . . heard? I married an angel!" The rich American women fainted with delight. For an encore, Larry did his Jolson—"Red Red Robin" and, on bended knee, "Mammy." By then Jimmy Rogers was looped enough to sit down at the piano and play an elaborate version of—what else?—"Blue Moon," which led the Chez Moi orchestra leader to assume he was Richard Rodgers. Rogers happily declined to correct the mistake. They all drank through the night and parted at 7 A.M., agreeing to meet in the hotel bar that afternoon for an eye-opener. After some sleep, Rogers arrived at the hotel to find Larry and Doc well under way. Suddenly Larry clapped a hand to his head and said, "Oh my God!" "What is it?" said Rogers, concerned. Bender, who knew Larry as well as anyone, only grinned. The museums were closing at three o'clock, Italian style, and Larry wanted to get to the Uffizi before he left Florence. So the party broke up for half an hour while Larry, half-sloshed, recharged by looking at great art.[34]

CHAPTER 19

Caring Too Much Is Such a Juvenile Fancy

R ODGERS AND Hart met up in London, as planned, though earlier than intended.

"We ran into each other at the Berkeley bar," Larry told the *New York Post*. "You mean I fell over you, you shrimp!" said Dick.

Dick and Dorothy Rodgers and Larry Hart and Doc Bender sailed from Southampton on December 18, 1937, on the *Normandie*, and were home in New York by December 23. Two weeks later they sat for a *Post* interview at Dinty Moore, the West Forty-Sixth Street steakhouse where proprietor James Moore—often hailed as "Dinty" by diners who didn't know him— corned his own beef. The *Post* reporter noted that Dick had ordered food and was not drinking; Larry was drinking brandy but not eating because, he explained, he was expecting his voracious friend George Tobias for dinner that night.[1] (Tobias played the Russian ballet master in *You Can't Take It with You* and might be remembered by a later generation as Abner Kravitz, the put-upon neighbor in the television series *Bewitched*.) *I Married an Angel* would be next, Dick and Larry told the *Post*, though it wasn't clear how much of the show was done.

The answer was: not much. Rodgers and Hart knew they would not use Moss Hart's 1933 script for the abortive MGM adaptation, but they hadn't come up with anything else except three or four songs, including that unas- sailable title song. And Larry needed a new project to occupy him. After Teddy Hart married Dorothy Lubow in January 1938, the newlyweds took an apartment on West Fifty-Fifth Street.[2] The household that Larry returned to each night was shrinking. Larry had spent his entire life sharing a bedroom with Teddy; the bedroom at the Beresford now seemed vast and unspeakably lonely. It was time to create a new musical, if only for the sake of distraction.

Fortunately, the boys had some serious financial backing, partly from Sam Goldwyn, who was determined to protect his investment in Vera Zorina, and partly from MGM, which retained a sizable stake in the show. Dwight Wiman intended to bring all this together. And Wiman had a young guy, an alumnus of Princeton's famous Triangle Club, who might be able to pull it off.

Joshua Logan was a curious choice to push Rodgers and Hart to finish *I Married an Angel*. Logan's theatrical accomplishments at Princeton had gotten him invited by David O. Selznick to come to Hollywood to direct dialogue for Selznick's first color film, *The Garden of Allah*. Even then, Logan was sensitive, maybe even oversensitive, to his position on the project. Writing to the film's director, Richard Boleslawski, a Pole whose limited command of English necessitated a dialogue director, Selznick described Logan as "most intelligent and most able," but that "the poor guy is worried sick for fear he is going to be in the way. I told him that he is only to try to help you and learn from you, and if anything, I think the danger now is that we have given him such an inferiority complex, and have frightened him so, that he will be afraid to contribute."[3] Logan's work on *Garden of Allah* led to similar dialogue coaching on *History Is Made at Night*, and then, back in New York, Wiman hired him to direct Paul Osborne's *On Borrowed Time*, which opened in early February 1938 to fantastic reviews. When Wiman told Logan he was the man for *I Married an Angel*, Logan's anxieties were right on the surface.

"Dick Rodgers hates me," he said. At Ciro's in Hollywood, Roger Edens, who was just beginning to put his stamp on MGM's musicals, had introduced Rodgers to Logan, and Logan was so drunk he could barely stand up.

Rodgers didn't hate Logan; if he was good enough for Wiman, he was good enough for Rodgers. Determined to get *something* done on *I Married an Angel*, Rodgers sent Logan down to Atlantic City, where Larry was pretending to be productive. "Just put your foot on his tail," Rodgers instructed Logan, "and get him to write the second act."[4]

Larry was comfortable in Atlantic City for several reasons. He loved the seashore. Atlantic City had been an important Broadway tryout city at least as far back as 1906, when the first *Ziegfeld Follies* debuted there, so there were always new shows to see. Movie palaces were erected each year. Bars had turned into speakeasies, then back into legitimate bars. "The combination of so many saloons and show business culture," Jonathan Van Meter has written in *The Last Good Time*, his cultural history of the New Jersey resort, "had turned Atlantic City into a kind of Times Square at the beach."[5] Larry was staying at the Traymore, of which he was especially fond. Built in the second decade of the twentieth century, the reinforced-concrete Traymore transformed the Boardwalk with its overwhelming size—it could accommodate up to three thousand guests—its early Art Deco touches, and its branded identity, in which everything (towels, martini glasses, you name the item) heralded the hotel's glamour. The design of the Traymore's Submarine Grill suggested you were dining under the sea. Larry, who had a talent for befriending bartenders, could while away hours at the Submarine Grill.

Aware of Larry Hart's reputation but otherwise not sure what he had signed up for, Josh Logan checked into the Traymore and fell for the lyricist immediately. Like so many people before him, Logan compared Larry to Toulouse-Lautrec and wanted to protect him. "His imagination worked endlessly," Logan wrote, "but only to make you laugh so he could laugh louder himself. Perhaps his pressured laughter covered something deeper. I never tried to penetrate it. I just learned to respect it."[6] For most of the week Hart and Logan did absolutely nothing about a second act for *I Married an Angel*. Larry was always in search of new restaurants, with special attention to the wine lists. When they weren't dining or walking, Larry wanted to play cards—not just any conventional card game, mind you, but something he called Cocksuckers' Rummy in which cheating was not only allowed but encouraged. Logan figured it was Larry's way, drunk or sober, of avoiding work.

Hours before they were to return to New York, Logan walked into Larry's hotel room to find him scribbling furiously on some foolscap—no more than three or four lines scratched on each sheet.

"Look at me!" hailed Larry. "I'm writing the second act!"

The frantic scribbling continued on the train to Penn Station. Halfway there Larry stuffed the pages into an envelope and pulled out the playing cards. It was back to Cocksuckers' Rummy. Later, Logan delivered the envelope to Rodgers, who extracted the pages and said, "What's all this?" Logan felt he had no choice but to report the week's most energetic activities—drinking and card playing—at the Traymore.[7] It was obvious to both men that nothing Larry had written was useable.

Rodgers wasn't surprised. "We'll go into rehearsal in two weeks," he reminded Logan, "and without a second act. I hope you can wing it."

Even without a second act, Wiman was putting the cast together. Vincent Price, who had expressed interest earlier, was never in serious consideration. Unable to sign the continental, darkly handsome Francis Lederer for the role of Willy, Wiman tried to get French singer Jean Sablon. That didn't happen either. Dennis King, known as a dependable juvenile before making his mark in *The Vagabond King* and other operettas, was available and could handle the material. The role of Willy's friend and benefactor Harry went to Walter Slezak. Larry's Los Angeles friend Chuck Walters won the role of Peter, assistant to Willy and lover of the conniving Anna, who was to be played by Audrey Christie. Act 1 dialogue for Peggy, Willy's sister, appeared to be written specifically for Vivienne Segal, with more to come. The show called for at least thirty dancers and, according to one of them, so many people came one day to audition for Balanchine that Shubert Alley became impassable, prompting the NYPD to block off Forty-Fourth and Forty-Fifth Streets west of Times Square.[8] The most crucial role of all, that of the angel—called Angel, in fact, by Willy and his friends—was already filled by Vera Zorina. Although she had developed a crush on Orson Welles, who was married, she was gradually being worn down by Balanchine's adoration.[9] She was mad about Larry Hart, whom she found to be "affectionate, with a sad look in his eyes."[10]

Zorina had a problem that had to be addressed: her diction sometimes made her difficult to understand. Unlike the European and Asian movie stars whose accents were amplified by microphones, Zorina was essentially a stage actress whose every word had to be heard clearly from the back of the house. Wiman assigned his longtime assistant, Lina Abarbanell, who had appeared in musicals as far back as *Madame Sherry* (1910), to coach her in English. A quick study, Zorina was soon reading New York newspapers aloud. Now all she needed to learn all her lines was the second act of *I Married an Angel*.

One morning in March, Rodgers phoned Logan. "Let's meet later at Larry's house and we'll write the second act." Logan had never worked this way before—certainly not on a project of this scale. He went up to Larry's apartment at the Beresford and, with coffee and booze in the cups and Larry's cigar smoke clouding the view of Central Park, they went to work. Dick and Larry paced and traded lines and dictated to Logan, and by the end of the day, impossibly, they had a second act. Logan couldn't believe it.

"But there's still no score," Logan reminded the boys.

"Ach," Larry said in his catarrhal, forget-about-it way, "we'll write that to-night."[11]

✤   ✤   ✤

In the second week of April, rehearsals were held at Boston's Wilbur Theatre, nearly opposite the Shubert Theatre and also operated and partly owned by the Shuberts. The plot of *I Married an Angel*, which retained the basic outline of the János Vaszary play, really was no more substantial than a popover.

Willy Palaffi runs his family's bank in Budapest. Wealthy and attractive, he's been jilted by his latest fiancée. His sister, Peggy, whose sexual awareness borders on the lewd, is always trying to fix him up; her latest prospect is the innocent-appearing Anna Murphy, who at first pretends to be a convent girl, then reveals herself to be an acquisitive gold digger. Disappointed, Willy vows to remain single.

A beautiful angel, seeing how unhappy Willy is, appears before him. Within minutes the two have fallen in love and eloped to Paris. During Boston rehearsals Larry realized that other angels couldn't address her as Angel, necessitating a more earthly name. "How about the name Brigitte?" said Larry, believing they couldn't do better than Zorina's real name.[12] (It's what everyone called her anyway.) Angel always tells the truth because, although she doesn't credit Keats's Grecian urn, she believes the truth is always beautiful. On their wedding night Willy, confessing he was never happy before, sings "I Married an Angel."

By morning, however, Angel has lost her wings because, well, to paraphrase Mae West, she's no longer an angel. Trying to fly, she ends up dancing. Willy is hardly upset; this means she can't fly away from him. In the "Bath and Dressmaking Sequence" that follows, the "I Married an Angel" lyrics are echoed and inverted ("The angel of whom he sings / Hasn't any wings"), and Larry uses the word *distingué*, rhyming it with *s'il vous plaît*. (This same year Billy Strayhorn famously employed it writing "Lush Life.")

The "Honeymoon Ballet," one of two ballets Balanchine created for act 1, takes place at Le Bourget Airport, with five male dancers moving together as a single airplane, each carrying a female dancer who sways slightly to the left, then to the right, simulating the motion of a plane. Some later listeners could hear in the ballet music stirrings of what would become "The Carousel Waltz."[13] The "Honeymoon Ballet" unfolds into the "Snow Ballet," Balanchine's homage to Zorina's Norwegian heritage, permitting her to ski, dance among snowflakes, then exit the stage on a sled pulled by Norwegian huskies.[14]

Willy's banking rival Harry arrives in Budapest. Peggy, who has been married four times, and Harry go way back. Harry pretends he didn't swoon over her when she was onstage in Sigmund Romberg's *Blossom Time*. It's an inside joke: Vivienne Segal, who played Peggy, was a twenty-four-year-old ingenue when she appeared in *Blossom Time* in 1921. Harry and Peggy sing the first of three versions of "I'll Tell the Man in the Street," one of Rodgers's loveliest melodies, with Larry's lyric to match:

> *I'll tell the man in the street*
> *And everyone I meet*
> *That you and I are sweethearts.*
> *I'll shout it out from the roof,*
> *I'll give the papers proof*
> *That we two are complete hearts.*

The impulse the lyric describes is the opposite of "I'd Like to Hide It" from *Dearest Enemy*: newly in love, we want to buttonhole strangers and tell them all about it—to speak, on the slightest of pretexts, the name of the beloved.

When Willy and Angel come home, Peter informs Willy there's a run on the Palaffi Bros. bank. The idea is to keep the largest depositors at Willy's house drinking and talking so they won't withdraw their money before close of business. Willy hopes to borrow from Harry to pay off the small investors. But after the truth-telling Angel reveals the extent of Willy's anxiety, their guests rush to the bank after all. Willy, feeling betrayed, keeps his distance from the bewildered Angel, who doesn't understand what she's done wrong.

Act 2 opens at the bank just as the wealthiest depositors are pulling up in their limousines. Missing Angel, but also wary of her truthfulness, which has offended several of his friends, Willy sings "Spring Is Here" and is soon joined by Peggy:

> *No desire,*
> *No ambition leads me.*
> *Maybe it's because*
> *Nobody needs me.*

Larry Hart wore such plaintiveness like an old coat. Spring, the season of rebirth and new love, when buds open and lovers stroll through the park, is also the season of disappointment and suicide. *Everyone else seems so happy! What's wrong with me?* The unmistakable silhouette of Cyrano hovers:

Oh I have no more
Illusions! Now and then—bah! I may grow
Tender, walking alone in the blue cool
Of evening, through some garden fresh with flowers
After the benediction of the rain;
My poor big devil of a nose inhales
April . . . and so I follow with my eyes
Where some boy, with a girl upon his arm,
Passes a patch of silver . . . and I feel
Somehow, I wish I had a woman too,
Walking with little steps under the moon,
And holding my arm so, and smiling. Then
I dream—and I forget . . .
And then I see
The shadow of my profile on the wall![15]

In "Spring Is Here" Larry might as well have been describing himself, as Cyrano did, even if his torment is expressed through the characters of the Count and Countess Palaffi. (More than a year later, in early May 1939, when *I Married an Angel* played the National Theatre in Washington, Vivienne Segal lost her mother. Unable to get through the song—*why doesn't the breeze delight me?*—she asked Dennis King to sing it solo. So he did.)

Angel learns that she can't go back to being an angel. She's mortal now, with all the heartbreak that might entail. To comfort her, and to coach her, Peggy speaks of herself in the third person. "Well, this girl was a bit naughty," Peggy tells Angel, "but a great artist. She had six lovers at one time and she was unfaithful to all of them." The dialogue suggests a flip side of Segal's future turn as the Queen in *Connecticut Yankee*, marrying many men but being "untrue to none of them." Peggy's advice to Angel: you can say just about anything to a man if only you keep "A Twinkle in Your Eye." Vivienne Segal owned such a twinkle, often accompanied by a leer.

Encouraged by Peggy, Angel makes amends to Willy's friends. For their amusement she plays "I Married an Angel" on the harp—the harpist was actually Caspar Reardon, who had played with the New York Philharmonic and Duke Ellington—and the guests move away from her, until she plays a swing version that brings them back. Meanwhile the dialogue contains a nod to Rodgers and Hart's old friend, composer Albert Sirmay; a plug for Chase & Sanborn coffee; and an affectionate reference in rhyme to the show's scenic designer, the gifted Jo Mielziner, who was responsible for the distinctive look of the show, organized around two conveyor belts running across the stage on which furniture was moved in dim blue light in front of the audience. Mielziner was determined to avoid the convention of the "scene-in-one," performed downstage while stagehands changed the set, which tended to halt the progress of the story. During Boston tryouts, the conveyor belts often lurched or stopped at the wrong spot, as in the machinery-works scene from Chaplin's *Modern Times*.[16]

To celebrate Willy's ruin, Harry throws a party. Yet the number that follows doesn't comment on Willy's fall, as might be expected, but instead serves as a wild, stand-alone extravaganza—what Larry likened to the European tradition of a midshow divertissement.[17] This involved not only a surrealist ballet—it went out of its way to poke fun at Salvador Dalí, who was now making not only the decor but a libretto for Balanchine's old colleague Léonide Massine—but an amalgam of Radio City Music Hall and the almost equally vast Roxy, at Fiftieth Street and Seventh Avenue. When the befuddled Logan asked Larry what surrealism had to do with Radio City—and what *either* had to do with Budapest—Larry looked up at Logan and said, "What the hell are you trying to do? Make this Ibsen?"[18]

The surrealist ballet included the Dalíesque vision of Zorina in a seashell rising like a papier-mâché Venus from a sea of green cheesecloth. Logan was only more puzzled when Balanchine explained that the ballet was inspired by *Othello*, with one of the dancers carrying his own head under his arm.

"Is this guy Othello or Iago?" asked Logan.

Balanchine gave his sniff of exhaustion and said, "Both."

"You're as crazy as Larry Hart," Logan said.

"Larry Hart is baby," said Balanchine. "I'm grown man."[19]

The ballet was part of the phantasmagoric show within the show in the cavernous Roxy Music Hall, where "the balcony's so high you get the fidgets" and "the actors seem to be a lot of midgets." It was during this number, "At the Roxy Music Hall," with Peggy and Anna serving as Rockettes, that *I Married an Angel* fluttered up into the clouds.

Earlier in that week of tryouts, Logan was rehearsing "At the Roxy Music Hall." (The anecdote has been told by several Rodgers & Hart chroniclers.) Noise from the back of the theater distracted him. Larry, who had evidently gotten good and tight somewhere near the Wilbur Theatre, was trying to light a cigar but kept bumping into aisle seats. Audrey Christie (as Anna) began to sing:

Now come with me,
And you won't believe a thing you see . . .

Larry shouted something that Logan couldn't make out. He continued to shout, his voice hoarse with alcohol.

"Everybody hold it!" said Logan. "What is it, Larry?"

Larry came babbling down the aisle, his cigar a noxious, wet sparkler.

"Slow down, Larry. Say it a little slower."

"No now-singers in this show!" shouted Larry. "No now-singers in this show!"

"What are now-singers?"

"*She's* a now-singer!" said Larry, pointing at Audrey Christie. "Did you hear how she began the chorus? It's 'Come with me' and she began '*Now* come with me'!"

Take the anguish of any writer who finds his or her words have been edited to mean something unintended, and double it for a lyricist. It's why W. B. Yeats, despite encouragement from friends and colleagues, shied away from song. "What was the good of writing a love-song," Yeats wrote, "if the singer pronounced love 'lo-o-o-o-o-ve,' or even if he said 'love,' but did not give it its exact place and weight in the rhythm?"[20] Like basketball players who must dribble the ball at least once before taking a shot, some singers need the extra beat provided by an added *now*, or a *well*, or an *oh*. Christie apologized. Larry told her to remember the proper lyric, then he took a seat close to the proscenium to monitor the rest of the rehearsal. He was asleep within minutes.[21]

In the final scene of *I Married an Angel*, Angel, taking a page from Peggy's book, delivers Harry to Willy so that he may write a check to save Willy's bank. When Willy asks Angel what she might have yielded to Harry in return, Angel is coy. "We must never let him know that nothing happened," she confides to Harry. "A man should never be too sure of a girl." Now the angels call out to Brigitte because they, too, want to lose their wings. Willy's heart is dancing because, at last, somebody needs him.

Treadmill problems were worked out, dialogue was revised, and songs were shifted around or dropped altogether. An intriguing lyric titled "Yodel If You Can" didn't make it to New York. The verse went:

Grandpa was a grand old man
Who lived without a worry,

And he had a happy plan:
"Never fret or hurry."
He never sighed or wrinkled up
That brow beneath his bowler—
Just opened his coat
And cleared his throat
And sang like a Tyroler.[22]

By the time *I Married an Angel* opened at the Shubert in New York, on May 11, 1938, it was still viewed by its authors as shaky. Ninety minutes before curtain time a storm broke over Manhattan, the thunder turning up the voltage on already jangled first-night nerves.[23] West Forty-Fourth Street turned into a lane of umbrellas. Ticket-holders huddled beneath the Sardi's awning to time their sprints across the street. Dorothy and Dick Rodgers sat in their usual first-night seats, on the aisle in the last row, and suffered through the long first act, which seemed to get minimal response from the audience. A much-needed intermission drink or two at the Astor bar made the second act more palatable.[24] Was it the booze?

It was the show. When the reviews came in, it had all proved worth it. Audrey Christie won raves. Dennis King was praised for becoming so dapper. With Fred Astaire working exclusively in Hollywood, Chuck Walters was widely considered to be the stage's ranking male dancer. George Balanchine's choreography demonstrated that he had affection for popular culture even as he spoofed it. The big surprise to both Dick and Larry was the effusive notice by Brooks Atkinson, who had previously deplored "the otiose spell of Hungarian dramaturgy."[25] *I Married an Angel* could easily have been swept up in Atkinson's wrath, but instead he praised "the extraordinarily beautiful production" and said the score would be placed "on the top shelf of the Rodgers and Hart music cabinet." Atkinson didn't gush like that more than once a decade. Citing the show for having "the ablest cast of performers since Hollywood cleaned us out," he had fulsome praise for the attractively wicked Segal singing "A Twinkle in Your Eye" "with enough impudent subtlety to stand an audience on its giddy head." And he called Zorina "a national treasure."[26]

Every critic referred to Zorina as charming or beautiful, or both. The only party-pooping words came from John Mason Brown in the *Post*, who suggested that Zorina looked like a cross between the actress Helen Gahagan and the actor Eric Wollencott, who specialized in portraying slow-witted boy-men. Brown's assessment wasn't inaccurate—you can see Zorina's face in both Gahagan (later Helen Gahagan Douglas) and Wollencott—which didn't make it any less provocative. If Zorina was aware of the comparisons, she didn't show it. In her autobiography, she described her feelings about those first weeks of *I Married an Angel* with a quote from a lyric sung by the German-English actress Lilian Harvey in the 1931 Ufa film *Der Kongress tanzt* (released in English under the title *The Congress Dances*):

> *Das gibts nur einmal, das kommit nicht wieder, das ist zu schön um wahr zu sein.* (This only happens once; it will never happen again; it's too beautiful to be true.)[27]

In the weeks that followed *I Married an Angel*'s opening, Leo Reisman and his Reismen recorded "Spring Is Here" and "I'll Tell the Man on the Street," and Larry Clinton and His Orchestra (with Bea Wain on vocals) recorded "I Married an Angel" and "How to Win Friends and Influence People," both on Victor. Audrey Christie went into the Liberty Music Shop and recorded "How to Win Friends and Influence People" and "At the Roxy Music Hall." The show's songs were heard all around the town.

There were reports that Larry had proposed marriage to Vivienne Segal. "Engaged?" asked one press item on the opening night of *I Married an Angel*, accompanied by a photograph of Segal. The item said Hart might make Segal his "angel by marriage." The follow-up went: "Intimate friends are willing to bet all kinds of dough that Vivienne Segal, of *I Married an Angel*, will become Mrs. Lorenz Hart before the summer is over."[28] Segal said Hart indeed proposed to her and that, never having kissed him, let alone anything more than that, she turned him down. If Larry proposed, it might have been because Teddy had married. Larry had recently turned forty-three, so, if not now, when? Otherwise it's hard to figure what he had in mind. Was he hoping to please Frieda, who probably knew her son's sexual preferences better than she was given credit for? To show the theater world that he could, like Cole Porter and so many other homosexuals in the theater, make a life with a woman? Perhaps Larry knew he was on safe ground: Segal had married actor-playboy Robert Ames in 1923 and divorced him in 1927, saying he was "too expensive" to keep, then reconciled with him briefly until Ames literally dropped dead.[29] After that, Segal had no interest in marrying anyone—not even Larry Hart.

Segal's rejection might have been the thing that sent Hart to his bed—or it might have been just plain overwork and exhaustion. In his "So This Is Broadway" column, George Ross reported that Larry was seriously ill with influenza. "Day and night nurses attend him and a physician has been present constantly. Among Hart's professed worries was Hitler's entrance into Austria, for it meant he had to speedily replace the 'Spring in Vienna' number in *I'd Rather Be Right* with another."[30] "Spring in Vienna" became "Spring in Milwaukee," probably because the new setting allowed Larry to retain references to lilacs and knockwurst.

When he recovered from the flu, Larry went downtown to visit the Shubert Theatre box office. Crossing Shubert Alley from Forty-Fifth Street, Larry could see that business was brisk—a line of ticket buyers snaked out onto the sidewalk. Midway through the alley he was accosted by a street urchin approximately his size but thirty years his junior.

"Larry, I seen you in a picture!" the kid said.

"Really? Was I any good?"

The kid had caught a revival of *Hallelujah, I'm a Bum!* at the Miami Theatre, on Sixth Avenue and Forty-Sixth Street. He advised Larry to go before noon so he could get in for a dime, then he ran off.[31] By then the Jolson picture was five years old, but Larry was grateful *somebody* had seen it.

The germ of a new Rodgers & Hart musical had appeared five months earlier, on a January train ride from Penn Station to Atlantic City, where they intended to work on *I Married an Angel*. Earlier that month, Maxwell Anderson had addressed the Modern Language Association:

> Old Greek Comedy was dedicated to the spirit of lust and riot and earth, spirits which are certainly necessary to the health and continuance of the race. . . . Our more ribald musical comedies are simply our approximation of the Bacchic rites of Old Comedy.[32]

That Old Comedy was co-opted by Shakespeare more than once. Larry had been steeped in Shakespeare since childhood. As a professional lyricist, he had quoted or alluded to Shakespeare—"The stuff that dreams are made on," for example, floats from *The Tempest* into the published verse of "Isn't It Romantic?," changing shape only slightly—dozens of times. But how would you adapt Shakespeare for an entire musical comedy? In decades to come, the creators of *Swingin' the Dream* (1939), *Kiss Me Kate* (1948), *West Side*

Story (1957), *Your Own Thing* (1968), and *Two Gentlemen of Verona* (1971) would approach the problem in different ways. In 1938, however, opera not-withstanding, there had been no successful musical-theater adaptation of Shakespeare for the stage. "Plots of operas are often more uninhibited than plots of plays," literary critic Northrop Frye wrote, "because the driving force of the opera is provided by the music. . . . The only place where the tradition of Shakespearean romantic comedy has survived with any theatrical success is, as we should expect, in opera. As long as we have Mozart or Verdi or Sulli-van to listen to, we can tolerate identical twins and lost heirs and love potions and folk tales: we can even stand a fairy queen if she is under two hundred pounds."[33] Ah, but Larry had Dick Rodgers. In Larry's mind, the musical fecundity of his partner, plus the very challenge presented by adapting Shake-speare, made an adaptation worth trying. Folded into the challenge was his chronic desire to help his brother, who might have been living in domestic bliss but—professionally, anyway—was on hiatus.

Larry thought of *A Comedy of Errors* because it had relatively little phi-losophy to contend with and, as Shakespeare goes, relatively little poetry. It was rarely performed, although Larry was probably aware of the production being planned by Komisarjevsky for Stratford, England, in early 1938.[34] It was also one of the Shakespeare plots featuring twins, in this case the Drom-ios.[35] With Larry's brother, Teddy, foremost in the minds of Rodgers and Hart, the obvious twin was the entertainer Jimmy Savo.

Savo was having a moment. He had recently popularized "One Meat Ball" ("You get no bread with one meat ball") and had developed an entire nightclub act around the Mort Dixon–Harry Woods song "River Stay Away from My Door." What was striking about Savo, though, was how closely his experience, as well as his appearance, paralleled Teddy Hart's. Savo was born on East Ninety-Seventh Street and attended the Church of Our Lady of Mt. Carmel on 116th Street before his family moved to the Bronx. He was essen-tially a Harlem boy, but with strong parental ties to Catholic Italy instead of Jewish Germany. Savo and Teddy had each been referred to as "pixies"; Savo was described as being about as tall "as a Hammacher-Schlemmer gnome." Each had played the vaudeville circuit for years, rolling through upstate cities like Utica, Syracuse, Buffalo, and Rochester, and had spent much of the mid-1930s living in Hollywood. Each comic could stir up mirth by remaining mute. They were practically twins already.[36]

Actually, *The Comedy of Errors* contains *two* sets of twins: the servant Dromio of Syracuse accompanies his master Antipholus to Ephesus, two seas away, where Dromio meets his twin and Antipholus meets *his* twin. Shakespeare had based *The Comedy of Errors* largely on Plautus's *The Menaechmus Twins*, staged some two thousand years earlier. Shakespeare's version had premiered on Christmas 1594 (some sources give the date as December 28), acted by the Lord Chamberlain's Men, as part of the revels at Gray's Inn at Court.[37]

With Teddy Hart and Jimmy Savo as part of the pitch, Dick and Larry took the idea to George Abbott. It excited Abbott enough to want to produce as well as direct—which automatically meant that Wiman would not be participating. "Originally the book was to be written by the three of us," Abbott said, "but I got to work first and finished a rough draft. Larry and Dick thought that it was so right that they withdrew as collaborators."[38] George Balanchine would make the dances. For the time being, Abbott, Balanchine, Rodgers, and Hart referred to the project as *Mixed Company*, a generic title that wouldn't last.[39]

There was so much going on that spring. With *I Married an Angel* about to open, Rodgers and Hart stayed quiet about the Shakespeare project, though they didn't stop thinking about it. The earliest press releases made it sound as if a musical version of *The Comedy of Errors* had been Abbott's idea. "If you run across something called the Gacoe Corporation," the *Times* reported on April 24, "it stands for 'George Abbott's "Comedy of Errors,"' or Shakespeare fixed up with music."[40] No mention of Rodgers and Hart. A few days later, Russel Crouse and Kurt Weill, bowing to Mr. Abbott's dominion, announced that they had dropped their detailed outline to adapt *Much Ado About Nothing*.[41]

In late May, to work on the songs, Dick and Larry returned to Atlantic City, staying at the Ritz instead of the Traymore, and began to draft a possible musical version. Larry, incidentally decrying high Broadway ticket prices and praising the WPA for its work in the theater, told a local reporter that he and Dick were using *The Comedy of Errors* simply "as a background for a crazy show."[42]

They were in danger of overextending themselves. Harry Kaufman, who had done right by them, persuaded them to consider writing a new show for Bea Lillie.[43] That always sounded appealing, particularly to Larry, for there was still nobody but she who could remain so attractive while laying waste to a stage set. But where would they find the time? Reaffirming his commitment to *Mixed Company*, Larry made plans to go on a South American cruise with

Balanchine. The idea was to sail on the Grace liner *Santa Paula* for two and a half weeks, the ocean air charging their creative impulses, then return to New York; Balanchine would be without Zorina, who was staying behind to conquer a thousand hearts each night at the Shubert Theatre, and Larry would be without Dick, the principal who flicked the hickory stick whenever Larry was tardy or drunk. Initially, Dick was fine with Larry's leaving for a couple of weeks because he'd be spending so much time at the family's summer house in Port Washington. Then he learned that Doc Bender would be tagging along on the South American cruise.

Dick was a master of what would come to be called passive-aggressive behavior. He had always been annoyed by the way Bender seemed to have cash of Larry's in his hand. There was a reasonable explanation for this: Doc took care of the things that Larry couldn't be bothered with. But Dick imputed only impure motives to Doc. He also knew that Bert Allenberg, the Los Angeles–based talent agent who had so courteously handled Larry's business affairs for years, no longer had the time or the inclination to pay every haberdasher and car-service bill that Larry sent him. Dick figured it was time for someone in New York to watch Larry's money. A few weeks before Larry went on the *Santa Paula* cruise, Dick introduced him to William Kron, who had been Rodgers's accountant for several years.

Born in Berlin in 1882, Willy Kron emigrated to New York in 1899. Wanting to be part of the theater, Kron appeared as an extra, carrying a spear, in the 1903 English-language version of the operetta *Old Heidelberg*. Having trained in Germany as an accountant, however, he spent the First World War in Washington, D.C., in the accounting department of the American Red Cross. In New York, he began to handle the books for Louis Blau, a Broadway tailor who made clothes for many songwriters, and was subsequently invited into Blau's backroom poker game, where he cemented his contacts in the music publishing world. Those contacts eventually helped make him executive secretary of music publisher Chappell.[44]

Officially becoming Larry's accountant, Kron took his royalty checks and banked them for him. He visited Larry at home, almost invariably at times when he knew neither Teddy nor Dorothy Hart would be around.

Hart and Balanchine, refreshed and ready to dig into Shakespeare, were back in New York by June 28. Abbott engaged Jo Mielziner for the new show's scenery and Irene Sharaff for the costumes. With Dick and Larry in attendance, casting began. All three men were impressed by Richard

Kollmar's audition as one of the Antipholus twins. That same week, Kollmar auditioned for Kurt Weill, Maxwell Anderson, and Josh Logan, who were preparing *Knickerbocker Holiday*; when that trio offered Kollmar the role of Brom Brock, the juvenile lead, he accepted so he could play alongside Walter Huston. So Abbott pulled Eddie Albert out of *Room Service* to play one Antipholus twin. Rudy Vallee was eager to play the other twin, though those negotiations quickly broke down; the role went to Ronald Graham. Nineteen-year-old Marcy Wescott was closing in *The Two Bouquets* and was considered absolutely right for Luciana, the young woman who fears she has fallen in love with the husband of her sister, Adriana. English soprano Muriel Angelus was engaged to play Adriana. It was almost unthinkable that anyone but Wynn Murray would play the saucy Luce who, like so many of Larry Hart's women, gives as good as she gets.[45]

On July 26 the Gacoe Corporation released the news that the *Comedy of Errors* show would be called *The Boys from Syracuse*.[46] Theater folk got the joke, for the most prominent boys from Syracuse around town were Lee and J. J. Shubert.

Dick and Larry continued to work through the dog days of August. One weekend, when Dick retired to the Port Washington house, Larry—with Doc Bender certainly, and maybe Doc's young new client, the poet-lyricist John Latouche—appeared in Cohasset, Massachusetts, to give a talk at Town Hall, where the repertory group The South Shore Players was in residence. Jacob Wilk's son Max, who had been introduced to Larry four years earlier during a Gilbert & Sullivan intermission, was in the audience. "He was erudite, witty, charming," Max Wilk wrote of Hart; "his head was crammed with fact and fancy, reflecting the remarkable scope of his learning. . . . As the afternoon wore on, he had quite a few drinks and his speech became somewhat slurred. But Larry's mind never went under the influence."[47]

On evenings in Manhattan, Larry would set up at a back table at Ralph's, on Forty-Fifth Street hard by the Imperial Theatre, frequently though not always with Doc Bender. (Barrymore's restaurant later occupied the building.) Ralph, Italian-American, and his Hungarian wife thought of themselves as running not just a restaurant but an actors' haven—a boozier, unbuttoned variation on Sardi's. Larry and Bender would drink gin from coffee cups and welcome anyone who wanted to sit down.[48]

Yet, possibly because so much of his present project involved promoting the career of his brother, Larry got his work done. By August 30, *The New York Times* reported that ten songs for *The Boys from Syracuse* had been completed, with two or three more to come, along with music for a ballet.[49] Ten days later the first chorus auditions were held. Abbott was turning out to be as commanding a producer as he was an inventive director. Dick and Larry bowed out of the Bea Lillie project—no hard feelings toward or from Harry Kaufman—so they could devote their time to *The Boys from Syracuse*.[50] There also seems to have been a swiftly aborted project called *Oddities*, based on Robert Ripley's "Believe It or Not" exhibition in Times Square.[51] Meanwhile Hans Spialek was orchestrating the completed *Boys* songs.

Hugh Martin was a twenty-four-year-old pianist from Alabama who had come to New York a couple of years earlier. Singing in *Hooray for What?*, he met his longtime professional partner, Ralph Blane, with whom he began to write songs. "Buckle Down, Winsocki," "The Boy Next Door," "The Trolley Song," and "Have Yourself a Merry Little Christmas" were still in their future; for now, though, Martin and Blane were both looking for work. Blane took a weekly radio gig. One day in the fall, Martin wrote to Richard Rodgers, care of ASCAP, to ask him why he tended to ignore the jazzier styles of the day. It was a nervy thing to say to one of the three or four most successful living Broadway composers.

So Martin was amazed when his telephone rang. It was Rodgers, asking him if he could come immediately to the Alvin Theatre. When Martin showed up, Rodgers put him to work arranging "Sing for Your Supper," a number for the three principal women to sing together—with a wink back at Gilbert and Sullivan's "Three Little Maids from School"—which, everyone hoped, would bring down the house.

During rehearsals Martin observed Larry paying close attention to what was going on, and to the way he hollered if a number wasn't working. "The great tragedy was that he never found anyone," Martin said. "He was convinced he was ugly. He was neurotic as hell."[52] Although Martin was nobody's idea of ugly, he identified with Larry. Both men were unutterably gentle and shy. As a rookie orchestrator, Martin answered to Rodgers and Spialek but, behind the swirls of cigar smoke and jokes, he couldn't help but feel Hart's suffering.

On days he appeared at the Alvin, Larry kept a car parked near the theater, with a chauffeur on call. Sometimes the chauffeur came into the theater to report on the races of the day so Larry could figure where his bets stood. "The astonishment I showed while watching Larry confer with his chauffeur," his sister-in-law said, "made Larry laugh, as he usually did when confronted with some bizarre behavior on his part. The racing interest seemed to be some extra excitement or stimulation that he was after. I wondered if his work in the theater was finally becoming merely a routine and too predictable."[53]

Increasingly, Larry failed to show up for rehearsals. Abbott knew that he was drinking heavily but ignored it for now because Larry was so fast when a new lyric was called for. On Wednesday night, October 26, Paul Whiteman played four songs from *The Boys from Syracuse* on his Chesterfield program.[54] The following week Abbott and Rodgers decided that Adriana needed a sewing-themed verse to the song in which she laments (mistakenly) the loss of the love of her husband, Antipholus of Ephesus, while she sits at her loom making a tapestry with her sister and servants in attendance. Whether one of them phoned Larry and insisted he come to the theater, or he simply showed up on his own, isn't clear. But Larry heard what they needed, grabbed a pencil and a discarded piece of paper, and, while Abbott and Rodgers conferred about other matters, worked out the verse to "Falling in Love with Love":

> *I weave with brightly colored strings*
> *To keep my mind off other things;*
> *So, ladies, let your fingers dance,*
> *And keep your fingers out of romance.*
> *Lovely witches,*
> *Let the stitches*
> *Keep your fingers under control.*
> *Cut the thread, but leave*
> *The whole heart whole.*
> *Merry maids can sew and sleep;*
> *Wives can only sew and weep!*

In much the same way, Larry wrote the lyric for "You Have Cast Your Shadow on the Sea," one of the more metaphorically resonant of all Rodgers & Hart songs.

Then Larry went AWOL again. "Dick was very concerned about Larry's growing addiction," Abbott wrote. "For one thing, he saw his collaborator gradually deteriorating; secondly, he knew from experience that when a show got on the road, it needed a lyric writer ready for emergencies. Dick's fears were realized; when we went to Boston there was no Larry. But everything in the show fell into place so easily that we didn't need him."[55]

❧   ❧   ❧

"Fell into place" is an understatement. In the way the incomparable beauty of the songs is complemented by the comedy, the costumes, and the sheer inventiveness of the whole enterprise, *The Boys from Syracuse* may be the greatest Rodgers & Hart show of all. The New York opening—at the Alvin Theatre, on November 23, 1938—was special because it was something of a family affair. Dick was seated in the back row on the aisle beside Dorothy. Teddy Hart would be onstage before the first scene was over. His brother was not in the theater.

Act 1's requisite exposition is cleverly handled in "I Had Twins," in which Aegeon and the Duke of Ephesus can be seen onstage but not heard. In *The Comedy of Errors*, Aegeon's monologue is long and detailed, but that would hardly do for a musical comedy that had to be up and running within a minute. Instead an E-flat clarinet (Aegeon) and a bass clarinet (the Duke) follow as their lips move, while a Policeman conveys their story to the crowd, and to us.[56]

Cut to more than twenty years later. Antipholus of Syracuse (Eddie Albert) and his servant Dromio of Syracuse (Jimmy Savo) arrive in Ephesus and instantly hate the place. In *The Comedy of Errors*, Antipholus acknowledges the city's reputation for:

> *Dark-working sorcerers that change the mind;*
> *Soul-killing witches that deform the body;*
> *Disguised cheaters, prating mountebanks;*
> *And many such-like liberties of sin:*
> *If it prove so, I will be gone the sooner.*[57]

In *The Boys from Syracuse*, Antipholus expresses his antipathy to Ephesus a bit less grimly, in what sounds like college fight-song style, in "Dear Old Syracuse":

> *You can keep your Athens,*
> *You can keep your Rome.*
> *I'm a hometown fellow*
> *And I pine for home.*
> *I wanna go back, go back*
> *To dear old Syracuse.*

Unbeknownst to him, Dromio of Syracuse has a twin, Dromio of Ephesus (Teddy Hart), who's married to Luce (Wynn Murray). In "What Can You

Do with a Man?," Dromio used to be five foot seven but Luce has gradually cut him down to four foot ten. On the other hand, Luce complains, "I wear my nicest negligee / And find him reading Plato." If Luce acts like a shrew, well, this Dromio, who behaves like a five-year-old by day and a ninety-seven-year-old at night, deserves it. Wynn Murray, Elliot Norton wrote, had "the kind of voice that might well stir a Liberty Bond rally."[58] Murray's eardrum-shattering was placed alongside Teddy Hart's lisping; it was a contrast that went back to American vaudeville of the late nineteenth century and the French revues of the early twentieth. As Luce, Murray smiled and grimaced and used that extraordinary mouth to convey heated emotion; Teddy used his dark eyes and impenetrable, goofy expression. (A decade earlier, Teddy had had the role of idiot gunman Stinkfoot Louie in a play called *Guns*. When he asked the director for advice about his makeup, the director said, "Just go on as you are. I think it'll ring the bell.")[59] For all their complaints, Luce and Dromio of Ephesus are a lusty couple holding conversations with flying plates.

Inside the house of Antipholus of Ephesus, his wife, Adriana—as melancholy here as she is in Shakespeare—sings the tapestry-weaving song, "Falling in Love with Love," which is filled with longing for her absent husband and regret that his love for her has not lasted. The scene more than faintly echoes Penelope waiting years for the return of Odysseus.[60] But Adriana's husband, passing through the streets of Ephesus, actually adores her and tells her so from afar—"The smallest smile on your face / Is the greatest kind of embrace"—in "The Shortest Day of the Year." The lyric is another example of Larry Hart's ability to repeat words to yield maximum emotion:

> *The shortest day of the year*
> *Has the longest night of the year,*
> *And the longest night*
> *Is the shortest night with you.*

Antipholus of Syracuse wanders into the house of his brother without knowing exactly where he is—or, as Northrop Frye put it in his analysis of *The Comedy of Errors*, "with almost a feeling of being initiated into a mystery."[61]

> *Am I in earth, in heaven or in hell?*
> *Sleeping or waking? mad or well-advis'd?*
> *Known unto these, and to myself disguis'd!*

Adriana is overjoyed that her husband has returned, and she leaves to prepare dinner for him. But this Antipholus, who is not her husband, gets one look at Adriana's sister, Luciana, and falls for her—and she for him. The lyric of "This Can't Be Love" was dictated by their respective need to stay away from each other: he knows her sister is treating him like a husband; she believes he *is* her sister's husband. The verses of "This Can't Be Love" make sly references to Romeo and Juliet, and the refrain supplies the negative image of "It's Got to Be Love" (which feels like neuritis) because the lovers *aren't* dizzy and their hearts *haven't* stood still ("Just hear it beat!"). Act 1 closes with Antipholus of Syracuse and Luciana in love but unable to do anything about it.

Backstage during intermissions, an oversize young actor would sometimes strum on a battered guitar and sing country ballads and old sea chanteys. Irritating as it sometimes was, nobody in the cast ever asked him to stop because the poor guy, not even identified in the program for his role as the Tailor's Apprentice, had only one line: "Master, they are coming!" In another decade or so, Burl Ives's recordings would be outselling anything by Rodgers and Hart.[62]

The Boys from Syracuse wouldn't have qualified as a genuine Larry Hart show without one particularly lewd lyric, and "Ladies of the Evening," early in act 2, fits the bill. It's another morning after the courtesans have taken rich men's money for services rendered, another morning when "a plum becomes a prune" and "daughters of the moon" squint in the light of day. Luce and Dromio of Ephesus sing "He and She," a chronicle of a marriage so nauseatingly harmonious that when the spouses died and went to heaven, "the angels moved to Hell." In "You Have Cast Your Shadow on the Sea," Antipholus of Syracuse and Luciana finally declare their love for each other. And in "Big Brother," Dromio of Ephesus wonders about his long-lost twin:

> Come to your twin,
> I'll treat you like a mother.
> Each little twin can have only
> One Brother,
> Big Brother! Big Brother!

Most Broadway audiences of 1938 were aware that Teddy might as well have been singing to his big brother. But in interviews he gave at the time, Teddy didn't think much of the parallel:

Some people think my brother wrote me a fat part, but that's wrong. This is the first time I've been in one of Larry's shows. I can't even get hold of the lyrics without going around to Abbott's office. I wouldn't even know when rehearsals started if I didn't watch the papers. That's the trouble working with relatives.[63]

But Larry's depth of feeling for his younger brother is even more evident in a recitation that was cut during rehearsals—cut not because it was bawdy (although it was) but because it took too much time:

> *You never had a childhood,*
> *You never had a chance.*
> *You never had a brother*
> *To kick you in the pants.*
> *And when you went a-fishing,*
> *Unhappy little fool,*
> *You never had a brother*
> *To take your place in school.*
> *And when you squeezed the chambermaid,*
> *Unhappy little man,*
> *You never had a brother*
> *To end what you began.*[64]

Like the "Big Brother" lyric, the recitation is an attempt to get at the joy brought by fraternal recognition, as well as the terror wrought by its absence.

Dromio of Ephesus's lament is answered by a ballet that Balanchine created for Dromio and Antipholus of Syracuse. Eddie Albert couldn't really dance—not yet, anyway—while Jimmy Savo's lack of agility became the basis for burlesquing Debussy's "Afternoon of a Faun," with Savo intermittently jumping as high as he could. "Sing for Your Supper," the number that Hugh Martin had worked on so closely, featured Marcy Wescott, Muriel Angelus, and Wynn Murray trilling, in harmonies that a nightingale would have envied, of the rewards of singing. It stopped traffic outside the Alvin Theatre. And Wynn Murray sent everyone home with the rousing "Oh, Diogenes!" appealing to the fourth-century B.C. philosopher to let her know should he and his lantern ever turn up an honest man.

"I think you have all drunk of Circe's cup," the Duke says in *The Comedy of Errors*.[65] The *Boys from Syracuse* patrons were not quite turned into swine, but most of them walked out onto West Fifty-Second Street utterly transformed.

❦ ❦ ❦

George Abbott's book was mostly original—the few lines he didn't write came from either Dick or Larry—and he had joked about it during tryouts, telling reporters that the Bard was too bawdy for Boston.[66] The one line Abbott retained from Shakespeare was "The venom clamours of a jealous woman / poisons more deadly than a mad dog's tooth," which the Seeress says in *The Boys from Syracuse* because its speaker in *The Comedy of Errors*, the Abbess (mother of the Antipholus twins), was cut out of the libretto. Rodgers wrote: "Lest anyone unfamiliar with the classics accept this as a sentence he had thought up all by himself, George had Jimmy Savo follow it by sticking his head out from the wings and proudly announcing to the audience: 'Shakespeare!'"[67]

Practically every critic in town regarded *The Boys from Syracuse* as a major achievement. *Variety* called it "a musical smash" and mentioned "the unusually canny casting job." In *Newsweek*, the perennially hostile George Jean Nathan was won over. In *The New Yorker*, Robert Benchley suggested it was the best score Rodgers and Hart had written in a long time, and added, "Without Mr. Savo's personality and Frère Hart's shadowing, my own personal laughter would have been confined to the lyrics." Perhaps the most extravagant notice came from the *Telegram*'s reviewer Sidney Whipple, who was inclined to like the boys' work anyway and wrote, "I believe it will be regarded as the greatest musical comedy of its time."[68]

Meanwhile, with Ira Gershwin more or less permanently situated in Hollywood and Oscar Hammerstein going through what was viewed as a slump, Larry was increasingly being compared to Cole Porter, whose *Leave It to Me* had opened two weeks prior to *The Boys from Syracuse*. Porter's "My Heart Belongs to Daddy" was as ribald as "What Can You Do with a Man?" and "Ladies of the Evening." Comparing the two musicals, *Variety* reported that the songs were "about even on laugh-and-blush lines."[69]

The reviews were gratifying to Larry, who read them from a hospital bed at Mt. Sinai. The flu he had suffered in early October had bloomed into pneumonia.[70] In mid-December Larry dictated to Dorothy Hart a letter to send to Mel Shauer, who had married again—to Rosita Moreno, an actress—and had since become Hollywood's most active proponent of the Good Neighbor Policy toward South America. Larry acknowledged that he was still recuperating and intended to go to Miami "with Mama" the following week.[71]

Larry and Frieda Hart settled in at the Roney Plaza in Miami, with Dorothy Hart coming down to trade places with Frieda after a few weeks. Larry missed the Christmas Eve wedding of his friend George Balanchine, who had withstood for more than a year the legions of men who came to court his beloved Zorina. "There was no jealousy in Balanchine's body," Ray Bolger said (surely a trait Balanchine shared with Larry Hart). Balanchine and Zorina married on Staten Island in a ceremony arranged by her frequent dance partner Charles Laskey, who lived nearby, far from Manhattan flashbulbs.[72]

Larry also missed Marcy Wescott entering the Stork Club one night and being serenaded, in quick-thinking Paul Shaffer style, by the orchestra's rendition of "This Can't Be Love" before she could be seated. And he missed Fiorello La Guardia, the Little Flower himself, showing up at the Alvin, where it was widely agreed he could serve as understudy to the Dromios. No, for the time being Larry was happy in Miami, where he could wear shorts and his admiral's cap all day, place bets at Hialeah, and—once Frieda returned to New York—keep company with a handsome young masseur who sat with him on the beach most afternoons.[73] What, if anything, was going on between the two men? Perhaps only Doc Bender knew. It was in Miami one night that Larry and Bender got their first look at the beaming, guitar-playing, twenty-one-year-old Cuban émigré Desi Arnaz.

CHAPTER 20

And Now I Know I Was Naïve

B Y THE early 1930s Miami Beach—in response to the ingrained segregation in American tourism, whether overt or covert—had become a predominantly Jewish town. If the Catskills were a Jewish paradise beckoning to New Yorkers and only two or three hours away by car, Miami Beach was a more distant Eden—two days by train or car but only a few hours, and considerably more cash, by airplane.

Larry Hart had the cash. The Roney Plaza, at Collins Avenue and Twenty-Third Street in Miami Beach, was completed in 1926 and marked by a tower that looked like the Giralda in Seville. It reminded Larry of the Beresford.[1] Larry liked being part of Miami Beach's Jewish community, which was assimilated but not straining to be Protestant as so much of the Hollywood community was. Friends from home were often at the Roney. The most prominent of these was Walter Winchell, who occupied the penthouse every winter, traded gossip with Larry, and, as he did wherever he pitched his tent, trawled the town's nightspots.[2]

Appearing at one of those nightspots was Desi Arnaz. Born Desiderio Alberto Arnaz y de Acha III, on March 2, 1917, Desi grew up in Cuba playing guitar passably and drums enthusiastically. His father was a pharmacist by profession but also a local politician. When the Machado regime, to which Desi's father was loyal, was overthrown in a coup in 1932, the family fled to Miami. Desi began to perform with the Siboney Septet, which followed the Buddy Rogers Orchestra in nighttime performances at the Roney. Buddy had been a movie star, starring in the film version of Rodgers and Hart's *Heads Up!*, but then moved into the more reliably lucrative field of radio and dance music. Miami's night creatures went to hear Buddy and instead found themselves marveling at Desi.[3]

Xavier Cugat either heard Desi or heard *about* him, and invited him to New York to sing. Desi made several important contacts while in New York but soon wanted to go back to Miami and start his own band. According to Marco Rizo, who became Desi's music director years later, Desi offered Cugat a licensing fee of twenty-five dollars a week to use Cugat's name. Out of their agreement came Desi Arnaz and His Xavier Cugat Orchestra, Direct from the Waldorf-Astoria Hotel in New York City.

When Larry Hart and Doc Bender got their first look at him, Desi was still shy of twenty-two but could already match them drink for drink. Larry knew this boy had extraordinary charisma, if not necessarily extraordinary musicianship. And if Doc Bender couldn't seduce him, he would do the next best thing—he would sign him.

Several weeks into his Miami holiday, Larry received two letters from the Theatre Guild's codirectors—one from Lawrence Langner, one from Theresa Helburn. The letters suggest a kind of tag-team strategy, with each correspondent hoping to get a commitment for a Rodgers & Hart musical for the 1939–40 season. "After having tried a book of Shakespeare and George Abbott in *The Boys from Syracuse*," Langner wrote, "we suppose that nothing less than the great classics would really appeal to you as being worthy of your mettle." Langner went on to suggest, among other sources, the Maurice Donnay version of *Lysistrata* and Congreve's *Way of the World* (which Langner had staged at the Westport Country Playhouse). Langner signed off with, "Hoping you have recovered from your recent illness—Sardi's is no longer Sardi's now that you are absent."[4] Helburn, "supplementing Lawrence's letter to you," recommended an adaptation of O'Neill's *Marco Millions*, or perhaps the Robert Sherwood comedies *The Road to Rome* or *Reunion in Vienna*.[5] Larry passed these suggestions on to his partner, though it's unlikely he was taking them seriously. They didn't sound like much fun.

Rested, he returned to New York in late February. *The Boys from Syracuse* was still running. Dick and Larry were still interested to see what Clare Boothe might come up with for Max Gordon—a project that had been put on hold for nearly two years. Naturally, they wanted something new for Vera Zorina. After Zorina and the transcontinental tour of *I Married an Angel*—a seven-car train to transport musicians, cast, crew, and sets—arrived in Chicago on March 5 for a six-week-long stay at the Grand Opera House, Dick and Larry went out to lend a hand.[6]

Reporting on a pre-opening party for *I Married an Angel*, *Chicago Tribune* columnist June Provines ignored Larry's lyric-writing and went right to the well-pounded subject of his diminutive size, inserting an old Dick Rodgers quote: "I take Larry by the hand, lead him into the children's department of any good store, and have him outfitted from head to foot—a short distance." The following night Dick and Larry went to the studios of Chicago radio station WBBM to prepare for the nine o'clock program *Tune Up Time*. Emceeing duties were handled by comedian and radio entertainer Walter O'Keefe, who had been on the Warners' songwriting staff with the boys in 1930. André Kostelanetz conducted the orchestra. Kay Thompson and her singers were routinely part of the program, and Ray Heatherton was brought on as special guest to help honor Rodgers and Hart.[7] It was a bizarre mix of styles. In between Kostelanetz's versions of "The Girl Friend" and "There's a Small Hotel," O'Keefe joked that he was so smitten by Hedy Lamarr that he paid to see her recently in nine pictures. "I saw *Algiers* once and then I saw her eight times in *Ecstasy*," he cracked, referring to the German film in which Lamarr appeared unabashedly nude, eroticized without being glamorized. O'Keefe introduced Dick and Larry as "the American Gilbert and Sullivan" and asked them to describe themselves.

"I'm Dick. I'm 152 pounds, height five-feet-eight, thirty-six years old—and I must have been a beautiful baby," said Rodgers.

"And you, Larry?" said O'Keefe.

"I'm Larry. I'm 125 pounds. I'm five feet tall, I'm fourteen years old, and I'm *still* a beautiful baby," piped Hart. "I may be little, but I'm *cute!*"

"Larry," O'Keefe chided, "I'm surprised to hear you plug somebody else's song like 'I Must Have Been a Beautiful Baby.' For a minute I was afraid you'd say, 'I'm five feet tall and I must have been a small hotel.' You know, if you had a black sombrero on I'd swear I was talking to Mayor La Guardia."

O'Keefe said his favorite Rodgers & Hart song was "Ten Cents a Dance" and asked how the boys came up with the idea for it.

"Larry got the idea from the women he hangs around with," Dick said.

"They charge me *five* cents a dance," Larry crowed.

At least it was a plug for *I Married an Angel*. Meanwhile, Zorina's husband, George Balanchine, was in Burbank navigating the labyrinthine process of moviemaking. Balanchine knew that his wife would come off the road tour of *I Married an Angel* to star in the Warner Bros. film version of *On Your Toes,* but he was less sure that Warners star James Cagney would play Junior, as announced. Balanchine's uncertainty proved justified when Cagney dropped out and Eddie Albert left *The Boys from Syracuse*—Ronald Graham, who had been playing his twin brother, stepped into the role—to play Junior. Balanchine would have preferred Cagney, if only because Cagney could really dance. "You know, of course, that there is a certain degree of sense in Balanchine's objection to Eddie Albert," wrote producer Robert Lord to Hal Wallis, Warners' head of production. "It is not easy to make a picture about a dancer played by an actor who can't dance at all."[8]

A big lug, perhaps, but a quick study, Albert took tap lessons, though not ballet lessons. Balanchine, the most encouraging of perfectionists, found Albert athletic enough to work with. One rush-hour morning in May, Balanchine and Albert set out together from Santa Monica in Balanchine's car, on their way to the Warners lot in Burbank. Balanchine was driving east along San Vicente Boulevard, past the broad median of beautiful coral trees, trying to explain how Albert was to execute a certain lift at the *On Your Toes* rehearsal later that day. Albert admitted that he didn't understand. Balanchine pulled the car over, got out, and said, "Come, I show you!" Signaling for Albert to follow, Balanchine lunged across two lanes of traffic to the median. While passersby gaped, the two men practiced lifting each other.[9]

In New York a new musical project emerged, considerably more appealing to Dick and Larry than Clare Boothe's idea. George Abbott held the option on a football-themed screenplay titled *The More the Merrier,* by George Marion, Jr. *The More the Merrier* had been available, in slightly different form, since 1931, when Paramount canceled plans to film it with Jack Oakie.[10]

Abbott often had great instincts for what was going on in American culture. Football's popularity was peaking. Beginning in the second decade of the twentieth century, colleges and universities began to use the tools of big business—accounting, advertising, sophisticated marketing strategies—to increase enrollment. Professional football enjoyed its first surge when Red Grange played for the Chicago Bears in the mid-1920s, then a second in 1933 when more teams were assigned to eastern metropolises. But then pro football stalled for many years, leaving all that space across the American plains and deltas for college football. In *King Football,* his detailed history of the sport, Michael Oriard wrote that football teams became the public symbols of universities—actors starring in a national drama. "Football power shifted westward in the 1920s and southward in the 1930s. Football regions became defined by major conferences: the Western (Big Ten), Pacific Coast, Southeastern, Southwest, and Big Six, more or less in that order of descending prestige." [11] Residing in those regions intensified the drama for fans, but you could also see what was happening across the country through newsreels: cameras could film entire football games, which were invariably played in daylight. On November 30, 1935, a crucial game between Southern Methodist University (SMU) and Texas Christian University (TCU) showcased their aerial offenses—a style of play then peculiar to the Southwest. When the clock ran out, SMU was the winner, but everyone in the nation seemed to know the name of TCU's quarterback, Sammy Baugh. [12] Even George Abbott, who preferred to relax on a dance floor or a putting green rather than in a stadium box, was aware of Slingin' Sammy Baugh.

Abbott lateraled *The More the Merrier* to Dick and Larry. After wandering through ancient Greece, the boys figured they could spend a few weeks on the American gridiron. Amicably, they dropped out of the Clare Boothe project (titled *Wedding Day*). [13] For a wince-inducing moment the football story was given the punning title *Yale Bait*. Dick and Larry went to work. The title changed to *Too Many Girls*. Abbott got his cast together.

The first cast member locked in (as Pepe) was a Puerto Rican dancer whose birth name was Juana de Dios Castrello and who danced under the name Diosa Costello. Raven-haired, pretty, with the ability—in Desi Arnaz's words—to "shake her ass better and faster than anyone I had ever seen," Costello was appearing that spring at the International Casino (at Broadway and Forty-Fifth), then the largest cabaret in the city. [14] She had also arranged to take her Echoes of Cuba orchestra into the new La Conga, where hers would be one of three nightly "native rhythm" acts. [15] How George Abbott was introduced to Diosa Costello is not known, though it's likely he first went to see her at one of the two clubs before he began to dance with her—the tall, rhumba-mad director from upstate New York partnering with the lovely Puerto Rican of the vibrating derriere. They referred to themselves as Abbott & Costello.

By the spring of 1939 Desi Arnaz was also in residence at La Conga. Desi was credited with introducing the conga rhythm to New York (possible but difficult to prove), and he credited himself with getting Diosa Costello noticed by Abbott and Rodgers and Hart (improbable). In any case, the magnetic looks and charisma that Larry and Doc saw in Desi in Miami Beach helped get him the role of Manuelito Lynch, an Argentine considered the best football player in South America, in *Too Many Girls.*

Manuelito was only one of the show's four major football-player roles, which added up to a singing and dancing equivalent of The Four Musketeers. After his run in *Knickerbocker Holiday*, Richard Kollmar was ready for one role. Eddie Bracken, a former child actor who grew up to specialize in comically bewildered characters, was plucked from the road company of *What a Life*, which Abbott had produced. Dancer Hal Le Roy had been so young when appearing in the 1932 *Follies* that he'd had to be escorted home each night by his father. Apart from Manuelito, who is desperate to attend a coeducational college (because you can never have "too many girls"), each football player has been connected to an Ivy League school.

Manuelito gets his wish when the father of beautiful Consuelo hires the four football players to serve as bodyguards as she heads off to Pottawatomie College, the father's alma mater, in Pottawatomie, New Mexico. The complication kicks in when Consuelo and Clint Kelly of Princeton (Kollmar) fall in love, then takes another turn when she discovers he's been *paid* to be near her. The Southwest was the right locale for a college desperate to have a football program, and for a touch of satire about its exoticism, for trainloads of New Yorkers were then arriving in Taos and Santa Fe to marvel at the landscape and buy goods from local Indians.

While *Too Many Girls* was being cast, Larry's lyrics were paid the honor of a WPA Federal Theatre revue opening with the title *Sing for Your Supper* (Bender's client John Latouche was one of the lyricists). But *The Boys from Syracuse* was weakened by competition from the World's Fair in Queens and shut down. So Abbott arranged for Marcy Wescott—blond, cool, Chicago Society—to take a summer vacation before she had to return to New York to play Consuelo, and for Mary Jane Walsh, who had danced so nimbly in *I'd Rather Be Right*, to play Consuelo's best friend at college.

In August 1939 Larry and Frieda Hart and Big Mary left the huge penthouse at the Beresford and moved eleven blocks north, to the Ardsley, at Ninety-Second Street and Central Park West. It was a matter of consolidation. Teddy was no longer in residence, and the Ardsley owners were inducing celebrated tenants with attractive rental terms. In the announcement of the Hart lease, Larry was listed as "author."[16] The new quarters at the Ardsley, yet another building designed by Emery Roth, were only slightly more modest—it was a twenty-first-floor duplex with a large terrace overlooking the park. The best thing about it was that it put mother and son on separate floors; Frieda wouldn't be disturbed by Larry and his guests in the wee small hours. (By then it was unlikely that Frieda was oblivious to her son's sexual preferences. In *Somewhere for Me*, Meryle Secrest wrote of Larry bringing the actor Peter Garey home to the Ardsley with him. Frieda hoisted herself onto the back of a sofa, up against the window, and warned Garey, "If you go out with my son, I'll jump." Garey went out with Larry anyway, though the evening was aborted after Larry made it clear he wanted sex.)[17] The apartment never quite felt lived-in. Larry slept on a couch pushed against the wall in the den, as though a bed signified sleep he hadn't earned. And books do furnish a room; Larry's books had warmed the Beresford apartment immeasurably. Dorothy Rodgers had decorated the Beresford apartment, but when she designed the interior of the new Ardsley penthouse she neglected to create space for the books.[18] Consequently, the books remained in boxes waiting to be unpacked. Except for a box or two, they never would be.

The Ardsley penthouse would later be occupied by Yip Harburg, who idolized Larry.[19] For now, Harburg was in Los Angeles writing songs with his partner Harold Arlen for *The Wizard of Oz*. "Avoiding the word 'integral,'" the *Los Angeles Times* reported, "they say their tunes are all a part of the plot. They also avoid referring to themselves as the American Gilbert and Sullivan, partly because of modesty and partly because a lot of people have already bestowed the title on Larry Hart and Richard Rodgers."[20]

An adulterated version of Arlen and Harburg's song "God's Country," originally written for *Hooray for What!*, figured prominently in MGM's version of *Babes in Arms*, released on September 19, 1939. The screenplay, by Hollywood veterans Kay Van Riper and Jack McGowan, retained the framework of the *Babes* book but threw out all the political commentary, every line concerning race, and the French aviator business. The movie also threw out all the songs but two, "Where or When" and the title song, and used patches of "The Lady Is a Tramp" only as underscoring. (The Hays Office would have permitted neither the lyrics of "Lady" on the sound track nor the title in the credits, anyway.) "The Lady Is a Tramp," "My Funny Valentine," "Johnny One Note," and "I Wish I Were in Love Again" were deemed too mature for the characters created in the screenplay, while the other numbers were jettisoned because they no longer fit the new story. The irony is that "Where or When" was still a song of breathtaking sagacity and might have seemed too wise for performers twice the age of the stars, Mickey Rooney and Judy Garland; it had become too popular to omit.

Babes in Arms was Mickey and Judy's third picture together, after *Thoroughbreds Don't Cry* and *Love Finds Andy Hardy*. (*Words and Music* would be their last.) Producer Arthur Freed was in his freshman year as a musicals producer and would soon become the most powerful producer on the lot; Busby Berkeley, who had an extensive history with Rodgers and Hart, directed; and the Texas transplant Roger Edens provided much of the underscore. Mickey plays Mickey Moran, and he's almost never off the screen, whether he's imitating Clark Gable, seen in a genuine film clip of him at five or so, doing his vaudeville routine—it fits nicely with the screen character's backstory as the child of vaudevillians—or pretending to play piano while Judy sings "Good Morning," written for the film by producer Freed and his longtime partner Nacio Herb Brown and eventually to become more popular when it was performed in *Singin' in the Rain*. Judy plays Patsy Barton, who loves Mickey and gives a flawless rendition of "I Cried for You" (Freed, Arnheim, and Lyman). June Preisser is the child movie star, now grown into an adolescent coquette, who decides to invest in the show. Douglas McPhail does good work as the tall boy baritone, striding through the studio-built small-town street in the title song, his voice resonating with no less depth than Alfred Drake's. And in her second witchlike turn that year, Margaret Hamilton is the county agent determined to put the kids on a work farm. The songs nudging Rodgers and Hart to the sidelines include Freed and Brown's "You Are My Lucky Star" and "Broadway Rhythm," with "God's Country" as the big finale. Although "Where or When" is an unsurpassable song, it's the movie's title song that stays with you, maybe because it's staged so cinematically, with a dollying camera and the juvenile characters coming together as a powerful chorus.

Larry could not have felt warm toward Metro's version of *Babes in Arms*. But he and Dick were immersed once again in a world almost as youthful in *Too Many Girls*. Most of the songs were completed by late September. Though Dick and Larry's musical sensibilities were already shaped, Desi Arnaz's style had an enormous impact on them. As the closing number for each performance at La Conga, Desi sang "Babalu," in which the African gods of rhythm descend on Havana, and La Conga patrons eagerly configured themselves into a happy-sweaty conga line, though by then it was two-thirty in the morning.[21] That kind of energy was worth capturing for Broadway.

When Desi was unable to negotiate the march beat of a song called "Look

Out," in which several prominent colleges are warned that Pottawatomie has a football team ("You're a ham, / Better scram, Notre Dame"), Rodgers rewrote it with a conga beat instead. "She Could Shake the Maracas" was written for Diosa Costello. So was "Spic and Spanish," a pun that would have been deemed politically incorrect only a couple of decades later. "Love Never Went to College," the first love song between Consuelo and Clint, has one of Larry Hart's most tightly constructed verses:

> *A pretty girl and a bright young man*
> *Try to be just friends but never can.*
> *That is what perplexes*
> *Young folks of opposite sexes.*
> *Love likes to pull their legs a bit,*
> *So they're either in love or out of it.*
> *Love doesn't make much sense*
> *But his technique's immense.*

"Too Many Girls" was written for Manuelito (Desi Arnaz) to express his love-'em-and-leave attitude. Even before the show opened on October 18, Hugh Martin heard a big-band recording of it and told Larry. "What? Already?" said Larry. "I've got to hear it!" Hart and Martin walked over to the Colony Record Shop on Broadway and Forty-Ninth Street and found a copy. Even without a vocal (i.e., Larry's lyrics) it was still exciting to hear your songs played out there in the world.[22]

As he had with "Sing for Your Supper," in *The Boys from Syracuse*, Hugh Martin arranged the complex ensemble piece "I Like to Recognize the Tune." The song is overstuffed with Larry's references to classical composers and pop tunesmiths—all victims of the explosive big bands, in which Gene Krupa plays the drums like thunder, burying "the melody six feet under." The song meant a lot to Dick, who couldn't abide the jazz musician's penchant for turning a composition inside out, and to Larry, who wanted his lyrics *heard*.

When a lyric was needed for "Heroes in the Fall"—it introduced the Pottawatomie football players, who loathed the humdrum summer jobs (bellboy, iceman, Fuller Brush man, etc.) that preceded seasonal stardom—Larry couldn't be found. "I had to supply the necessary lyric myself," Rodgers wrote.[23] The lyric isn't bad, suggesting that Rodgers had something of a gift for the craft—he would put it to arresting use more than twenty years later writing *No Strings*—and one couplet sounds too Hart-like to ignore:

We hate the signs of spring
Because it makes bums of us all.

Another ensemble piece, "Give It Back to the Indians," seemed to be one of Larry's divertissements—a number that didn't advance the show's story so much as stop it cold. Written 313 years after the purchase of Manhattan Island, "Give It Back to the Indians" celebrates the city's corruption-slicked chaos, spinning ever faster out of control. The verse suggests that "old Peter Minuit" was taken for a ride when he paid "twenty-six dollars and a bottle of booze" for Manhattan. "We've tried to run the city, / But the city ran away" leads into the first refrain:

Broadway's turning into Coney,
Champagne Charlie's drinking gin,
Old New York is new and phony,
Give it back to the Indians!

Champagne Charlie may be a reference to Cholly Knickerbocker (Maury Paul) the Society columnist, but it could also be harking back to the popular nineteenth-century song "Champagne Charlie," by Alfred Lee and George Leybourne.[24] A subsequent refrain, rarely sung since the show was first produced, goes:

Shakespeare doesn't get a showing
When those striptease girls begin,
Yet Tobacco Road keeps going;
Give it back to the Indians.

And its rarely heard bridge:

Bound on the north
By the Bronx—a pretty view.
East by Long Island—smoke.
West by New Jersey—pots of glue.
South Brooklyn's asleep,
Chief no wanna keep!

Try to rein it in and the city just gallops off.

"I Didn't Know What Time It Was," the second love song in *Too Many Girls*, was the one that stuck in the public's mind, and for good reason. In it Larry Hart employs yet another idiomatic title phrase, as well as his characteristic repetition ("[I] never was naïve" is subsequently corrected as "I *know* I was naïve") with an emotional kick. "I Didn't Know What Time It Was" is one of Rodgers's most beautiful melodies, but its beauty also derives from the lyric's arc, from self-delusion and befuddlement to clarity and contentment. Once again the song's setting deepens its meaning: when Consuelo (Marcy Wescott) sings it to Clint (Richard Kollmar), she thinks she's revealing herself to him at last; but he already knows all about her. The song steers clear of bathos by having the other football players, who have overheard their singing, reenact the episode to Manuelito (Desi Arnaz). Manuelito is properly amused, but for us in the audience the laughter carries a lump in the throat.

Too Many Girls tried out in Boston in early October. Larry was trying to stay sober, and once again his lyrical cleverness in "I Like to Recognize the Tune" made the audience hungry for more. Desi Arnaz, misremembering the setting as New Haven, wrote that George Abbott asked Larry for two more choruses. Larry borrowed a pencil and, placing an old envelope on top of the piano, began to write. The cast and crew left him there, a little boy forced to do his homework, while they all attended a party at the restaurant across the street. "In about half an hour Larry came in," Arnaz recalled, "went to Mr. Abbott and Dick Rodgers and said, 'What do you think of this?' as he handed them the envelope. He had written three more choruses as good as, if not better than, the ones he had written before. Unbelievable mind!"[25]

By the time *Too Many Girls* opened in New York, at the Imperial Theatre on October 18, 1939, there was added interest because the college football season had become high drama. For the first time in years the Big Ten was up for grabs. Texas A&M and Tennessee were looking unbeatable (though Tennessee would lose to powerhouse USC in the Rose Bowl). And UCLA proudly started four great black players—Kenny Washington, Woody Strode, Johnny Wynne, and an "antelope in human form," Jackie Robinson— to override the minimal tokenism of the era.[26]

Too Many Girls ran with its high expectations and made it all the way downfield for a touchdown. Mary Jane Walsh took charge of each scene she appeared in. Eddie Bracken was on his way to stardom. Hal Le Roy, whose dancing style suggested that his limbs might be detachable, wowed just about everybody. Richard Kollmar and Marcy Wescott charmed with their love songs. During that first performance Kollmar, distracted because his new girlfriend, Dorothy Kilgallen, was in the house, drew in his stomach and sang:

> Once I was young
> Yesterday perhaps
> Danced with Jim and Paul
> And kissed some other chaps. . . .

He remained oblivious to the audience's hysteria until Wescott sang the same words back to him.[27] One of the male students of the chorus was a tall red-head named Van Johnson, and when it became apparent that audience members couldn't take their eyes off him, Doc Bender signed him, too.

Ultimately, however, the evening belonged to Desi Arnaz and Diosa Costello. When Brooks Atkinson expressed reservations about Costello's "imitation of the less engaging side of Lupe Velez's abandon," Costello admirers could only ask for more.[28] The Atkinson review was read at La Conga, where everyone had repaired after the opening performance because Desi and Diosa had another show to do. Dick and Dorothy Rodgers were there, as well as Dick Kollmar and Dorothy Kilgallen. Larry brought Frieda. The *New Yorker* cartoonist Peter Arno brought Debutante Number One, Brenda Frazier. Polly Adler, the most notorious madam in Gotham, approached their table and bellowed to Desi that he was "the biggest fucking hit in town" as she dropped on their table the morning's papers, most of them attesting to Desi's magnetism. Adler's craggy Russian-Jewish appearance (John O'Hara wrote that Adler looked like restaurateur Mike Romanoff in drag) and gruff manner prompted Dorothy Rodgers to raise an exquisite eyebrow. "Who is she?" asked Dorothy. Larry laughed. Peter Arno explained the facts of life to Dorothy.[29]

Three days after *Too Many Girls* opened, the film version of *On Your Toes* was released. It was one of a new wave of musicals: Warner Bros. was also releasing *The Desert Song*; MGM had *Balalaika* and *Broadway Melody of 1940*; and Twentieth Century-Fox was going out with *Swanee River*.[30] *On Your Toes* remains watchable for Zorina's aura, which can be maddeningly contradictory: sylphlike one moment, voluptuous the next; light on her feet and then surprisingly heavy-footed; Teutonically brittle in one scene, and in the next one luminous. Zorina remained the focus of Rodgers and Hart for whatever they did next. And that already seemed to be in preparation: a musical about the annual Butler's Ball, held at the Waldorf-Astoria.

The idea had come from Irvin Pincus, who ran the Alvin Theatre with his brother Norman. (Alex Aarons and Vincent Freedley had sold the theater to the Pincus family in 1932.) Late one night in the fall, while *Too Many Girls* was in rehearsal, Pincus met Larry Hart at Ruby Foo's (then at Broadway and Fifty-Second Street). The two men had been at Brant Lake Camp at the same time and saw each other occasionally in the city. Pincus conveyed to Larry his idea of the Butler's Ball, which suggested not only an upstairs-downstairs story but a terrific role for Zorina, as a scullery maid who masquerades as a debutante. Larry was drunk to the point of incoherence, so Pincus figured his idea hadn't registered. But the next day Pincus arrived at the Alvin to find that Dick Rodgers wanted to speak to him. "We'd like to buy the idea you told Larry last night," Rodgers said. Because Josh Logan had handled Zorina so well in *I Married an Angel*, he was the boys' choice to direct. Logan brought in his close friend Gladys Hurlbut to write the book for the musical.[31] Since Dick, Larry, and Pincus were all represented by Howard Reinheimer, it was easy to come to terms. For the time being the Butler's Ball musical was called *Nice Work*.[32] Dwight Wiman would produce.

Zorina was on Dick's mind while he worked on *Ghost Town*, a ballet for the Ballet Russe de Monte Carlo, and he was only too happy not to have to think about Larry for a few weeks. The art-collecting socialite, painter, and ballet patron Gerald Murphy, whose fame came from close proximity to Scott Fitzgerald in the 1920s and whose fortune came from Mark Cross, had made the introductions. As performing arts companies went, the Ballet Russe had Society's stamp of approval, and Rodgers wanted a little of that action. Dancer-choreographer Marc Platt had an idea for a ballet about the Gold Rush. Rodgers's music for *Ghost Town* sounds more like Respighi than anything we've come to think of as American Western. The ballet would be presented at the Metropolitan Opera House, with the composer conducting, for five performances in mid-November.[33]

Zorina was also on Larry's mind in the last week of October, when he performed one of his vanishing acts. Frieda and Mary Campbell—and implicitly Teddy and Dorothy Hart, less than two miles away—were accustomed to Larry's stumbling in at all hours, before and after dawn, but now his absence was more protracted than usual—thirty-six hours and counting. Phone calls went back and forth to decide whether to declare Larry missing. When he showed up on October 28, he explained he'd flown to Indianapolis to see

Zorina's final appearance in the road show of *I Married an Angel* before the ballerina Karen Van Ryn took over; he'd just neglected to tell anyone.[34]

Then came the huge letdown: Zorina would not be available after all. She was still under contract to Samuel Goldwyn, who hated how Warners had used her in *On Your Toes* and, in a rebuke to Warners, decided to lend her to Fox to star in *European Plan*, which had an original screenplay by Milton Lazarus.[35] *European Plan* was eventually abandoned, but the damage to *Nice Work* had been done. Zorina was out; after Wiman and the songwriters briefly considered Rosita Moreno (the Hollywood singer-actress married to Mel Shaver) as the leading lady, the Hungarian singer Marta Eggert (formerly Eggerth) was in; and so was a seal named Sharkey, a graduate of Huling's Seal College at Kingston-on-the-Hudson, whose act had excited the show's book writer, Gladys Hurlbut, when she saw him at an animal fair in Woodstock.[36]

As the 1939 football season rushed toward the bowl games, Desi Arnaz worked "Spic and Spanish" into his La Conga act. The RKO film version of *Too Many Girls*, which George Abbott would direct, wouldn't be ready for release for another eleven months, but it's worth mentioning here because it comes closer to re-creating the spirit of the original stage production than any other movie adaptation of a Rodgers & Hart show. For the movie, Richard Kollmar's role was taken by Richard Carlson, but Arnaz, Bracken, and Le Roy were retained; the decidedly Latina Diosa Costello was replaced by the consummately Hollywood Ann Miller; the big-band singer Frances Langford took over for Mary Jane Walsh; and Marcy Wescott gave way to the willowy redhead Lucille Ball. On the set Ball and Arnaz fell in love. Out of that partnership would come the long-running television series *I Love Lucy*; Desilu, one of the most formidable television production entities of the twentieth century; and marriage, on November 30, 1940, a week after the picture was released. (Larry Hart was asked to stand up for Lucy and Desi at their Connecticut wedding, but he never made it to the ceremony.)[37] Conspicuous throughout the film is Van Johnson, who towers over the other chorus men. Of the songs, the most important change was the addition of Rodgers and Hart's "You're Nearer." "You're nearer," sings Trudy Erwin (dubbing Ball) to a faraway former boyfriend,

> *Than my head is to my pillow,*
> *Nearer*

Than the wind is to the willow,
Dearer
Than the rain is to the earth below.
Precious as the sun to the things that grow.

The first time it's sung, every guy in earshot gets moony over Consuelo. Later, when Consuelo and Carlson are on the outs, each reprises the song alone. Part of the impact of the lyric is that the love object is nowhere nearby; its metaphoric intimacy is conveyed by images of only a few inseparable pairs and must have influenced Dorothy Fields while she was writing "Close as Pages in a Book" (music by Sigmund Romberg).

On December 1, 1939, Larry Hart submitted an application for admission to the Lambs Club. If Dick Rodgers wanted entry to the Four Hundred, Larry wanted entry to a bar where he could find someone to drink and play cards with. The bar at the Lambs Club, at 130 West Forty-Fourth Street, suited those desires just fine. Truthfully claiming membership in Phi Sigma Delta, Larry had his playwright pal Harry Irving second him for admission. "He is a great writer, a swell host and a loyal friend," Irving wrote. Through December, testimonial letters supporting Larry's candidacy poured into the Lambs Club. Asked the reasons for the applicant's eligibility, *Variety* editor Joe Laurie, Jr., answered, "He is a fine artist and a grand gentleman." Bandleader Fred Waring commanded, "Get him in!" Answering the question "Do you think he would make a desirable Lamb?" Victor Moore wrote, "Yes yes yes!" Under Remarks, Moore wrote only, "No remarks necessary." Larry was admitted. He paid a $75 initiation fee, $11.66 in dues, $8.67 in a War Tax (to support the war in Europe), and $1.00 to the Flower Fund, for a total of $96.33. To a man terrified of being alone, it was worth every penny.[38]

As 1939 ended, it was painfully apparent to Dwight Wiman and his associate producer Tom Weatherly that they would have to make *Nice Work* attractive to Broadway audiences without Zorina's supernova. The first order of business was to lose that title. Wiman placed announcements in most of the New York dailies admitting as much. One announcement, signed by Weatherly, offered a pair of first-night tickets to any reader who came up with a new title.[39] Weatherly didn't have to pay up, though, because the winning title, *Higher and Higher*, was submitted by "a Hindu student" named Sregdor

Drahcir—Richard Rodgers spelled backward.[40] In the meantime Gladys Hurlbut was writing the book. Josh Logan was spending his mornings mapping out the Nancy Hamilton–Buddy Lewis revue *Two for the Show* (remembered, if at all, for "How High the Moon") and his afternoons working with Hurlbut.[41] It was a strain.

By mid-February 1940 Jack Haley, more recognizable since the release of *The Wizard of Oz*, and Shirley Ross had been signed to star in *Higher and Higher* alongside Marta Eggert. Jo Mielziner was designing the sets. Each day Logan struggled to tailor the show to Eggert and her vocal talents. But Zorina's absence had left everyone bedraggled. There was a rumor going around that Dick and Larry had become more interested in returning to a musical adaptation of Molnár's *The Play's the Thing*, and that Wiman was encouraging them to update *The Merry Widow* for Deanna Durbin and Desi Arnaz—a bizarre pairing that nevertheless might have proved interesting.[42]

There was also a nice surprise from Lee Wiley, the Oklahoman whose jazz-inflected interpretations rarely missed the heart of a song. Larry could not have been displeased when Wiley, recording an album of Rodgers & Hart songs at Rabson's Music Shop at 111 West Fifty-Second Street, included the diabolically sensuous "As Though You Were There," which had been jettisoned from *Heads Up!* eleven years earlier and neglected ever since. The album would not be released until April, but Dick and Larry must have heard the acetates. There have never been better readings of "As Though You Were There" or "A Ship Without a Sail."

But there was still *Higher and Higher* to mount. Lucinda Ballard, who had worked on *Babes in Arms* without credit, was brought in to design the costumes. Ballard's ex-husband, Bill, had built Wiman's house in Bermuda, so initially she felt secure in the job.[43] But Logan was suffering a depression that would not lift, and he channeled much of that mental anguish into reproaching his cast and crew, particularly Ballard, nearly every day. "[Josh] made trouble with Dwight [Wiman]," Ballard wrote to Rodgers years later, "and all of a sudden from having been everybody's dream girl nobody would speak to me except Larry Hart and he, poor darling, couldn't do much for me."[44]

In early March, Ballard went with the show to New Haven for its first tryout performances. Tension between her and Logan had not broken. Ballard was at the Shubert Theatre when Larry accosted her.

"Come over to Casey's, baby," he said, referring to the bar next to the theater, where a table had been reserved for him. "I'm so lonesome."

Ballard went over to keep Larry company and have a drink. Buffeted by her recent divorce and a love affair that earned her friends' scorn, Ballard let her hair down. Larry, who could be judgmental about a friend's stupidity but not about her emotional state, listened. Doc Bender suddenly appeared at the bar with a sheaf of papers for Larry to sign. One paper gave him pause. "What's this?"

"Life insurance," Bender said. "We have to put someone in as beneficiary."

"We'll put Lucinda [Ballard] in, who else?"

A look of terror, Ballard remembered, came over Bender's face. Larry laughed. Ballard laughed, too, more in appreciation of Larry's clowning than because it was funny. Doc didn't think it was funny at all.[45]

On orders from Wiman (who had evidently consulted with Logan), Ballard was asked not to accompany the show to Boston. It would be years before she worked again with Rodgers, and it was the last opportunity she had to work with Hart.

But Larry was barely in Boston himself. In her column in the *Journal American*, Dorothy Kilgallen reported that Larry was commuting so he could spend nights at various Manhattan clubs and bars.[46] This might have been cover for Larry's absence altogether. By the end of March, when tryouts ended, he seemed to have lost interest in the show.

Curiously, a letter John O'Hara sent from Hollywood to Rodgers in Boston would grip Larry's interest.[47]

> I don't know whether you happened to see any of the series of pieces I've been doing for *The New Yorker* in the past year or so. They're about a guy who is master of ceremonies in cheap night clubs, and the pieces are in the form of letters from him to a successful band leader. Anyway, I got the idea that the pieces, or at least the character and the life in general could be made into a book show, and I wonder if you and Larry would be interested in working on it with me. I read that you two have a commitment with Dwight Wiman for this Spring but if and when you get through with that I do hope you like my idea.

O'Hara was then under contract at Twentieth Century-Fox, taking a stab at the scenario for *South American Way*, the title based on a hit song by Jimmy McHugh and soon to be changed to *Down Argentine Way*. A week or two before O'Hara wrote the letter, George Oppenheimer, the peripatetic playwright–movie executive, had suggested to O'Hara that his recent *New Yorker* stories about a nightclub entertainer named Joey would adapt well for the stage. At first, O'Hara didn't think so, but then he warmed to the idea. That's when he approached Rodgers. After consulting with his partner— Larry was rubbing his hands and already exploding with lyric fragments— Rodgers wired O'Hara that they were indeed interested. Their collaboration would have to wait, however, until O'Hara fulfilled his Fox contract and the boys saw *Higher and Higher* onto Broadway.[48]

Higher and Higher went into the Shubert Theatre in New York on April 4, 1940. Robert Alton had done the choreography, which received praise even from those critics who dismissed both the book *and* Sharkey the seal. Among the dancers were Vera-Ellen and June Allyson. The score included the lovely, long-neglected "Nothing But You," which harks back to Larry Hart's preoccupation with dreams as romantic signposts. The verse goes:

> *This may seem queer to you,*
> *The meaning unclear to you.*
> *Have you ever dreamed of someone*
> *Very dear to you?*

But only two *Higher and Higher* songs became standards, "Disgustingly Rich" and "It Never Entered My Mind."

"Disgustingly Rich" is sung by several servants to launch maid Minnie (Eggert) on her masquerade as a high-flying debutante, with references to "21," the glamorous Fifty-Second Street night spot Tony's, and Larry's beloved Roney Plaza. The verse features a kind of invocation of debutante Brenda Frazier, who was known to comb her hair at her nightclub table, to watch the show through the mirror in her compact, and to have been given a 1938 allowance of $52,000.[49] The melody to "It Never Entered My Mind" has been accurately described as "haunting," and the title is yet another example of Larry Hart's use of a colloquialism teetering on the edge of cliché. The lyric, shaped by the shock of losing a love, is rife with remarkable couplets:

> *You have what I lack myself*
> *And now I even have to scratch my back myself.*

And:

You were my barometer,
And now my only friend is my thermometer.

That last line derives from Larry's post-pneumonia preoccupation with taking his own temperature. And the phrase "uneasy in my easy chair" is deceptively spare—elegant, vivid, and eminently singable. But the song may be finally too self-pitying to be great. Shirley Ross put it across in her characteristically dry delivery, but few other singers can navigate it without sounding whiny or, to quote the lyric itself, mopey.

"It Never Entered My Mind" includes one phrase Hart might have meant more literally than most interpreters take it for:

Once you warned me that if you scorned me
I'd sing the maiden's prayer again . . .

Is "the maiden's prayer" something Larry concocted to connote loneliness? Or is it possible he had in mind the mid-nineteenth-century Polish composition "The Maiden's Prayer," which adorned so many pianos in Europe and America and was often ridiculed for ornamentation that rendered its performances maudlin? If so, he probably meant that the doleful singer, rejected by her lover, fears returning to a humdrum existence. In the Brecht-Weill opera *Rise and Fall of the City of Mahagonny*, a pianist plays a bit of "The Maiden's Prayer," prompting another character to declare sarcastically, "That's what I call eternal art!" The great Texas bandleader Bob Wills, who was taught by his father to play it on the fiddle, recorded "Maiden's Prayer" in Dallas in 1935.[50]

Neither "It Never Entered My Mind" nor "Disgustingly Rich" was enough to keep *Higher and Higher* running longer than three months and one week. Performances were suspended through August 5, when Marie Nash, who had also played a maid, replaced Eggert in the leading role. But this second iteration didn't last three weeks. Robert Alton took most of the *Higher and Higher* dancers and put them right into Cole Porter's *Panama Hattie*.[51] Shirley Ross told the *World-Telegram* that there were too many changes made in rehearsal, too much plot for a musical comedy, and too much stage time spent in a kitchen—even if it was the kitchen of a mansion.[52] Except for heroine Minnie, the servants never made it out of the pantry.

When *Higher and Higher* was made at RKO, it still had Irvin Pincus's original idea, but all that was left of the Rodgers & Hart score was "Disgustingly Rich." The other songs were by Jimmy McHugh and Harold Adamson, and most of them were very good. Jack Haley was still the male lead, with Michele Morgan in Eggert's role, and both of them got billing over the movie's real star, Frank Sinatra, who was playing himself in one of the most self-assured acting debuts in screen history. A bevy of welcome guests shows up at the party—Mel Tormé, Dooley Wilson (seated, as he was in *Casablanca*, at a piano he couldn't really play), Leon Errol, Mary Wickes, and the one-of-a-kind Victor Borge. But it's Sinatra you watch and listen to. He sings "I Couldn't Sleep a Wink Last Night," "I Saw You First," and "A Lovely Way to Spend an Evening"—three strong numbers that compensate for the deletion of the Rodgers & Hart songs, including "It Never Entered My Mind," which Sinatra recorded later for Columbia Records (substituting "lonely prayer" for "maiden's prayer"). Larry Hart would surely have found Sinatra as charming in *Higher and Higher* as so many moviegoers did. Alas, the picture was released two weeks too late for him to see it.

During the brief summer entr'acte of the *Higher and Higher* run, Dick and Larry had other commitments to ponder. The John O'Hara project, referred to then as *Your Pal Joey*, could begin as soon as O'Hara came home from the West Coast. At the end of June, the boys agreed to write songs for the upcoming RKO picture *They Met in Argentina*, yet another Good Neighbor Policy production.[53] On weekdays Dick and Larry still met in each other's apartments to work, though Larry was becoming increasingly dilatory and, as the afternoons wore on, increasingly impatient for a drink. ("When a person accustomed to a certain amount of alcohol every day doesn't get those carbohydrates," Truman Capote declares in *Tru*, "why, the body just sets up this demand.")[54] It took less alcohol now to get Larry feeling good and numb, which meant that he was pretty far along by mid-evening. As Meryle Secrest pointed out, Rodgers would have described his own drinking as "being one of the boys, almost a proof of manhood, as long as it did not happen too often," whereas Larry rarely stopped until he had passed out. Besides, Rodgers hated chiding Larry about booze. "I didn't feel that it was my business particularly," he said. "I may have been the keeper of his lyrics but not his morals."[55]

After one work session in the third week of July, Larry went off to one of his regular midtown haunts. Dick and Dorothy drove up to the Westport Country Playhouse at the behest of Lawrence Langner to see a revival of the 1931 play *Green Grow the Lilacs*. The revival had been planned as something of a novelty because John Ford had agreed to direct it, with Ford's young star John Wayne starring as Curly. But neither showed up. (Ford would still be listed as producer.) Instead, Ford regular Ward Bond made the trip east to play Curly.[56] The gears of one's imagination might lock at the projection of Ward Bond, the perennially gruff and overgrown sidekick in Ford's movies, as the character who would subsequently sing "Oh, What a Beautiful Mornin'," but the gears in Dick Rodgers's mind clicked into operation that very night.

CHAPTER 21

To Write I Used to Think Was Wasting Ink

*T*HE INVITATION to Westport was probably another attempt by the Theatre Guild to get Rodgers and Hart on board to write a new musical under its auspices. It was a curious choice, because *Green Grow the Lilacs* had been hardly received as a masterpiece when it premiered in 1931. "It makes up into a rather pleasant entertainment," Robert Benchley reported in *The New Yorker* a couple of weeks after the 1931 opening, "interspersed with an olio of folk dancing (they were great ones for dancing 'round and 'round) and recitations. After a while it gets just a little tiresome, just as the fun following a 'church sociable' in Massachusetts used to get tiresome, and for exactly the same reasons."[1] But something made Dick Rodgers think he could turn *Green Grow the Lilacs* into a musical. The title alone connoted a sunniness that was a hemisphere away from Larry Hart's shadow-darkened outlook. "The more smiling aspects of life . . . are the more American," William Dean Howells wrote near the end of the nineteenth century.[2] Larry didn't buy that, but Dick thought Larry could warm to the material anyway.

There was some dancing in the Westport production. The choreographer was a young actor named Gene Kelly, who had been greatly impressed with, even inspired by, "Slaughter on Tenth Avenue" four years earlier. Kelly had caught theatergoers' attention in early 1939 in a substantial role in the Nancy Hamilton–Buddy Lewis revue *One for the Money*, and then again in a smaller but no less significant role in William Saroyan's *The Time of Your Life*, which went on to win the Pulitzer Prize for drama and the New York

Drama Critics' Circle Award. Both shows had been housed in the Booth Theatre, on Forty-Fifth Street, and after an evening's performance Kelly often walked down the block to Larry Bergin's, where Larry Hart was sometimes holding forth.[3] (Bergin's was adjacent to Ralph's; Hart patronized both establishments.) "He loved the actors," Kelly said of Hart, "and he loved to hang around with them, and I got to know him, not closely, but in a fun kind of way. He'd come in, and we'd be around the bar, and he'd tell stories, usually chomping on a cigar."[4] During this period Kelly began to choreograph other people's shows, including *Green Grow the Lilacs*. By then Kelly had auditioned for Rodgers and John O'Hara, for *Your Pal Joey*—Kelly didn't remember Larry Hart or George Abbott in attendance—by singing "I Didn't Know What Time It Was," a choice that Rodgers might have regarded as obsequious except that he liked hearing his songs performed if they were performed well. Primed by Larry to appreciate Kelly's gifts, Rodgers and O'Hara—probably after consulting by telegram with Abbott—agreed that Kelly was the guy to play Joey.[5] Vivienne Segal and Leila Ernst were signed next. Now it was just a matter of O'Hara sitting at his typewriter to adapt his "Pal Joey" stories into a book musical and Dick and Larry sitting down to write the songs.

Would that it were so easy. O'Hara was still putting his *New Yorker* short stories first. He was also trying to mastermind the autumn publication of *Pal Joey*, a collection of the Joey stories. Dick and Larry were waiting for O'Hara to give them something and for Abbott to return from Los Angeles. In the gossip columns Abbott was quoted as thinking of putting Desi Arnaz, Lucille Ball, and Ann Miller—three members of the *Too Many Girls* film cast—in his upcoming Broadway show.[6] Desi as Pal Joey? Abbott was toying with his collaborators. He was also telling the press he would begin rehearsals for *Your Pal Joey* in early October.

With the pressure on but no script from O'Hara, Dick and Larry knocked out about six songs, all of them keyed to the main characters they knew from the Joey stories. At the same time, *They Met in Argentina* producer Lou Brock was waiting for the songs Dick and Larry had contracted to write for that picture—more specifically for the Argentine baritone Alberto Vila. It had become increasingly difficult for the boys to rouse themselves for such an assignment. The Universal Pictures version of *The Boys from Syracuse* had been released in August, and although some of the notices were surprisingly enthusiastic—"riotous fun," said the *Los Angeles Times'* industry-boosting reviewer—it was the familiar Hollywood adaptation recipe of squeezing the music dry to make room for low comedy, the lower the better.[7] Neither Rodgers nor Hart could have liked it much.

The director was Eddie Sutherland, who had handled *Mississippi,* and one of the screenwriters was Larry's friend Leonard Spigelgass. In the movie Allan Jones plays the Antipholus twins, and Joe Penner the Dromio twins, with Irene Hervey as Adrianna (now spelled with two *n*'s) and the canyon-mouthed Martha Raye as Luce. (Raye is now remembered mostly as a screen comedienne, but she was a terrific singer.) Those always-amusing character actors Charles Butterworth (as the Duke) and Alan Mowbray and Eric Blore (as royal tailors) were also on hand. Retained from the stage show were "This Can't Be Love," "Sing for Your Supper," "He and She," and "Falling in Love with Love"; two songs, the love song "Who Are You?" and the madcap "The Greeks Have No Word for It," appeared to have been written for the movie but were probably recycled after being dropped from the show two years earlier. The lyric for "The Greeks Have No Word for It" (an inversion of the title of a Zoë Akins play about New York gold diggers) suggested that "It" was that special something you couldn't define. "The African slaves call it hi-de-ho." The verse harks back to Larry's poems written at Columbia Grammar, when he was already folding classical references into contemporary show business:

> When Orpheus started the Orpheum circuit
> Me and Romeo used to work it;
> One day we danced for the great Achilles
> And gave Achilles the willies.

Unimpressed by the entire enterprise, *The New Yorker*'s reviewer Sally Benson made it sound like a chore to sit through. "One more word of warning: Allan Jones sings a duet with himself."[8]

Nevertheless, Rodgers and Hart knew they had to get to work on *They Met in Argentina.* With Abbott not arriving in New York until just before Labor Day, and O'Hara still missing in action, they set the *Your Pal Joey* songs aside and wrote ten songs for Alberto Vila alone.[9] Vila was a special talent, but there always had to be an American leading man, and in this case it was James Ellison, who had made half a dozen westerns in the preceding years. Starring opposite Ellison was the decidedly non-Latina Maureen O'Hara, with the boys' old friend Diosa Costello paired with Buddy Ebsen as a more comical couple. Added to the mix was the already legendary Joseph

Buloff, of the Yiddish Art Theatre in New York. Principal photography on *They Met in Argentina* began in November.

In its formulaic way the story had possibilities. A Texan (Ellison) commissioned to buy a fabulous racehorse goes to Argentina and falls in love with a senorita of Irish lineage (O'Hara), unaware that her father owns the horse he covets. The film includes a long sequence showing Pan-American Day at the racetrack in Buenos Aires, and several references to *El Pato*, the polo-like game played with an inflated ball with six handles (banned for years in Argentina because the play proved so dangerous to riders).

But the possibilities went unrealized. Half of the boys' songs were tossed out. "It is all very unfunny and is even denied the saving grace of catchy music," the *Hollywood Reporter* said. "Richard Rodgers and Lorenz Hart wrote for *They Met in Argentina* their most undistinguished score."[10]

In mid-September of 1940, Dick and Larry went to work on the remaining songs for *Your Pal Joey*, the title soon shortened to *Pal Joey*. They were seen having lunch at Dinty Moore with Abbott, who was still scheduling rehearsals for late October. A reporter wanted to know if there was any truth to the rumor that, once they were through with *Your Pal Joey*, the songwriters would dissolve their partnership.

"We've been parting for twenty-two years and we still are," Dick said.

"It's ridiculous," said Larry.[11]

O'Hara, who was accustomed to having editors but not collaborators waiting for his copy, remained silent for weeks at a time. Dick wired O'Hara: SPEAK TO ME JOHN SPEAK TO ME. Larry's line "If they asked me, I could write a book" was his way of nudging the novelist to get busy.[12] O'Hara's stories were usually pared to the bone, but how to choose from all that Joey material?

Joey's voice in his letters combines Ring Lardner's peculiar Broadway desedems-and-dose flavor with *Variety*-speak. Sometimes Joey refers to himself in the third person. "It's hard to believe that under two months ago Joey was strictly from hunger as they say but I was," Joey writes to his pal Ted, a jazz violinist, in the opening story, "Pal Joey." Auditioning for a club date, he tosses off Gershwin, Kern, and Hoagy Carmichael—but not Rodgers and Hart. In the fourth story in the series, "Bow Wow," Joey tells Ted about Betty Hardiman, a "mouse"—every woman he might date is a "mouse"—whom he picks up by pretending to love a dog they both see in a store window.[13]

After several drafts, O'Hara used all of "Bow Wow" and most of a later story called "A Bit of a Shock." O'Hara strayed from the stories to construct the frame of Joey's involvement with the wealthy Vera Simpson, whose name echoes not only that of the most notorious American divorcée of the era, Wallis Simpson, but that of Vivienne Segal, another V.S., whose knowing sauciness O'Hara appreciated as much as Hart did. Vera's blackmail by the thuggish Ludlow Lowell was also added. An early working draft had Joey redeemed by the love of Linda English, an innocent among the gallery of tough dames, but that was thrown out in favor of an ending showing the unregenerate Joey pursuing a new mouse.[14] What O'Hara retained from the short stories was the seedy nightclub ambience and Joey's character as an All-American *heel* (the word evolved as a polite form of *shit-heel*).[15] This was a guy Larry Hart knew; this was a character he could write lyrics for.

Still, as Gerald Mast has pointed out, there was a technical challenge that Rodgers and Hart—and, by extension, O'Hara—hadn't encountered since *Chee-Chee:* how do you get such unsavory characters to *sing?*[16]

Even in the weeks in which they failed to communicate, O'Hara shared another problem with Rodgers: neither one was getting along with George Abbott. Rodgers began to think of Abbott as a cheap producer. Abbott told Jo Mielziner to spend as little money on the sets as possible because he didn't have much faith in the show. And he told Robert Alton that if he really needed two more girls in the chorus, he should get Rodgers to pay their salaries. O'Hara was indulging one of his funks by drinking mightily and, determined not to be a nuisance, keeping his distance from the theater—which in Abbott's mind amounted to unprofessional behavior. Larry took it upon himself to make an unannounced visit to O'Hara's place one morning to rouse him out of bed and implore him to come to the theater. "Get up, baby," Larry said. "Come on, you're hurting George's feelings."[17] O'Hara told the story on himself years later, and he must have been in truly lousy shape to have Larry Hart, who was usually the one sleeping it off, come shake him awake.

Rodgers confronted Abbott and suggested that he turn over the reins to someone else. You're joking, said Abbott. Rodgers wasn't joking. "Abbott may not have been wild about doing *Pal Joey*," Rodgers wrote, "but, by God, he wasn't about to let anyone else get his hands on it."[18] Soon everything was back on track. "John O'Hara has been sending George Abbott scenes of *Pal Joey* filled with private jokes," the *Times* reported in mid-October, "the idea apparently being to keep Mr. A in a good humor at all costs. According to Lorenz Hart, *Pal Joey* can best be described as 'comedy with songs.' It will be intimate, no big production numbers."[19] "No big production numbers" was probably part of a compromise Rodgers worked out with Abbott, but the lower budget also enabled Hart to inject the nightclub numbers with a seediness he found not only amusing but authentic. The budgetary limit would also distinguish the show from the season's more extravagant competitors, including *Panama Hattie* and *Lady in the Dark*.

These theatrical matters were by no means first in the minds of most Americans, who were focused on the dire events transpiring in Europe. During the spring of 1940, Winston Churchill had succeeded Neville Chamberlain as British prime minister, and it was Churchill's stirring words during the escalating war with Germany—the famous "We shall fight" speech in early June, when he promised that the British "shall never surrender," and the House of Commons speech of August 20, when he praised the RAF's turning back of the Luftwaffe—that moved American readers and radio listeners. On August 23 the London blitz had begun; three weeks later Hitler launched an all-out air attack on England. On September 27 the Axis—Germany, Italy, and Japan—was created, bonding the three nations in a ten-year alliance. The Nazis had already taken France and moved its capital to Vichy; now they wanted England.

Noël Coward reproved his fellow British actors for remaining in America while England needed them most. Reacting to Europe's rapidly changing map, Jerome Kern and Oscar Hammerstein II wrote the wistful "The Last Time I Saw Paris," which, unlike their other songs, was unconnected to any show. But Dick and Larry were too preoccupied to address events in Europe. On October 29, 1940, as America continued to watch from the sidelines, the nation instituted its first peacetime military draft. On the same day, the Rodgers-Hart-O'Hara show, its title officially shortened to *Pal Joey*, held its first chorus call at the Biltmore Theatre.

The Biltmore was one of two theaters used by the *Pal Joey* cast and crew when rehearsals began on November 11. Robert Alton and the dancers worked at the Biltmore; Abbott worked with the actors at the Longacre. Gene Kelly scurried back and forth between the theaters. Because Joey was conceived as promiscuous and amoral, feeling no guilt that an older woman is keeping him and building him a nightclub, Kelly knew he had to dance well to make Joey attractive.[20] Without Kelly's charm, Joey would be unpalatable. Kelly's high, sandpapery tenor worked wonders with "I Could Write a Book," which he sings less than sincerely to Linda (Leila Ernst), the mouse he picks up at the pet shop, only to have the unworldly Linda sing it back to him with genuine feeling:

> Used to hate to go to school,
> I never cracked a book;
> I played the hook.
> Never answered any mail;
> To write I used to think
> Was wasting ink.
> It was never my endeavor
> To be clever and smart.
> Now I suddenly feel
> A longing to write in my heart.

Linda could really write that book about Joey, but Joey will later express his independence and indifference in the song "Pal Joey" ("What do I care for the skirts?").

Vera Simpson (Vivienne Segal) falls hard for Joey. When she sings "Bewitched, Bothered and Bewildered," she takes us through the entire arc of their romance—the sleepless agitation that transforms into exhilaration and possessiveness, the unremitting lust, and (to quote earlier Hart) the self-deception that believes the lie—all of which is familiar to anyone who's loved hard. In the middle of their affair Vera and Joey sing "Our Little Den of Iniquity," which is so hospitable to the illicit lovers that even "The Overture of 1812" on the radio sounds dreamy. After Vera has been unsuccessfully blackmailed and the affair with Joey has run its course, she encounters Linda—the once naïve girlfriend meeting the seasoned former mistress—and together they sing "Take Him," which predates Irving Berlin's marvelous "You Can Have Him" (*Miss Liberty*) by nearly a decade. Both of them burned by Joey, Vera and Linda catalogue his deficiencies—he snores, he never picks up a check, and he's illiterate. "I know a movie executive / Who's twice as bright," sings Vera, a line Stephen Sondheim once cited as an example of Hart's sloppiness in the way his lyrics can sit awkwardly on the music. In Sondheim's view there are many examples.[21] Yet it's an odd choice because the line from "Take Him" rings with wit and truth.

In a reprise of "Bewitched, Bothered and Bewildered," a benumbed Vera celebrates the end of her feelings for Joey. In all of American song there is no more mordant summary of romantic closure.

Wise at last,
My eyes at last
Are cutting you down to your size at last . . .

And:

Couldn't eat—
Was dyspeptic,
Life was so hard to bear;
Now my heart's antiseptic
Since you moved out of there.

Of the two rehearsal theaters the Biltmore was the more exciting because it pulsated with music and dance. June Havoc was playing the nightclub dancer Gladys Bumps, and practically everyone connected with the show already knew Havoc as the sister of the highly literate ecdysiast Gypsy Rose Lee and knew of their burlesque circuit upbringing. Originally a minor role, Gladys was the character that linked her blackmailing boyfriend Ludlow Lowell (Jack Durant) to Vera.[22] Already a part of the ensemble number "You Mustn't Kick It Around," Havoc shoved her way into "That Terrific Rainbow," a blues lampoon about the red-hot-mama-with-the-heart-of-gold who burns with an orange flame. And then, calling up cheap lessons she had taken from a vocal coach, Havoc sang for Rodgers while she was on point so she would be assigned "The Flower Garden of My Heart," an imagined nightclub floor show that would have made Flo Ziegfeld blush.[23]

All the *Pal Joey* numbers were meant to delight and wound. But the one consistent showstopper was "Zip," sung by the newspaper columnist Melba Snyder (Jean Casto). In O'Hara's story collection, Joey refers to Melba as "Lesbo" and is surprised that she's "terrific in bed"; but that was too much for Broadway, even in the determinedly groundbreaking *Pal Joey*, so Melba is portrayed instead as a bespectacled, brainy type.[24] "Zip" is Melba's one long quotation from an "interview" with Gypsy Rose Lee. "What do you think of while you work?" asks Melba, and Gypsy answers:

Zip! Walter Lippmann wasn't brilliant today.
Zip! Will Saroyan ever write a great play?
Zip! I was reading Schopenhauer last night.
Zip! And I think that Schopenhauer was right.

The lyric remains as arrestingly salacious as a great striptease while exemplifying Larry Hart's lifelong penchant for dropping names that connect with the audience: Zorina is rhymed with Cobina (as in Cobina Wright, Jr., a New York debutante who demanded almost as much ink as Brenda Frazier); Salvador Dalí; Arturo Toscanini; Larry's old friend Tyrone Power, at last a movie star; and the Mickeys Mouse and Rooney are given their due, while Gypsy makes it clear that her professional rivals Margie Hart, Sally Rand, and Lili St. Cyr simply aren't in her league.

"The song's appeal became plainly evident at the very first out-of-town preview," wrote Stanley Donen's biographer Stephen Silverman. Donen, who would work so rewardingly with Gene Kelly for the next dozen years, and Van Johnson were both in the cast that night, December 16, 1940, at Philadelphia's Forrest Theatre. "'The next day,' said Donen, 'Larry Hart came into the theater and everybody wanted more choruses to "Zip!" only there weren't any, so Hart said, "Okay." He sat down in the back of the house and wrote two more choruses on a piece of paper.'"[25]

The young photographer Mary Morris, who had chronicled the rehearsal process in New York for the newspaper *PM*, joined the company in Philadelphia and kept shooting. One of her more famous photographs is of Larry revising "Bewitched, Bothered and Bewildered" on the mirror in Gene Kelly's dressing room. Whenever he spotted Morris, Larry would rub his hands together and implore her to come to the bar with him.[26]

Larry was also drinking nightly with O'Hara and Budd Schulberg, who was correcting proofs of his first novel, *What Makes Sammy Run?* Sharing a suite at the Warwick Hotel in Philly, the novelists sometimes had to go in search of the lyricist, who had drunkenly wandered off. "Once they found Hart in an after-hours joint and took him back to the Warwick," O'Hara biographer Matthew Bruccoli wrote, "but Hart refused to leave the cab and went into a fetal position. O'Hara and Schulberg picked up the diminutive lyricist by the arms and carried him into the hotel."[27]

Six days of Philadelphia tryouts were instructive to the authors and to Abbott. Audiences were excited through every performance except the Wednesday matinee, when disapproving ladies predominated. "They would not accept Vivienne Segal and myself," Kelly said.[28] *PM* previewed the out-of-town tryout as "the dirtiest show you ever hope to see," and ran Mary Morris's picture story on *Pal Joey* on the night of the last Philadelphia performance.[29] The same night brought word that F. Scott Fitzgerald, a Rodgers & Hart booster throughout the team's career, had died of a heart attack in Los Angeles.

❧   ❧   ❧

Pal Joey opened at the Ethel Barrymore Theatre on Christmas Day 1940. On his way to the theater, John O'Hara, suffering through his first bout of opening night butterflies, vomited out his cab's window. Larry paced. The Rodgerses were in their usual last-row orchestra seats to take it all in. "Approximately one half of the first night audience applauded wildly while the other half sat there in stony, stunned silence," Rodgers recalled.[30]

But everyone seemed to know that the American musical was being turned inside out, led by a unique actor-dancer playing a protagonist who was disreputable not because he was mean—O'Hara might have worked on that role, but Larry Hart could not have—but because he was selfish. The book and lyrics were, in Clifton Fadiman's words, "brass dissolved in vitriol [and] really ticked off the end of the gag-and-girlie show." Fadiman compared that Christmas 1940 opening night to May 29, 1913, when Stravinsky's *Le Sacre du Printemps* outraged the audience at the Théâtre du Châtelet in Paris with its modern dissonances and fiery rhythms. "If, as someone has said, vulgarity conceals something whereas coarseness reveals something, then these lyrics [are] coarse but not vulgar, being supreme examples of what can only be termed single *entendre*."[31]

Ready to celebrate, many in the cast and crew gathered at Larry's apartment in the Ardsley. Mary Campbell had prepared the usual abundance of food, augmented by a groaning board of whitefish and lox from Barney Greengrass. The telephone was ringing. The bar was open. Somebody was playing the piano. Shortly after midnight Larry was called to the phone; he listened for a few minutes, his eyes filling, then hung up, went into his bedroom, and closed the door. Someone had called from the *Times* to read him Brooks Atkinson's review of *Pal Joey*. "And we couldn't get him out of his room all night," Gene Kelly remembered. "He was that hypersensitive a man. And with all that success he was that easily affected by that kind of diatribe."[32]

It might be stretching to call Atkinson's review, one of the most notorious in the annals of theater history, a diatribe. But it was a lance that went right through Larry's heart. As Frederick Nolan put it so beautifully, "Brooks Atkinson's reaction mattered most because Larry believed him to be the critic who best understood what he and Rodgers were trying to do."[33] Atkinson wrote:

> If it is possible to make an entertaining musical comedy out of an odious story, *Pal Joey* is it. The situation is put tentatively here because the ugly topic that

is up for discussion stands between this theatergoer and real enjoyment of a well-staged show. Taking as his hero the frowsy night club punk familiar to readers of a series of sketches in *The New Yorker*, John O'Hara has written a joyless book about a sulky assignation.

Atkinson went on to praise much about the show, including Dick and Larry's songs. But his closing line wounded in a way that couldn't be cauterized: "Although *Pal Joey* is expertly done, can you draw sweet water from a foul well?" [34]

Given *Pal Joey*'s subsequent reputation as a groundbreaking musical—not to mention its undeniable box office success, running for 374 performances—it's been tempting for the past seventy years to dismiss Atkinson's review as the viewpoint of a buttoned-up schoolmaster decrying this very modern show's "scabrous lyrics," its "depravity," and the "dreariness of night club frolics." Dirty, perhaps, but *foul?* The adjective wasn't applicable to either Rodgers *or* Hart. Otherwise, was Atkinson's reaction all wrong? While declining to take the assignment of adapting *Pal Joey* for Columbia Pictures, Moss Hart confessed that he found the musical's book "off-hand and ambling"—a succinct analysis of the failure of its second act. [35] It's been said that movies demand that a character's bad behavior be punished for moral reasons, but experienced moviemakers know it's more crucial that it be punished for *dramatic* reasons—to provide the audience with a catharsis and resolution that would be otherwise missing. "If you want to enlist sympathy for your characters," Arnold Bennett wrote, "be as hard as nails on them." Maybe O'Hara, Rodgers, and Hart weren't hard enough on Joey. Or maybe sympathy for Joey was not what they had in mind.

A dozen years later, when Jule Styne mounted a successful revival of *Pal Joey*, with Segal in the same role and Harold Lang as Joey, John Lardner wrote that the original *Pal Joey* had paved the way for *Guys and Dolls* (1950), which in turn made the *Pal Joey* revival more acceptable to a wider audience. [36] On its face this was probably true, except that *Guys and Dolls*' Broadway types were funny and warm, even if they gambled and had a hard time committing to their dames; *Pal Joey*'s seedy characters were lusty but not necessarily warm, and only sour humor was squeezed from their illiteracy.

On the morning of December 26, with the *Times* actually in his hands, Larry's reaction to the Atkinson review got a bit more complicated: alongside *Pal Joey*, Atkinson had given a kind notice to the Hollywood-born revue *Meet the People*. "While the ermine and mink were pushing their way into *Pal Joey*,"

Atkinson wrote, "Union Label was across the street at the Mansfield, and having a marvelous time, thank you." Atkinson recommended the ermine cross the tracks and meet the people. The revue's satirical targets—the movie industry, psychiatry, Congress—could easily have been Larry's targets, and its creators were his friends—Henry Myers in particular. Larry wanted *Meet the People* to succeed, just not at the expense of his own show.

Sixty-five years before *Pal Joey* opened, W. S. Gilbert had completed his play *Broken Hearts*—up to that time the work closest to him. Soon after *Broken Hearts* opened on December 9 at the Royal Court Theatre, the playwright F. C. Burnand referred to it as *Broken Parts*, which subsequently morphed into *Broken Tarts*. Gruff and tough-skinned though Gilbert usually was, the puns stung him to the quick, and for years he remained bitter toward Burnand and all those other critics who had laughed at him.[37]

Gilbert eventually got over Burnand's crack. Hart, nowhere near as well-defended as Gilbert, eventually got over Atkinson's negative notice. *Pal Joey* kept pulling in audiences who wanted to see what the fuss was about. Recordings of "Bewitched, Bothered and Bewildered" were necessarily bowdlerized because no radio station would have allowed a line like "Until I could sleep where I shouldn't sleep" to be sung on the air. And yet it was practically moot because ASCAP had been in conflict with the National Association of Broadcasters since the spring, and popular music on the air had been reduced to a whisper while the two factions duked it out.[38] In response to ASCAP's perceived monopoly on popular music licensing, the broadcasters had begun BMI (Broadcast Music, Inc.), which tried to sign up new authors and composers and claimed public domain material as its own. (Suddenly there was a lot of Stephen Foster being played on the air.) Broadway was ASCAP turf—Cole Porter, Irving Berlin, and Rodgers and Hart were all ASCAP stalwarts—and there was a theory that, after January 1, 1941, when the networks planned to cease playing all ASCAP compositions, Broadway would get a lift from radio listeners starved for the music of their favorite composers. When Bob Rice of *PM* asked Larry Hart if this theory was sound, Larry waved it away. "Nobody cares anymore whether a song is good or not," he said. "People just listen to bands."[39]

Despite their songs' limited airplay in the winter of 1941, the *Pal Joey* team was encouraged enough to attempt another project. By mid-February it was reported that John O'Hara was working on the dialogue for a new musical, probably set in Florida, to be scored by Rodgers and Hart and produced by

George Abbott.[40] Nothing came of it, however, and O'Hara's relationship with Rodgers devolved from collegiality to hostility. One curious project that surfaced some years later, intended for Rodgers and Hammerstein, was an O'Hara idea for a musical about Toulouse-Lautrec. Did O'Hara have Larry Hart in mind? He certainly had Larry in mind when he intended to title his 1951 novel *A Small Hotel*, in homage to his former collaborators; but when Rodgers reminded him that the song was actually called "There's a Small Hotel," O'Hara perceived the correction as ingratitude and changed the title to *The Farmers Hotel*.

Pal Joey was received with excitement but not much ardor. *Cabin in the Sky*, which had opened two months earlier, was received with ardor but not much excitement. Doc Bender had raised money for *Cabin in the Sky* before dropping out as a producer; two of his clients, Vernon Duke and John Latouche, had written the score, which included "Taking a Chance on Love." In fact, it was Bender, using Rodgers and Hart as his models, who had put Latouche and Duke together in the first place, forcing the dissolute Latouche to work with the more disciplined Duke. In the early weeks of 1941, Bender, Duke, Latouche, and Larry Hart often gathered at the Essex House to play music and read lyrics.[41]

Around the same time, the Rodgerses bought a house in Fairfield, Connecticut. They wouldn't move in for another few months. In the interim the mother of Zoe d'Erlanger, an English refugee child they had taken in the previous summer, was killed in a German air raid. The Connecticut house could easily accommodate the adults, the three girls in the household (their own two and Zoe), and servants, with plenty of acreage for sports activity and gardens. It had a massive oak tree in the front yard.[42] The grand house signaled a shift in Rodgers's identity as a man of the theater. Composing would always come first, but now, after observing Dwight Wiman and other producers in action, he wanted to have control as a producer as well. Rodgers would soon turn thirty-nine and increasingly felt he could no longer depend for the rest of his life on Larry, who had come to the point where he found work as tedious as sobriety. Through the winter of 1941 Hart was often impossible to locate. Sometimes he was playing cards or drinking at the Lambs, where he had taken the young Alan Jay Lerner under his wing, or in one of the bars on Forty-Fifth Street. If not there, he might have been holed up someplace with a new companion, whether arranged by Doc Bender or picked up on his own.

Of course he might have been at one of a dozen bathhouses. In his poem "Lorenz," Brad Leithauser put it this way:

> Now and then he would drop from sight,
> days at a stretch. No doubt he found his way
> to drink—some suitcase full of spirits—
> and, likely, to some paid romance;
> he knew the poignancy of *that*
> from both sides of the street—the dwarfish man
> who wrote "Ten Cents a Dance." [43]

After another troubling week when Dick could not reach Larry by telephone, the partners of twenty-three years finally met for lunch at Tony's, on Fifty-Second Street. Larry's face was bruised, his jaw so swollen that he could swallow only scrambled eggs and coffee. Dick asked him what happened. Larry went into a story about a stranger who showed up at his apartment with a letter of introduction, drank too much, and then wouldn't leave unless Larry came out with him. On the sidewalk on Central Park West, the stranger suddenly knocked Larry to the ground, bloodying him, and the ensuing fight was eventually broken up by an acquaintance of Larry's, who ushered him back up to his apartment and, taking pains to avoid Frieda so she wouldn't worry, put him to bed.

Dick, winded just from listening, said, "I hope somebody called the police and they put this character in jail!"

"As a matter of fact I feel sorry for him," Larry said. "I broke his wrist, knocked out his front teeth, and kicked him where it hurt the most, and he won't be out of the hospital for a week."

Telling the story on radio more than sixteen years later, Rodgers explained the punch line by reminding his on-air host that Larry's elevator shoes were "deadly weapons"; it made sense to him that Larry, the gentlest of men, would put the other guy in the hospital. The anecdote, Frederick Nolan has pointed out, illustrates Rodgers's "almost willful blindness to its real content." [44]

With episodes like that one mounting, "I had to think about the unthinkable," Rodgers wrote in his autobiography. "I had to think about a life without Larry Hart." [45]

One day Rodgers went to lunch with Lawrence Spivak, his cousin by marriage. Spivak would subsequently be better known as the creator and host of

Meet the Press, but at the time he was publishing or editing several magazines, including *The American Mercury*. Rodgers unloaded some of his Hart-aches to Spivak.

"Do you think Larry misbehaves this way," Spivak speculated, "because he's such a short man and it bothers him? Getting in the way of his work, his life . . ."

Rodgers couldn't help laughing. Spivak was as short as Hart but seemed to be managing a perfectly happy, productive life.[46]

In March 1941 Preston Sturges's *The Lady Eve* was booked at the Paramount for a three-week engagement. Although Larry had been to Sturges's Players restaurant in Hollywood, and the lyricist and the director certainly admired each other, they were not close. But Larry must have been curious, and ducked in one afternoon to see the film—one of the most sparkling of all American comedies. When beer heir Charles (Henry Fonda) first escorts con artist Jean (Barbara Stanwyck) to her stateroom aboard an oceanliner, the underscoring leaks out strains of the verse to "Isn't It Romantic?," a Paramount-owned song, followed by its better-known chorus. Dick and Larry had added the verse for the song's publication after *Love Me Tonight* had been filmed. There were no lyrics sung on the *Lady Eve* sound track, but then most moviegoers in 1941 knew at least the lyrics of the chorus. Later, Charles and Jean fall in love, much to the astonishment of each of them, and stand together after a ride through Connecticut pastures. Listening to the dialogue, Larry sat up in recognition of the theme of "Where or When," if not of the words themselves:

CHARLES

(to JEAN)

Every time I've looked at you here on the boat
it wasn't only here I saw you: you seemed to go
way back . . . I know that isn't clear but I saw
you here and at the same time further away, and
then still further away, and then very small . . .
way back there a little boy is standing with you,
holding your hand, and in the middle distance
I'm still with you, not holding your hand any
more because it isn't manly, but wanting to . . .

what I'm trying to say, only I'm not a poet, I'm
an ophiologist, is that I've always loved you . . .
I mean I've never loved anyone but you . . . I
suppose that sounds as dull as a drug store
novel, and what I see inside I'll never be able to
cast into words . . . but that's what I mean.[47]

CHAPTER 22

Wait Till You Feel
the Warmth of Her Glance

*I*NCREASINGLY, THE clothes Larry Hart was wearing were the clothes he wore—he was often so drunk and disheveled now that his friends shied away from him. Dick Rodgers implored him to seek professional treatment. Larry resisted. Further encouraged to do so by Dorothy Hart, Larry finally checked himself into Doctors Hospital—more to get everyone off his back than because he agreed he needed to dry out. Even as Rodgers was mentally unhitching himself from a future with his professional partner, he was looking out for him. On the q.t. he went to see Dr. Richard Hoffman, a psychiatrist who specialized in treating alcoholism. Among Hoffman's more celebrated patients had been F. Scott Fitzgerald. Fitzgerald's lover Sheilah Graham described Hoffman as "a soft-spoken man with piercing dark eyes and great charm."[1] Hoffman listened to Rodgers's concern about his partner, and to his warning that Larry would never willingly submit to psychoanalysis. Accustomed to such resistance, Hoffman assured Rodgers he'd "simply pass himself off as a hospital staff member and drop in" to see Larry now and then.

Larry was having none of it. Although he had always been fascinated by Freud and the interpretation of dreams, he laughed at the glaze he saw in the eyes of psychoanalysis's most ardent proponents. When he was twenty-one he had attended, along with several Columbia Journalism classmates, the one-act comedy *Suppressed Desires*, by Susan Glaspell and George Cram Cook. *Suppressed Desires*, one of the plays produced during the Great War

that established modern theater in America, was about a married couple living on Washington Square and temporarily hosting the wife's sister, whose
mania for psychobabble wears them down. Glaspell and Cook wrote the play
the previous winter in their apartment in Milligan Place, off Sixth Avenue.
"You could not go out to buy a bun without hearing of someone's complex,"
Glaspell complained at the time.[2]

Larry had been jesting about the whole business ever since. No, he was not
going to be psychoanalyzed—not even surreptitiously. Hoffman checked in
on him but apparently dropped the charade as a hospital staff member. "Why
do you like oversized chairs?" was one question Hoffman asked Larry. "Why
do you like oversized rooms?" "Do you have a Napoleon complex?"[3] If Hoffman believed the lyricist would put himself under his psychiatric care after
questions like those, he was a fool.

Work usually helped Larry find his bearings, but the project that came
up now would prove far less tonic than any he'd previously undertaken. In
mid-April 1941 Alex Yokel purchased the dramatic rights to Richard Shattuck's comedy-mystery novel *The Snark Was a Boojum*. The novel's teaser
goes like this:

> Sandy was beginning to realize that she should have listened to mother. "Don't
> look up your father's people," she had warned, "they'll get you into trouble."
>
> Aunt Maud wasn't turning out to be *odd*, exactly, but there was a matter of
> carrying Uncle Wilson around in a brief case . . .

A little of this goes a long way, and *The Snark Was a Boojum* has a lot of
it. The plot has to do with some barmy New Englanders—Sandy's father's
people—and the family legacy that will go to the first baby who emerges
from one of three women, one of whom is in the family way without a family.
The title was drawn from Lewis Carroll's "The Hunting of the Snark," but the
farcical tone of the novel probably reminded Yokel of *Arsenic and Old Lace*,
which was proving to be one of the more durable comedies of mid-century
Broadway. It also reminded Yokel of his only true hit, *Three Men on a Horse*,
in which he had cast—or claimed credit for casting—Teddy Hart. Larry had
made it clear he was indebted to Yokel for that.

Yokel came to collect.

So Larry, professing enthusiasm for the novel, went to work on an adaptation. As always, though, he went looking for ways to distract himself. There

were the usual haunts: Lindy's, Reuben's, Tony's, Larry Bergin's, Sardi's, and Ralph's. He was as hungry for company as he was thirsty for booze.

"Sometimes you would be sitting [at Ralph's] late at night and this little person would walk by," said the actress Betty Garrett:

> He'd stand there with his chin practically on your table just to listen to your conversation. That was Larry Hart. He was not much taller than the table and would look from one person to the other and smile while you talked.

One night Garrett was having a bite with the comic Jack E. Leonard. Larry came up to listen and rested his chin on the table.

"Who ordered John the Baptist?" said Jack E.[4]

While Larry was caught in the familiar cycle of work and drink, then more drink and less work, Rodgers was scouring the town for a new project he could write with him. John O'Hara was presumably writing the new Florida musical, but nobody was waiting for him. Rodgers, still determined to get some producing experience, accepted George Abbott's invitation to coproduce the new musical *Young Man's Fancy*, set at a prep school and written by John Cecil Holm, who, whatever Abbott claimed, was the original author of *Three Men on a Horse*. There were no songs yet; there were no songwriters. This was fine with Rodgers because: (a) he had worked with Abbott several times before and, despite their tussle on *Pal Joey*, he respected him; and (b) *Young Man's Fancy* would be cast largely with performers eighteen or under, which meant that Rodgers was back in *Babes in Arms* land and wouldn't have to contend with so many grown-up demands and commands. He was further pleased when, in the first week of May, Abbott signed Hugh Martin and Ralph Blane to write the music and lyrics. Rodgers had liked playing mentor to Martin, and now it was the younger man's turn to get his name on the marquee. The one proviso Rodgers made to Abbott was that he be permitted to produce with no press releases referring to him and no program listing. Rodgers was hardly indifferent to credit, but having his name on the show, which would eventually be retitled *Best Foot Forward*, would fuel rumors of the breakup, at long last, of Rodgers and Hart. Abbott agreed; Rodgers would apprentice as a producer.[5]

In mid-May 1941 the Dramatic Workshop of the New School presented a revival of the 1932 comedy *The Warrior's Husband* at the Friendship House on Park Avenue. William Liebling, a casting and play agent, attended the first of two performances to get a look at an actress he was considering signing.

Impressed by the musical possibilities of the play, he contacted Dwight Wiman, who either attended the second performance or read the play and began to think it might be right for Rodgers and Hart.[6]

What could all this activity mean for songwriters who were sick of each other? In the first week of July, *Arsenic and Old Lace* reached its two hundredth performance.[7] How was Larry faring, Yokel wondered, with *Snark*? Expecting a comic riot from the incomparable Lorenz Hart, Yokel still had every intention of staging *Snark* in the 1941–42 season.

Rodgers, also contemplating the new season, put out word that he and Larry were thinking of reviving *A Connecticut Yankee*, with William Gaxton (the original Broadway lead) and Gaxton's old friend Victor Moore (presumably as Merlin).[8] Gaxton and Moore would lend the revival a more knockabout vaudeville tone than the 1927 show had.

That idea was shoved into a corner to make room for *Saratoga Trunk*, the new Edna Ferber novel, which Ferber was keen to see adapted for the musical stage as soon as possible. *Cosmopolitan* was serializing the novel; Warner Bros. paid a record-shattering $175,000 for it eight months prior to publication by Doubleday, Doran. Ferber, who was also a client of Willy Kron's, put out feelers. One was to Dick Rodgers, who was interested but wasn't certain Larry could handle the libretto and suggested they talk to Oscar Hammerstein. Ferber was hardly averse to this—Hammerstein and Jerome Kern had turned her *Show Boat* into what many theatergoers regarded as the most important musical play ever staged—so on June 29 they both wired Hammerstein. The Rodgers telegram said, LARRY AND I SIT WITH EVERYTHING CROSSED HOPING THAT YOU WILL DO SARATOGA TRUNK WITH US.

The project was soon dropped, but it had the effect of putting Rodgers, whose best work with Larry Hart tended to be topical (even when it was about medieval England or ancient Greece), jazzy, and witty, in direct communication after all these years with Hammerstein, who was drawn to grander, more serious themes. Acknowledging that they wouldn't be adapting *Saratoga Trunk*, Rodgers wrote to Hammerstein: "Even if nothing further comes of this difficult matter it will at least have allowed us to approach each other professionally. Specifically, you feel that I should have a book of 'substance' to write to. Will you think seriously about doing such a book?"[9] As Frederick Nolan has written, the letter "was a direct overture toward partnership. Since Rodgers was well aware that Oscar Hammerstein had rarely written a book for which he did not also provide the lyrics, any such partnership would of necessity exclude Larry Hart."[10]

The *Best Foot Forward* score by Martin and Blane was coming along nicely. After a mid-September week of tryouts in New Haven, Rodgers went with the show to Philadelphia. Gene Kelly, who had finally pulled out of *Pal Joey* after eight months in the title role, was there to oversee his choreography for *Best Foot Forward*, and to get married. The bride was Betsy Blair, who had recently appeared in Saroyan's *The Beautiful People*. Kelly would soon head west to fulfill a Hollywood contract, his first, with David O. Selznick.[11] Rodgers wished Kelly and Blair well, but it was Larry Hart who was on his mind. Hammerstein's farm was only an hour from downtown Philadelphia, and Rodgers went out to see him. Hammerstein—regal in his bearing where Larry was usually unkempt; dependable where Larry was undependable—assured Rodgers that he would be there for him if and when Larry was no longer able to work; until then, Hammerstein said, Rodgers should try to keep the partnership going. Hammerstein knew Hart well, of course, and loved him; his counsel was as much with Hart's welfare in mind as Rodgers's career.[12]

Gene Kelly's replacement in *Pal Joey* was Georgie Tapps, who had had a couple of roles in *I'd Rather Be Right*. Hart hated the way Tapps interpreted the part, but that was only one of the things oppressing Larry that September. He certainly did not want to do *Hotel Splendide*, which Rodgers planned to co-produce with Dwight Wiman. The project was based on Ludwig Bemelmans's stories in *The New Yorker* about a busboy who becomes a waiter; Donald Ogden Stewart, riding high after winning an Oscar for adapting *The Philadelphia Story*, had written the book and changed the protagonist into a bellhop.[13] Larry thought it was precious.

"Why so downcast, my soul," asks the forty-second Psalm, "why do you sigh within me?" Like a man who senses, but can't prove, that his spouse is being unfaithful, Larry was becoming what Frieda Hart would have called *farbissen*—bitter, dour, suspicious—the kind of guy he had never had much use for. In the first week of September he sat down and, intending to place it in one of the New York dailies, typed out an essay of what turned out to be pitiable vitriol:

> There isn't a good lyric-writer alive. There are smart lyric-writers, sweet boys and commercial boys, but there isn't a decent one trying to find another rhyme with love today. The dodo has nothing on the man with the singing words.
>
> There should be a reason and there is. The modern lyric-writer knows too much about his craft. If Richard Burbage had asked Shakespeare for a

polysyllabic rhyme, the Swan would have thrown Yorick's skull at the Eliza-
bethan ham. Bobbie Burns never heard of repeating a title three times and
wouldn't have done it for any publisher. Heinrich Heine never gave a *verdammt*
whether or not his words sounded hot over a microphone and I don't think
Homer knew much about punch lines.

The old singers sang free and easy and sang pretty thoughts with pretty
sounds. The new singers are Tin Pan Alley scientists. Science doesn't come
from the heart.

When George Abbott signed Mr. Rodgers and me to write the lyrics for
his *Pal Joey* (at the Shubert Theatre, matinees Saturday and Sunday at a newly
reduced three dollar top), I was told that I had to get laughs right at the end of
some of our songs, so that the electrician could blackout on the scenes without
embarrassment. Imagine Virgil worrying about a spot-light.

Pal Joey, moreover, is a cad and a scoundrel and something else unprintable
right here, and he has to sing out words that Henry Wadsworth Longfellow
never would have used. In fact, Joey is so unsanctimonious that even the publisher would not print his songs, let alone the independent radio stations who
are scabbing on the B.M.I. I was forced to write "Nice Nelly" versions for the
radio. How can the modern lyric-writer approach the divinity of the Psalms?
He hasn't a chance.

The nice-nelly versions of "Bewitched, Bothered and Bewildered" replaced
"Until I could sleep where I shouldn't sleep" with "Then love came and told
me I shouldn't sleep," or with "And what would I do if I shouldn't sleep?" It
was no less grating to Larry than having Georgie Tapps replace Gene Kelly as
Joey. Larry went on:

In the old days, Byron, Scott and even Kipling were public idols. Today, people
imagine that the actors make up the lyrics as they go along. I'm sure nobody
has ever even heard of me—and while a little anonymity is a good thing, it is
hard to be the forgotten man before one has even been remembered.

Sir William Shwenk [*sic*] Gilbert (author of "Box and Cox" [*sic*: actually
Cox and Box]) never had to write words for music. Sir Arthur Sullivan (composer of "Seated One Day at the Organ") had to fit music to Gilbert's words.
Today, even the composer who writes the music for the second movement of
Tchaikowski's Fifth or the music for the swing version of "Swanee River," even
such a slightly unoriginal music, makes all his music first. Then and then only
can the lyric-writer plot his weary way.

No wonder the schedule of radio recordings in the daily newspaper lists "My Heart Stood Still" as by Richard Rodgers and "Trees" by Oley Speaks. Yet let me try to go to my publisher with

Under the Greenwood tree
Who loves to lie with me!

my publisher would inform me that the radio censors will not permit such things to be heard.

As for the movies, they will never accept a lyric unless it is either like "The Broadway Melody," "Singing in the Rain," or "Jeannie with the Light Brown Hair." And there are even higher hurdles for the poor jumping lyricist (a high class Hollywood word). He must be proficient in jive-talk and be able to write lines such as "I Want Some Seafood, Mama" and "A Rillora Is a Stream" and other deathless jabberwockys that Lewis Carroll could never have invented.

Perhaps that is why there are no fine lyric-writers anymore. And perhaps you care less about it than I do.[14]

Apparently, there were no takers for the essay. Still, apart from Larry's embittered tone, there are a few things worth reviewing here. The couplet he quotes, you will recall, is from *As You Like It*. Oley Speaks was, at the time of the essay's composition, a director of ASCAP and a popular song-writer whose most durable song is probably "On the Road to Mandalay" (to Kipling's verse), its survival ensured by Frank Sinatra. And the mention of Heine might have been Larry's only written reference to his ancestor, who not only was among the greatest literary figures of nineteenth-century Europe but moved about, it was said, hobbled by either a humped back or a clubfoot. "The life of literature was from the springs of the best common speech," William Dean Howells wrote of Heine's literary credo, "and the nearer it could be made to conform, in voice, look, and gait, to graceful, easy, picturesque and humorous or impassioned talk, the better it was."[15] Howells might as well have been describing the work of Larry Hart.

Did Larry believe he was already on his own? In October 1941 Simon & Schuster published *A Treasury of Gilbert & Sullivan*, which collected most of the songs from the operettas, with arrangements by Dr. Albert Sirmay. In the book's introduction Deems Taylor recounts how neither Sullivan nor Gilbert was especially successful on his own. "The 'and' in Gilbert and Sullivan is important; for it is what made the whole greater than the sum of the parts.

Gilbert as a playwright, without Sullivan, was a prolific writer of farces, a few of which are still faintly amusing, and of pompous Victorian dramas, none of which was particularly successful even in its day, and all of which are, by contemporary standards, terrible."[16] And what would Hart be without Rodgers?

Why was he even bothering with *The Snark Was a Boojum?* Although Alex Yokel had put out word that Lee Patrick, the rosy-cheeked blonde who had recently appeared as Sam Spade's can-do secretary in *The Maltese Falcon*, would star, Larry was unable or unwilling to revise what he'd completed of the adaptation. Yokel also announced that he had sent the novel—but not, tellingly, a partial script—to actress-author Patricia Collinge.[17] It was as if he was already casting about for a new writer.

One day Yokel arrived at the Ardsley determined to remove Larry to a place where he could finish the adaptation without distraction. Larry—exhausted, drunk, or both—resisted, even as the belligerent Yokel tried physically to pull him out of the apartment. Fortunately, Teddy, back in Manhattan after an upstate tour, happened to be there and intervened.[18] Larry was so indisposed that he probably wouldn't have made it to the elevator.

The specter of war finally summoned the boys. The Fight for Freedom organization, formed in April 1941, had been challenging the stance of American isolationists—Charles A. Lindbergh most prominent among them—and promoting the nation's entry into the war in Europe. Fight for Freedom persuaded the Office of Emergency Management to sponsor a new radio program, *Keep 'Em Rolling*, broadcast from the Mutual network's rooftop studio at the New Amsterdam Theatre, beginning at ten thirty Sunday night, November 9, 1941.[19] Dick and Larry turned out the theme song, "The Flame of Freedom Is Burning" (later, with a verse added, retitled "Keep 'Em Rolling"). A patriotic call to industry, if not yet to arms, it has a touch of the familiar Hart wordplay:

> *In town and country,*
> *Lowland and mountain ridge,*
> *Let's build bridges*
> *Instead of playing bridge.*

On that first program, broadcast in New York on Mutual's flagship station WOR, Ethel Merman belted out the theme song. In the months to come, other big, ear-popping contraltos—Wynn Murray among them—would handle that chore. Clifton Fadiman was master of ceremonies. Maurice Evans led a reading of Maxwell Anderson's *Valley Forge*, punctuated by a medley of American tunes conducted by Morton Gould.

Ten days after *Keep 'Em Rolling* premiered, Dick and Larry were scheduled to be guests on the final Canadian War Savings Show, broadcast from Toronto on the CBC. It was probably André Kostelanetz, for whom they had hawked Canadian war bonds the previous year on the air, who had the idea of making that final broadcast an all–Rodgers & Hart show.[20] Also booked for the show was the singer Jane Froman.

A few hours before the broadcast, Larry was on his way into a reception at the Toronto hotel where he and the Rodgerses were staying when he suddenly bent double and vomited every drop of booze, and then some, that he'd drunk since the night before. Later, upstairs, Dorothy Rodgers confronted a cleaned-up, embarrassed Larry.

"Give me the bottles," Dorothy said.

"What bottles?" said Larry. But he was so stunned she knew what was in his suitcase—he had long since traded the morocco-bound collected works of Shakespeare for fifths of Schenley's—that he complied. Still, he could not stop shaking. Bashfully, he asked Dorothy if he could have one drink—just one—right now.

"Tonight," Dorothy said, protecting her husband's interests as much as Larry's health, "when the show is over."

The War Savings show that night was an exhortation to Canadians to buy war bonds and *more* war bonds. "We Canadians must not fail in our national war weapons drive!" the announcer asserted. Before a live studio audience, André Kostelanetz opened the program with his orchestral rendition of "The Girl Friend." Jane Froman came to the microphone to sing "I Didn't Know What Time It Was." A native of Columbia, Missouri, Froman had worked on the air in Cincinnati and in Chicago. She was pretty enough to have been invited to New York in 1933 to appear in the *Ziegfeld Follies*. Froman stuttered when she spoke but sang with clarity and emotional credibility—both Dick and Larry admired her work—and was soon voted the number one female vocalist on radio.[21] Kostelanetz and his orchestra went into "Where or When," closing with the evocative ping of a triangle, the chime of memory. Then, while Dick and Larry waited backstage, the maestro and the choir of CBC Singers gave a surprisingly moving rendition of "Blue Moon." Larry, listening to the lyric he'd been so wisely encouraged to write, could only lick his lips, practically tasting the promised drink, and wait. The choir was making the song twinkle like a star, and poor parched Larry was about to go on.

"For sixteen years they've been the talk of the country," said the announcer. "Here they are—Dick Rodgers and Larry Hart!"

The requisite small talk led to the announcer asking if the boys' music-making ever bothered the neighbors.

"Whenever someone comes up to complain," Dick said, "I just pick Larry up, put a bottle in his mouth, and walk the floor with him. 'Little Junior needs to be fed.'" (They used the material several times on the air. An alternate tagline was "The little darling is teething.") The studio audience roared. Larry was used to this theme. And yet it must have grated.

Froman returned to sing "My Heart Stood Still," and then Rodgers went to the piano to play "Falling in Love with Love." "Ah, we had some grand experiences doing that show," said Larry, ever the professional, betraying no audible sign of suffering. Rodgers began the verse of "With a Song in My Heart" and, as Froman and Kostelanetz prepared to join in, the announcer asked Larry what his favorite Rodgers & Hart song was. "Well, if I were a businessman," Larry replied in his singsong way, "I'd say my favorite was from our latest show. But I think Richard's best tune is the one he's playing now." The refrain of "With a Song in My Heart" burst forth—a powerful number with which to end the program.

"Hats off to our fighting men!" praised the announcer, once more stirring the radio audience to buy bonds for arms to prevent "free Canadians from becoming Nazi slaves!"

Dick and Larry exited the broadcast studio. Dorothy, as promised, handed Larry a tumbler of whiskey. "He drank it down in one gulp," Richard Rodgers said.[22]

The announcement that *Hotel Splendide* had collapsed was delayed until co-producers Wiman and Rodgers could confidently say what the next Rodgers & Hart show would be: a musical adaptation of *The Warrior's Husband*, the Julian Thompson play that Wiman had been told about by William Liebling the previous spring, and the one that made Katharine Hepburn a Broadway star in 1932. The producers were "reasonably confident" that Twentieth Century-Fox, which produced the film version with Elissa Landi as Hippolyta, Queen of the Amazons, would transfer the rights to them.[23] In any case, *The Warrior's Husband* was what Larry wanted to do next. It was even possible that, by the first week in December, Dick and Larry had resumed convening every day, as they had for twenty-three years, at one or the other's apartment to talk over the libretto, which they would write themselves.

Wiman and his office, sprinkling the town with public relations fairy dust, let it be known that Joan Blondell and Dick Powell were "interested" in playing Hippolyta and Sapiens, her husband, on Broadway.[24] But only Ray Bolger was seriously considered for Sapiens. This was partly because Bolger had been so fine in *On Your Toes* and would be available, and partly because *Pal Joey* had confirmed Rodgers and Hart's belief that a male lead who could dance was intrinsically more interesting than a male lead who could only sing.

On Sunday, December 7, 1941, at 1:20 in the afternoon in New York (7:50 A.M. in Honolulu), three hundred sixty Japanese planes attacked the American Navy fleet in Pearl Harbor, sinking five battleships and killing more than 2,300 men. It wasn't until 9:00 P.M. that the Japanese foreign minister advised the U.S. embassy in Tokyo that the two countries were at war. When *Keep 'Em Rolling* came on at 10:30—the guests that night were soprano Risë Stevens and the actors Sylvia Sidney and Jeffrey Lynn—"The Flame of Freedom Is Burning" packed an extra wallop. By the following evening, America would be finally, officially in it.

Practically everyone on or near Broadway wanted to be part of the war. Dick Rodgers, months away from turning forty, hoped for a civilian commission. His father, Will, now widowed and retired from his medical practice, volunteered to examine draftees. Among the draftees were actors, directors, producers, and designers. The USO, organized the previous year to boost the morale of soldiers being trained at camps across the country, kicked into high gear, drawing performers from the theater, radio, and the movies. Two USO circuits were formed: the Red White and Blue Circuit was equipped with theaters and hosted Broadway shows, which usually included new gags and lots of girls; the Stars and Stripes Circuit featured smaller acting units. Condescending to the servicemen was a common mistake; these boys wanted no half-sincere salutes to their courage and sacrifice but the best entertainment available. "Popular music they like fast and furious," *The New York Times* reported. "Legitimate plays are such a novelty to most of the boys that the two dramas now on the circuits have been playing to packed and cheering houses."[25]

It was a very American way to be sent off to war. Doing their part as 1941 turned into 1942, Dick and Larry immersed themselves in adapting *The Warrior's Husband* and its subject—the ancient, mythic war between the

Amazons and the Greeks. The Press Matter attached to the Samuel French edition boils down the plot to four sentences:

> Here is an Amazonian queendom in which man is naught but a racial necessity and a domestic convenience. The women do the fighting and ruling—and look extraordinarily attractive in armor. To their Caucassian [*sic*] land comes an army of Greek warriors, sight-seeing on their way to besiege Troy and lending a hand to poor half-wit Hercules, who has promised his publicity man (Homer) to steal the sacred girdle of the Amazons' queen. The opposing warriors line up for battle, but call a truce for the night—and in the morning are the best of friends.

The kisses of Greek warrior Theseus subdue the Amazon huntress Antiope, whose magnificent, twenty-year-old legs are meant to signify strength—and draw the attention of every ticket-holder in the theater.

The tone of *The Warrior's Husband* is established early and boldly. Three middle-aged Amazons are at the palace, gossiping:

CAUSTICA
Husband. What's a husband?

HEROICA
A husband is what you call a man you can't get
rid of.

POMPOSIA
These Greeks have a system they call marriage,
whereby you make a contract to live for life with
the man who is the father of your children.

CAUSTICA
Oh, ye Gods! You don't expect to start *that*
here, do you?

Lines like these were nectar to Larry. For the libretto, he and Dick made only minimal changes to Julian Thompson's play.

Once *The Warrior's Husband* had a book, it needed songs to attract financing. But Larry got too sick to get out of bed. Admitted to Dr. Harold Hyman's care at Doctors Hospital on January 22, 1942, Larry received a diagnosis of acute alcoholism. He was treated with vitamin B complex and physiotherapy.[26] "Talks continuously about having to get out of hospital to finish new play," noted one of his doctors.

The mountain came to Muhammad. Rodgers showed up with newspapers for the news-starved patient, and staff paper and pencils. Hyman suggested to Rodgers that he and Larry work in the interns' quarters, where Cole Porter had had a piano rolled in the previous autumn while receiving treatment for his shattered left leg. The smell of ether was in the air.[27] Larry, wearing pajamas, paced the corridors and frequently stopped to write.

At Doctors Hospital, Rodgers and Hart completed four or five songs for the *Warrior's Husband* adaptation. "Jupiter Forbid" was a paean, sung by Queen Hippolyta, to Pontus, the capital city of the Amazons:

> *Maybe there's a place where people never laugh,*
> *Maybe there's a place where kids don't kid,*
> *Maybe there's a place for just the upper half,*
> *Not here,*
> *Jupiter forbid!*

"Here's a Hand" was a love song between Antiope and Theseus, the romantic leads of the show. "The Gateway of the Temple of Minerva" put a new frame on "A College on Broadway," which the boys had written at Columbia more than twenty years earlier, and added a boogie-woogie beat. "Careless Rhapsody" satirized love songs. "Nobody's Heart" was to be sung by the sexually inexperienced Antiope before she falls in love with Theseus. "Nobody's heart belongs to me, / Heigh-ho, who cares?" she sings with feigned indifference, while echoing the call of the hunt. The lyric seems to reflect Larry's view of himself as an undesirable, middle-aged man—nobody's Hart—who goes everywhere stag. "Nobody's Heart" removes the attractively anthropomorphic consciousness of the moon in "Blue Moon," which can see the subject standing alone and hearing her prayer, for a clear-eyed perspective that imputes no significance to it:

> *I admire the moon*
> *As a moon,*
> *Just a moon.*

Larry Hart "had few observable illusions," Yip Harburg said. After a while the glow always dimmed, like a gas lamp turned way down. And yet no matter how much self-pity or self-reproach a character expressed, Hart knew it would be leaden to do so without humor. In the comic reprise of "Nobody's Heart," Sapiens, the delicate (but not effeminate) son of the Amazon Pomposia, sings:

> I've had no trial in the game of man and maid.
> I'm like a violin that no one's ever played.
> Words about love are Greek to me.
> Nice girls won't speak to me.
> I despise the moon
> As a moon,
> It's a prune.
> Nobody's heart belongs to me today.

The lyric was composed between the harsh hospital lighting and the cold-to-the-step floors. "Morning care," said the hospital notes on Larry:

> oral hygiene, bath, walking around room, appears to be anxious to go home—shaved by barber and facial massage—back to bed—appears to be sleeping—seen by Dr. Fischl and intravenous medication given by him. Resting, ate fairly well. Reading newspaper. Is very loquacious. Afternoon visitors . . . [he] . . . says he feels fine. Dinner, complains of feeling tired.

On February 11 the entry on Larry said "Much improved." Larry went home. In the three weeks he had been hospitalized, Alex Yokel removed *The Snark Was a Boojum* from the season's production schedule.[28] Eventually he induced Owen Davis to try his hand at an adaptation. Davis's version was staged the following year and lasted five performances.

As junior producer, Rodgers knew he would have to shoulder such unglamorous responsibilities as arranging for orchestra chairs, negotiating with music publishers, providing expenses to auditors, and commissioning lobby displays. But Dwight Wiman was gone a lot—Rodgers wrote it off to Wiman's clubbiness, though Wiman was in fact unwell—so Rodgers, with a few songs in hand, also had to find an angel, or two or three. He got lucky when he induced Howard S. Cullman, whose considerable fortune came from his family's cigar-manufacturing company Cullman Bros., to invest in the new show, which was now called *All's Fair* (presumably as in "in love and war").

Cullman was that rare breed of New Yorker whose career seems to be canopied by the financial, political, and cultural fabrics of the city. At the time of Rodgers's courting of him, Cullman was vice-chairman of the Port of New York Authority (he would eventually become chairman) and sat on a dozen corporate boards, but Rodgers really wanted Cullman's money because, with the drama-savvy counsel of his wife, Margaret Wagner Cullman, he had invested in an awe-inspiring string of hit shows, including *Life with Father* and *Arsenic and Old Lace*. By early 1942 Cullman was widely known as a theatrical angel who rushed in where fools—and other investors—feared to tread. He likened the business of the theater to a baseball game in which there are only home runs and strikeouts; walks and base hits—shows that break even after a brief run—were no longer part of the game.[29]

Richard Kollmar, who had married Dorothy Kilgallen since his *Too Many Girls* days, had set himself up in January as a producer, with a capitalization of $100,000 to produce musicals; he put in $35,000 with no expectation of having any creative input. "The veterans of the game were Dwight Deere Wiman and Richard Rodgers," Kollmar wrote, "so I made a resolution to keep my eyes open and my mouth shut."[30]

Once again Bob Alton would choreograph, taking dancers from the School of American Ballet and several from Hollywood. Irene Sharaff would design the costumes, Jo Mielziner the scenery. *All's Fair* would be Mielziner's last show before closing his office to enter the Air Force and then serve in the Office of Strategic Services.[31] Josh Logan was the producers' choice to direct, even though he had come through a nervous breakdown in the winter of 1940–41. Just when his psyche was feeling sturdy again, he received his draft notice. Wiman intervened to get Logan a deferment until the new show was up and running.[32]

Then Larry Hart relapsed with liver and kidney trouble and went back into the hospital. Treated with Nembutal, he began to sleep regularly and was home by the second week of March.

With *All's Fair* rehearsals scheduled to commence a month later, the cast had to be filled out. For Antiope, the producers signed movie starlet Constance Moore, who had been spending 1942 as an honorary master sergeant in the U.S. Army entertaining at USO Camp Shows. Bertha Belmore, who had played Caustica in the 1932 *The Warrior's Husband* on Broadway, was signed to play Pomposia, Sapiens's mother, in *All's Fair*. Rodgers and Wiman passed on signing Benay Venuta, a blond dynamo, for Hippolyta; but Larry had seen Venuta around town several times—at another USO Camp Show in late March, she had sung "Deep in the Heart of Texas" and brought the boys to their feet—and persuaded the producers to have another look. At her second audition, with Dick and Larry listening from the orchestra, Venuta sang the first twelve bars of "Jupiter Forbid!"

Larry leaped up and said, "I *told* you she should play it!"

"It was the first time I met him," Venuta said of Hart. "He had a big white handkerchief with which he was always blowing his nose or wiping his eyes."[33]

Rodgers, Mielziner, and Alton were game to try something new for a musical comedy with dance: the *All's Fair* set would include a ramp slanting from the footlights to a gradual three-foot rise. The set was built in Fort Lee, where it would stay until right before the New York opening, so the Ladies and Gentlemen of the Ensemble were bused across the Hudson each week to practice walking on the set. The dancers got seasick until, after many rehearsals under Alton's supervision, they became so acclimated to the ramp effect that they had a hard time readjusting to flat surfaces. Ray Bolger, on the other hand, took to the ramp immediately.[34]

For musical director, Rodgers had brought in the young composer-conductor Johnny Green. The son of an architect, Green was descended from German, Hungarian, and Dutch Jews who regarded Yiddish as a language not to be spoken by refined people. Green had gone to Harvard and was considering a career on Wall Street, but music called. "Body and Soul" was one of four songs he sold to Gertrude Lawrence for $250. After signing a 1941 contract to write the music for a musical called *Hula Honeymoon*, which Rodgers had under option, and later writing music for a 1941 flop called *Hi Ya, Gentlemen!*, Green took the *All's Fair* job to pull himself out of debt.[35] Green and Larry Hart never developed much of a rapport.

Green had a Leonard Bernstein–like tendency—though without Bernstein's lion's mane of hair—to mug when putting the orchestra through its paces at the St. James Theatre, where rehearsals brought a new song every week or so. "Life with Father" was written for Sapiens (Bolger) to sing about his beloved dad, Sapiens Major; the title might have been a nod to the long-running Broadway hit, but several lines in the song—"a louse in the house was he" was one—could have easily applied to Max Hart. Dick and Larry constructed a reprise of "Life with Father" for Bertha Belmore, as Sapiens's buxom Amazon mom, to sing and dance with Bolger, and the reprise never failed to delight everyone. "The Boy I Left Behind Me" was a smart lyric about an Amazon warrior pining for the boy—the one who knitted socks for her—waiting for her back home.

Boston tryouts were only two weeks away when Larry discovered Mabel Mercer at Tony's on Fifty-Second Street. "Recommended: Mabel Mercer singing 'You Are Too Beautiful,'" swooned the *New York Amsterdam News*. "*So* continental." Mercer sang with an insuperable diction in which every word shone like a pearl. Unlike so many nightclub singers, she did not use a microphone but sang to the room with unerring clarity. Larry was grateful to be hearing his and his friends' lyrics without strain.[36]

Listening to Mercer at Tony's late one night, Larry was introduced to the songwriter Alec Wilder, who had moved to Manhattan from Rochester, New York, where he'd haunted the halls of the Eastman School of Music long past his student days, and had taken up more or less permanent residence at the Algonquin. Hart and Wilder had at least three things in common: music, a sexuality veiled to the public, and booze. While Mercer took a break, the two men talked.

> Hart was warm and congenial—a special delight, considering my own prac-
> tically anonymous position in the songwriting world. He said that he and
> Rodgers never tried to write hit songs. Their income came from the theater, not
> hits. Should a song break loose from a show and live an independent life, the in-
> come from it was regarded by the two as an extra dividend, a luxury. He told me
> that all his lyrics were concerned with character delineation and plot. He con-
> sidered a lyric that ignored either of these to be unprofessional and untheatrical.

This was revelatory for Wilder, who was used to hearing the Rodgers & Hart songs unmoored from the contexts of their shows. Wilder later wrote that the two lyricists who nourished him most were Hart and Johnny Mercer:

> And I believe that the reason for this is by no means that they were such mas-
> ters of their craft but that in their craft they were vulnerable to the point of self-
> revelation. And in revealing themselves they also revealed their profound need
> to put on paper their attitudes toward love, life, irony, absurdity, loneliness and
> loss. The other lyricists wrote well, but I never sensed that need, that hunger.[37]

✣   ✣   ✣

A couple of weeks before *All's Fair* was ready to try out at the Shubert The-atre in Boston, Dick and Larry wrote "The Bombardier Song" for the Army Air Corps. The song was written at the behest of Colonel Hans Christian Adamson, of the War Department, who wanted the song to "create the feeling of the air crew and the spirit of the team." [38] It did so by having the members of a bomber crew—bombardier, pilot, navigator, and engineer—talk to each other as they prepare to drop their payload on "the target, the lovely target." The song was published the week of the first Broadway blackout, when the Great White Way went semi-dark between 9:30 and 9:50 P.M., drawing New Year's Eve–sized crowds to Times Square. The Civilian Protection Agency deemed the blackout insufficiently dark; subsequent blackouts would turn the city ghostly. [39]

Early in the morning of May 11, 1942, the *All's Fair* company headed for Boston by train. Aleen Robinson was then working as one of the Ladies of the Ensemble under the name Toni Stuart. Robinson was seated in the dining car across from Mark Dawson, who was playing a herald, and his first wife, and Larry Hart. (Robinson and Dawson would later marry.) She remembered Dick Rodgers dashing into the car to say they needed a four- or five-minute number for a set change early in the second act. "So little Larry took a pad out of his pocket, and his pencil," Robinson said. "And that's the way they would throw out a number, put a number in. You were in awe of these people!" [40]

Larry wanted to get Dawson, a baritone, "in the show," so he wrote him the lusty drinking song "Bottoms Up," in which Homer prompts him to tell the story of Hercules and the command for Hercules to purloin Hippolyta's girdle. [41] (Key plot points, Larry knew, go better in song, and with wine.) "For Jupiter and Greece," in which the plot is laid out by Achilles, appears to have been reworked on the train to Boston for Dawson and the male ensemble. It turned into the perfect opening number.

In Boston next afternoon the producers were seated in the orchestra of the Shubert Theatre watching Josh Logan direct a scene when Larry bounded down the aisle, took a seat next to Dick, and handed him a piece of paper with some verse scribbled on it.

"What's this?" said Dick.

"For that spot toward the end of the first act. Ray and Benay could do it in-one." Larry had promised Benay Venuta that he would write her a great comic number; this was the fulfillment of that promise.

Rodgers read the lyrics and smiled. He stood up and said to Larry, "Don't leave the theater." Rodgers went upstairs to a dressing room, sat down at a rehearsal piano, and had a melody in ten minutes. He returned to the auditorium with a lead sheet of "Ev'rything I've Got."[42] It was one of the few times Rodgers composed a melody to lyrics Larry had already drafted without whip-cracking supervision. The song, written for Sapiens and Hippolyta, catches the sparring couple in the romantic inebriation so longingly recalled by the youngsters of "I Wish I Were in Love Again." The fearsome warrior queen is committed, in her way, to her delicate but challenging new lover:

> I've a powerful anesthesia in my fist,
> And the perfect wrist to give your neck a twist.
> There are hammerlock holds,
> I've mastered a few,
> And everything I've got belongs to you.

The love-by-insult tone of the song was meant to evoke laughter with each line; when the couplet "Off to bed we will creep / Till the birdies start to peep" failed to get a response, Ray Bolger suggested that he repeat a phrase:

> Off to bed we will creep,
> Then we'll sleep and sleep and sleep
> Till the birds start to peep.
> I'll give you plenty of nothing.

Naughty but nuanced, the repetition produced the laugh Larry wanted.[43]

That same day Richard Ainley, who had been trying to fit into the role of Theseus, was paid $4,000 to bow out of the show and was replaced by Ronald Graham, who had played Antipholus of Ephesus in *The Boys from Syracuse*.[44] Within a couple of days the producers were alerted to the existence of another musical show titled *All's Fair*, a revue that had been produced three seasons earlier at the Wharf Theatre in Provincetown. So Dick and Larry renamed the show *By Jupiter*.

The producers and songwriters were staying at the Ritz-Carlton. One night Kollmar, who had become invaluable as coproducer while Wiman was ill, invited Larry Hart to dinner. The show looked pretty good, although songs were being revised and reshuffled after every performance. A particular headache to Josh Logan was the placement of "Wait Till You See Her," a song for Theseus to sing about Antiope, which combined the best of Rodgers—those beautifully carpentered waltzes—with the best of Hart—his idiomatic phrasing and, not incidentally, his focus on the appearance of the beloved. Hart, who had a keen instinct for a show's timing, and Kollmar talked about where "Wait Till You See Her" might work. After the entrée Kollmar, who knew Hart's reputation as a compulsive check-grabber, excused himself and quietly took the maître d'hôtel aside.

"Mr. Hart is my guest," Kollmar said. "Don't let him give you any nonsense about paying the check."

The maître d' looked at Kollmar imperiously and said, "I am sorry, Mr. Kollmar. Mr. Hart spoke to me after the appetizer. I have accepted his gratuity. *C'est fini.*"[45]

It was the last night Larry was out for dinner in Boston. Fearful that bronchitis would turn into pneumonia, he went into the hospital there for the rest of the tryout period, which ran till the end of May. He must have read about the equally hard-drinking John Barrymore entering Hollywood Presbyterian Hospital with hypostatic pneumonia, his organs failing by the hour.[46] In Larry's absence Dick wrote the lyrics to a song for Sapiens, "Now That I've Got My Strength," and, after consulting with Logan, was prepared to throw out "Wait Till You See Her," though the title had already been printed for the New York program.[47]

Nearing the end of the tryout period, what had been apparent to Larry was soon common knowledge: conductor Johnny Green and Constance Moore (Antiope) had begun a romance, their heat warming the entire company. When Moore sang "Nobody's Heart," according to Aleen Robinson, everyone inside the Shubert could feel her aiming the song at Green.[48] The orchestra pit's configuration prompted Green to conduct while sitting atop a brass rail, balancing himself by curling his toes around a lower rail. Musicians and performers half-expected the lovelorn maestro to fall off any minute. Julia Warren Tucker, whose father photographed the *By Jupiter* Boston tryouts, was nine years old when he took her to the show one night, and she saw Green's baton fly out of his hand and almost hit the ceiling. "He looked up," Tucker recalled, "but didn't miss a beat."[49]

On May 31 the company returned to New York, arriving to the news that British forces had temporarily turned back Field Marshal Rommel in Libya, and that John Barrymore had died the previous night in Hollywood. Although Barrymore had spent the last few years mostly on radio, often pickled in self-parody, the American theater was almost unimaginable without him. Two weeks earlier the city had undergone its second major dimout, but once again Times Square was deemed too light to meet wartime regulations.[50] Manhattan would have to become darker to protect itself.

Larry Hart attended the June 2 opening of *By Jupiter* at the Shubert on Forty-Fourth Street. It was considered the first musical show of the new 1942–43 season. (The Equity contract calendar begins on June 1.) The sloping stage was in place. Constance Moore and Johnny Green were still in love—great for the show, disastrous for their marriages. "Wait Till You See Her" was performed one last time before Rodgers ruthlessly—and probably effectively—pulled it from the show because it simply didn't fit.[51] But Mabel Mercer began to sing it at Tony's, and it would soon become a cabaret and nightclub standard.

Reviews for *By Jupiter* were mostly positive without being terribly enthusiastic, with just about every critic saving their praise for Ray Bolger. Nobody suggested it was anything close to Rodgers and Hart's best score. Writing in the *Mirror*, Walter Winchell welcomed the boys back to Broadway but didn't find much except Bolger to get excited about. "That is to report," Winchell wrote, "their familiar genius appeared arid last night, with not one ditty in the score staying in these ears. More rhythm, you might say, than melody, and more rhymes than rhythm." Writing in *PM*, which on May 29 had published a set of Mary Morris photographs taken during the show's rehearsals, Louis Kronenberger liked only the rueful "Nobody's Heart." Brooks Atkinson, aware how much his *Pal Joey* notice had wounded Larry, probably pulled his punch in the *Times*: "a fistful of Lorenz Hart's casually complicated lyrics . . . Mr. Hart has made a reasonably close free-hand transcription of the Julian F. Thompson comedy, pausing only to put in some normal Rodgers and Hart moments of their own from the classics—boogie-woogie and gags. . . . [Constance] Moore is more attractive than vocal." The *Wall Street Journal* praised the music as "expert, if not outstanding, and its dancing generally superior. People who liked *The Boys from Syracuse* will enjoy it more than those who particularly doted on *Pal Joey*." True to form, the *Daily Worker* chided the boys for not writing "the war show they have in them," and recommended they consider adapting Chaplin's *The Great Dictator* for the stage. George Jean Nathan found the gags as old as antiquity:

For fifty years one of the standbys of the burlesque shows was the episode involving a statuesque blonde and an effeminate comedian. It usually ran about ten minutes. In this case we engaged it again, the only difference being that it ran about two hours and a quarter and that the scene, instead of being the familiar beach at Monte Carlo, was ancient Greece. In place of Mrs. Gotrox it was Hippolyta the Amazon, and in place of Percy it was Sapiens.[52]

The theme of the Amazons' men's effeminacy riled some critics. Richard Watts, Jr., in particular admonished Rodgers and Hart for a preoccupation with "humor that springs from homosexuality and kindred forms of degeneracy." When Sapiens's mother speaks of her son, who might give the Amazon queen an heir, she says, "My son has not been taught any of our warlike feminine ways. In fact he is, if I may say so, an example of our best traditions of delicate masculine grace," and half the audience roared while the other half squirmed. This was now, after all, wartime, and the imputation that some men were too delicate to fight offended some people. In his column in the *Journal American*, John Anderson repudiated Watts's accusation, as though Rodgers and Hart needed defending, asserting that the songwriters were not exploiting homosexuality at all.[53] The perennially diplomatic Brooks Atkinson suggested that Ray Bolger was able to remain outside his character and make fun of the whole conception.[54] Bolger's rubbery footwork suggested a fragility that everyone knew he didn't really possess. He wasn't really such a sentimental sap; he was only playing one.

After its first or second Saturday night performance, *By Jupiter* underwent a major alteration that upset Larry Hart no end: it became the first Broadway musical to have an electrical amplification system installed. Radio had become the dominant medium, utterly reliant on the microphone; but since the mid-1930s, during the post-Prohibition entertainment boom, clubs were designed to have the seating capacity of a football stadium, and most club performers also needed a microphone to reach patrons seated far away. In that technological climate, placing microphones in theaters was inevitable.

"We had to stay after the show," Aleen Robinson recalled, "and they were going to mike it, so we all had to run through it again."

The electricians and engineers installed the mikes in the footlights. So, of course, all you heard was the feet—not only the walking on stage but the taps on our shoes, creating a deafening discomfort! We waited while the mikes were moved to the front of the balcony's rail. Now the audience sounds could be picked up, and of course the orchestra was far louder than desired, drowning out the voices on stage. There were adjustments throughout the long night. Larry Hart, having returned at 2 A.M. after his escaping for a long walk and a much needed drink, was seated in the left-stage box declaring his opinion. "You'll never hear pure sound in the theater again!" he said. "It's ruination!" But nobody would listen to him.[55]

It was true that everyone who attended *Knickerbocker Holiday* had been able to hear Walter Huston's parlando singing of "September Song." And from any Broadway stage, Ethel Merman could be heard as far away as Pittsburgh. But amplification minimized the anxiety that the audience wouldn't be able to hear a performer, especially someone singing a crucial lyric. As the lyricist Sheldon Harnick has pointed out, "The audience has to be able to hear it the first time around."[56]

Imposition of the microphone did not affect Larry Hart's lyric-writing—it was too late for that—but it would contribute to the erosion of the part of a song in which Hart had no equal as a writer: the verse. On Broadway the verse had come into its own in the 1920s as a signal to the audience that a formal song was about to begin. Over the years the verse generally became shorter, partly because orchestrators (the underrated Don Walker orchestrated *By Jupiter*) were increasingly clever about underscoring, providing instrumental music played during the dialogue as it moved into a song. A microphone installed in a Broadway theater removed the need for that get-ready transition in musical comedy, just as it had already made verses moot in songs performed in the movies. In addition, Sheldon Harnick suggested, as musical librettos became stronger and tighter, as they would shortly after 1942, the narrative need for a verse seemed superfluous; the verse doesn't carry the melody, Harnick said, and it's the melody that gets played on the air and sold on recordings.[57]

By Jupiter was said to be the last extravagant musical show produced for the duration of the war.[58] Although the show itself had cost more than $90,000 to get on the boards, conditions for the performers were anything but grand. Aleen Robinson remembered being backstage between scenes and squeezing packets of margarine, which had been recently introduced to American households because of severe butter rationing, onto chunks of bread.[59] The war was everywhere on Broadway and in Times Square—in news kiosks, in nightclubs, and on storefronts. Dimouts, casting a twilight patina, continued intermittently. "I wonder if anyone could describe this Broadway June, 1942, to a Broadwayite who had not been home since war started," wrote Dorothy Kilgallen:

> Anyone can imagine total darkness, but this peculiar spotty dimness is a thing you have to walk through and see: the blue and red bulbs on the undersides of the marquees spilling patches of glow along the sidewalk; white caps of sailors bobbing through the dark of the throng like vanilla cupcakes; khaki going by and gold braid going by and bright summer skirts getting into taxis and white shoes stepping off the curbs into thin traffic, and overhead a sudden sharpness in the stars you never noticed before because they had too much competition.[60]

The high-gloss MGM film *Mrs. Miniver*, heralding the British spirit in wartime, opened at Radio City Music Hall on June 5. The action picture *Remember Pearl Harbor*, factory-made only months after the date which lives in infamy, opened a few blocks away. The Rodgers & Hart song "Keep 'Em Rolling" supplied the title of a Hollywood-made patriotic short subject, the theme turned over to opera star Jan Peerce. On July 9, MGM's version of *I Married an Angel*, starring Jeanette MacDonald and her longtime professional partner Nelson Eddy, fluttered into the Capitol Theatre. The plot was reworked so that Eddy, as the banker from Budapest, falls asleep during his thirty-fifth birthday party and *dreams* of meeting an angel (MacDonald), whose real-life counterpart turns out to be a secretary at his bank. Scraps of Rodgers & Hart were wedged in—just enough to suggest that it had once been theirs. Anita Loos (*Gentlemen Prefer Blondes*) officially took the blame for the script. The young songwriters Chet Forrest and Robert Wright, under contract at Metro some years before their own Broadway successes *Song of Norway* and *Kismet*, couldn't escape the indignity of being ordered to embellish and revise Larry Hart's lyrics. Forrest and Wright, like so many other practitioners of the craft, had regarded Hart's work as unimprovable.[61]

In a climate agitated by war, the film version of *I Married an Angel* was quickly forgotten. But *By Jupiter* was still doing strong business.

Johnny Green, fifteen pounds skinnier after all that illicit passion, resigned his captaincy in the New York State Guard and accepted a commission in the Air Corps; but he was also preparing a new musical, *Beat the Band*, with Rodgers and George Abbott producing, and he was about to turn over the *By*

Jupiter baton to Harry Levant.[62] Rodgers had *Beat the Band* to oversee, but he needed a new musical to compose, too. "If you're intent enough on your work," he once told a British radio interviewer, "you want to do it more, and you want to do it better." But the Rodgers & Hart partnership was in a state of advanced decay.

Larry certainly wasn't interested in adapting *Green Grow the Lilacs*, which Rodgers, after further lobbying by Theresa Helburn and Lawrence Langner, had decided would be his next musical. The Theatre Guild was in danger of sliding into bankruptcy, with half of Broadway second-guessing Langner and Helburn, and badly needed a hit. In the musical theater Rodgers and Hart had the most consistently high batting average of the past seven years. But Larry kept shaking his head.

Frustrated, Dick phoned Oscar Hammerstein and asked to meet him for lunch at the Barberry Room in the Hotel Berkshire, on East Fifty-Second Street. "Oscar, remember when you said you'd be there if Larry became unable to work? Well, we have finally reached that point."[63] By the time they left the Barberry Room that afternoon, they had agreed that Hammerstein would attempt to write a libretto for *Green Grow the Lilacs*, leaving open the possibility that Larry might change his mind and write the lyrics.

Fat chance. Larry, more frightened than ever of being alone, began spending an increasing amount of time at the Lambs Club. That summer the Lambs launched William S. Hart's Famous Cowboy Movie Party, which entertained soldiers from various forts in the northeast—a kind of USO and Stage Door Canteen combined. Irving Berlin and Edgar Bergen each hosted an evening; so did Larry.[64] At the Lambs he drank and played gin rummy with Alan Jay Lerner. The Lambs that summer was where the twenty-four-year-old Lerner met Frederick Loewe, a Viennese composer whose father had originated the role of Prince Danilo in *The Merry Widow* in Berlin. When Loewe asked Lerner to write new lyrics for an earlier musical of his titled *Salute to Spring*, Larry encouraged Lerner to take the job. "To be a writer you've got to be brutal," Larry told Lerner.

"He didn't mean you must hurt people," Lerner explained. "He meant you must be ruthless with yourself; you must concentrate on your writing to the exclusion of everything and everyone else; you must devote yourself to learning it, improving it, working at it constantly without ever giving yourself an out, without ever settling for less." *Do as I say, not as I do.* It was too late for Larry to take his own counsel. During another evening at the Lambs bar he said to Lerner, "I've got a lot of talent, kid. I probably could have been a genius. But I just don't care."[65]

"Good work has a fair chance to be recognized in the end," the novelist George Meredith wrote to a friend in 1881, "and if not, what does it matter?"[66] Meredith was fifty-three at the time and already talking as though he were finished. Larry had recently turned forty-seven and was already insisting, "Heigh-ho, who cares?"

"Somewhere along the line," Lerner wrote, "there obviously did come a time when the joy of his professional success became drowned in the lost misery of his handicapped life."[67]

In the first week of August, Dick and Larry agreed to allow Billy Rose to use "The Circus Is on Parade," written for *Jumbo*, in his new show *Mrs. Astor's Pet Horse* at his Diamond Horseshoe club. (The show was about a Central Park hansom horse stationed outside the Plaza Hotel.) But Dick could not get Larry to discuss *Green Grow the Lilacs*. It was frustrating because the Theatre Guild had jumped the gun and announced that the folk play would soon be adapted by Rodgers, Hart, and Hammerstein.[68] Running out of patience, Dick asked Larry to meet him later in the week at the offices of their publisher Chappell, in the RKO Building near Rockefeller Center. It was a carefully considered meeting place. To the boys, Chappell was practically another home. Its chairman, Max Dreyfus, pushing seventy, still behaved like a father to them. Willy Kron, financial adviser to each of them, had served as a Chappell officer for years. Dr. Albert Sirmay kept a desk there. Hans Spialek and Robert Russell Bennett shared an office there, too.

In the meantime Larry had made arrangements to go to Mexico—far from Dick, from Frieda, from anyone who might scold him. He knew the partnership was broken, but he couldn't see repairing it with *Green Grow the Lilacs*. He must have laughed at that week's news report that a van carrying Rosie the elephant, now billed as Jumbo and appearing for another circus, had two flat tires on the George Washington Bridge; Jumbo was kept cool at the corner of 178th Street and Broadway, drawing squeals of delight from children in the neighborhood, while the tires' inner tubes were repaired.[69] If Larry resisted the item's all-too-easy metaphor, perhaps it took him back seven years earlier, when he and Dick were reconquering New York and the city was as merry as a carousel.

On the appointed day Larry, pale and haggard, arrived at Chappell. Max Dreyfus, sensitive to the high stakes of the meeting, had arranged for the boys to use the company's boardroom. Dick opened the meeting by saying he needed to get to work on a new musical, though it was apparent that Larry was in no shape to do so.

"I want you to have yourself admitted to a sanitarium," Dick said. "I'll get myself admitted, too. We'll be there together and work together. But you've got to get off the street."

"I know, I know. I'm sorry." Larry kept looking away. But he made it clear that he was not checking himself into any sanitarium—that he was on his way to Mexico.

"Larry, if you walk out now, someone else will do the show with me."

"Anyone in mind?"

"Oscar will write the lyrics."

"There's no better man for the job," Larry said. "I don't know how you put up with me all these years. The best thing would be for you to forget about me."

"Oh, please. I'm not going to forget about you."

Larry stood and moved to the door, pausing there for a moment. His coal-black eyes finally met Dick's eyes. "I still think *Lilacs* is a mistake. But I wish you luck with it." He went out and gently closed the door behind him.

In so many deaths, relief and grief play off each other in counterpoint. Alone in the boardroom Dick sighed, the burden of tolerating an increasingly truant, irresponsible partner over the course of twenty-four years having been lifted in an instant. And then he wept.[70]

After years of rumors and denials, the conclusion of Rodgers and Hart's partnership was not immediately publicized. On the last day of August 1942, *The New York Times* reported that Rodgers, Hart, and Hammerstein were all working together at Rodgers's Connecticut home on their adaptation of *Green Grow the Lilacs*. "The Theatre Guild plans the resultant musical for Fall presentation."[71]

But Larry was long gone. He arrived in Laredo, Texas, on August 25. The mercury there had climbed to well past a hundred degrees. On the other side of the Rio Grande the mescal could knock out your back teeth. Young men sold sex cheaply and anonymously; you couldn't get more anonymous. Larry filled out the U.S. border crossing certificate, giving his occupation as Writer, his address as 320 Central Park West, New York City, and his height at an absurdly generous five feet four. He lit a cigar and took a taxi into Mexico.

CHAPTER 23

Nobody Writes His Songs to Me

*T*HE THEATRE Guild soon corrected the impression that Larry Hart had a hand in the musical version of Lynn Riggs's *Green Grow the Lilacs*. The tone of the new collaboration was being set by reports that Rodgers and Hammerstein were writing this week in Fairfield, Connecticut, next week in Bucks County, Pennsylvania—bucolic settings in which to transpose turn-of-the-century Americana to the musical stage. "Although Mr. Hart will not help with the musical version of the Lynn Riggs folk play," *The New York Times* reported in mid-September, "he is not loafing. Presently he is in Mexico gathering local color for a Rodgers-Hart musical to be known as *Muchacho*, a sort of good-will musical they plan for Broadway some time next season." [1] In 1935 Larry had published a lyric called "Muchacha" (though it was probably written earlier at MGM), which evokes the Latin-flavored sounds of castanets and stomping heels, but it wasn't clear whether the proposed *Muchacho* emerged from anything other than a face-saving remark made by Rodgers or someone at the Theatre Guild.

No, Larry was not loafing. He had labored hard to lose himself in Mexico—in drink, certainly; in sex, perhaps—and, according to Rodgers, had to be carried off the train on a stretcher when he returned to New York. [2]

For a while Larry had no communication with Rodgers, who, despite his new collaborator's relatively slow writing pace, was characteristically quick composing music to the *Green Grow the Lilacs* lyrics that Hammerstein had delivered. "If Oscar said he'd be there at three, he'd be there at three—with a lyric in his hand!" said Rodgers.

Word spread that Larry was available. Taking the matter in hand, Doc Bender made an approach to Jerome Kern in Los Angeles. After *Show Boat* Kern had worked for years, off and on, with Hammerstein, and although none of their shows came close to *Show Boat*'s achievement, they had produced many memorable songs, including "All the Things You Are," which was among the top money-earners in the ASCAP catalogue. Kern, like everyone else, knew of Larry's reputation for disorganization, disappearances, and drink. So it came as a surprise at the Ardsley one day when a telegram from Holly-wood arrived: WHEN CAN YOU COME OUT HERE AND START A PICTURE WITH JEROME KERN? Milton Pascal, who was at the apartment playing cards with Larry and writer Phil Charig, marveled, "Not bad: from Rodgers to Kern."

"Larry looked at the telegram," Pascal remembered, "then tore it up and said, 'Deal the cards.'"[3]

There were several possible connections to Emmerich Kalman, the Hungarian-born practitioner of the Viennese school of operetta. Whether sung in German, Yiddish, or English, Kalman's operettas—*Countess Maritza, Parisian Love, The Circus Princess,* and *The Duchess of Chicago* among them— were widely beloved. Kalman had fled Vienna in 1938 and spent two years in Paris before coming to New York. Bender may have known Kalman was looking for a show to do, and made the introductions. More likely, the con-nection came from Columbia alumnus Paul Gallico. For twenty years Gallico had kept up with Rodgers and Hart, and he might have had some additional encouragement from his literary agent, Harold Ober, who had represented Scott Fitzgerald and knew of Fitzgerald's admiration for Hart's lyrics. Gal-lico's career was close to peaking. He had recently completed his famous story "Joe Smith, American" and the novel *The Snow Goose;* he had worked on several drafts of a Lou Gehrig biopic for Goldwyn and written the book *The Pride of the Yankees,* its publication timed to coincide with the release of the Goldwyn picture. He was writing at top rates for *Cosmopolitan* and *The Saturday Evening Post,* and his Hollywood agent, H. N. Swanson (known by friends and enemies as Swanee), was negotiating lucrative screenwriting con-tracts for him. In 1942 Gallico and his wife, Pauline Garibaldi, bought a farm in Stockton, New Jersey, a bike ride away from Colligan's and that damned wishing well. When they weren't in Hollywood, they lived on the farm during warm months and at the Hotel Navarro, on Central Park South, during the winter.

In one of those residences, the Gallicos had cooked up an outline for a musical comedy they were calling *Here Comes the Circus*. It revolved around "the type of Cirque Medrano or the Cirque d'Hiver playing in Paris at the time of the German invasion."[4]

Emmerich Kalman warmed to the idea because it was all about Nazi-occupied Paris, which he knew well. Larry wanted to work on it, too, maybe because the circus setting was familiar. Or maybe because Paris of May 1942 was far away from the turn-of-the-century "Indian territory" setting of Dick Rodgers's current project. Larry also liked the idea of not traveling so far to work—Gallico's Central Park South apartment and Kalman's Park Avenue apartment were both not far from the Ardsley. And then, as *Here Comes the Circus* turned into *Miss Underground*, Larry could see Vivienne Segal in the title role. Segal was ready to follow Larry anywhere. Pending a completed script, she was on board, and so was George Balanchine. They'd begin work that winter, after other commitments had been met.

By Jupiter, meanwhile, was acquiring some notoriety from the City of New York. With his reformer's zeal, Mayor La Guardia was determined to protect the virtue of America's military personnel from vice on the street and in Broadway theaters. Toward that end he had Paul Moss, his longtime Licensing Commissioner, shut down the revue *Wine, Women and Song*, which, in the burlesque tradition of pairing a comic headliner with a stripper, featured Jimmy Savo and the striptease artist Margie Hart. La Guardia claimed that theatergoers were confusing *Wine, Women and Song* with the Strauss waltz "Wine, Woman and Song," and often entered the theater believing they were about to see a clean show scored with Viennese music. Archbishop Francis J. Spellman attacked the revue and several other shows as indecent. The Catholic Theatre Movement listed *By Jupiter* among the shows it deemed "wholly objectionable." *Star and Garter*, starring Bobby Clark and Gypsy Rose Lee, was shut down, prompting producer Mike Todd to quit the League of New York Theatres for its failure to rush to his defense. The Lindsay and Crouse show *Strip for Action* was in trouble, and so was Paul Osborn's searing adaptation of Richard Wright's *Native Son*. The last time a Broadway show had been shuttered for indecency was 1928, when the police raided Mae West's *Pleasure Man*. Almost everyone was intimidated by La Guardia's finger-shaking prudery, and by Commissioner Moss, who, weirdly, had once been an executive with the Theatre Guild. Becoming the city's chief vice-hunter, Moss had proclaimed, "The stage, dancehalls, and poolrooms are scheduled for a clean-up whenever there is any indication of commercial filth." Moss found enough commercial filth even in the Ringling Brothers circus to threaten to close it.[5]

Confronted with written and verbal threats from the Mayor's Office, the Catholic Theatre Movement, and other attack-dog agencies, the understandably skittish producers modified elements in their shows. In *By Jupiter*, this task fell mostly to Rodgers because Wiman, eager to assist in the war effort, was packing up to go to England to become director of entertainment for the Red Cross.[6] Of the producers put on the defensive for their shows' supposed indecency, only Louis and George W. Brandt, gatekeepers of *Native Son*, refused to alter a syllable.[7] The producers of *Wine, Women and Song* were hauled into court, and the prosecution's hypocrisy was exposed when a Justice Stephen S. Jackson attended the show as a "reviewer" for the Catholic Theatre Movement, and then forced himself—*forced himself!*—to attend two additional times to make sure Margie Hart was completely nude onstage.[8]

Larry Hart was amused by much of this, but censorship in general made him sore. When Broadway columnist Leonard Lyons went on vacation the following year, he cobbled together politically tinged contributions from a few songwriters—Harold Rome, Richard Rodgers, Frank Loesser, Irving Berlin, and Lorenz Hart—writing on the theme "If I Could Write the Nation's Laws," to appear during his absence in his syndicated column "Lyons Den." Larry's contribution went:

> (*If I could write the nation's laws*)
> *I would exclude the Peeping Toms—*
> *The men who think they're clerics—*
> *From jolly entertainments and*
> *To save them from hysterics.*
>
> *This world has been much more distressed*
> *From men attired than girls undressed.*[9]

Larry didn't demand that everyone embrace the ribald, but he resented being prevented from doing so himself.

The season's traditional Christmas tree, a thirty-five-foot Douglas fir, was put up in Madison Square but bereft of its usual 3,500 lights. "Carolers sang out beneath it in a forestlike darkness," writes New York City historian Mark

Caldwell.[10] For New Year's Eve 1942, Larry took Frieda and sister-in-law Dorothy to Miami—Teddy Hart was touring in *Three Men on a Horse* and unable to join them—but the U.S. Army had taken over the Roney Plaza, so the Hart contingent had to be satisfied with less opulent accommodations at a smaller hotel. Dorothy was identified by hotel staff and guests as Mrs. Hart and was widely presumed to be Larry's wife. The mistake emphasized what Larry *didn't* have—a romantic partner, never mind a wife, or anyone outside his family he could devote himself to. His friends were dropping away— some of them because his cycle of boozing and crashing had become repellent, some because they now had families that took priority, and some, like Josh Logan, because they'd entered military service. Doc Bender, whatever others thought of him, remained a concerned friend, but he'd been carefully monitoring his own blood pressure since his brother Charles had suffered a fatal heart attack in December 1939, at forty-seven, and now Bender avoided late nights fueled by liquor in massive quantities. Drinking more secretively than usual, Larry lost his temper one night in a Miami restaurant when his food selection couldn't be accommodated. He took it out on Frieda, who surely knew by then that her brilliant older son was not going to marry and give her the grandchild she coveted. Heartsick to see Larry become so unhinged, Frieda went home to New York. Larry was contrite but declined Dorothy's familiar entreaties to see a psychiatrist.[11]

Returning to New York a couple of weeks later, Larry threw himself into the Gallico-Hart-Kalman musical project *Miss Underground*. Doc Bender intended to produce. The story revolves around Susan Jones (to be played by Vivienne Segal), an American who infiltrates a French circus to spirit American blueblood Nicky Malden out of Paris and back to America, as his family has paid her to do. The main complication is that she's wanted by the Gestapo; but she's also unaware that Nicky has been engaged in crucial undercover work for years.

Through the winter Larry completed more than a dozen lyrics. In act 1, "Alexander's Blitztime Band" is led by Otto Schulz, a corporal in the Reichswehr and formerly a waiter at Lüchow's on Fourteenth Street in Manhattan. Otto keeps making asides to the audience about how much he loves New York, but as soon as his (Nazi) Boys bring him back to the business at hand—that is, singing the song—he "*Heil*"s away.

> *You think that I'm a Nazi?*
> *Vat Vinchell calls a Ratzi?*

But don't throw any mud, son,
I come from the banks of the Hudson,
This joint could not be drearer.

"Vot?" say the Boys, and Otto throws in: "*Ich heil mein Fuehrer!*" Otto tells us he was waiting tables at Lüchow's ("Where they sure serve you chow") when he decided to go to France on holiday; then the Nazis arrived in Paris and forcibly inducted the German native.

No garden spot is flowery
If it's too far from the Bowery
I wish that I could swim out
And look at that lousy dimout.

Nostalgia for Manhattan is mixed with a brazen nose-thumbing at the Nazis, with more than a touch of Spike Jones's rude and very funny 1942 hit "Der Fuehrer's Face." Frederick Nolan has likened the tone of the lyrics to that of "Springtime for Hitler" from the Mel Brooks movie *The Producers*, several years before Brooks's Broadway version became the hottest ticket in town.[12]

As the plot develops, the circus family the Victorias have been invited to New York to appear with the Ringling Circus at Madison Square Garden, but the Nazis won't permit them to leave Paris. Susan Jones says wistfully, "New York—Madison Square Garden—Eighth Avenue—in May—and all the kids and the crowds pushing along the streets to get to the circus!" The circus includes an elephant called Baby, which the Nazis intend to requisition so they can eat her.

In act 2, Otto, disguised as a dowager, identifies himself as Duchess de Tête de Veau Bonaparte Bourbon De Luxe D'Appolinaris du Perrier de Coca Cola—widowed by Counte de Brazier-Zipper Rip. Her second husband, she explains, was Lt. Saazerac de Bouillabaisse, the father of their daughter Éclair, who attended the riding academy Bois de Boloney. Is there any doubt that Larry Hart came up with these gags? In a subsequent scene, Susan, decked out with a blond wig and a fan, is announced by a footman as the Countess Braziere Saazerac Chateaubriand.

After Nicky and Susan escape the Gestapo at the Folies Bergère, they're separated at the French-Spanish border in the Alps [*sic*: actually the Pyrenees]. The closing scene is set on a Portuguese freighter carrying Otto, the entire Victoria family, and a moody-looking Susan, coming into New York

Harbor. Susan appears to be pining for Nicky, as though he's absent, but Nicky is actually in the crow's nest disguised as a sailor. He and Susan reprise the declaration "I'm not in love with you!" and sing, "Do I Love You? (No, I Do Not!)." Curtain.

Larry often appeared at his collaborators' apartments too drunk to work. Dick Rodgers was not around to discipline him. Nor did the collaborators have the use of Rodgers's ruthless editing, which could help shape a libretto as well as the lyrics. Given wartime reluctance to invest in a new Broadway show, Doc Bender couldn't raise the money, though he kept announcing *Miss Underground*, "an adventure with music," as a spring 1943 production. There was an infusion of enthusiasm when Vinton Freedley came aboard as producer. Freedley re-signed Vivienne Segal and the Christianis, the twenty-six-member circus troupe, with Balanchine, Boris Aaronson (scenic design), and Billy Livingston (costumes) still ready to participate.

But Freedley "lost his nerve," Paul Gallico wrote, and *Miss Underground* was never produced. Kalman used at least two of the melodies he'd written for the show in *Marinka*, his 1945 operetta revisiting the melodramatic 1889 suicide-murder at the Mayerling hunting lodge.[13]

During those late winter weeks of the Gallico-Hart-Kalman collaboration, Constance Moore left *By Jupiter*, which was then recouping its costs, and was replaced by Nanette Fabray, who had been appearing in the long-running *Let's Face It*, by Cole Porter and Dorothy and Herb Fields. Taking over the role of Antiope, Fabray wasn't sure if Larry Hart was alive because he was nowhere on the scene.[14] Larry must have spent at least an hour one day with Dick working on the song "The Girl I Love to Leave Behind," for Ray Bolger to sing in United Artists' *Stage Door Canteen*. The lyric was a takeoff not only on *By Jupiter*'s "The Boy I Left Behind Me" but on "The Girl I Left Behind Me," the Irish folk tune popular in mid-nineteenth-century America. Not for Larry an all-American girl waiting demurely for her soldier boy to return home; this one wears her hair like Veronica Lake and makes the scene "silly for soldiers and mad for marines." Again, one thinks of a Preston Sturges character—of Trudy Kockenlocker (Betty Hutton) in *The Miracle of Morgan's Creek*, which completed filming early in the year (though its release was held up by the Hays Office), and concerned Trudy's drunken tryst, resulting in pregnancy, with a soldier whose identity she can't recall. Larry might have had the picture in mind because Eddie Bracken was the costar.

In late February 1943 Jane Froman was aboard the Pan-Am flying boat *Yankee Clipper*, traveling to entertain GIs under the auspices of the USO, when the aircraft crashed off the Lisbon coast, killing several passengers and leaving her badly crippled. Trouping through dozens of bone grafts, Froman would take Rodgers and Hart's "With a Song in My Heart" as her signature song. Wasn't the song schmaltz? she was subsequently asked. "Yes," she agreed, "but schmaltz with a sock!"[15] Three weeks after the *Yankee Clipper* crash, *Away We Go!*, the working title for the Rodgers and Hammerstein adaptation of *Green Grow the Lilacs*, was scheduled to try out in New Haven. Larry Hart got a ride up with Billy Rose. Rose was now married to Eleanor Holm, whom Larry had known when he was hosting come-one-come-all pool parties in Beverly Hills in the summer of 1932.

Helene Hanff, an aspiring playwright who had been put to work in the Theatre Guild press office, remembered trying to generate some effective publicity for *Away We Go!* "This was, they told us, the damndest musical ever thought up for a sophisticated Broadway audience," Hanff wrote. "It was so pure you could put it on at a church social. It opened with a middle-aged farm woman sitting alone on a bare stage churning butter, and from then on it got cleaner."[16]

It was the kind of Americana that Larry Hart distrusted. But at the New Haven tryout he tried to keep an open mind. Of the songs in *Away We Go!*'s first act, five of them—"Oh, What a Beautiful Mornin'," "The Surrey with the Fringe on Top," "Many a New Day," "People Will Say We're in Love," and "Out of My Dreams"—were destined to become instant classics, with "All Er Nuthin'" and "Oklahoma!" delighting the audience in the second act. But Larry wasn't so delighted. He might have regarded "We know we belong to the land" as a professionally crafted line, as resonant to recent immigrants as to *Mayflower* descendants; but "The land we belong to is *grand*"? Every now and then Larry would lean over and whisper to Rose, "It's a flop, isn't it?" and Rose would answer, "Sure, it's a flop," though the Bantam Barnum had never seen anything like it.[17]

The first reports from New Haven, however, were closer to Larry's assessment than those of the critics who weighed in later. The most famous of these originated, according to Helene Hanff, with Walter Winchell's secretary, Rose, who saw the show and then wired her boss: NO LEGS NO JOKES NO CHANCE. The wire got around.[18] Controlling the damage, Winchell swore that Mike Todd was overheard in the lobby of the Shubert Theatre in New Haven saying, "No jokes, no tits, no chance."[19]

For eleven days the Rodgers & Hammerstein show went to Boston, where it was decided that *Away We Go!* was too generic a title. Rodgers, according to Hanff, wanted to call it *Yessiree!* Lawrence Langner's wife, Armina Marshall, came up with *Oklahoma!* In an enthusiastic squib about the show, *The Boston Globe* made a passing reference to Larry Hart, "who used to be a colorful figure on Broadway." [20]

When the show opened at the St. James Theatre in New York on March 31, snow was on the ground. Larry took Frieda to opening night and, as most accounts had it, applauded and bravoed from their box. The show had integrated its libretto and songs in a way that no Rodgers & Hart show—not even the elegantly tapestried *The Boys from Syracuse*—had quite managed.

Half an hour after the curtain, at Sardi's, Larry, with Frieda hanging back, found his way to Dick Rodgers, who had been accepting extravagant praise from half a dozen friends per minute. Seeing Larry approach, Dick released himself from the grip of one gushing fan, and the two songwriters embraced. "This is one of the greatest shows I've ever seen," Larry said, "and it'll be playing twenty years from now!" [21]

Larry made excuses about attending the opening night party—he had to get Frieda home, after all—and stepped back to make way for another wave of gushers. As Larry took his mother's arm, he passed beneath Alex Gard's caricature of him. It had been Gard's practice to refrain from drawing spouses or theatrical collaborators, in case they broke up; but in the years to come, he would make an exception for Rodgers and Hammerstein. [22]

Larry's return to the Ardsley penthouse with Frieda must have been no less lonely than the night of the *Pal Joey* opening and the advance word on Brooks Atkinson's review. Oscar Hammerstein had been Larry's friend since college, and had, in a way, shown him up, marrying a clear and optimistic worldview with idiomatic, highly singable lyrics. *Oklahoma!*'s director was Rouben Mamoulian, with whom Dick and Larry had collaborated to revolutionize the film musical eleven years earlier in *Love Me Tonight*. And all of it was produced with the undying support of Lawrence Langner and Theresa Helburn, who had given Rodgers and Hart their break in 1925. Larry might have felt betrayed; more likely, he felt obsolete.

Oklahoma! was lauded by the theatergoing public as well as the critics. "The union of two sympathetic temperaments," Cecil Smith wrote, "created the first all-American, non-Broadway musical comedy (or operetta; call it what you will) independent of the manners or traditions of the Viennese comic opera or French opéra-bouffe on the one hand, and Forty-Fourth Street clichés and specifications on the other. *Oklahoma!* turned out to be a people's opera, unpretentious and perfectly modern, but of interest equally to audiences in New York and in Des Moines." [23] Larry Hart's work was of no interest in Des Moines? Ouch. Clifton Fadiman, who had become Hart's friend, attempted to get at the fundamental difference between Rodgers and Hammerstein and Rodgers and Hart:

> It is not only that Mr. Hammerstein's temperament is naturally sunnier than was Larry Hart's. The difference has to do with a change in our temper as a people. With the coming of the forties (and the war) the whole idea of "sophistication" had the air let out of it. We were now compelled to grow up for real. The "knowingness" of *Pal Joey* began to seem very unlike true knowledge. The slick wisdom of the opportunist began to seem inopportune. . . . The Rodgers-Hammerstein purified musical comedy, with its stress on the wholesome, has weaned us away from the indiscretions, with their mild suggestion of the street corner, of the Larry Hart school. One feels some embarrassment, too, the embarrassment that comes of listening to the small boy saying something shocking in the drawing room. [24]

It's as if Larry Hart's work had been consigned to a prewar drawer—smart, clever, bawdier than it needed to be, and now utterly irrelevant. Meanwhile the airwaves were abuzz with *Oklahoma!* On a "Millions for Defense" radio program, featuring Dick and Larry's friend and patron André Kostelanetz, the announcer welcomed special guest Richard Rodgers and grandly placed *Oklahoma!* alongside two previous milestones of American musical theater, *Show Boat* and *Porgy and Bess.* Allan Jones, Mr. Johnny One Note himself, sang "Oh, What a Beautiful Mornin'," stretching the word out as "byoo-teeful." On "Texaco Time," host Fred Allen told special guest Oscar Levant that he'd written a new musical along the lines of *Oklahoma!* "It's called *North Dakota*," Allen drawled. Allen had his chorus sing a few bars. "But Fred, that's 'Oklahoma!'" said Levant. And so it was. The studio audience ate it up. [25]

On April 17, Frieda Hart—daughter of Sophie Moses and Benjamin Isenberg—went into Doctors Hospital suffering intense pain. Just shy of seventy-six, she died eight days later, Easter Sunday. Larry was at first too distraught, then too drunk, to handle any of the funeral arrangements, so Dorothy and Teddy took control. Frieda's funeral was scheduled for 3:00 P.M., April 27, at the Midtown Chapel at Eighty-Fifth Street and Columbus Avenue. That afternoon it took a while to find Frieda's older son, who was pulled out of a local bar.[26] Befogged during the ride out to the Mt. Zion Cemetery plot, Larry saw his mother buried beside his father, his grandfather, an uncle, and two aunts. On the ride back to Manhattan, Larry, seated across from his ninety-two-year-old uncle William Herman, was sober enough to murmur to Teddy, "There's hardly any point to Uncle Willie's going home."[27] (William Herman outlived Larry Hart but died before probate of Larry's will.)

"After the funeral," Mary Campbell remembered, "Lorenz Hart came to the house and went out again unbeknown to anyone. When he returned he was still in a paralyzed condition. Mrs. Theodore Hart took his clothes off and tried to get him to bed, and when she was unable to do so she had him removed to the hospital in his pajamas. . . . I believe he stayed in the hospital four days and then got away again."[28]

After that hospital stay, Larry would never again be sober for twenty-four hours straight, except for those times he returned to the hospital. Frieda's death had snapped his tenuous hold on even the most minimal decorum. Dorothy Hart wrote that Larry had never before had trouble sleeping, no matter where he was or how much he drank, but now he struggled against sleep like a child who equates sleep with death.[29] The booze-induced black-outs became more frequent. Mary Campbell said that Larry now had to drink in the morning to still his shaking hands, and he often remembered nothing about the previous night. "For instance, he would bring men home during the night, men whom he did not know and who were chance acquaintances whom he had picked up at the bars, and on the following day when I spoke to him about those men he denied having had anybody there. Due to the use of alcoholics [*sic*] his mind seemed to wander. He could not carry conversations. He would repeat the same thing many times over."[30]

Now that Frieda was dead, Willy Kron lobbied for Larry to let Big Mary go, after twenty years of employment with the Harts.[31] Although Larry's income in 1941 had amounted to more than $200,000, he was borrowing money from the bank. Kron also said it was imperative that Larry change his will. It was odd: Larry had accepted Kron as his accountant and financial adviser in the first place because Dick Rodgers had said Larry needed Kron. And where was Dick now?

Rodgers was producing—he would do so for another two decades—and writing, but without Larry. In the afterglow of *Oklahoma!*, Oscar Hammerstein had set up his dream musical play, a contemporary, all-black version of Bizet's *Carmen* that he had written on spec a year or so earlier and titled *Carmen Jones*; Billy Rose offered to produce it. This left Dick free for other activities, including trying his hand at a screenplay for *By Jupiter*, which Twentieth Century-Fox had bought. The transfer from stage to screen was being piloted by producer Sol Wurtzel, who had his own ideas—a cast that at one point included Laurel and Hardy, Martha Raye, and Laird Cregar, and new songs by Lew Pollack and Charley Newman.[32] (The project was eventually dropped.)

Larry Hart's name is not on the Rodgers screenplay, and one wonders if he even knew about it. Did Willy Kron bank Larry's share of the Fox movie rights? Kron was monitoring Larry, but was anybody monitoring Kron? Larry seemed dimly aware that the bottle had taken precedence over everything else. Irving Eisenman, a young friend about to join Army intelligence, accompanied Larry one day to Atlantic City. A few weeks earlier Larry had written a letter of recommendation for Eisenman, referring to the subject's "pith, piquancy, and erudition" as well as the "indubitable proof of his patriotism."[33] Now, walking with Eisenman on the Boardwalk after drinking all morning, Larry stopped and clutched his friend's arm. "It's finally happened! I'm having the DTs! I see pink elephants!" The sober Eisenman looked where Larry was looking and saw the same pink elephants etched into the stucco facade of a hotel.[34]

Even waking to a throbbing hangover, Larry had been a news junkie. But it's not clear whether he could still follow the events of the day, or even cared to. In early June, for instance, was he aware that most of Broadway and Hollywood was convinced—correctly, it turned out—that actor Leslie Howard's plane had been shot down? As a horseplayer from way back, did he know that Count Fleet had won at Belmont, taking the Triple Crown? Did he realize that *Stage Door Canteen* had just been released, and that Ray Bolger had not only sung Rodgers and Hart's "The Girl I Love to Leave Behind" in it but danced an elaborate travesty of a close-order drill?[35]

On the evening of June 13, Larry planned to give a birthday dinner for his playwright friend Harry Irving, with Doc Bender joining them. While Larry was out that afternoon, Mary Campbell prepared the meal. Larry arrived home drunk and proceeded to talk, and talk, about Willy Kron's insistence that he change his will.[36] Could Larry have been too preoccupied to notice *By Jupiter* was closing, and not for lack of ticket sales?

Ed Sullivan's column in the *Daily News* reported: "For the first time in 54 weeks, Ray Bolger won't go to work tonight (*By Jupiter* is shuttered, so Bolger is a loafer)."

Dick Rodgers, the supervising producer since Wiman's defection to the Red Cross, saw red. He fired off a letter to Sullivan, who printed it two days later:

> *"By Jupiter is shuttered, so Bolger is a loafer."*
> *I read it in your column, and it's stuff you shouldn't go fer.*
> *Let's read the line correctly—*
> *Here's the way it should be uttered,*
> *Bolger is a loafer, so By Jupiter is shuttered.*
> *P.S.: Gross last week, $21,655. Performers out of work, nearly one hundred.*
> *Love, Richard Rodgers.*[37]

With his terrible tongue and a temper for two, Rodgers was publicly airing his fury at a presumably egotistical leading man for placing his own interests before the show's. He was also probably venting some long-swallowed anger at Bolger from six years earlier when the star of *On Your Toes* sued unsuccessfully to be allowed to leave the road company so he could report to MGM.

In the case of *By Jupiter*, the irreplaceable Bolger had maintained that he was ill and was leaving the show on doctor's orders. In fact he'd given notice more than a month earlier, and the disappointed producer and theater owners had tried to come up with a replacement. "Regarding Ray Bolger leaving the show and not coming back to it next season," J. J. Shubert wrote to his brother, Lee, on May 5, 1943, "it is a pity these people are always starred instead of featuring them. I think Buster West would do very well indeed as he is a nice dancer and has a very pleasant personality."[38] Buster West was nice-looking and could entertain audiences by dancing on ice skates or roller skates, but he was not Ray Bolger. Word went around that Bolger simply wanted more money. For a few weeks Bolger, whose departure swelled the ranks of the unemployed, was the most resented man in the theater district. "There were red faces on Broadway a little later," Deems Taylor wrote, "when it transpired that at the request of the USO he had made a secret flight to the South Seas to entertain the troops."[39]

That third week in June was a rough one for Bolger. For Larry Hart, too, though he must have been convinced he was doing the right thing. On June 17, at 1:00 P.M., Larry went to see his attorney Abe Wattenberg at Wattenberg's office at 1250 Sixth Avenue. It was the meeting Willy Kron had pushed for. As Wattenberg would later testify, Larry's will was rewritten to add bequests to two aunts and an uncle (Willie Herman), with no mention of what else might have been altered. Wattenberg then called in two women, Helen Schoen and Sadie Rosenfeld, each in the employ of Chappell, to witness Hart's signature. Larry said he wanted to phone his physician Jacques Fischl, who had been treating him recently whenever he was checked into Doctors Hospital, because Fischl was now a patient there recuperating from a June 10 automobile accident. "In my presence Mr. Hart called said hospital," Wattenberg remembered in a deposition at the end of that year, "and spoke to Dr. Fischl inquiring about the latter's health and stating that he would visit him. He then left my office."[40]

Jacques Fischl confirmed that Larry visited him in the middle of the afternoon at Doctors Hospital. "Without any hesitation," Dr. Fischl testified, "I can state that at the time of his visit Mr. Hart was sober and showed not the slightest trace of intoxication."[41]

Perhaps Fischl was telling the truth. Perhaps Wattenberg was also telling the truth, altering Larry Hart's will only as he was directed to. When Larry next went home, however, it was the early morning of June 18; his hands were shaking, his eyes were bloodshot, and he needed Big Mary to settle him down. Larry told her that Willy Kron had promised he would see to it that Teddy and Dorothy Hart would never put him in an insane asylum.[42] An effective gaslighting depends, of course, not only on the victim's being spooked by things invisible and insidious, but on the illusion that the agent perpetrating the spooking should be the victim's savior. Teddy and Dorothy were being forcibly removed from Larry's largesse, if not his affections, by people outside the family, and the trick had been to make it appear that Larry himself was removing them.

By the time Henry Myers ran into Larry that summer, Mary Campbell had been removed, too. She retreated to Harlem, leaving Larry alone to roam around the Ardsley penthouse. That he had probably never boiled a pot of water, let alone prepared a meal, was far less of a handicap than his bottomless need to be around people. To a man who had grown up in a houseful of merrymaking relatives, friends, and servants, he might as well have been stranded in the Sahara Desert. "I don't remember precisely where or how I happened to encounter him," Myers wrote; "I only recall that he was staggeringly, incoherently drunk. That's when I was first aware of his compulsion to keep talking. He had liked, a long time before, to sing songs he was writing, but this was not the same thing. Now his words made no sense." Myers, who had known Larry for more than thirty years, got him to tell him where he

420 ★ A Ship Without a Sail

was living. Myers took him home and put him to bed. Larry mumbled something about lunch next day at Lindy's. Sure, Larry, sure.

Naturally, Myers was surprised when Larry showed up. Myers was already seated at the table that Lindy's had set aside for Larry. The waiter, well-acquainted with his customer, served Larry two beers at once, while Myers, a nondrinker, ordered food. At the end of the meal the waiter declined to let Myers pay—no one else paid when Larry Hart was in the restaurant—so Myers stopped near the cashier to buy Larry his favorite brand of cigars. But by the time Myers had the cigars in hand, Larry had vanished.[43]

CHAPTER 24

And Yet I Was Untrue to None of Them

THE EARLY summer evenings of 1943 seemed to go on forever because of the dimouts. Some Broadway theaters routinely cheated the dimout rules by lighting up their marquees in the half hour before the curtain went up. But most New Yorkers adhered to regulations—Londoners had been doing so for four years—and adjusted, though not always easily. In Manhattan there were more traffic fatalities. "Had he worn white, he might be back," went a cautionary verse, "But now he's gone. His friends wear black." Drivers often couldn't see pedestrians, who sometimes bumped into other pedestrians, alternately antagonizing and finding each other. It was warm, exciting, and a little dangerous.

It was on one of these long, sultry evenings of semidarkness, approximately three months after *Oklahoma!* began its trot into musical theater history, that Larry Hart joined Alan Jay Lerner and Frederick Loewe at Loewe's apartment on East Fifty-Seventh Street. The three men were drinking and talking when a blackout turned the room pitch dark; some electricity remained, however. As Lerner remembered it:

The only light came from Larry's cigar. Fritz [Loewe] turned on the radio and an orchestra was playing something from *Oklahoma!* The end of the cigar flashed brighter and brighter with accelerated puffs. Fritz immediately switched to another station. Again someone was playing a song from *Oklahoma!* And Larry's cigar grew brighter and the puffs became faster. It happened three times and then Fritz turned off the radio. The glow from the cigar sub-sided and the breathing so slow the cigar almost went out. The whole incident probably took less than two minutes and during it not a word was said, but I wept for him in the dark. The moment the lights came on Larry continued the conversation that had been interrupted by the blackout without a trace of what had happened in his voice or on his face.[1]

Despite Rodgers's chronic disapproval of him, Larry had never bad-mouthed his former partner, and he wouldn't do so now. But his pain was evident to Lerner and Loewe.

So a phone call from Dick in that last week of June came as something of a lifebuoy thrown to a drowning man. Dick and Herb Fields were talk-ing again about updating *Connecticut Yankee*: William Gaxton and Victor Moore wouldn't be part of it, but how about Vivienne Segal as Queen Mor-gan Le Fay? Segal's participation was no less alluring to Larry than a case of Châteauneuf-du-Pape.

Rodgers had a press release prepared. On July 1 *The New York Times* re-ported that *Connecticut Yankee* was scheduled for a September revival, with Rodgers producing solo for the first time. "The book will be tinkered with by Mr. Fields and Mr. Hart," said the *Times*.[2]

Rodgers's timing was curious. He explained it with a charming story about being invited by the boys' old friend Jacob Wilk to a Warner Bros. screening of *The Adventures of Mark Twain*. The film was a production of Jesse Lasky, who had announced that he was devoting the remainder of his career to mak-ing pictures of outstanding Americans; his previous film had been the Acad-emy Award–winning *Sergeant York*; his current production was *Rhapsody in Blue*. Rodgers was interested in *The Adventures of Mark Twain* because Fred-ric March, who had been a close friend since his appearance in *The Melody Man*, had the title role. Rodgers was moved by the film. When the lights came up in the screening room, his eyes were blurred with tears, but he could still make out Charles Tressler Lark, the attorney who had sold Rodgers, Hart, and Fields the rights to produce *A Connecticut Yankee* sixteen years earlier. Rodgers said he approached the lawyer with the idea of restaging the show.[3] *The Adventures of Mark Twain* had actually completed filming several months earlier and would not be released until May 1944. But Rodgers used that serendipitous sighting of Lark to publicly mark the beginning of his renewed interest in reviving *Connecticut Yankee*—interest that he'd actually been expressing, off and on, for years.

A cynical view of Rodgers's timing would be that, having urged Kron and Wattenberg to persuade Larry to make a new will and name Rodgers and Kron as executors, Rodgers needed to keep Larry serene. When Dorothy and Teddy Hart heard that Rodgers had called Larry about *Connecticut Yankee*, they believed this to be a delusion of Larry's. After all, the runaway numbers of *Oklahoma!* dwarfed any commercial achievement by a Rodgers & Hart show; why would Rodgers want to return to the less successful collaboration? A more generous view would be that Rodgers wanted to work with Larry because he still loved him and knew it could be beneficial to his health. It might even be argued that, by suggesting they revive *Connecticut Yankee* and write something new for Vivienne Segal, Rodgers was prolonging Larry's life.

In midsummer Larry moved out of the Ardsley and set up quarters at the Hotel Delmonico, at Park Avenue and Fifty-Ninth Street. Dorothy Hart wrote that the move was at Willy Kron's insistence, presumably as another cost-cutting measure, for Larry no longer needed a large apartment and certainly not a penthouse.[4] But he could not have continued to endure the loneliness of the Ardsley anyway. Barring a hideaway he might have leased at one time or another—Meryle Secrest wrote that Larry kept a place at the Ritz—it was Larry's first residence on the East Side.[5]

The updating of *A Connecticut Yankee* took Rodgers, Hart, and Fields longer than Rodgers had anticipated, so a September opening was out of the question. New scenes had to be constructed. Larry worked with Herb Fields to make the contemporary references reflect 1943 rather than 1927. By now Fields had written as many shows with Cole Porter as he had with Dick and Larry; he still idolized Larry, but he was no less successful and, like Dick, had shown Larry that he could produce a hit show in collaboration with someone else.[6] In 1943 the war could not be ignored, so for the prologue (still set in Hartford), the protagonist became Lt. Martin Barrett, USN, and the principal female role (Segal's) became Lt. Fay Merrill, WAVE.

At least four songs from the 1927 production, including "My Heart Stood Still" and "Thou Swell," would be used for the 1943 production. To write the others, Larry was driven up to Connecticut to stay a few days with the Rodgers family, where both Dick and Dorothy could watch over him. "I don't think he took a drink the entire time," Dick recalled, incidentally buttressing the Surrogate's Court testimony he would give over the next few years. One story, possibly apocryphal, is that Larry, bored by their working sessions, bribed young Linda Rodgers to hide him in her tree house and swore her to secrecy so he wouldn't be found.[7] Of the new songs Dick and Larry wrote in Connecticut, a few of them were close to top-drawer Rodgers & Hart. Lyrically, "Camelot Samba," like "Thou Swell," wove Arthurian language and syntax into contemporary vernacular:

> *Forsooth, old Camelot is like Brazil,*
> *So we can Samba, 'tis a thrill*
> *'Twill kill thee.*
> *In truth, ye Latin lovers be not wrong*
> *To dance their merry way along—*

Musically, according to Hart scholar Scott Willis, the song moved from a Mozartian daintiness to a swinging samba style. "Ye Lunchtime Follies" was a radio program heard by workers at a munitions factory, circa A.D. 543. "You Always Love the Same Girl" is Martin and King Arthur agreeing that each love object, despite vast differences, turns out to have something similar that the lover is inevitably drawn to. "The moment that you meet her / You know you've met before," Arthur sings, harking back to "Where or When." When George Jean Nathan heard the song, he wondered if Larry's lyrics didn't owe a debt to the French revue writer, active during the Great War, who called himself simply Rip. Under contract to the Théâtre des Capucines, M. Rip wrote a popular show titled *As You Were*, which was about a man trying to escape unfaithful women and war, but no matter where he went he kept encountering both. (Charles B. Cochran produced an English version at the Pavilion Theatre in London.)[8] Perhaps Larry knew the show.

While these songs were being written, Rodgers was doing his bit as producer of *Connecticut Yankee*'s revival. He got Warner Bros. to put up 50 percent of the backing in exchange for 25 percent of the profit—a deal so sweet it was rumored the studio wanted Dick Powell to star as Martin. Rodgers filled out the remaining 50 percent of the budget with investments from his wife, Dorothy; from Mrs. Marshall Field; once again from Howard S. Cullman, who had been modestly rewarded for his *By Jupiter* investment; from Adele R. Levy, whose money came from Sears, Roebuck; and from Al Greenstone, whose money came from printing and selling souvenir programs in Broadway theaters.[9] By early September, with the *Connecticut Yankee* financing in place, Dick and Larry were ready to look at chorus girls and boys, who were asked to appear at the Martin Beck Theatre to audition. Dick

Foran, a big-band singer turned cowboy-movie actor, was engaged to star as Martin opposite Vivienne Segal. There had been talk of Elia Kazan, one of the driving forces of the Group Theatre, directing; but John C. Wilson was brought in to stage the show when Kazan elected to direct the new Kurt Weill musical *One Touch of Venus*, with lyrics by Ogden Nash and a book by S. J. Perelman.

One Touch of Venus starred Mary Martin. One of Martin's costars was Teddy Hart, who took Dorothy with him to Boston on September 16 for the show's tryouts. The Harts felt pretty good—hey, look at us! swank hotel accommodations!—until Larry phoned from Doctors Hospital. He was there to be treated for "alcoholic excess," and probably did not reveal to his brother and sister-in-law that he was also being treated for gonorrheal urethritis (suggesting he'd been sexually active in recent weeks).[10] Over the phone Larry merrily sang some of the lyrics he'd written for the revival. The lyric he was proudest of was "To Keep My Love Alive," in which Queen Morgan Le Fay (Segal) recounts how she disposed of each of her husbands. The whole idea is presented in the verse:

> *I've been married and married,*
> *And often I've sighed,*
> *I'm never a bridesmaid,*
> *I'm always the bride.*
> *I never divorced them—*
> *I hadn't the heart.*
> *Yet remember these sweet words,*
> *"Till death do us part."*

As he so often did, Larry laughed at his own work. But he was just getting started. The first refrain begins:

> *I married many men,*
> *A ton of them,*
> *And yet I was untrue to none of them*
> *Because I bumped off ev'ry one of them*
> *To keep my love alive. . . .*

Larry supplied several more choruses, each one detailing the demise of a royal spouse:

I thought Sir George had possibilities,
But his flirtations made me ill at ease,
And when I'm ill at ease
I kill at ease
To keep my love alive. . . .

I caught Sir James with his protectoress,
The rector's wife,
I mean the rectoress.
His heart stood still—angina pectoris
To keep my love alive.

And:

Sir Ethelbert would use profanity,
His language drove me near insanity,
So once again I served humanity
To keep my love alive.

From the first note, Rodgers's melody was playful and characteristic of their old sugar-and-spice combination—the razor-edged words sweetened by the golden honey music.

Rehearsals began September 27 at the Martin Beck and were under way when Larry was released from Doctors Hospital. He wrote at least one more lyric, "Can't You Do a Friend a Favor?" for Segal and Dick Foran. Its verse, though not technically dazzling by Hart standards, shows Larry stripped almost naked:

You can count your friends
On the fingers of your hand.
If you're lucky you have two.
I have just two friends,
That is all that I demand.
Only two—just me and you.
And a good friend heeds a friend
When a good friend needs a friend.

Rehearsing "To Keep My Love Alive," Segal quickly made the song her own. But she was irked when Rodgers pushed for her to end each successive chorus on an increasingly lower, nearly impossible D.

"Dick," Segal complained, "if I go any lower I'll grow balls!"

"Then you'll be the only one in the company who's got 'em," said Rodgers, taking a swipe, Segal recalled, at "these flaming chorus boys who could fly through windows."[11]

With Rodgers preoccupied with getting *A Connecticut Yankee* onstage, and Teddy and Dorothy consumed with *One Touch of Venus*, Larry had no supervision to stop him from drinking himself blind. In Philadelphia *A Connecticut Yankee* settled into the Forrest Theatre. Dorothy Hart came down at the behest of Dick Rodgers to keep an eye on Larry, who was sharing a hotel suite with Herb Fields. Fields was irritated that Rodgers's name was all over the revival as its producer; Fields remembered a time when his father was the most important person on a show and Dick was the hired melodist. Oscar Hammerstein was in town to oversee tryouts of *Carmen Jones* at the Erlanger Theatre, and the contrast between the dignified, quietly commanding Hammerstein and the frantic, confused Hart was striking to everyone—even to Larry. More pathetic than puckish, all he seemed to look forward to was the next drink. He mislaid his latest custom-made overcoat. Dorothy took him to Wanamaker's and got him a coat off the rack—in the boys' department. She knew this one, too, would be lost any day now.[12]

Kron, promising to look after Larry, advised Dorothy to return to New York, where Teddy was appearing in *One Touch of Venus*. The "chief comedian" of the show, as *The New York Times* called him, Teddy still had no idea that his brother feared being institutionalized by his own family.

In Philadelphia *A Connecticut Yankee* went through the usual growing pains. Dick Foran was smooth and likable onstage but, after eleven years in Hollywood, was having trouble projecting without a microphone.[13] Vera-Ellen, who had appeared as a dancing Minerva in *By Jupiter*, was playing Mistress Evelyn La Rondelle, to whom the deliberately treacly "Evelyn" is crooned during "Ye Lunchtime Follies"; but "Evelyn" seems to have been cut at the Forrest Theatre. A week into tryouts, Rodgers became president of the Dramatists Guild—the first author of musicals to be named to the position. It was another event in which Larry, lyricist and lifelong dramatist, was overlooked.

Even if he were genuinely inclined to do so, Willy Kron couldn't control Larry. At some point near the end of the Philadelphia tryouts, Larry sprained his ankle. Exasperated with this man who was still, in effect, his writing partner, Dick asked Jacques Fischl to come to Philadelphia. Dick wouldn't phone the one person, Mary Campbell, who might have been able to calm Larry and keep him sober for a few hours. Fischl arrived with a nurse and, with Harry Irving accompanying them on the train, took Larry to New York and checked him into Doctors Hospital.[14]

On Tuesday, November 16, with *A Connecticut Yankee* scheduled to open at the Martin Beck the following night, Larry phoned Dorothy Hart and asked her to arrange with Jules Glaenzer to buy a gold cigarette case for Herb Fields and "something special" for Vivienne Segal, and to charge it to Larry's account with Cartier. Worried about this extravagance, however, Dorothy first checked with Willy Kron.

"Don't buy anything!" said Kron. "He can't afford it!" That was the end of that.[15]

Expensive or not, Larry arranged for orchids to be sent to Dorothy Rodgers for opening night.

By the following afternoon, with the sky threatening rain, Larry was well into the bottle. He showed up at Teddy and Dorothy's Fifty-Seventh Street apartment with a dozen pairs of opening night tickets to be passed out to friends and relatives. Larry had every intention of being there, which could only mean trouble for Dick, who in fact had instructed the Martin Beck's stage manager to remove him from the theater if necessary. Since the tryouts in Philadelphia—no, really since Frieda died in April—Larry had become a runagate drunk whose behavior was no longer predictable.

Larry invited Helen Ford to attend opening night with him. Ford, volunteering as a mistress of ceremonies at the Stage Door Canteen (housed in what was formerly the Little Theatre, in the Forty-fourth Street Theatre Building, in a space donated by Lee Shubert), went to fetch him at the Hotel Delmonico. Ford found Larry, already plastered, in the hotel's dining room sitting with a young couple. Showing no interest in food, he ordered more drinks and assessed himself "still the best lyric writer in town." Ford steered him out onto a rainy Park Avenue and into a cab to West Forty-Fifth Street.[16]

The first-night crowd was huddled beneath the Martin Beck marquee. Years earlier Larry would have taken immense pleasure in having the theater district so alive with the work of his friends and family. At the St. James,

Oklahoma! was still the toughest ticket in town to procure. Teddy was making *One Touch of Venus* audiences laugh at the Imperial. At the Broadway Theatre, Lou Walters was presenting *Artists and Models*, a revue with songs by Danny Shapiro and Larry's old pals Milton Pascal and Phil Charig; in her first stage appearance since the Lisbon plane crash, Jane Froman, unable to walk on her own power but as lovely as ever, sat in billowing gowns and sang. But all this neighborhood activity didn't much matter to Larry anymore.

Dorothy Hart had asked Harry Irving and Larry's cousin Billy Friedberg, a Broadway publicist who maintained an office on Forty-Second Street, to keep an eye on Larry. But the marquee's lights were dim, open umbrellas blocking perspectives high and low, and Larry managed to duck through the crowd. In the next few minutes he checked his overcoat without being detected by the management. Helen Ford and Dorothy Hart went backstage to find Dick Rodgers, who was stunned to learn Larry was in the theater.

A few minutes later, when the *Connecticut Yankee* overture began, Dick coiled himself into his usual last-row-center-aisle seat next to his wife.

"Larry's here," he whispered.

Dorothy Rodgers's hand went to her mouth. A few minutes later she felt Larry's hand brush the top of her head. He was in *his* usual opening night spot, in the gangway in the back of the theater, pacing and jingling the coins in his pocket. "Is very nervous at his own opening nights," Sidney Skolsky had written of Larry more than fifteen years earlier, and it was still true. "Paces the back aisles continuously. . . . During intermission he shaves himself to look neat for the second act." [17] This was not the night for Larry to be wielding a razor. Dorothy Rodgers turned and caught Larry's eyes, which stared at her emptily before he moved away.

Larry began to sing along with Segal on "To Keep My Love Alive"—not yet loud enough to be intrusive, just enough to be supporting his favorite actress in his own way. After a reprise of "My Heart Stood Still," he hurried out of the theater, not bothering with his overcoat, in advance of the intermission crowd. He went to a nearby bar—it could have been Larry Bergin's or Ralph's, which were both on the block—and returned to the theater soaked by rain and still more drink. As "Ye Lunchtime Follies" gave way to "Can't You Do a Friend a Favor?" his unsolicited accompaniment grew increasingly loud and began to draw shushes from theater patrons. "Give me a man who sings at his work," wrote Dorothy Fields in her diary—perhaps Larry was simply singing at his work. [18] Acting on orders he'd received from Dick, the Martin

Beck stage manager had two men escort Larry out to the lobby. He was soon out on the street.

Dorothy Hart took Larry back to the Harts' apartment, where he fell asleep in his clothes on the couch. She waited for Teddy to come home from the Imperial Theatre. She was just then experiencing the overwhelming nausea she feared was symptomatic of an ulcer but was actually morning sickness. When Teddy walked in, she could tell he'd already been alerted by the doorman, who had been tipped often and well during previous visits by the little man on the couch. Checking intermittently on Larry, who was sweating through what appeared to be a very troubled sleep, the Harts talked about how to address this latest episode. Doctors Hospital again? Another psychiatrist? Should they consult with Kron? Could Larry *afford* a psychiatrist these days? The Harts finally fell asleep.

When they awoke, the couch was empty.

Larry couldn't be found—not at the Delmonico, not at Lindy's, not in any of the bars he was known to patronize. It's not clear whether he saw any of the *Connecticut Yankee* reviews, most of them admiring, particularly of Segal and the lyric for "To Keep My Love Alive." Yet Robert Garland, writing in the *Journal American*, mentioned Segal and Rodgers but not Hart.[19] It was painful enough to be patronized for one's physical stature but thoroughly unacceptable to have one's professional stature neglected.

By midafternoon on Tuesday there was a break in the rain. But as evening approached, the wind kicked up: pedestrians leaned into it; in an alleyway a garbage can flipped over, its metallic clatter heard a block away. Still searching for Larry, Dorothy Hart phoned Billy Friedberg, who phoned Fritz Loewe. Knowing Larry as well as he did, Loewe went out and found him sitting in the gutter outside a bar on Eighth Avenue.

"Larry?" said Loewe, leaning down to him. Larry's eyes were so glassy, it was difficult to tell if he recognized Loewe. "Come on, Larry, let's get you home."

Loewe hailed a cab and got him back to the Delmonico. "[Fritz] made Larry promise he would go upstairs and go to bed," Lerner wrote of that night, "and he stayed in the cab until he saw him enter the hotel. Then he went home. Larry, true to his promise, went up to his room and got into bed."[20]

Next day the Harts got him into Doctors Hospital. Larry was assigned a room on the fourth floor. Jacques Fischl arrived before 5:00 P.M. to examine him.

❧   ❧   ❧

"This is a readmission of a forty-eight-year-old chronic alcoholic who has been drinking heavily for the past week," began the illness report:

> He reenters with a history of chilly sensations, generalized myalgia, dyspnoea and weakness and fever of 102.
>
> Physical examination reveals a well-developed and nourished white male, appearing acutely ill. Face flushed, alcoholic breath, profuse sweating, and a slight cyanosia. Head and neck grossly negative. Lungs bilateral dullness at base. Abdomen distended.

Larry's breathing was so labored that it was decided he needed an oxygen tent. Disoriented and restless, he tried to kick the tent off. Demerol was administered to sedate him and sulfa therapy was begun. One of the doctors sent a tube down Larry's trachea to aspirate mucus that sounded as though it was strangling him. Friends and relatives gathered on the fourth floor, though the Harts were perplexed that they weren't permitted to see him. On Saturday night Dick and Dorothy Rodgers attended the opening of *Winged Victory*, Moss Hart's show about the Army Air Corps, as well as the opening night party atop the Hotel Astor.[21] Life went on. Others continued the vigil at Doctors Hospital. Larry was sedated but could not rest, his agitation apparent to the nurses and doctors monitoring him. Maybe he had a new lyric on his mind, or maybe this old one:

> *My friend the night*
> *Looks down on me*
> *And watches while I sleep.*
> *He holds me tight,*
> *My friend the night.*

He wrote it at Metro in 1933. It was never used in a film, but he hadn't forgotten it.

On Sunday Larry's white blood count plummeted, so sulfa therapy was discontinued. His breathing remained labored. Irene Gallagher, of Chappell, asked producer John Golden to phone his friend Eleanor Roosevelt, who interceded with the War Production Board and arranged to have the new wonder drug penicillin, developed a couple of years earlier at Oxford University but still scarce, flown in. In the middle of the afternoon of November 22, 80,000 Oxford units of penicillin were administered intravenously.[22]

Larry began to mumble. A nurse—possibly a Miss Sandberg, whose name appears on the hospital document—made sure he didn't kick off his oxygen tent. What was he saying? Larry's ancestor Heinrich Heine was known to say on his deathbed, "*Dieu me pardonnerai, c'est son métier.*" "God will forgive me because it's His job to." (In the Jewish version of Heine's last remark, there is often the tagline, "He has something else to do?") In 1929 Larry's friend Oscar Hammerstein had written a lyric that is perched on the nexus of all philosophical inquiry:

> *Why was I born?*
> *Why am I living?*
> *What do I get?*
> *What am I giving?*

Larry's final question, as reported by the nurse, was a variation on the theme. "What have I lived for?" he said.

At 9:08 P.M. on November 22, air raid sirens howled, signaling a full-scale blackout. Streetlights were extinguished, shop window curtains drawn. The oxygen feeding Larry had its own generator in the hospital. At 9:30, however, he stopped breathing. Fischl emerged from Larry's room and shook his head. "He's gone," he said. Seven minutes later, lights returned to the city, and at 9:57 the all-clear signal was sounded.[23]

Officially, Larry Hart died of bilateral bronchopneumonia. His death notice, signed by Fischl, contains a curious detail that contradicts Dorothy Hart's claim that she and Teddy had been kept out of Larry's room in the last four days of his life. "Brother at Bedside," the notice says. Had Teddy been there after all, comforting his brother? Or was Fischl conspiring with the estate's executors to show that the Harts were included in Larry's final hours?

The body was removed to the Universal Chapel at 597 Lexington Avenue (at Fifty-Second Street). Through the evening of November 23 mourners came to view Larry lying in a small casket—a ritual he would have shunned if he'd thought of it, for he hated funerals and all they entailed. Teddy went on that night in *One Touch of Venus*, so Dorothy Hart, still contending with nausea, was at the chapel representing the family. Dick and Dorothy Rodgers, each dressed in perfectly tailored mourning clothes, went up to the casket. Dick had come to resent his dead partner to the point of revulsion. Many years later, after writing his own lyrics for the musical *No Strings*, Dick, in a rush of self-satisfaction, sighed to Diahann Carroll, "You can't imagine how wonderful it feels to have written this score and not have to search all over the globe for that little fag."[24] And yet, whatever animosities had bloomed between them, the two men had once been dearer to each other than the rain is to the earth below. Now, at the Universal Chapel, the normally undemonstrative Dick took one last look at his partner of twenty-five years, then turned away and collapsed, sobbing, into his wife's arms.[25]

Vivienne Segal wasn't there because she was appearing as Queen Morgan Le Fay in *A Connecticut Yankee*. Distraught, as so many of Larry's friends were, Segal the trouper was playing to a sold-out house. She managed to get through her first number, "This Is My Night to Howl." Her second number was "To Keep My Love Alive."

"I blew one of the couplets," Segal recalled, "and I dragged in a name from another chorus and filled it in. Then I couldn't remember what I had done when it came time for the second chorus. And all I could do was—being the Queen—I just stopped singing and I said, 'I'm so sorry' to the audience and I walked offstage." The audience murmured, not with disapproval but with a kind of support, coaxing her back to try once more. Segal had written on a proscenium wall the names of the several husbands Larry Hart had eliminated so cleverly in rhyme; after scanning them for a moment, Segal returned to the stage and, with the audience's encouragement, started the number all over again. "And I remembered every bit of it. But oh, what a horrible moment it was!"[26]

The New York funeral, presided over by Nathan Perilman, associate rabbi at Temple Emanu-El, began at 12:30 on the twenty-fourth and proceeded without music. Perilman read Psalm 19, whose opening lines—"The heavens are telling of the glory of God / and the firmament proclaims his handiwork"—are echoed by "Mountain Greenery." Psalm 121, a Song of Ascents, was followed by John Greenleaf Whittier's "Snow-bound":

A careless boy that night he seemed;
    But at his desk he had the look
And air of one who wisely schemed,
    And hostage from the future took
    In trained thought and lore of book.

It was a quick service—perhaps too quick for anyone to eulogize Larry in any depth. In less than half an hour the funeral cortege departed for Queens.[27]

When the mourners returned to Manhattan, somebody shared his copy of that day's *Variety*:

Larry Hart's Death in N.Y. at 47 [*sic*] Ends G&S Partnership with Rodgers: Rodgers and Hart's expertness as songwriting artisans was w.k. in the music business. They did their stuff from a business viewpoint with no chi-chi about the "muse" or inspiration.[28]

Someone else picked up the *Journal American*; inside, there was dependable Dorothy Kilgallen riffing on Thanksgiving eve:

We could, in turning to the lighter things, give thanks for the romance-laden sighs caused by every breath Frank Sinatra takes in public. . . . For the way Vivienne Segal sings "To Keep My Love Alive."[29]

The Harts went home to Fifty-Seventh Street. In the next few days they would clean out Larry's quarters at the Delmonico, although there wasn't much, and contend with "the awful reverberating thunder of his absence," a line that F. Scott Fitzgerald had tried out in the unfinished *The Last Tycoon*.[30] Two days later, at Temple Israel in Hollywood, a memorial service for Larry was attended by a hundred people, the majority of them songwriters. While the mourners greeted each other and took their seats, an organist played Rodgers & Hart songs, and it didn't matter that nobody was singing the lyrics because everyone knew them anyway. Rabbi Max Nussbaum read the eulogy in English and the cantor sang in Hebrew.[31] When the service was over the mourners emerged from the synagogue and lingered, talking about Larry and how he'd helped so many of them years ago, when he was at Paramount and Metro. Beginning at sundown some of them would be observing the Sabbath. Eventually they got into their cars and drove home.

Perhaps because Hart was only forty-eight, and perhaps because his decline was protracted and not subtle, his death has acquired barnacles of myth. Josh Logan wrote, "Larry was found dead in a gutter, having drowned in his own regurgitation."[32] Marjorie Jane, one of the youthful gang in *Babes in Arms*, remembered Hart as committing suicide "just after the opening of one of his shows, and he thought it was going to be a failure and it was such a success."[33] Both memories are false, yet both are fundamentally true. Larry had been slowly killing himself over the past half decade, and when Fritz Loewe found him in the early morning hours of November 19, he was probably past saving. "Larry was a fey creature," said Rouben Mamoulian, surely intending to describe him as elfin, visionary, out of this world; but did Mamoulian also intend to invoke the ancient Scottish meaning of "fey": *fated to die?*[34] Perhaps he did.

At the dawn of the twentieth century Larry Hart was receiving an excellent classical education, but he was of the wrong pedigree required for most American professions; he was, after all, Jewish and the issue of Max Hart, career con artist. Fortunately, Hart came of age in an era when the music and movie businesses were young and wild and not yet structured to bar anyone who could put on a show. "Society at large is less particular about those who *entertain* it," Parker Tyler wrote (the italics are his), "than about those it *receives at home.*" Tyler referred to the creed of show business as the Universal Church. Show business, according to Gerald Mast, was "the risky crapshoot shunned by both the moral and fiscal establishment," open to talented immigrants or the children of immigrants—in Larry Hart's time a preponderance of them Jews. This made it a quick way out of the ghetto and onto that new neon-blazed avenue of abundance known as Broadway.[35] Jews were welcome in the musical theater if they could delight an audience; and, much later, homosexuals were welcome, too. In the first third of the twentieth century, Jews and homosexuals began to shape musical theater.

"The two pioneering forces of modern sensibility are Jewish moral seriousness and homosexual aestheticism and irony," Susan Sontag wrote in her essay "Notes on Camp."[36] Jewish moral seriousness (goes the simplified version of the argument) emerged first from the Diaspora, then from the Holocaust; homosexual aestheticism and irony are the natural outgrowth of being forced to hide, or to at least live on the margins of a culture, and view the straight world through lenses that have been of necessity ground into unusual sharpness. But Sontag's aphorism might apply more to herself than to others who happened to be Jewish and homosexual, including Larry Hart. Hart was sincere but rarely serious; he worked in the days of musical *comedy*, before Rodgers and Hammerstein made the phrase seem outmoded, and he believed in it; he was moral without ever being morally serious. He sidestepped the ponderables of "taste," gay or straight, and he'd be the first to advise going easy on the irony, especially in the theater. England's is a culture of irony, but Larry knew that irony had—still has—limited theatrical traction in America.

When Larry Hart began to write lyrics, in the second decade of the twentieth century, most American musical comedies took as their models the often numbingly witless lyrics of operetta. Even as a boy Larry knew he could do better by following Yeats's directive to take our stories from the ancients and our speech from our contemporaries. It took him awhile—he and the perennially fertile Dick Rodgers had to find each other first—but he finally hauled musical theater into the 1920s.

"Hammerstein pointed out something to me," said Stephen Sondheim, whose criticisms of Hart's laziest work were not prompted, he insisted, by his being raised by the Hammersteins, "which at the tender age of fourteen I didn't fully comprehend, which is that Larry Hart freed American lyrics from the stilted middle-European operetta technique, into a natural form of speech."[37]

"Larry Hart made all lyricists a little braver," said Fred Ebb (*Cabaret*, "New York, New York").[38] After Hart's lyrics were heard on Broadway, the old high-flown words just wouldn't do anymore. The characters Larry wrote for were rarely the extravagant, swooning sweethearts of operetta but women and men who argued and kissed and frequently felt sorry for themselves. Sometimes they were German, sometimes Chinese; most often they were American. Sometimes they were middle-aged ("Old Enough to Love") though more often they were young. They were not only lovers but frisky playmates ("Manhattan," "Mountain Greenery") and they could have a great time even when they were furious with each other ("I Wish I Were in Love Again").[39] They were furious with themselves, too, whether descending into self-torture ("Glad to Be Unhappy") or paralyzing perplexity ("Spring Is Here"). The emotions Hart coaxed from his characters were rarely simple, and yet they continue to touch us because they're so recognizable. We prize Oscar Hammerstein's lyrics for their optimism and the imputation of decency to all women and men. We admire Ira Gershwin's lyrics for their unmatchable combination of vividness and understatement, Johnny Mercer's for their personal and evocative imagery, and Yip Harburg's for their playfulness and political passion. Of the lyricists who consistently showed what Richard Rodgers called that "pinwheel brilliance," however, only Cole Porter was seen as Larry Hart's equal.

And yet Porter runs cooler than Larry Hart. "Cole Porter was all about sex," Hugh Martin said. "Larry was about love."[40] Porter's lyrics greet you at the party, and it's endlessly amusing to sit with him as he pokes fun at his fellow guests, all of them well turned out and comfortable. Hart's lyrics disclose what it's like to be excluded from that party: to be standing outside looking in; to feel slovenly, no matter how nattily you might be dressed; to feel undesirable and insignificant. No other lyricist has ranged so intelligently—or emotionally—between the extremes of enthralling new romance and lonely, unforgiving desolation.

The architect Louis Kahn famously said, "The creation of art is not the fulfillment of a need but the creation of a need. The world never needed Beethoven's Fifth Symphony until he created it. Now we could not live without it." In much the same way, a world without the songs of Rodgers and Hart now seems unimaginable. Their catalogue occupies the core of the Great American Songbook, which, in this twenty-first century, is gradually becoming America's classical music.

Larry Hart is buried near his parents in the family plot in Mt. Zion Cemetery in Maspeth, Queens. To get there from Manhattan you can take any one of several subways to Queens Plaza and then hop the Q-67 bus to Maurice and Fifty-Fourth Avenues; the cemetery entrance is up the block. By car, take the Long Island Expressway exit at Maurice Avenue. In fact, Mt. Zion is close enough to the L.I.E. to hear, practically around the clock, the scrannel, trafficky sounds in the distance. But if you're there to see the lyricist's grave, none of that clamor can make you forget the beauty and wit of so many Rodgers & Hart songs. And you know that, several feet beneath the headstone marked *Lorenz Hart*, the plain, undersized casket contains a giant.

In Appreciation

Researching Lorenz Hart's life and work and making this book, I was helped by many people—many at the New York Public Library (NYPL), where much of *A Ship Without a Sail* was written, and several at the Margaret Herrick Library, Academy of Motion Picture Arts & Sciences (AMPAS). Inevitably, I will have omitted some names; the omissions are inadvertent.

Warm thanks to: Debby Applegate, Peter Asch (Bobst Library, NYU), David Atchison (20th Century Fox), Kevyne Baar (Tamiment Library, NYU), Stephen Barr (Writers House), Susan Brady (Beinecke Library, Yale University), Charlie Chu, Kenneth Cobb (New York Municipal Archives), Tara Craig (Butler Library, Columbia University), Lisa Darms (Fales Library, NYU), Lynne DeGiacomo (Cohasset Historical Society), Jim Di Giovanni, Ted Dodd (20th Century Fox), David Ehrenstein, Wayne Furman, Robyn Gaines (Columbia Grammar School), Susan Gamer, Bob Gersten, Libbie Gersten, and Rich Gersten (Brant Lake Camp), Tracey Guest (Simon & Schuster), Mary Rodgers Guettal, Nicole Harman (Rodgers & Hammerstein Organization), Sheldon Harnick, Carrie Hintz (Butler Library, Columbia University), Caronae Howell (Butler Library, Columbia University), Rick Hunter (NYPL), Melanie James (General Society of Mechanics and Tradesmen Library), Diane Jaust (Radio City Music Hall Archives), Leah Jehan (Beinecke Library, Yale University), Mary Jones (NYPL), Michael Jones (20th Century Fox), Gare Joyce, Christine Karatnytsky (NYPL), Diane Kiesel, Karen Knickeson (NYPL), Mary Morris Lawrence, Ruth Lee-Mui (Simon & Schuster), Mimi Muray Levitt, Tom Lisanti (NYPL), Howard Mandelbaum and Ron Mandelbaum (Photofest), Dan Marmorstein, Rebecca Marsh (Simon & Schuster), Hugh Martin, Louise Martzinek (NYPL), Steve Massa (NYPL), Jeremy Megraw (NYPL), Michael Nash (NYU), Dave Newhouse, Gerald Pelisson (DeWitt Clinton Alumni Association), Bruce Pomahac (Rodgers & Hammerstein Organization), Bill Reed, Emily Remes (Simon & Schuster), Aleen Robinson, Malena Rogers (General Society of Mechanics and Tradesmen Library), David Rosner, Jackie Seow (Simon & Schuster),

Kenneth Shauer, Thomas Z. Shepard, David Smith, Joseph Struble (George Eastman House), Mark Swartz (Shubert Archive), Susan Tell (Surrogate's Court Archives, New York County), Faye Thompson (AMPAS), Julia Warren Tucker, Bill Waldman, Robin Walton (Rodgers & Hammerstein Organization), and Sarah Ziebell (NYPL).

Special gratitude to: Jay Barksdale (NYPL), Stacey Belhmer (AMPAS), Bob Bender (Simon & Schuster), Sue Bernstein, Maryann Chach (Shubert Archive), Ted Chapin (Rodgers & Hammerstein Organization), Dan Conaway (Writers House), Tina de Varon, Sebastian Fabal (Williamson Music), Barbara Hall (AMPAS), Larry Hart II, Muriel Jorgensen, Johanna Li (Simon & Schuster), Anthony Newfield, Sybil Pincus (Simon & Schuster), Troy Schreck (Alfred Music), Sylvia Wang (Shubert Archive), and Leslie Whitney.

I am forever indebted to the supreme triumvirate of Lorenz Hart scholars: Dennis Moore, Frederick Nolan, and Scott Willis. Each has been exceedingly generous with his counsel and support.

Notes

Note: Full references for all books cited can be found in the Bibliography.

Prologue: I'm a Sentimental Sap, That's All

1. Abraham M. Wattenberg, deposition to Surrogate's Court, New York County, Dec. 20, 1943.
2. Sardi, Sr., and Gehman, *Sardi's*, pp. 84–85.
3. "Lorenz Hart's Will Filed," *The New York Times*, Nov. 30, 1943, p. 22.
4. Dorothy Rodgers, quoted in Block, ed., *Richard Rodgers Reader*, p. 38.
5. Richard Rodgers, interviewed by Kenneth Leish, 1968–69, Columbia Center for Oral History, Columbia University, p. 179.
6. Nolan, *Lorenz Hart*, p. 252. Hart, *Thou Swell*, p. 116.
7. Mary Campbell, deposition to New York Surrogate's Court, Jan. 8, 1944.
8. Milton Bender, deposition to New York Surrogate's Court, Jan. 9, 1944.
9. The order is dated Nov. 2, 1944.
10. "Lorenz Hart's Will Fought by Brother," *The New York Times*, Dec. 29, 1943, p. 19.
11. Ibid.
12. Lucinda Ballard, interviewed by Ronald L. Davis, SMU Oral Histories, January 1985–March 1987.
13. Secrest, *Somewhere for Me*, p. 223. John Lahr, "Walking Alone," *The New Yorker*, July 1, 2002, p. 86.
14. Rodgers, deposition to New York Surrogate's Court, Dec. 17, 1944. Lahr, "Walking Alone," p. 86.
15. Hans Christian Adamson, letter to Richard Rodgers, Feb. 19, 1944. Rodgers, letter to Adamson, Feb. 25, 1944, New York Public Library. "Memorial Tribute Paid Lorenz Hart," *The New York Times*, March 6, 1944, p. 16.
16. Louis Brodsky, letter to Theodore Hart, New York Surrogate's Court Papers, April 28, 1944.
17. L. Arnold Weissberger, letter to James A. Delehanty, New York Surrogate's Court Papers, Dec. 19, 1944.

18. Wilder, *American Popular Song*, p. 164.
19. Notes for lecture, Buster Davis Papers, New York Public Library. Richard Rodgers, interviewed by Stanley Green, Feb. 6, 1973, New York Public Library.
20. 193 Misc. 884, 83 N.Y.S. 2d 635.
21. Sheed, *The House That George Built*, p. 166.
22. Block, ed., *Richard Rodgers Reader*, p. 79, quoting Foreword in Darrell, *The Rodgers and Hart Song Book*.
23. 193 Misc. 884, 83 N.Y.S. 2d 635.
24. Mast, *Can't Help Singin'*, p. 166.
25. Henry Myers, "Portrait of Larry Hart," unpublished memoir, p. 65.
26. *Words and Music* papers, p. 4, Turner Files, AMPAS. Ray Bolger, interviewed by Ronald Davis, SMU Oral History, p. 19.

Chapter 1: Life Is More Delectable When It's Disrespectable

1. Nolan, *Lorenz Hart*, p. 3.
2. James M. Hart died March 26, 1893; NYC death certificate no. 10964. Silver, *Lost New York*, p. 140.
3. Reznikoff, *By the Waters of Manhattan*, p. 138. Gurock, *When Harlem Was Jewish*, p. 44.
4. Gurock, *When Harlem Was Jewish*, p. 30.
5. Max Meyer Hertz, application for naturalization, June 23, 1893, and for U.S. passports, June 24, 1893.
6. Whitman, "Crossing Brooklyn Ferry," stanza 8.
7. Cahan, *The Rise of David Levinsky*, p. 486.
8. "Laurence" Hart, Certificate of Birth, reported July 25, 1895, granted Aug. 20, 1895. Nolan, *Lorenz Hart*, p. 6.
9. Mayer, quoting the *New York Herald*, Aug. 3, 1903, in *Once Upon a Time*, p. 212.
10. Hart, *Thou Swell*, p. 13.
11. Some sources suggest that Frieda Isenberg, not Max Hertz, was Heine's descendant. Max's mother's maiden name, however, was Heine.
12. Richard Rodgers, Columbia Oral History.
13. Marx and Clayton, *Rodgers & Hart*, p. 18. Nolan, *Lorenz Hart*, p. 11.
14. 37 Misc. 412, 75 N.Y.S. 781.
15. 87 A.D. 632, 84 N.Y.S. 1119.
16. "Lottery Prisoners Remanded," *New York Tribune*, Feb. 23, 1903, p. 4.
17. "Charges Big Larceny," *New York Tribune*, Nov. 18, 1903, p. 8. "Dr. Carlos Martyn Held," *New York Tribune*, Jan. 4, 1905, p. 3.
18. "The Passing Throng," *New York Tribune*, Aug. 4, 1902, p. 7.
19. "Plans for Theatrical Season," *New York Tribune*, June 4, 1905, p. 9. "Stageland Incidents in Comment and Gossip," *New York Tribune*, June 11, 1905, p. 13.
20. Michael Tilson Thomas, interviewed by Michael Kantor in 2003 for PBS documentary *Broadway: The American Musical*. "Hebrew Actors Out on Strike,"

New York Tribune, Nov. 7, 1904, p. 1. "Ushers Unionized," *New York Tribune*, Oct. 21, 1905, p. 16.

21. Clayton Hamilton, "In the Starlight of the Nineties," in *The Thirtieth Birthday of Vogue*, p. 152.
22. 20 N.Y. Crim. R. 199, 114 A.D. 9, 99 N.Y.S. 758. Dos Passos, *The Best Times*, p. 7.
23. Richard Rodgers, Columbia Oral History.
24. Mark Sullivan, "The Mobbed Metropolis," *Boston Evening Transcript*, June 4, 1904, unpaged.
25. *The Magpie*, DeWitt Clinton High School, 1910, pp. 354–355.
26. Nasaw, *Going Out*, pp. 3, 6, and 9.
27. Hart, *Thou Swell*, p. 17.
28. Fordin, *Getting to Know Him*, p. 24.
29. Hart, *Thou Swell*, p. 19.
30. Ibid., p. 20.
31. Abraham Jacoby, "The Three Musketeers," *New York World*, Sept. 20, 1928.
32. Fields and Fields, *From the Bowery to Broadway*, p. 289. Hart, *Thou Swell*, p. 15.
33. "No Holes Bard," *Stage*, November 1938, p. 17.
34. Nolan, *Lorenz Hart*, p. 10.
35. Boas, *Changes in Bodily Form*, p. 62.
36. Hall, *Size Matters*, p. 7.
37. Kanter, *The Jews on Tin Pan Alley*, p. 162. Hart, *Thou Swell*, p. 14. Nolan, *Lorenz Hart*, p. 7. Henry Myers, Columbia Oral History, unpaged.
38. Henry Myers, "Portrait of Larry Hart," unpublished memoir, p. 16.
39. Kanter, *The Jews on Tin Pan Alley*, p. 162.
40. Nolan, *Lorenz Hart*, p. 7.
41. Wolff, *The Duke of Deception*, p. 9.
42. George Kibbe Turner, "Daughters of the Poor," *McClure's Magazine*, November 1909, pp. 45–61. "Traffic in Slaves," *New York Tribune*, Oct. 22, 1909, p. 4.
43. Trattner, *Understanding the Talmud*, p. 163.

Chapter 2: I Read My Plato

1. *Columbia Grammar School: A Historical Log*, pp. xiii and 38.
2. *The Columbia News*, November 1911, p. 8.
3. Hart and Kimball, eds., *The Complete Lyrics of Lorenz Hart*, p. 4. Hart, *Thou Swell*, p. 23. "The Friars' Frolic," *New York Tribune*, June 4, 1911, p. C3. *The New York Times*, May 28, 1911, p. X1. Trager, *The New York Chronology*, p. 332.
4. *The Columbia News*, December 1911, pp. 3–5.
5. "Gaby Deslys Here in Startling Gown," *The New York Times*, Sept. 17, 1911, p. 11. "Play Stops, Students Riot," *The New York Times*, Nov. 19, 1911, p. 1.
6. *The Columbia News*, January 1912, pp. 8, 9.
7. *The Columbia News*, April 1912, p. 7.

8. *The Columbia News*, December 1912, pp. 7 and 16. Hart, *Thou Swell*, p. 26.
9. *The Columbia News*, December 1912, pp. 1–3.
10. *The Columbia News*, January 1913, p. 8. Fowler, *Skyline*, p. 47.
11. *The Columbia News*, February 1913, p. 5.
12. *The Columbia News*, March 1913, pp. 6–7.
13. Hart, *Thou Swell*, p. 25.
14. Hart and Kimball, eds., *The Complete Lyrics of Lorenz Hart*, p. 8.
15. Herbert Marks, Columbia Oral History, interviewed Fall 1957, p. 20.
16. "No Holes Bard," *Stage*, November 1938, p. 17.
17. Henry Myers, "Portrait of Larry Hart," unpublished memoir, p. 45.
18. Toohey, *A History of the Pulitzer Prize Plays*, p. 36. Marx and Clayton, *Rodgers & Hart*, p. 22. Myers, "Portrait of Larry Hart," p. 4.
19. Robbins journal, p. 233, John Jacob Robbins Papers, New York Public Library. Myers, "Portrait of Larry Hart," p. 6. Hart, *Thou Swell*, p. 22.
20. Hart, *Thou Swell*, p. 22.
21. Myers, "Portrait of Larry Hart," p. 7.
22. Ibid., p. 18.
23. Hart, *Thou Swell*, p. 22.
24. Max Lincoln Schuster, interviewed by Dr. Louis Starr, April 1956; further interviews by Neil Newton Gold, Columbia Oral History, November 1964.
25. Huneker, *New Cosmopolis*, p. 112.
26. Gelb and Gelb, *O'Neill*, p. 271.
27. "Necrology," in Mantle, ed., *The Best Plays of 1928–1929*, p. 524. Myers, "Portrait of Larry Hart," p. 6. Blum, *A Pictorial History of the American Theatre*, p. 93.
28. Amberg letters, May 1914, Shubert Archive.
29. "U. S. Seeks Wreckers of Bayonne Bank," April 17, 1914, p. 9. "Witness Wilson Now for Swann," *New York Tribune*, Jan. 20, 1917, p. 4.

Chapter 3: The Rhyme Is Hard to Find, My Dears

1. Secrest, *Somewhere for Me*, pp. 16–17.
2. Rodgers, *Musical Stages*, pp. 4–5.
3. Richard Rodgers, Columbia Oral History. Rodgers, interviewed on video by Stanley Green, New York Public Library, 1973.
4. New York College of Dentistry records, Bobst Library, New York University.
5. George W. Clarke, "Man About Boston," *The Boston Record*, May 11, 1942..
6. Amberg Letters, Shubert Archive.
7. Ryskind, *I Shot an Elephant in My Pajamas*, p. 26. "Election Row at Columbia," *The New York Times*, May 16, 1916, p. 13.
8. *Columbia Spectator* review of 1916 student journal *Challenge*, quoted in "Finds Challenge Dull," *The New York Times*, Feb. 24, 1916, p. 5.
9. Max Lincoln Schuster, Columbia Oral History.

10. Dietz, *Dancing in the Dark*, p. 28.

11. Meryman, *Mank*, p. 29.

12. Nolan, *Lorenz Hart*, p. 15. Fordin, *Getting to Know Him*, p. 28. Marx and Clayton, *Rodgers & Hart*, p. 23.

13. "Peace Pirates Some Punkins," *Columbia Spectator*, April 15, 1916, p. 1.

14. "Madcap Dolly Opens Yorkville Theatre," *New York Tribune*, Oct. 24, 1916, p. 7. "Broadway and Elsewhere," *New York Tribune*, Oct. 29, 1916, p. C4.

15. Kenneth Shauer, telephone interview with author, July 8, 2008. Zukor, *The Public Is Never Wrong*, p. 45.

16. *Hello Central*, copyright 1917, Shubert Archive.

17. "Professors Dana and Cattell Are Removed from Faculty," *Columbia Spectator*, Oct. 2, 1917, p. 1. See also *Columbia Spectator*, Oct. 9, 1917, p. 1, and Oct. 15, 1917, p. 2.

18. Hall, *Size Matters*, p. 15.

19. Helene Stapinksi, "For Ft. Lee, Film Moments of 100 Years," *The New York Times*, May 10, 2009, p. NJ5. "Entire East Is Snowbound," *The New York Times*, Feb. 6, 1918, p. 20.

20. Hamm, *Music in the New World*, pp. 346–347. Rodgers, *Musical Stages*, p. 20.

21. *The Jester*, May 1918, p. 35.

22. Ibid. Rodgers, *Musical Stages*, p. 19.

23. Bob and Libbie Gersten, interview with author, Nov. 5, 2008.

24. Glendon Allvine, "Round About the Camp That Is Right in Our Midst," *New York Tribune*, Oct. 27, 1918, p. B5.

25. *Columbia Spectator*, Nov. 8, 1918, p. 5.

26. Larry Hart II, e-mail to author, May 13, 2011.

27. Seldes, *Witness to a Century*, p. 93.

28. *Going Up*, Shubert Archive.

29. "Gym Show Is Advised by Major," *Columbia Spectator*, Nov. 20, 1918, p. 4.

30. "Downtown Stars Win Applause at Big Army Show," *Columbia Spectator*, Dec. 3, 1918, p. 8.

31. Fitzgerald, "My Lost City," in *The Crack-Up*, p. 25. Ferber, *A Peculiar Treasure*, p. 233.

32. Brown, *Champagne Cholly*, pp. 278–279.

33. Stanley Green, *The World of Musical Comedy*, pp. 142–143. *Richard Rodgers Fact Book*, p. 4.

34. Philip Leavitt, unpublished memoir, p. 3.

35. U.S. Census 1920. Rodgers, *Musical Stages*, p. 28.

36. Rodgers, *Musical Stages*, p. 27.

37. Richard Rodgers, "How to Write Music in No Easy Lessons," *Theatre Arts Monthly*, October 1939, p. 742.

38. Philip Leavitt, unpublished memoir, p. 5.

39. Richard Rodgers, Columbia Oral History, pp. 48–49.

Chapter 4: I'll Go to Hell for Ya

1. *Take a Chance* sheet music, cover by T. L. Fowler; "Sandman" copyright by Roy Webb. Hart and Kimball, eds., *Complete Lyrics of Lorenz Hart*, p. 10. *Columbia Spectator*, April 28, 1919, p. 1.
2. Richard Rodgers, Columbia Oral History, p. 173.
3. Fields and Fields, *From the Bowery to Broadway*, p. 381.
4. Sobel, *Burleycue*, p. 42. Edward Thompson, "Don't Push Me Myer," *Los Angeles Times*, April 14, 1940, p. I3.
5. Heywood Broun, "Lew Fields Very Funny in *A Lonely Romeo* at the Shubert," *New York Tribune*, June 11, 1919, p. 13.
6. Davis, *I'd Like to Do It Again*, pp. 131–133.
7. Dorothy Fields, Columbia Oral History, p. 1.
8. Fields and Fields, *From the Bowery to Broadway*, pp. 382–383. Hart and Kimball, eds., *Complete Lyrics of Lorenz Hart*, p. 12.
9. "Actors' Walk-Out Closes 12 New York Theatres," *New York Tribune*, June 8, 1919, p. 1.
10. The joke was an old standby of the author's grandfather David Saperstein (1901–90).
11. "Chorus Forms Union to Back Actors' Strike," *New York Tribune*, Aug. 13, 1919, p. 1.
12. Ibid.
13. Minnie Maddern Fiske, "The Purpose and Promise of the Actors' Fidelity League," *The Washington Post*, Aug. 31, 1919, p. A2.
14. *The Century in Times Square*, p. 75.
15. "Managers Meet to End Strike on Actors' Terms," *The New York Times*, Sept. 3, 1919, p. 1.
16. Fowler, *Skyline*, p. 296. "Managers Meet to End Strike on Actors' Terms."
17. Rodgers, *Musical Stages*, p. 30.
18. "Plays and Players," *New York Tribune*, Oct. 3, 1919, p. 13.
19. Henry Myers, "Portrait of Larry Hart," unpublished memoir, p. 15. "'Fair Helen' Sung at the Majestic," *Boston Daily Globe*, Oct. 21, 1919, p. 10.
20. Brieux, *Three Plays*, p. xxiv.
21. Ibid., pp. 240–241. A copy of *The Reality* can be found in the Shubert Archive.
22. Blumenthal, *Stork Club*, p. 198.
23. Behr, *Prohibition*, p. 3.
24. Muray and Gallico, *The Revealing Eye*, pp. viii–ix.
25. Richard F. Shepard, "First Rodgers and Hart Show Revived," *The New York Times*, April 21, 1980, p. C18.
26. *Columbia Songs, 1754–1924*. Wood, *The Development of Song Forms in the Broadway and Hollywood Musicals of Richard Rodgers, 1919–1943*. Lee Adams,

notes to *Fly with Me* CD. Hart and Kimball, eds., *Complete Lyrics of Lorenz Hart*, pp. 12–17. Taylor, *Some Enchanted Evenings*, p. 11.

27. Fields and Fields, *From the Bowery to Broadway*, p. 388.
28. Ibid., p. 389.
29. Rodgers, *Musical Stages*, p. 37. Secrest, *Somewhere for Me*, p. 43.
30. *The Violet* 1921, yearbook of New York University. Huneker, *New Cosmopolis*, p. 114.
31. Arthur Schwartz, Columbia Oral History, November 1958, p. 8.
32. Myers, "Portrait of Larry Hart," p. 48.
33. Rose, *Wine, Women and Words*, p. 66.
34. Hecht, *A Child of the Century*, pp. 398–399.
35. Rodgers, *Musical Stages*, p. 38.
36. Fields and Fields, *From the Bowery to Broadway*, p. 393. Rodgers, *Musical Stages*, pp. 38–39.
37. Grace LeBoy Kahn, Oral History, American Jewish Committee, New York Public Library, p. 77.
38. Heywood Broun, "Jokes at Last Have a Place in Musical Shows," *New York Tribune*, July 29, 1920, p. 6.
39. Mordden, *Make Believe*, pp. 114–119.
40. Myers, "Portrait of Larry Hart," p. 46.

Chapter 5: The Great Big City's a Wondrous Toy

1. *New York Clipper*, June 13, 1923, p. 14.
2. Rodgers, *Musical Stages*, p. 44.
3. Irwin, *Highlights of Manhattan*, p. 240. Burrows and Wallace, *Gotham*, p. 500. Trager, *The New York Chronology*, pp. 33–34.
4. The Hart version of *The Lady in Ermine* is copyrighted by United Plays, 1920, and can be found in the Shubert Archive.
5. Schildkraut, *My Father and I*, pp. 158–159. Molnár, *Liliom*, p. ix.
6. Helburn, *A Wayward Quest*, p. 172. Molnár, *Fashions for Men and The Swan*.
7. Marx and Clayton, *Rodgers & Hart*, pp. 33–34.
8. Frederick Nolan, e-mail to author, July 4, 2008. Hart, *Thou Swell*, p. 28.
9. J. J. Geller, "They Had a Show for Sale," *The Dance Magazine*, August 1929, p. 38.
10. "Akron Club to Stage Its Musical Comedy Tonight," *New York Tribune*, Feb. 12, 1921, p. 8.
11. Richard Rodgers, "Mr. Rodgers' Yankee," *The New York Times*, Nov. 21, 1943, p. X1. O'Dell, *Modern Authorship*, p. 249. "On the Screen," *New York Tribune*, March 16, 1921, p. 8. "Writing Titles for Twain Film Is a Delicate Job," *New York Tribune*, March 27, 1921, p. C6.
12. "Pension for Minnie Hauck," *The New York Times*, Dec. 25, 1925, p. 17. "Will Drawn by Expert Barred," *The New York Times*, Oct. 13, 1946, p. 15.

13. Muray and Gallico, *The Revealing Eye*, p. 242.
14. *Columbia Spectator*, April 25, 1921, page number obscured.
15. Henry Myers, Columbia Oral History.
16. Duberman, *Paul Robeson*, p. 58.
17. Henry Myers, "Portrait of Larry Hart," unpublished memoir, p. 31.
18. Nolan, *Lorenz Hart*, p. 40. Nolan's language is more refined.
19. Myers, "Portrait of Larry Hart," p. 36.
20. Alexander Woollcott, "The Play," *The New York Times*, March 14, 1922, p. 20. Percy Hammond, "The First Fifty Years Is an Interesting, If Gloomy, Inspection of Matrimony," *New York Tribune*, p. 8.
21. Myers, "Portrait of Larry Hart," p. 9.
22. Ibid., p. 39.
23. Mantle, ed., *The Best Plays of 1921–1922*, p. 558. "The Season's Runs," *The New York Times*, June 11, 1922, p. 80.
24. Hart and Kimball, eds., *The Complete Lyrics of Lorenz Hart*, p. 28.
25. Georgie Price, letter to Herbert Fields, Nov. 25, 1949, joking about agreement for written material in 1922. "Since poor Larry is no longer available I might settle for some lyrics by your sister Dorothy, or if she is too busy, then you might get Irving Berlin." [Photostat below]: "August 2, 1922. Received in advance from George Price one hundred dollars, for full rights to number and dialogue to 'Shakespeares of 1922.' Balance due, $200.00. [Signed] Herbert L. Fields, Lorenz M. Hart, Richard C. Rodgers" (Richard Rodgers Papers, New York Public Library).
26. Rodgers, *Musical Stages*, p. 50.
27. Marx and Clayton, *Rodgers & Hart*, p. 49. Secrest, *Somewhere for Me*, p. 51. Richard Rodgers, Columbia Oral History, p. 76.
28. Henry F. Pringle, "Words and Music," *Collier's*, Feb. 18, 1933, p. 28.
29. Mair, *The Chappell Story*, p. 36. Rodgers, *Musical Stages*, p. 51.
30. "Musical Shows Getting Most of Broadway's Theatre Money," *The Clipper*, Sept. 13, 1922, p. 1.
31. Teague, *Mrs. L.*, p. 114.
32. "Legality of Sunday Shows a Fight to the Finish," *New York Clipper*, Feb. 21, 1923, p. 4.
33. "Wagner's Widow in Want," *The New York Times*, March 3, 1923, p. 9. "News and Gossip of the Rialto," *The New York Times*, Feb. 25, 1923, p. X1. Henry Myers, Columbia Oral History, unpaged. Nolan, *Lorenz Hart*, p. 44.
34. "Gossip of the Rialto," *The New York Times*, Dec. 16, 1923, p. X1. Rodgers, *Musical Stages*, p. 49.
35. "Mme. Galli-Curci's Return," *The New York Times*, Jan. 9, 1924, p. 25.
36. Nolan, *Lorenz Hart*, p. 47.
37. "Mill Girl Heroine in New Dance Show," *The New York Times*, June 20, 1923, p. 22.

38. "Broadway Musical Shows Getting Big Share of Theatre Money," *New York Clipper*, July 11, 1923, p. 1.
39. Chauncey, *Gay New York*, p. 146 and p. 455, n. 54.
40. Mantle, ed., *The Best Plays, 1923–1924*, p. 337. Myers, "Portrait of Larry Hart," p. 52.
41. Secrest, *Somewhere for Me*, p. 53. Nolan, *Lorenz Hart*, p. 55. Fields and Fields, *From the Bowery to Broadway*, p. 419. Rodgers, *Musical Stages*, pp. 52–53.
42. "Dr. Albert Sirmay, Composer, Editor," *The New York Times*, Jan. 17, 1967, p. 35.
43. Rodgers, *Musical Stages*, p. 80. Fields and Fields, *From the Bowery to Broadway*, p. 421.
44. Name change petition to City of New York, Jan. 16, 1925, Actors Equity Papers, Tamiment Library, NYU.
45. Toohey, *A History of the Pulitzer Prize Plays*, p. 36.
46. Fields and Fields, *From the Bowery to Broadway*, p. 433.
47. J. J. Geller, "They Had a Show for Sale," *The Dance Magazine*, August 1929, p. 49.
48. Ford reminisced for the University of Southern California celebration of Lorenz Hart, *The Hart of the Matter*, Sept. 30, 1973, program, p. 7.
49. Harold Clurman, "What Was Broadway's All-Time Best Season?" *The New York Times*, March 9, 1980, p. D1.
50. Theatre Guild Papers, Beinecke Library, Yale University. "Theatre Guild to Come to Garrick Theatre," *New York Tribune*, March 9, 1919, p. C1. Helburn, *A Wayward Quest*, p. 209.
51. Secrest, *Somewhere for Me*, p. 62.
52. Helburn, *A Wayward Quest*, pp. 215–216.

Chapter 6: You Mustn't Conceal Anything You Feel

1. Hart, *Thou Swell*, p. 41.
2. Morrie Ryskind Papers, New York Public Library. *New York Herald*, May 17, 1925, part IV, p. 16.
3. Clurman, *The Fervent Years*, pp. 10–11.
4. Hart, *Thou Swell*, p. 41.
5. "Garrick Gaieties Spoofs Mamma Guild," *Daily News*, May 19, 1925, p. 26.
6. "Mayor Hylan's Party Reaches Palm Beach," *The New York Times*, Feb. 2, 1925, p. 3.
7. "A Try-out," *The Wall Street Journal*, May 28, 1925, p. 3.
8. Helburn, *A Wayward Quest*, p. 216.
9. "Lyrics Made While You Wait," *New York Amusements*, July 6, 1925, p. 15.
10. "Revise Their Editions Because Bryan Died," *The New York Times*, July 28, 1925, p. 13.
11. *Richard Rodgers Fact Book*, p. 29.

12. Wilson, *Classics and Commercials*, p. 30.

13. Nathan, *The Autobiography of an Attitude*, p. 66.

14. Coward, *The Noël Coward Diaries*, p. 374. Secrest, *Somewhere for Me*, p. 66.

15. Richard Rodgers, letter to Sheridan Morley, June 28, 1968, Richard Rodgers Papers, New York Public Library.

16. Dorothy Fields Columbia Oral History, p. 4. Fields and Fields, *From the Bowery to Broadway*, p. 128.

17. Nolan, *Lorenz Hart*, p. 68. *Who's Who in America, 1934–35*, vol. 18, p. 1264.

18. *Evening Graphic* clipping, Aug. 17, 1927, page number missing. Walter Winchell Scrapbooks, New York Public Library.

19. Sullivan, *Our Times*, p. 690. Caldwell, *New York Nights*, p. 228.

20. J. Brooks Atkinson, "The Play," *The New York Times*, Sept. 19, 1925, p. 9. Percy Hammond, "The Theater," *The Herald Tribune*, Sept. 19, 1925, p. 8.

21. Secrest, *Somewhere for Me*, p. 70. Nolan, *Lorenz Hart*, p. 68.

22. Wood, *Song Forms*, p. 190.

23. Ibid., p. 192.

24. *Boston Herald*, March 28, 1937.

25. "Garrick Gaieties Music," *The Music Trade Review*, July 18, 1925, p. 44. Rayno, *Paul Whiteman*, p. 545.

26. Wilson, *The Twenties*, p. 220.

27. Schulberg, *Writers in America*, p. 117.

28. Barnett, *Writing on Life*, pp. 286–287.

29. Dorothy Rodgers, interviewed by David C. Berliner, May 17, 1976, for the William E. Weiner Oral History Library of the American Jewish Committee, New York Public Library (transcript unpaged). Secrest, *Somewhere for Me*, p. 75.

30. Fields and Fields, *From the Bowery to Broadway*, p. 441.

31. Marx and Clayton, *Rodgers & Hart*, pp. 86–87. Rodgers, *Musical Stages*, pp. 74–75.

Chapter 7: *It's So Good It Must Be Immoral*

1. Taylor quoted by Rose, *Wine, Women and Words*, p. 13.

2. Ibid., p. 12. Conrad, *Billy Rose*, p. 87.

3. Green, *The World of Musical Comedy*, p. 149.

4. Darrell, *The Rodgers and Hart Song Book*, p. 16.

5. "If You Must Write Lyrics," *Herald Tribune*, March 21, 1926, sec. 5, p. 4.

6. Yeats, "Adam's Curse," *Selected Poems*, p. 28.

7. Robert Benchley, "The Drama," *Life*, April 8, 1926, p. 27.

8. Gaines, *Wit's End*, p. 37.

9. Behr, *Prohibition*, pp. 89, 221.

10. Arthur Schwartz, letter to Howard Dietz, Feb. 24, 1926, Howard Dietz

Papers, New York Public Library. In Dietz's autobiography, *Dancing in the Dark*, p. 69, Schwartz's letter is quoted but "Lorry" had been changed to "Larry."

11. T. Goldsmith, "One Hart Would Not Stand Still," *Theatre Magazine*, April 8, 1931, p. 56.

12. J. Brooks Atkinson, "Theatre Guild Cut-ups," *The New York Times*, May 11, 1926, p. 25. "Revues and Revues," *The New York Times*, June 13, 1926, p. X1.

13. Nathan, "Judging the Shows," *Judge*, June 5, 1926.

14. Dennis Moore, letter to author, Oct. 14, 2009. "'The Light Blues' at the Shaftesbury," *The Manchester Guardian*, Sept. 15, 1916, p. 4. "The Light Blues," *The Observer*, Sept. 17, 1916, p. 7.

15. Nolan, *Lorenz Hart*, p. 81.

16. Rodgers, *Musical Stages*, pp. 86–89.

17. "Says America Leads the World in Dancing," *The New York Times*, Aug. 3, 1926, p. 7.

18. Dorothy Rodgers, interviewed by David C. Berliner, May 17, 1976, for the William E. Weiner Oral History Library of the American Jewish Committee, New York Public Library (transcript unpaged). Nolan, *Lorenz Hart*, p. 84.

19. Taylor, *A Pictorial History of the Movies*, p. 42.

20. "Innocents Abroad," *The New York Times*, Oct. 17, 1926, p. X4.

21. Freedman, *Mendel Marantz*, p. 9. Freedman, *The Intellectual Lover and Other Stories*, p. vii.

22. Mantle, ed., *The Best Plays of 1926–1927*, p. 450.

23. Mary Carstairs, "Belle of Broadway," *Popular Song*, September 1936, p. 7. Whitcomb, *Irving Berlin and Ragtime America*, pp. 176–177.

24. Harry Ruby, Columbia Oral History, p. 2029.

25. Much of the material about November–December 1926 is drawn from Richard Rodgers's letters to Dorothy Feiner, Richard Rodgers Papers, New York Public Library. Nolan, *Lorenz Hart*, p. 87. Dietz, *Dancing in the Dark*, p. 70.

26. Richard Rodgers, letter to Dorothy Feiner, Nov. 21, 1926, Richard Rodgers Papers, New York Public Library.

27. Rodgers letters, Nov. 23, 1926.

28. Silver, *Lost New York*, p. 215.

29. H. H., "Lido Lady," *Observer*, Dec. 5, 1926, p. 16.

30. Duke, *Listen Here!* p. 257. Agate, "Lido Lady," *The Sunday Times* [London], Dec. 12, 1926.

31. Baral, *Revue*, p. 219.

32. Richard Rodgers, letter to Dorothy Feiner, Dec. 5, 1926, Richard Rodgers Papers, New York Public Library.

33. Ziegfeld and Ziegfeld, *The Ziegfeld Touch*, p. 136. Rodgers, *Musical Stages*, p. 95.

34. Arthur Mann, "Harmonica King: The Story of Borrah Minevich," *Literary Digest*, Nov. 17, 1924, p. 24. Some sources spell the surname with two *n*'s.

35. Gross, *Nize Baby*, p. 24.

36. Marx and Clayton, *Rodgers & Hart*, p. 103. Ziegfeld and Ziegfeld, *The Ziegfeld Touch*, p. 136.

37. "Irving Berlin Takes a Bride," *Best of the World*, Jan. 5, 1926, pp. 305–306.

38. Richard Rodgers, letter to Dorothy Feiner, Jan. 7, 1927, Richard Rodgers Papers, New York Public Library.

Chapter 8: A House in Iceland Was My Heart's Domain

1. Ganzl, *The British Musical Theatre*, pp. 264–265. Nolan, *Lorenz Hart*, p. 96.

2. Baral, *Revue*, pp. 219–222. Lillie, *Every Other Inch a Lady*, p. 200.

3. Richard Rodgers, interviewed by Douglas Cooper, WKTC-FM, Hartford, Conn., Feb. 2, 1971. Rodgers, *Musical Stages*, p. 101. Nolan, *Lorenz Hart*, p. 97. Secrest, *Somewhere for Me*, p. 103. Marx and Clayton, *Rodgers & Hart*, p. 106.

4. J. Brooks Atkinson, "The Play," *The New York Times*, March 11, 1927, p. 24.

5. Richard Rodgers, letter to Dorothy Feiner, March 27, 1927, Richard Rodgers Papers, New York Public Library.

6. Henry Myers, "Portrait of Larry Hart," unpublished memoir, p. 66.

7. Jeans, *Writing for the Theatre*, p. 180.

8. Graham and Frank, *Beloved Infidel*, p. 98. Cochran, *Showman Looks On*, p. 27.

9. *Richard Rodgers Fact Book*, p. 73. "At Random," *The Observer*, May 1, 1927, p. 15. Sir J. E., "The Week's Theatres," *The Observer*, May 22, 1927, p. 15. "Mr. Cochran's New Revue," *The Manchester Guardian*, May 21, 1927, p. 14.

10. Richard Rodgers, Columbia Oral History, p. 129. Marx and Clayton, *Rodgers & Hart*, p. 108.

11. Nolan, *Lorenz Hart*, p. 103.

12. Charles B. Cochran, "Stage Decoration and Fantasy," *Creative Art*, November 1927, pp. 394–397.

13. Reik, *From Thirty Years with Freud*, p. 232.

14. Hart, *Thou Swell*, p. 63.

15. Gurock, *When Harlem Was Jewish*, pp. 139–143.

16. Graham, *New York Nights*, p. 14.

17. Walter Winchell, *Evening Graphic*, Nov. 14, 1927, unpaged clipping.

18. Walter Winchell, *Evening Graphic*, Aug. 20, 1927, unpaged clipping.

19. Ganzl, *British Musical Theatre*, p. 263.

20. Nolan, *Lorenz Hart*, p. 105. Ganzl, *British Musical Theatre*, p. 263.

21. A.R., "A New Musical Comedy," *The Manchester Guardian*, Sept. 9, 1927, p. 5.

22. "Buy Their Own Hit Song," *The New York Times*, Sept. 16, 1927, p. 21. Fields and Fields, *From the Bowery to Broadway*, p. 467.

23. *The Complete Lyrics of Lorenz Hart*, p. 105, spells Glyn's name as "Glynn."

24. Wood, *Song Forms*, p. 203.

25. Robert M. W. Vogel, interviewed by Barbara Hall, AMPAS Oral History Program, April 13–Aug. 13, 1990, p. 226.
26. Wood, *Song Forms*, p. 200.
27. Richard Rodgers Papers, New York Public Library.
28. The history of the life insurance policy is provided in material accompanying *Theodore Hart v. New York Life Insurance Co.*, Court of Appeals, argued Nov. 26, 1946.
29. Richard Rodgers, interviewed by Stanley Green, 1973.
30. Dietz, *Dancing in the Dark*, pp. 17–19.
31. E. Y. Harburg, Columbia Oral History, p. 12.
32. Adams, *Diary of Our Own Samuel Pepys*, p. 759.
33. *The Hart of the Matter*, pp. 7–8. Beatty, *The Rascal King*, pp. 172–173.
34. Wilson, *The Twenties*, p. 514.

Chapter 9: You've Cooked My Goose

1. Charles Collins, "She's My Baby," *The Chicagoan*, April 21, 1928, p. 20.
2. Mordden, quoted in Block, ed., *Richard Rodgers Reader*, p. 15.
3. Sidney Skolsky, "Times Square Tintypes," *The Sun*, Jan. 30, 1928, p. 13.
4. Whitcomb, *Irving Berlin and Ragtime America*, pp. 198–199.
5. Rodgers, *Musical Stages*, p. 114.
6. Berkeley, quoted in Thomas and Terry, *The Busby Berkeley Book*, p. 21.
7. George Jean Nathan, "Judging the Shows," *Judge*, May 26, 1928, p. 28.
8. Croce, "The Two Trocaderos," in *Afterimages*, p. 80.
9. "Songs for High or Low Brows," *Evening Post*, May 19, 1928, sec. 3, p. 6.
10. Nolan, *Lorenz Hart*, p. 118.
11. Marx and Clayton, *Rodgers & Hart*, p. 127.
12. Vincent Sardi, Jr., interviewed by Michael Kantor for documentary *Broadway*, New York Public Library. Abraham Jacoby, "Three Musical Musketeers," *New York World*, Sept. 20, 1928.
13. Lorenz Hart, "Renaissance of Musical Shows Due, Hart Feels," *New York American*, July 5, 1928.
14. Richard Rodgers, letter to Dorothy Feiner, Sept. 1, 1928, Richard Rodgers Papers, New York Public Library. Richard Rodgers, interviewed by Stanley Green, 1973, New York Public Library.
15. J. Brooks Atkinson, "The Play," *The New York Times*, Sept. 26, 1928, p. 36. *Richard Rodgers Fact Book*, pp. 105–107. Nolan, *Lorenz Hart*, p. 121.
16. Mordden, quoted in Block, ed., *Richard Rodgers Reader*, pp. 18–19.
17. Hart, *Thou Swell*, p. 63. Nolan, *Lorenz Hart*, p. 122. Max Hart, Standard Certificate of Death, Reg. No. 25292.
18. Trager, *New York Chronology*, p. 328.
19. In the Matter of the Application for Letters of Administration upon the Goods, Chattels, and Credits of Max M. Hart, Deceased, 1928, Surrogate's Court Archives.

20. Ellington, quoted by Stanley Dance in Gammond, ed., *Duke Ellington*, p. 18.

21. Mantle, ed., *The Best Plays of 1928–1929*, p. 478.

22. Davis, *I'd Like to Do It Again*, p. 205.

23. Mary Cleere Haran, "Hart's Heart and Rodgers's Glorious Soul," *The New York Times*, June 23, 2002, p. A5.

24. Nolan, *Lorenz Hart*, p. 78.

25. George Jean Nathan, "Judging the Show," *Judge*, April 6, 1929, p. 18.

26. Lief, *Hangover*, p. 142.

27. Chesterton, quoted in Silver, *Lost New York*, p. 73.

28. Wilson, *The Twenties*, p. 536.

Chapter 10: My Head Is Just a Hat Place

1. Darrell, *The Rodgers and Hart Song Book*, p. 22.

2. "Rialto Gossip," *The New York Times*, April 7, 1929, p. X1.

3. Nolan, *Lorenz Hart*, p. 118. Secrest, *Somewhere for Me*, pp. 56–57.

4. Hamilton, *Writers in Hollywood*, p. 46.

5. Schickel, *The Stars*, p. 80.

6. Lief, *Hangover*, p. 7.

7. Charles Collins, "Holiday Death-Watch on the Drama," *The Chicagoan*, June 8, 1929, p. 26.

8. "Westchester Deals," *The New York Times*, March 31, 1929, p. 46. "Future Musical Shows," *The New York Times*, June 2, 1929, p. X4.

9. Wood, *Song Forms*, pp. 142–143. Mordden, quoted in Block, ed., *Richard Rodgers Reader*, p. 16.

10. Richard Rodgers, letter to Dorothy Feiner, July 3, 1929, Richard Rodgers Papers, New York Public Library.

11. Nolan, *Lorenz Hart*, p. 133.

12. "Gossip of the Rialto," *The New York Times*, June 23, 1929, p. X1.

13. Sardi, Sr., and Gehman, *Sardi's*, p. 21. Sardi, Jr., and West, *Off the Wall at Sardi's*, p. 57.

14. Vincent Sardi, Jr., interviewed by Michael Kantor for PBS documentary *Broadway*, Jan. 16, 1997. Some material following is also drawn from this interview.

15. Sardi, Sr., and Gehman, *Sardi's*, p. 172.

16. Lief, *Hangover*, pp. 21–23.

17. "Chatter in New York," *Variety*, July 24, 1929, p. 58.

18. Darrell, *The Rodgers and Hart Song Book*, p. 22.

19. George Jean Nathan, "Judging the Shows," *Judge*, Dec. 7, 1929, p. 20. "*Heads Up!* Proves Lively Diversion," *The New York Times*, Nov. 12, 1929, p. 37. Darrell, *The Rodgers and Hart Song Book*, p. 22.

20. George Jean Nathan, "Judging the Shows," *Judge*, Dec. 21, 1929, p. 29.

21. "Songwriters Really Live High," *New York Sun*, Nov. 18, 1929, p. 19.

22. Lorenz Hart, "A Lesson in Song Writing," *The World*, Dec. 1, 1929, p. M3.
23. Richard Rodgers, Columbia Oral History, p. 123.
24. Actors' Equity Papers, Tamiment Library, New York University.
25. Ed Wynn, Oral History, interviewed by Max Wilk for the American Jewish Committee, Aug. 9, 1960, New York Public Library.
26. Nolan, *Lorenz Hart*, p. 138.
27. "To Write 'Revue Operette,'" *The New York Times*, Jan. 13, 1930, p. 26. Rodgers, *Musical Stages*, p. 130. Nolan, *Lorenz Hart*, p. 136.
28. Isaac Goldberg, "Men of Notes, of Parts and Tuneful Puns," *Boston Evening Transcript*, Feb. 1, 1930, part four, p. 4.
29. Rodgers, *Musical Stages*, p. 132.
30. *College Humor*, June 1930, p. 56.
31. Charles Collins, "Simple Simon," *Chicago Daily Tribune*, Dec. 8, 1930, p. 23.
32. "Other Weddings," *The New York Times*, March 6, 1930, p. 15.
33. Dorothy Feiner, interviewed by David C. Berliner for the American Jewish Committee, May 17, 1976, New York Public Library.
34. Ross, "Taxi-Dance," *The Strangest Places*, pp. 81–83.
35. Richard Rodgers, letter to Dorothy Rodgers, June 25, 1930, Richard Rodgers Papers, New York Public Library.
36. *Variety*, Dec. 10, 1930, p. 11.
37. *Zit's Theatrical Newspaper*, April 25, 1931, p. 16.
38. Cochran, *Showman Looks On*, pp. 292–293.
39. Skinner, *Our Changing Theatre*, pp. 179–180.
40. Mantle, ed., *The Best Plays of 1930–1931*, p. 8.
41. Nolan, *Lorenz Hart*, p. 141. Rodgers, *Musical Stages*, pp. 136–137.

Chapter 11: I Try to Hide in Vain
1. "Writing Trio's First," *Variety*, April 2, 1930, p. 65.
2. Caldwell, *New York Nights*, p. 252.
3. "Fields on a Horse," *Variety*, June 18, 1930, p. 81.
4. Some of this paragraph is culled from material found throughout Gebhard and Von Breton, *Los Angeles in the Thirties*.
5. "Warners Get Control of 61 More Theatres," *The New York Times*, June 19, 1930, p. 31. *Zit's Theatrical Newspaper*, Nov. 15, 1930, p. 15.
6. Davis, *I'd Like to Do It Again*, p. 215.
7. "Theme Song Writer Arrives," *Los Angeles Times*, Feb. 9, 1930, p. A8.
8. Richard Rodgers, letters to Dorothy Rodgers, June 1930, Richard Rodgers Papers, New York Public Library.
9. Richard Rodgers, letter to Dorothy Rodgers, June 24, 1930, Richard Rodgers Papers, New York Public Library. In *Musical Stages*, pp. 138–139, Rodgers, at a remove of more than forty years, remembers the episode only slightly less elaborately.

10. Sennett, *Warner Brothers Presents*, p. 25. See also *Variety*, June 25, 1930.
11. *Variety*, June 25, 1930, p. 242.
12. Gottlieb, *Funny, It Doesn't Sound Jewish*, p. 9, n. 17.
13. Ona Munson Papers, New York Public Library.
14. Richard Rodgers, letter to Dorothy Rodgers, June 27, 1930, Richard Rodgers Papers, New York Public Library.
15. *Zit's Theatrical Newspaper*, April 12, 1930, p. 1.
16. Edwin Schallert, "Tin-Pan Alley Still Wobbly," *Los Angeles Times*, Sept. 7, 1930, p. B9.
17. "Ducking Musicals and Crying for Comedies," *Variety*, July 9, 1930, p. 27.
18. Wilson, letter to Perkins, quoted by Leon Edel in Wilson, *The Twenties*, p. 459.
19. Murray, *Life on a Pogo Stick*, p. 11. "Final Effort Released," *Los Angeles Times*, June 15, 1930, p. B11. "War Pictures Enter Realm of Burlesque," *Los Angeles Times*, July 20, 1930, p. B13. "Sunday School Lesson," *Los Angeles Times*, Sept. 21, 1930, p. B12.
20. Henry Pringle, "Words and Music," *Collier's*, Feb. 18, 1933, p. 44. "Authors East for New Jobs," *The Washington Post*, Sept. 7, 1930, p. A3.
21. "Warners Stage Musical," *Variety*, Aug. 13, 1930, p. 6. "Warners Off B'way Shows," *Variety*, Aug. 20, 1930, p. 4.
22. "New York Still Sweltering," *The Manchester Guardian*, Aug. 8, 1930, p. 9.
23. Ben Washer, "Lorenz Hart Visions New Type of Musical Show on Broadway," *New York Telegram*, Aug. 20, 1930.
24. "Authors East for New Jobs."
25. Richard Rodgers, letter to Dorothy Rodgers, Aug. 23, 1930, Richard Rodgers Papers, New York Public Library.
26. Richard Rodgers, letters to Dorothy Rodgers, Aug. 29, 1930, and Sept. 3, 1930, Richard Rodgers Papers, New York Public Library.
27. Adler, *It Ain't Necessarily So*, p. 72.
28. "Divorce for Miss Evelyn Laye," *Manchester Guardian*, July 12, 1930, p. 20.
29. *Zit's Theatrical Newspaper*, Nov. 8, 1930, p. 3.
30. Richard Rodgers, letter to Dorothy Rodgers, Sept. 19, 1930, Richard Rodgers Papers, New York Public Library.
31. Richard Rodgers, letters to Dorothy Rodgers, Sept. 14, 1930, and Sept. 30, 1930, Richard Rodgers Papers, New York Public Library.
32. Richard Rodgers, letter to Dorothy Rodgers, Sept. 19, 1930, Richard Rodgers Papers, New York Public Library.
33. "Dramatis Personae," *The Observer*, Sept. 21, 1930, p. 13.
34. Richard Rodgers, letter to Dorothy Rodgers, Oct. 1, 1930, Richard Rodgers Papers, New York Public Library.
35. *Zit's Theatrical Newspaper*, Nov. 8, 1930, p. 3. Nolan, *Lorenz Hart*, p. 145.

36. Philip K. Scheuer, "Music Aids Romance in *Heads Up*," *Los Angeles Times*, Oct. 3, 1930, p. A9. "Buddy Rogers in Drama of Coast Guard," *Hartford Courant*, Nov. 10, 1930, p. 6. Mae Tinée, "Society Rum Running Yacht, Girl and Ensign," *Chicago Daily Tribune*, Nov. 18, 1930, p. 19. "Comedy and Bootlegging," *The New York Times*, Oct. 13, 1930, p. 33.

37. I.B., "Ever Green," *The Manchester Guardian*, Dec. 4, 1930, p. 11.

38. Secrest, *Somewhere for Me*, p. 143.

39. "Mason Theater Leased," *Los Angeles Times*, Oct. 3, 1929, p. A9. Muriel Babcock, "Producer Here for *Follow Thru*," *Los Angeles Times*, Oct. 20, 1929, p. B13. "It Seems They Always Come Back," *The New York Times*, Feb. 22, 1931, p. 96.

40. Green, *The World of Musical Comedy*, pp. 151–153.

41. Hart and Kimball, eds., *The Complete Lyrics of Lorenz Hart*, p. 329. Nolan, *Lorenz Hart*, p. 149. Marx and Clayton, *Rodgers & Hart*, p. 164. All three of these sources place the meeting between Hart and Adler in Hollywood in 1933, when Adler was appearing at Grauman's Chinese Theater.

42. "A Musical in Pittsburgh," *The New York Times*, Jan. 25, 1931, p. X2.

43. Secrest, *Somewhere for Me*, pp. 145–146.

44. Dorothy Parker, *The New Yorker*, Feb. 21, 1931, pp. 26–28.

45. Dorothy Parker, *The New Yorker*, March 21, 1931, p. 36.

46. *Richard Rodgers Fact Book*, p. 138.

47. Davis, *I'd Like to Do It Again*, p. 64.

48. Barnett, *Writing on Life*, p. 300.

49. Nolan, *Lorenz Hart*, p. 296. Adler's biographer Debby Applegate wrote, however, that there was "not even a hint that she was hiring out men or boys."

50. Rorem, *The New York Diary*, p. 15. Mast, *Can't Help Singin'*, p. 168.

51. *Vanity Fair*, February 1931, pp. 314–318. Sidney Skolsky, "Tintypes," *Daily News*, April 2, 1931, p. 41.

52. Carroll, *In Your Hat*, p. 151.

53. Vining, *How Can You Come Out?* pp. 53–56.

54. Mast, *Can't Help Singin'*, p. 168.

55. "Boy" Solmson, "On and Off Broadway," *Zit's Theatrical Newspaper*, Sept. 26, 1931, p. 8.

56. "Leads Chosen for *Love of Michael*," *Los Angeles Times*, March 26, 1931, p. A11.

57. J.C.M., "The Current Cinema," *The New Yorker*, March 14, 1931, p. 81.

58. Walker, *The Night Club Era*, p. 231.

59. "Lewis Warner Out of Danger from Tooth," *Los Angeles Times*, March 3, 1931, p. 5. "Lewis Warner Gravely Ill," *The New York Times*, April 3, 1931, p. 39. "Son of Warner Slightly Better," *Los Angeles Times*, April 4, 1931, p. A3. Display Ad 35, *Los Angeles Times*, April 7, 1931, p. A9.

60. "Chatter," *Variety*, June 16, 1931, p. 44. "Theatre Notes," *Daily News*, June 23, 1931, p. 35. Howard Barnes, "The Playbill," *Herald Tribune*, June 28, 1931, sec. 8, p. 1.
61. Richard Rodgers, Columbia Oral History, p. 112.
62. "Theater News," *New York Post*, July 13, 1931, p. 10.
63. "Boy" Solmson, "On and Off Broadway," *Zit's Theatrical Newspaper*, Oct. 31, 1931, p. 8.

Chapter 12: I'm Not Afraid of My Own Creation

1. Damase, *Les Folies du Music-Hall*, p. 25.
2. Behr, *The Good Frenchman*, p. 136.
3. Alma Whitaker, "Foreign Stars Outlook Cited," *Los Angeles Times*, Aug. 25, 1929, p. B9.
4. Dorothy Rodgers, interviewed by David C. Berliner, May 17, 1976, for the William E. Weiner Oral History Library of the American Jewish Committee, New York Public Library. Secrest, *Somewhere for Me*, p. 148.
5. "Hollywood Boulevard Decorated," *Los Angeles Times*, Dec. 6, 1931, p. D2.
6. Harry Ruby, Columbia Oral History, p. 2042.
7. Block, ed., *Richard Rodgers Reader*, pp. 34–35. Nolan, *Lorenz Hart*, pp. 156–157.
8. Secrest, *Somewhere for Me*, p. 156. Secrest, with Dorothy Rodgers her probable source, identifies the jazz band as Count Basie's; but there's no evidence Basie was in Los Angeles that early, and he was then playing piano for Benny Moten rather than leading a band under his own name.
9. Block, ed., *Richard Rodgers Reader*, p. 35.
10. Makinson, *Greene & Greene*, p. 185. Smith, *Greene and Greene*, p. 178. Nolan, *Lorenz Hart*, p. 158.
11. Henry Myers, "Portrait of Larry Hart," unpublished memoir, p. 69. Nolan, *Lorenz Hart*, p. 161.
12. "*Kiki* Starring Pickford on Loew's Bill," *Hartford Courant*, July 13, 1931, p. 7. Nolan, *Lorenz Hart*, p. 41.
13. Will Rogers, "Will Rogers Finds the Nation Has but a Single Thought," *The New York Times*, March 4, 1932, p. 21.
14. "Fear Kidnapers," *Zit's Theatrical Newspaper*, March 12, 1932, p. 1.
15. Taylor, *Some Enchanted Evenings*, pp. 52–53. Nolan, *Lorenz Hart*, p. 158.
16. Abbott, *Mister Abbott*, p. 131.
17. Rodgers, *Musical Stages*, p. 152.
18. Llewellyn Miller, "Hays Fever," *Zit's Theatrical Newspaper*, Feb. 14, 1931, p. 16.
19. Wilkerson and Borie, *The Hollywood Reporter*, p. 40.
20. Jason Joy, letter to B. P. Schulberg, March 2, 1932, included in special material in DVD of *Love Me Tonight*. The commentary is by Miles Kreuger.
21. Heyward and Heyward, *Porgy*, pp. 2–3. Nolan, *Lorenz Hart*, p. 160. Rodgers, *Musical Stages*, p. 151.

22. Kotsilibas-Davis and Loy, *Myrna Loy*, p. 74.

23. Parcq, *Crime Reporter*, p. 20.

24. Arce, *The Secret Life of Tyrone Power*, pp. 60–70.

25. John Scott, "Comedy Tricks Open Film Door," *Los Angeles Times*, May 22, 1932, p. B13.

26. Myers, "Portrait of Larry Hart," p. 64. Nolan, *Lorenz Hart*, p. 162.

27. Coslow, *Cocktails for Two*, pp. 99–100.

28. "Mankiewicz Quits Par., May Join Radio Lot," *Variety*, July 12, 1932, p. 4. "Hollywood," *Variety*, July 19, 1932, p. 31.

29. Taylor, *Some Enchanted Evenings*, pp. 52–53. "Screen Job Suits Swim Star," *Los Angeles Times*, Oct. 29, 1932, p. A1.

30. "Cohan Here to Appear in Picture," *Los Angeles Times*, June 1, 1932, p. A1.

31. Mast, *Can't Help Singin'*, p. 35.

32. Mollie Merrick, "George M. Cohan Makes Discovery in Hollywood," *Los Angeles Times*, June 12, 1932, p. B11.

33. Richard Rodgers, letter to Dorothy Feiner, Aug. 14, 1929, Richard Rodgers Papers, New York Public Library.

34. Durante and Kofoed, *Night Clubs*, p. 34. Richard Rodgers, Columbia Oral History, p. 166. Rodgers, *Musical Stages*, p. 154.

35. Coslow, *Cocktails for Two*, p. 154.

36. Ibid., p. 137.

37. Financial analysis made by Sam Hawkins of Paramount Music Dept., recorded in memo to A. C. Martin, Aug. 10, 1932.

38. Dorothy Parker, interviewed by Marion Capron, in Cowley, ed., *Writers at Work*, p. 81.

39. Edwin Schallert, "*Hullabaloo*, Novel Revue," *Los Angeles Times*, July 12, 1932, p. 9.

40. "New Hollywood Café Planned," *Los Angeles Times*, July 10, 1932, p. 15. "Don't Quote Me," *Los Angeles Times*, July 17, 1932, p. B13.

41. McGuire, *Lullaby of Broadway*, p. 115.

42. Richard Rodgers, Columbia Oral History, p. 187.

43. "Abreast of the Market," *The Wall Street Journal*, Jan. 28, 1933, p. 2. Zukor, *The Public Is Never Wrong*, p. 262.

44. Mollie Merrick, "Hollywood in Person," *Los Angeles Times*, April 15, 1932, p. 13. "Music," *Variety*, May 24, 1932, p. 77.

45. Ben Hecht letter to Mary Pickford, June 16, 1942, AMPAS. Edward Watz, "*Hallelujah, I'm a Bum!* A Reappraisal," *Classic Film Collector*, Fall 1975, pp. 37–38.

46. Sidney Skolsky, "Tintypes," *Daily News*, Aug. 12, 1932, p. 34. "Pictures," *Variety*, Aug. 16, 1932, p. 3.

47. Philip K. Scheuer, "A Town Called Hollywood," *Los Angeles Times*, Aug. 14, 1932, p. B15. "'Photographic Music' Latest," *Los Angeles Times*, Aug. 27, 1932, p. 5. "Song Romance Delightful," *Los Angeles Times*, Sept. 2, 1932, p. 13.

48. "The Current Cinema," *The New Yorker*, Aug. 20, 1932, p. 58.
49. "New Films Reviewed," *The Boston Globe*, Aug. 27, 1932, p. 15. Mordaunt Hall, "Maurice Chevalier and Jeanette MacDonald in Charming Romantic Musical Fantasy," *The New York Times*, Aug. 18, 1932, p. 20.
50. Secrest, *Somewhere for Me*, p. 157.
51. "Rogers-Hart [*sic*] Doing a Rover Boys on 2 Films," *Variety*, Aug. 8, 1932, p. 3. Ad, *Variety*, Sept. 13, 1932, p. 44.
52. "Pictures," *Variety*, Aug. 30, 1932, p. 3. The friend was Irving Lesser.

Chapter 13: I Am Too Drunk with Beauty

1. *Variety*, Oct. 11, 1932, p. 6.
2. Richard Rodgers, letter to Dorothy Rodgers, Oct. 17, 1932, Richard Rodgers Papers, New York Public Library.
3. Richard Rodgers, letter to Dorothy Rodgers, Nov. 6, 1932, Richard Rodgers Papers, New York Public Library.
4. Nolan, *Lorenz Hart*, p. 172.
5. "Miss Carrington a Bride," *The New York Times*, July 8, 1934, p. N3.
6. Nolan, *Lorenz Hart*, p. 192. "News of the Cafes," *Los Angeles Times*, Sept. 16, 1932, p. A5. "News of the Cafes," *Los Angeles Times*, Sept. 21, 1932, p. A7.
7. Arce, *The Secret Life of Tyrone Power*, pp. 69–70. "Chatter," *Variety*, Jan. 19, 1932, p. 46.
8. Meyerson and Harburg, *Who Put the Rainbow in the Wizard of Oz?* p. 64. Brooks Atkinson, "The Play," *The New York Times*, Oct. 6, 1932, p. 19. "Drama Music Pictures," *The Boston Globe*, Nov. 6, 1932, p. A48.
9. Sillman, *Here Lies Leonard Sillman*, pp. 149–150.
10. *Theodore Hart, Appellant, v. New York Life Insurance Company et al., Respondents, et al., Defendants*, Court of Appeals, New York, 296 N.Y. 991; 73 N.E. 2d 568; 1947 N.Y. Lexis 1929, argued Nov. 26, 1946, decided April 17, 1947.
11. Nolan, *Lorenz Hart*, p. 177.
12. Elizabeth Abel, "Shadows," *Representations*, November 2003, p. 170.
13. "NBC Says Jolson Too Warm, but CBS OK's," *Variety*, Feb. 7, 1933, p. 55.
14. "Jolson Film Flops; So U.A. Yanks It," *Zit's Theatrical Newspaper*, Feb. 25, 1933, p. 1.
15. Schatz, *The Genius of the System*, p. 106.
16. Henderson, *Mielziner*, pp. 117–118.
17. MGM reader's report by Alexander G. Kenodi, April 17, 1932. *I Married an Angel* files, AMPAS.
18. James Wingate, letter to Eddie Mannix, May 4, 1933. *I Married an Angel* files, AMPAS.
19. Rodgers, *A Personal Book*, p. 126.
20. "Scores Perish in Southland Quake," *Los Angeles Times*, March 11, 1933, p. 1. Nolan, *Lorenz Hart*, p. 174.

21. Nolan, *Lorenz Hart*, p. 174.
22. "Roosevelt Calls Will Hays," *Zit's Theatrical Newspaper*, April 8, 1933, p. 1.
23. "Nazis Halt U.S. Films," *Zit's Theatrical Newspaper*, April 15, 1933, p. 1.
24. "Studios Put Salaries Back," *Zit's Theatrical Newspaper*, April 22, 1933, p. 1.
25. Dietz memo, May 15, 1933. *Hollywood Revue* files, AMPAS.
26. Richard Rodgers, letter to Dorothy Rodgers, June 8, 1933, Richard Rodgers Papers, New York Public Library.
27. Richard Rodgers, letter to Dorothy Rodgers, June 3, 1933, Richard Rodgers Papers, New York Public Library.
28. Richard Rodgers, letter to Dorothy Rodgers, May 31, 1933, Richard Rodgers Papers, New York Public Library.
29. Sillman, *Here Lies Leonard Sillman*, p. 152. Carr, *Los Angeles: City of Dreams*, p. 313.
30. *Manhattan*, Feb. 11, 1939, p. 5. Charles Walters, interviewed by Ronald L. Davis, Malibu, Aug. 21, 1980, SMU Oral History, p. 9. AMPAS.
31. Richard Rodgers, letter to Dorothy Rodgers, June 10, 1933, Richard Rodgers Papers, New York Public Library.
32. James Wingate, letter to Eddie Mannix, June 23, 1933. *Hollywood Party* files, AMPAS.
33. "Pictures," *Variety*, Sept. 5, 1933, p. 4.
34. "Jack Pearl's Film Prices," *Variety*, Feb. 14, 1933, p. 3.
35. Nolan, *Lorenz Hart*, p. 186.
36. Miles Kreuger, interviewed by Janice Ross and Claude Conyers, March 25, 2001, Popular Balanchine Dossier for *I Married an Angel*, New York Public Library.
37. Richard Rodgers, letter to Dorothy Rodgers, June 24, 1933, Richard Rodgers Papers, New York Public Library.
38. John T. McManus, "Book by Rodgers and Hart," *The New York Times*, Feb. 14, 1937, p. 164.
39. Cole Porter, "Anything Goes."
40. Richard Rodgers, letter to Dorothy Rodgers, June 28, 1933, Richard Rodgers Papers, New York Public Library.
41. Richard Rodgers, letter to Dorothy Rodgers, July 1, 1933, Richard Rodgers Papers, New York Public Library.
42. Oppenheimer, *The View from the Sixties*, p. 110.
43. Richard Rodgers, letter to Dorothy Rodgers, June 25, 1933, Richard Rodgers Papers, New York Public Library.
44. Richard Rodgers, letter to Dorothy Rodgers, June 27, 1933, Richard Rodgers Papers, New York Public Library.
45. Fordin, *Getting to Know Him*, p. 92n. Richard Rodgers, letter to Dorothy Rodgers, July 14, 1933, Richard Rodgers Papers, New York Public Library.
46. Richard Rodgers, Columbia Oral History, pp. 199–200. "Restaurateur and Publisher Wilkerson Dies," *Los Angeles Times*, Sept. 3, 1962, p. A1.

47. "M-G Wants *Love Parade* Trio for *Merry Widow*," *Variety*, Oct. 12, 1930, p. 3.
48. "Technicolor *Merry Widow*," *Variety*, Dec. 19, 1933, p. 2.
49. Edwin Schallert, "New *Merry Widow* Tunes Refused by Lehár," *Los Angeles Times*, Dec. 21, 1933, p. 7. "Tamara Geva, Stage Actress and Dancer, Signed for Films," *Los Angeles Times*, Dec. 26, 1933, p. 5. "Chevalier and Jeanette Mac-Donald Kiss, Make Up, Decide to Play in Film Together," *Los Angeles Times*, Feb. 14, 1934, p. 13.
50. "Legal Liquor Due Tonight! City Ready to Celebrate; Liquor Stores Open To-morrow!" *The New York Times*, Dec. 5, 1933, p. 1.
51. O. O. McIntyre, "Once Overs," *Los Angeles Examiner*, Dec. 22, 1933, part 2, p. 1. Mosedale, *The Men Who Invented Broadway*, p. 184. Richard Rodgers, Columbia Oral History, p. 155.

Chapter 14: I Heard Somebody Whisper, "Please Adore Me"

1. Rodgers, *Musical Stages*, p. 165.
2. Richard Rodgers, Columbia Oral History, p. 155.
3. Behr, *The Good Frenchman*, p. 183.
4. Joseph L. Breen, letter to Louis B. Mayer, March 27, 1934, *Merry Widow* file, AMPAS.
5. Behrman, *People in a Diary*, p. 162.
6. Robert M. W. Vogel, AMPAS Oral History Program, p. 62.
7. "Lilyan Tashman Dies in Hospital," *The New York Times*, March 22, 1934, p. 21.
8. Rodgers, *Musical Stages*, p. 165. Fitzgerald, *The Last Tycoon*, p. 3.
9. William B. Chase, "Who's New in the Opera," *The New York Times*, Nov. 4, 1923, p. SM8. Marx and Clayton, *Rodgers & Hart*, p. 191. "*Faust* and *The Jest* Sung," *The New York Times*, March 21, 1926, p. 26. F. O. Perkins, "Nanette Guilford Merits Acclaim at Metropolitan," *Herald Tribune*, March 21, 1926, p. 18. "Nanette Guilford, Opera Star, A Secret Bride," *The New York Times*, Nov. 30, 1928, p. 1. "Nanette Guilford to Seek a Divorce," *The New York Times*, Feb. 13, 1930, p. 25. "Miss Guilford Files as Bankrupt," *The New York Times*, March 15, 1930, p. 9.
10. Hart, *Thou Swell*, p. 70.
11. "Dillinger Case Stirs Nation's Press to Sarcasm," *The New York Times*, May 5, 1934, p. 9.
12. Joseph I. Breen memo to Hon. Will Hays, April 10, 1934. *Hollywood Party* files, AMPAS.
13. Marx and Clayton, *Rodgers & Hart*, p. 193.
14. Brooks Atkinson, "The Play," *The New York Times*, June 8, 1934, p. 19.
15. Rodgers, *Musical Stages*, p. 169.
16. Richard Rodgers, letter to Dorothy Rodgers, July 18, 1934, Richard Rodgers Papers, New York Public Library.

17. *Variety*, April 24, 1935, p. 12. Mantle, ed., *The Best Plays 1923–1924*, pp. 309–310.
18. *Mississippi* files, AMPAS.
19. Richard Rodgers, letter to Dorothy Rodgers, July 23, 1934, Richard Rodgers Papers, New York Public Library.
20. Tip Poff, "That Certain Party," *Los Angeles Times*, July 22, 1934, p. A1.
21. Richard Rodgers, letter to Dorothy Rodgers, July 26, 1934, Richard Rodgers Papers, New York Public Library.
22. Max Lief, "Words and Music," *The Saturday Evening Post*, March 25, 1933, p. 11.
23. Rostand, *Cyrano de Bergerac*, p. 252.
24. O'Hara, "I Could Have Had a Yacht," in *Here's O'Hara*, p. 93.
25. Richard Rodgers, letter to Dorothy Rodgers, July 27, 1934, Richard Rodgers Papers, New York Public Library.
26. Richard Rodgers, "Words Without Music," *The New York Times*, June 14, 1936, p. X1. Rodgers, *Musical Stages*, p. 171.
27. Richard Rodgers, letter to Dorothy Rodgers, Aug. 7, 1934, Richard Rodgers Papers, New York Public Library.
28. "*Peggy-Ann* Has Premiere Today on Local Stage," *Los Angeles Times*, Aug. 9, 1934, p. 19.
29. "Diva, Composer to Marry," *New York Evening Journal*, Aug. 11, 1934, p. 3.
30. Richard Rodgers, letter to Dorothy Rodgers, Aug. 11, 1934, Richard Rodgers Papers, New York Public Library.
31. *Hollywood Reporter*, Aug. 10, 1934, p. 1.
32. "Rambling Reporter," *Hollywood Reporter*, Aug. 13, 1934, p. 2. "Composers Leave," *Los Angeles Times*, Aug. 23, 1934, p. 18.
33. Hallas, *You Play the Black and the Red Comes Up*, pp. 207–208.
34. "Movie Theatres Inaugurate Fall Season with Labor Holiday Boom," *The Wall Street Journal*, Sept. 4, 1935, p. 1.
35. "Ex-Opera Star Plans to Marry Wealthy Briton," *Los Angeles Times*, Sept. 3, 1934, p. 1.
36. Wilk, *They're Playing Our Song*, p. 51.
37. Manager and Authors' Agreement, dated Dec. 19, 1934, Shubert Archive. Richard Rodgers, Columbia Oral History, p. 158. Liebling, "The Boys from Syracuse," *The Telephone Booth Indian*, pp. 73–74. Maurice Zolotow, "The Co-ordinator of Shubert Alley," *The New York Times*, Sept. 19, 1943, p. X1.
38. Richard Rodgers, "Words Without Music," *The New York Times*, June 14, 1936, p. X1.
39. Rodgers, *Musical Stages*, p. 171.
40. "Balaban and Katz Showing in Red," *The Wall Street Journal*, Jan. 18, 1933, p. 1. "Paramount Bankruptcy," *The Wall Street Journal*, March 15, 1933, p. 1. "Paramount Publix," *The Wall Street Journal*, July 6, 1933, p. 17. "Plan of Reorganization Prepared for Paramount," *The Wall Street Journal*, Nov. 21, 1934, p. 2. "Ten

Million Profit Cited," *Los Angeles Times*, Feb. 7, 1935, p. A1. Edwin Schallert, "Inside Story of Paramount Studio Shakeup Told," *Los Angeles Times*, Feb. 10, 1935, p. A1.

41. Carroll Nye, "Kingsford-Smith to Be Initiated into Breakfast Club," *Los Angeles Times*, Nov. 7, 1934, p. 12. *Mississippi* files, AMPAS.

42. Analysis of Loss in Schedule, *Mississippi* files, AMPAS. Giddins, *Bing Crosby*, p. 405.

43. Marc Connelly, "For Services Rendered," *The New York Times*, Feb. 24, 1935, p. X2.

44. Caldwell, *New York Nights*, p. 258. Hawes, *New York, New York*, p. 233.

Chapter 15: The World Was Younger Than I

1. "Yale Professor Who Turned Actor," *The Boston Herald*, March 22, 1936. "D. D. Wiman Unusual Person," *The Boston Post*, March 21, 1936, p. 37. Unpaged clippings from the Dwight Deere Wiman Papers, New York Public Library.

2. Kahn, *The World of Swope*, p. 209.

3. Richard Maney, "The Bantam Barnum," *Stage*, November 1938, p. 18. "Boris Would Sell Costly Elephants," *The New York Times*, Dec. 17, 1934, p. 21. "King Loses One Elephant and Will Keep the Other," *The New York Times*, Dec. 21, 1934, p. 20. "Rialto Gossip," *The New York Times*, Dec. 30, 1934, p. X1.

4. Caldwell, *New York Nights*, p. 176.

5. Conrad, *Billy Rose*, p. 118.

6. Maney, "The Bantam Barnum," p. 33.

7. Ibid.

8. Van Doren, ed., *The Borzoi Reader*, p. 400.

9. Robbins, *Inka Dink A Doo*, p. 108.

10. "They Stand Out from the Crowd," *Literary Digest*, April 4, 1934, p. 12.

11. DeLong, *Pops*, p. 240. Rayno, *Paul Whiteman*, p. 545.

12. Maney, "The Bantam Barnum," p. 33.

13. Darrell, *Rodgers and Hart Songbook*, p. 27. Maney, "The Bantam Barnum," pp. 33–34.

14. Maney, "The Bantam Barnum," pp. 33–34. Baral, *Revue*, pp. 202–203.

15. Abbott, *Mister Abbott*, p. 177.

16. Philip K. Scheuer, "Independents Go on Periodic Picture Spree," *Los Angeles Times*, Jan. 19, 1936, p. C1.

17. *Dancing Pirate* files, AMPAS.

18. *Richard Rodgers Fact Book*, pp. 161–162.

19. Maney, "The Bantam Barnum," p. 20.

20. Hodges, *The Play That Changed My Life*, frontispiece. Patrick Healy, "Falling, Falling, Falling for the Footlight Parade," *The New York Times*, Dec. 22, 2009, p. C8.

21. "Theater to Have Three Features," *Los Angeles Times*, May 6, 1936, p. A17.
22. Richard Rodgers, letters to Dorothy Rodgers, Dec. 12, 1935, and Dec. 13, 1935, Richard Rodgers Papers, New York Public Library.
23. Faderman and Timmons, *Gay L.A.*, p. 45.
24. Pitkin, *Careers After Forty*, p. 201.
25. Gary Marmorstein, "Lorenz Hart at 100," *Performing Arts*, May 1995, p. 20.
26. *Zit's Theatrical Newspaper*, Jan. 11, 1936, p. 5.

Chapter 16: Unrequited Love's a Bore

 1. Kilgallen, "Dancer Kicks at Critics of Jazz Ballet," *New York Evening Journal*, Dec. 30, 1935.
 2. Lee Shubert agreement with George Balanchine, Aug. 13, 1935, Shubert Archive.
 3. "Business Records," *The New York Times*, Jan. 14, 1936, p. 39.
 4. Comden and Green, *Bells Are Ringing*, pp. 85–87.
 5. Duke, *Passport to Paris*, p. 311.
 6. Emily Coleman, "The Musical Takes a Giant Step," 1968 *On Your Toes* revival program, included in Popular Balanchine Dossier compiled by Lynn Garafola, New York Public Library.
 7. John T. McManus, "Book by Rodgers and Hart," *The New York Times*, Feb. 14, 1937, p. 164. Rodgers, *Musical Stages*, p. 178. Hart, *Thou Swell*, p. 121.
 8. Hart and Kaufman, *You Can't Take It with You*, p. 164.
 9. Mielziner, *Designing for the Theatre*, p. 21.
10. Cohen, ed., *Dictionary of Modern Ballet*, pp. 56–57.
11. Richard Rodgers, letter to Dorothy Rodgers, Feb. 6, 1936, Richard Rodgers Papers, New York Public Library. Rodgers, *Musical Stages*, p. 175.
12. Darrell, *The Rodgers and Hart Song Book*, p. 8.
13. Aleen Robinson, interviewed by author, May 28, 2008. Dietz, *Dancing in the Dark*, p. 120. Abbott, *Mister Abbott*, p. 177. Rodgers, *Musical Stages*, p. 174.
14. Ray Bolger, interviewed by Ronald Davis, SMU Oral History, August 1976, p. 20.
15. *The Boston Globe*, March 28, 1937, p. A46.
16. Grace Kaye, interviewed by Lynn Garafola, Dec. 4, 2000, Popular Balanchine Dossier, New York Public Library.
17. Richard Rodgers, letter to Dorothy Rodgers, March 20, 1936, Richard Rodgers Papers, New York Public Library.
18. David Raksin, interviewed by Lynn Garafola, Nov. 29, 2000, and Dec. 5, 2000, Popular Balanchine Dossier, New York Public Library.
19. Richard Rodgers, letter to Dorothy Rodgers, March 22, 1936, Richard Rodgers Papers, New York Public Library.
20. Abbott, *Mister Abbott*, p. 177.
21. Rodgers, *Musical Stages*, p. 174.

22. Ray Bolger, interviewed by Ronald Davis, SMU Oral History, August 1976, pp. 23–24.

23. Nolan, *Lorenz Hart*, p. 211.

24. *Cue*, April 16, 1936, pp. 12–14.

25. Rodgers, *Musical Stages*, p. 178.

26. Jon Pareles, "What Is the Sound of Broadway? Hans Spialek Knows," *The New York Times*, April 17, 1983, p. A4.

27. Sharaff, *Broadway and Hollywood*, p. 30. Popular Balanchine Dossier compiled by Lynn Garafola, p. 12.

28. Wolcott Gibbs, "The Theatre Success Story," *The New Yorker*, April 18, 1936, p. 28.

29. Wilk, *They're Playing Our Song*, p. 60.

30. Coward, *Private Lives*, act 1.

31. Nolan, *Lorenz Hart*, p. 212. Hart, *Thou Swell*, p. 93.

32. Walter Holbrook, "Ex-Wrestler Pirouettes Daintily on Ballet; So There, Mr. Ripley!" *Herald Tribune*, April 9, 1939, sec. VI, p. 5.

33. Barnett, *Writing on Life*, p. 307.

34. Salinger, *The Catcher in the Rye*, p. 35.

35. John O'Hara, letter to Bennett Cerf, Jan. 18, 1963, in *Selected Letters of John O'Hara*, p. 415.

36. Jon Pareles, "What Is the Sound of Broadway? Hans Spialek Knows," *The New York Times*, April 17, 1983, p. A4.

37. "Theater Notes," *Daily News*, April 29, 1936.

38. Danton Walker, "Broadway," *Daily News*, Oct. 6, 1939, p. 58. Hart, *Thou Swell*, p. 86.

39. Sobol, *The Longest Street*, pp. 296–297. Clark, *Damon Runyon*, p. 203. Carroll, *In Your Hat*, p. 179.

40. "Fifty Children Will Play in Forthcoming Musical," *Los Angeles Times*, July 27, 1936, p. 15.

41. Duke, *Passport to Paris*, p. 369. Hart, *Thou Swell*, p. 93. Taper, *Balanchine*, p. 195. Frederick Nolan, e-mail to author, June 1, 2008.

42. "Pair Through with Broadway but Maybe Not 'Positively,'" *Los Angeles Times*, Aug. 3, 1936, p. 10.

43. Schulberg, *Writers in America*, p. 143.

44. Edwin Schallert, "Lloyd Recruits Trio of Gag Men," *Los Angeles Times*, Sept. 17, 1936, p. A17.

45. "The Story of Richard Rodgers," air check of *The Singing Story Lady*, Oct. 4, 1936, Richard Rodgers Papers, New York Public Library.

46. "Musicals Pall, So Rodgers, Hart Turn 'Serious,'" *World-Telegram*, Nov. 23, 1936. Richard Rodgers, Columbia Oral History, pp. 204–205.

47. Harrison, *The Day Before Yesterday*, p. 297.

48. Richard Rodgers, letter to Dorothy Rodgers, Feb. 6, 1936, Richard Rodgers Papers, New York Public Library.
49. Nolan, *Lorenz Hart*, p. 216.
50. Brooks Atkinson, "The Play," *The New York Times*, Dec. 26, 1936, p. 14.
51. Contract between *On Your Toes, Inc.*, and Warner Bros., Dec. 30, 1936.
52. Krafsur and Munden, eds., *American Film Institute Catalogue*, p. 1558.
53. Nolan, *Lorenz Hart*, p. 217.
54. "News of the Stage," *The New York Times*, Jan. 5, 1937, p. 19. "Gossip of the Rialto," *The New York Times*, Jan. 24, 1937, p. 149.
55. "Miss Lawrence Gets New Role," *The New York Times*, Jan. 14, 1937, p. 17.
56. Glenn C. Pullen, *Cleveland Plain-Dealer*, Feb. 3, 1937. "News of the Stage," *The New York Times*, Feb. 22, 1937, p. 12.
57. "How Screen Star Became Vera Zorina," *World-Telegram*, May 7, 1938, p. 8.
58. Vivienne Segal, interviewed by Ronald Davis, SMU Oral History, Sept. 23, 1981, p. 28.

Chapter 17: Is Your Figure Less Than Greek?

1. Mordaunt Hall, "An Hour at a Rehearsal of the Musical Comedy, 'Babes in Arms,'" *Boston Transcript*, March 27, 1937.
2. Gerry Thompson, "Young Man of Manhattan," *Popular Song*, September 1936, p. 16.
3. Behrman, *People in a Diary*, p. 172.
4. *The Boston Globe*, March 28, 1937, p. A46.
5. "Kid Actor's Billing Holdout Causes 'Babes' to Switch Its Script," *Variety*, March 17, 1937, p. 53.
6. Richard Rodgers, letters to Dorothy Rodgers, March 15, March 16, March 18, and March 19, 1937, Richard Rodgers Papers, New York Public Library.
7. "Wynn Murray New Face in Musical Comedy," *The Boston Post*, April 4, 1937.
8. Mordaunt Hall, "An Hour at a Rehearsal of the Musical Comedy, 'Babes in Arms,'" *Boston Transcript*, March 27, 1937.
9. Nolan, *Lorenz Hart*, p. 218.
10. Reed, *Hot from Harlem*, p. 177. W.C.C., "Entertainment World," *New York Amsterdam News*, April 17, 1937, p. 16.
11. *Babes in Arms* Dossier, Popular Balanchine Dossier, compiled by Constance Valis Hill, May 2002, George Balanchine Foundation, New York Public Library.
12. Greene, *The Pleasure Dome*, p. 276. "Damages for Shirley Temple," *The Manchester Guardian*, March 23, 1938, p. 5.
13. Dennis Moore, letter to author, March 4, 2010.
14. Sinclair Lewis, "Hobohemia," *The Saturday Evening Post*, April 7, 1917, p. 3. Schorer, *Sinclair Lewis*, pp. 150, 191.

15. Stirling Bowen, "The Theatre: Youthful Spontaneity," *The Wall Street Journal*, April 16, 1937, p. 13. Brooks Atkinson, "The Play," *The New York Times*, April 14, 1937, p. 30. Robert Benchley, "The Theatre," *The New Yorker*, April 24, 1937, p. 28.
16. Nathan, *The Theatre Book of the Year, 1942–1943*, p. 5.
17. Charles E. Dexter, "Mighty Little Lorenz Hart Does a Show with Dick Rodgers," *Daily Worker*, April 19, 1937.
18. "Breaking Down Caste," *New York Amsterdam News*, July 10, 1937, p. 14.
19. "Theatre," *Time*, April 26, 1937, p. 26.
20. *New York Journal American*, March 22, 1937. Helen Worden, "Eerie Story of Skeleton Stirs Party," Akron, Ohio, *Times Press*, April 15, 1937.
21. Leonard Lyons, "Lyons Den," *New York Post*, April 15, 1937, p. 21.
22. Sidney Phillips, report to Eddie Knopf, April 15, 1937. Turner Files, AMPAS.
23. Douglas Gilbert, "Theatres' Standards Uplifted by Movies," *World-Telegram*, April 21, 1937.
24. Richard Rodgers, letter to Dorothy Rodgers, April 27, 1937, Richard Rodgers Papers, New York Public Library. Rodgers, *Musical Stages*, p. 183.
25. Richard Rodgers, letter to Dorothy Rodgers, May 2, 1937, Richard Rodgers Papers, New York Public Library.
26. Ryskind, *The Diary of an Ex-President*, p. 55.
27. Richard Rodgers, letter to Dorothy Rodgers, May 5, 1937, Richard Rodgers Papers, New York Public Library.
28. Richard Rodgers, letter to Dorothy Rodgers, May 6, 1937, Richard Rodgers Papers, New York Public Library.
29. Richard Rodgers, letter to Dorothy Rodgers, May 7, 1937, Richard Rodgers Papers, New York Public Library.
30. Richard Rodgers, letter to Dorothy Rodgers, May 12, 1937, Richard Rodgers Papers, New York Public Library.
31. Larry Walters, "News of the Radio Stations," *Chicago Tribune*, May 15, 1937, p. 20. Carroll Nye, "Johnny Green to Take Over Astaire Show," *Los Angeles Times*, May 20, 1937, p. 14.
32. Agate, *The Later Ego*, May 5, 1937.
33. Agate, *Here Is Richness!* p. 211.
34. Richard Rodgers, letter to Dorothy Rodgers, June 26, 1937, Richard Rodgers Papers, New York Public Library.
35. The air check can be heard on the CD of *Command Performance*, Harbinger Records HCD2501.
36. *On Your Toes* inventory, April 30, 1937, Shubert Archive.

Chapter 18: All at Once I Owned the Earth and Sky

1. Beerbohm, *Around Theatres*, p. 53.
2. Irving Kolodin, *Brooklyn Eagle*, April 25, 1937.

3. George Ross, "Hart Calls Producers Optimists," *World-Telegram*, July 31, 1937, p. 8.

4. Orville Prescott, "Broadway Duet," *Cue*, May 1, 1937, pp. 6–7.

5. Nolan, *Lorenz Hart*, p. 229.

6. John Peter Toohey, "Regarding Those Who Would Rather Be Right," *The New York Times*, Nov. 7, 1937, p. 182.

7. Rodgers, *Musical Stages*, p. 182.

8. Richard Rodgers, letter to Dorothy Rodgers, July 10, 1937, Richard Rodgers Papers, New York Public Library.

9. Fitzgerald, *The Letters of F. Scott Fitzgerald*, p. 63.

10. Rodgers, *Musical Stages*, p. 183.

11. "On the Air from Hollywood," *Los Angeles Times*, July 11, 1937, p. H3. Richard Rodgers, letter to Dorothy Rodgers, July 12, 1937, Richard Rodgers Papers, New York Public Library.

12. "Gershwin Death Stuns," *Hollywood Reporter*, July 12, 1937, p. 1. Richard Rodgers, Letter to Dorothy Rodgers, July 15, 1937, Richard Rodgers Papers, New York Public Library.

13. "American Negro Girl to Entertain in London," *New York Amsterdam News*, Oct. 26, 1935, p. 6. Roi Ottley, "Hollywood's Chocolate Princess," *New York Amsterdam News*, Nov. 21, 1936, p. 12.

14. Nolan, *Lorenz Hart*, p. 224.

15. *Judge*, Jan. 14, 1928, back of front cover.

16. Runyon, "A Call on the President," in *Take It Easy*; the story appeared in *The Saturday Review*, Aug. 21, 1937. Clark, *Damon Runyon*, p. 228.

17. Richard Rodgers, Columbia Oral History, p. 209. Rodgers, *Musical Stages*, pp. 186–187. Nolan, *Lorenz Hart*, p. 233.

18. Bankhead, *Tallulah*, p. 25.

19. Bert Andrews, "Budget Balance Pledged Again by 'President,'" *Herald Tribune*, Oct. 12, 1937, p. 23. Nolan, *Lorenz Hart*, p. 232. Green, *The World of Musical Comedy*, p. 157.

20. "When All Night Long" from *Iolanthe*, by Gilbert and Sullivan.

21. "Spoofing the Great," *The New York Times*, Oct. 14, 1937, p. 24.

22. Lucius Beebe, "Going to It," *Stage*, December 1937, pp. 60–65.

23. Nolan, *Lorenz Hart*, p. 234.

24. Brooks Atkinson, "The Play," *The New York Times*, Nov. 3, 1937, p. 28. Atkinson, "I'd Rather Be Right," *The New York Times*, Nov. 14, 1937, p. 181.

25. *Richard Rodgers Fact Book*, pp. 195–196.

26. Brown, *Two on the Aisle*, pp. 286–287.

27. Richard Rodgers, letter to Fanny E. Holtzmann, Feb. 10, 1964, Richard Rodgers Papers, New York Public Library.

28. "News and Gossip of Broadway," *The New York Times*, Nov. 14, 1937, p. 181.

29. "Rodgers and Hart: A Theater Team 18 Years Old," *The Boston Herald*, May 1, 1938.

30. Michel Mok, "Did You Ever Hear That One About Budapest?" *New York Post*, Jan. 10, 1938, p. 13. Nolan, *Lorenz Hart*, pp. 234–235.
31. Green, *Ring Bells! Sing Songs!*, p. 147.
32. Nolan, *Lorenz Hart*, p. 239.
33. Michel Mok, "Hoot Owls, Indeed! It Was Blind Moles, Forsooth!" *New York Post*, March 2, 1938, p. 15.
34. Ibid.

Chapter 19: Caring Too Much Is Such a Juvenile Fancy
1. Michel Mok, "Did You Ever Hear That One About Budapest?" *New York Post*, Jan. 10, 1938, p. 13.
2. Hart, *Thou Swell*, p. 118.
3. Selznick, *Memo from David O. Selznick*, p. 101.
4. Logan, *Josh*, p. 118.
5. Van Meter, *The Last Good Time*, p. 28.
6. Logan, *Josh*, p. 119.
7. Marx and Clayton, *Rodgers & Hart*, p. 202. Logan, *Josh*, p. 119.
8. Nancy Knott, interviewed by Marilyn Hunt, Dec. 8, 2000, Popular Balanchine Dossier, New York Public Library.
9. Zorina, *Zorina*, p. 203.
10. Ibid., p. 210.
11. Josh Logan, interviewed by Raymond Daum, July 1980, Columbia Oral History, pp. 220–221.
12. Zorina, *Zorina*, p. 210.
13. Nancy Knott, interviewed by Marilyn Hunt, Dec. 8, 2000, Popular Balanchine Dossier, New York Public Library.
14. Ibid.
15. Rostand, *Cyrano de Bergerac*, p. 53.
16. Mielziner, *Designing for the Theatre*, p. 21. Zorina, *Zorina*, pp. 213–214.
17. Josh Logan, Columbia Oral History, p. 221.
18. Logan, *Josh*, pp. 122–123.
19. Ibid., p. 123.
20. Yeats, "Speaking to the Psaltery," *Essays and Introductions*, p. 14.
21. Josh Logan, Columbia Oral History, p. 223. Logan, *Josh*, pp. 123–124. Nolan, *Lorenz Hart*, p. 248. Secrest, *Somewhere for Me*, p. 199.
22. Lyric courtesy Scott Willis.
23. Zorina, *Zorina*, p. 219.
24. Rodgers, *Musical Stages*, p. 189. Nolan, *Lorenz Hart*, p. 249.
25. Brooks Atkinson, "The Play," *The New York Times*, Sept. 27, 1937, p. 24. Atkinson's irritation was prompted by sitting through the play *The Lady Has a Heart* by Ladislaus Bus-Fekete.

26. Brooks Atkinson, "The Play in Review," *The New York Times*, May 12, 1938, p. 26. Brooks Atkinson, "Marrying an Angel," *The New York Times*, May 22, 1938, p. 151.

27. Zorina, *Zorina*, p. 220.

28. *Chicago Times*, May 11, 1938. Press item, May 16, 1938.

29. Grant Hughes, "Orchids to Vivienne," *Popular Song*, October 1935, p. 12.

30. George Ross, "So This Is Broadway," *World-Telegram*, May 16, 1938, p. 10.

31. "After Dark," *Stage*, October 1938, p. 52.

32. Maxwell Anderson's "The Essence of Tragedy" was read at the MLA conference in New York City, January 1938.

33. Frye, "Mouldy Tales," in *A Natural Perspective*, pp. 23–25.

34. Ivor Brown, "The Week's Theatres," *The Observer*, April 17, 1938, p. 9.

35. Richard Rodgers, Columbia Oral History, p. 202.

36. H. Allen Smith, "Teddy Hart to Play a Dromio in Abbott's Musical Burlesque," *World-Telegram*, July 9, 1938. Douglas W. Churchill, "Hollywood Convenes a Congress of Comics," *The New York Times*, Aug. 8, 1937, p. 137. Edward L. Eustace, "Full Measure in a Half-Pint Juggler," *The New York Times*, Nov. 14, 1937, p. 186.

37. Harrison, *Introducing Shakespeare*, p. 71.

38. Abbott, *Mister Abbott*, pp. 186–187.

39. Jo Mielziner Papers, New York Public Library.

40. "News and Gossip of the Rialto," *The New York Times*, April 24, 1938, p. 147.

41. "Gossip of the Rialto," *The New York Times*, May 22, 1938, p. 151.

42. Charlotte Johnson, "I Cover the Beachfront," *Atlantic City Press*, May 31, 1938.

43. "News of the Stage," *The New York Times*, June 9, 1938, p. 26.

44. "William Kron, 83, Broadway Figure," *The New York Times*, May 21, 1965, p. 35. "Week's Playhouse Bills," *The New York Times*, Oct. 11, 1903, p. 21.

45. Richard Kollmar, liner notes to *Girl Crazy/By Jupiter* by Jackie Cain and Roy Kral. Abbott, *Mister Abbott*, pp. 186–187. "Bard's Lines Tossed Out of Musical," *Daily News*, May 18, 1938, p. 49.

46. "News of the Stage," *The New York Times*, July 26, 1938, p. 22.

47. Wilk, *They're Playing Our Song*, p. 51.

48. Dennis Moore, letter to author, March 24, 2010. *Manhattan*, March 11, 1939, p. 5.

49. "Miller's Defiance Stirs Dramatists," *The New York Times*, Aug. 30, 1938, p. 15.

50. *New York Herald Tribune*, Sept. 7, 1938, p. 19. "News of the Stage," *The New York Times*, Sept. 10, 1938, p. 20.

51. "Team Works," *Chicago Daily Tribune*, Oct. 23, 1938, p. E3.

52. Hugh Martin, telephone interview with author, May 19, 2008.

53. Hart, *Thou Swell*, p. 124.

54. *Variety*, Oct. 26, 1938, p. 38.

55. Abbott, *Mister Abbott*, pp. 186–187.
56. Jack Gould, "Rodgers and Hart Do the Words and Music," *The New York Times*, Dec. 4, 1938, p. X5.
57. Shakespeare, *The Comedy of Errors*, act 1, scene 2.
58. Elliot Norton, *The Boston Post*, Nov. 8, 1938.
59. "Diminutive Dromio," *Manhattan*, April 1, 1939, p. 9. "No Holes Bard," *Stage*, November 1938, p. 17.
60. *The Boys from Syracuse* Dossier, Popular Balanchine Dossier, compiled by Camille Hardy, May 2003, New York Public Library. Wood, *Song Forms*, p. 216.
61. Frye, "The Triumph of Time," in *A Natural Perspective*, p. 78.
62. George Church, from his unpublished memoir, "Dancing Amongst the Stars," p. 100, Popular Balanchine Dossier, New York Public Library.
63. "No Holes Bard," *Stage*, November 1938, p. 17.
64. Hart lyric courtesy Scott Willis.
65. Shakespeare, *The Comedy of Errors*, act 5, scene 1.
66. Marjory Adams, "Shakespeare Lines Too Spicy for Boston, Quips Mr. Abbott," *The Boston Globe*, Nov. 7, 1938, p 6.
67. Rodgers, *Musical Stages*, p. 191. Shakespeare, *The Comedy of Errors*, act 5, scene 1.
68. Sidney B. Whipple, *World-Telegram*, Nov. 25, 1938. *Richard Rodgers Fact Book*, pp. 215–216.
69. *Variety*, Nov. 9, 1938, p. 40.
70. Nolan, *Lorenz Hart*, p. 254.
71. Philip K. Scheuer, "Talent Exchange Hypos Good-Neighbor Policy," *Los Angeles Times*, April 15, 1941, p. A10. Hart, *Thou Swell*, p. 126.
72. Ray Bolger, interviewed by Dawn Lille Horwitz, in *I Remember Balanchine*, p. 158. Zorina, *Zorina*, p. 223.
73. "But Nobody Likes to Sip Champagne from a Slipper Now," *New York Herald Tribune*, Jan. 22, 1939, sec. VI, p. 5. *New York Herald Tribune*, Feb. 18, 1939. Nolan, *Lorenz Hart*, p. 254.

Chapter 20: And Now I Know I Was Naïve

1. Lejeune and Shulman, *The Making of Miami Beach: 1933–1942*, pp. 22, 33.
2. Blumenthal, *Stork Club*, p. 168. Kofoed, *Moon over Miami*, p. 103.
3. Some of the material on Desi Arnaz is taken from an unpublished memoir, Marco Rizo, as told to C. David Younger, "The Desi I Knew," Marco Rizo Papers, New York Public Library.
4. Lawrence Langner, letter to Lorenz Hart, Jan. 31, 1939, Theatre Guild Papers, Beinecke Library, Yale.
5. Theresa Helburn, letter to Lorenz Hart, Feb. 2, 1939, Theatre Guild Papers, Beinecke Library, Yale.

6. *Hollywood Reporter*, Oct. 2, 1939.

7. *Chicago Tribune*, March 9, 1939, p. 19. June Provines, "Front Views and Pro-files," *Chicago Tribune*, March 8, 1939, p. 14.

8. Edwin Schallert, "Young Actors Win Big Roles in Lincoln Film," *Los Angeles Times*, March 7, 1939, p. A17. Warners' Interoffice Communication, Warner Bros. Archives, University of Southern California, quoted in Popular Balanchine Dossier, New York Public Library.

9. Eddie Albert, telephone interview with Camille Hardy, Sept. 19, 2002, Popular Balanchine Dossier, New York Public Library. "Hedda Hopper's Hollywood," *Los Angeles Times*, May 17, 1939, p. 12.

10. "Par's Musical in June," *Variety*, March 4, 1931, p. 4.

11. Oriard, *King Football*, p. 7.

12. Ibid., pp. 95–96.

13. "*The Hot Mikado* Closes Tonight," *The New York Times*, June 3, 1939, p. 17.

14. Arnaz, *A Book*, p. 73. "Le Roy Will Appear in Abbott Musical," *The New York Times*, June 26, 1939, p. 17.

15. *Manhattan*, April 8, 1939, p. 4. Nolan, *Lorenz Hart*, p. 258.

16. "Demand Reported for Large Suites," *The New York Times*, Aug. 5, 1939, p. 29.

17. Secrest, *Somewhere for Me*, p. 101.

18. Hart, *Thou Swell*, p. 123.

19. Henry Myers, "Portrait of Larry Hart," unpublished memoir, p. 76.

20. Philip K. Scheuer, "Studios Theater Gossip," *Los Angeles Times*, Aug. 13, 1939, p. C3.

21. Rizo, "The Desi I Knew."

22. Hugh Martin, telephone interview with author, May 19, 2008.

23. Rodgers, *Musical Stages*, p. 192. Hart and Kimball, eds., *Complete Lyrics*, p. 258.

24. Spaeth, *Read 'Em and Weep*, pp. 108–109.

25. Arnaz, *A Book*, p. 87.

26. Oriard, *King Football*, p. 9.

27. Israel, *Kilgallen*, pp. 126–127.

28. Brooks Atkinson, "The Play," *The New York Times*, Oct. 19, 1939, p. 26.

29. Arnaz, *A Book*, p. 94. Nolan, *Lorenz Hart*, p. 262. John O'Hara, letter to William Maxwell, July 9, 1963, in *Selected Letters of John O'Hara*, p. 434.

30. "The Return of the Musical," *Los Angeles Times*, Oct. 22, 1939, p. C1.

31. Logan, *Josh*, p. 145.

32. "Musical May Arrive as a Play," *Daily News*, Nov. 12, 1939, p. C32.

33. *Ghost Town* can be heard on *Richard Rodgers: Three Ballets*, conducted by John Mauceri, CDJAY 1349.

34. Cecil Smith, "*The White Steed* Will Begin Three Week Run Tomorrow," *Chicago Tribune*, Nov. 22, 1939, p. E2. George Ross, "So This Is Broadway," *World-Telegram*, Oct. 30, 1939.

35. *Variety*, New York, Nov. 8, 1939. Ted Dodd, e-mail to author, April 7, 2009.
36. Taylor, *Some Enchanted Evenings*, pp. 84–85.
37. Hart, *Thou Swell*, p. 142.
38. Lambs Club Papers, New York Public Library.
39. Cecily Hathaway, "It All Comes Out in the Wash," *Gotham Life*, Dec. 31, 1939.
40. *The New York Times*, Jan. 15, 1940, p. 18.
41. Logan, *Josh*, p. 146.
42. "Durbin, Arnaz Bid to Broadway," *Telegraph*, Feb. 17, 1940.
43. Cholly Knickerbocker, *New York Journal American*, April 9, 1940.
44. Lucinda Ballard, letter to Richard Rodgers, June 18, 1944, Richard Rodgers Papers, New York Public Library.
45. Lucinda Ballard, interviewed by Ronald L. Davis, January 1985–March 1987, SMU Oral History, pp. 44–45.
46. Dorothy Kilgallen, "The Voice of Broadway," *New York Journal American*, March 19, 1940.
47. Rodgers, *Musical Stages*, p. 198.
48. O'Hara, *Selected Letters of John O'Hara*, p. 158. Bruccoli, *The O'Hara Concern*, p. 175. Ted Dodd, e-mail to author, May 4, 2010.
49. Jean Bach, introduction to *The Erteguns' New York Cabaret Music*, Atlantic 7 81817-1. Walter Winchell, *Daily Mirror*, March 11, 1940. Wilkerson and Borie, *The Hollywood Reporter*, p. 101.
50. *Bob Wills and His Texas Playboys*, compilation produced by Gregg Geller, Sony Legacy 82796 93858 2. *Rise and Fall of the City of Mahagonny*, Audra McDonald, Patti LuPone, Anthony Dean Griffey, James Conlon, and the Los Angeles Opera, EuroArts DVD 2056258.
51. William Skipper, unpublished memoir, p. 21, William Skipper Papers, New York Public Library.
52. Elliott Arnold, "Shirley Ross Wiser but Not Sad as Play Ends," *World-Telegram*, Aug. 24, 1940.
53. Edwin Schallert, "Power, Darnell Attain Third Feature as Team," *Los Angeles Times*, July 1, 1940, p. A10.
54. Jay Presson Allen, *Tru*. At this writing the play is unpublished. A videotaped version starring Robert Morse is available at the New York Public Library.
55. Secrest, *Somewhere for Me*, pp. 222–223. Richard Rodgers, Columbia Oral History, p. 174.
56. Carter, *Oklahoma!* pp. 24–25.

Chapter 21: To Write I Used to Think Was Wasting Ink

1. Robert Benchley, "The Theatre," *The New Yorker*, Feb. 7, 1931, p. 26.
2. Howells, "Criticism and Fiction," in *My Literary Passions*, p. 252.
3. *The Hart of the Matter*, p. 10. Gene Kelly, interviewed on *Words and Music* DVD.

4. Nolan, *Lorenz Hart*, p. 273.

5. "Rialto Gossip," *The New York Times*, June 23, 1940, p. X1. Nolan, *Lorenz Hart*, p. 273.

6. "Tattletale," *Los Angeles Times*, Aug. 18, 1940, p. D6.

7. John L. Scott, "*Boys from Syracuse* Riotous Fun," *Los Angeles Times*, Aug. 24, 1940, p. 7.

8. Sally Benson, "The Current Cinema," *The New Yorker*, Aug. 10, 1940, p. 43.

9. Edwin Schallert, "Alberto Vila to Break Film Warbling Record," *Los Angeles Times*, Oct. 19, 1940, p. 11.

10. " 'Met in Argentina' . . . Why?" *Hollywood Reporter*, June 13, 1941, p. 3.

11. "Equity to Discuss Sunday Show Pay," *The New York Times*, Sept. 10, 1940, p. 26.

12. Bruccoli, *The O'Hara Concern*, p. 175.

13. O'Hara, *Files on Parade*, pp. 122–159.

14. Bruccoli, *The O'Hara Concern*, p. 176.

15. Beale, ed., *Concise Dictionary of Slang and Unconventional English*, p. 215.

16. Mast, *Can't Help Singin'*, pp. 177–178.

17. John O'Hara, "Some Fond Recollections of Larry Hart," *The New York Times*, Feb. 27, 1944, p. X1. Nolan, *Lorenz Hart*, p. 276.

18. Rodgers, *Musical Stages*, p. 200.

19. "Gossip of the Rialto," *The New York Times*, Oct. 13, 1940, p. 123.

20. Gene Kelly, interviewed by Marilyn Hunt, Beverly Hills, Calif., March 10–14, 1975, New York Public Library.

21. Stephen Sondheim, talk at National Theatre: Platform Papers, March 1990.

22. Smith, *Musical Comedy in America*, p. 307.

23. Nolan, *Lorenz Hart*, p. 275.

24. Mast, *Can't Help Singin'*, p. 180.

25. Silverman, *Dancing on the Ceiling*, p. 24. See also Stephen Holden, "An Old-Fashioned Girl Playing Dress-Up Games," *The New York Times*, Oct. 8, 2009, p. C5. Reviewing Jane Krakowski's cabaret show, Holden refers to the updating of "Zip" as "Tweet," with "up-to-date new lyrics" by Marc Shaiman and Scott Wittman.

26. Mary Morris Lawrence, telephone interview with author, Dec. 3, 2008.

27. Budd Schulberg, e-mail to author, June 17, 2008. Bruccoli, *The O'Hara Concern*, p. 178.

28. Gene Kelly, interviewed by Marilyn Hunt, Beverly Hills, Calif., March 10–14, 1975, New York Public Library.

29. "How a Musical Is Made," a picture report by Mary Morris, words by Robert Rice, *PM*, Dec. 22, 1940, pp. 51–56.

30. Bruccoli, *The O'Hara Concern*, p. 179. Richard Rodgers, "*Pal Joey*: History of a 'Heel,' " *The New York Times*, Dec. 30, 1951, p. X1.

31. Fadiman, "Reflections on Musical Comedy," *Party of One*, pp. 280–281.

32. *The Hart of the Matter*, p. 11.
33. Nolan, *Lorenz Hart*, p. 281.
34. Brooks Atkinson, "The Play," *The New York Times*, Dec. 26, 1940, p. 22.
35. Moss Hart to George Cukor, May 20, 1954. *Pal Joey* production files, AMPAS.
36. "John Lardner's New York," *Look*, Jan. 29, 1952, p. 4.
37. Goldberg, *The Story of Gilbert and Sullivan*, p. 163. Ellis, introduction to W. S. Gilbert, *The Bab Ballads*, p. 9.
38. "ASCAP Prepares for New Contract," *The New York Times*, March 23, 1940, p. 8.
39. Robert Rice, "Rice and Old Shoes," *PM*, Dec. 5, 1940, p. 12.
40. Bruccoli, *The O'Hara Concern*, p. 219. "News of the Stage," *The New York Times*, Feb. 21, 1941, p. 16.
41. Duke, *Passport to Paris*, pp. 400–401.
42. Rodgers, *Musical Stages*, p. 203.
43. Leithauser, *Curves and Angles*, p. 14.
44. Richard Rodgers, interviewed by Arnold Michaelis, WBAI, Dec. 18, 1957. Nolan, *Lorenz Hart*, p. 289.
45. Rodgers, *Musical Stages*, pp. 206–207.
46. Richard Rodgers, Columbia Oral History, p. 176.
47. Sturges, *The Lady Eve*, scene C-31, pp. 65–66, of script, Oct. 18, 1940, in Sturges, *Five Screenplays by Preston Sturges*, pp. 419–420.

Chapter 22: Wait Till You Feel the Warmth of Her Glance

1. Graham, *Beloved Infidel*, p. 272.
2. Parry, *Garrets and Pretenders*, p. 278.
3. Hart, *Thou Swell*, p. 160.
4. Garrett and Rapoport, *Betty Garrett and Other Songs*, p. 101.
5. "The Guild Cancels Premiere of May 7," *The New York Times*, May 1, 1941, p. 26. "Geo. Abbott Gets a New Song Team," *The New York Times*, May 8, 1941, p. 20. Rodgers, *Musical Stages*, p. 208.
6. *New York News*, Dec. 28, 1941. "Students to Give *Wozzeck*," *The New York Times*, May 11, 1941, p. 19.
7. "News of the Stage," *The New York Times*, July 2, 1941, p. 18.
8. "Cornell Ponders Film Offer from Pascal to Act in Shaw's Work," *The New York Times*, June 26, 1941, p. 26. "De Sylva Raids Eastern Field for Playwrights," *Los Angeles Times*, July 21, 1941, p. A14.
9. Nolan, *Lorenz Hart*, pp. 286–287. Fordin, *Getting to Know Him*, p. 174. Rodgers, *Musical Stages*, p. 207.
10. Nolan, *Lorenz Hart*, p. 287.
11. "Gene Kelly Weds Today," *The New York Times*, Sept. 22, 1941, p. 17.
12. Rodgers, *Musical Stages*, pp. 208–209.
13. "Ginger Rogers and James Stewart Take Top Film Academy Awards," *Los Angeles Times*, Feb. 28, 1941, p. 1. *Herald Tribune*, Oct. 17, 1941.

14. Lorenz Hart, essay, Sept. 7, 1941, Shubert Archive.
15. Howells, *My Literary Passions*, p. 128.
16. Gilbert and Sullivan, *A Treasury of Gilbert & Sullivan*, p. 7.
17. "Carnovsky Named for *Crown Café*," *The New York Times*, Dec. 15, 1941, p. 25. "Hedda Hopper's Hollywood," *Los Angeles Times*, Nov. 11, 1941, p. 9.
18. Hart, *Thou Swell*, p. 173. Nolan, *Lorenz Hart*, p. 286.
19. R. W. Stewart, "One Thing and Another," *The New York Times*, Nov. 2, 1941, p. X12.
20. Kostelanetz and Gammond, *Echoes*, p. 90.
21. DeLong, *Pops*, pp. 159–160.
22. Tape of CBC War Savings Show, Nov. 19, 1941, Rodgers and Hammerstein Archive, New York Public Library. Rodgers, *Musical Stages*, p. 210. Nolan, *Lorenz Hart*, p. 292.
23. "News of the Stage," *The New York Times*, Nov. 24, 1941, p. 11.
24. Dwight Deere Wiman Scrapbooks, New York Public Library.
25. Jean Block, "Entertaining Soldiers," *The New York Times*, March 1, 1942, p. X1.
26. Notes by Dr. Harold Hyman and others on Hart's hospitalization can be found in Surrogate's Court Papers, Municipal Archives, New York City.
27. Richard Rodgers, letter to Lincoln Barnett, April 12, 1950, Richard Rodgers Papers, New York Public Library. Fordin, *Getting to Know Him*, p. 186.
28. "News of the Stage," *The New York Times*, Feb. 26, 1942, p. 14.
29. Richard P. Cooke, "The Theatre," *The Wall Street Journal*, Oct. 14, 1947, p. 10.
30. Louis Sobol, "New York Cavalcade," *New York Journal American*, June 3, 1942, p. 17. *The Boston Globe*, May 11, 1942. "News of the Stage," *The New York Times*, April 9, 1942, p. 24. *By Jupiter* and *Girl Crazy*, Jackie Cain and Roy Kral, notes by Richard Kollmar, Roulette Records R 25278. Israel, *Kilgallen*, p. 148. Rodgers, *Musical Stages*, p. 211.
31. Mielziner, *Designing for the Theatre*, p. 230.
32. Logan, *Josh*, pp. 164–165. "Vaudeville Draws Gaxton and Moore," *The New York Times*, April 6, 1942, p. 18.
33. Secrest, *Somewhere for Me*, p. 221. Brooks Atkinson, "The Play," *The New York Times*, March 30, 1942, p. 20. *The Hart of the Matter*, p. 17.
34. "What a Lovely Party," unpublished memoir by Aleen Robinson [Toni Stuart].
35. Johnny Green, interviewed by Ann Burk, July 1975, SMU Oral History, p. 65.
36. Bill Chase, "All Ears," *New York Amsterdam News*, April 25, 1942, p. 8. Balliett, "A Queenly Aura," in *American Singers*, p. 150.
37. Alec Wilder, "Orange Juice for One," *The New Yorker*, Oct. 18, 1976, pp. 181–185.
38. Hans Christian Adamson, letter to Richard Rodgers, March 6, 1943, Richard Rodgers Papers, New York Public Library.
39. Inez Robb, "Blackout over Broadway," *New York Journal American*, May 1, 1942, p. 1.

40. Aleen Robinson [Toni Stuart], Oral History, Oct. 26, 2005, Shubert Archive.

41. "What a Lovely Party," unpublished memoir by Aleen Robinson [Toni Stuart].

42. *By Jupiter and Girl Crazy*, Jackie Cain and Roy Kral, notes by Richard Kollmar, Roulette Records R 25278.

43. Ray Bolger, interviewed by Ronald Davis, August 1976, SMU Oral History, p. 19.

44. "*Keep 'Em Laughing* Gets Miss Fields," *The New York Times*, May 12, 1942, p. 17.

45. *By Jupiter and Girl Crazy*, Jackie Cain and Roy Kral, notes by Richard Kollmar, Roulette Records R 25278.

46. "John Barrymore Ill; His Condition Grave," *The New York Times*, May 22, 1942, p. 26.

47. Benay Venuta, interviewed by Ronald Davis, Jan. 5, 1979, SMU Oral History, pp. 15–17.

48. Aleen Robinson, telephone interview with author, May 28, 2008.

49. Julia Warren Tucker, e-mails to author, March 24, 2010, and April 18, 2010.

50. *New York Journal American*, April 19, 1942, p. 11.

51. Logan, *Josh*, p. 187.

52. Nathan, *The Theatre Book of the Year, 1942–1943*, p. 3. Richard P. Cooke, "June Musical," *The Wall Street Journal*, June 5, 1942, p. 8. Ralph Warner, "Rodgers, Hart Go to Greeks for Comedy," *Daily Worker*, June 11, 1942, p. 7. Louis Kronenberger, "A Great Dancer Heads a Fair Show," *PM*, June 4, 1942, p. 23. Brooks Atkinson, "The Play," *The New York Times*, June 4, 1942, p. 22. Walter Winchell, "Ray Bolger Returns to Light Up *By Jupiter*," *Daily Mirror*, June 4, 1942.

53. Richard Watts, Jr., "The Theater: Latest, Perhaps Last," *The Washington Post*, June 14, 1942, p. L3. John Anderson, "The Drama," *New York Journal American*, June 21, 1942.

54. Brooks Atkinson, "One for the Book," *The New York Times*, Aug. 30, 1942, p. X1.

55. "What a Lovely Party," unpublished memoir by Aleen Robinson [Toni Stuart]. Oral History, Oct. 26, 2005, Shubert Archive.

56. Sheldon Harnick in unused footage for documentary *Broadway*, by Michael Kantor, New York Public Library.

57. Sheldon Harnick, letter to author, Dec. 17, 2008. Wood, *Song Forms*, pp. 84–88. Hamm, *Yesterdays*, p. 360.

58. "*By Jupiter* May Be Last Broadway Musical in Grand Pre-War Style," *Life*, June 1, 1942, p. 82.

59. "What a Lovely Party," unpublished memoir by Aleen Robinson [Toni Stuart].

60. Kilgallen, "The Voice of Broadway," *New York Journal American*, June 12, 1942, p. 9.

61. Miles Kreuger, interviewed by Janice Ross and Claude Conyers, March 25, 2001, Popular Balanchine Dossier, New York Public Library.

62. Johnny Green, interviewed by Ann Burk, July 1975, SMU Oral History, p. 65. Louis Sobol, "New York Cavalcade," *New York Journal American*, June 11, 1942, p. 17. Dorothy Kilgallen, "Voice of Broadway," *New York Journal American*, June 29, 1942, p. 7.
63. Taylor, *Some Enchanted Evenings*, p. 165.
64. Hardee, *The Lambs Theatre Club*, p. 179.
65. Lerner, *The Musical Theatre*, p. 86. Jablonski, *Alan Jay Lerner*, pp. 146–147.
66. George Meredith, letter to André Raffalovich, November 1881, in *Letters of George Meredith*, vol. 1, p. 326.
67. Lerner, *The Musical Theatre*, p. 86.
68. "Lynn Riggs Play to Be a Musical," *The New York Times*, July 23, 1942, p. 15.
69. "Circus Is Forced to Give Free Show," *The New York Times*, Aug. 18, 1942, p. 16.
70. Rodgers, *Musical Stages*, pp. 216–217. Lerner, *Musical Theatre*, p. 151.
71. "Mystery Comedy Off till Thursday," *The New York Times*, Aug. 31, 1942, p. 12.

Chapter 23: Nobody Writes His Songs to Me

1. "*Let Freedom Sing* Delays Premiere," *The New York Times*, Sept. 17, 1942, p. 20.
2. Rodgers, *Musical Stages*, p. 217.
3. Nolan, *Lorenz Hart*, p. 305.
4. *Here Comes the Circus* file, Gallico Papers, Box 23, Butler Library, Columbia University.
5. Caldwell, *New York Nights*, p. 281. *Zit's Theatrical Newspaper*, Jan. 27, 1934, p. 1. "3 Charged for *Wine, Women, Song*," *Daily News*, Nov. 3, 1942, p. 10. "City Renews Fight for Clean Stage; Burlesque-Type Show Summoned," *The New York Times*, Nov. 3, 1942, p. 1. "Producer Todd Quits League of Theatres," *The New York Times*, Nov. 6, 1942, p. 26.
6. Wilella Waldorf, "Forecasts and Postscripts," *New York Post*, Nov. 13, 1942, p. 34. "Wiman Leaving Broadway," *The New York Times*, Nov. 13, 1942, p. 28. "Wiman to Assist Troops Overseas," *The New York Times*, Dec. 13, 1942, p. 28.
7. Nathan, *Theatre Book of the Year, 1942–1943*, p. vii.
8. "Jurist Describes Nudity," *The New York Times*, Dec. 1, 1942, p. 27.
9. Leonard Lyons, "If I Could Write the Nation's Laws," "Lyons Den," *New York Post*, Aug. 27, 1943, p. 20.
10. Caldwell, *New York Nights*, pp. 278–279.
11. Hart, *Thou Swell*, pp. 170–171.
12. Nolan, *Lorenz Hart*, p. 301.
13. Gallico note, appended to copy of *Here Comes the Circus*, Gallico Papers, Box 23, Butler Library, Columbia University. "Freedley Will Produce *Miss Underground*," *Los Angeles Times*, May 14, 1943, p. A14. Nolan, *Lorenz Hart*, p. 301. Frederick Nolan, e-mail to author, June 25, 2008.

14. Nanette Fabray, interviewed by Ronald C. Davis, Pacific Palisades, Aug. 5, 1975, SMU Oral Histories.
15. Bert Schwartz, "Jane Froman: Schmaltz with a Sock," *The New York Times*, Feb. 15, 1953, p. X13. "24 Lost in Clipper Crash," *Chicago Tribune*, Feb. 23, 1943, p. 1.
16. Hanff, *Underfoot in Show Business*, p. 93.
17. Marx and Clayton, *Rodgers & Hart*, p. 256.
18. Hanff, *Underfoot in Show Business*, p. 94.
19. Winchell, *Winchell Exclusive*, p. 181.
20. M.L.A., "Composers of Music as Variously Imagined," *The Boston Globe*, March 21, 1943, p. C44.
21. Richard Rodgers, Columbia Oral History, p. 245.
22. Sardi, Sr., and Gehman, *Sardi's*, p. 172.
23. Smith, *Musical Comedy in America*, pp. 343–344.
24. Fadiman, "Reflections on Musical Comedy," in *Party of One*, p. 283.
25. These and other post-*Oklahoma!* radio programs can be heard in the Rodgers and Hammerstein Archive, New York Public Library.
26. Mary Campbell, deposition to New York Surrogate's Court, Jan. 8, 1944.
27. Nolan, *Lorenz Hart*, p. 305.
28. Mary Campbell, deposition to New York Surrogate's Court, Jan. 8, 1944.
29. Hart, *Thou Swell*, p. 177.
30. Mary Campbell, deposition to New York Surrogate's Court, Jan. 8, 1944.
31. Hart, *Thou Swell*, p. 177.
32. *Hollywood Reporter*, June 3, 1943. Ted Dodd, e-mail to author, May 2, 2009.
33. Hart, *Thou Swell*, p. 178.
34. Marx and Clayton, *Rodgers & Hart*, p. 260. Marx and Clayton, Dorothy Hart, and the Hart letter of recommendation all refer to Irving *Eisman*, but New York Surrogate's Court documents list the name as *Eisenman*.
35. Burns Mantle, "Leslie Howard Was Definite Force for Good in the Theatre," *Daily News*, June 8, 1943, p. M37. Ed Sullivan, "Little Old New York," *Daily News*, June 13, 1943, p. 60.
36. Mary Campbell, deposition to New York Surrogate's Court, Jan. 8, 1944.
37. Ed Sullivan, "Little Old New York," *Daily News*, June 16, 1943, p. 40. Nolan, *Lorenz Hart*, p. 306. Ed Sullivan, "Little Old New York," *Daily News*, June 14, 1943, p. 17.
38. J. J. Shubert, letter to Lee Shubert, May 5, 1943, Shubert Archive.
39. Taylor, *Some Enchanted Evenings*, p. 89.
40. Abraham Wattenberg, deposition to New York Surrogate's Court, Dec. 20, 1943.
41. Jacques Fischl, deposition to New York Surrogate's Court, Dec. 18, 1944.
42. Mary Campbell, deposition to New York Surrogate's Court, Jan. 8, 1944.
43. Henry Myers, "Portrait of Larry Hart," unpublished memoir, p. 78.

Chapter 24: And Yet I Was Untrue to None of Them

1. Lerner, *The Street Where I Live*, pp. 25–26. Nolan, *Lorenz Hart*, p. 304.
2. "Old Musical Hit Will Be Revived," *The New York Times*, July 1, 1943, p. 13.
3. Fred Stanley, "Jesse L. Lasky Again on Biographical Trail," *The New York Times*, Aug. 8, 1943, p. X3. Richard Rodgers, "Mr. Rodgers' Yankee," *The New York Times*, Nov. 21, 1943, p. X1.
4. Hart, *Thou Swell*, p. 177.
5. Secrest, *Somewhere for Me*, p. 101.
6. Mordden, *Broadway Babies*, pp. 78–79.
7. Jablonski, *Alan Jay Lerner*, p. 204.
8. Nathan, *The Theatre Book of the Year, 1943–1944*, pp. 134–135. "The International *As You Were*," *The New York Times*, Feb. 8, 1920, p. XX2.
9. "Warners to Back Musical Revival," *The New York Times*, Aug. 5, 1943, p. 19. "Gossip of the Rialto," *The New York Times*, Aug. 15, 1943, p. X1.
10. Physician's statement no. 2 accompanying Hart death notice, Nov. 22, 1943, in New York Surrogate's Court Papers.
11. Vivienne Segal, interviewed by Ronald C. Davis, SMU Oral History, p. 33. In *Lorenz Hart*, p. 309, Frederick Nolan attributes the line to Hart.
12. Hart, *Thou Swell*, p. 177.
13. Robert Sensenderfer, "Connecticut Yankee Back in Camelot," *Philadelphia Evening Bulletin*, Oct. 29, 1943.
14. Milton R. Bender, deposition to Surrogate's Court, Jan. 9, 1944.
15. Hart, *Thou Swell*, p. 178.
16. Nolan, *Lorenz Hart*, p. 310.
17. Skolsky, "Times Square Tintypes," *New York Sun*, Jan. 30, 1928, p. 13. Rodgers, *A Personal Book*, pp. 116–117.
18. Dorothy Fields Papers, New York Public Library. Buster Davis Papers, New York Public Library.
19. Robert Garland, "Connecticut Yankee Back After 16 Years," *New York Journal American*, Nov. 18, 1943, p. 14.
20. Lerner, *The Street Where I Live*, p. 26.
21. Radie Harris, "New York Runaround," *Variety*, Nov. 24, 1943, p. 2.
22. Final illness report, New York Surrogate's Court Papers, Nov. 22, 1943. Nolan, *Lorenz Hart*, p. 312.
23. "New Raid Test Turns City 'Brownout' Black," *The New York Times*, Nov. 23, 1943, p. 1. Nolan, *Lorenz Hart*, p. 312. Hart, *Thou Swell*, p. 181.
24. Carroll and Firestone, *Diahann*, p. 109.
25. Dorothy Hart, *The Rodgers and Hart Story: Thou Swell, Thou Witty*, PBS Great Performances, 1995.
26. Vivienne Segal, interviewed by Ronald C. Davis, SMU Oral History, p. 30.
27. Nolan, *Lorenz Hart*, p. 313.

28. "Larry Hart's Death in N.Y. at 47 [*sic*] Ends G&S Partnership with Rodgers," *Variety*, Nov. 24, 1943, p. 53.

29. Dorothy Kilgallen, "The Voice of Broadway," *New York Journal American*, Nov. 24, 1943, p. 12.

30. F. Scott Fitzgerald, *The Last Tycoon*, p. 162.

31. *Variety*, Dec. 1, 1943, p. 37.

32. Logan, *Josh*, p. 188.

33. Marjorie Jane, interviewed by Constance Valis Hill, June 4, 2000, Popular Balanchine Dossier, New York Public Library.

34. Marx and Clayton, *Rodgers & Hart*, p. 154.

35. Mast, *Can't Help Singin'*, pp. 35–37. Tyler, *The Three Faces of the Film*, pp. 96–97.

36. Sontag, "Notes on Camp," in *A Susan Sontag Reader*, p. 118.

37. National Theatre, Platform Papers, March 1990.

38. Ebb, quoted in *The Hart of the Matter*, p. 17.

39. See Dan Sullivan, "Larry Hart: Lyrical Laureate of Musical Theater," *Los Angeles Times*, Sept. 30, 1973, p. N27.

40. Hugh Martin, telephone interview with author, May 19, 2008.

Bibliography

Abbott, George. *Mister Abbott*. New York: Random House, 1963.

Adams, Franklin P. *The Diary of Our Own Samuel Pepys*. Vol. 2. New York: Simon & Schuster, 1935.

Adler, Larry. *It Ain't Necessarily So*. London: Collins, 1984.

Agate, James. *Here Is Richness!* London: George G. Harrap, 1942.

———. *The Later Ego*. New York: Crown, 1951.

Alldritt, Keith. *W. B. Yeats: The Man and the Milieu*. New York: Clarkson Potter, 1997.

Anderson, Maxwell. *The Essence of Tragedy*. Washington, D.C.: Anderson House, 1939.

Arce, Hector. *The Secret Life of Tyrone Power*. New York: William Morrow, 1979.

Arnaz, Desi. *A Book*. New York: William Morrow, 1976.

Balliett, Whitney. *American Singers*. New York: Oxford University Press, 1979.

Bankhead, Tallulah. *Tallulah: My Autobiography*. New York: Harper and Brothers, 1952.

Baral, Robert. *Revue: The Great Broadway Period*. New York and London: Fleet Press Corporation, 1962.

Barnett, Lincoln. *Writing on Life: Sixteen Close-ups*. New York: Sloane Associates, 1951.

Barrios, Richard. *A Song in the Dark*. New York: Oxford University Press, 1995.

Batterberry, Michael, and Ariane Batterberry. *On the Town in New York*. New York: Charles Scribner's Sons, 1973.

Beale, Paul, ed. *Concise Dictionary of Slang and Unconventional English*. London: Routledge, 1991.

Beatty, Jack. *The Rascal King*. Reading, Mass.: Addison-Wesley 1992.

Beerbohm, Max. *Around Theatres*. New York: Simon & Schuster, 1954.

Behr, Edward. *The Good Frenchman*. New York: Villard Books, 1993.

———. *Prohibition: Thirteen Years That Changed America*. New York: Arcade Publishing, 1996.

Behrman, S. N. *People in a Diary*. Boston and Toronto: Little, Brown, 1972.

Bennett, Arnold. *Critical Writings of Arnold Bennett*. Ed. Samuel Hynes. Lincoln: University of Nebraska Press, 1968.

Bent, Silas. *Ballyhoo: The Voice of the Press*. New York: Horace Liveright, 1927.

Blair, Betsy. *The Memory of All That: Love and Politics in New York, Hollywood, and Paris*. New York: Alfred A. Knopf, 2003.

Block, Geoffrey, ed. *The Richard Rodgers Reader*. New York: Oxford University Press, 2002.

Blum, Daniel. *A Pictorial History of the American Theatre, 1900–1956*. New York: Greenberg, 1956.

Blumenthal, Ralph. *Stork Club: America's Most Famous Nightspot and the Lost World of Café Society*. Boston: Little, Brown, 2000.

Boas, Franz. *Changes in Bodily Form of Descendants of Immigrants*. New York: Columbia University Press, 1912.

Brady, John. *The Craft of the Screenwriter*. New York: Simon & Schuster, 1981.

Brieux, Eugene. *Three Plays*. New York: Brentano's, 1914.

Brown, Eve. *Champagne Cholly: The Life and Times of Maury Paul*. New York: E. P. Dutton & Company, Inc., 1947.

Brown, Henry Collins. *Valentine's Manual of Old New York: New York in the Elegant Eighties*. Hastings-on-Hudson, N.Y.: Valentine's Manual, 1927.

Brown, John Mason. *Two on the Aisle: Ten Years of the American Theatre in Performance*. New York: W. W. Norton, 1938.

Bruccoli, Matthew J. *The O'Hara Concern: A Biography of John O'Hara*. New York: Popular Library, 1977.

Burrows, Edwin G., and Mike Wallace. *Gotham: A History of New York City to 1898*. New York: Oxford University Press, 1999.

Cahan, Abraham. *The Rise of David Levinsky*. New York: Harper and Brothers, 1917.

Caldwell, Mark. *New York Nights: The Mystique and Its History*. New York: Scribner, 2005.

Carr, Harry. *Los Angeles: City of Dreams*. New York and London: D. Appleton-Century Company, Inc., 1936.

Carroll, Diahann, and Ross Firestone. *Diahann! An Autobiography*. Boston: Little, Brown, 1986.

Carroll, Renee. *In Your Hat*. Caricatures by Alex Gard. New York: Macauley, 1933.

Carter, Tim. *Oklahoma! The Making of an American Musical*. New Haven, Conn.: Yale University Press, 2007.

The Century in Times Square. New York: Bishop Books, 1999.

Cerf, Bennett. *At Random*. New York: Random House, 1977.

Chase, W. Parker. *New York, The Wonder City: 1932*. New York: New York Bound, 1983.

Chauncey, George. *Gay New York: Gender, Urban Culture, and the Making of the Gay Male World, 1890–1940*. New York: Basic Books, 1994.

Clark, Tom. *Damon Runyon*. New York: Harper and Row, 1978.

The Clintonian 1910. Annual of DeWitt Clinton High School.

The Clintonian: Sixteenth Annual of the DeWitt Clinton High School, June 1916.

Clurman, Harold. *The Fervent Years: The Group Theatre and the Thirties*. New York: Da Capo Press, 1975.

Cochran, Charles B. *Showman Looks On*. London: J. M. Dent and Sons, 1946.

Cohen, Marilyn. *Reginald Marsh's New York*. New York: Whitney Museum of Art, 1983.

Cohen, Selma Jeanne, American ed. *Dictionary of Modern Ballet*. New York: Tudor, 1959.

Coit, Margaret L. *Mr. Baruch*. Boston: Houghton Mifflin, 1957.

Columbia Grammar School, 1764–1964: A Historical Log. New York: Columbia Grammar School, 1965.

Columbia Songs, 1754–1924. New York: Alumni Federation of Columbia University, 1924.

Comden, Betty, and Adolph Green. *Bells Are Ringing*. New York: Random House, 1957.

Committee of Fourteen—Annual Report 1907. New York: The Committee, 1908.

Conrad, Earl. *Billy Rose: Manhattan Primitive*. New York: Paperback Library, 1969.

Cook, George Cram, and Susan Glaspell. *Suppressed Desires*. Included in *The Provincetown Plays*, 2nd ser. New York: Frank Shay, 1916.

Coslow, Sam. *Cocktails for Two: The Many Lives of Giant Songwriter Sam Coslow*. New Rochelle, N.Y.: Arlington House, 1977.

Covarrubias, Miguel. *The Prince of Wales and Other Famous Americans*. New York: Alfred A. Knopf, 1925.

Coward, Noël. *The Noël Coward Diaries*. Ed. Graham Payn and Sheridan Morley. London: Weidenfeld and Nicolson, 1982.

Cowley, Malcolm, ed., *Writers at Work: The Paris Review Interviews*. New York: Viking Press, 1959.

Cripps, Thomas. *Slow Fade to Black*. New York: Oxford University Press, 1977.

Croce, Arlene. *Afterimages*. New York: Alfred A. Knopf, 1977.

Crowninshield, Francis W. *Manners for the Metropolis: An Entrance Key to the Fantastic Life of the 400*. New York: D. Appleton, 1908.

Crowther, Andrew. *Contradiction Contradicted: The Plays of W. S. Gilbert*. Madison and Teaneck, N.J.: Fairleigh Dickinson University Press, 2000.

Damase, Jacques. *Les Folies du Music-Hall*. London: Hamlyn Publishing Group, 1970.

Darrell, Margery. *The Rodgers and Hart Song Book*. New York: Simon & Schuster, 1951.

Davis, Owen. *I'd Like to Do It Again.* New York: Farrar and Rinehart, 1931.

DeLong, Thomas A. *Pops: Paul Whiteman, King of Jazz.* Piscataway, N.J.: New Century Publishing, 1983.

Dickinson, Thomas H., ed. *Chief Contemporary Dramatists.* Boston: Houghton Mifflin, 1915.

Dietz, Howard. *Dancing in the Dark.* New York: Quadrangle, 1974.

Diner, Hasia R. *In the Almost Promised Land: American Jews and Blacks: 1915–1935.* Westport, Conn.: Greenwood Press, 1977.

Dolkart, Andrew S. *Morningside Heights: A History of Its Architecture and Development.* New York: Columbia University Press, 1998.

Dos Passos, John. *The Best Times.* New York: New American Library, 1966.

Duberman, Martin. *Paul Robeson.* New York: Ballantine Books, 1989.

Duke, Vernon. *Listen Here!* New York: Ivan Obolensky, 1963.

———. *Passport to Paris.* Boston: Little, Brown, 1955.

Dunning, John. *Tune in Yesterday: The Ultimate Encyclopedia of Old-Time Radio 1925–1976.* Englewood Cliffs, N.J.: Prentice-Hall, 1976.

Durante, Jimmy, and Jack Kofoed. *Night Clubs.* New York: Alfred A. Knopf, 1931.

Everett, William A. *Sigmund Romberg.* New Haven, Conn., and London: Yale University Press, 2007.

Eyman, Scott. *Ernst Lubitsch: Laughter in Paradise.* New York: Simon & Schuster, 1993.

Faderman, Lillian, and Stuart Timmons. *Gay L.A.: A History of Sexual Outlaws, Power Politics, and Lipstick Lesbians.* New York: Basic Books, 2006.

Fadiman, Clifton. *Party of One: The Selected Writings of Clifton Fadiman.* Cleveland: World Publishing, 1955.

Ferber, Edna. *A Peculiar Treasure.* Garden City, N.Y.: Doubleday, 1960.

Fields, Armond, and L. Marc Fields. *From the Bowery to Broadway: Lew Fields and the Roots of American Popular Theater.* New York: Oxford University Press, 1993.

Fitzgerald, F. Scott. *The Crack-Up.* Ed. Edmund Wilson. New York: New Directions, 1956.

———. *The Last Tycoon.* New York: Charles Scribner's Sons, 1941.

———. *The Letters of F. Scott Fitzgerald.* Ed. with an introduction by Andrew Turnbull. New York: Charles Scribner's Sons, 1963.

Ford, Charles Henri, and Parker Tyler. *The Young and Evil.* New York: Obelisk Press, 1933.

Ford, Corey. *The Time of Laughter.* Boston: Little, Brown, 1967.

Fordin, Hugh. *Getting to Know Him: A Biography of Oscar Hammerstein II.* New York: Ungar Publishing, 1977.

Fowler, Gene. *Skyline.* New York: Viking Press, 1961.

Freedman, David. *The Intellectual Lover and Other Stories.* Introduction by Konrad Bercovici. New York: Harper and Brothers, 1940.

————. *Mendel Marantz.* New York: Harper and Brothers, 1926.

Frommer, Myrna Katz, and Harvey Frommer. *It Happened in Manhattan: An Oral History of Life in the City During the Mid-Twentieth Century.* New York: Berkley Books, 2001.

————. *It Happened on Broadway: An Oral History of the Great White Way.* New York: Harcourt, Brace, 1998.

Frye, Northrop. *A Natural Perspective: The Development of Shakespearean Comedy and Romance.* New York: Columbia University Press, 1965.

Fuller, Samuel. *New York in the 1930s.* Paris: Hazan Pocket Archives, 1997.

Gaines, James R. *Wit's End.* New York: Harcourt Brace Jovanovich, 1977.

Gammond, Peter, ed. *Duke Ellington: His Life and Music.* New York: Da Capo Press, 1977. Reprint of 1958 ed. published by Phoenix House, London.

————, ed. *The Oxford Companion to Popular Music.* Oxford and New York: Oxford University Press, 1991.

Ganzl, Kurt. *The British Musical Theatre.* Vol. 2: *1915–1984.* New York: Oxford University Press, 1986.

Garrett, Betty, and Ron Rapoport. *Betty Garrett and Other Songs.* Lanham, Md.: Madison Books, 1998.

Gebhard, David, and Harriette Von Breton. *Los Angeles in the Thirties: 1931–1941.* Los Angeles: Hennessy and Ingalls, 1989.

Gelb, Arthur, and Barbara Gelb. *O'Neill.* New York: Dell, 1964.

Gershwin, Ira. *Lyrics on Several Occasions.* New York: Viking Press, 1973.

Giddins, Gary. *Bing Crosby: Pocketful of Dreams: The Early Years, 1903–1940.* New York: Little, Brown, 2001.

Gilbert, W. S. *The Bab Ballads.* Ed. James Ellis. Cambridge, Mass.: Belknap Press of Harvard University Press, 1970.

Gilbert, W. S., and Arthur Sullivan. *A Treasury of Gilbert & Sullivan.* Ed. Deems Taylor. Illus. Lucille Corcos. Arrangements by Dr. Albert Sirmay. New York: Simon & Schuster, 1941.

Goldberg, Isaac. *The Story of Gilbert and Sullivan.* New York: Simon & Schuster, 1928.

Goldman, Herbert. *Jolson: The Legend Comes to Life.* New York: Oxford University Press, 1988.

Gottfried, Martin. *Sondheim.* New York: Harry N. Abrams, 1993.

Gottlieb, Jack. *Funny, It Doesn't Sound Jewish: How Yiddish Songs and Synagogue Melodies Influenced Tin Pan Alley, Broadway, and Hollywood.* Washington, D.C.: State University of New York in association with the Library of Congress, 2004.

Graham, Sheilah, and Gerold Frank. *Beloved Infidel: The Education of a Woman.* New York: Henry Holt, 1958.

Graham, Stephen. *New York Nights.* New York: George H. Doran, 1927.

Green, Abel, and Joe Laurie, Jr. *Show Biz, from Vaude to Video.* New York: Holt, 1951.

Green, Stanley. *Ring Bells! Sing Songs! Broadway Musicals of the 1930's.* New Rochelle, N.Y.: Arlington House, 1971.

———. *The World of Musical Comedy.* South Brunswick, N.J., and New York: A. S. Barnes, 1968.

Greene, Graham. *The Pleasure Dome: The Collected Film Criticism, 1935–40.* Ed. John Russell Taylor. New York: Oxford University Press, 1980.

Gross, Milt. *Nize Baby.* New York: George H. Doran, 1926.

Gurman, Joseph, and Myron Slager. *Radio Round-ups: Intimate Glimpses of the Radio Stars.* Boston: Lothrop, Lee and Shepard, 1932.

Gurock, Jeffrey S. *When Harlem Was Jewish, 1870–1930.* New York: Columbia University Press, 1979.

Hall, Carolyn. *The Thirties in Vogue.* New York: Harmony Books, 1985.

Hall, Stephen S. *Size Matters: How Height Affects the Health, Happiness, and Success of Boys—and the Men They Become.* Boston and New York: Houghton Mifflin, 2006.

Hallas, Richard [Eric Knight]. *You Play the Black and the Red Comes Up.* New York: Robert M. McBride, 1938.

Hamilton, Ian. *Writers in Hollywood.* New York: Harper and Row, 1990.

Hamm, Charles. *Music in the New World.* New York: W. W. Norton, 1983.

———. *Yesterdays.* New York: W. W. Norton, 1979.

Hanff, Helene. *Underfoot in Show Business.* New York: Harper and Row, 1962.

Hapgood, Hutchins. *The Spirit of the Ghetto: Studies of the Jewish Quarter in New York.* With drawings from life by Jacob Epstein. New edition—preface and notes by Harry Golden. New York: Funk and Wagnalls, 1965. Originally published in 1902.

Hardee, Lewis J., Jr. *The Lambs Theatre Club.* Jefferson, N.C.: McFarland, 2006.

Harris, Reed. *King Football.* New York: Vanguard Press, 1932.

Harrison, G. B. *The Day Before Yesterday: Being a Journal of the Year 1936.* London: Cobden-Sanderson, 1938.

———. *Introducing Shakespeare.* Harmondsworth, Middx.: Penguin Books, 1957.

Hart, Dorothy, and Robert Kimball, eds. *The Complete Lyrics of Lorenz Hart.* Expanded Edition. New York: Da Capo Press, 1995.

———. *Thou Swell, Thou Witty: The Life and Lyrics of Lorenz Hart.* New York: Harper and Row, 1976.

The Hart of the Matter: A Celebration of Lorenz Hart. Los Angeles: University of Southern California Libraries, 1974.

Hart, Moss, and George S. Kaufman. *You Can't Take It with You: A Play.* New York and Toronto: Farrar and Rinehart, 1937.

Hawes, Elizabeth. *New York, New York: How the Apartment House Transformed the Life of the City (1869–1930).* New York: Alfred A. Knopf, 1993.

Haynal, André. *Depression and Creativity.* New York: International University Press, 1985.

Hecht, Ben. *A Child of the Century.* New York: Simon & Schuster, 1954.

Helburn, Theresa. *A Wayward Quest: The Autobiography of Theresa Helburn*. Boston: Little, Brown, 1960.

Henderson, Mary C. *The City and the Theatre*. New York: Back Stage Books, 2004.

———. *Mielziner: Master of Modern Stage Design*. New York: Back Stage Books, 2001.

Heyward, Dorothy, and DuBose Heyward. *Porgy: A Play in Four Acts*. Garden City, N.Y.: Doubleday, Doran & Company Inc., 1928.

Hines, Duncan. *Lodging for a Night*. Bowling Green, Ky.: Adventures in Good Eating, Inc., 1941.

Hodges, Ben, ed. *The Play That Changed My Life*. Milwaukee: Applause Theatre & Cinema Books, 2009.

Howells, William Dean. *My Literary Passions/Criticism and Fiction*. New York: Harper and Brothers, 1968.

Huneker, James. *New Cosmopolis: Intimate New York*. New York: Charles Scribner's Sons, 1915.

Hutchens, John K., and George Oppenheimer, eds. *The Best of the World*. New York: Viking Press, 1973.

Irwin, Will. *Highlights of Manhattan*. Illus. E. H. Suydam. New York: Appleton-Century, 1937.

Israel, Lee. *Kilgallen*. New York: Dell, 1979.

Jablonski, Edward. *Alan Jay Lerner*. New York: Henry Holt, 1996.

James, Rian. *Dining in New York*. New York: John Day, 1931.

———. *Hat-Check Girl*. New York: Grosset & Dunlap, 1932.

Jeans, Ronald. *The Review of Revues*. London: Samuel French, 1925.

———. *Writing for the Theatre*. London: Edward Arnold, 1949.

Kahn, E. J. *The World of Swope*. New York: Simon & Schuster, 1965.

Kanfer, Stefan. *A Summer World: The Attempt to Build a Jewish Eden in the Catskills from the Days of the Ghetto to the Rise and Decline of the Borscht Belt*. New York: Farrar, Straus & Giroux, 1989.

Kanter, Kenneth Aaron. *The Jews on Tin Pan Alley: The Jewish Contribution to American Popular Music, 1830–1940*. New York: Ktav Publishing House, 1982.

Kaufman, George S., and Moss Hart. *I'd Rather Be Right*. New York: Random House, 1937.

Kaufman, George S., and Morrie Ryskind. *Of Thee I Sing*. New York: Samuel French, 1935.

Kiernan, John. *A Natural History of New York City*. Boston: Houghton Mifflin, 1959.

Knox, Herman W., ed. *Who's Who in New York—1918*. 7th ed. New York: Who's Who Publications, 1918.

Kofoed, Jack. *Moon over Miami*. New York: Random House, 1955.

Kostelanetz, André, and Gloria Gammond. *Echoes: The Memoirs of André Kostelanetz*. New York: Harcourt Brace Jovanovich, 1981.

Kotsilibas-Davis, James, and Myrna Loy. *Myrna Loy: Being and Becoming.* New York: Alfred A. Knopf, 1987.

Krafsur, Richard, and Kenneth W. Munden, eds. *American Film Institute Catalogue of Motion Pictures Produced in the United States.* Berkeley: R. R. Bowker, 1971.

Kristeva, Julia. *Black Sun: Depression and Melancholia.* Trans. Leon S. Roudiez. New York: Columbia University Press, 1989.

Langner, Lawrence. *The Magic Curtain: The Story of Life in Two Fields, Theatre and Invention, by the Founder of the Theatre Guild.* New York: Dutton, 1951.

Laning, Edward. *The Sketchbooks of Reginald Marsh.* Greenwich, Conn.: New York Graphic Society, 1973.

Leithauser, Brad. *Curves and Angles: Poems.* New York: Alfred A. Knopf, 2006.

Lejeune, Jean-François, and Allan T. Shulman. *The Making of Miami Beach, 1933–1942.* Miami Beach: Bass Museum of Art, 2000.

Lerner, Alan Jay. *The Musical Theatre: A Celebration.* New York: McGraw-Hill, 1986.

———. *The Street Where I Live.* New York: Norton, 1978.

Levy, Newman. *My Double Life.* Garden City, N.Y.: Doubleday, 1958.

Lewis, David Levering. *When Harlem Was in Vogue.* New York: Oxford University Press, 1982.

Liebling, A. J. *The Telephone Booth Indian.* San Francisco: North Point Press, 1990.

Lief, Max. *Hangover.* New York: Horace Liveright, 1929.

Lillie, Beatrice. *Every Other Inch a Lady.* New York: Doubleday, 1972.

Logan, Joshua. *Josh: My Up and Down, In and Out Life.* New York: Delacorte Press, 1976.

Lonsdale, Frederick. *Plays One.* London: Oberon Books, 2000.

The Magpie 1910. Literary publication of DeWitt Clinton High School.

Mair, Carlene. *The Chappell Story: 1811–1961.* London: Chappell & Co., Limited, 1961.

Makinson, Randell L. *Greene & Greene: Architecture as a Fine Art.* Salt Lake City, Utah: Peregrine Smith Books, 1977.

Mallen, Frank. *Sauce for the Gander.* White Plains, N.Y.: Baldwin Books 1954.

Mantle, Burns, ed., *The Best Plays of 1921–1922.* New York: Dodd, Mead and Company, 1930.

———, ed., *The Best Plays of 1923–1924.* New York: Dodd, Mead and Company, 1930.

———, ed., *The Best Plays of 1926–1927.* New York: Dodd, Mead and Company, 1928.

———, ed., *The Best Plays of 1928–1929.* New York: Dodd, Mead and Company, 1930.

———, ed., *The Best Plays of 1930–1931.* New York: Dodd, Mead and Company, 1931.

———, ed., *The Best Plays of 1931–1932.* New York: Dodd, Mead and Company, 1932.

Mantle, Burns, and Garrison P. Sherwood, eds., *The Best Plays of 1909–1919*. New York: Dodd, Mead and Company, 1943.

Marsh, Reginald. *East Side, West Side, All Around the Town: A Retrospective Exhibition of Paintings, Watercolors and Drawing*. Introduction by William E. Steadman. Tucson: University of Arizona Museum of Art, 1969.

Marx, Samuel, and Jan Clayton. *Rodgers & Hart: Bewitched, Bothered and Bedeviled: An Anecdotal Account*. New York: G. P. Putnam's Sons, 1976.

Masefield, John. *ODTAA*. London: William Heinemann, 1926.

Mason, Francis. *I Remember Balanchine: Reflections on the Ballet Master by Those Who Knew Him*. New York: Doubleday, 1991.

Mast, Gerald. *Can't Help Singin': The American Musical of Stage and Screen*. Woodstock, N.Y.: Overlook Press, 1987.

Matthews, Jessie. *Over My Shoulder*. As told to Muriel Burgess. New Rochelle, N.Y.: Arlington House, 1974.

Mayer, Edwin Justus. *A Preface to Life*. New York: Boni and Liveright, 1923.

Mayer, Grace. *Once Upon a Time*. New York: Macmillan, 1958.

McGuire, Patricia Dubin. *Lullaby of Broadway: A Biography of Al Dubin*. Secaucus, N.J.: Citadel Press, 1983.

McNamara, Daniel I., ed. *ASCAP Biographical Dictionary of Composers, Authors, and Publishers*. New York: Thomas Y. Crowell, 1948.

Meredith, George. *Letters of George Meredith*. 2 vols. New York: Charles Scribner's Sons, 1912.

Meryman, Richard. *Mank: The Wit, World, and Life of Herman Mankiewicz*. New York: William Morrow, 1978.

Meyerson, Harold, and Ernie Harburg. *Who Put the Rainbow in the Wizard of Oz?* Ann Arbor: University of Michigan Press, 1993.

Mielziner, Jo. *Designing for the Theatre: A Memoir and a Portfolio*. New York: Atheneum, 1965.

Millichap, Joseph R. *Lewis Milestone*. Boston: Twayne Publishers, 1981.

Molnár, Ferenc. *Fashions for Men and The Swan*. New York: Boni and Liveright, 1922.

———. *Liliom: A Legend in Seven Scenes and a Prologue*. English text by Benjamin F. Glazer. New York: Boni and Liveright, 1921.

Mordden, Ethan. *Broadway Babies: The People Who Made the American Musical*. New York: St. Martin's Press, 1981.

———. *Make Believe: The Broadway Musical in the 1920s*. New York: Oxford University Press, 1997.

Morehouse, Ward. *Forty-five Minutes Past Eight*. New York: Dial Press, 1939.

Mosedale, John. *The Men Who Invented Broadway: Damon Runyon, Walter Winchell and Their Worlds*. New York: Richard Marek Publishers, 1981.

Muray, Nickolas, and Paul Gallico. *The Revealing Eye: The Personalities of the 1920's in Photographs*. New York: Atheneum, 1967.

Murray, Ken. *Life on a Pogo Stick: Autobiography of a Comedian*. Philadelphia: John C. Winston, 1960.

Nasaw, David. *Going Out: The Rise and Fall of Public Amusements*. New York: Basic Books, 1993.

Nathan, George Jean. *The Autobiography of an Attitude*. New York: Alfred A. Knopf, 1925.

————. *The Bachelor Life*. New York: Reynal and Hitchcock, 1941.

————. *The Intimate Notebooks of George Jean Nathan*. New York: Alfred A. Knopf, 1932.

————. *The Popular Theatre*. New York: Alfred A. Knopf, 1923.

————. *The Theatre Book of the Year, 1942–1943*. New York: Alfred A. Knopf, 1943.

————. *The Theatre Book of the Year, 1943–1944*. New York: Alfred A. Knopf, 1944.

New York Standard Guide. New York: Foster and Reynolds, 1912.

Nolan, Frederick. *Lorenz Hart: A Poet on Broadway*. New York: Oxford University Press, 1994.

O'Connell, Shaun. *Remarkable, Unspeakable New York: A Literary History*. Boston: Beacon Press, 1995.

O'Dell, Scott. *Modern Authorship: Representative Photoplays Analyzed*. Hollywood, Calif.: Palmer Institute of Authorship, 1924.

O'Hara, John. *Butterfield 8*. New York: Harcourt, Brace, 1935.

————. *Files on Parade*. New York: Harcourt, Brace, 1939.

————. *Here's O'Hara*. New York: Duell, Sloan and Pearce, 1946.

————. *Selected Letters of John O'Hara*. Ed. Matthew Joseph Bruccoli. New York: Random House, 1978.

Oppenheimer, George. *The View from the Sixties: Memories of a Spent Life*. New York: David McKay, 1966.

Oriard, Michael. *King Football: Sport and Spectacle in the Golden Age of Radio and Newsreels, Movies and Magazines, the Weekly and the Daily Press*. Chapel Hill: University of North Carolina Press, 2001.

Parcq, Georges. *Crime Reporter*. New York: Robert M. McBride, 1934.

Parry, Alfred. *Garrets and Pretenders: A History of Bohemianism in America*. New York: Covici-Friede, 1933.

Pettit, Charles. *Son of the Grand Eunuch*. New York: Boni and Liveright, 1927.

Pitkin, Walter. *Careers After Forty*. New York: Whittlesey House, 1937.

Powell, Dawn. *The Diaries of Dawn Powell 1931–1965*. Ed. Tim Page. South Royalton, Vt.: Steerforth Press, 1995.

Ramkalawon, Jennifer. *Toulouse-Lautrec*. London: British Museum Press, 2007.

Rankin, Hugh F. *The Theatre in Colonial America*. Chapel Hill: University of North Carolina Press, 1965.

Raymond, Jack. *Show Music on Record*. New York: Frederick Ungar, 1982.

Rayno, Don. *Paul Whiteman: Pioneer in American Music*. Vol. 1: *1890–1930*. Lanham, Md., and Oxford: Scarecrow Press, 2003.

Reed, Bill. *Hot from Harlem: Twelve African American Entertainers, 1890–1960*. Rev. ed. Jefferson, N.C.: McFarland, 2010.

Reik, Theodor. *From Thirty Years with Freud*. Trans. Richard Winston. New York: Farrar and Rinehart, 1940.

Reznikoff, Charles. *By the Waters of Manhattan*. New York: Albert and Charles Boni, 1930.

Richard Rodgers Fact Book. New York: Lynn Farnol Group, 1965.

Rivkin, Allen, and Leonard Spigelgass. *I Wasn't Born Yesterday*. New York: Macauley, 1935.

Robbins, Jhan. *Inka Dink A Doo: The Life of Jimmy Durante*. New York: Paragon House, 1991.

Rodgers, Dorothy. *A Personal Book*. New York: Harper and Row, 1977.

Rodgers, Richard. *Musical Stages*. New York: Random House, 1976.

Rorem, Ned. *The New York Diary of Ned Rorem*. New York: George Braziller, 1967.

Rose, Billy. *Wine, Women and Words*. Illustrated by Salvador Dalí. New York: Simon & Schuster, 1948.

Ross, Leonard Q. [Leo Rosten]. *The Strangest Places*. New York: Harcourt, Brace, 1939.

Rostand, Edmond. *Cyrano de Bergerac: An Heroic Comedy in Five Acts*. Trans. Brian Hooker. New York: Henry Holt, 1923.

Runyon, Damon. *Take It Easy*. New York: Frederick A. Stokes, 1938.

Ryskind, Morrie. *The Diary of an Ex-President*. New York: Minton, Balch, 1932.

Ryskind, Morrie, with John H. M. Roberts. *I Shot an Elephant in My Pajamas: The Morrie Ryskind Story*. Lafayette, La.: Huntington House Publishers, 1994.

Salinger, J. D. *The Catcher in the Rye*. Boston: Little, Brown, 1951.

Sandburg, Carl, ed. *The American Songbag*. New York: Harcourt, Brace and World, 1990. (Originally published 1927.)

Sardi, Vincent, Jr., and Thomas Edward West. *Off the Wall at Sardi's*. New York: Applause Books, 1991.

Sardi, Vincent, Sr., and Richard Gehman. *Sardi's, the Story of the Famous Restaurant*. New York: Henry Holt, 1953.

Savo, Jimmy. *I Bow to the Stones: Memoirs of a New York Childhood*. New York: Howard Frisch, 1963.

Schatz, Thomas. *The Genius of the System: Hollywood Filmmaking in the Studio Era*. New York: Pantheon Books, 1988.

Schickel, Richard. *The Stars*. New York: The Dial Press, 1962.

Schildkraut, Joseph, as told to Leo Lania. *My Father and I*. New York: Viking Press, 1959.

Schoener, Allon. *The American Jewish Album: 1654 to the Present*. New York: Rizzoli, 1983.

Schorer, Mark. *Sinclair Lewis: An American Life*. New York: McGraw-Hill, 1961.

Schulberg, Budd. *Writers in America: The Four Seasons of Success*. New York: Stein and Day, 1983.

Secrest, Meryle. *Somewhere for Me.* New York: Alfred A. Knopf, 2001.

Seldes, George. *Witness to a Century.* New York: Ballantine Books, 1987.

Selznick, David O. *Memo from David O. Selznick.* Ed. Rudy Behlmer. New York: Viking Press, 1972.

Sennett, Ted. *Warner Brothers Presents.* New Rochelle, N.Y.: Arlington House, 1972.

Sharaff, Irene. *Broadway and Hollywood: Costumes Designed by Irene Sharaff.* New York: Van Nostrand Reinhold, 1976.

Shattuck, Richard. *The Snark Was a Boojum.* New York: William Morrow, 1941.

Sheed, Wilfrid. *The House That George Built: With a Little Help from Irving, Cole, and a Crew of About Fifty.* New York: Random House, 2007.

Sillman, Leonard. *Here Lies Leonard Sillman (Straightened Out at Last).* New York: Citadel Press, 1959.

Silver, Nathan. *Lost New York.* New York: Schocken Books, 1972.

Silverman, Stephen M. *Dancing on the Ceiling: Stanley Donen and His Movies.* New York: Alfred A. Knopf, 1996.

Simon, Robert A. *Bronx Ballads.* With 11 Illustrations and 11 Gags by Harry Hershfield. New York: Simon and Schuster, 1927.

Skinner, R. Dana. *Our Changing Theatre.* New York: Dial Press, 1931.

Smith, Bruce. *Greene & Greene: Master Builders of the American Arts and Crafts Movement.* London: Thames and Hudson, 1998.

Smith, Cecil Michener. *Musical Comedy in America.* New York: Theatre Arts Books, 1950.

Sobel, Bernard. *Burleycue: An Underground History of Burlesque Days.* New York: Farrar and Rinehart, 1931.

Sobol, Louis. *The Longest Street.* New York: Crown, 1968.

Sontag, Susan. *A Susan Sontag Reader.* New York: Farrar, Straus & Giroux, 1982.

Spaeth, Sigmund. *Read 'Em and Weep: The Songs You Forgot to Remember.* Garden City, N.Y.: Doubleday, Page, 1927.

Stigand, William. *Anthea: Poems and Translations (The Latter Chiefly from the German Poet Heine, with Sketch of His Life).* London: Kegan Paul, Trench, Trubner, 1907.

Sturges, Preston. *Five Screenplays by Preston Sturges.* Ed. Brian Henderson. Berkeley and Los Angeles: University of California Press, 1985.

Sullivan, Mark. *Our Times: America at the Birth of the Twentieth Century.* Ed. and with new material by Dan Rather. New York: Scribner, 1996.

Suskin, Steven. *Show Tunes: The Songs, Shows, and Careers of Broadway's Major Composers.* New York: Oxford University Press, 2000.

Taper, Bernard. *Balanchine: A Biography.* Berkeley and London: University of California Press, 1996.

Taylor, Deems. *A Pictorial History of the Movies.* New York: Simon & Schuster, 1950.

———. *Some Enchanted Evenings: The Story of Rodgers and Hammerstein.* New York: Harper and Brothers, 1953.

Teague, Michael. *Mrs. L.: Conversations with Alice Roosevelt Longworth.* New York: Doubleday, 1981.

Teichmann, Howard. *George S. Kaufman: An Intimate Portrait.* New York: Atheneum, 1972.

The Thirtieth Birthday of Vogue, 1892–1922. New York: Vogue Company, 1923.

Thomas, Tony, and Jim Terry with Busby Berkeley. *The Busby Berkeley Book.* New York: New York Graphic Society, 1973.

Thompson, Julian. *The Warrior's Husband.* New York: Samuel French, 1932.

Thornton, Michael. *Jessie Matthews: A Biography.* London: Hart-Davis, MacGibbon, 1974.

Toohey, John L. *A History of the Pulitzer Prize Plays.* New York: Citadel Press, 1967.

Tovey, Donald Francis. *The Main Stream of Music and Other Essays.* Cleveland and New York: Meridian Books, 1959.

Trager, James. *The New York Chronology.* New York: HarperResource, 2003.

———. *The People's Chronology.* New York: Henry Holt, 1994.

Trattner, Ernest R. *Understanding the Talmud.* New York: Thomas Nelson and Sons, 1955.

Turk, Edward Baron. *Hollywood Diva: A Biography of Jeanette MacDonald.* Berkeley: University of California Press, 1998.

Tyler, Parker. *The Three Faces of the Film.* Cranbury, N.J.: A. S. Barnes, 1960.

Vacha, Keith. *Quiet Fire: Memoirs of Older Gay Men.* Trumansburg, N.Y.: Crossing Press, 1985.

Van Doren, Carl, ed. *The Borzoi Reader.* New York: Alfred A. Knopf, 1936.

Van Meter, Jonathan. *The Last Good Time.* New York: Crown, 2003.

Vining, Donald. *How Can You Come Out If You've Never Been In? Essays on Gay Life and Relationships.* Trumansburg, N.Y.: Crossing Press, 1986.

The Violet 1921. Yearbook of New York University.

Walker, Stanley. *The Night Club Era.* Baltimore: Johns Hopkins University Press, 1999. (Originally published 1933 by Frederick A. Stokes Company.)

Weinstock, Matt. *My L.A.* New York: Current Books, 1947.

Wheeler, Leigh Ann. *Against Obscenity: Reform and the Politics of Womanhood in America, 1873–1935.* Baltimore: Johns Hopkins University Press, 2004.

Whitcomb, Ian. *Irving Berlin and Ragtime America.* London: Century, 1987.

Who's Who in America 1934–1935. Chicago: A. N. Marquis Company, 1934.

Wilder, Alec. *American Popular Song: The Great Innovators 1900–1950.* New York: Oxford University Press, 1972.

Wilk, Max. *They're Playing Our Song.* New York: Atheneum, 1973.

Wilkerson, Tichi, and Marcia Borie. *The Hollywood Reporter: The Golden Years.* New York: Arlington House, 1986.

Williams, Adriana. *Covarrubias.* Austin: University of Texas Press, 1994.

Wilson, Edmund. *Classics and Commercials: A Literary Chronicle of the Forties.* New York: Farrar, Straus, 1950.

———. *The Thirties*. Ed. Leon Edel. New York: Farrar, Straus & Giroux, 1980.

———. *The Twenties*. Ed. Leon Edel. New York: Farrar, Straus & Giroux, 1975.

Winchell, Walter. *Winchell Exclusive: Things That Happened to Me—and Me to Them*. Englewood Cliffs, N.J.: Prentice Hall, 1975.

Wodehouse, P. G., and Guy Bolton. *Bring on the Girls! The Improbable Story of Our Life in Musical Comedy with Pictures to Prove It*. Pleasantville, N.Y.: Akadine Press, 1997.

Wolff, Geoffrey. *The Duke of Deception: Memories of My Father*. New York: Vintage Books, 1990.

Wood, Graham. *The Development of Song Forms in the Broadway and Hollywood Musicals of Richard Rodgers, 1919–1943*. Doctoral dissertation, University of Minnesota, 2000.

Yeats, W. B. *Essays and Introductions*. London: Macmillan, 1961.

———. *Selected Poems and Two Plays*. Ed. with an introduction by M. L. Rosenthal. New York: Macmillan, 1962.

Ziegfeld, Richard, and Paulette Ziegfeld. *The Ziegfeld Touch: The Life and Times of Florenz Ziegfeld, Jr*. New York: Harry N. Abrams, 1993.

Zorina, Vera. *Zorina*. New York: Farrar, Straus & Giroux, 1986.

Zukor, Adolph, with Dale Kramer. *The Public Is Never Wrong: The Autobiography of Adolph Zukor*. New York: G. P. Putnam's Sons, 1953.

Selected (and Highly Idiosyncratic) Discography

Rodgers & Hart recordings, including a few instrumentals and one not by R & H but referring only to Hart, appear below in various formats. Catalogue numbers, when available, are provided.

Alive and Kickin': Big Band Sounds at M-G-M. Rhino R2-72721, CD. "I Like to Recognize the Tune," written for Rodgers and Hart's *Too Many Girls*, was used to rousing effect in the MGM musical *Meet the People* (1944), with Vaughn Monroe's band and June Allyson and Virginia O'Brien among the singers. Additional lyrics, written after Hart's death, are by MGM's resident music sorceress, Kay Thompson.

Dorothy Ashby. *In a Minor Groove.* Prestige 24120-2, CD. The jazz harpist's rendition of "There's a Small Hotel" is like no one else's.

Babes in Arms. DRG CD 0-21471-4769-2. Recording of the 1999 City Center Encores! revival of the 1937 show, with David Campbell, Erin Dilly, and Melissa Rain Anderson. The Coffee Club Orchestra—the best in the business—is conducted by Rob Fisher.

Ben Bagley and Michael McWhinney. *Rodgers and Hart Revisited.* World of the Theatre Series M 3001, vinyl. Among the fifteen Rodgers & Hart tracks, Dorothy Loudon's version of "This Funny World" (1926) and Danny Meehan and Charlotte Rae's duet on "Send for Me" (1930) and "I Must Love You" (1928) will make your hair stand up.

Tony Bennett. *Duets II.* RPM Records Columbia 88697 66253 2. Recorded in Bennett's eighty-fifth year, "The Lady Is a Tramp," with Lady Gaga, is surprisingly lively. *Tony Bennett Sings Rodgers & Hart.* Concord CCD-2243-2. The most touching Rodgers & Hart interpretation by Bennett may be of "You're Nearer," accompanied by the most influential of all jazz pianists, Bill Evans, on *Together Again* (Rhino R2 75837, CD).

The Boys from Syracuse. Sony Broadway SK 53329. A 1993 reissue, produced by Didier Deutsch, of the 1953 long-playing Columbia album produced by Goddard Lieberson and starring Portia Nelson, Jack Cassidy, and Bibi Osterwald.

Jackie Cain and Roy Kral. *By Jupiter & Girl Crazy.* Roulette R 25278, vinyl. Six Rodgers & Hart songs, with Cain's version of "Nobody's Heart" perhaps the most moving of all.

The Magic of Diahann Carroll, with the André Previn Trio. Recorded on United Artists in 1960, shortly before Carroll appeared on Broadway in Richard Rodgers's *No Strings,* the CD was released in 2005 on DRG Records/EMI. There are three excellent Rodgers & Hart songs: "Spring Is Here," "Glad to Be Unhappy," and "Nobody's Heart."

Betty Carter. *Social Call.* Columbia, a 1980 rerelease, vinyl. In May 1955, the incomparable jazz singer, with Quincy Jones arranging and Ray Bryant on piano, recorded "Thou Swell" at breakneck speed and a straight-ahead, adoring version of "I Could Write a Book." On *Inside Betty Carter* (Capitol Jazz CDR 0777 7 89702 2 4), she does "Isn't It Romantic?" as a rhumba.

Rosemary Clooney. *Some of the Best.* Laserlight 12633. Probably the definitive version of "Yours Sincerely," arranged by Nelson Riddle.

John Coltrane and Johnny Hartman. Impulse A-40, vinyl. If there is a lovelier rendition of "You Are Too Beautiful" (1932), in which Hartman is backed by the John Coltrane Quartet of 1963, we'd all like to know about it.

Chris Connor. Atlantic 1228, vinyl. Hers may be the most haunting reading of "He Was Too Good to Me." Also hear Connor's "Spring Is Here" on *The Finest of Chris Connor* (Bethlehem 2BP-1001, vinyl).

A Connecticut Yankee. Decca Broadway CD. Songs from the 1943 revival, with Dick Foran and Vivienne Segal, plus Shirley Ross singing songs from *Higher and Higher* (1940) and Hildegarde covering *By Jupiter* (1942).

Sammy Davis, Jr. *It's All Over But the Swingin'.* Decca DL 8641, vinyl. Excellent studio musicians help make Davis's versions of "It Never Entered My Mind," "Spring Is Here," and "Where's That Rainbow?" first-rate. Sammy's *Sammy Davis Jr.* (Vocalion 73827, vinyl) includes a fine "Glad to Be Unhappy," arranged by Sy Oliver.

Blossom Dearie, Soubrette, Sings Broadway Hit Songs. Verve VS 62133. If Vivienne Segal sang "To Keep My Love Alive" as a bawdy queen, Blossom handles the great Hart lyric like a coquette hiding a knife behind her back.

Matt Dennis. *She Dances Overhead . . .* RCA 74321898312, CD. Matt Dennis, piano and vocal; Harry Geller and His Orchestra. Recorded in Hollywood, 1955. Still among the best of all Rodgers & Hart albums.

Frank D'Rone Sings. Mercury SR 60064, vinyl. Particularly pleasing versions of "I Could Write a Book" and "Spring Is Here."

Anita Ellis. *The World in My Arms.* Collectibles COL-CD-6392. Ellis does the neglected "A Lady Must Live" (1931).

Bill Evans Trio. *Waltz for Debby*. Riverside OJCCD-210-2. You can hear the surprise and delight of every Hart syllable in two instrumental takes of "My Romance," recorded on June 25, 1961.

Ella Fitzgerald. *The Rodgers and Hart Songbook* Vols. 1 and 2. Verve CD 422-821579-2/Verve CD 422-821580-2. For a generation of listeners, this was the first—and still unsurpassed—wide exposure to the songs of Rodgers and Hart. The string-heavy, swelling arrangements are by Buddy Bregman.

Fly with Me. Original Cast Records. The Rodgers & Hart Varsity Show of 1920, recorded at Columbia University on April 26, 1980.

Classic Judy Garland: The Capitol Years 1955–1965. Capitol CDP 7243 5 39281 2 4. When Garland sings "Two feet are ever cold; / Four feet are never cold" on "Why Can't I?" (1929), you might agree it's a shame she didn't record more of Hart's lyrics. Of course there's always the propulsive Garland–Mickey Rooney duet on "I Wish I Were in Love Again," from the 1948 MGM biopic *Words and Music*. It's on *That's Entertainment!* (Rhino R2 72182).

Buddy Greco. "*My Buddy.*" Epic LN 3660, vinyl. Through the 1960s, Greco's finger-popping rendition of "The Lady Is a Tramp" evoked the cocktail lounge and the penthouse.

Mary Cleere Haran. *There's a Small Hotel*. Columbia CK 52403. In addition to the title track, Haran gives a brief lecture on Rodgers and Hart. Haran's *This Funny World* (Varese Sarabande 5584) contains one of the clearest readings of "Manhattan."

The Hi-Lo's. *Love Nest*. Collectibles COL-CD-6694. Reissue of the 1959 Columbia album, including three fine Rodgers & Hart interpretations. On *Suddenly It's the Hi-Lo's* (Columbia CL 952, vinyl), they perform the definitive version of "I Married an Angel."

Hollywood Party. Warner Archives DVD. This 2011 release of the 1934 MGM film includes bonus audio tracks of unused Rodgers & Hart songs, including some unpublished Hart lyrics. Recommended by Scott Willis.

Keep 'Em Rolling. Original Old Radio. KR-002. Air check of the 1941–42 radio program, for which Rodgers and Hart wrote the theme song.

André Kostelanetz. *The Columbia Album of Richard Rodgers*. EN2 13725, vinyl. Fine orchestral versions of many Rodgers & Hart songs.

Maude Maggart. *With Sweet Despair*. www.maudemaggart.com, CD. The song "Beyond Compare," written by Marshall Barer and David Ross, includes a charming reference to Larry Hart, whose work greatly influenced lyricist Barer.

Mary Martin Sings, Richard Rodgers Plays. RCA LPM-1539 RE, vinyl. Orchestra conducted by John Lesko; orchestrations by Robert Russell Bennett.

Mabel Mercer. *Midnight at Mabel Mercer's*. Collectibles COL-CD-6603. One of Larry Hart's favorite singers interprets "Wait Till You See Her" and "He Was Too Good to Me."

The Merry Widow/The Love Parade. La Nadine du Disco 260 (Canada). The two Jeanette MacDonald–Maurice Chevalier films on which Rodgers and Hart worked. Recommended by Frederick Nolan.

Joe Mooney. *Lush Life*. Koch KOC CD 8524. Originally released on Atlantic LP 1255. Mooney was among the most relaxed of American singers. Once you've heard his rendition of "Have You Met Miss Jones?," most other versions sound stiff. Here he accompanies himself on the Hammond organ.

On Your Toes. Columbia COS 2590. Another early Goddard Lieberson production with Portia Nelson and Jack Cassidy.

Pal Joey. Columbia 4364, vinyl. The recording featured several cast members of the 1952 Broadway production, including Vivienne Segal again and Harold Lang, which became one of the few musical comedy revivals more commercially successful than the original. Orchestra conducted by Lehman Engel.

John Pizzarelli. *With a Song in My Heart*. Telarc. The singer-guitarist covers Rodgers, with mostly Hart and some Hammerstein. "Johnny One Note" is a blast. The legendary arranger Don Sebesky wrote six of these charts.

Kenny Rankin. *A Song for You*. Verve 314 589 540-2. Like so many male singers, Rankin—whose deep speaking voice belied his high singing voice—changes the pronoun for "He Was Too Good to Me," but it hardly diminishes the lyric. His version is among the best.

Nelson Riddle Interprets Great Music Great Films Great Sounds. Reprise R-6138, vinyl. The ace arranger puts his orchestra through five songs from *Jumbo* (1935), including the infrequently recorded "Over and Over Again."

Richard Rodgers. *Command Performance*. Harbinger Records HCD2501. Rodgers's 1920s piano rolls, plus demos and air checks—one including Larry Hart's speaking voice—from 1934 through 1971. Also Rodgers: *Three Ballets: Slaughter on Tenth Avenue, Ghost Town*, and *La Princess Zenobia*. CDJay 1349. Orchestrations by Hans Spialek. Conducted by John Mauceri.

Rodgers and Hart in Hollywood Vol. 1 1929–1935. Box Office JJA 1976. *Rodgers and Hart in Hollywood* Vol. 2 1934–1943. Box Office JJA1982. *Rodgers and Hart in Hollywood* Vol. 3. Box Office JJA 1982. The team's movie work, from *Makers of Melody* to *Words and Music*. Recommended by Frederick Nolan.

The Songs of Rodgers & Hart. Various artists. Warner Bros., Williamson Music, RH-1/2, CD. A compilation of mostly familiar but still welcome versions of forty-eight songs.

Hugh Shannon. *True Blue Hugh*. Audiophile ACD-140. Recorded in 1977, the CD includes what may be the most amusing version of "Disgustingly Rich" (1940).

Frank Sinatra Sings Rodgers & Hart. Capitol W1825. The greatest of all pop singers sets the bar impossibly high for other Rodgers & Hart interpreters. *Sinatra at the Sands*. Reprise 1019, vinyl. Backed by Count Basie & His Orchestra and Quincy Jones's arrangements (many of which are built on earlier Nelson Riddle charts), Sinatra takes "Where or When" up-tempo and the result is fantastic. Sinatra's

Ring a Ding Ding (Reprise F/R9 1001; reissued on Concord) includes him working out "Have You Met Miss Jones?," which was left off the 1961 vinyl release.

Jimmy Smith. *The Sermon.* Blue Note CDP 7 46097 2. The jazz organist had, among his sidemen, the extraordinary trumpeter Lee Morgan, but it's the trombonist Curtis Fuller who shines on "Blue Room."

Jeri Southern. *You Better Go Now!* Decca DL 8214, vinyl. The singer-pianist dispenses with the verse of "Dancing on the Ceiling," but hers was probably the most popular interpretation on record for several decades.

Jo Stafford. *No Other Love.* The Entertainers CD 359. A favorite reading of "It Never Entered My Mind." Stafford's husband, Paul Weston, did the arrangements.

The Barbra Streisand Album, Columbia CS 8807, vinyl. Streisand's is still the best version of "I'll Tell the Man in the Street." Arranged and conducted by Peter Matz. A shimmering "Quiet Night" is on *My Name Is Barbra, Two* (Columbia CK 9209).

Elaine Stritch. *Stritch.* Dolphin Records 3, vinyl. Portia Nelson's arrangement of "You Took Advantage of Me" showcases Stritch's wry, faux-tipsy delivery.

Too Many Girls. Painted Smile PS 1368. This is a very efficient Ben Bagley production, with the actor Anthony Perkins singing on several tracks.

The Best of Mel Tormé. EMI-Capitol 72435-20578-2-5, CD. Fine versions of "Blue Moon" and "Bewitched, Bothered and Bewildered." Tormé sings a particularly memorable "My Romance" on *That's All* (Columbia/Legacy CK 65165).

The Ultimate Rodgers & Hart Vols. I–III. Pavilion Records, CD. Many songs, beginning with *Dearest Enemy* (1925) through *Young Man with a Horn* (1950).

Dawn Upshaw Sings Rodgers & Hart. Nonesuch Records. Wonderful interpretations, but the most fun may be "Sing for Your Supper," based on Hugh Martin's 1938 arrangement.

Dinah Washington: The Jazz Sides. EmArcy Jazz Series, EMS-2-401, vinyl. The legendary blues singer handles "I Could Write a Book" and "This Can't Be Love" (both arranged by Quincy Jones) as if she owned them.

Wesla Whitfield. *Nice Work.* Landmark Records LCD 1544-2. Of the four Rodgers & Hart songs, "Where's That Rainbow?" is particularly fine.

Lee Wiley Sings Rodgers & Hart and Harold Arlen. Monmouth Evergreen, MES 6807. Includes the unforgettable "As Though You Were There" and the rarely recorded "A Little Birdie Told Me So."

Credits and Permissions

Text

"Lorenz," from *Curves and Angles: Poems,* by Brad Leithauser, copyright © 2006 by Brad Leithauser. Used by permission of Alfred A. Knopf, a division of Random House, Inc.

Lorenz Hart quote, pp. 383–85 of *A Ship Without a Sail: The Life of Lorenz Hart,* courtesy of The Estate of Lorenz Hart.

Photographs

Courtesy Larry Hart II: 1, 4. By permission of Larry Hart II.

Photo by Nickolas Muray, courtesy Beinecke Library, Yale University: 2. By permission of Nickolas Muray Archives LLC.

Photo by Nickolas Muray, courtesy Photofest: 3. By permission of Nickolas Muray Archives LLC.

Courtesy Academy of Motion Picture Arts and Sciences: 5, 11, 12

Courtesy Photofest: 6, 9, 13, 15, 19, 21, 29

Courtesy Jim Di Giovanni: 7, 25

Courtesy United Artists/Photofest: 9

Photo by Pritchard Studios. Courtesy Photofest: 14, 28

Photo by World-Telegram staff photographer. Courtesy Photofest: 16, 18

Photo by De Mirjian Studios: 8

Courtesy New York Public Library: 17, 20, 23

Photo by Vandamm Studios. Courtesy Shubert Archive: 22, 24

Photo by Mary Morris. Courtesy New York Public Library: 26, 27. By permission of Mary Morris Lawrence.

Photo by Frederick Nolan. Courtesy Frederick Nolan: 30

Key to Chapter Titles

Prologue: "I'm a Sentimental Sap, That's All" is from "You Took Advantage of Me" (*Present Arms*, 1928), by Rodgers and Hart.

Chapter 1: "Life Is More Delectable When It's Disrespectable" is from "Mountain Greenery" (*The Garrick Gaieties*, 1926), by Rodgers and Hart.

Chapter 2: "I Read My Plato" is from "My Heart Stood Still" (*One Dam Thing after Another*, 1927, and *A Connecticut Yankee*, 1927), by Rodgers and Hart.

Chapter 3: "The Rhyme Is Hard to Find, My Dears" is from an untitled poem (written at Brant Lake Camp, New York, 1918), by Lorenz Hart.

Chapter 4: "I'll Go to Hell for Ya" is from "Any Old Place with You" (*A Lonely Romeo*, 1919), by Rodgers and Hart.

Chapter 5: "The Great Big City's a Wondrous Toy" is from "Manhattan" (*The Garrick Gaieties*, 1925), by Rodgers and Hart.

Chapter 6: "You Mustn't Conceal Anything You Feel" is from "On with the Dance" (*The Garrick Gaieties*, 1925), by Rodgers and Hart.

Chapter 7: "It's So Good It Must Be Immoral" is from "Mountain Greenery" (*The Garrick Gaieties*, 1926), by Rodgers and Hart.

Chapter 8: "A House in Iceland Was My Heart's Domain" is from "My Heart Stood Still" (*One Dam Thing after Another*, 1927, and *A Connecticut Yankee*, 1927), by Rodgers and Hart.

Chapter 9: "You've Cooked My Goose" is from "You Took Advantage of Me" (*Present Arms*, 1928), by Rodgers and Hart.

Chapter 10: "My Head Is Just a Hat Place" is from "A Ship Without a Sail" (*Heads Up!*, 1929) by Rodgers and Hart.

Chapter 11: "I Try to Hide in Vain" is from "Dancing on the Ceiling" (*Simple Simon*, 1930, and *Ever Green*, 1930) by Rodgers and Hart.

Chapter 12: "I'm Not Afraid of My Own Creation" is from "Isn't It Romantic?" (*Love Me Tonight*, 1932), by Rodgers and Hart.

Chapter 13: "I Am Too Drunk with Beauty" is from "You Are Too Beautiful" (*Hallelujah, I'm a Bum!*, 1933), by Rodgers and Hart.

Chapter 14: "I Heard Somebody Whisper, 'Please Adore Me'" is from "Blue Moon" (1934), by Rodgers and Hart.

Chapter 15: "The World Was Younger Than I" is from "Little Girl Blue" (*Jumbo*, 1935), by Rodgers and Hart.

Chapter 16: "Unrequited Love's a Bore" is from "Glad to Be Unhappy" (*On Your Toes*, 1936), by Rodgers and Hart.

Chapter 17: "Is Your Figure Less Than Greek?" is from "My Funny Valentine" (*Babes in Arms*, 1937) by Rodgers and Hart.

Chapter 18: "All at Once I Owned the Earth and Sky" is from "Have You Met Miss Jones?" (*I'd Rather Be Right*, 1937), by Rodgers and Hart.

Chapter 19: "Caring Too Much Is Such a Juvenile Fancy" is from "Falling in Love with Love" (*The Boys from Syracuse*, 1938), by Rodgers and Hart.

Chapter 20: "And Now I Know I Was Naïve" is from "I Didn't Know What Time It Was" (*Too Many Girls*, 1939), by Rodgers and Hart.

Chapter 21: "To Write I Used to Think Was Wasting Ink" is from "I Could Write a Book" (*Pal Joey*, 1940), by Rodgers and Hart.

Chapter 22: "Wait Till You Feel the Warmth of Her Glance" is from "Wait Till You See Her" (*By Jupiter*, 1942), by Rodgers and Hart.

Chapter 23: "Nobody Writes His Songs to Me" is from "Nobody's Heart" (*By Jupiter*, 1942), by Rodgers and Hart.

Chapter 24: "And Yet I Was Untrue to None of Them" is from "To Keep My Love Alive" (revival of *A Connecticut Yankee*, 1943), by Rodgers and Hart.

Index